Italian Cinema: From the Silent Screen to the Digital Image

Italian Cinema: From the Silent Screen to the Digital Image

Edited by
Joseph Luzzi

BLOOMSBURY ACADEMIC
NEW YORK · LONDON · OXFORD · NEW DELHI · SYDNEY

BLOOMSBURY ACADEMIC
Bloomsbury Publishing Inc
1385 Broadway, New York, NY 10018, USA
50 Bedford Square, London, WC1B 3DP, UK

BLOOMSBURY, BLOOMSBURY ACADEMIC and the Diana logo are trademarks of
Bloomsbury Publishing Plc

First published in the United States of America 2020

Cover design by Eleanor Rose
Cover photograph: Marcello Mastroianni and Anita Ekberg in a scene from
La Dolce Vita, 1960, dir Federico Fellini © Mary Evans Picture Library

Library of Congress Cataloging-in-Publication Data
Names: Luzzi, Joseph, editor.
Title: Italian cinema from the silent screen to the digital image /
edited by Joseph Luzzi.
Description: New York: Bloomsbury Academic, 2019. |
Includes bibliographical references and index.
Identifiers: LCCN 2019026358 (print) | LCCN 2019026359 (ebook) |
ISBN 9781441195616 (paperback) | ISBN 9781441174932 (hardback) |
ISBN 9781441147561 (epub) | ISBN 9781441186423 (pdf)
Subjects: LCSH: Motion pictures–Italy–History and criticism.
Classification: LCC PN1993.5.I88 I7255 2019 (print) | LCC PN1993.5.I88
(ebook) | DDC 791.430945–dc23
LC record available at https://lccn.loc.gov/2019026358
LC ebook record available at https://lccn.loc.gov/2019026359

ISBN: HB: 978-1-4411-7493-2
PB: 978-1-4411-9561-6
ePDF: 978-1-4411-8642-3
eBook: 978-1-4411-4756-1

Typeset by Deanta Global Publishing Services, Chennai, India
Printed and bound in the United States of America

To find out more about our authors and books visit www.bloomsbury.com and
sign up for our newsletters.

To Scott McGill

CONTENTS

CHRONOLOGY

Mattia Acetoso

1890s: A Silent Beginning

On November 11, 1895, Filoteo Alberini (1865–1937), a pioneering director of Italian cinema, patented the Kinetografo Alberini, an early device for the production of motion pictures. Using this invention, in 1896 the director Vittorio Calcina (1847–1916) filmed the documentary *Umberto e Margherita di Savoia a passeggio per il parco (King Umberto and Margherita of Savoy Strolling in the Park)*. This film is arguably the beginning of Italian cinema. As in France, the prevalent genre in the early days of Italian cinema was documentary. Using mobile structures for projection, the earliest screenings were in piazzas and other public spaces, but by the end of the 1890s, film theaters began appearing across the peninsula.

1910–14: The Golden Age of Italian Silent Cinema

On September 20, 1905, Alberini presented the first Italian feature film with a complex plot, *La presa di Roma (The Capture of Rome)*, a historical work that portrayed the Piedmontese conquest of Rome in 1870. An important series of silent films was released in the following years: the period between 1910 and 1914 is generally acknowledged as the Golden Age of Italian Silent Cinema. The Italian film industry gained prestige as Italian films reached wide popularity both at home and abroad, seriously challenging the more powerful Hollywood productions. Many early films were literary adaptations (see Glossary), and the industry saw the direct involvement of such prominent intellectuals as Gabriele D'Annunzio (1863–1938) and Luigi Pirandello (1867–1936). However, while the first full-length film—Giuseppe de Liguoro's *Dante's Inferno* (1911)—was a loose adaptation of Dante's *Divine Comedy*, the historical epic rapidly became the most popular genre of the time. Among the most famous films of the period were Mario

Caserini's *Gli ultimi giorni di Pompei* (*The Last Days of Pompeii*, 1913), Enrico Guazzoni's *Marc'Antonio e Cleopatra* (*Antony and Cleopatra*, 1913), and Giovanni Pastrone's *Cabiria* (1914).

1920s: The First World War and the Decline of Italian Silent Cinema

The sacrifices demanded by the First World War gravely impacted film production in Italy, and the postwar period was one of decline for the nation's cinema. After the war, the film industry was crippled, and Italian filmmakers struggled to produce films. Those films that were made did not become as successful as the films of the earlier years. In turn, American and other foreign productions supplanted the Italian market and garnered wide popular interest. The influx of powerful foreign production companies in Rome further complicated the situation for Italian filmmakers. In 1919, a union of the most prominent Italian production companies, the Unione Cinematografica Italiana (UCI), attempted to create a consortium to compete against Hollywood production companies, but it failed and the union was dismantled in 1926.

1928–43: Sound Film, Fascist Cinema, and Cinecittà

The most important event to reverse the decline of the Italian film industry was the direct support of film companies by the Fascist government. The dictator Benito Mussolini (1883–1945) was well aware of the importance of cinema for government propaganda and for the promotion of Fascist cultural values worldwide. Among the most significant actions taken by the government was *autarchy*, a self-imposed policy of national self-sufficiency and nonreliance on imports, which also impacted the film industry and partially halted the intrusion of foreign productions. Many new Italian film companies were formed and became the engine for the development of a national cinema.

The first Italian sound film was Gennaro Righelli's *La canzone dell'amore* (*The Song of Love*), based on a novel by Pirandello and first screened in Rome on October 8, 1930. The film was produced by a joint venture of CINES (see Glossary), the most famous Italian production company, and Stefano Pittaluga (1887–1932), an entrepreneur and film producer. Pittaluga also supported the two most popular and successful directors of the era, Alessandro Blasetti (1900–87) and Mario Camerini (1895–1981), early in their careers.

From August 6 to 21, 1932, Venice hosted the first European Film Festival, which quickly became one of the most prestigious international festivals and boosted worldwide recognition of Italian cinema. Even after Pittaluga's death, the Fascist government kept supporting the film industry, and in 1935 special state funds were assigned to Italian film productions. Galeazzo Ciano (1903–44), at the time Minister of Press and Propaganda, encouraged the formation of film clubs all over Italy, with the intent of educating Italians on world cinema. In 1936, the Italian publisher Ulrico Hoepli (1847–1935) founded the journal *Cinema*, later directed by Vittorio Mussolini (Benito's son), which attracted a cohort of young and talented filmmakers, intellectuals, and film theorists. And on April 28, 1937, Benito Mussolini inaugurated Cinecittà, the largest and most prominent of Italian film studios, and to many the very symbol of Italian cinema to this day. Mussolini famously considered cinematography the most powerful of all communicative weapons: Cinecittà was intended to be yet another expression of Fascist power.

Not incidentally, during Fascism the Italian film industry thrived. Keen on the power of film to divulge ideas, the Fascist government mostly relied on the LUCE Institute (see Glossary) for propaganda and exercised relatively limited censorship on film production. Despite a sizable number of propagandistic films, which aimed at celebrating the core values of Fascism and its accomplishments, most Italian directors enjoyed relative artistic freedom, although they avoided directly challenging the regime with their works. Most white telephone films (see Glossary), depicted escapist and glamorous situations, while expressing conservative ideas of Italian society and exalting the social status quo.

Another popular genre during the Fascist era was historical cinema: colossal movies that narrated either biblical or mythological episodes. However, in the last years of the regime, some films began challenging Fascism with a new worldview, one that showed the less flattering aspects of Italian society by insisting on an aesthetics of reality, and anticipating many characteristics of neorealism (see Glossary). Among these films were Vittorio De Sica's *I bambini ci guardano* (*The Children Are Watching Us*, 1944) and Luchino Visconti's *Ossessione* (*Obsession*, 1943), an adaptation of James M. Cain's novel *The Postman Always Rings Twice* (1934).

1945: Italian Neorealism and the Rebirth of Italian Cinema

After the Second World War, the Italian film industry was decimated, and the Allied government had no interest in reviving what had become a Fascist symbol. However, in 1944, ANICA (see Glossary), a national association of film companies, was established: it was one of the first attempts to revive a moribund Italian cinema. Producers asked the Italian government for direct financial support, in order to confront the pressure, power, and obstructionism of American film production companies that flooded the Italian market with their works. In addition, after the Second World War, insurmountable issues and technical problems hindered national film production to such an extent that Cinecittà was turned into an emergency hospital and a warehouse. As a consequence, directors began to shoot on location and with limited means, using nonprofessional actors and focusing on the portrayal of real-life situations. All this contributed to the beginning of Italian neorealism.

Between 1945 and 1952, neorealist cinema defined the rebirth and the international reappraisal of Italian cinema, becoming the most successful movement in Italian film history. In October 1945, Roberto Rossellini's *Roma città aperta (Rome, Open City)* premiered in Milan. An international success, *Rome, Open City* represented a watershed for both Italian cinema and the history of film as a whole. While some critics question the nature and legitimacy of the term *neorealism*, Rossellini's masterpiece is generally accepted as the harbinger of a new aesthetic. The directors of this period—including the acclaimed triumvirate De Sica, Rossellini, and Visconti—showed Italians in dire need and a nation in ruin, but at the same time the movement restored dignity and prestige to the country after twenty years of Fascism. Neorealist directors overcame the technical difficulties and limitations of Italy's postwar struggle and devised a so-called aesthetics of reality that influenced generations of directors both in Italy and abroad, most notably the French Nouvelle Vague (New Wave) in the 1950s and 1960s.

Many politicians and cultural conservatives harshly criticized neorealism. The most vocal was possibly the Christian Democrat politician Giulio Andreotti (1919–2013), who famously bristled at the portrayal of Italian daily life in De Sica's *Umberto D.* (1952) in *Libertas*, the weekly newspaper of the Christian Democrat Party. Despite his skepticism, Andreotti was well aware of the importance of Italian cinema for the rebirth of Italian culture, and on December 29, 1949, he successfully endorsed a law that would freeze revenue of American films in Italy. With this special decree, Italy was able to fund its own film industry, reaffirm the role of Cinecittà as a production center, and create a vibrant film community. During the postwar reconstruction, Italian cinema helped rehabilitate Italy's image abroad, from a country in ruins to a symbol of elegance, fashion, and culture.

1950s: Pink Neorealism and Comedy Italian Style

In the early 1950s, the artistic potential of Neorealist cinema began to fade, and producers and spectators alike drifted toward lighter forms of entertainment. These newer films showed how the economic and social conditions of the country were slowly improving. The social engagement of Neorealist cinema made room for what was later labeled *neorealismo rosa* (pink neorealism; see Glossary). The first example of the new filmic trend was Luigi Comencini's *Pane, amore e fantasia* (*Bread, Love, and Dreams*, 1953). This film was very popular and inspired many imitations. Pink neorealism paved the way for the genre that defined Italian postwar cinema up to the present day, the *commedia all'italiana* (comedy italian style; see Glossary). The comedic register already hinted at by pink neorealism found more defined contours: it abandoned the lighter tone of previous comedies and cast a satirical lens on Italian society. The portrayal of contemporary Italy veered toward the bittersweet, while the judgment on Italians' shortcomings became ruthless and disenchanted, through the use of a comedic register in treating dramatic situations and themes. The beginning of this filmic trend is usually considered *I soliti ignoti* (*Big Deal on Madonna Street*, 1958) by Mario Monicelli, which featured a large cast of brilliant actors. The success of Italian comedies contributed to the consolidation of a new star system, including such prominent figures as Vittorio Gassman, Alberto Sordi, and Marcello Mastroianni, as well as Sophia Loren and Gina Lollobrigida, two female sex symbols who rapidly reached the heights of international stardom.

1960s: Auteurist Cinema

At the same time as the *commedia all'italiana*, the genre of art cinema developed in Italy in the late 1950s. In 1960, three seminal films were released almost simultaneously: Luchino Visconti's *Rocco e i suoi fratelli* (*Rocco and His Brothers*), Michelangelo Antonioni's *L'avventura*, and Federico Fellini's *La dolce vita*, which was awarded that year's Academy Award for Best Foreign Film. These directors began to attract critical success and set a new gold standard for Italian film. The intellectual roots of Visconti, Antonioni, and Fellini extend back into neorealism, but compared to the previous generation these directors explored more personal ways of filmmaking. Their cinema was characterized by an "auteur" or authorial approach that reflected their unique artistic worldviews and developed into what many consider the most aesthetically accomplished period of Italian cinema ever.

Visconti focused on ambitious storytelling, from the family drama *Rocco and His Brothers* to filmic adaptations of such works of literature as *Senso* (1954), *Il Gattopardo* (*The Leopard*, 1963), and *Morte a Venezia* (*Death in Venice*, 1971). The first two films explore interpersonal dramas against the backdrop of European conflicts, giving Visconti the opportunity to articulate his political views on history and national identity. During the same period, Antonioni considered the conflicted human condition in modern society in his so-called trilogy of alienation: *L'avventura* (1960), *La notte* (1961), and *L'eclisse* (1962). Antonioni also analyzed similar themes in more approachable English-language productions: *Blow-Up* (1966), *Zabriskie Point* (1970), and *Professione: reporter* (*The Passenger*, 1975).

Fellini's uniquely personal artistic vision continued to evolve out of his early contribution to neorealism as a screenwriter and into autobiographical films influenced by psychoanalysis and an ambition to probe the very nature of filmmaking. His work was immediately influential: the autobiographical film *I vitelloni* (1953), a coming-of-age tale of a group of friends in Fellini's hometown of Rimini, would shape the work of such later directors as Martin Scorsese and George Lucas, while *La strada* (1954) and *Le notti di Cabiria* (*The Nights of Cabiria*, 1957) received the Academy Award for Best Foreign Film. *La dolce vita* (1960), a break with conventional filmic storytelling, explored the glamour and contradictions of Italy's economic boom, and the brilliant *8 1/2* (1963) brought to full fruition the director's search into the nature of the creative process and psychoanalysis. In the following years, Fellini emphasized his authorial approach to filmmaking, expanding his interest into politics, sexuality, and the role of the media in contemporary society. Awarded an honorary Oscar for Lifetime Achievement in 1993, Fellini has been for many—both inside and outside of Italy—the preeminent symbol of Italian cinema.

Pier Paolo Pasolini, a more controversial but equally celebrated figure, fits less easily into the canon of Italian cinema, even though he was a major player in the 1960s auteurist movement. At the intersection of film, literature, art, and politics, his cinema evolved from his early post-neorealist films such as *Accattone* (1961) and *Mamma Roma* (1962), which portray the underworld of Rome's poorest neighborhoods, to a psychoanalytic examination of human nature through myth in films including *Edipo Re* (*Oedipus Rex*, 1967), *Teorema* (*Theorem*, 1968), and *Medea* (1969). Pasolini also explored the theme of sexuality as a form of revolution against social dogmas in his critically acclaimed "trilogy of life," a filmic adaptation of literary masterpieces from the Middle Ages: *Il Decameron* (*The Decameron*, 1971), *I racconti di Canterbury* (*Canterbury Tales*, 1972), and *Il fiore delle Mille e una notte* (*Arabian Nights*, 1974).

1958–68: A Profusion of Genres

During the golden years of Italian comedy, Italian filmmakers experimented with several other genres, often mimicking and revising the clichés of larger American and international productions. In the 1950s, the historical epic genre, also labeled "peplum" or "sword and sandal" (see Glossary), reached new popularity. Another crucial development that led to international success was a new take on the Western. Beginning with Sergio Leone's *Per un pugno di dollari* (*A Fistful of Dollars*, 1964), Italian-directed Westerns, known as Spaghetti Westerns (see Glossary), brought back the genre's popularity and remain influential to this day in the films of Quentin Tarantino and many other contemporary American directors. Another important genre was the Italian *Giallo* (see Glossary), supremely embodied in Dario Argento's stylized thriller *Profondo rosso* (*Deep Red*, 1975). In the 1970s, Italian comedy developed into a peculiar style that would be later known as *commedia sexy* (see Glossary), popular in the 1970s and early 1980s.

1970s: The Cinema of *Impegno*

The spring of 1968 and the social unrest of the 1970s eventually led to a period of turmoil in Italy, conventionally labeled as the *anni di piombo* (Years of Lead). Terrorist attacks and gruesome events such as bombings and kidnappings became regular occurrences and defined this historical moment and its political tensions. The climactic event of this era was the 1978 kidnapping and murder of former prime minister, Aldo Moro (1916–78), by the terrorist organization known as the Red Brigades—a tragedy that shocked Italy and left an impression on public opinion for generations. This political situation prompted a cinema of political and civic engagement, usually defined as *cinema d'impegno civile* (engaged cinema; see Glossary). Francesco Rosi, Elio Petri, Gillo Pontecorvo, and the Taviani brothers were among the leading figures of a generation of Italian filmmakers that used cinema as a means to interpret the country's social distress and uncertainty.

Rosi (1922–2015) undertook biographical films and the analysis of documented historical facts in such works as *Salvatore Giuliano* (1962), *Il caso Mattei* (*The Mattei Affair*, 1972), and *Lucky Luciano* (1973). In other films, including *Le mani sulla città* (*Hands Over the City*, 1963) and *Cadaveri eccellenti* (*Illustrious Corpses*, 1976), he sought to expose and denounce Italy's ongoing tendency for political corruption. A similar attitude characterizes the films of Petri (1929–82), known for his visionary and grotesque take on the deformities of Italian society, especially in his so-called trilogy of neurosis: *Indagine su un cittadino al di sopra di ogni sospetto* (*Investigation of a Citizen Above Suspicion*, 1970), *La classe operaia va in paradiso* (*Lulu the Tool*, 1971), and *La proprietà non è più un furto* (*Property Is No Longer a Theft*, 1973). Pontecorvo (1919–2006) is best known for his masterpiece *La battaglia di Algeri* (*The Battle of Algiers*, 1966), which documented the Algerian struggle for independence from France and contributed to the development of critical interest toward the political realities of economically developing countries.

1980s: A New Crisis Looms

On July 15, 1976, a court decision recognized the monopoly of RAI, the Italian state broadcast company, and de facto allowed for the liberalization of private television in Italy, thus paving the way for what would become the media empire of the tycoon Silvio Berlusconi. In the following decade, private television companies became the most prominent distributors of entertainment for Italians. Commercial broadcast networks began buying films and TV series from the United States and other foreign countries, delivering cheap entertainment directly into the households of average Italian families. This change to the media landscape reduced the number of spectators in movie theaters. Italian cinema entered into a new crisis that crippled the whole industry, as Italian film production was split in two between films that sought popular appeal and art films that looked back to the older generation of masters.

1990s: Old and New Masters

In the 1990s, a series of tragedies and scandals hit the Italian world of politics, and the international credibility of the country was once again shaken. In 1992, two bombs killed, respectively, Giovanni Falcone (1939–92) and Paolo Borsellino (1940–92), magistrates working against organized crime in Italy. The First Republic—the political order established at the end of the Second World War, with the Christian Democrat Party largely in power and with the Italian Communist Party as its main opposition—collapsed in a period of endless scandal and corruption called Tangentopoli, or Bribesville. Italy went through a political and social renewal, and a new cast of characters from the worlds of industry and culture came to prominence. The media mogul Berlusconi, who would dominate Italy's political life and divide public opinion for the following twenty years, rose to power. Nonetheless, it was during this turbulent historical phase that Italian cinema seemed finally to experience a rebirth.

Many productions of this decade received the praise of both critics and the general public. In 1990, Giuseppe Tornatore's *Nuovo Cinema Paradiso* (*Cinema Paradiso*, 1988) was awarded the Academy Award for Best Foreign Film, the first Italian film in twenty years to attain this honor. Meanwhile, an older generation of directors, including Ettore Scola, Mario Monicelli, and Marco Bellocchio, continued to exercise artistic influence, just as a new generation was emerging. Besides Tornatore, other directors including Nanni Moretti, Gabriele Salvatores, Roberto Benigni, and Ferzan Ozpetek took the artistic lead in a new era of Italian cinema. Salvatores and Benigni received Academy Awards, respectively, for *Mediterraneo* (1991) and *La vita è bella* (*Life Is Beautiful*, 1997).

2000s: Italian Cinema in the Present Tense

The 2000s continued the rebirth of Italian cinema. Matteo Garrone's *Gomorra* (*Gomorrah*, 2008) and Paolo Sorrentino's *Il divo* (2008) met with popular success, received international praise, and garnered critical recognition. Italians began to return to movie theaters and pay attention to contemporary Italian productions. And new filmic trends emerged while old ones were revived. An evolving, more multicultural society inspired films that focus on such themes as national identity, unemployment, immigration, and changes in the Italian family structure. Earlier genres such as the *poliziottesco* (Italian crime film; see Glossary) were revisited in an attempt to blur the divide that long separated entertainment and art films.

Though still affected by issues of declining spectatorship, poor international distribution, and the lack of proper funding, Italian cinema is returning to prominence. In 2014, Sorrentino's *La grande bellezza* (*The Great Beauty*, 2013) was awarded that year's Academy Award for Best Foreign Film. While portraying Italy's cultural and moral decline, Sorrentino channeled the greatness of Fellini, Scola, and other masters of the past. *The Great Beauty* explored the contradictions of present-day Italian society, and lingered on a sense of lost grandeur, but also confirmed the liveliness of contemporary Italian cinema and its relevance to the international film scene. Revisiting the foundations of past Italian cinema, Sorrentino and his contemporaries are paving the way for its future.

Introduction

Joseph Luzzi

Early in Ettore Scola's masterpiece *Una giornata particolare* (*A Special Day*, 1977), the ominous unfolding of a Nazi swastika is followed by a low-angle shot of the looming Palazzo Federici apartment complex on Rome's Viale XXI Aprile. The camera pans to the entrance of the building and a man taking out the trash. It is a "particular" day, May 6, 1938, to be exact, the infamous date when Hitler visited Mussolini in Rome, and yet it is also just another day in the life of the nation. The camera continues its pan to the interior lights glowing in the dawn windows, and the stirring of daily routines in the anonymous-looking flats: children dressing, wives cleaning, and husbands heading out to work to the chirping of birds.[1] Finally, the camera settles on the window of a decidedly unglamorous-looking Sophia Loren, a diva of the Italian screen in a most unexpected role: the haggard housewife Antonietta, who will fall in love with her disgraced neighbor, the gay Gabriele (memorably played by Marcello Mastroianni), a former Fascist radio announcer who is now persona non grata because of the regime's intolerance of his sexuality. Not a word is spoken in this sequence of establishing shots. And yet the cinematography could not be more eloquent: here are Italy and the Italians, at a given time in their complicated history, in an ordinary day that will telescope into a *giornata particolare*, with all the ambiguity of that term. The day will be "special" because of two extraordinary, star-crossed meetings: the two tyrants who seek to consolidate their brutal hold over their subjugated peoples; the two lovers who are a bit like Dante's Paolo and Francesca, condemned to passions they can never truly consummate, yoked as they are in a story of love that can only have the most unhappy of endings. Scola's opening shot thus sets the stage for multiple revelations, without a word and, fittingly enough for this nation of painters, sculptors, and architects, in a series of images.

If the following pages of *Italian Cinema: From the Silent Screen to the Digital Image* can be said to have a single overriding theme and article of faith, it may very well be the relation between cinematic expression and the representation of Italian identity *(italianità)* that features so strongly in Scola's *A Special Day* and countless other Italian films. Perhaps the eminent film historian Gian Piero Brunetta said it best, when he diagnosed the astonishing intensity of exchange between cinematic language and the construction of the national self—or better, selves:

> Non solo nei momenti critici della sua storia il cinema italiano ha agito di straordinario luogo di percezione e rappresentazione di ciò che unisce il paese nella sua molteplicità di luoghi e di comportamenti, ma ha anche agito da modificatore di comportamenti, da oracolo in grado di emettere profezie o più o meno catastrofiche sul futuro. (*Identikit del cinema italiano*, 19)

> Not only has Italian cinema in crucial periods of its history played a mighty role in perceiving and representing all that unites Italy in its multiplicity of sites and behaviors, but it has also served to modify these behaviors as a kind of oracle capable of issuing varying types of prophecies, more or less dire, about the future.

Perhaps, again, such a daunting burden on filmmakers—defining the nation!—was to be expected, in a country as young as Italy (it was unified, and only tenuously so, as recently as 1861), and as varied linguistically, culturally, even emotionally as the amalgam of ancient regions, worldviews, and customs permeating the Italian peninsula. Charles De Gaulle once asked famously of the French, how can you govern a country that has over 200 varieties of cheeses? And yet France had already been a sovereign nation with a massively influential capital city and dominant language for centuries before Italian unification; if France was a country divided by a dairy product, then Italy, much more formidably, was the ultimate "geographical expression" in the notorious words of Metternich after the 1815 Congress of Vienna, whose lack of a unifying cultural discourse has been exacerbated by a historic North-South divide and the exodus of millions of its inhabitants to "Little Italies" throughout the world. Certainly, Italian cinema in all its regional and dialectal variety has reflected the kaleidoscope of *italianità* in its full diversity. Yet just as powerfully the nation's cinema has also been a place where the citizens of this remarkably diverse, often divided peninsula could discover their unifying "Italian-ness"—and not just on screen, but in the theaters themselves, which provided access to culture and a public forum for social exchange to all manner of Italians, especially the lower and less educated classes who would never dream of setting foot in an aristocratic opera house, or turning the pages of a literary classic.

Of course, the flip side of Italian film directors' drive for an understanding of the larger cultural and identity discourses driving their nation was their interest in those hidden, unspoken, and unseen spaces that also constituted the national drama. In Scola's *A Special Day*, the subject matter is in some respects supremely public, as a delirious Roman people prepares for the ceremonial handshake between Mussolini and Hitler. And yet the movie's interest is also in the irreducibly private and individual. Sophia Loren's Antonietta is the suppressed *casalinga*, housewife, whose yearnings are alien to both her husband and the masculinist regime; Marcello Mastroianni's Gabriele is the discarded "undesirable" to the Fascists because of his desires that dare not declare themselves in the homophobic air of the ruling party. The brilliance of the film, and of Italian cinema at its finest, is its ability to discover the macrocosmic understanding of what makes the Italian nation tick, while never losing sight of the individual and often discordant voices who either refused to conform to public categories or were brutally expulsed from them in the name of some revered, repressive social construct. In one of the most poignant scenes in the film, after Antonietta and Gabriele make love, he tells her that it changes nothing: he can physically perform the act of love with a woman, but never emotionally give himself over to her. Outside their apartment window, a city rejoices in the mob hysteria that attends the détente of two of the world's most powerful men; inside, a man and a woman surrender their loneliness to a kind stranger, both understanding that once they separate from each other's arms, the shadow of sorrow that brought them together will return. From the domestic space to the public sphere—from close-up to long shot, from intimate portrait to overhead pan—the images of a nation are, true to the etymology of cinema, written with light in Scola's film.

The capaciousness of this volume's subject matter is reflected in the nature of the film medium itself. From its origins, whether it was Luigi Pirandello wondering in 1929 if *il film parlante*, "the talking film," would abolish theater, or Walter Benjamin musing on the mechanical reach of film as a medium without "aura" in 1935, the new cinematic medium was both celebrated and feared for its capacity to synthesize existing art forms into a new aesthetic whole. As the chapters in this volume attest, this totalizing art form had an especially long interdisciplinary reach in Italy, as it has long engaged the talents of some of the nation's most celebrated writers, musicians, artists, and intellectuals. Perhaps Raymond Williams said it best when he described the *cinematic* as a "new mode," one that not only recast existing art forms but through its particular alchemy established new ones (*The Sociology of Culture*, 202). And perhaps it is no surprise that a culture such as Italy's, one deeply committed to interdisciplinary artistic exchange since at least the Renaissance, would prove to be such fertile ground for the cross-pollination of cinematic forms and countless other artistic media and methods.

The desire to write *Italian Cinema: From the Silent Screen to the Digital Age* sprang from a conviction that the study of Italian cinema remains the rare academic subject that is of broad interest to three usually disconnected groups: the undergraduate student, the advanced scholar, and the nonspecialist film enthusiast. Cinema continues to occupy a privileged status in the Italian cultural landscape, as evidenced by the comparatively large number of festivals and conferences held there each year.[2] Indeed, in the view of many, filmmaking represents Italy's most influential contribution to the global art scene of the last century. And so this volume reaches out to the nonacademic audience as well as the scholarly one, since a great number of people outside of the academy are lifelong connoisseurs of directors like Michelangelo Antonioni, Vittorio De Sica, Federico Fellini, Roberto Rossellini, and Luchino Visconti, as well as a plethora of Italian cinematic genres ranging from the *commedia all'italiana* to the Spaghetti Western. This volume marshals the talents and expertise of some of the world's leading scholars of Italian cinema, as well as scholars in the earlier stages of their careers, to create a comprehensive guide that covers the range of essential topics and concerns in Italy's fabled film history. Readers can expect an immersive exploration of the issues, films, and filmmakers that have given Italian cinema its enduring appeal.

Using the resources of this guide, the reader will be able to

- identify the major periods, filmmakers, films, and issues in the history of Italian cinema;
- develop a vocabulary and set of methodological approaches for studying and enjoying film in general;
- understand the historical and cultural contexts that helped shape the films and filmmakers under discussion;
- explore the abiding influence of the Italian screen by showing its impact in other arts, including literature, painting, and music;
- consider such new developments in Italian film studies as the role of documentary and television, the increased presence of women in the Italian film industry, and the wealth of social and cultural concerns that have shaped the history of the nation's cinema.

The heart of this book is the set of specially commissioned chapters by experts who offer scholars and specialists indispensable new contributions to the critical literature on their respective topics. By the same token, the chapters can also serve as a valuable research guide for undergraduates and as a logical choice for course adoption for the many instructors throughout the anglophone world who teach Italian film.

After providing a Chronology of key dates, the volume's Part 1, "Periods and Movements," covers some of the major historical issues in the study of Italian film. In Chapter 1, "Italian Silent Film," Antonio Costa examines the illustrious origins of *cinema muto*, silent cinema, and the early Italian film industry, a time of important studios like Cines in Rome and Ambrosio and Itala Film in Turin, as well as historical blockbusters like Filoteo Alberini's *La presa di Roma* (*The Taking of Rome*, 1905) and Giovanni Pastrone's *La caduta di Troia* (*The Fall of Troy*, 1910) that helped establish Italian film as a serious international rival to Hollywood. In Chapter 2, "Futurism and Film," Michael Syrimis provides a comprehensive account of the practical and theoretical issues involved in this avant-garde movement's storied interest in the emerging film medium. Vito Zagarrio's Chapter 3, "*Vincere:* The Never-Ending Story of Film and Fascism," considers the role of Benito Mussolini's Fascist government in the development of the Italian film industry as a cultural and political force. In Chapter 4, "Neorealism," Giuliana Minghelli examines the most important and influential "movement" (if one can hazard to label it with this controversial tag) in the history of Italian cinema, neorealism, the documentary-style approach to filmmaking after the Second World War that sought to record the nation's physical and moral reconstruction after twenty years of Fascism. Jumping ahead, Chapter 5, "The Orphaned Generation: Cinema of the 1980s and 1990s" by Alessia Ricciardi, surveys the films made during a period that many believe coincided with the sharp commercial and aesthetic decline of the nation's cinema. And in Chapter 6, "Persistence of Vision: Realism and the Popular in Italian Cinema of the New Millennium," Millicent Marcus discusses the ongoing relevance of Italian cinema in today's global village, by focusing on how certain contemporary directors have sought to revitalize the sense of ethical engagement that defined neorealist film.

Part 2, "Gender, Genre, and Theory," begins in Chapter 7 with Stephen Gundle's meditation on the "femme fatale," which analyzes this figure from its appearance in early works like *Cabiria* to its afterlife in more recent film. In Chapter 8, "Italian Women's Cinema and the Wounded Filmic Body," Dana Renga examines the work of major Italian woman directors, an increasingly powerful artistic group that is redefining what has historically been the nation's male-dominated film industry. In Chapter 9, "The Cinematic Evolution of *Commedia all'Italiana*," Marcia Landy analyzes a profoundly influential category of Italian film whose comic and commercial aspirations often masked sharp sociopolitical commentary on such abiding problems as the North-South divide, organized crime, and political corruption. Chapter 10, Catherine O'Rawe's "Popular Italian Cinema," contemplates the manifold ways in which supposedly "popular" cinematic forms have both accrued significant aesthetic value and provided an invaluable lens on key social issues defining the nation. In the final chapter of the section, "Italian Film Theory, 1907–2015," Gabriele Pedullà surveys the major theorists and thinkers who have advanced compelling insights into the nature of the medium and its social impact as well its broader contribution to the history of aesthetics.

Part 3, "Relations and Debates," ponders the extraordinary inter-disciplinary energy at the heart of Italian film since its inception.

In Chapter 12, "Film Music: *Kaos* and the Tavianis," Daniela Bini reads the Taviani brothers' landmark adaptation of Luigi Pirandello's work in the broader context of film's rich historical relation to music. The next chapter, Sarah Carey's "Photography and Film," analyzes how the history of photography has shaped that of cinema and discusses the ways in which Italian filmmakers have incorporated photographic techniques. In Chapter 14, "Film and Television in Italy," Stefano Baschiera discusses the historical relationship between the two media, with a focus on how the emergence of television as a powerful force in Italian life in the 1970s and up to the present has shaped the evolution of film. Chapter 15, Luca Caminati and Mauro Sassi's "Italian Documentary and the Predicaments of the Auteur," charts the historical development of Italian film documentary and argues on behalf of the inherent aesthetic values of the genre, especially in the hands of directors who produced fabled fictional works for the screen as well. Finally, in Chapter 16, Laura E. Ruberto and Kristi M. Wilson's "The Global Impact of Italian Neorealism," the authors discuss how this eminently Italian postwar film movement went on to have an international, even global, influence.

The following section, Part 4, "Films in Focus," offers specially commissioned chapters on carefully chosen masterpieces of Italian cinema, as well as on lesser-known works that represent important trends, themes, and techniques: Chapter 17, Robert Rushing on Giovanni Pastrone's *Cabiria* (1914); Chapter 18, Charles L. Leavitt IV on Giuseppe De Santis's *Bitter Rice* (1949); Chapter 19, Brendan Hennessey on Luchino Visconti's *Senso* (1954); Chapter 20, Federico Pacchioni on Federico Fellini's *La strada* (1954); Chapter 21, John David Rhodes on Michelangelo Antonioni's *L'avventura* (1960); Chapter 22, Mary Ann McDonald Carolan on Sergio Leone's *Once Upon a Time in the West* (1966); Chapter 23, Robert S. C. Gordon on Pier Paolo Pasolini's *Theorem* (1968); Chapter 24, Michael Cramer on Bernardo Bertolucci's *The Conformist* (1970); Chapter 25, Bernadette Luciano on Lina Wertmüller's *Love and Anarchy* (1973); and Chapter 26, Alan O'Leary on Marco Tullio Giordana's *The Best of Youth* (2003).

The final section, Part 5, "Behind the Scenes," analyzes elements that have not always received their due in film studies, but which are now increasingly acknowledged for their undeniable centrality to scholarship on the medium. Monica Facchini's Chapter 27 focuses on landmark developments in "Sound and Soundtrack in Italian Cinema"; Cosetta Gaudenzi's Chapter 28 discusses the capacious topic of "Screenwriting" from both a practical and a theoretical perspective; and Allison Cooper's Chapter 29, "Outdoor Cinema," considers the actual physical theaters where Italian films were screened, along with the sociocultural issues surrounding these public events and spaces.

Of course, when one is approaching a subject as vast and complex as the history of Italian film, any attempt at "comprehensiveness" is perforce doomed to incompleteness and omission. Begging the reader's understanding for any particularly glaring lacuna or absence, I ask also that the present volume be considered as much a sketch as a guide. However selective or unfinished, the contours of Italian cinema that are mapped out here will hopefully show, or at least suggest, the magnitude of what film has meant and continues to mean to Italy and all those who study its culture, especially those cinematic forms that both express the mysteries of Italian life and in no small way may even help create them.

Notes

Translations are my own.

1 I am indebted to Millicent Marcus for alerting me to the importance of perspective in Scola's film.

2 See Ricci, *Cinema and Fascism*, 30.

Bibliography

Brunetta, Gian Piero. *Identikit del cinema italiano oggi: 453 storie*. Venice: Marsilio, 2000.

Ricci, Steven. *Cinema and Fascism: Italian Film and Society, 1922–1943*. Berkeley: University of California Press, 2008.

Williams, Raymond. *The Sociology of Culture*. Chicago: University of Chicago Press, 1995.

PART ONE

Periods and Movements

1

Italian Silent Film

Antonio Costa

For a long time in Italy, little was done to deepen and spread the knowledge of silent film. Italians have neglected to set a serious policy for the recovery, conservation, and restoration of the film heritage from that era. In general, film critics seem more focused on interpretive issues, discussing, say, how Giovanni Pastrone's *Cabiria* (1914) influenced D. W. Griffith's *Intolerance* (1916). And while much has been written on how neorealism was anticipated by such works as Nino Martoglio's *Sperduti nel buio* (*Lost in the Dark*, 1914) or Gustavo Serena's *Assunta Spina* (1915), the original copies of those films have been lost. Fortunately, the situation has changed in recent decades. Film libraries and major festivals have done great recovery work on lost or forgotten films, or on films that are now close to disappearing.[1] The possibility of viewing under optimal conditions many works that had long fallen out of historical memory now enables us to revisit long-held critical clichés. The bibliography on Italian silent film has become truly impressive, and at the same time there are various editions of silent films on restored versions in DVD format.

1 The Invention of Italian Cinema

Italian cinema was born in Rome, one evening in the late summer of 1905. On September 20, the thirty-fifth anniversary of the Breach of Porta Pia, the military capture of Rome and a decisive event in the decadelong process of Italian unification known as the Risorgimento. Filoteo Alberini, cofounder and artistic director of the Primo Stabilimento di Manifattura Cinematografica Alberini and Santoni, had the idea of projecting his first film, *La presa di Roma (The Capture of Rome)*, on a large screen set up at the site where soldiers had entered the Papal State, forcing Pope Pius IX to surrender.[2] In the very place where the final event of the Risorgimento took place, the film commemorating it was shown. Cinema, which was then still considered a vaudeville sideshow, thus evolved into an instrument capable of capturing an episode that had produced lacerations in the social conscience. Although the Porta Pia breach evoked "memories of an outrage" for the church, for the Italian state it was "a sign of victory."[3] Italian cinema was born, therefore, as a public event that called into question historical memory, social conscience, and opposing passions that were lived in a collective dimension, in the "public square."[4]

Many of the hallmarks of Italian cinema, which would gather momentum over time, were present in this inaugural event, from its technical means of production to its mix of public ritual, scenic installation, and publicity stunt. In the wake of this "media event" that the historian Aldo Bernardini (*Cinema muto*, 26) defined as the true masterpiece of Alberini, his production company realized that they were on to something. The following year, thanks to new financial contributions, the company became a joint stock venture called Cines, destined to become one of the most prestigious and enduring brands in the history of Italian cinema. But at the time it was only one of several production companies of the nascent film industry.

2 The Production System

What we can call *polycentrism* was a characteristic feature of Italian filmmaking in the era of silent film. Unlike what would happen with the centralizing policy of Fascism, which culminated in the creation of Cinecittà in 1937, the Italian film industry's origins were shaped by the presence of several production centers located in various cities, even small ones, in a kind of productive federalism. This situation would attenuate, if not disappear altogether, in the 1930s. But before then, many cities of differing cultural and economic characteristics contributed to the growth of Italian film: Turin, Naples, Milan, and naturally Rome, but also such smaller urban centers as Genoa and Catania. Yet at the same time this disjointed polycentrism was also a weakness of the Italian economy because of the fragmented nature of the investments held by a myriad of small companies with limited business skills. In the beginning of the century, it was actually Turin, and not Rome, that had the largest film production center, which was aided by the entrepreneurial activism of a city that also developed the first Italian car industry. Fiat was created in Turin in 1899, and its rapid growth would soon intertwine with the rising fortunes of the city's film industry. If Turin achieved its international success through large, spectacular films that reached their apex with *Cabiria* in 1914, Naples rose to prominence as a film center with strong regionalist and "vernacular" traits.[5] Naples was also the home of Gustavo Lombardo, future founder of the important production company Titanus.[6] Cultured and progressive, Lombardo developed a coherent promotion policy for cinema through his magazine *Lux* and distributed films such as *Dante's Inferno* (1911) as well as Futurist works including *Vita futurista* (*Futurist Lifestyle*, 1916) by Arnaldo Ginna (now lost) and *Thaïs* (1917) by Anton Giulio Bragaglia.

3 Birth of the Feature Film and the Epic-historical Genre

The first Italian feature film was *Dante's Inferno*, produced by Milano Films and directed by Adolfo Padovan, Francesco Bertolini, and Giuseppe de Liguoro. It was inspired by the first canticle of Dante's *Divine Comedy* and had a decisive impact on the artistic and industrial development of Italian cinema. At the very moment it started to undertake complex and challenging productions, the early film industry turned to Dante's text, a work that was surrounded like no other by an aura of prestige and classicism, while also being deeply rooted in the popular imagination. In the film version of Dante's *Inferno*, Italian cinema found an original way to access the themes and iconography of the fantasy genre, imbuing it with a unique civil and political dimension. *Dante's Inferno*, which premiered at the Teatro Mercadante in Naples on the fiftieth anniversary of the proclamation of the Kingdom of Italy (1861–1911)—and which was projected in the presence of such prestigious intellectuals as Benedetto Croce and Matilde Serao—ended with an image of the monument to Dante in the city of Trento, then still under Austrian rule. This evocation of Dante's universe acquired a great political significance: the screening took place on the eve of the outbreak of the First World War, at the end of which would come the annexation of Trento and Trieste to Italy.[7]

Though it broke away from current productions, *Dante's Inferno* had some affinity with the historical costume genre. From *Gli ultimi giorni di Pompei* (*The Last Days of Pompeii*), directed by Luigi Maggi in 1908 for Ambrosio Film of Turin and based on the novel by E. G. Bulwer-Lytton, Italian cinema achieved great success abroad, reaching its peak with *Cabiria*. Other titles that contributed to the great fortune of the epic-historical genre include: *L'Odissea* (*The Odyssey*, 1911), Giuseppe de Liguoro's adaptation of the Homeric epic (Milano Films); *La Gerusalemme liberata* (*Jerusalem Delivered*, 1911), a Cines production by Enrico Guazzoni, who also directed *Quo vadis?* (1913) based on the eponymous novel by Henryk Sienkiewicz; and *La caduta di Troia* (*The Fall of Troy*, 1911), an Itala Film production also by Pastrone.

There are various reasons for the good fortune and strategic importance of this popular genre in the development of Italian film. The genre had its roots in a past rife with historical, artistic, and literary riches, traces of which are still evident in the Italian cultural landscape today. The increasing length of films made cinema competitive with the more established media of theater and opera. Moreover, early cinema's iconographic references, literary sources, and artistic ambitions attracted a large middle- and upper-class audience, which had originally rejected the supposed lowbrow of film spectacle. Filmgoers were seduced by the magnificent scenic innovations, accuracy of the productions, and technical innovations of the historical cinematic blockbusters. Among these films, the most important techniques were the expressive use of light and the systematic use of camera movements that enhanced the impressive scenery and crowd scenes, and which also gave the sequences a rhythmic and spatial organization. Such were the extraordinary artistic and spectacular results of *Cabiria*, for example, that the film exerted great influence in the United States in scenes like the Babylonian episode of *Intolerance* by D. W. Griffith in 1916.

In Italy, the epic-historical genre was a rather composite phenomenon. On the one hand, it brought together literary aspects that were exploited with entrepreneurial flair, drawing on the success of a very popular narrative genre. But the epic-historical film also contained an educational and pedagogical intent, as it reflected the basic classics of the Italian school curriculum. So the cinematic historical blockbuster became a kind of experimental laboratory as well as a lucrative cultural product for mass consumption, which undoubtedly explains the involvement of the poet Gabriele D'Annunzio in the making of *Cabiria*.

4 D'Annunzio and Pirandello

The presence of the larger-than-life D'Annunzio on the public and literary scene in Italy's first two decades of the twentieth century was so pronounced that it also influenced the birth and development of movie stardom. The links between cinema and the most famous Italian writer of the time were long-standing. Many of D'Annunzio's works (literary and theatrical) were often brought to the screen, and his efforts for the film *Cabiria* involved him directly in a production of great artistic and economic value. Fame and the force of attraction were irresistible for D'Annunzio, the authentic cultural star of his era, and not only in the literary field. In 1911–12, Ambrosio Film of Turin presented six films based on his writings: *Jorio's Daughter* (1911); *La fiaccola sotto il moggio* (*Blood Vengeance*, 1911); *An Autumn Sunset Dream* (1911); *La Gioconda* (*Love Reconquered*, 1912); *L'innocente* (*The Innocent*, 1912); and *La nave* (*The Venetian Tribune Marcus*, 1912). The peak of D'Annunzio's fame in Italian film was in *Cabiria*, which he agreed to sign as his own work, although his participation was rather marginal. The film posters in Italy read, *Cabiria. visione storica del III sec. a.C. di Gabriele D'Annunzio* (*Cabiria, Historical Vision of the Third Century B.C. by Gabriele D'Annunzio*), while the French advertising headlines ran, *Cabiria, Admirable œuvre de Gabriele D'Annunzio* (*Cabiria, Acclaimed Work of Gabriele D'Annunzio*).[8] D'Annunzio, in fact, merely imposed his own seal on the film's verbose captions and helped choose the names of the principal characters, including the heroine and title character, Cabiria. So he behaved like the latest fashion designers who merely "sign" a production that is not entirely their own, and who only contribute their marketing strategy or some idea about the name of the product and its packaging.

The advantages for Itala Film because of the involvement of D'Annunzio, who was paid the astronomical sum of 50,000 gold lire, were palpable. The film, whose technical means and special effects have no precedent either in Italy or abroad, was enhanced by the aura of his literary, cultural, and artistic prestige. There were, on the other hand, negative effects: the seal of D'Annunzio and his literary aura obscured for a long time the most innovative aspects of the film, especially the authentic cinematic brilliance of Pastrone.

D'Annunzio announced, for merely promotional reasons, his deep interest in film in a famous interview with *Corriere della Sera* (February 28, 1914), later incorporated into the *Del cinematografo come strumento di liberazione e come arte di trasfigurazione* (*On Cinematography as an Instrument of Liberation and Art of Transfiguration*). The interview represented D'Annunzio's attempt to insert film into his own personal and poetic mythology. But otherwise he remained artistically aloof from the medium.

In addition to D'Annunzio, the early Italian film industry sought to involve other writers, adapting their texts for the screen as well as seeking their direct collaboration as screenwriters. Those who took part included Roberto Bracco, Lucio D'Ambra, Salvatore Di Giacomo, Antonio Fogazzaro, Guido Gozzano, and Giovanni Verga. An author with a complex relation to cinema was Luigi Pirandello, a legendary writer on the level of his contemporary D'Annunzio. Pirandello viewed movies, foremost, as a source of inspiration for his literary work. Set in the world of cinema is his *Si gira (Shoot!)*, the novel published in the journal *Nuova Antologia* in 1915 and eventually reprinted as *Quaderni di Serafino Gubbio operatore* (*The Notebooks of Serafino Gubbio, Cinematograph Operator*) in 1925. The novel tries to render accurately the various aspects of film production. It reveals an early interest in the cinematic objects, techniques, and situations of a universe that were totally new to the literary field. The work is by far the only occasion in which film is fully absorbed into Pirandello's poetics, and historically it is a major text in showing how the new aesthetic and technological reality of cinema evolved into an object of literary treatment.

And yet, it was not until the 1920s that Pirandello's writings were brought to screen. The best adaptation of his work appeared during that decade: Marcel L'Herbier's *Feu Mathias Pascal* (*The Late Matthias Pascal*, 1925), based on Pirandello's novel *Il fu Mattia Pascal* (1904). Before that date, Pirandello-derived films relied almost exclusively on his short stories.[9] Ironically, just as Pirandello was developing the idea of the superiority of silent film, or rather a film without words based on the pure power of images and their rhythmic organization, Italian cinema produced its first *sound* film, *La canzone dell'amore* (*The Song of Love*, 1930) by Gennaro Righelli, based on the short story "In silenzio" ("Silence") by Pirandello.[10]

5 Star-system Italian Style

"D'Annunzio is for literature what Lyda Borelli is for superstardom": this statement by Pietro Bianchi (*Francesca Bertini*, 4) perfectly sums up the D'Annunzian character of Italian stardom. Even female stardom felt his effect, as D'Annunzio created the prototypical diva with Elena Muti, protagonist of the novel *Il piacere* (*Pleasure*, 1889). Italian cinema's female star system is full of names and prominent figures: Lyda Borelli, Francesca Bertini, Pina Menichelli, Italia Almirante, Diana Karenne, Rina de Liguoro, Soava Gallone, and last but not least—even with only one active film, *Cenere* (*Ashes*, 1917) by Febo Mari—Eleonora Duse, D'Annunzio's lover and the most prominent figure of the Italian stage, who migrated to screen late in her career. Among the divas of Italian cinema, Borelli was certainly the one who had the most influence in the history of film costume, even though her career lasted only five years, from 1913, when she debuted with *Ma l'amore mio non muore* (*Love Everlasting*) by Mario Caserini, to 1918, when she abandoned the screen after her marriage to the nobleman Count Vittorio Cini.[11] Such was her renown that terms like *borellismo* (Borelli-ism) and *borelleggiare* (to imitate Borelli's style) were included in dictionaries of the Italian language. The acting technique of Borelli was essentially based on the body's ability to produce signs of troubled inner life, imbuing her gestures with undulations and gestures that suggest the expressive lines of Symbolist painting or, better, the graphics of Art Nouveau (known as *Stile Liberty* in Italy). It is difficult for today's audience not to feel as though Borelli is "forcing it" with her exaggerated acting, which can now seem ridiculous. But as with any film from the silent era, it is necessary to interpret the gestures according to the expressive code of the time, which was obviously not in the realistic key of much modern sound cinema.

Other actresses were more realistic in their technique. Bertini had a more versatile range than Borelli, evidenced by her ability to move from the rarefied and lunar figure of Pierrot in *Histoire d'un Pierrot* (*Pierrot the Prodigal*, 1914) by Baldassarre Negroni to the passionate commoner of

Assunta Spina a year later. Bertini also soon left the set for marriage in 1921, but unlike Borelli she never entirely abandoned film.[12] Yet even Bertini had many D'Annunzio-like gestures. In *Mariute* (1918), a film of self-promotion and nationalistic propaganda, she dedicated herself to grueling nighttime readings that wreaked emotional havoc, causing her to arrive late to the set on the following day. What kind of literature this could be, the film caption does not say. But perhaps the star herself lets us know. In one of her autobiographical articles published in the magazine *Film*, she recalled her joy when she received some books by D'Annunzio from her friend, the great Neapolitan poet Salvatore Di Giacomo: "I stole hours from my work and sleep, and I spent long days and long nights in those books trying to decipher their mysteries, discover their hidden beauties, and savor their precious scent."[13]

Italian silent film was permeated with femme fatales of incomparable life trajectories and disturbing passions. The female star system offered models far from the reality of subordination and marginalization in which most Italian women lived in Italy's inveterately patriarchal society. In the paroxysms of desire that riled the femme fatale, Italian female moviegoers were given a vision—if only at the level of the imagination—of possible escape from their traditional roles. The actresses who played these characters were not only divas and actresses; they became de facto directors of themselves, thus changing the very nature of the Italian star system. This is particularly true in the cases of Bertini, Karenne, and Duse.[14] Few male actors reached this level of stardom. The exception was probably Amleto Novelli, who, in the course of a brilliant career that ended with his untimely death at thirty-eight, played some of the most fascinating characters in the era's historical films, especially Tancredi in the two adaptations of *Gerusalemme liberata* (1911 and 1918) by Guazzoni. In speaking about the male star system, one must single out *i forzuti* (the strongmen), such heroes of athletic acrobatic films as Bartolomeo Pagano, the Maciste of *Cabiria*, and the inimitable figure of Emilio Ghione, famous for the romantic and gloomy pulp hero Za La Mort. Through his irregular behavior and transgressions, Ghione revived the myth of the tragic artist, whose dramatic traits merged with those of his actual life.[15]

6 Strongmen and Clowns

Beginning with the Carthaginian strongman Maciste played by Pagano in Pastroni's *Cabiria* in 1914, a series of mythological characters with equally exotic names appeared: Sansone or Samson (Luciano Albertini), Ajax (Carlo Aldini), and Saetta (Domenico Mario Gambino). These *forzuti* were the masculine opposite of the D'Annunzian diva. Before Pagano's success in *Cabiria*, this unlikely actor had been a dockworker in Genoa.[16] His burly character owed his name, Maciste, to D'Annunzio, who personally chose it (Maciste, D'Annunzio noted, "was the ancient name of the demigod Hercules"). One might even consider the mythology of the strongman as a popular version of D'Annunzio's myth of the superman.

A mixture between real life and fiction, so typical of the star system, defines the Maciste-Bartolomeo Pagano films. *Maciste alpino* (*The Warrior,* 1916), directed by Luigi Maggi and Luigi Romano Borgnetto (with the supervision of Pastrone), brings the star Maciste to the front of the First World War, as if to suggest that Pagano could abandon the ancient clothes he wore in *Cabiria* and now don the uniform of an *alpino* (alpine) soldier. Links exist between the military variants of the Maciste franchise and D'Annunzio's exploits at the time, as the ideologies of the *forzuti* and the militarism of D'Annunzio seemingly converge in his celebrated occupation of the city of Fiume during the First World War.[17] But the fame of the *forzuti* and D'Annunzio would be eclipsed by the Fascist dictator Benito Mussolini, who in propaganda changed with incredible ease and speed from the clothes of a statesman to those of a peasant dedicated to the harvest, or from an airplane pilot to a horseman and even a good family man.

Much less original are the Italian comedy films of the silent era, which were largely derivative of their French antecedents. But nevertheless they had great popular success. Kri Kri, Cretinetti, Robinet, Fricot, Tontolini, and Polidor were the bizarre nicknames of characters in slapstick comedies, which were essentially based on gestural comedy effects, with their spasmodic movements and scenes of disaster induced by their rambling behaviors. The creators of these characters were actors who came from the circus, variety shows, and popular theater. Film added to all of this its magical ability to play on rhythmic effects and change them at will through editing.

Italian companies attempted to beat the French at their own comedic game by taking away their best comedians, eliminating the competition by offering them advantageous contracts. It is for this reason that the most famous actors of early Italian comic film were given such Gallic names as André Deed, the creator of the cheerfully destructive character Cretinetti; Ferdinand Guillaume, creator first of Tontolini and then Polidor; and Marcel Fabre, the creator of Robinet. Some of the films in this genre were quite original, especially a curious film adaptation of Carlo Collodi's famous novel *Pinocchio* by Giulio Antamoro in 1911, which featured the mimic-gestural performance of Ferdinand Guillaume in the role of the wooden puppet as well as spurious elements from the surging world of American film: Pinocchio and Geppetto end up in America, where the first is worshiped as a god and the second is likely to end up roasted. A typically American happy ending is assured by the arrival of Canadian soldiers, who rescue the puppet from Indian tribes. In recent times, thanks to the rediscovery and restoration of silent films, it is possible to appreciate the mixture of slapstick comedy and fantastic adventures in many of this era's comic works.[18]

7 The Crisis of the 1920s and the Rise of Fascism

In the 1920s, Italian cinema experienced a long and difficult crisis caused, among other things, by the bankruptcy of the Unione Cinematografica Italiana (UCI), which had failed, in a mix of megalomania and entrepreneurial ineptitude, to transform the production company into a trust. As a consequence, Italian cinema failed to innovate and ended up recycling old ideas like the historical-mythological genre and the diva film, which had ceased to be an artistic force before the First World War.[19] The advent of Fascism in 1922 made the situation even more difficult, partly because the new regime initially did not pay particular attention to the film industry. In fact, the relationship between cinema and Fascism during the silent period remains an underdeveloped area of scholarship. This relationship has been studied mainly for the period of the 1930s, and in particular since 1934, when Fascism began to intervene actively in the field of film. It is, instead, crucial to study the earlier period, especially in relation to the climate of conservatism that dominated most of the Italian culture of the 1920s, including cinema.[20] For example, in *Il grido dell'aquila* (*The Eagle's Cry*, 1923) by Mario Volpe, the themes of Fascism's political culture are already well defined.[21] These themes would be more formally refined in the more technically complex works of Alessandro Blasetti, Giovacchino Forzano, and Luis Trenker.[22]

Overall, Italian cinema stalled in the 1920s after a decade of growth in the 1910s, especially in the historical-mythological genre that encompassed Italy's literary and theatrical tradition. There was also growth in the diva film, where new modes of acting were developed and new lifestyles portrayed on screen, and in the vital relation between film and literature through the adaptation of literary classics like Dante's *Inferno* and the contemporary writings of D'Annunzio and Pirandello. Popular entertainment acts, relying on such "strong men" as Maciste and a cohort of popular comedians, also played a major role in the growth of Italian film industry. Unfortunately, Futurism, the artistic movement developed in Italy in the 1910s, failed to leave a mark on Italian film, although it influenced movie making in other countries, especially France and Russia, with its glorification of technology, speed, rhythm, and the myths of the modern city. As a consequence, silent films of the 1920s were in full bloom in various European countries, as well as in the United States, while Italian cinema experienced one of the greatest crunches in its illustrious history. This situation was a direct consequence of a profound crisis in Italian society, as it experienced the rise of Fascism and its reactionary turn. Other, connected reasons explain the implosion of Italian film industry. For example, early cinema in Italy was based on dated production modes, tied to preindustrial forms of organization, and incapable of handling competition from more advanced foreign cinematography. Yet, as we saw in the 1910s, Italian cinema succeeded then in discovering elements of originality that have long been internationally recognized. Such innovative feats of Italian early film production deserve further investigation. Fortunately, significant progress is being made in the recovery and restoration of the silent film heritage, bringing us ever more deeply inside the achievements of this remarkable cinematic era.

Notes

1 Organizations dedicated to restoring and studying Italian silent film include the Cineteca di Bologna and its annual event "Il cinema ritrovato"; the Pordenone Silent Film Festival, organized by the Cineteca del Friuli in Gemona; and the Museo Nazionale del Cinema in Turin.

2 On the film by Alberini, see Canosa, *La Presa di Roma*; Musumeci and Toffetti, *From "La presa di Roma" to "Il piccolo garibaldino."*

3 Caracciolo, *Rome*, 165–72.

4 Bondanella sees in this event the first example of that "civic function" that Italian cinema would play in the years of neorealism and beyond (*History of Italian Cinema*, 5).

5 Among the prominent exemplars of this trend was Elvira Notari, one of the first female directors in the history of cinema. Her films were often inspired by the themes of Neapolitan songs and reached a wide audience, both in the south of Italy and abroad, especially in countries with a strong presence of Italian immigrants.

6 The company Gustavo Lombardo (CODE) became Titanus in 1928 and moved fromNaples to Rome. After the death of Lombardo in 1951, and under the guidance of his son Goffredo, it became one of the most important Italian production companies, producing films of Federico Fellini, Luchino Visconti (including *Rocco and His Brothers* and *The Leopard*), Dino Risi, Valerio Zurlini, and Ermanno Olmi. See Bernardini and Martinelli, *Titanus*.

7 This image, which originally concluded the film, does not appear in the copy preserved in the Cineteca Nazionale of Rome, as censors eliminated it for the film's re-release in 1914, when Italy had not yet entered the war and Italians did not want to provoke Austria. The monument to Dante is instead visible in the English copy of the National Film and Television Archive in London, where, however, it appears at the beginning of the film and not at the end. See Canosa, *La presa di Roma*, 36.

8 See the extraordinary iconographic documentation collected in Alovisio and Barbera, *Cabiria & Cabiria*.

9 Films based on Pirandello's short works include: *Il crollo* (*The Crack-Up*, 1920) by Mario Gargiulo; *Il lume dell'altra casa* (*The Light of the Other House*, 1920) by Ugo Gracci; *Lo scaldino* (*The Heater*, 1920) by Augusto

Genina; *Ma non è una cosa seria* (*But It Isn't Serious*, 1921) by Augusto Camerini; *La rosa* (*The Rose*, 1921) by Arnaldo Frateili; and *Il viaggio* (*The Voyage*, 1921) by Gennaro Righelli.

10 For Pirandello's opinions on the relationship between silent films and talkies, see Callari, *Pirandello e il cinema*, 120–27.

11 The major achievements of Borelli's career include *Marcia nuziale* (*Wedding March*, 1915); *Fior di male* (*Flower of Evil*, 1915); and *Malombra* (1917).

12 In the film *Novecento* (1976) by Bernardo Bertolucci, she appeared in a brief role in the guise of a nun. In 1982, she appeared in the documentary *The Last Diva* by Gianfranco Mingozzi. The Mingozzi documentary and the film *Assunta Spina* were collected in the DVD *The Queen of Italian Silent Screen: Francesca Bertini* (Kino Video, New York). Among her silent films are *Idillio tragico* (*Tragic Romance*, 1912); *Lagrime e sorrisi* (*Tears and Smiles*, 1912); *La maestrina* (*The Teacher*, 1913); *Tramonto* (*Sunset*, 1913); *Fedora* (1916); *Malia* (*Enchantment*, 1917); and *La serpe* (*The Poison Mood*, 1919).

13 The quotation is from *Art and Life of Francesca Bertini*, the second episode of an autobiographical writing appeared in *Cinema*, no. 29, August 13, 1938.

14 See, in this regard, the contributions of Dall'Asta (Bertini), Jandelli (Karenne) and Dagrada (Duse) in Dall'Asta, *Non solo dive*. See also Jandelli, *Le dive italiane*.

15 The cycle in six episodes entitled *I topi grigi* is one of the rare Ghione works available today. Ghione is also the author of a curious autobiography that does not distinguish between his role as author and character. See Ghione, *L'ombra di Za la Mort*; and Lotti, *Emilio Ghione*.

16 See the book with an enclosed DVD edited by Dagna and Gianetto, *Maciste*.

17 In 1919, after the end of World War 1, D'Annunzio led an expedition of several thousand Royal Army rebels and occupied the city of Fiume (now Rijeka in Croatia), declaring its annexation to the Kingdom of Italy. The Italian government opposed him in every way, and in December 1920 put an end to the expedition, which in many ways anticipated the methods and ideology of Fascism.

18 See, for example, *Le avventure straordinarissime di Saturnino Farandola* by Marcel Fabre (*The Extraordinary Adventures of Saturnino Farandola*, 1914) and *L'uomo meccanico* by André Deed (*The Mechanical Man*, 1921), which combines burlesque with fantasy and science fiction.

19 Brunetta, *Il cinema muto*, 279–91.

20 See Costa, *Impossible Voyages*, 300–323.

21 See Sorlin, *Il grido dell'aquila*, 251–57.

22 Volpe connected the Risorgimento, populism, and the exaltation of the rural world, in opposition to that of the blue collar workers. His recovery of popular traditions, including the masks of *commedia dell'arte*, aimed at celebrating an exasperated nationalism.

Bibliography

Alovisio, Silvio and Alberto Barbera, eds. *Cabiria & Cabiria*. Turin and Milan: Museo Nazionale del Cinema and Il Castoro, 2006.

Bernardini, Aldo and Vittorio Martinelli, eds. *Titanus: La storia e tutti i film di una grande casa di produzione*, Milan: Coliseum, 2006.

Bernardini, Aldo. *Cinema muto italiano*. Vol. 2. *Industria e organizzazione dello spettacolo 1905-1909*. Bari: Laterza, 1981.

Bianchi, Pietro. *Francesca Bertini e le dive del cinema muto*. Turin: UTET, 1969.

Bondanella, Peter. *A History of Italian Cinema*. New York: Continuum, 2009.

Brunetta, Gian Piero. *Il cinema muto italiano. Da "La presa di Roma" a "Sole," 1905-1929*. Bari: Laterza, 2008.

Callari, Francesco, ed. *Pirandello e il cinema*. Venice: Marsilio, 1991.

Canosa, Michele, ed. *A nuova luce: Cinema muto italiano 1*. Atti del Convegno Internazionale. Bologna, November 12-13, 1999. Bologna: CLUEB, 2000.

Canosa, Michele, *1905. La presa di Roma*. Recco: Le mani, 2006.

Canosa, Michele, *Cento anni fa. Inferno di Francesco Bertolini, Adolfo Padovani e Giuseppe de Liguoro*. Bologna: Cineteca di Bologna, 2011.

Caracciolo, Alberto. "Roma." In *I luoghi della memoria: Simboli e miti dell'Italia unita*. Ed. Mario Isnenghi. Bari: Laterza, 1996.

Caracciolo, Alberto. "Impossible Voyages and Extraordinary Adventures in Early Science Fiction Cinema: From Robida to Méliès and Marcel Fabre." In *Fantastic Voyages of the Cinematic Imagination: Georges Méliès' Trip to the Moon*. Ed. Matthew Solomon. Albany: State University of New York Press: 2011.

Dagna, Stella and Claudia Gianetto, eds. *Maciste l'uomo forte*. Bologna: Cineteca di Bologna, 2009. Book and DVD.

Dall'Asta, Monica. *Un cinéma musclé: Le surhomme dans le cinéma muet italien 1913-1926*. Crisnée: Yellow Now, 1992.

Dall'Asta, Monica, ed. *Non solo dive: Pioniere del cinema italiano*. Bologna: Cineteca di Bologna, 2008.

Ghione, Emilio. *L'ombra di Za la Mort*. Milan: Bietti, 1930.

Jandelli, Cristina. *Le dive italiane del cinema muto*. Palermo: L'Epos, 2006.

Lotti, Denis. *Emilio Ghione l'ultimo apache: Vita e film di un divo italiano*. Bologna: Cineteca di Bologna, 2008.

Musumeci Mario and Sergio Toffetti, eds. *From "La presa di Roma" to "Il piccolo garibaldino": Risorgimento, massoneria e istituzioni: l'immagine della nazione nel cinema muto (1905-1909)*. Roma, Gangemi, 2007. Book and DVD.

Sorlin, Pierre. "Il grido dell'aquila": Ultima tappa del primo cinema italiano." In *A nuova luce: Cinema muto italiano 1*. Ed. Michele Canosa, Atti del Convegno Internazionale. Bologna, November 12-13, 1999. Bologna: CLUEB, 2000.

2

Futurism and Film

Michael Syrimis

The notion of Futurist cinema has always posed a challenge to critics: though the Futurists celebrated the medium's structural and ideological affinities to their movement, they experimented with filmmaking only transiently.[1] "Cinematografia futurista," the first Futurist manifesto on film, written in 1916 by the movement's founder Filippo Tommaso Marinetti and five of his collaborators—Bruno Corra, Emilio Settimelli, Arnaldo Ginna, Giacomo Balla, and Remo Chiti—proclaims Futurism's affinity with the young and growing medium: "Il cinematografo, nato da pochi anni, può sembrare già futurista, cioè privo di passato e libero di tradizioni . . . Noi vediamo in esso la possibilità di un'arte eminentemente futurista" (Cinema, born only a few years ago, may already seem Futurist, that is, lacking a past and free of traditions. . . . We see in it the possibility of an art that is eminently Futurist).[2]

Defying the expectations created by the manifesto's vigorous endorsement of the medium, the filmic material that the Futurists produced consists of only three projects. I am referring to the works completed by artists working within the movement and remaining faithful to its program, specifically, the 1916 film *Vita futurista* (*Futurist Life*), the late 1910s filmscript *Velocità* (*Speed*), and the early 1930s film *Velocità*. To be sure, in a broader view, Futurist cinema may be discussed in relation to artists working independently, whether in Italy or abroad, whose projects resonate with Futurist aesthetics. Some notable examples are the experiments in *cinepittura* (cine-painting) of the brothers Arnaldo Ginna and Bruno Corra prior to their affiliation with the movement, Aldo Molinari's 1914 film *Mondo Baldoria* (*World Revelry*), and films from the later European avant-gardes. Particularly noteworthy in this respect is the work of Anton

Giulio Bragaglia, whose affiliation with the Futurist movement was short-lived. Bragaglia's remarkable film *Thaïs* (1916) is to my knowledge the only extant Italian film from the 1910s made by an artist with strong—if temporary—ties to the movement, which explains perhaps why readers often characterize it as the exemplary film of Futurism despite its rather indirect or subtle Futurist attributes.[3]

In 1916, while writing the manifesto, the Futurists also made *Vita futurista*, the single film officially launched as Futurist during the movement's early, most revolutionary or "heroic" phase.[4] Except for a few short fragments, the film is now lost.[5] Probably written in the late 1910s, Marinetti's script *Velocità* was never made into a film.[6] Finally, in 1930–31, the Futurist artist Pippo Oriani collaborated with writers Tina Cordero and Guido Martina in making *Velocità*, the only surviving Futurist film. Though unrelated to Marinetti's script bearing this title, *Velocità* actualizes some of the stylistic objectives of the 1916 manifesto.[7] This material does not approach the Futurists' volume of work in other areas, such as literature, theater, or painting. The same is true of theory. Against their more rigorous reflections on other cultural phenomena, the Futurists' other writings on cinema add little, if anything, to the 1916 manifesto, which remains the single substantial delineation of Futurist film aesthetics.[8] I will discuss the Futurists' views on cinema and their major collaborative project, *Vita futurista*, and offer some remarks on their failure to further exploit the medium that they themselves praised as "eminently Futurist."[9]

Driven by the rapid advancements in technology at the turn of the century, the Futurists embarked on voicing the effects of technology on sensibility and the new demands imposed upon culture. The dynamism of daily life associated with the era's revolutionary scientific developments—the high pace of industrial production, the spatiotemporal relations established by new means of transportation such as automobiles and airplanes, the transformed image and invigorating rhythm of urban centers, and the awe inspired by modern weaponry—gave rise to a new sensibility tied to such things as movement, speed, innovation, vitality, and belligerence. This new sensibility in turn fostered hostility to rest, slowness, tradition, apathy, pacifism, and analytical thinking. To honor the era's new sensibility, Futurism devised an avant-garde aesthetic in defiance of traditional art and thought, with its supposedly dismal sanctuaries—museums and libraries—all of which the Futurists disdainfully labeled as *passéist*. The first Futurist manifesto, whose publication in the Parisian newspaper *Le figaro* in February 1909 marked the founding of the movement in an international platform, enumerates the drives of the Futurist mind-set: rebellion, movement, speed, and war; the destruction of museums and libraries; and modern urbanity embodied in large crowds, railway stations, steamers, and airplanes (*TIF*, 10–11). Such notions recurred in different contexts in the numerous manifestos and works of various aesthetic forms that the Futurists produced for three decades, tackling every manifestation of cultural, social, and political life: architecture, literature, music, the visual arts, education, fashion, and more.

A young medium arising amid the technological inventions of the new era, cinema quickly claimed a large and diverse audience and became a vital component of modern experience. For Futurism, film provided the ideal means to envision a decisive flight from an asphyxiating cultural tradition, while it stood as the aesthetic paradigm of the modern technological era that sparked Futurism's conception in the first place. Its significance for Futurism was not merely symbolic. The 1916 manifesto, in defining the innovative techniques that would culminate in Futurist cinema, paid close attention to the possibilities offered by the medium's specific technology, which encapsulated montage, animation, and multiple exposure.

The mere ability to show moving photographs spoke to Futurism's attraction to movement as a driving force of modern experience. Yet it was montage, the filmic property par excellence, that provided the visual counterpart to analogy, previously launched by Marinetti as Futurism's foremost literary technique: "L'analogia non è altro che l'amore profondo che collega le cose distanti, apparentemente diverse ed ostili" (Analogy is nothing more than the deep love that connects distant, seemingly different, and hostile things) (*TIF*, 48). In poetry, analogy involves the successive presentation of nouns with no evident link between them. Its aptness is born out of modernity's spatiotemporal relations: "Siccome la velocità aerea ha moltiplicato la nostra conoscenza del mondo, la percezione per analogia diventa sempre più naturale per l'uomo. Bisogna dunque sopprimere il *come*, il *quale*, il *così*, il *simile a*" (Since aerial speed has multiplied our knowledge of the world, perception by analogy becomes ever more natural for man. It is therefore necessary to suppress the *like*, the *which*, the *thus*, the *similar to*) (47). In cinema, analogy is achieved through montage, in successive images the relations among which are ambiguous: "Se vorremo esprimere lo stato angoscioso di un nostro protagonista invece di descriverlo nelle sue varie fasi di dolore daremo un'equivalente impressione con lo spettacolo di una montagna frastagliata e cavernosa" (If we want to express the anguished state of one of our protagonists, instead of describing him in his various stages of pain, we will give an equivalent impression with the sight of a jagged and cavernous mountain) (141). The indefinite link between the image of the man and that of the mountain, heightened by the medium's muteness, is in no way inferior to the narrative linearity and transparency found in traditional performances. Rather, the ambiguity is meant to direct the spectators' imagination toward the articulation of multiple meanings, as the authors imply in an ironic appeal to "comprehensibility": "In tal modo i nostri personaggi saranno perfettamente comprensibili come *se parlassero*" (In this way, our characters will be perfectly comprehensible *as if they spoke*) (142).[10]

Film technology offers unique ways of making a bizarre spectacle out of tradition. Metaphors found in canonical poetry could be directly transcribed into images. A filmic rendering of Giosuè Carducci's verse "il cor mi fuggì su 'l Tirreno" (My heart fled to the Tyrrhenian Sea) would show the poet whose heart "gli sbotta fuori dalla giacca e vola come un enorme pallone rosso sul golfo di Rapallo" (pops out of his jacket and flies like a huge red balloon over the Gulf of Rapallo) (*TIF*, 142). As the hilarious scene delights a public that craves innovation and yawns at the old esoteric verses, the gesture announces that in today's world, where technology permits the material imaging of anything imaginable, conventional literary tropes lose their cultural relevance. The manifesto proposes numerous techniques relying on film specificity. The *simultaneity* and *interpenetration* of diverse times and places—two recurrent motifs in Futurism, where modernity's mobility heightens the ability to perceive different times and places all at once—are possible through montage or multiple exposures, while animation gives life to dramatic events between objects. The authors envisage further astonishing effects: the harmonies and symphonies of gestures, colors, and lines; unrealistic recreations of the human body; scenes of disproportion, such as a man drinking up an entire lake through a gigantic straw; and dramas of humanized or animated letters.[11]

The pursuit of an abstract style in defiance of photographic verisimilitude and narrative transparency aims at something more specific than the Futurists' usual attack on tradition. It promotes an alternative to the realist style that dominated film production at that time. In reading the manifesto, one must distinguish between two notions of *cinematografo*. At times it refers to a technological apparatus in its pure form, a tabula rasa sort of thing, available to a diverse range of aesthetic actualizations and social applications. At other times it refers to an institution, the deployment of the apparatus for a particular set of aesthetic and social uses by the Italian film industry of the mid-1910s—when cinema had grown into a pervasive form of mass entertainment, with claims to cultural legitimacy, an edifying mission, and a diverse audience across socioeconomic and educational boundaries. The manifesto advocates the film apparatus's radical expressive potential, while attacking how commercial practices had compromised the medium's inherent artistry. Lacking a past and free of traditions, cinema could be a true Futurist medium. However, "sorgendo come *teatro senza parole*, ha ereditate tutte le più tradizionali spazzature del teatro letterario . . . [I]l cinematografo sino ad oggi *è stato e tende a rimanere profondamente passatista*" (emerging as a *theater without words*, it has inherited all the most traditional rubbish of the literary theater. . . . Cinema, until this moment, *has been and tends to remain deeply passéist*) (*TIF*, 139–40). The "theater without words" represents not the medium's whole history (as the manifesto seems to imply) but the particular style that prevailed when the manifesto was written—namely, the feature-length narrative film.

During the first two decades of its life, cinema made crucial changes in its aesthetic choices and modes of exhibition. For about a decade after its inception in the mid-1890s, films of a brief duration—initially a single shot aiming primarily to astonish with the ability to show moving photographs—appeared occasionally as "attractions" in a live variety show.[12] Following this initial phase, cinema grew into an autonomous form of diversion. The film auditorium proper expanded, along with the formation of Italy's major production houses, while public polemics attacking cinema as dangerous and immoral—as a school of pornography and corruption—pushed the industry to implement measures of cultural legitimization, such as making films on serious subjects that qualified as artistic and edifying.[13] The need for respectability also led to many literary adaptations, the hiring of prestigious writers for original screenplays, and the marketing of films by genre. Some of the more "serious" genres of the 1910s were the *film storico*, costume dramas styled on nineteenth-century theater and opera; the *cinema in frac*, tragic melodramas unfolding in contemporary decadent upper-class milieus; the *verista*, melodramatic realism with emphasis on the Neapolitan working class; and the *diva film*, which despite its significant overlaps with any genre was distinguished by its focus on the plights of an alluring and morally complex female protagonist. And while the earlier historical films were shorts, production in the early to mid-1910s marked the industry's adoption of the feature-length narrative, exemplified in some epics and the other genres mentioned in the chapter.[14]

This kind of cinema—with its epics and sentimentality, reverence to history and high literature, and obsession with photographic realism and narrative form—is what "theater without words" represents. Thanks to the apologists of traditionalism who flooded an industry in need of cultural legitimacy, cinema's Futuristic potential yielded to stagnant theatrical gesticulations. And this kind of cinema is what the Futurists hoped to subvert in practice with *Vita futurista*, made in 1916 in Florence. Although the film is not extant, we know of its content from various sources, such as testimonies by its creators, advertisements and reviews related to it, plus some surviving stills and brief fragments as well as a treatment submitted to the authorities for censorship clearance. The existing sources vary with regard to its length and the exact number, order, and titles of the individual episodes. We know, however, that it consisted of ten to twelve episodes, adding up to a total duration of at least forty minutes. The episodes were independent of one another with respect to storyline and differed significantly in narrative transparency and visual style.[15]

Parts of the film exhibit an abstract style similar to the kind described in the manifesto. An episode about a sentimental man who wastes his virility by falling in love portrays his surrender to traditionalist psychic forces and ensuing troubled mental state with scattered dots in the air around him. Evidently, during development the film was exposed to dust, which sprinkled the image with white dots. Ginna, who served as the film's director, profited from the incident by hand-coloring the dots, thus portraying the protagonist's mental disturbance more creatively.[16] Another segment shows the love affair between Balla and a chair, out of which a footstool is born. In the surviving stills believed to derive from this episode, an ethereal female figure that possibly represents the spirit of the chair is portrayed against a striped backdrop through double exposure, while the man's partial figure seen in the right of the frame is distorted through the use of special mirrors (Figure 2.1).[17] Moreover, a segment about a "drama of objects" apparently showed the "exploration" of herrings, carrots, and eggplants, a ball falling on the head of a statue and staying still, and the "discussion" between a foot, a hammer, and an umbrella.[18]

Inasmuch as the film's abstract style actualized the manifesto's search for a radical future, it also recalled an earlier phase of cinema. As in later avant-garde movements, it evoked the "marvelous," the absurd and nonsensical, that distinguished the films of Georges Méliès at the turn of the century.[19] A tribute to that era is also suggested by the episode that Ginna described as the dynamic-rhythmic dance of women dressed in tinfoil, against which the gleams of bright reflectors created the peculiar effect of intersecting flashes.[20] Giovanni Lista views this segment as a filmic interpretation of the "Dance of Steel," staged in 1914 in Paris by Loïe Fuller, whose "serpentine" dances had been the thrill of some of the earliest moving pictures.[21] The tribute to early cinema is also suggested by episodes that display a realist rather than abstract style. One of the surviving stills is from a scene filmed at an outdoors restaurant in Florence. A group of Futurists are mocking the passéist eating style of an old man sitting nearby. Of course, the old man was himself played by a young Futurist, who wore a white beard and sat at a table alone, and is discernible in the background of the image (Figure 2.2). During the shooting, however, an Englishman mistook the fiction for reality and reproached Marinetti for insulting the elderly.[22] The on-location shooting combined with the fortuitous incident evokes the Italian actualities filmed around 1900 by such pioneers as Filoteo Alberini and Rodolfo Remondini, who adopted the Lumière tactic of shooting in populated streets and piazzas to recruit potential clients who hoped to see themselves on screen.[23] The episode may also be compared to the Lumière actualities themselves, some of which showed people socializing or eating outdoors, or reality intruding into a staged event.[24]

This gaze backward characterized not only the film's content but also its mode of exhibition. *Vita futurista* was shown for the first time in Florence on January 28, 1917, and again in Rome on June 14 and 15 of that year. Its Florentine screening, on which the contemporary press gives more detail, was part of a longer show that included Futurist plays, or "syntheses," and poetry readings.[25] This Futurist "variety" show represented a later (or tamer, as we will see) phase of the notorious *serate futuriste* (Futurist evenings),

FIGURE 2.1 *An ethereal female and a distorted male in* Vita futurista.

Source: The image was previously printed in Verdone, *Cinema e letteratura del futurismo*. Copyright unknown.

FIGURE 2.2 *A scene at a Florentine restaurant, from* Vita futurista.

Source: Previously printed in Verdone, *Cinema e letteratura del futurismo*.

which had epitomized Futurism's relationship with the public during its earliest years.

The *serate* were public gatherings in major theaters, moving from city to city, and consisting of diverse performances, such as manifesto or poetry readings, or presentations of paintings. They typically elicited a violent reaction from the audience, thanks to their audacious social or political affirmations or experimental aesthetics. Hence, with *Vita futurista*, an episodic film inserted in a series of live performances, the Futurists defied the modes of film exhibition typical in those years, which involved the presentation of a feature-length narrative in a film auditorium proper. Instead, they provided a viewing experience similar to that of the earliest years of cinema, what is now known as "cinema of attractions." In coining this term, Tom Gunning disputes a teleological view of early cinema as a primitive phase of the feature-length narrative. He addresses the specificities of early cinema—its film content and mode of exhibition—that make it a distinct experience. Unlike narrative cinema, which seeks to absorb the spectator in its illusionary realism by disavowing the materiality of the apparatus, the auditorium, and the spectator's reality, early cinema flaunted the presence of the apparatus, its ability to *show* things. Its purpose was to shock, surprise, assault, incite visual curiosity, and create spectacle for spectacle's sake, thus addressing the audience directly, drawing attention to the material conditions of projection and the audience's role therein. And so films were often included as attractions in vaudeville programs, in a series of diverse, narratively unrelated performances.

The Futurist film manifesto, while defining an alternative style, does not discuss exhibition or spectator address. Marinetti's preference for the ways of early attractions, however, is suggested by his 1913 manifesto on the variety theater. He celebrates this form of diversion for its "Futuristic" qualities: tradition-less, comic, astonishing; based on instinct, laughter, muscular agility; averse to grief, academics, the sublime in art; and especially, replacing old theater's *psicologia* (psychology) with *fisicofollia* (body madness). The latter is not restricted to the physical eccentricity of the performers—comedians, dancers, jugglers, or gymnasts—but includes the spectator's participation. No longer a passive voyeur, the spectator is noisy, sings along, chats with the actors, quarrels with the musicians, and flirts with the stars.[26] Marinetti praises the variety theater also for using cinema, "che lo arricchisce d'un numero incalcolabile di visioni e di spettacoli irrealizzabili" (which enriches it with an incalculable number of unrealizable visions and shows) (*TIF*, 81).[27] Gunning cites this manifesto in defining the mood of attractions: "Writing on the variety theatre, Marinetti not only praised its aesthetics of astonishment and stimulation, but particularly its creation of a new spectator who contrasts with the 'static,' 'stupid voyeur' of traditional theatre."[28] With *Vita futurista*, an episodic and heterogeneous film presented in a variety-like format, the Futurists did not just refute the present-day institution with its drawn-out narratives and exclusive film auditoriums. They did so specifically by paying homage to early cinema, to its vitality, spontaneity, physicality, and by the thrill of releasing modernity's public from an age-old literary-theatrical dreariness.[29]

Any discussion of Futurist cinema, however, must also address national politics and the Futurists' stance vis-à-vis the Great War. Politics permeated the content of *Vita futurista* and influenced its reception. Moreover, the politics of the film's reception in relation to cinematic reception in Italy at that time led to the Futurists' reluctance to further experiment with film.[30] At the outbreak of war in 1914, Italy declared neutrality, while public opinion was divided between neutralists and interventionists. The latter group, aspiring to liberate the northeastern territories of Trento and Trieste from Austria, advocated Italy's siding with the Entente of Britain, France, and Russia. The Futurists were fervent interventionists. When Italy finally declared war on Austria in May 1915, some Futurist artists fought and sacrificed their lives in the name of patriotism. But the meaning of war for Futurism was not a matter of defeating Austria and restoring peace. The Futurists abhorred peace and pacifism. For them, war was a fundamental drive of man, an ongoing state of combat essential to vitality. For Marinetti, "La Guerra non può morire, poiché è una legge della vita. Vita = aggressione. Pace universale = decrepitezza e agonia delle razze" (War cannot die, since it is a law of life. Life = aggression. Universal peace = decrepitude and death throes of races) (*TIF*, 334). This spirit fueled the violence of the *serate*, where the Futurists unfailingly engaged their public in auditorium "battles," and where audiences arrived, as it were, equipped with vegetables to use as projectiles, while performers persisted in their provocations or ran away to protect themselves.[31] Writing on theater, the Futurists expressed vehemently their loathing of any traditional type of success, and their desire instead "to be booed," proof of the artist's ability to touch the souls of modernity's restless masses.[32]

War was a central theme in Futurist writings, and the film manifesto was no exception. Its discourse on technique is framed by a nationalistic sermon established in its opening remarks: "La nostra grande guerra igienica, che dovrà soddisfare *tutte* le nostre aspirazioni nazionali, centuplica la forza novatrice della razza italiana" (Our great hygienic war, which must satisfy *all* our national aspirations, is increasing the revitalizing power of the Italian race a hundredfold) (*TIF* 138-39). Avant-gardism, the manifesto concludes, will multiply the power of the creative Italian genius and its world supremacy. *Vita futurista* exemplified Futurist politics. According to one source, it began with the projection of text—something like opening credits—that presented the participants' names and aesthetic aspirations, along with their views on war. And it portrayed in comical fashion the Futurists' superior stamina over the neutralists. A still from "How a Futurist Sleeps" shows a neutralist sleeping on a normal (horizontal) bed, while a Futurist sleeps vertically, thus remaining alert (Figure 2.3). Other scenes showed gymnastics, fencing, boxing, and more contests between Futurists and neutralists, such as Marinetti's sword fight with Chiti, his "discussion with boxing gloves" with Ungari, and the mockery of the neutralist walk against the Futurist "interventionist" step (cxxix-cxxx).

Remarkably, the film's reception was wholly lacking in that belligerent spirit, ceremonially pursued by the Futurists, especially in their earlier *serate*.

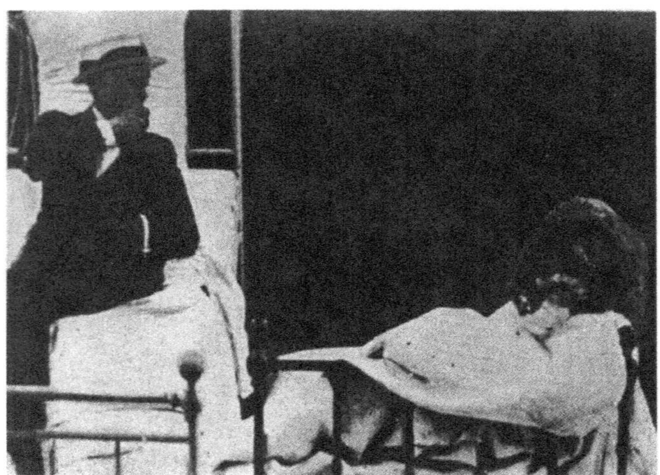

FIGURE 2.3 *A Futurist sleeps vertically, in* Vita futurista.
Source: Previously printed in Verdone, *Cinema e letteratura del futurismo*.

Contemporary reviews of the Florentine premiere noted that the atmosphere was peaceful and the audience amused, with no desire for brawls.[33] Ironic as it may seem, the evening's peacefulness was an outcome of the war climate that permeated it. *Vita futurista* was not the only politicized part; so were the syntheses preceding it, on uplifting, military, anti-Austrian themes.[34] Furthermore, as Florence's *La nazione* and *Il nuovo giornale* announced on the day before the premiere, the event was a fundraiser for the families of recalled servicemen, thus sustaining a patriotic wartime institution. Indeed, the patriotic sentiment of the war years resulted in an overall taming of the *serate*. With Italy at war, the politics now shared by Futurism and the general public alleviated the tension between the radical style of Futurist performances and the spectators' traditional cultural background, which had inspired the violence of the *serate* in the prewar years.[35] The clash between performance and audience now gave way to another kind of clash: between the worship of war as a concrete state of affairs and war as symbol, as a model for audience response.

The audience's identification with the spectacle at the expense of their sought-after collision also reflected *Vita futurista*'s patriotic resonances with narrative cinema, which cultivated patriotism diligently during the First World War. The rivalries between Futurists and neutralists displayed a slapstick element, as suggested by the surviving still of a boxing match, which shows Ungari's body submitting to Marinetti's blow, while both men are wearing tails (Figure 2.4). The amalgamation of slapstick, nationalism, and aggressiveness evoked a crucial element of the *forzuto* (strongman). Rising during the war years, this thriving genre celebrated the feats of a

FIGURE 2.4 *A boxing match between Marinetti and Ungari, in* Vita futurista.
Source: Previously printed in Verdone, *Cinema e letteratura del futurismo*.

working-class hero who used his bulging muscles only to protect the weak and righteous from the villains.[36] Most exemplary was the sensational character of Maciste, invented for Giovanni Pastrone's colossal Roman epic *Cabiria* (1914). Many Maciste films followed, well into the 1920s, where slapstick informed the punishment of villains, usually foreign weaklings. In *Maciste alpino* (*The Warrior*, 1916), Maciste saves his compatriots from the Austrians, whom he handles with both hilarity and violence: bodies tossed about and slamming against each other, kicked off steep cliffs, or tied together by the neck and hurled down snowy mountains.

The recourse to early attractions unites *Vita futurista* and the *forzuto*. Although the *forzuto* exemplifies the 1910s feature-length narrative, its manifestations of strength, when considered in isolation from the rest of the narrative, resemble early attractions. They functioned like inserts, brief variety numbers, which suspended narrative progression, summoning the viewer's fascination with the actor outside the narrative constraints of any given film. *Vita futurista*'s slapstick resonated with the *forzuto*'s exaggerated virility. Thus Futurism elicited a response characteristic of narrative cinema. By aligning virility (a thematic element) with attractions (a stylistic element), Futurism appealed to that same kind of theme-style alignment that narrative cinema, thanks to its high popularity and exposure, had already stored in the audience's collective imagination.

To be sure, live performance seems to be more pertinent to Futurism than film is, given the priority ascribed to the audience's physical encounter with the stage. We must not, however, attribute the Futurists' short-lived film practice to the medium's technical specificity. The mere fact that cinema involves an ongoing projection of images, which remain impervious to the spectator's behavior, does not restrict the spectator's function to that of a passive voyeur. Let us recall our distinction between cinema as pure apparatus and cinema as institution. It is the manner in which the apparatus is deployed—the aesthetic choices made for it and the social configuration within which films are exhibited—that determines the spectator's function. The early attractions, like the experience that Marinetti finds in the variety theater, attest to the fact that the film spectator need not remain "static like a stupid voyeur," but may also experience the type of encounter that the Futurists envisioned.

Indeed, the notion of cinema as pure apparatus, as opposed to cinema as institution, is an abstraction, because technology does not exist in a vacuum. Once technology is deployed, especially in cinema, which engages the spectator through astonishing images and everything that those images conjure up for that spectator— dreams, memories, habits, fears, and so on—an institution is already being created. Thus, an audience begins to be formed and patterns of representation, exhibition, and reception begin to be established. Therefore, with the radical aesthetics of the 1916 manifesto, which would rescue film from traditionalism and restore its purer, "eminently

Futurist" form "free of traditions," the Futurists were articulating an *ideal* rather than a realizable vision. Futurism was not "free" of anything: not of politics nor the institution of cinema, both of which pervaded daily life. For all its traditionalism, cinema touched the restless souls of modernity more than Futurism did. With its epics, melodramas, seductive divas, feisty strongmen, slapstick, war films, and multiple other forms, it entered the sphere of culture quite vigorously, recoloring experience with an exuberant layer of mobility and formal polyphony, reshaping sensibility at its core—the sensibility that inspired the conception of Futurism itself. It is cinema's pervasiveness and the ideological bind it placed on the Futurists that undermined their wish to make films. The peaceful reception of *Vita futurista*, which unwittingly reaffirmed the political and aesthetic program of narrative cinema, made the Futurists aware that, by grappling with this robust phenomenon, they were found within its loop (much to their chagrin). They honored cinema's *symbolic* Futuristic significance, but in practice they essentially put aside its practical realities in order to preserve the radical ideals of Futurism.

Notes

1 The Futurists' both delayed and short-lived engagement with cinema has concerned critics. See, among others, Lindvall, "Futurist Fears of the Machine"; Lista, *Cinema e fotografia futurista*, 11–18 and *Il cinema futurista*, 15–19; Strauven, *Marinetti e il cinema*, 20–24, 54–59; and Verdone, *Cinema e letteratura del futurismo*, 118–19.

2 Marinetti, *Teoria e invenzione futurista*, 139–40 (hereafter *TIF*). The manifesto first appeared in the November 15, 1916 issue of the Florentine biweekly *L'Italia futurista*. All translations of Futurist texts are mine, with consultation of Marinetti, *Let's Murder the Moonshine* and/or *Critical Writings*.

3 For more on Bragaglia's role in the Futurist movement and commentaries on *Thaïs*, see Marcus, "Anton Giulio Bragaglia's *Thaïs*"; and Re, "Futurism, Film, and the Return of the Repressed." For comprehensive studies of Futurist cinema, see Lista, *Cinema e fotografia futurista* and *Il cinema futurista*; Verdone, *Cinema e letteratura del futurismo*; and edited volumes by Catanese, *Futurist Cinema: Studies on Italian Avant-Garde Film*; and Sainati, *Cento anni di idee futuriste nel cinema*.

4 See De Maria's periodization of the "heroic" phase (*TIF*, xxxi).

5 On the existing fragments, see Lista, *Il cinema futurista*, 51–60.

6 For extensive commentaries and reprints of the script, see Lista, *Il cinema futurista*, 65–69, 209–18; Strauven, *Marinetti e il cinema*, 188–204, 255–61; and Syrimis, *Great Black Spider*, 106–36. For the script in both Italian and English translation, see Boschi and Manzoli, "Oltre l'autore," 15–25, 143–47.

7 See Lista's study in *Il cinema futurista*, 81–112.

8 For discussions and reprints of additional writings on cinema, see Lista, *Il cinema futurista*; and Strauven, 82–121, 228–38.

9 Earlier treatments of this topic appear in Syrimis, "Film, Spectators, and War" and *Great Black Spider*, 27–105.

10 For more on analogy, see Somigli, *Legitimizing the Artist*, 141–44; Strauven, *Marinetti e il cinema*, 59–73; and Syrimis, *Great Black Spider*, 33–39.

11 See *TIF*, 143–44.

12 See Gunning, "Cinema of Attractions." On Italy specifically, see Bernardini, *Cinema muto 1896/1904*, 65–136.

13 See Bernardini, *Cinema muto 1905/1909*, esp. 15–55, 79–108, 194–223.

14 For more on these developments, see Bernardini, *Cinema muto 1910/1914*, 40–97, 192–211; and Brunetta, *Storia del cinema italiano*, 71–106, 130–230. On the *diva film* as a genre, see Dalle Vacche, *Diva*, 2–3.

15 For analyses of the film's content see Innamorati, "Un 'manifesto' fatto d'immagini" and "Nuovi documenti"; Kirby and Kirby, *Futurist Performance*, 120–42; Lista, *Il cinema futurista*, 45–65, 199–208; Strauven, *Marinetti e il cinema*, 161–88; Syrimis, *Great Black Spider*, 45–61; and Verdone, *Cinema e letteratura del futurismo*, 103–109.

16 Ginna, "Note sul film," 157–58; Innamorati, "Un 'manifesto' fatto d'immagini," 34–35.

17 See Kirby and Kirby, *Futurist Performance*, 127–31; and Lista, *Il cinema futurista*, 57–60.

18 This segment is described in "Alcune parti del film *Vita futurista*," an advertisement appearing in all issues of *L'Italia futurista* between October 15 and December 1, 1916 (reprinted in *TIF*, cxxviii–cxxx).

19 Gunning, "An Unseen Energy," 357; Strauven, *Marinetti e il cinema*, 77–79.

20 Ginna, "Note sul film," 158.

21 Lista, *Cinema e fotografia*, 11–13, 47.

22 On the surviving images, see Lista, *Il cinema futurista*, 55.

23 It also anticipates later styles, such as *cinéma vérité* (Verdone, *Cinema e letteratura del futurismo*, 107). On Alberini, Remondini, and actualities, see Bernardini, *Cinema muto 1896/1904*, 155–71, 229–34.

24 For more on this comparison, see Syrimis, *Great Black Spider*, 50–52.

25 See reprints of contemporary newspaper reviews in Antonucci, *Cronache del teatro futurista*, 115–16. See also Innamorati, "Nuovi documenti," 47–51. Against the "analytic" (detailed and tedious) narratives of traditional theater, the "synthesis" epitomized the Futurist style of live drama, marked by extreme brevity, and often in the form of a single act lasting a few minutes, thus embodying the ideals of speed and laconicism. See the "synthetic theater" manifesto (*TIF*, 113–22).

26 See *TIF*, 83–84.

27 Marinetti evidently added this remark in the manifesto's longer version (1914), now mistakenly listed in many anthologies as the original 1913 version (Strauven, *Marinetti e il cinema*, 46).

28 Gunning, "Cinema of Attractions," 59.

29 The Futurists also attempted to market *Vita futurista* through the industry's distribution network (Strauven, *Marinetti e il cinema*, 185). This effort, however, indicates less their endorsement of the industry's aesthetic principles than their wish to reach a larger audience.

30 Syrimis, *Great Black Spider*, 62–105.

31 See Antonucci, *Storia del teatro futurista*, 14–45; and Berghaus, *Italian Futurist Theatre*, 85–155.

32 See "La voluttà d'esser fischiati" (*TIF*, 310–13).

33 Antonucci, *Cronache*, 115–16.

34 On the Futurist "synthesis," see note 25 above.

35 See Innamorati, "Nuovi documenti," 48–49.

36 On the *forzuto* see Dall'Asta, *Un cinéma musclé*; Farassino and Sanguineti, *Gli uomini forti*; and Reich, *The Maciste Films of Italian Silent Cinema*.

Bibliography

Antonucci, Giovanni. *Cronache del teatro futurista*. Rome: Abete, 1975.

Antonucci, Giovanni. *Storia del teatro futurista*. Rome: Studium, 2005.

Berghaus, Günter. *Italian Futurist Theatre, 1909-1944*. Oxford: Clarendon Press, 1998.

Bernardini, Aldo. *Cinema muto italiano: Ambiente, spettacoli e spettatori 1896/1904*. Bari: Laterza, 1980.

Bernardini, Aldo. *Cinema muto italiano: Industria e organizzazione dello spettacolo 1905/1909*. Bari: Laterza, 1981.

Bernardini, Aldo. *Cinema muto italiano: Arte, divismo e mercato 1910/1914*. Bari: Laterza, 1982.

Brunetta, Gian Piero. *Storia del cinema italiano I: Il cinema muto 1895-1929*. Rome: Riuniti, 1993.

Boschi, Alberto and Giacomo Manzoli, eds. "Oltre l'autore 1." *Fotogenia* 2 (1995): 15-25.

Catanese, Rossella, ed. *Futurist Cinema: Studies on Italian Avant-Garde Film*. Amsterdam: Amsterdam University Press, 2017.

Dall'Asta, Monica. *Un cinéma musclé: Le surhomme dans le cinéma muet italien (1913-1926)*. Trans. Franco Arnò and Charles Tatum, Jr. Crisnée. Belgium: Editions Yellow Now, 1992.

Dalle Vacche, Angela. *Diva: Defiance and Passion in Early Italian Cinema*. Austin: University of Texas Press, 2008.

Farassino, Alberto and Tatti Sanguineti, eds. *Gli uomini forti*. Milan: Mazzotta, 1983.

Ginna, Arnaldo. "Note sul film d'avanguardia '*Vita futurista*.' " *Bianco e nero* 26.5–6 (1965): 156–58.

Gunning, Tom. "The Cinema of Attractions: Early Film, Its Spectator and the Avant-Garde." In *Early Cinema: Space, Frame, Narrative*. Ed. Thomas Elsaesser. London: BFI, 1990. 56–62.

Gunning, Tom. "An Unseen Energy That Swallows Space: The Space in Early Film and Its Relation to American Avant-Garde Film." In *Film before Griffith*. Ed. John L. Fell. Berkeley: University of California Press, 1983. 355–65.

Innamorati, Isabella. "Un 'manifesto' fatto d'immagini." In *Il "Fronte interno" de L'Italia Futurista (Firenze 1916–1918)*. Ed. Luciano Caruso. Florence: S.P.E.S., 1992. 31–36.

Innamorati, Isabella. "Nuovi documenti d'archivio su 'Vita Futurista': Peripezie di una pellicola d'avanguardia." *Quaderni di teatro* 9.36 (May 1987): 47–64.

Kirby, Michael and Victoria Nes Kirby. *Futurist Performance*. New York: PAJ Publications, 1986.

Lindvall, Daniel. "Futurist Fears of the Machine." *Film International* 1.3 (2003): 16–24.

Lista, Giovanni. *Cinema e fotografia futurista*. Milan: Skira, 2001.

Lista, Giovanni. *Il cinema futurista*. Recco, Genoa: Le Mani, 2010.

Marcus, Millicent: "Anton Giulio Bragaglia's *Thaïs*, or, The Death of the *Diva* + the Rise of the *Scenoplastica* = The Birth of Futurist Cinema." *South Central Review* 13.2–3 (1996): 63–81.

Marinetti, Filippo Tommaso. *Critical Writings*. Ed. Günter Berghaus. Trans. Doug Thompson. New York: Farrar, Straus and Giroux, 2006.

Marinetti, Filippo Tommaso. *Let's Murder the Moonshine: Selected Writings*. Ed. R. W. Flint. Trans. R. W. Flint and Arthur A. Coppotelli. Los Angeles: Sun and Moon Press, 1991.

Marinetti, Filippo Tommaso. *Teoria e invenzione futurista*. Ed. Luciano De Maria. 3rd ed. Milan: Mondadori, 1996.

Re, Lucia. "Futurism, Film, and the Return of the Repressed: Learning from *Thaïs*." *MLN* 123.1 (2008): 125–50.

Reich, Jacqueline. *The Maciste Films of Italian Silent Cinema*. Bloomington: Indiana University Press, 2015.

Sainati, Augusto, ed. *Cento anni di idee futuriste nel cinema*. Atti del convegno di studi. Naples: Università Suor Orsola Benincasa, April 21–22, 2010. Pisa: ETS, 2012.

Somigli, Luca. *Legitimizing the Artist: Manifesto Writing and European Modernism. 1885–1915*. Toronto: University of Toronto Press, 2003.

Strauven, Wanda. *Marinetti e il cinema: Tra attrazione e sperimentazione*. Pasian di Prato: Campanotto, 2006.

Syrimis, Michael. "Film, Spectators, and War in Italian Futurism." In *Italian Cultural Studies 2001: Selected Essays*. Ed. Anthony Julian Tamburri et al. Boca Raton: Bordighera Press, 2004. 168–85.

Syrimis, Michael. *The Great Black Spider on Its Knock-Kneed Tripod: Reflections of Cinema in Early Twentieth-Century Italy*. Toronto: University of Toronto Press, 2012.

Verdone, Mario. *Cinema e letteratura del futurismo*. Rome: Centro Sperimentale di Cinematografia, Edizioni di Bianco e Nero, 1968.

Filmography

Cabiria, Dir. Giovanni Pastrone. Italy: Itala Film. 1914.
Maciste alpino, Dir. Giovanni Pastrone. Italy: Itala Film. 1916.
Velocità, Dir. Tina Cordero, Guido Martina, Pippo Oriani. Italy: Futurista Film. 1930.
Vita futurista, Dir. Arnaldo Ginna. Italy: Italia Futurista. 1916.

3

Vincere: The Never-Ending Story of Film and Fascism

Vito Zagarrio

This chapter borrows its title from *Vincere* (Marco Bellocchio, 2009), which brilliantly represents Fascism and its icons through the secret affair of Benito Mussolini's wife and her secret, illegitimate son. Like many films of the 2000s—including *Sanguepazzo* (*Crazy Blood*, Marco Tullio Giordana, 2008), *Il papà di Giovanna* (*Giovanna's Father*, Pupi Avati, 2008), *L'uomo che verrà* (*The Man Who Will Come*, Giorgio Diritti, 2009), *Il sangue dei vinti* (*The Blood of the Defeated*, Michele Soavi, 2008), and the sarcastic *Fascisti su Marte* (*Fascists on Mars*, Corrado Guzzanti, 2006)—Bellocchio's work shows how filmmakers felt the need to stage the years of the Fascist regime. Such films point out how Fascism produces an appeal that over the years has transformed but not waned.

Allow me to start from my personal experience as a scholar of Fascism (and in particular of Fascist cinema), and also as an academic.[1] When I teach the relationship between culture and regime, between cinema and Mussolini's Italy, I am compelled to declare my anti-Fascism and cover my back. But I fear sometimes that my claim to be not a Fascist, despite some of my positive evaluations of the policies and aesthetics of cinema of the 1930s and 1940s, sounds like a Freudian denial. The dilemma arises when one is forced to sketch an analysis, like the one I try to do with this essay, within a broader political and cultural debate. The risk is that if you analyze the Fascist film policy with an analysis devoid of ideology, you may be associated with a pervasive nostalgic revisionism. Instead, if you reaffirm the primacy of historical judgment, you may be branded as nostalgic for an "old" kind of ideology. In a jungle of controversial positions that recur corrosively, I will try to synthesize those reasons that, in my opinion, are the most essential in the debate over Fascism in the new millennium.

1 The Cultural Policy

How much did Fascist "cultural intervention" apply to cinema and influence the birth of neorealism? And which elements of continuity can be traced between the film policy of the regime and that of the postwar governments? If *historia non facit saltus* (history makes no jumps), it must be acknowledged that the often contradictory state policy of Fascism may have contributed, unconsciously, to producing the professionalism, personality, technological and linguistic tools, motivations, and basic theoretical contexts that became essential to the generation that rose to prominence with neorealism. The neorealist generation (i.e., such directors as Roberto Rossellini, Vittorio De Sica, Luchino Visconti, and Giuseppe De Santis) found arguably fertile ground for their new stylistic and ideological elaborations thanks at least in part to Fascism. They grew as directors and had their film education in a period that was influenced by Fascist cultural politics. Benito Mussolini's idea of cinema as the "strongest weapon" (a slogan that he borrowed from Lenin!) brought much investment to the film industry, and the Italian state helped the film world by following the model of such pivotal foreign industries as those of the United States, Soviet Union, and Germany. And the Fascist regime created institutions of great importance, founding Cinecittà and the Centro Sperimentale di Cinematografia, which nourished artistic talents, technical staff, and skilled workers (directors, cinematographers, editors, set designers, and so on). In short, Fascist cultural politics helped create the creative soil in which neorealism could develop.

Let us turn to a famous example: the experience on set of the "Fascist" Rossellini (I use the word in quotation marks to denote the pre-neorealist "war trilogy" ironically referred to by Serri) must have shaped this same director when he made his legendary film *Rome, Open City* after the end of the Second World War. The issue of continuity, rather than rupture, of the different phases of Rossellini's work has been repeatedly addressed.[2] But should not the technical and professional training that came from the years of Fascism also be considered? The neorealist filmmakers learned their craft and shaped their own authorial personalities precisely under or during (even despite) the Fascist regime, as did the hundreds of technicians, machinists, and other skilled workers in the film industry.

A similar claim can be made with regard not so much to the authorship of postwar films, but to their institutional and legislative contexts, their productive models. As in the many other areas of the Italian economy permeated by Fascist modernization, Mussolini's regime created the premises that would largely influence the choice of managers for film policy of the 1940s and 1950s. Even the 1965 Italian law regulating the cinema industry was partially influenced by Fascist film politics (see the so-called *ritorni* [rebates] that enabled films that earned more money from the box office to receive financial help from the state).

During the 1920s you could not talk of a Fascist film policy.[3] It did not exist as a coherent line of intervention, nor did it have any structures and organizations capable of harmonizing a possible program of the regime that was not, for the time being, fully aware of the importance of the cinema as an instrument for communication and consensus building. The Fascism of that first decade had not substantially affected film production. The main intervention of the government in the film industry had focused, on the one hand, on strengthening censorship, and on the other hand, on the foundation of the Istituto LUCE, an organization that would soon become one of the main instruments of propaganda and consensus building to the regime.[4] Among state interventions designed to stimulate film production, there was only ENAC, the National Agency for Cinematography (1929), a semi-private entity funded by the state with the aim of influencing the activities of distributors and regulating relations with foreign producers.

The Italian film industry of the 1920s was floundering in a deep crisis characterized by organizational weakness, lack of planning, increased production costs, loss of foreign markets, and an inadequacy of resources. In 1926, Stefano Pittaluga founded SASP (Società Anonima Stefano Pittaluga) with the support of Banca Commerciale Italiana, and he incorporated Unione Cinematografica Italiana and all its equipment. The following year, he further strengthened his position by buying Cines, a well-known film company specializing in the production and distribution of films that was founded in 1906 and destined to play a major role in the introduction of sound equipment throughout Italy. Pittaluga hoped to take the film industry in an artistically serious direction, while at the same time making it commercially viable. He combined the roles of producer and distributor, and was motivated by the idea that the creation of an efficient film industry, focused and well-organized at the national level, would win state assistance. Cines, managed by Ludovico Toepliz, appointed as artistic director the renowned critic Emilio Cecchi, who had established close relationships with such fellow authors as Luigi Pirandello, Corrado Alvaro, Aldo De Benedetti, and Umberto Barbaro. Pittaluga died prematurely in 1931, but his example would influence other Italian entrepreneurs and also shape the future input of the government in the film sector.

By the early 1930s, the film policy of Fascism began to take shape, and at that time one also begins to glimpse the gap between either direct or indirect intervention of the state into private industry. The regime approved in June 1931 a plan to revitalize the national film industry. The movie system was facing declining revenues, the closure of numerous movie theaters, and the failure or inability of manufacturers to achieve adequate profits; the production of domestic films was just seven movies in 1930. A strong move was necessary. Such a measure provided a subsidy to producers that corresponded to 10 percent of the proceeds from their movies in Italy, and at the same time increased the taxation of imported and dubbed films. In truth, this measure was a direct aid in favor of Pittaluga, and did not help improve film quality or artistic strength, but rather pushed the Italian film production business in the direction of entertainment and escapism. In October 1933, a new law (which repealed the previous measure) dealt more broadly with the whole sector: the aim was to strengthen domestic production at the expense of foreign production, and reward the "quality" of films as well as their commercial success. It established the obligation to schedule one Italian film for every three foreign ones and to dub non-Italian films. The non-Italian films were also burdened by a special tax whose proceeds went to support domestic producers. If the previous law had created a mechanism of automatic help based on the proceeds, now there was a law establishing a financial support system centered on the alleged artistic and technical merits of a film, a program that allowed parties to intervene in a selective manner that was often motivated by political intentions.

In any case, while they provided some stimulus to production, the actual impact of these laws was modest. So in the early 1930s, the intervention of the state was still limited to censorship and some measures of financial assistance, which confirms that the cinema in those years was less of a priority in the politics of Fascism. The regime did not appear particularly aware or concerned with cinema's possible uses as an effective political, cultural, and propaganda tool, and the main concern of the film industry was to produce films that suited popular taste and cashed in at the box office. Despite this duplicity of attitude, Giuseppe Bottai was among the first to understand the importance of cinema to the regime: he became a supporter of Augustus, the company for the production and exploitation of films promoted by the journals of the legendary director Alessandro Blasetti. Then he headed the delegation that in 1930 discussed with Mussolini the role of government in the cinema. Bottai was initially in favor of the law of 1931 that favored private industry for the cinema. Then from 1932 to 1933, he was more and more convinced of the government's need to focus on cinema as a "powerful means for the dissemination of ideas," and therefore he saw film as closely aligned with the political and cultural levels of the regime.

But if one wishes to trace the institutional and legislative framework for Italian film's presence in Fascism and locate an Italian mode of production in the mid-1930s, then one should consider the turning point in film policy represented by the creation of Direzione Generale per la Cinematografia. Because of the pressure of industrialists who demanded more government intervention, and because certain personalities and party leaders were convinced that cinema was an important means to influence public opinion, the need arose for a specific administrative structure that could systematically deal with the whole film industry. The creation of Direzione Generale represented a crucial turning point that is also important from a purely historical point of view. In fact, a major phase of Fascism ended at that time, accompanied by a lively political and economic debate. The years 1932–33, in particular, were a period that theorized the so-called left wing of Fascism, a crucial issue in which "corporatist" attempts to marry "revolutionary" instances of Fascism with the organization—to quote Aquarone—of the totalitarian state.[5] It was a time when both the intellectuals who dealt with cinema and the managers that the regime was forming looked to foreign models to forge their own path, especially in Soviet Russia, the United States, and a little later even in Hitler's Germany. Between Soviet "collectivism" and capitalist "individualism," the regime sought its own "third way." Upstream, of course, there was the Depression, which indirectly affected this theoretical framework during a period of extreme importance for cultural policy in general and film policy in particular.[6]

An important Fascist film strategy was the so-called genre policy. Cinecittà started producing its own film styles and its own studio system. Such genres as the colonial and war movies, the historical and costume films, the screwball and sophisticated Italian comedies, and finally the films of "white telephones" made for an interesting cinematic ecosystem that some scholars have attempted to redefine as an example of *deco* cinema.[7] In this complex scenario, the general director of cinematography Luigi Freddi played a major role. His relationship with cinema had already begun at the end of the 1920s, but the birth of his passion for the medium took place during a famous trip to Hollywood—a journey that he transformed into a study of the production style of American filmmaking, based on the integrated cycle of production-distribution-exhibition known as the studio system. Galvanized by the American model, Freddi returned to Italy to write a series of reports on cinema, including one commissioned by Mussolini. The adventure of Freddi as manager of Fascist cinema starts here: with a decree on September 18, 1934, Galeazzo Ciano created the General Directorate for Film at the Undersecretariat of the Press and Propaganda, a body responsible for the coordination of state policies toward the film industry, which until then were "not in harmony with the aims and ideals of the regime." Three days later, Freddi was appointed director of the new organization. And from that moment on, he was one of the greatest creators of symbolic imagery in Fascist cinema, and one of the leaders of the regime's massive contribution to cinema in the second half of the 1930s, as described in his postwar book *Cinema*. It was essentially a diary—although it has an ambiguous relation to the genre of autobiography—that reconstructed the theory and practice of so-called Fascist cinema.[8] One does well to start with Freddi for rethinking the institutional and legislative frameworks of the Fascist period. He believed that the state had the duty to influence directly the formidable social reach of cinema, which found its parallel only in the press. His ambitious project was to build a state cultural and industrial policy for cinema. Freddi believed that the state must not only direct but also conceive, design, and manage the national film industry (even with protectionist measures) by defending culture against the invasion of foreign monopolies. The strong demand for state intervention in the economy of cinema led him, however, to a different position from that of the official regime, which did not intend to clash with the interests of private producers. Mussolini in fact called for a strong control on film policy but did not wish to stand in the way of entrepreneurs, since this would create, as in Germany, a state cinema. But Freddi dreamt of a total state-guided cinema as in UFA, the German state industry dominated by the Nazis after Hitler's ascent to power. Here one can see a contradiction in Freddi, who, on the one hand, looked to Germany and Russia for their strongly oriented state control (although he did not like the German censorship system); but, on the other hand, subscribed to the myth of Hollywood, where the industry was instead controlled by an oligopoly of private producers. Basically this was the same contradiction in much of Fascism, which sought a "third way" between Moscow and New York, Berlin and Los Angeles.

On the key issue of censorship, Freddi's central idea was to make it not an essentially negative practice, but rather something capable of provoking ideas and intervening in a positive way in national cinema. In his reports to the Ministry and in his book *Cinema*, Freddi was often annoyed by the idea of an exclusively police-type censorship and denounced the shortcomings of a system that was limited to a purely formal control exercised by the officials of the Ministry of the Interior. For him, censorship had a highly political role, but it also had to function as a cultural and productive stimulus in order to bring Italian cinema out of its crisis. Freddi's position on censorship brings up a whole political-cultural and aesthetic criterion: a cinema that has a "predisposition that is essentially spectacular and evocative," in other words, Hollywood. The construction of the studios at Cinecittà went hand in hand with the establishment of censorship. In his American study trips, Freddi must have observed and weighed the rules of the already outlined Hays code, established in 1932. One should also note the bond between the Fascist state and the Catholic Church: in the first two weeks following his taking office as director general, Freddi had a series of meetings with Father Tacchi Venturi, a highly influential Vatican figure (ironically enough, when the left-wing writers Alberto Moravia and Elsa Morante married, it was this same priest who celebrated the Mass).

Two film institutions occupy a central role in the construction of the identity of Fascism: the Istituto LUCE and the Venice Film Festival. LUCE (an acronym for L'Unione Cinematografica Educativa, or Educational Film Unit) was created in 1924 and specialized in documentaries and propaganda newsreels. In the 1930s, LUCE strengthened its profile as an instrument of ideological propaganda. This was especially true during the Ethiopian war, when it produced the feature film *Il cammino degli eroi* (*The Path of the Heroes*, Corrado d'Errico, 1936), which won the award for best documentary at the Venice Film Festival. The film exalts the ideological elements that are the basis of the conquest: the civilizing mission of Italy and its need for land to cope with demographic pressures. The film also emphasizes the preparations for war, devoting to the conflict itself no more than five minutes, and thus rendering it something abstract and distant. The Venice Film Festival was inaugurated in 1932 and organized not only by the state but also by the local authorities, the Institute of Cinematography and the Venice Biennale. After a few years of relative autonomy, the festival gradually came under the control of the regime. It remained an important symbol of the cultural ambitions of the regime and a showcase for Fascist Italy abroad.

Education and training were other tools that the system used to improve the quality of Italian productions and strengthen simultaneously its presence and influence on film. In 1933, at Ciano's initiative, the Gruppi universitari fascisti (GUF), which since 1920 had dealt with the ideological education of university students, created film sections. By the end of the decade, more than half of the GUF had film sections, even if they lacked adequate financial resources and qualified staff to be able to keep them functioning fully within the expectations of the regime. In effect, the activities of Cineguf would remain mostly confined to the amateur level. However, these centers of debate and formation would prove to be important training centers and sources for cultural exchange, thus linking young anti-Fascist intellectuals to the activities of the national film school, the Centro Sperimentale di Cinematografia (CSC, Experimental Film Center).

The Centro Sperimentale was established in Rome in October 1935, after several previous similar attempts had not been as successful as hoped (e.g., a school headed by Bottai, Corrado Pavolini, and Luciano Doria was born in 1932 and organized by Blasetti as part of the Conservatory of Santa Cecilia). The courses had a duration of two years, the first focused on theoretical preparation with classes in acting, set design, techniques of photography, sound and lighting, and directing; and the second on their practical application. The school was formally independent and initially funded by the Ministry of Popular Culture. But in 1941, it became a public institution dependent on that ministry. The Centro Sperimentale welcomed about one hundred students each year, published the magazine *Bianco e nero* (*Black and White*), established a library, and produced numerous educational documentaries. Among its teachers were Umberto Barbaro, Blasetti, Francesco Pasinetti, and Antonio Valente. And its students included Michelangelo Antonioni, Clara Calamai, Giuseppe De Santis, Pietro Germi, Pietro Ingrao, Alida Valli, and Luigi Zampa. The school was led by Luigi

Chiarini, an important intellectual who, in spite of his link with the regime, engaged in the best cultural practices (sometimes even anti-Fascist).

In the mid-1930s, state intervention in the film industry was even directed toward strengthening technical infrastructure. At the end of 1935, Carlo Roncoroni, president of Cines at the recommendation of Freddi, submitted to Mussolini a project for the creation of a new complex of cinema establishments distributed over an area of 60 hectares on the Tuscolana on the outskirts of Rome—after a fire destroyed the studios that had stood on Via Veio, his property. The state intervened with substantial financing (four million lire) and Cinecittà was inaugurated April 21, 1937, the anniversary of the founding of Rome. Read symbolically, the walls of Cinecittà, launched with great fanfare by the Duce and his administration, were meant to remind people of the walls of Eternal City and its ancient glories. All this was to be connected to the modern cinematic medium. "Urbis condendae, ad effigiendas per cinematographi artem, imagines se moventes, solemnitur positus,"[9] read the parchment attached to the first stone of Cinecittà, with a double neologism suggestively used to define cinema in Latin. It belonged to a private company, the SAISC of Roncoroni, and only after his death in 1938 did Cinecittà become the property of the state, in October 1939.

It is important to note that more than half of the films produced in Italy between 1937 and 1943 were crafted at Cinecittà, confirming the importance of the new structure, which became one of the largest production centers in Europe. But with regard to production hubs run by the state, one should not forget another place: Pisorno, a synthesis between Pisa and Livorno, located in Tirrenia, home of the studios desired by Gioacchino Forzano in the early 1930s. The Tirrenia facilities were the first to comprise the entire cycle of film processing.

In short, there was a certain schizophrenia in Fascism's approach to the film industry: on one side, there was the will and desire to bring to bear the power of the state on production choices, and the need to apply to cinema that theoretical third way between Moscow and Hollywood, which then necessarily passed through Berlin. On the other side, there was a tendency to favor indirectly industry and industrialists, limit ideological control, and promote as in the United States the self-censorship of the producers rather than state censorship. And it was obvious that this "soul divided in two" of Fascism is reflected in the products: on one side, propaganda films; on the other, comedies and other works devoid of explicitly nationalist rhetoric.

Schizophrenia is also applicable to Freddi. Although it is true that he was convinced of the need for action and direct control by the state (the German way) and its tendency toward censorship, he was overall much softer and opted for indirect control and self-policing of the industry (on the American model). Brunetta is right when he speaks of the Cinecittà as a "Renaissance workshop": "Besides being a place of dreams, Cinecittà became a kind of gigantic late-Renaissance workshop, unparalleled in the rest of Europe:

an emporium where thousands of objects of the collective desire were put on display and paraded."[10] Thanks to designers, architects, costume designers, tailors, operators, craftsmen, technicians, and other talents, a new generation of future cinema was born. That generation arrived during Fascism and developed intellectually throughout the period and despite the regime, thanks to university organizations and cultural periodicals that were originally conceived as instruments of "consent" but ultimately functioned as engines of renewal. One of the most famous reviews was *Primato*, directed by Bottai, who wanted to bring together the youngest and most brilliant intellectuals. In this important review, founded in 1940 (when Italy entered into the Second World War), cinema and the visual arts played a central role in addition to history, politics, and theater.[11] Similar to *Primato*, the film review *Cinema* became a place and an opportunity to experiment with anti-Fascist attitudes in the waning days of the regime.

2   The Revision of Fascism

Of course, the risk of my previous interpretations of Fascism and its cultural policies is that they are implicitly proposing—perhaps unconsciously—a fascination for the achievements of the regime, as we have seen in recent television. For example, a controversial episode of *Porta a porta (Door to Door)*, the talk show hosted by Bruno Vespa, was entirely dedicated to the Mussolini family. The pretext was a book by Benito's son Romano, who reconstructed the figure of his notorious father: *Il Duce mio padre* (My Father, the Duce).[12] Guests of the episode included Romano Mussolini, Benito's granddaughter Alessandra Mussolini, Lucio Villari, Arrigo Petacco, Roberto Gervaso, and the actors of a work about Edda Ciano, Massimo Ghini, and Alessandra Martines.[13] "Soap opera Mussolini," commented one observer, on the ease of the conversation in the Vespa living room about Mussolini "the man," his relationship with his family, and even with his lovers.[14] It all had the effect of humanizing the powerful dictator, bringing him closer to the common man. "Fascism was a dictatorship, of course," Roberto Cotroneo said ironically:

> Mussolini had a temper, but he was a loving father, a man who respected institutions, and woe betide anyone who spoke badly of the Pope in front of him. In addition, poor fellow, what could he do with that traitor, Galeazzo Ciano? His son in law, after all, had betrayed him, and therefore he had no choice but to have him shot at dawn, hoping that poor Edda would not take it badly. I think it is entirely legitimate . . . that if you invite to your talk show a man who is nearly eighty years old, who has lived in the memory of a father like Benito Mussolini, it can only result in a portrait that is moving and intimate.[15]

Prime-time television thus legitimized Fascism, drawing a private and homespun portrait of Mussolini as father, husband, lover—in short, it made Mussolini into one of us. The same pattern was at work in another episode of the same television show, this time in an episode dedicated to the Savoia family, with the last descendant as a guest, Emanuele Filiberto, who became a hero of the tabloids after his wedding turned into a media event.

Television, after all, had already begun in the 1980s to come to terms with Fascism. Memorable, in this sense, was a program of Beniamino Placido broadcast by RAI on July 4, 1983: *Serata Mussolini* (Mussolini Evening), which deliberately mixed the theoretical and the spectacular, the analysis of professors and politicians with archival footage, songs, and performances, all of which combined to produce a show that was not just enjoyable but also questionable from a historical point of view. This kind of program signals how the media were and are essential to the reevaluation of the regime, and its place in the imagination. Audiovisuals, in fact, still strongly make their presence felt in the ongoing reinterpretation of the period, as we see in the interactive documentary edited by Chiara Ottaviano on the "Italic race."[16] Just as noteworthy is how the history of the twentieth century, and in particular that of the Fascist period, is filtered through the photographs by a specialist on Fascism such as John De Luna, one of the principal figures in the current debate on the regime.[17] One of the major themes of the current debate on the "modernity" of Fascism, as evidenced in a conference in Turin entirely dedicated to the *Contessa di Parma* (*Countess of Parma*, Alessandro Blasetti, 1936).[18] This seemingly minor film by Blasetti asks us to reconsider the alleged modernity of Fascism, which emerged strongly—perhaps even more so—in the films of Mario Camerini, also recently celebrated on the twenty-fifth anniversary of his death.[19]

My impression is that different concepts are often confused: "modernization," which is a fact linked to the social progress of technology; "modernism," a formula tied to the history of art from the late nineteenth century and early twentieth century; and "modernity," a concept that draws on linguistic and stylistic issues, and that is ultimately highly subjective and in the eye of the beholder. What is modernity? It was recently asked at a conference in Milan—the relationship with industrial production, technological progress, or multiple points of view, the complexity of the gaze, or an awareness of crisis?[20] Pure historians interpret it as modernization: for example, the original title of the book by Ruth Ben-Ghiat, which later become *La cultura fascista*, was *Fascist Modernities*, in the plural, as if to underline that there are several kinds of modernity of Fascism.[21] "Cinema," the American scholar writes in a chapter called "Visions of Modernity," "in the thirties attracts many members of the journalistic and literary world seeking the means to articulate the images and behaviors intended to mark the national models of modernity." Modernity is thus understood as a project of transformation of the customs and taste in the public sphere and the private sphere, a sort of reclamation in the metaphorical sense that points to the conquest of souls rather than the earth. Nicola Tranfaglia understands it differently: "By *modernization* I mean—following the definition of the sociologist Luciano Gallino—social change on a large scale involving major economic, political, administrative, family, and religious structures of a society that demonstrably proceed in gradual steps to a model of modern society."[22] This view is echoed by Patrizia Dogliani: "The term *modernization* has been used in multiple fields, from society to the economy, to wonder about the nature of Fascism."[23] Another variable, and another gap between modernization and modernity, is in the informative booklet by Emilio Gentile, *Il fascismo in tre capitoli* (*Fascism in Three Chapters*): "To study *Fascism* also means to reflect on the nature of politics in the era of modernization and mass society, on the role of the individual and the community, and on the meaning of modernity."[24]

Among the most important contributions on the theme of modernity, I would refer to two volumes: one is dedicated to the architect and designer Antonio Valente, who worked with Gioacchino Forzano, creator of the buildings of the Experimental Centre of Cinematography in Rome. The volume, edited by Lucia Cardone and Lorenzo Cuccu, is an example of how one can deal with film from the point of view of its production methods and factual components, in this case the artistic collaborators, technicians, and craftsmen that enriched the panorama of film production even in the most humble roles, creating—as in the case of Cinecittà or Pisorno—a network of uniquely skilled workers who shaped postwar cinema.[25] The other volume I recommend is *Stile Cines* (*Cines Style*) by Vincenzo Buccheri, a study of the famous Cines studio that investigates its method of production in the light of the individual directors who worked there.[26] Buccheri tracks, in such films as *La canzone dell'amore* (*The Love Song*, Gennaro Righelli, 1930), *Resurrectio* (*Resurrection*, 1931), and *Acciaio* (*Steel*, Walter Ruttmann, 1933), "A high rate of stylistic eclecticism, so as to frame the entire formal repertoire available to a director of the period, from the most daring long take to the imperceptible editing, from the naturalist sound to the metaphorical one, from the daily register to the intellectual symbolism."[27] Aside from those cases, however, there is a feeling that the reader probably needs to move out of Italy in order to breathe a different critical air, as interest in Italian Fascism, especially from the point of view of society and culture, has flourished in the field of Anglo-American studies (see especially *Italian Fascism* by Philip Morgan and *Liberal and Fascist Italy*, edited by one of the pioneers of research on Fascism, Adrian Lyttelton).[28] I am thinking again about the development of American cultural studies and their interest in cinema during Fascism: in addition to Ruth Ben-Ghiat, one does well to recall James Hay and his investigation of the popular models; Marcia Landy, attentive to the dual concept of genre and gender (i.e., genre as both a form of expressive typology and sexual differentiation); Angela Dalle Vacche, an

Italian scholar living in the United States who wrote an important chapter on the body in Fascist iconography[29]; and Piero Garofalo and Jacqueline Reich, who research new methodological trends.[30] The debate over Fascism has thus become the key to a more general question about the role of historians and intellectuals in relation to contemporary history as they face a political present on which they cannot be neutral observers.[31] Fascism—its interpretations and its relation to cultural policy—is always a hot topic that brings back issues of ideology long after their apparent death.[32]

"Anti-fascism seems to correspond to a horizon of values that belongs to the past," writes Sergio Luzzatto. "Also because the Fascist period has ended for sixty years . . . it is as if fascism and anti-fascism should no longer relate to the younger generation. . . . But is anti-fascism really useless?" Yes, is the answer of Luzzatto, whose polemic "against the clichés now widely circulating on fascism and anti-fascism is relentless," writes Claudio Pavone in a vigorous review in favor of Luzzatto in *la Repubblica*.[33] You cannot grind all historical subjects in the same mortar without distinction and without making judgments: this kind or revisionism ends up demonstrating that there are no differences in historical memory between the anti-Fascist partisans and the pro-Fascist soldiers fighting for the Mussolini's Salò Republic. The "unique and shared memory," invoked by many, only produces a "negotiated forgetfulness," or a "memory of compromise."

The only solution, according to Luzzatto and Pavone, is to distinguish between history, historiography, and memory, a process without which you create a melting pot made of confused absolutions, a "de-fascisation of fascism." This ahistorical trend is in line with the protocol of "fascism with a human face," as seen in the examples mentioned in the chapter: the biographies of Mussolini, its hierarchy and its "actors," its reconstruction of his "enterprises" and his "works"—all of which risk sugarcoating his brutal legacy with the warm patina of nostalgia.

"We hope," Pavone continued, "that this book will circulate fresh air in the increasingly stale debate on so-called revisionism." This is also my wish: that in the end field studies as well as textual and archive analysis will prevail in addition to the usual ideological debates and interventions. It is very significant, however, that a new generation has been devoting its interests to the history of Fascism. This is demonstrated also by the project of Einaudi's *Dizionario del fascismo* (*Dictionary of Fascism*), edited by Luzzatto, a vast work of new ideas and interpretations that I would put alongside an older classic text.[34] I am speaking of the "lessons of fascism" of Togliatti, recently reedited.[35] With these two texts of the new millennium, and with these two specular testimonies of generations distant from each other, I would like to close, even metaphorically, my mapping of the age-old debate on Fascism and cinema. It is a "Never-Ending Story," which seems to doze off every now and then, but then reemerges corrosively under the pressure of complicated Italian politics.

Notes

1 See my *Cinema e Fascismo* and *L'immagine del fascismo.*

2 See Serri, *I redenti*, who proposes that Rossellini was an "opportunist" like many other intellectuals of his generation.

3 For an overview of state intervention in the twenties and thirties, see Brunetta, *Storia del cinema italiano*; and Cannistraro, *La fabbrica del consenso.*

4 See *Bianco e nero.*

5 See Aquarone, *L'organizzazione dello stato totalitario.*

6 On the relations between the state and Fascist film, see Argentieri, *L'occhio del regime* and *Risate di regime*; Gili, *L'Italie de Mussolini et son cinéma*; and Redi, *Cinema italiano sotto il fascismo* and *Cinecittà 1.*

7 See Casadio et al., *Telefoni bianchi*; and Casadio, *Il grigio e il nero,* esp. 15.

8 See the portrait by Catania in Biondi and Borsotti, *Cultura e fascismo.*

9 "Established [i.e., Cinecittà], it is consecrated to making moving pictures through the art of cinematography for the building of the city."

10 Brunetta, *Storia del cinema italiano.*

11 See Zagarrio, *"Primato" degli intellettuali e neorealismo.*

12 See Mussolini, *Il duce mio padre.* The episode of "Porta a Porta" was broadcast on October 20, 2004.

13 *Edda,* produced by Rai Fiction-Lux, directed by Giorgio Capitani, and aired on May 23–24, 2005.

14 See Maltese, "Soap opera Mussolini."

15 See Cotroneo, *l'Unità,* October 22, 2004.

16 See *La "stirpe italica."* On the relationship between the media and Fascism, see D'Angelo, *Fascismo e media.* For a discourse on the media and the imaginary of the mass of Fascism, see Pinkus, *Bodily Regimes.* Even the film posters are being studied, in another initiative in Turin: see Ventavoli, *Il cinema del ventennio raccontato dai manifesti.*

17 See De Luna et al., *L'Italia del Novecento*; and Romano, *Una biografia per immagini.*

18 See "Contessa di Parma di Alessandro Blasetti."

19 See the conference *Alla ricerca di Mario Camerini.*

20 See *La modernità controversa.*

21 Ben-Ghiat, *La cultura fascista.*

22 Tranfaglia, *Fascismi e modernizzazione in Europa.* See also his *Un passato scomodo.*

23 See Dogliani, *L'Italia fascista 1922–1944.*

24 See Gentile, *Il fascismo in tre capitoli.* On Fascist modernity, see also De Bernardi, *Una dittatura moderna*; and Jeffrey, *Il modernismo reazionario.*

25 See Cardone and Cuccu, *Antonio Valente*; and Baldi and Cardone, *Antonio Valente.*

26 See Buccheri, *Stile Cines*; and *Bianco e Nero 2005.*

27 See Buccheri, *Stile Cines.*

28 See Morgan, *Italian Fascism, 1915–1945*, esp. 137ff.; Lyttelton, *Liberal and Fascist Italy, 1900–1945*; and Braun, "The Visual Arts: Modernism and Fascism."

29 See Hay, *Popular Film Culture in Fascist Italy*; Landy, *Fascism in Film* and *The Folklore of Consensus*; Dalle Vacche, *The Body in the Mirror*; and Pickering-Iazzi, *Politics of the Visible.*

30 Garofalo and Reich, *Reviewing Fascism: Italian Cinema, 1922–1943.* See in particular the reading attuned to homosexual themes of *Ossessione* (*Obsession*, Luchino Visconti, 1943) by Van Watson; the analysis in Hay, *Popular Film Culture in Fascist Italy*; and the discussion of female spectatorship in Pickering-Iazzi, *Politics of the Visible.* Other essays in Garofalo and Reich's edited volume deal with the usual theme of Fascism's relationship with neorealism, or that of the influence of Soviet cinema, investigating a possible Italian star system and notions of theatricality, impersonation, identity, modernity.

31 See a discussion between Giovanni De Luna and Franco Cardini on the craft of the historian in *Porta a porta con la storia.*

32 Sometimes this ideology is used almost instrumentally to talk about other things, especially concerns of cultural memory. In this vein, see especially the work of a younger generation of scholars on Fascism, including Luzzatto, *La crisi dell'antifascismo.*

33 See Pavone, *Resistenza.*

34 De Grazia and Luzzatto, *Dizionario del fascismo.*

35 See Togliatti, *Corso sugli avversari.*

Bibliography

Alla ricerca di Mario Camerini. Conference. Università di Roma Tor Vergata, February 28, 2006.

Aquarone, Alberto. *L'organizzazione dello stato totalitario.* Turin: Einaudi, 1965.

Argentieri, Mino. *L'occhio del regime.* Florence: Vallecchi, 1979.

Argentieri, Mino, ed. *Risate di regime. La commedia italiana 1930–1945.* Venice: Marsilio, 1991.

Baldi, Alfredo and Lucia Cardone, eds. *Antonio Valente: Cinema, architettura, arti figuraive.* In *Bianco e nero* 553 (March 2005).

Ben-Ghiat, Ruth. *La cultura fascista.* Bologna: Il Mulino, 2000.

Bianco e nero. Special Issue: *I tesori del Luce.* Ed. Silvio Celli, nos. 1–3, vol. 5479. Winter 2003.

Bianco e nero. Special issue dedicated to the actor Sergio Tofano: *Sergio Tofano, il cinema a merenda.* Ed. Alessandro Faccioli and Francesco Pitassio, in *Bianco e nero*, no. 552, February 2005.

Braun, Emily. "The Visual Arts: Modernism and Fascism." In *Liberal and Fascist Italy, 1900-1945*. Ed. Adrian Lyttelton. Oxford: Oxford University Press, 2002. 196-215.

Brunetta, Gian Piero. *Storia del cinema italiano. Il cinema del regime, 1929-1945*. Rome: Editori Riuniti, 1993.

Buccheri, Vincenzo. *Stile Cines. Studi sul cinema italiano, 1930-1934*. Milan: Edizioni Vita e Pensiero, 2004.

Cannistraro, Philip V. *La fabbrica del consenso: Fascismo e mass-media*. Bari: Laterza, 1975.

Cardone, Lucia and Lorenzo Cuccu, eds. *Antonio Valente: Il cinema e la costruzione dell'artificio*. Pisa: Edizioni ETS, 2005.

Casadio, Gianfranco, Ernesto G. Laura, and Filippo Cristiano. *Telefoni bianchi. Realtà e finzione nella società e nel cinema degli anni Quaranta*. Ravenna: Longo, 1991.

Casadio, Gianfranco, Ernesto G. Laura, and Filippo Cristiano. *Spettacolo e propaganda nel cinema italiano degli anni Trenta (1931-1943)*. Ravenna: Longo, 1989.

Catania, Alessio. "Luigi Freddi e il libro della solitudine." In *Cultura e fascismo*. Ed. Marino Biondi and Alessandro Borsotti. Florence: Ponte alle Grazie, 1996.

"Contessa di Parma di Alessandro Blasetti. Una commedia nella Torino anni trenta." Turin, October 6, 2005.

Cotroneo, Roberto. *l'Unità*, October 22, 2004.

D'Angelo, Giuseppe. "Fascismo e media: Immagini, propaganda e cultura nell'Italia fra le due guerre," In *Storia contemporanea* 6 (November–December 2003).

Dalle Vacche, Angela. *The Body in the Mirror: Shapes of History in Italian Cinema*. Princeton: Princeton University Press, 1992.

De Grazia, and Sergio Luzzatto. *Dizionario del fascismo*. 2 vols. Turin: Einaudi, 2002.

De Luna, Giovanni, Gabriele D'Autilia, and Luca Criscenti. *L'Italia del Novecento: Le fotografie e la storia*. Turin: Einaudi, 2005.

De Bernardi, Alberto. *Una dittatura moderna. Il fascismo come problema storico*. Milan: Mondadori, 2001.

Dogliani, Patrizia. *L'Italia fascista 1922-1944*. Milan: Sansoni, 1999.

Gentile, Emilio. *Il fascismo in tre capitoli*. Bari: Laterza, 2004.

Gili, Jean A. *L'Italie de Mussolini et son cinéma*. Paris: Éditions Henri Veyrier, 1985.

Hay, James. *Popular Film Culture in Fascist Italy*. Bloomington: Indiana University Press, 1987.

Herf, Jeffrey. *Il modernismo reazionario: Tecnologia, cultura e politica nella Germania di Weimar*. Bologna: Il Mulino, 1988.

Landy, Marcia. *Fascism in Film: The Italian Commercial Cinema, 1931-1943*. Princeton: Princeton University Press, 1986.

Landy, Marcia. *The Folklore of Consensus: Theatricality in the Italian Cinema, 1930-1943*. New York: New York University Press, 1998.

Luzzatto, Sergio. *La crisi dell'antifascismo*. Turin: Einaudi, 2004.

Maltese, Curzio. *Soap opera Mussolini, la Repubblica*. October 22, 2004.

La modernità controversa. Cinema, media e processi di modernizzazione in Italia nei primi quattro decenni del Novecento. Milan: Università Cattolica del Sacro Cuore. September 26-27, 2005.

Morgan, Philip. *Italian Fascism, 1915–1945.* New York: Palgrave Macmillan, 2004.

Mussolini, Romano. *Il duce mio padre.* Milan: Rizzoli, 2004.

Pavone, Claudio. Resistenza. La memoria inquinata. *La Repubblica,* October 6, 2004.

Pickering-Iazzi, Robin. *Politics of the Visible: Writing Women, Culture, and Fascism.* Minneapolis: Minnesota University Press, 1997.

Pinkus, Karen. *Italian Advertising Under Fascism.* Minneapolis: University of Minnesota Press, 1995.

Porta a porta con la storia, in Ttl, supplement to *La Stampa.* October 23, 2004.

Redi, Riccardo, ed. *Cinema italiano sotto il fascismo.* Venice: Marsilio, 1979.

Redi, Riccardo, ed. *Cinecittà 1: Industria e mercato nel cinema italiano tra le due guerre.* Venice: Marsilio, 1985.

Reich, Jacqueline and Piero Garofano, eds. *Re-Viewing Fascism. Italian Cinema, 1922–1943.* Bloomington: Indiana University Press, 2002.

Romano, Sergio. *Una biografia per immagini.* Milan: Longanesi, 2000.

Serri, Mirella. *I redenti: Gli intellettuali che vissero due volte, 1938–1948.* Milan: Il Corbaccio, 2005.

La *"stirpe italica." Vita quotidiana durante il fascismo. Giovani e mamme prolifiche,* The DVDs of Focus Storia. Special issue, Summer 2005. Ed. Chiara Ottaviano.

Togliatti, Palmiro. *Corso sugli avversari. Lezioni sul fascismo.* Turin: Einaudi, 2010.

Tranfaglia, Nicola. *Fascismi e modernizzazione in Europa.* Turin: Bollati Boringhieri, 2001.

Tranfaglia, Nicola. *Un passato scomodo. Fascismo e postfascismo.* Milan: Baldini Castoldi and Dalai, 2006.

Ventavoli, Lorenzo, ed. *Il cinema del ventennio raccontato dai manifesti.* Turin: Bolaffi, 2001.

Zagarrio, Vito. "'Primato' degli intellettuali e neorealismo." In *Il neorealismo cinematografico italiano.* Ed. Lino Miccichè. Venice: Marsilio, 1975.

Zagarrio, Vito. *Cinema e Fascismo. Film, modelli, immaginari.* Venice: Marsilio, 2004.

Zagarrio, Vito. *L'immagine del fascismo: La re-visione del cinema del regime.* Rome: Bulzoni, 2008.

4

Neorealism

Giuliana Minghelli

Neorealism describes a powerfully innovative phenomenon in Italian and world cinema emerging from the Second World War in 1943–45 and coming to a close in the early 1950s. The use of the word "phenomenon" is not casual. Neorealism was not, in my view, a school or a movement; it did not produce any manifestos, and despite being described as a project of national reconstruction or social justice, it can hardly be subsumed under a single political agenda.[1] What unites a certain cluster of filmmakers (Luchino Visconti, Roberto Rossellini, and Vittorio De Sica, as well as the younger Giuseppe De Santis, Michelangelo Antonioni, and Federico Fellini) as "neorealists" is a confused yet urgent commitment to represent "what is," the wounded world emerging from Fascism and the war.[2]

"Why Italy first?" philosopher Gilles Deleuze asked in his two-volume study of cinema: why of all countries did the postwar revolution of the cinematic image start there? "Cinema had to begin again from zero," observes Deleuze, "yet without illusions."[3] Italy's historical position was unique. It was a defeated Fascist nation, the homeland of Fascism. But after the Armistice of 1943, it also became an ambiguous partner of the Allies and had a small yet well-organized Resistance movement. As a result, Italy, unlike Germany, never came to terms officially, through public trials or a process of reconciliation, with its twenty years of dictatorship. These conflicting experiences opened a fertile ground, at once "liberated" and yet highly charged with the unspoken, for a new cinema.[4] Neorealism, a makeshift and imprecise, even generic and reductive label, signifies the first and arguably most visually powerful new way of processing the historical trauma of Fascism and the war.

1 Journey in a Primordial Chaos

During his return trip from Auschwitz, Jewish-Italian writer Primo Levi described the Europe he saw in the immediate aftermath of the war as a primordial chaos. Frontiers were erased, as masses of survivors, displaced civilians, and soldiers moved across the Continent to escape from or return to what they used to know as home. To Levi this seemed like the beginning

FIGURE 4.1 *In the ruins of Florence. From* Paisan.

FIGURE 4.2 *A battle on the River Po. From* Paisan.

of a new world: Nazism and Fascism, with their virulent militarism and racism, lay in ashes, while older values, norms, and allegiances were also (temporarily) dissolved, freeing space and time in an unprecedented way. In this environment—radically open, magmatic, yet weighed down with loss, shame, and mourning—neorealism pursued, in the words of Pier Paolo Pasolini, "the rediscovery of Italy . . . without rhetorical filters or falsities."[5] "Reality hidden under myths slowly reemerged," Cesare Zavattini noted, "cinema started its creation of the world" (*Opere*, 681).

One way to tell the story of neorealist cinema would be to relate its feverish journeys, in its attempt to film the diversity of what Fascism had suppressed, starting with the restlessness of Visconti's 1943 road movie *Ossessione* (*Obsession*), and finding repeated expression in the work of Rossellini: from the journey up a war-torn peninsula in *Paisà* (*Paisan*, 1946) and the odyssey of a woman displaced by the war in *Stromboli* (1951), to his modern revisiting of the Grand Tour in *Viaggio in Italia* (*Voyage to Italy*, 1954).[6] On a more intimate and everyday scale, the restless walking of urban streets sets the rhythm of neorealist storytelling in Rossellini's *Roma città aperta* (*Rome, Open City*, 1945), and De Sica's *Sciuscià* (*Shoeshine*, 1946), *Ladri di biciclette* (*Bicycle Thieves*, 1948), *Miracolo a Milano* (*Miracle in Milan*, 1950), and *Umberto D.* (1952), even echoing well beyond the neorealist period in the early work of Fellini (*Luci del varietà* [*Variety Lights*, 1950]; *La strada*, 1954; *Le notti di Cabiria* [*Nights of Cabiria*, 1957]); Antonioni (*Il grido*, 1956; *L'avventura*, 1960; *La notte*, 1961; *L'eclisse*, 1962); and Pasolini (*Accattone*, 1961; *Uccellacci e Uccellini* [*Hawks and Sparrows*, 1966]). This bodily kinetics, which informs the filming and what critic Siegfried Kracauer defines as the camera's "permeability" to the streets, speaks of neorealism's earthbound point of view, radically immersed in the real. "When history is made in the streets, the streets tend to move unto the screen,"[7] and what enters the screen is the *now* of the postwar moment, a ruinous, defamiliarized landscape inhabited by a struggling humanity (tramps, children, unemployed workers) and traversed by overwhelming historical emotions—the experience of twenty years of Fascism, war, Resistance, and liberation as well as the hopes of a new democracy.

2 What Is "Neo" in This "Realism"? Early Insights from Cesare Zavattini and André Bazin

Although lacking a manifesto, neorealism had a most conscious proponent in Cesare Zavattini, writer and longtime collaborator of De Sica. Early on, Zavattini articulated the tasks of postwar cinema starting from a basic recognition that cinema had fallen short of its duties when faced with Fascism and its horrors ("1895–1945, fifty years of cinema; it seems a tombstone . . . Cinema did not help us").[8] Zavattini felt that to atone for the past and reground the medium ethically—"Neorealism is by now the conscience of cinema" (*"Neorealismo, ecc.,"* 768)—cinema had to return to the documentary-style roots of early cinematography: not simply to represent social reality, but to stand in a relation of openness to the world, what Zavattini called "la poetica dell'incontro" (the poetics of the encounter). For Zavattini, "the banal doesn't exist" (*"Neorealismo, ecc.,"* 730): any anonymous everyday act can be the point of departure. "What is at stake is to give humanity in every minute its historical importance" (*"Neorealismo, ecc.,"* 725).

Zavattini understood such a cinema as inseparable from the pedagogic mission of developing a new spectator: "Few have the patience to look and listen" (*"Neorealismo, ecc.,"* 743), he noted, so cinema's chief task was "allevare il nostro guardatore" (to educate/raise our viewer; *"Neorealismo, ecc.,"* 762) by cultivating attentiveness. This ongoing reminder of the materiality and contingency of our looking—"*Now, here, you,* are watching these things"[9]—gives a sense of how neorealism, one, reinvented nineteenth-century realism in terms of a documentary-style practice that blurred the boundary between the spectacle of life and the cinematic spectacle; and two, fostered an idea of seeing as an ethical practice.

The stories of the Italian postwar films are so simple and minimal (a partisan is killed, children struggle to earn money, a man's bike is stolen) that for a long time neorealism was stereotyped as populist social realism. Nonetheless, as early as 1946 one of neorealism's subtler interpreters, French film critic André Bazin, hailed the "Italian cinema of the Liberation" as a revolution both of content and form. If Zavattini voiced neorealism's general ethos and aspirations, Bazin's seminal work inaugurated the close study of the aesthetic achievements of the new cinema.[10] The material conditions of postwar film production, which pushed the filmmakers, Bazin noted, out of the gutted studios and into the streets, spurred neorealism's commitment to "the portrayal of actuality" (*What Is Cinema?* 2:20), and forced "the elimination of all cinematic conventions,"[11] stimulating a radical new way of seeing and telling. Thus, the concern with everyday events meshed with a preference for on-site shooting and "the rejection of the star concept" in favor of an "amalgam" (*What Is Cinema?* 2:23) of professional actors and common people. The Neorealist camera's consistent use of long takes and depth of field projected a "concrete point of view" (*What Is Cinema?* 2:33), flowing with the events and adhering to reality to the point of creating what Bazin called, using an archaic sensual meaning of the word, a "cinematic tact" (*What Is Cinema?* 2:32), the ability to make us feel the material texture of the world, its tactility. The belief that reality cannot be scripted but must be revealed to the camera in its "factual integrity" through startling, undeciphered encounters gives rise, for Bazin, to a new narrative unit of neorealist storytelling, the "image-fact," in which the "fact," concrete, fragmentary, and ambiguous, takes the place of the traditional shot's abstract sectioning of reality.

A floating partisan, a man shooting himself, a child crying next to the bodies of his slaughtered parents: these are shards of reality from Rossellini's film *Paisan*: small, indivisible units of expression. For Bazin, these images, elliptical and fragmented, impose their own narrative organization that gives rise to a new cinematic syntax where nothing is brought into arbitrary

FIGURE 4.3 *A partisan executed by the Germans.*
Source: From the sixth episode of *Paisan*.

FIGURE 4.4 *A partisan killing himself to escape capture.*
Source: From the sixth episode of *Paisan*.

FIGURE 4.5 *A child crying after his family has been shot by the Germans.*
Source: From the sixth episode of *Paisan*.

relief, "everything . . . is of a like importance" (*What Is Cinema?* 2:36). Bazin highlights a new idea of authorship and spectatorship arising from this cinematography: the authorial presence is erased, as if the film had made itself; the spectator, on the other hand, is asked to step up and engage with the world represented, actively questioning perception and interpretation. Bereft of a traditional linear narrative, the viewers are plunged into an unknown landscape where following the story is like hopping from stone to stone to cross a river (Bazin, *What Is Cinema?* 35).

While criticism within Italy for a long time focused mainly on content and ideology (neorealism being identified tout court with the Resistance and postwar reconstruction), Bazin's understanding of neorealism as both the "cinema of the Liberation" and a radical break from established codes of cinematic coherence and readability helped establish neorealism's international status and its importance as a radical beginning in the history of cinema.[12] His momentous insight into postwar Italian cinema, and hence cinema in general, as an ongoing process of opening new fields of visibility would also spur future theoretical developments that we will return to at the close of this chapter.

3 The Beginnings: Neorealism under Fascism, *Ossessione*

Despite their association with the Resistance, liberation, and the new Italy, the majority of neorealist filmmakers were neither partisans nor victims of persecution. Rossellini, De Sica, and Zavattini already had full-fledged careers under Fascism. Rossellini directed nature documentaries and a series of feature films (referred to as his Fascist trilogy: *La nave bianca* [*The White Ship*, 1941]; *Un pilota ritorna* [*A Pilot Returns*, 1942]; *L'uomo dalla croce* [*The Man of the Cross*, 1943]); De Sica had been a film star in light comedies in the 1930s and started directing in the 1940s. And Zavattini had been a successful writer for magazines, radio, and cinema since the 1930s. The continuity of personnel, techniques, and infrastructure between Fascist and the postwar cinema has been widely remarked upon.[13]

In 1924, Mussolini founded Istituto LUCE to centralize propaganda through newsreels, but it was only in the 1930s that the regime invested heavily in cinema: the Venice Biennale of cinema started in 1932, the Centro Sperimentale di Cinematografia was founded in 1935, and the Cinecittà studios were opened in 1937. All the while film magazines flourished. Yet ironically cinema would become Italy's "strongest weapon," according to Mussolini's famous dictum, only after Fascism was vanquished.

The case of *Cinema*, the most advanced of the cinema journals and edited by Mussolini's son Vittorio, sheds light on this complex story of continuity and change. From the late 1930s, young film critics and future directors (De Santis, Visconti, Antonioni) worked toward a new idea of cinema on its pages, an aesthetic pursuit that for many coincided with political dissidence.[14] Looking to earlier literary and cinematic traditions of realism— for example, the nineteenth-century naturalist and regionalist literature of Giovanni Verga, the American short story and New Deal photography,[15] Soviet and French films of the 1920s and 1930s—these young critics strove to articulate an aesthetic that would move beyond both Fascist propaganda and Hollywood-style melodramas (known in Italy as *telefoni bianchi* [white telephones] for their obsession with fashion and consumerism).[16] In "For an Italian Landscape," the future assistant director of *Ossessione*, Giuseppe De Santis, argued that the filming of an actual environment was the key to the rebirth of a national cinema.[17] Landscape was not only a setting for telling new stories, but also an occasion for a radical rethinking of the medium itself. As Antonioni theorized in a 1939 article "For a Film on the River Po," the goal was a cinematography emerging from nature.[18] Upsetting the conventional hierarchy between figure and background, the landscape was proposed as the protagonist of a story of passage and movement, a vision Antonioni realized in his documentary *Gente del Po* (*People of the Po*), shot in 1942 (though released only in 1947).

Ossessione, Luchino Visconti's directorial debut in which many of the young critics of *Cinema* participated, was the first feature film to articulate this aesthetic. According to cinema lore, it was upon seeing the film rushes that editor Mario Serandrei coined the term "neorealism" to describe the striking materiality of the images. Shot in the Po Valley, Ferrara and Ancona, *Ossessione* is a journey in a submerged, provincial Italy, previously unseen. This unclaimed, politically virgin ground ruptured the

FIGURE 4.6 *Opening titles, on the road to the inn.*

FIGURE 4.8 *Gino and Lo Spagnolo resting in front of the Duomo in Ancona.*

FIGURE 4.7 *Actors and director on the set of the movie. © Coll. Museo Nazionale del cinema Torino.*

conventionality of both linear narrative and the Fascist social order by suggesting a critique of the everyday and the possibility of an alternative space of experience.

Within *Ossessione* coexist a formulaic crime story (an adaptation of James Cain's novel *The Postman Always Rings Twice* [1934]) and an innovative way of looking at the world. It tells the story of Giovanna, a black-clad femme fatale unhappily married to an older innkeeper, and Gino, an indecisive tramp who kills her husband and ends up bound to a house conquered through violence. Gino and Giovanna's obsession to find a way out from their stories of homeless wandering and silent submission ends tragically. With the exception of the husband Bragana, all the characters of *Ossessione*—Giovanna, Gino, his bohemian friend lo Spagnolo (the Spaniard), the ballerina Anita—are exiles with shady pasts of *vagabondaggi* (vagabondage) and destitution. Inhabiting a home, and by extension, belonging to a country, is the true "obsession" and a confused utopian yearning in the film. If the unhappy and restless characters are imprisoned in an inescapable plot—an apt expression of the predicament of the human subject under Fascism—the profilmic space (i.e., all that is placed in front of the camera captured in the image) opens a deep surface that breaks the fatality and conventionality of the story. Far from simply expressing a heightened realism, this visual depth opens up what Walter Benjamin called the "optical unconscious," to describe the unspoken historical substrata of images. This aesthetic choice grants the cinematic image a freedom that intimates the presence within Fascist society of other stories, the suggestion of artistic and social liberations yet to come.[19]

Ossessione sits on the cusp of a major historical upheaval. Shot between June and November 1942, it was first screened in Rome on May 16, 1943, and immediately sequestered by the censors. A few months later on July 25, Mussolini was arrested, and on September 8, General Badoglio announced that Italy had joined the Allies. As the Allied army slowly advanced up the Peninsula, a brutal civil war raged in the occupied north as the Resistance battled against the Nazis and a retrenched Fascist Republic of Salò. It was on this liberated territory that the new cinema would thrive.

Visconti's films marked equally important moments in Italy's tumultuous postwar. In 1945, he codirected with Serandrei, De Santis, and Marcello Pagliero *Giorni di Gloria* (*Days of Glory*, 1945) a documentary on the Resistance. His neorealist masterpiece, *La terra trema* (1948), an adaptation and rereading in terms of class struggle of Giovanni Verga's 1881 novel *I Malavoglia* (*House by the Medlar Tree*), was commissioned by the Communist Party during the fierce 1948 political elections. Shot on site, acted by local fishermen, and spoken in Sicilian dialect, the film is at the same time the "purest" example of the neorealist aesthetic and its greatest financial flop. After Visconti's final contribution to neorealism, *Bellissima* (1951), which portrayed the cruel world of Cinecittà, his 1954 *Senso*, a highly stylized costume drama of an episode in the Risorgimento, was hailed by critics as the official close of the neorealist movement.[20]

4 Cinema as National Epic: Roberto Rossellini

The filmmaker who fully embodied neorealism's complex engagement with history and inaugurated a powerful visual epic for the new nation was Roberto Rossellini (1906–77). As Italy emerged from Fascism, Rossellini's work succeeded "not only to imagine a new Italy for Italians, but also a new Italy to be exported to the world."[21] In the summer of 1944, as the war was still raging north of a recently liberated Rome, that new Italy found its first powerful cinematic articulation in *Rome, Open City*. A dramatic portrayal of life in an occupied city, the first "liberated" film was aptly described as "a mythical reconstruction of the past in which good memories are made to drive out bad."[22] The "bad memories" marking the six months of German occupation loom large in the history of the nation: the October 1943 mass deportation of the Jews and the 1944 Fosse Ardeatine massacre of 335 civilians in reprisal for a partisan attack in Via

Rasella. In the words of screenwriter Ugo Pirro, this history "was too raw to become a film. . . . Nobody had the courage. Neorealism could not start at Via Rasella."[23] Steering away from troubling and politically polarizing memories, the Catholic Rossellini, together with communist screenwriter Sergio Amidei and conservative journalist Alberto Consiglio, focused on stories of everyday heroism and resistance.

Set in the working-class neighborhood of Prenestino, the film tells the story over two days time of a cell of resistors: the communist leader Manfredi who comes to hide in a comrade's apartment; Francesco, a typographer about to be married to the feisty *popolana* Sora Pina (Anna Magnani); the priest Don Pietro (played by popular theater actor Aldo Fabrizi), who supports the Resistance by delivering messages; and Marcello, the son of Sora Pina and a member of a band of child partisans who carry out a daring bombing of a depot only to be spanked by their terrified parents upon returning home. The film is a mélange of registers ranging from comedy to high drama and horror.

The most iconic images from the film are based on real events: Anna Magnani being mowed down as she runs after the truck taking away Francesco during a roundup on the eve of their wedding was fashioned after the actual shooting of a working-class woman, Teresa Gullace. Manfredi tortured in the offices of the Gestapo was modeled on the horrors of the actual SS headquarters in Via Tasso. And the shooting of Don Pietro was

FIGURES 4.9–4.12 *The sequence of Francesco's arrest: Pina runs after the truck; after she is mowed down, Marcello runs to her help and is held back by Don Pietro.*

inspired by the execution of the partisan priest Don Giuseppe Morosini. The movie is a story of betrayal—Manfredi handed over to the Germans by his cocaine-addicted girlfriend Marina—and resilience against the Fascist and German occupying forces. As both communist and Catholic resistors die, the movie closes with a haunting image of the band of child partisans as they walk back toward the city, the cupola of San Pietro looming on the horizon, an image of mourning and hope for the new nation.

Rome, Open City was immediately hailed in Italy and abroad as epoch-making for its unprecedentedly raw cinematic representation of the brutality and heroism of the war.[24] Unlike other canonical neorealist works, the film was a great success both with the reviewers and at the box office.[25] Later critics, however, objected to the melodramatic tone, the conventional storytelling, and the Manichean representation of the politics, pitting the good partisans and their innocent supporters (priests, women, and children) against Nazi-Fascists painted as traitors, drug addicts, or sadistic homosexuals (especially the Gestapo chief, Major Bergmann). Recently, more nuanced readings have tried to account for the emotion that the film elicited in postwar audiences. Thus, Restivo sees a hybrid tension in the film between "the tyranny of classical enunciation" (a tightly plotted drama aligned with the master narrative of Nazi occupation) and the subversive eruption of documentary-like footage (for example, the sequence of Pina's death) that "allegorizes the birth of the aesthetic of reality out of the bankruptcy of the Fascist aesthetic" and prepares the viewer for the full-fledged visual revolution of *Paisan* (27).

Paisan is divided into six episodes, framed by documentary footage with voice-over narration. Starting with the landing in Sicily on July 10, 1943, the film follows the advance of the American army, revealing a country that had lost any immediate political and historical point of reference. The episodic structure foregrounds the film's tension between unity and fragmentation.[26] The reassuring image of the *paese* (country) contained on the military map, descends within each episode into a landscape of *spaesamento* (disorientation).[27]

Every story revolves around an encounter between Allied soldiers and Italians, the ensuing cultural clash and the effort to understand each other: Joe, an American GI just landed in a nocturnal Sicily and a local girl Carmela; an African American MP and a street urchin in the ruins of Naples; a soldier and a Roman girl in a story of love and prostitution in the newly liberated Rome; a British nurse and an Italian crossing a Florence under siege. After an awkward meeting of American chaplains and Franciscan monks, the film closes on the solidarity of Office of Strategic Services (OSS) men and partisans struggling for survival along the Po River. In each story the camera is engaged in an act of witnessing and memorialization of the loss and heroism in the everyday reality of the war.

Paisan has come to exemplify the formal revolution inaugurated by neorealism. Rossellini's technique catches the events unawares in their shocking unfolding, creating a film language marked by ellipses. The camera adheres to the profilmic environment: from the darkness that envelops the newly landed American soldiers in the first episode and the ruins that dominate Naples and Florence to the final labyrinthine waterways of the Po.[28] Immersed, even hidden, in the landscape, Rossellini's gaze is detached and unobtrusive. As a cinematic materialization of what writer Italo Calvino

FIGURE 4.13 *Carmela and Joe in the first episode.*

FIGURE 4.14 *Nurse Harriet listening to the dying partisan in Florence.*

FIGURE 4.15 *American OSS men and partisans burying their dead in the Po episode.*

called "the anonymous voice of the age" (1186), the impersonal gaze of the camera suspends conventional authorship recalling instead the time-honored figure of the storyteller.

These stylistic features are intimately connected with the ambiguity of postwar Italian identity. *Paisan* is almost exclusively narrated from the perspective of the Anglo-American characters (at once participants, chroniclers, bystanders, or involuntary tourists on a strange new type of Grand Tour). This narrative choice filters our witnessing of the emergence of a new nation and helps unify the great variety of regional, linguistic, and cultural differences that Rossellini represents. The title fully encapsulates this operation. A word of recognition between immigrants, reimported to Italy by the American army, *paisà* (countryman) works as a talisman, heralding the possibility of contact, communication, and community in the midst of wartime chaos. At the same time, the word papers over both the divisions between Italians and Allied troops and, more importantly, between Italians enmeshed in a civil war. As the film moves north, where the civil war is raging, *paisà* gives way to a different word: *partigiano*. The unresolved tension between "partigiano" (the one who takes political sides) and "paisà" (fellow countryman, from the same village), a tension that only the mediation of the American presence holds in check, epitomizes the uncertainty surrounding the question of national identity. *Partigiano*, a word that points upriver to the ongoing struggle with Fascism, though also ideally to the future of the new nation, disappears like the partisans swallowed up by water at the end of the film. Like the word *Paisan* chiseled on stone in the opening titles, the film stands as an ironic memorial to the unresolved politics of war and Resistance.[29]

5 Neorealism and the Religion of the Everyday: De Sica and Zavattini

While neorealism marks the beginning of the cinema of auteurs, its greatness can be best understood as a complex, collective endeavor, and the collaboration of De Sica and Zavattini reveals the importance of this teamwork. De Sica's visual genius is at work behind the camera and, as an actor himself, in his intense interaction with the nonprofessional performers. But his films are unthinkable without Zavattini's poetic and critical input into the overall conception, storytelling, and editing. This collaboration was well established by the time of their first postwar feature, *Shoeshine* (1946), about the struggle for survival in Rome of two shoeshine boys. Key aesthetic choices, fully emerging in *Shoeshine*, were already in place in their 1943 film *I bambini ci guardano* (*The Children Are Watching Us*): the lowering of the camera-eye to the level of children as witnesses/protagonists dramatizes the act of seeing and the idea of a new spectator.[30] Simultaneously, the everyday working-class neighborhoods and forgotten peripheries of Rome and Milan in *Shoeshine*, *Bicycle Thieves*, *Umberto D.*, and *Miracle in Milan* also emerge as a new protagonist/spectator.

The simple story of a man's bicycle being stolen, De Sica's legendary *Bicycle Thieves* was described as an example of "pure cinema." Shot with nonprofessional actors in the streets of Rome, it suggested "the perfect aesthetic illusion of reality."[31] Yet nothing was improvised in the 1948 film: the production was minutely planned and lavishly funded,[32] and the apparent simplicity of story, image, and montage—easily condensed into a moral aphorism (in an unjust world, the poor are doomed to suffer) or an exposé of social evils (unemployment and a lack of social solidarity in postwar Italy)—disguises a consummate work of art that poses ongoing challenges to criticism.

Told over the space of three days, *Bicycle Thieves* is the story of an unemployed worker in Rome, Antonio Ricci (played by factory worker Lamberto Maggiorani), who at the start of his new job as a bill-hanger

FIGURES 4.16–4.18 *Bruno and Antonio getting ready to go to work and the ride toward the center of Rome.*

has his bicycle stolen. The film opens as Antonio and his wife Maria (the journalist Lianella Carell cast in her role extemporaneously by De Sica) upon notification of a new job, go to redeem their old bike from the pawnshop. The next day a new character appears as if by magic, Bruno (Enzo Stajola), Antonio's older son, as he lovingly shines the battered bike. With Bruno, a steady reservoir of hope and energy in the stark unfolding of the story, Antonio rides triumphantly into the city only to return by foot that evening in despair.

There are two movies in *Bicycle Thieves*: the one just recounted, with the bike, and one without it. The opening bicycle-themed story—covering two days yet lasting only thirty minutes of cinematic time—is a textbook of classical montage, with cuts and dissolves to indicate great temporal condensation, and classical narrative modes ranging from realism to romantic comedy, musical, melodrama, and tragedy.[33] The second part, the erratic Sunday spent by Antonio and Bruno walking through a hostile and indifferent Rome in search of the bike, takes a full hour of cinematic time. "What is a bicycle?" asks Zavattini at the opening of his final treatment for the film, a question that reveals the importance of the marginal object as the dramatic focus of the story.[34] The missing bicycle works as a powerful narrative device and a highly charged element in the symbolic economy of the film. With its disappearance, not only Antonio but also the narrative is left without a means of locomotion, and the story loosens, becomes episodic, utterly immersed in contingency. The sustained focus on the rich interaction between the man and the child gives the sense that the story is elapsing in real time. Skipping along with his father and looking at him insistently, Bruno's presence works as an "internal chorus,"[35] an actor-spectator who expressively or mutely comments on the action. Mature and responsible while his father is lost and confused, Bruno sees and judges, occasionally acts, and most importantly forgives.

Bicycle Thieves has the somewhat crippling reputation of being the most realistic, and therefore least adventurous of neorealist movies. Its conventional camera movements and classical montage set it apart from the exhilaratingly disruptive and fragmented forms of Rossellini's modernist cinematography. But *Bicycle Thieves* does something unexpected and complex: it theorizes two ways of making cinema. Through the trick of the present/absent bicycle, De Sica and Zavattini dramatize, under the spectator's very eyes, the transition from an older (faster) Hollywood cinema to the newer (slower) cinema of neorealism, a passage from what one might term "realism with wheels" to one without. The disappearance of the bike tears the smooth surface of the realist image so that common everyday objects become dreamlike, hallucinatory. De Sica's film retrains the viewer to perceive reality as a foreign territory.

Unlike *Paisan*, *Bicycle Thieves* has virtually no date markers, a fact that fosters a sense of its being a generic postwar scenario. Too thorough to be casual, the erasure of time hides the film's intimate and dramatic entwinement with history.[36] The planning and location searches for the film took place in the fall and winter of 1947–48 in a Rome dominated by a fierce electoral campaign between the Popular Front coalition led by the Communist Party and a Christian Democratic Party backed by the Vatican and the United States. The Cold War had redefined the United States' alliances: long gone were the days when American soldiers fought side by side with the partisans in *Paisan*; it was *Paisan*'s episode of the encounter with the monks and allied chaplains that had held the key to the nation's future.[37] On April 16, 1948, two days before Zavattini completed the screenplay and a month before the shooting of the film began, the Christian Democrats won, marking the end of the revolutionary era that had begun in 1943 and the beginning of a "restoration" of old values and power relations.[38] To the extent that neorealism was associated with the very forces that had earned Italy a "renewed" moral standing, this electoral defeat was a defeat for the new cinema. Through the loss of the bike, the anguished face of Lamberto Maggiorani, and the oppressive presence of Rome, *Bicycle Thieves* mourns the loss of the postwar dream.

Yet the sense of resignation and marginalization has far more profound roots in the past, as Rome's geography and architecture testify.[39] Sorlin notes how "distance is a fundamental feature in [*Bicycle Thieves*]" (*European Cinemas*, 119). At the start, we find Antonio and his family exiled from the city in the faraway Val Melaina, one of the *borgate* (suburbs) built between 1935 and 1940 by Mussolini to house the population displaced by the *sventramenti* (disembowelings) of Rome's central working-class neighborhoods. Then throughout the film, Fascist architecture physically thwarts Antonio and underscores his most anguished moments right through to his final humiliation in front of the Stadio Nazionale built by Mussolini in 1927. Thus, the profilmic space powerfully yet silently portrays the

FIGURE 4.19 *Antonio, seated in front of his apartment building in Val Melaina.*

FIGURE 4.20 *Ponte Duca d'Aosta in Rome where Antonio loses Bruno.*

FIGURE 4.21 *The Stadio Nazionale, in front of which Antonio's story ends in defeat.*

forgotten history of Fascism, adding a further layer to the seeming simplicity and immediacy of the story.

While *Bicycle Thieves*, like many neorealist masterpieces, did poorly in Italy, it triumphed internationally with popular audiences and critics alike. Subsequently, ongoing accusations of easy sentimentality and superficiality have tarnished the film's standing in the cinematic canon.[40] *Bicycle Thieves* might be "weepy," but the tears that seal its closing images are far from mawkish: they bring no easy consolation or cheap promise.

In this sense, the film fully embodies the secular, unsentimental task of the new cinema as stated by Zavattini: "To follow everything that is there, letting people understand that beyond this there is nothing else" (*Opere*, 691). That "nothing else," contained in Bruno's final gesture of reaching for the hand of his defeated father to take him home, interrogates us to this day.

6 The Legacies of Neorealism: Finished and Unfinished

Like its beginning, the close of neorealism is a matter of differing opinions and ongoing discussion. Most agree on the *courte durée*, which has neorealism coinciding with the immediate postwar season and concluding with *Umberto D.* in 1952.[41] After the 1948 elections and the onset of Cold War politics, the country froze over culturally, economically, and socially. neorealist directors were attacked for projecting a degraded image of the country and excluded from state subsidies. The controversy surrounding *Umberto D*, famously labeled by Giulio Andreotti (later seven times the prime minister for the Christian Democrats, and at the time the all-powerful czar of Italian cinema) as "washing dirty linen in public," gives a measure of the political backlash.[42] In this general atmosphere of intimidation and retrenchment, the time of neorealism, that view from the streets, seemed over. De Sica and Zavattini's 1951 fable *Miracle in Milan* seems an apt allegory. The film tells the story of the childlike Totò and a utopian community of beggars living in a shantytown on the outskirts of Milan, who, after being evicted by the capitalist Mr. Mobbi, fly away from Piazza Duomo on the brooms of the street sweepers in search of a better country. Soon after 1948 each of our filmmakers would similarly mount on their figurative broom and fly away.

De Sica was called to Hollywood; Visconti returned cinema to a theater of historical melodramas; Rossellini, after existentialist films with Ingrid Bergman including (*Stromboli*, 1951), *Europa '51* (1952), and *Voyage to Italy* (1954), abandoned traditional filmmaking for the popular appeal of RAI, the national television network where he made historical documentaries.

Generally, cinema retreated to the studios and embraced forms of escapism. Already in 1949, Giuseppe De Santis pushed neorealism in a more popular and traditional direction with *Riso amaro* (*Bitter Rice*), a portrayal of the life of the rice pickers and the Americanization of Italian postwar society built around Hollywood elements of sex appeal and crime. Later, De Sica would be instrumental in the wholesale popularization of neorealism with his 1950s work both as director in *L'oro di Napoli* (*The Gold of Naples*, 1954) and as actor in the successful series started with *Pane amore e fantasia* (*Bread, Love, and Dreams*, 1953) directed by Luigi Comencini.

FIGURE 4.22 *Publicity poster of* Miracle in Milan *with the tramps leaving on their brooms to find a better place.*

FIGURE 4.23 *Publicity poster of* Riso amaro *with its focus on conventional sex appeal.*

This latter taming of neorealism came to be known as *neorealismo rosa* (pink neorealism), its hardships, beggars, and *il popolo* redeemed in facile manner by sentimentality and happy endings.[43] The national body politic, so central to neorealist cinema, came to be substituted with the very earthly bodies of the *maggiorate*, divas like Silvana Mangano, Sophia Loren, and Gina Lollobrigida.[44]

FIGURE 4.24 *In* Accattone, *Vittorio, nicknamed Accattone (beggar), walking in the periphery of Rome.*

Alternatively, however, neorealism can be thought in a *longue durée*, its vision continuing and changing throughout the 1950s, into the Italian Economic Miracle of the 1960s and beyond. A look at the work of poet and filmmaker Pier Paolo Pasolini will afford a sense of a longer periodization. In a seminal 1966 essay entitled "Cinema di Poesia" ("Cinema of Poetry"), Pasolini sketched a history of cinema divided into two main moments. The first phase, roughly coinciding with classical Hollywood production, uses narrative to subordinate and tame the irrational and dreamlike nature of cinematic images. Then, starting with the 1960s, and specifically with his films and those of Antonioni, Bernardo Bertolucci, and Jean-Luc Godard, a new lyrical cinema emerged in which the images, freed from a narrative imperative, give rise to a mixed enunciation, at once "objective" and dreamlike, documentary-driven, and visionary. Pasolini's *Accattone* (1961) is a case in point: a portrayal of the Roman sub-proletariat, highly stylized and allegorical, and at the same time steeped in the profilmic reality of the slums. Although this first film of Pasolini's is at once a recuperation (as a dark remake of *Bicycle Thieves*) of neorealism and its eulogy, Italian postwar cinema is virtually erased from his 1966 periodization. Yet, the neorealist camera—which tells a (realist) story and dwells in (the lyrical mystery of the) images, displaying a contamination of gazes between character, environment, and author—is a clear point of reference for the *cinema di poesia* (cinema of poetry). But an anxiety of influence prevents

Pasolini from recognizing it as such.[45] Nevertheless, his view of the new cinema, inspired by semiotics and linguistics, as the "written language of reality" can be read as the first sustained Italian theorization of the neorealist revolution in cinematic language, and one that has had lasting impact.

Pasolini's reflection had a great influence on Gille Deleuze's work on cinema. The notion of the cinematic image suspended between visibility and invisibility, profilmic materiality and mental processes (memory, dream, and thought), became the cornerstone of his theory in his dyptich *Cinema 1: The Movement-Image* and *Cinema 2: The Time-Image*. For Deleuze, neorealism is the groundbreaking moment in the history of cinema when this radically different regime of vision emerges, the transformation from a cinema of action to a cinema of time, from a focus on events to the act of seeing and perceiving itself. The change from the movement-image of prewar cinema to the time-image of neorealism, the French Nouvelle Vague, and other avant-garde cinemas that followed is defined by the slackening of plot and a giving way to wandering and contemplation. Stressing the oneiric and mental dimension of the image, Deleuze moves beyond Bazin's reading of neorealism. He highlights the dissolution of realist milieus and the "mounting of optical and sound situations," pointing to the emergence of a new lacunary perception of space ("any-space-whatever"). Neorealism marks the passage from "films that had riveted spectators to their seats . . . to features encouraging reflection on the relation of the medium to what it cannot represent."[46] In Deleuze's study, neorealism was transformed into the first manifestation of a cinema of invisibility, the time-image being a site of loss, disorientation, and amnesia. Visconti's *Ossessione* was one of the films that marked this momentous change for Deleuze. Gino and Giovanna spend much of their time wandering, uncertain about what action to take (whether to escape from the husband, kill him, or simply leave each other), lost in daydreaming. For this reason, Giovanna, "closer to a visionary, a sleepwalker, than to a seductress or a lover" (3), represents the first protagonist of the cinema of the time-image.

As its best critics have argued, once neorealism is defined not by its content but by its way of seeing, its duration and scope as a movement are greatly enlarged. From this perspective, Rossellini, De Sica, and the younger Antonioni and Fellini belong to the same era because they all make the same choice, that of immersing themselves in the materiality of the world. While the background changes—in 1945, reality was the war; in 1948, the everyday hardships and the shortcomings of reconstruction; in 1950, the year of Antonioni's *Cronaca di un amore* (*Story of a Love Affair*), the ennui of a bourgeois society without memory; in 1954, the year of Fellini's *La strada*, the sleepy Italian provinces—the open structure of neorealist storytelling and vision remain the same.

Despite neorealism's global canonical status, in Italy the reception of postwar cinema has been at once enthusiastic and fraught with reservations.

"Is neorealism dead or alive?" was the cliché that structured much of the Italian debate on cinema from the 1950s into the 1960s. Federico Fellini had a journalist ask this question of the American actress Sylvia (Anita Ekberg) in *La dolce vita* (1960). Evoked next to the full-figured Sylvia, the vast un-sexiness of the topic suddenly fills the room. "Say alive," someone curtly suggests, and Sylvia's baffled smile seems to bury the stale issue once and for all. This scene gives an iconic articulation to a persistent affect—a mix of annoyance, impatience, and bored dismissal—which, as early as 1950, revealed an anxious desire in Italy to archive the cinematic phenomenon of neorealism by declaring its death. Even if historical and geopolitical worlds apart, a recent call for a moratorium on the study of neorealism to "challenge its hegemonic position" within Italian studies and cinematic culture expresses a similar annoyance.[47] The persistence of the same affect over seventy years of critical pronouncements suggests a compulsive and unresolved discomfort with the legacy of postwar cinema and its politics that is worth closer examination.

In the twenty-first century, the questioning of neorealism's place within the canon echoes the resurgent right's political critique of the supposed hegemony of the liberation and Resistance narratives within Italian postwar democracy. From the start, however, both the histories of the Resistance and the stories of neorealism marked a contested ground where the realities of a Fascist past and the aspirations to a democratic future confronted one another. That this confrontation remains to be adjudicated in the context of a national and global reemergence of white supremacy and Fascism is alarming. Riddled as the politics of neorealism may be with shortcomings and contradictions (the moral compromise of its auteurs with Fascism, the fact that neorealism like the Resistance was a minority phenomenon), the aspirations they embodied represent a democratic legacy that, in my view, now more than ever needs to be critically analyzed and reclaimed. What I believe deserves particular scrutiny is how the movement has been historicized and co-opted, even reduced to expedient clichés, in ways that have silenced not only alternative voices and narratives but the events associated with the neorealist films themselves. Neorealism has been beset by repeated acts of outright censorship (e.g., its excommunication by Andreotti in the 1950s) and disavowal, ranging from the impatience to shelve the past to open contestations.

What is then the meaning of such unabated eagerness to archive postwar cinema? Perhaps a misunderstanding lies behind this state of things. What is considered to be neorealism's oppressively hegemonic presence is rather, I would argue, the powerful persistence of an unreconciled and traumatic history. Like the shapeless, archaic monster fished out of the sea at the end of *La dolce vita*, whose glassy cinematic eye keeps staring, to the annoyance of the protagonist Marcello, at the party revelers, neorealism keeps interrogating the present and, most urgently, a still-unresolved relation with the Fascist past.

Seen in this light, Sylvia's baffled smile might suggest less dismissal than another silently lingering question, namely, "What is neorealism?" Despite a massive body of criticism, this question is still generating answers. "There is no other movement of twentieth-century Italian art and culture (not even Futurism) which modified a system on a global scale with equal reach and duration," Brunetta concludes in his *Storia del cinema italiano* (367). The understanding of the historical and artistic import of neorealism remains elusive precisely because it is bound to a still-developing understanding of postwar history and the unfolding of artistic modernism in the wake of Fascism.[48] Martin Scorsese in his film tribute to neorealism, *My Voyage to Italy* (1999), compared neorealism to a big tree from which all following cinemas developed as different branches. The cinematic and ethical reach of the Neorealist vision, from the French Nouvelle Vague to directors as different as the Indian Satyajit Ray, Glauber Rocha (founder of the Brazilian Cinema Nõvo Movement), and the Iranian Abbas Kiarostami, is indisputable evidence of its impact.[49]

Notes

1 For a general introduction, see Bondanella, *Italian Cinema from Neorealism to the Present*, 31–73; and Marcus, *Italian Film in the Light of Neorealism*, 3–29.

2 A shared moral commitment and an all-absorbing attention to "reality" are the most often mentioned features of neorealism. There are many points of reference for the genealogy of the term: internationally, the German *Neue Sachlichkeit* of the 1930s; American literary and photographic realism of the New Deal; and Italian debates on realism from the nineteenth century to the 1930s. The understanding of neorealism itself changed and evolved over the years. For an overview of the early debate, see Milanini, *Neorealismo*; and for the evolving discussion in the 1970s, see Miccichè, *Il neorealismo cinematografico italiano*, 1999. Finally for a general history of the term and more contemporary views, see Marcus, *Italian Film in the Light of Neorealism*, 1986; and Parigi, "Neorealismo," 2003.

3 Deleuze, *Cinema 1*, 211.

4 Brunetta, *Identità italiana e identità europea nel cinema italiano*; Ben-Ghiat, "Liberation."

5 Interview with Pasolini on *Rai-TV Cultura*.

6 On the journey as a search for identity in Neorealist cinema, see Brunetta, *Identità italiana e identità europea nel cinema italiano*.

7 Kracauer, *Theory of Film*, 98.

8 *Il cinema e l'uomo moderno*, Relazione al convegno internazionale di cinematografia (Presentation at the International Congress of Cinematography), Perugia, 24–27, September, 1949; now in Zavattini, 2002, 678–79. These statements resound profoundly at another fifty years distance with Jean-Luc

Godard's reflection on cinema and the history of the twentieth century in *Histoire(s) du cinéma* (1998): "Cinema totally fell short of its duty . . . By not filming the concentration camps cinema forfeited itself. It is like the parable of the good servant who died from not being utilized. Cinema is a means of expression from which expression disappeared. Only the medium remained" (336).

9   Bernardi, *Il paesaggio*, 89.

10   The main essay here quoted is "An Aesthetic of Reality: Cinematic Realism and the Italian School of the Liberation" (1948). Bazin wrote as well a series of important reviews of, among others, *Ladri di biciclette* (1948), *La terra trema* (1948), *Europa '51* (1952), *Umberto D.* (1952), Federico Fellini's *Nights of Cabiria* (1957) and a later appraisal "In Defense of Rossellini" (1955).

11   Brunetta, *Storia del cinema italiano*, 354.

12   See Milanini and Miccichè.

13   On this institutional and ideological continuity, see Cannella; Cannistraro; and Forgacs.

14   De Santis, Visconti, the Puccini brothers, Massimo and Gianni, Carlo Lizzani and the future Communist leader Pietro Ingrao were eventually arrested as members of a Communist cell. On the *Cinema* group, see Vitti, 7.

15   See Grespi.

16   For a discussion of the eclecticism in content and style of Fascist film production, see Landy.

17   "Per un paesaggio italiano" ("For an Italian Landscape"), Overbey, *Springtime in Italy*, 125–29; originally in *Cinema*, v.s., 116, April 25, 1941.

18   Michelangelo Antonioni, "Per un film sul fiume Po" ("Concerning a Film About The River Po"), Overbey, *Springtime in Italy*, 79–82; originally in *Cinema*, v.s., 68, April 25, 1939.

19   For in-depth readings of *Ossessione*, see Quaresima and Minghelli.

20   The 1954 Venice Film Festival was polarized between the supporters of Visconti, led by film critic Guido Aristarco, who believed it was time to overhaul neorealism and return to historical representation and traditional nineteenth-century realism, and supporters of Fellini's *La strada*, a film which arguably revitalizes the Neorealist poetic with a dreamlike vein that will soon become the signature of Fellini's cinema.

21   Restivo, *The Cinema of Economic Miracles*, 25.

22   Forgacs, *Rome, Open City*, 12. Forgacs's volume provides an excellent introduction to the film; for more recent assessments, see Restivo; Rancière; and the special issue on *Rome Open City* of *Journal of Italian Cinema and Media Studies*, 2018.

23   Ugo Pirro, *Celluloide* (Milan: Rizzoli, 1983), 72; translation is mine. *Celluloide* offers a detailed reconstruction of the adventurous rebirth of Italian cinema in Rome in the aftermath of the liberation.

24   See Schoonover for an analysis of the imperiled body in Neorealist films and its connection to the global context of the World War and the postwar economic intervention of the Marshall Plan.

25 See Wagstaff for box office data on Neorealist films.

26 See Brunette.

27 For an illuminating introduction to the film, see Parigi.

28 On the importance of the postwar profilmic environments in the articulation of a new cinematic language and the ethos of a post-Fascist nation, see Bernardi; Steimatsky; and Minghelli.

29 For a reading of the poetics and politics of memory, see Steimatsky; and Minghelli. With *Germania anno zero (Germany Year Zero* [1947]), the story of a doomed childhood in the ruins of Berlin, Rossellini will close his postwar trilogy by displacing his most pessimistic representation of the destructive legacy of the war and Fascism unto foreign ground. Other important films inspired by the war and Resistance belonging to the orbit of the Neorealist moment are Aldo Vergano, *Il sole sorge ancora (The Sun also Rises* [1946]), De Sanctis, *Caccia tragica (Tragic Hunt* [1947]), Carlo Lizzani, *Achtung! Banditi!* (1951) and *Cronache di poveri amanti (Chronicle of Poor Lovers* [1954]).

30 Deleuze observed that, because of their limited mobility and inability to act, children embody pure perception, hence their centrality in neorealist cinema.

31 Bazin, "De Sica: Metteur en Scène" [1953], 60.

32 Marcus, *Italian Film*, 56.

33 For an insightful introduction to the film, see Marcus; and Gordon.

34 The idea for the film came from the homonymous novel by the painter Luigi Bartolini. For a reconstruction of the film's genesis, see Wagstaff.

35 Marcus, *Italian Film*, 58.

36 The three exceptions are the poster for the 31st Giro d'Italia bicycle race (May–June, 1948), the poster for Rita Hayworth's *Gilda* (1946; Italian release 1948) that Antonio is assigned to hang (Gordon, 13), and a pro-American election poster which peeks out from a billboard. See Minghelli for a reading of the historical optical unconscious in *Ladri*.

37 See Gennari on the intersection of American and Vatican interests in postwar cinema.

38 For an account of "the postwar settlement," see Ginsborg 72–120.

39 See Rhodes, *Stupendous, Miserable City.*

40 For a reassessment of the formal importance of emotions in the film, see Gordon 99–114; and Minghelli.

41 For the "short" periodization, see Marcus, *Italian Film in the Light of Neorealism*; and Bondanella.

42 For a discussion of the government heavy intervention in postwar cinema see Brunetta 2001, "La censura," 73–96.

43 Another important representative of this trend is Renato Castellani, *Sotto il sole di Roma (Under the Roman Sun* [1948]) and *Due soldi di speranza (Two Cents Worth of Hope* [1952]).

44 See Gundle and Landy 2008.

45 See Rhodes, *Stupendous, Miserable City.*

46 Conley, "Facts and Figures of History," 9.

47 See O'Leary and O'Rawe 2011.

48 For an overview of the critical debates which surrounded neorealism in Italian culture, see the chapter "Lo sguardo del neorealismo" in Brunetta (2001) and Miccichè (1999). In the introduction to *Il neorealismo cinematografico italiano,* Miccichè noted that coming to terms with neorealism was the great missing act of post-neorealist Italian cinema and criticism ("nobody till now took it upon her/himself to draft a comprehensive picture of that season") ix, xxi.

49 For an assessment of the ongoing legacy of neorealism in global cinema, see Miccichè (1999) who reads neorealism as the fist "cinema of underdevelopment," inspiring many postcolonial cinematographies (xiv-xvi); and, more recently, Ruberto and Wilson.

Bibliography

Journal of Italian Cinema and Media Studies. Special issue on *Rome, Open City.* 6.3 (July 2018).

Alonge, Giaime. *Vittorio De Sica. Ladri di biciclette.* Turin: Lindau, 1997.

Aprà, Adriano. Interview. In Criterion DVD of *Paisan,* 2010.

Bazin, André. *What Is Cinema?* 2 vols. Berkeley: University of California Press, 1971.

Ben-Ghiat, Ruth. "Liberation: Italian Cinema and the Fascist Past, 1945–50." *Italian Fascism: History, Memory and Representation.* Ed. Richard Bosworth and Dogliani, Patrizia. New York: St. Martin's Press, 1999: 83–101.

Benjamin, Walter. "The Work of Art in the Age of Its Technological Reproducibility." In *Selected Writings.* Ed. Howard Eiland and Michael Jennings. Vol. 4 (1938–1940). Cambridge, MA: Harvard University Press, 2003: 251–83.

Bernardi, Sandro. *Il paesaggio nel cinema italiano.* Venice: Marsilio, 2002.

Bondanella, Peter. *Italian Cinema from Neorealism to the Present.* New York: Continuum, 2002.

Brunetta, Gian Piero. *Identità italiana e identità europea nel cinema italiano.* Ed. Gian Piero Brunetta. Turin: Edizioni della Fondazione Agnelli, 1996: 11–68.

Brunetta, Gian Piero. *Storia del cinema italiano: Dal neorealismo al miracolo economico, 1945–1959.* Vol. 3. Rome: Editori Riuniti, 2001.

Brunette, Peter. "Unity and Difference in *Paisan.*" *Studies in the Literary Imagination* 16.1 (1983): 91–111.

Brunette, Peter. *Roberto Rossellini.* New York: Oxford University Press, 1987.

Calvino, Italo. "Prefazione 1964 al *Sentiero dei nidi di ragno.*" *Romanzi e racconti.* Vol. 1. Milan: Mondadori, 1991: 1185–204.

Cannistraro, Philip. "Ideological Continuity and Cultural Coherence." *Bianco e nero* 36.9 (12 September–October 1975).

Cannella, Mario. "Ideology and Aesthetic Hypothesis in the Criticism of Neo-Realism." *Screen* 14 (Winter 1973): 5–60.

Conley, Tom. "Facts and Figures of History: *Paisan*." In *Film Hieroglyphs, Ruptures in Classical Cinema*. Minneapolis: University of Minnesota Press, 1991: 102–29.

Conley, Tom. *Cartographic Cinema*. Minneapolis: University of Minnesota Press, 2007.

Deleuze, Gilles. *Cinema 1: The Movement-Image*. Minneapolis: University of Minnesota Press, 1986.

Deleuze, Gilles. *Cinema 2: The Time-Image*. Minneapolis: University of Minnesota Press, 1989.

Forgacs, David. "Post-War Italian Culture: Renewal or Legacy of the Past?" In *Reconstructing the Past: Representations of the Fascist Era in Post-War European Culture*. Ed. Graham Bartram, Maurice Slawinski, and David Steel. Keele: Keele University Press, 1996: 49–63.

Forgacs, David. *Roberto Rossellini Magician of the Real*. Ed. Sarah Lutton and Geoffrey Nowell-Smith. London: BFI, 2000.

Forgacs, David. *Rome Open City*. London: BFI, 2000.

Gennari, Daniela Treveri. *Post-War Italian Cinema: American Intervention, Vatican Interests*. New York: Routledge, 2009.

Ginsborg, Paul. *A History of Contemporary Italy: Society and Politics, 1943–1988*. New York: Palgrave Macmillan, 2003.

Godard, Jean-Luc. "Le cinéma n'a pas su remplir son role." In *Jean-Luc Godard par Jean-Luc Godard, II. 1984–1998*. Paris: Cahiers du Cinéma, 1995.

Gordon, S. C. Robert. *Bicycle Thieves*. New York: Palgrave Macmillan, 2008.

Grespi, Barbara. "Italian Neo-Realism between Cinema and Photography." In *Stillness in Motion: Italy, Photography and the Meanings of Modernity*. Ed. Sarah Patricia Hill and Giuliana Minghelli. Toronto: University of Toronto Press, 2014: 87–117.

Gundle, Stephen. *Bellissima: Feminine Beauty and the Idea of Italy*. New Haven: Yale University Press, 2007.

Kracauer, Siegfried. *Theory of Film*. Princeton: Princeton University Press, 1997.

Landy, Marcia. "Fascism in Film." In *Reviewing Fascism: Italian Cinema 1922–1943*. Ed. Jaqueline Reich and Piero Garofalo. Bloomington: Indiana University Press, 2002.

Landy, Marcia. *Stardom, Italian Style: Screen Performance and Personality in Italian Cinema*. Bloomington: Indiana University Press, 2008.

Marcus, Millicent. *Italian Film in the Light of Neorealism*. Princeton: Princeton University Press, 1986.

Marcus, Millicent. *After Fellini: National Cinema in the Postmodern Age*. Baltimore: Johns Hopkins University Press, 2002.

Miccichè, Lino. *Visconti e il neorealismo*. Venice: Marsilio, 1998.

Miccichè, Lino. *Il neorealismo cinematografico italiano*. Venice: Marsilio, 1999.

Milanini, Claudio. *Neorealismo: Poetiche e polemiche*. Milan: Saggiatore, 1980.

Minghelli, Giuliana. *Landscape and Memory in Post-Fascist Italian Film: Cinema Year Zero*. New York: Routledge, 2013.

O'Leary, Alan and Catherine O'Rawe. "Against Realism: On a 'Certain Tendency' in Italian Film Criticism." *Journal of Modern Italian Studies* 16.1 (2011): 107–28.

Overbey, David, ed. *Springtime in Italy: A Reader on Neo-Realism*. Hamden: Archon Press, 1978.

Quaresima, Leonardo. "*Ossessione*: Il teatro dei rapporti." In *Il cinema di Luchino Visconti*. Ed. Veronica Pravadelli. Venice: Marsilio, 2000: 37–52.

Parigi, Stefania. "Neorealismo: Le avventure di una parola." In *Storia del cinema Italiano*. Vol. 7 (1945–48). Ed. Callisto Cosulich. Venice: Marsilio, 2003: 82–96.

Parigi, Stefania. *Paisà*. Venice: Marsilio, 2005.

Pasolini, Pier Paolo. "Cinema di poesia." In *Saggi sulla letteratura e sull'arte*. Vols. 1–2. Ed. Walter Siti and Silvia De Laude. Milan: Mondadori, 1999. Translated in *Pier Paolo Pasolini. Contemporary Perspectives*. Ed. Patrick Rumble and Bart Testa. Toronto: University of Toronto Press. 1994.

Pasolini, Pier Paolo. Intervista Rai-TV Cultura. https://www.youtube.com/watch?v=rZps5sqkFNw. Accessed May 18, 2013.

Pirro, Ugo. *Celluloide*. Milan: Rizzoli, 1983.

Rancière, Jacques. "Falling Bodies: Rossellini's Physics." In *Film Fables*. Oxford: Berg, 2006.

Restivo, Angelo. *The Cinema of Economic Miracles: Visuality and Modernization in the Italian Art Film*. Durham: Duke University Press, 2002.

Rhodes, John David. *Stupendous, Miserable City: Pasolini's Rome*. Minneapolis: University of Minnesota Press, 2007.

Ruberto, Laura and Kristi Wilson, eds. *Italian Neorealism and Global Cinema*. Detroit: Wayne State University Press, 2007.

Schoonover, Karl. *Brutal Vision: The Neorealist Body in Postwar Italian Cinema*. Minneapolis: University of Minnesota Press, 2012.

Sitney, P. Adams. *Vital Crises in Italian Cinema: Iconography, Stylistics, Politics*. Austin: University of Texas, 1995.

Sorlin, Pierre. *European Cinemas European Society, 1939–1990*. New York: Routledge, 1991.

Steimatsky, Noa. *Italian Locations: Reinhabiting the Past in Postwar Cinema*. Minneapolis: University of Minnesota Press, 2008.

Thompson, Kristin. *Breaking the Glass Armor: Neoformalist Film Analysis*. Princeton: Princeton University Press, 1988.

Vitti, Antonio. *Giuseppe De Santis and Postwar Italian Cinema*. Toronto: Toronto University Press, 1996.

Wagstaff, Christopher. *Italian Neorealist Cinema: An Aesthetic Approach*. Toronto: University of Toronto Press, 2007.

Zavattini, Cesare. *Opere. Cinema. Diario cinematografico. Neorealismo, ecc*. Ed. Valentina Fortichiari and Mino Argentieri. Milan: Bompiani, 2002.

Filmography

Antonioni, Michelangelo. *Cronaca di un amore* (Story of a Love Affair) [1950]. No Shame Films. DVD. 2005.

Antonioni, Michelangelo. *Il grido* [1956]. Kino Video, DVD. 2000.

Antonioni, Michelangelo. *L'avventura* [1960]. New York: The Criterion Collection, DVD. 2014.

Antonioni, Michelangelo. *La notte* [1961]. New York: The Criterion Collection, DVD and Blue Ray. 2013.

Antonioni, Michelangelo. *L'eclisse* [1962]. New York: The Criterion Collection, DVD. 2005.

Antonioni, Michelangelo. *Gente del Po* (People of the Po) [1943–1947]. New York: The Criterion Collection, Blue Ray Special Edition Features. 2010.

Antonioni, Michelangelo. *N.U.—Nettezza Urbana* (Trash Collection) [1948]. New York: The Criterion Collection, Blue ray Special Edition Features. 2010.

Comencini, Luigi. *Pane, amore e fantasia* (Love, Bread and Dreams) [1953]. Mustang Entertainment.

De Santis, Giuseppe. *Riso amaro* (Bitter Rice) [1949]. New York: The Criterion Collection, DVD. 2016.

De Sica, Vittorio. *I bambini ci guardano* (The Children Are Watching Us) [1943]. New York: The Criterion Collection, DVD. 2006.

De Sica, Vittorio. *Sciuscià* (Shoeshine) [1946]. Sony Pictures, DVD. 2011.

De Sica, Vittorio. *Ladri di biciclette* (Bicycle Thieves) [1948]. New York: The Criterion Collection, DVD. 2007.

De Sica, Vittorio. *Miracolo a Milano* (Miracle in Milan) [1950]. Multimedia San Paolo, DVD. 2002.

De Sica, Vittorio. *Umberto D.* [1952]. New York: The Criterion Collection, DVD. 2003.

De Sica, Vittorio. *L'oro di Napoli* (The Gold of Naples) [1954]. CATCOM, DVD. 2006.

Fellini, Federico. *Luci del varietà* (Variety Lights) [1950]. Janus Film, DVD. 2009.

Fellini, Federico. *La strada* [1954]. New York: The Criterion Collection, DVD. 2010.

Fellini, Federico. *Le notti di Cabiria* (The Nights of Cabiria) [1957]. New York: The Criterion Collection, DVD. 2007.

Fellini, Federico. *La dolce vita* [1960]. New York: The Criterion Collection, Multi-format. 2014.

Rossellini, Roberto. *La nave bianca* (The White Ship) [1941]. CG Entertainment, DVD. 2008.

Rossellini, Roberto. *Un pilota ritorna* (A Pilot Returns) [1942]. Terminal Video Italia, DVD. 2009.

Rossellini, Roberto. *L'uomo dalla croce* (The Man of the Cross) [1943]. Terminal Video Italia, DVD. 2009.

Rossellini, Roberto. *Roma città aperta* (Rome, Open City) [1945]. New York: The Criterion Collection, DVD. 2009.

Rossellini, Roberto. *Paisà* (Paisan) [1946]. New York: The Criterion Collection, DVD. 2009.

Rossellini, Roberto. *Stromboli* [1950]. New York: The Criterion Collection, DVD. 2013.

Rossellini, Roberto. *Europe '51* [1952]. New York: The Criterion Collection, DVD. 2013.

Rossellini, Roberto. *Viaggio in Italia* (Voyage to Italy) [1954]. New York: The Criterion Collection, DVD. 2013.

Pasolini, Pier Paolo. *Accattone.* [1961]. Water Bearer Films, DVD. 2003.

Pasolini, Pier Paolo. *Uccellacci e Uccellini* (Hawks and Sparrows) [1966]. Water Bearer Films. DVD. 2003.

Scorsese, Martin. *My Voyage to Italy*. Buena Vista Home Video, DVD. 1999.

Visconti, Luchino with Mario Serandrei, Giuseppe De Santis, and Marcello Pagliero. *Giorni di gloria* (Days of Glory) [1945].

Visconti, Luchino. *Ossessione* [1942]. Chatsworth, CA: International Media Films, DVD. 2001.

Visconti, Luchino. *La terra trema* [1948]. Entertainment One, DVD. 2012.

Visconti, Luchino. *Bellissima* [1951]. Entertainment One, DVD. 2012.

Visconti, Luchino. *Senso*. New York: The Criterion Collection, DVD. 2011.

5

The Orphaned Generation

Cinema of the 1980s and 1990s

Alessia Ricciardi

A frank appraisal of Italian cinema in the 1980s and 1990s can hardly avoid starting with a glance at the triumph of Hollywood spectacle during the same decades. The era witnessed the international hegemony of special effects-laden action "franchises" such as the first *Star Wars* trilogy (1977–83), the first three *Indiana Jones* features (1981–89), the first three *Rambo* productions (1982–88), *Terminator* (1984) and *Terminator 2* (1991), the first three *Die Hard* movies (1988–95), *Batman* (1989) and *Batman Returns* (1992), and *Mission: Impossible* (1996), among others. Italy's moviegoing audience consequently was often relegated to the role of a consumer of blockbusters from the United States. In other countries, Italian film was measured by the artistic glories of its golden age of neorealism and cinematic modernism from the 1940s through the 1960s as well as the sentimental appeal of such award-winning melodramas as Giuseppe Tornatore's *Nuovo Cinema Paradiso* (*Cinema Paradiso*, 1989), Gabriele Salvatores' *Mediterraneo* (1991), and Roberto Benigni's *La vita è bella* (*Life Is Beautiful*, 1997), which traded in nostalgic fantasies of Italy from around the Second World War and its immediate aftermath.

Gian Piero Brunetta argues that from the early 1970s through the early 1990s the Italian film industry underwent a "dramatic and irreversible process of marginalization" in the global market.[1] He points out that, from an all-time high of just over 500 million tickets sold worldwide at the end of the 1960s, annual box office sales of Italian films dropped steadily until average annual sales hovered below 100 million by the early 1990s.[2] He observed as well that changes in the financing of motion pictures led in Italy to the replacement of traditional Italian movie producers with "individuals who have more in common with brokers and traders" and to a risk-averse distribution system dominated by RAI and Fininvest that "has weakened creativity and has begun to transform cinematic products into made-for-television products."[3]

In Italy, the political tumult of the so-called *anni di piombo* (Years of Lead)—which started in the late 1960s and culminated with the murder of the prominent Christian Democrat politician Aldo Moro at the end of the 1970s—was followed by a period of relative economic prosperity fueled by the increasing decentralization of production that began in the early 1980s. Popularly labeled the "Second Economic Miracle" in an optimistic evocation of Italy's fabled economic miracle from the late 1950s to the 1960s, the subsequent boom of the 1980s enabled Italy to briefly displace Great Britain as fifth largest economy in the world in terms of GDP, an event referred to as *Il grande sorpasso* (The Great Overtaking). The business tycoon Silvio Berlusconi solidified control of the media in the 1980s thanks to deregulation and the success of his American-style commercial broadcasting empire. In 1994, Berlusconi founded a new party, Forza Italia, and won the election for prime minister following the revelation of widespread corruption among Christian Democrats and Italian Socialist Party members through the judicial investigation dubbed *Mani pulite* (Clean Hands). After the fall of the Berlin Wall, the Partito Comunista Italiano (PCI; Italian Communist Party), which for decades had been the largest and strongest party of the political left in Western Europe, changed its name in 1991 to the Partito Democratico della Sinistra (PDS; Democratic Party of the Left) and drifted away from its original raison d'être. Throughout the period, from the climax of the *anni di piombo* through Berlusconi's ascension to power, Italy's filmmakers were unable to respond with conviction to the major historical traumas of the years following the Second World War.

By the start of the 1980s, Italian cinema had lost Vittorio De Sica, Pietro Germi, Pier Paolo Pasolini, Elio Petri, Roberto Rossellini, and Luchino Visconti from the ranks of its most famous living practitioners. Of the directors who were alive and well in the decade, only Federico Fellini, Bernardo Bertolucci, and arguably Ermanno Olmi—who won the Venice Film Festival's Leone d'argento (Silver Lion) and Leone d'oro (Golden Lion) awards for, respectively, the films *Lunga vita alla signora!* (*Long Live the Lady!* 1987) and *La leggenda del santo bevitore* (*The Legend of the Holy Drinker*, 1988)—made significant creative and imaginative contributions. Other established masters such as Michelangelo Antonioni, Ettore Scola, and the brothers Paolo and Vittorio Taviani ceased to produce works of note. At the same time, the filmmakers that came of age in the 1980s and 1990s were not able to set new aesthetic directions for the medium as the nation's directors had done in earlier decades, with the possible exception of Nanni Moretti.[4] Because the cinema for many decades provided a compelling critical window on Italy's collective imaginative life, starting with neorealism's ambitious attempt to spur a national-popular rebirth of society, the regression of the 1980s and 1990s can be read as an ominous symptom for the culture at large.[5]

Most serious critics indeed view these years as a time of cinematic impoverishment. The very idea of comparing these decades to the golden age of neorealism and modernism strikes Mario Sesti as "sadistic."[6] On a similar note, Lino Miccichè associates the period with a *cinecidio* or killing of the film medium, while Brunetta likens it to the mathematical concept of Cantor Dust (*polvere di Cantor*), which he defines as points in space that proliferate around the absence of a common plane.[7] Although the Italianist Manuela Gieri takes a more approving view, she admits to not having sufficient "critical distance" from the era to judge its productions and acknowledges that, unlike their predecessors, Italian filmmakers of the 1980s and 1990s lacked a common aesthetic or ethical project.[8]

In Gieri's opinion, the so-called new Italian cinema began in 1978, when Maurizio Nichetti, Nanni Moretti, and Gianni Amelio entered the scene as directors. While Nichetti to a degree, and Moretti in particular, experimented with the possibilities of new methods of storytelling on screen, Amelio intelligently revisited the legacy of such great directors of the past as Bertolucci and Visconti and succeeded in reviving neorealist critical concerns without nostalgia. In fact, some of the best films of the 1980s and 1990s evoked the language and, at times, the aesthetics of neorealism, for example Nichetti's extraordinary, comic *mise-en-abîme* of Italian neorealism *Ladri di saponette* (*Icicle Thief*, 1989) and Amelio's *Il ladro di bambini* (*Stolen Children*, 1992), both of which echoed De Sica's *Ladri di biciclette* (*Bicycle Thieves*, 1948) in very different narrative registers. Along similar lines, Ricky Tognazzi's *Ultrà* (1991) and *La scorta* (*The Escort*, 1993), followed the stories of protagonists who come into conflict with their social milieus in a manner that recalled the narratives of the great screenwriter Cesare Zavattini, who wrote the scripts for, among many others, *Bicycle Thieves*, *Miracolo a Milano* (*Miracle in Milan*, 1951), *Umberto D.* (1952), and *Il giardino dei Finzi-Contini* (*The Garden of the Finzi Continis*, 1970).[9]

The starkest index of the condition of Italian cinema in the years of the second economic miracle, however, may be the decline undergone by the genre of comedy from the heights that it enjoyed in earlier times. The examples of the *commedia all'italiana* (so called in homage to the 1961 hit *Divorzio all'italiana* or *Divorce Italian Style*) that directors such as Mario Monicelli, Pietro Germi, and Dino Risi concocted throughout the 1950s and 1960s succeeded in blending acute sociological and critical observations with an appetite for the drolly absurd, resulting in brilliant lampoons of the culture's unexamined conventions. During the 1980s and 1990s, however, this sophisticated mix of satire and farce vanished from the screen. In its place, we find represented in the productions of Carlo Vanzina, Neri Parenti, and Enrico Oldoini a brand of spectacular buffoonery that dominated the box office thanks to its relentless privileging of appearance, vulgarity, and wealth over substance. A list of the popular titles of the day might give us an idea of how vacuous the comic imagination had grown in Berlusconi's Italy: *Una vacanza bestiale* (*A Beastly Holiday*, 1980), *Sapore di mare* (1982; released in the United States as *Time for Loving*, but literally "taste of the sea," which happens to be the direct quotation of a line from Gino Paoli's pop song "Sapore di sale"), *Vacanze di Natale* (1983), *Yuppies* (1986), *Vacanze in America* (1984), and *Miliardi* (*Millions*, 1990). The films are filled with male characters whose only interests appear to be status symbols, scantily clad women, and killing time while on vacation by telling jokes.

1 The "Old" Authors: Fellini, Antonioni, Bertolucci

Of the few remaining auteurs of an earlier generation who were still active in the 1980s and 1990s, Fellini ought to be praised for his enduring creativity and critical acumen. He may not have had a smash hit during these years, but he directed vibrant films such as *Prova d'orchestra* (*Orchestra Rehearsal*, 1978), *E la nave va* (*And the Ship Sails On*, 1983), *Ginger e Fred* (*Ginger and Fred*, 1985), and *La voce della luna* (*The Voice of the Moon*, 1990) that arguably are as good as any of his more celebrated masterpieces of the 1950s and 1960s. Yet most commentators are indifferent or hostile to the productions of his later career.[10] Such neglect is, I believe, all the more deplorable given both the visual brio of the films and their cogency in reflecting on the historical conditions of the time, with its terrorism and political disorder (*Orchestra Rehearsal* and *The Ship Sails On*), Berlusconi's hegemony over mass media (*Ginger and Fred*), and the pervasiveness of consumerism (*The Voice of the Moon*).

The Voice of the Moon inaugurated a new decade by evoking the lunar imagery of the great nineteenth-century poet Giacomo Leopardi (1798–1837). In the spirit of Leopardi's moral writings, the film confronted Italy with a parable of its own vanity. A free adaptation of Ermanno Cavazzoni's novel *Il poema dei lunatici* (*The Poem of Lunatics*, 1987), *The Voice of the Moon* tells the surreal story of the three Micheluzzi brothers' mad quest to capture the moon, a mission that mirrors the futile efforts of the self-deluded Ivo Salvini (played by Roberto Benigni) to seduce a blonde beauty. The director's lyrical camera work and editing frame both storylines against a dystopian backdrop of the contemporary Italian society of spectacle, which appears to be an inexhaustible farrago of television commercials, beauty pageants, disco music, and other vulgar rites of an increasingly anarchic constellation of power. The film won three David di Donatello Awards (the Italian equivalent of Academy Awards) for best editing, best actor, and best producer as well as nominations for best director and best film, but was not a popular success. Notwithstanding Fellini's status at the time of production as a *vecchio*, or old man, as Zagarrio puts it, *The Voice of the Moon* is one of the most lucid and visionary statements on contemporary Italy made during the 1990s.[11]

While Fellini managed to stay relevant to the end of his career, the same unfortunately cannot be said of Antonioni, who, after making *Professione: reporter* (*The Passenger*) in 1975, produced disappointing films in the ensuing two decades. Even before suffering a stroke in 1985 that left him unable to direct on his own, he surrendered to the growing coarseness of Italian culture in *Identificazione di una donna* (*Identification of a Woman*, 1982).[12] The story of a search conducted by a celebrated Italian movie director named Niccolò for the ideal lead actress of his next production is arguably an embarrassment when considered in light of its regressive gender politics and voyeuristic sex scenes.

The treatment of women in this production stands in marked contrast to their representation in Antonioni's sublime tetralogy of films starring Monica Vitti, which includes *L'avventura* (1960), *La notte* (1961), *L'eclisse* (1962), and *Il deserto rosso* (*Red Desert*, 1964). In the films of the tetralogy, Antonioni portrays women protagonists as the crucial visual and ethical witnesses of the stories in which they take part. This willingness to question narrative conventions, especially as they relate to the depiction of feminine subjectivities, is lost in *Identification of a Woman*, which views women as objects of male desire in the most banal ways. As a result, the strategies of visualization adopted by the film are less compelling than those at work in the tetralogy, where, for example, Antonioni studiously avoids the familiar dialectic of shot and countershot and the rhetorical device of the flashback, both of which he relies on in *Identification of a Woman*. His eye for visually arresting landscapes in urban and natural settings, a key characteristic of his films of the 1960s, is notably absent from the later production with the exception of a sequence that involves a beautiful and disorienting drive through the fog, during which the main characters disappear and reappear in the mist. Yet even here the film suffers in comparison to the director's earlier accomplishments, as the scene implicitly pays homage to a similar and more noted sequence in *Red Desert*.

Antonioni made one last full-length feature film, *Al di là delle nuvole* (*Beyond the Clouds*, 1995), for which he shared the director's credit with Wim Wenders, although most of Wenders's footage wound up on the cutting floor. An adaptation by Tonino Guerra, Antonioni, and Wenders of four stories selected from Antonioni's collection, *Quel bowling sul Tevere* (*That Bowling Alley on the Tiber*, 1997), the film is visually more arresting than *Identification of a Woman*, but often comes across as too self-regarding and, in order to unify the four episodes, resorts to an awkward voice-over delivered by the portentous figure of a famous film director played by John Malkovich.

Bertolucci managed to advance his already considerable international standing in the 1980s and 1990s, starting with the critical and commercial success of *The Last Emperor* (1987), which recounts the spectacular story of Puyi, the final ruler of China's Qing Dynasty. Thanks to the director of photography, Vittorio Storaro, who assigned a specific chromatic tone to every phase and aspect of the protagonist's life, the film was a visual triumph and went on to win nine Academy Awards including Best Picture, Best Director, Best Art Direction, and Best Cinematography. With the exception of *Io ballo da sola* (*Stealing Beauty*, 1996), a clumsy attempt to imagine a young American woman's coming of age in Tuscany that starred the inexperienced Liv Tyler, Bertolucci's other movies of the 1990s are all visually arresting and original, if at times coolly received by audiences. Bertolucci inaugurated the decade with *Il tè nel deserto* (*The Sheltering Sky*, 1990), an adaptation of a novel by Paul Bowles. Although the theme of the voyage to an exotic locale as the supreme test of a couple's vitality and mutual understanding may not be original, the director managed to charge every image of the film with resonance. As Vincent Canby wrote in *The New York Times*, "*The Sheltering Sky* is stunning to look at . . . but it is never simply picturesque. It mesmerizes."[13]

After the relative failure of *The Sheltering* Sky at the box office, Bertolucci regained a measure of worldwide attention in 1993 with *Little Buddha*, the story of an American family's initiation into Buddhism when Tibetan monks identify their son, Jesse, as the potential reincarnation of a revered sage, the Lama Dorje. The film exemplified Bertolucci's abiding curiosity for other cultures, a trait that may seem to have been in short supply among other Italian directors of the time.

2 The International Success of Sentimental Stereotypes

In the years from the end of the Second World War through the 1960s, Italy produced a long run of complex and critically demanding works of cinematic art, chiefly in the films of Rossellini, De Sica, Fellini, Visconti, Pasolini, and Antonioni. Of this tradition, the last two figures, in particular, continue to exert an influence on international filmmakers.[14] As Zagarrio notes, however, the current generation of Italian directors is indebted to other cinematic "fathers," including Scola, Monicelli, Luigi Comencini, Francesco Maselli, and Carlo Lizzani, as well as such "uncles" as Bertolucci, Marco Bellocchio, and Pupi Avati.[15]

Three titles belonging to the latter genealogy stand out for having won the acclaim of non-Italian audiences, especially in the United States: Tornatore's *Cinema Paradiso*, Salvatores' *Mediterraneo*, and Benigni's *Life Is Beautiful*. Due in no small part to marketing efforts by the movies'

American distributor, Miramax, all three productions won the Academy Award for Best Foreign Language Film following their releases.

Cinema Paradiso rehearses the glory days of Italian cinema immediately following the Second World War through the eyes of a young boy named Salvatore, who frequents the sole movie theater in the poor Sicilian village of Giancaldo, where he strikes up an enduring friendship with Alfredo, the theater's projectionist. In the framing sequences at the beginning and ending of the narrative, Salvatore reminisces about these experiences from the vantage point of his adulthood as a famous movie director. Although visually seductive, as Gieri observes, Tornatore's film did not pursue a new direction for Italian cinema, relying instead on a nostalgic rhetoric of confession that seems one-dimensional by comparison to, say, the irony and poetry of Fellini's masterpiece *Amarcord* (1973).[16]

Mediterraneo (1991) opens with a quote from the scientist Henri Laborit' *In Praise of Flight* (*Éloge de la fuite*, 1976): "In times like these, fleeing is the only way to stay alive and to continue dreaming." Indeed, Salvatores' film may well be regarded as the most sophisticated exemplar of the escapism of Italian film during the 1980s and 1990s. Set in 1941, the story follows a group of Italian soldiers who establish their base on a Greek island that the original inhabitants at first seem to have abandoned in the wake of the German invasion. The Italians, however, have no interest in their military duties and quickly succumb to the charms of reading poetry, painting, and the local prostitute, Vassilissa, who, along with the rest of the Greek population, soon emerges from hiding when it becomes evident that the occupiers pose no threat. Their assimilation into the leisurely life of the island continues until the day that an Italian military plane makes an emergency landing three years later. Informed of the Armistice, the soldiers must all reluctantly go home, except for one who has married the prostitute. Over the years, however, several of them grow disenchanted with Italy and return to the island. Along with the other two titles in the director's so-called *Trilogia della fuga* (Trilogy of Escape), *Marrakech Express* (1989) and *Turné* (*On Tour*, 1990), as well as the later *Puerto Escondido* (1992), which concerns a Milanese banker's flight from police corruption to Mexico, *Mediterraneo* responds to a deep malaise in Italian culture that, Salvatores implies, it may be best to avoid through quasi-touristic experiences of travel.

Life Is Beautiful closed the decade by winning the Grand Prix at the Cannes Film Festival in 1998, five Nastri d'argento (Silver Ribbons, which are the annual honors conferred by the National Syndicate of Italian Film Journalists; 1998), nine David di Donatello awards (1998), and three Academy Awards (1999). Written by Benigni and Vincenzo Cerami, the movie tells a story divided into halves. The first part recounts the fairy-tale romance between Guido, a humorous Jewish bookshop owner, and the schoolteacher Dora, whom he marries and has a son with, Giosuè, in Fascist Italy in the 1930s. In the second part, Guido and Giosuè are sent by the authorities to a concentration camp during the German occupation of the country, while Dora, who is a gentile, voluntarily accompanies them. To protect Giosuè, Guido teaches him that the brutality of the camp is a game in which prisoners compete for the prize of a tank. The father thus prevails on his son to avoid any attention or undue risk that might eliminate him from the game and maintains the ruse for Giosuè's benefit even when being led away to his own death.

Despite its many industry accolades, *Life Is Beautiful* created a controversy on its release that continues to frame critical reflections on its narrative. Numerous detractors have condemned Benigni for sacrificing historical veracity with respect to the Holocaust in favor of comic solace, while supporters have countered that artists such as he should be free to use any methods, including those of the clown and the fabulist, to explore the topic.[17] To substantiate their argument, Benigni's defenders often cite accepted examples of irreverent approaches to Nazism such as Ernst Lubitsch's *To Be or Not to Be* (1942), Mel Brooks's *The Producers* (1968), and Lina Wertmüller's *Pasqualino Settebellezze* (*Seven Beauties*, 1975), a list to which one might add Quentin Tarantino's *Inglourious Basterds* (2009). By affirming Benigni's right to "laugh in the face of the unthinkable," however, enthusiasts of *Life Is Beautiful* generally fail to examine the film's claims to an ostensibly more serious enterprise in its latter half.[18] Lawrence L. Langer aptly questions the legitimacy of such claims:

> Through the nostalgia of a manufactured memory, Benigni restores to the imagination the one factor most missing in the concentration- and death-camp environment: the freedom to choose. . . . If it were true that unwavering parental love could have insured the survival of one's child, even at the price of one's own life, then thousands of Jewish martyrs would have been honored after the war by their spared children. History, of course, tells a darker story.[19]

Rather than helping to expose the reality of the Holocaust, Langer clearly implies, the production's transformation from comic fable to sentimental drama obfuscates the truth. The result may well be what one reviewer scathingly called the illusion of a "Walt Disnified concentration camp."[20]

3 From the 1980s to the 1990s: Moretti and Amelio

When asked in 1981 if a new Italian cinema had emerged, Moretti candidly replied: "I do not believe that a new Italian cinema exists: there are no new authors, nor a new way of making movies."[21] Yet it may well be argued that his own efforts point toward just such a "new way." By eschewing the populist vulgarity of mass-market genre conventions, Moretti has reinvented the forms and methods of Italian film comedy, making of these devices a uniquely ironic rhetoric. His distinctive observations of Italy's politics and culture reject the often overly commercial nature of the *commedia all'italiana* in pursuit of a more self-critical mode of satire.[22]

Starting with his debut feature, *Io sono un autarchico* (*I Am Self-Sufficient*, 1976), and continuing through at least four of his next five films, *Ecce bombo* (1978), *Sogni d'oro* (*Sweet Dreams*, 1980), *Bianca* (1984), and *Palombella rossa* (*Red Lob*, 1989), Moretti fashioned the character of an alter-ego named Michele Apicella, played in each case by himself, into "a generational signifier," as Millicent Marcus puts it.[23] In *La messa è finita* (*The Mass Is Ended*, 1985), the director again performed the role of the protagonist, a young priest named Don Giulio, who, Moretti hinted in interviews, might be interpreted as another incarnation of the Apicella persona.[24] Caught between the doldrums that followed the events of 1968 and the terrorism of the *anni di piombo*, the figure of Apicella, whom Moretti depicts as a different individual with a different profession in each film, reflects the alienation, moral outrage, and neuroses of a generation denied the comforting bliss of shared ideological commitments.

Of these early productions, the last three are the most substantive. *Bianca* sardonically diagnoses the pathologies of contemporary Italian men by chronicling Apicella's sexual frustrations as he assumes a new job as a high school math teacher, frustrations that eventually lead him to murder his friends. *The Mass Is Ended*, which won the Grand Jury Prize at the Berlin Film Festival of 1986, recounts Don Giulio's ongoing struggles to connect with his parishioners in Rome, until his own family's troubles (namely, his father's affair with a younger woman, his mother's suicide, his sister's decision to have an abortion) lead him to renounce this assignment for a distant mission in Tierra del Fuego. *Red Lob* (1989) depicts Apicella's trials during a critical match as an amnesiac water polo player who also happens to be a Communist Party member in the Italian Parliament and whose loss of memory thus literalizes the PCI's symbolic loss of identity in the 1990s. This last film won the film critics' Bastone Bianco Award of the Venice Film Festival of 1989, *Cahiers du cinéma*'s best film of 1989, the Nastro d'argento for best story of 1990, and the critics' award of the São Paolo International Film Festival of 1990, in addition to receiving front-page coverage in both *Cahiers du cinéma* and the leftist French daily *Libération*. Moretti's following among French film critics and journalists attests to the long history of France's critically productive relation to Italian cinema, which dates back to the enthusiasm for neorealism among the filmmakers of the Nouvelle Vague. Unlike American viewers, the French have shown almost no interest for Italy's more populist and sentimental productions of the 1980s and 1990s, instead preferring to celebrate Moretti's originality.

As a director, Moretti reinforced his central place in Italian filmmaking with *Caro diario* (*Dear Diary*, 1993) and *Aprile* (*April*, 1998), for both of which he dropped the guise of Michele Apicella and assumed the role of a perplexed film director by the name of Nanni Moretti. Winner of the Cannes Film Festival prize for best director, the David di Donatello for best film, and the Nastro d'argento for best director, *Dear Diary* is generally regarded as Moretti's most original film to date. The paratactic narrative unfolds in three distinct "chapters," the first of which, entitled "In vespa" (On My Vespa), follows Moretti as he rides a Vespa through Rome and its suburbs and shares his thoughts with the audience in voice-over, until he finally arrives at the memorial in Ostia that marks the site where Pier Paolo Pasolini was murdered. The end of the sequence, in which the narration fades away and leaves the viewer to absorb in strictly visual terms the completion of Moretti's unplanned pilgrimage, pays fit tribute to one of Italy's most daringly outspoken filmmakers. The second section, "Isole" ("Islands"), rehearses Moretti's absurd and increasingly futile search for refuge from contemporary culture during an excursion to the Aeolian Islands. In the final segment, "Medici" ("Doctors"), Moretti faces a mysterious illness symptomatized by constant itching and insomnia that none of his doctors can diagnose. An X-ray eventually reveals a treatable tumor indicating Hodgkin's lymphoma, and Moretti is cured, but not before discovering that his symptoms, which he has recited to all of the experts, are clearly included in the medical dictionary entry on his ailment. In each episode, Moretti confronts an exemplary problem: the individual's relation to history in the first, to culture in the second, and to authority in the third. As Zagarrio puts it, Moretti plays the critical conscience of his generation as an uneasy, even antipathetic uncle, an obsessive moralist who is nevertheless right about the need to fight cynicism.[25]

After Moretti, Gianni Amelio might well be regarded as the most important director in Italy to have emerged in the 1980s, an auteur who has completed several subtle and at times difficult films. Although for reasons of space I cannot cover his entire corpus of the 1980s and 1990s, we should at least consider four crucial works: *Colpire al cuore* (*A Blow to the Heart*, 1982), *Il ladro di bambini* (*The Stolen Children*, 1992), *Lamerica* (1994), and *Così ridevano* (*The Way We Laughed*, 1998). With a screenplay by Vincenzo Cerami, *A Blow to the Heart* is one of the few Italian productions to explore the social and psychological violence that erupted during the *anni di piombo*. Set in Milan in the early 1980s, the film depicts the growing estrangement of Emilio, an introverted teenager, from his father, Dario, a leftist professor who may or may not be involved in supporting a terrorist organization. The conflict between father and son simmers until Emilio finally denounces Dario, sending him to prison.

In *The Stolen Children*, two children, Rosetta and Luciano, whose mother has been arrested for selling the girl's services as a prostitute, are turned over to the care of the *carabiniere* (military policeman) Antonio, who accompanies them from a suburb of Milan to Sicily in the hope of finding them somewhere to live. The film's emphasis on the children's points of view and attention to the particularities of landscape and local culture revive some of the key concerns of neorealism, especially as exemplified by the works of Rossellini and De Sica. Clearly echoing in a melancholic register the title of De Sica's paradigmatic masterwork, the wording of the title that Amelio gives his own film, "*il ladro di bambini*" (literally, "the thief of children"), seems to insinuate that nowadays what has been stolen is nothing less than the very being of children, as they meet with the neglect of all the institutions—from the family to the state—that are supposed to care for them. As Marcus cannily observes, the film also may be viewed as a part of the tradition of the "journey" film inaugurated by Rossellini's *Paisà* (*Paisan*, 1946), in which a trip across the Peninsula takes on the symbolic importance of an attempt to reclaim national identity.[26] In their movement across the country from north to south, however, Antonio, Rosetta, and Luciano in fact reverse the trajectory taken by Rossellini's characters in *Paisan* and plunge themselves into ever greater depths of isolation and destitution, which are relieved only by the bond of solidarity that gradually asserts itself between the two children and the *carabiniere*.

Amelio's most important film of the era is *Lamerica* (1994). At a time when thousands of Albanians had reached the coasts of Puglia, *Lamerica* was one of the first films in Italy to give a serious account of the reality of contemporary immigration against the background of the nation's own history of emigration. The story opens on the efforts of a pair of Italian hustlers, Fiore and Gino, to set up a bogus company in Albania in order to dupe the state into paying them a subsidy. Needing an Albanian figurehead for their venture, they conscript a deranged old man named Spiro who has just been released from a labor camp. When Spiro disappears by train, Gino sets out in pursuit, only to discover on catching up with him that the old man is a Sicilian named Michele who deserted the Italian Army during World War II. In order to return to their initial meeting place, the two men begin a trek through the Albanian countryside that is interrupted when Gino is arrested and jailed because the police have uncovered the fraudulent business.

Sometime later, Gino and Michele are reunited on an Albanian ship that is sailing to Italy, but that the old man in his delusional state of mind imagines to be destined for America. Through the play of mistaken identities and disappointed hopes that resonates in the film's conclusion, Amelio ironically underscores the historical parallel between the contemporary Albanian flight to Italy and a bygone Italian exodus to the United States.

The director's final production of the 1990s, *The Way We Laughed*, recounts the struggles of two Sicilian brothers, Giovanni and Pietro, to fashion a new life for themselves in the northern industrial city of Turin during the years 1958 to 1964, at the height of the economic miracle.

The brothers' story hinges on Pietro's decision to abandon his potential career as a schoolteacher, which Giovanni has worked to support with money from his job as a labor boss, and instead to take all of the blame for a murder committed by Giovanni during a fight, including the eventual prison sentence. With this troubling vision of the reality underlying postwar Italy's promise of growing prosperity, Amelio crowned his creative achievements of the 1980s and 1990s by winning the Leone d'oro at the Venice Film Festival of 1998.

4 Generation Moretti: The 1990s

Perhaps the most interesting filmmaker to emerge in the 1990s is Mario Martone, who started his career in the theater as the director of an avant-garde troupe called Falso Movimento (False Movement), a name that takes its inspiration from Wim Wenders's movie, *Falsche Bewegung* (*The Wrong Move*, 1975), and neatly emblematizes Martone's penchant for combining methods from cinema and stage. Martone proceeded to hone his directorial talents in the late 1980s on several stage productions for Teatri Uniti, a collective of theatrical artists that one critic recently has called "the principal point of reference for Neapolitan production over the last two decades."[27] He then made his debut as a filmmaker with *Morte di un matematico napoletano* (*The Death of a Neapolitan Mathematician*, 1992), which relates the story of Renato Caccioppoli, a musician and professor of mathematics who committed suicide in 1959 at age fifty-five. The film won the Grand Special Jury Prize at the Venice Film Festival of 1992. After this initial effort, Martone shot one of five segments for an anthology film, *I vesuviani* (*The Vesuvians*, 1997), and the full-length feature, *Teatro di guerra* (*Rehearsal for War*, 1998). In the style of the experimental approaches to performance space taken by companies such as the Living Theatre, the film captures a theatrical rehearsal of Aeschylus's *Seven Against Thebes* in the *quartieri Spagnoli* or Spanish Quarter of Naples. It was screened as part of the series Un Certain Regard at the Cannes Film Festival of 1998.

It would be hard to argue, however, that any of Martone's works from the same period are more original or accomplished than his cinematic reimagining of Elena Ferrante's novel, *L'amore molesto* (1995). Although the film's English-language distributor mistranslated its title as "Nasty Love," which misses the proper sense of "molesto" as disturbing or troubling, Martone grippingly reinterprets in cinematic terms the complex problematics of Ferrante's narrative, in which questions concerning the body, sexuality, vulgarity, and language all become crucial to the efforts of the protagonist, Delia, to make sense of her mother's suicide. A single woman returning to her childhood home of Naples from her present-day residence of Rome, Delia is assailed by unpleasant memories and associations as, under a persistent and unwelcoming rain, she explores the city where her mother took her own life. In fact, the inscrutable realities of the sprawling, urban environment repeatedly thwart Delia's search for answers, creating a visual tension that drives the dramatic logic of Martone's thriller. Anna Buonaiuto's affecting performance as Delia, sound mixer Alberto Doni's arresting use of ambient noise, and director of photography Luca Bigazzi's evocative camerawork make *L'amore molesto* one of the most memorable Italian films of the decade.

By an odd coincidence, some of Italy's best-known directors of the 1980s and 1990s happened to be the children of well-known directors or actors. For example, Marco Risi, the son of Dino Risi, the director of many popular *commedie all'italiana*, helmed a series of realist dramas focused on problems of social witnessing, including *Mery per sempre* (*Forever Mery*, 1988), *Ragazzi fuori* (*Boys on the Outside*, 1990), *Nel continente nero* (*On the Dark Continent*, 1992), *Il branco* (*The Gang*, 1994), and *L'ultimo capodanno* (*The Last New Year*, 1998), the last of which was based on a short story by Niccolò Ammaniti. Similar ethical concerns motivated films such as *Ultrà* and *La scorta* by Tognazzi, the son of the celebrated actor Ugo Tognazzi. And, in one of the few signs of life for contemporary Italian cinema, the daughters of director Luigi Comencini, Cristina and Francesca Comencini, joined an emerging generation of women filmmakers who had artistic impact during this period.

Notable women directors of the era also include Francesca Archibugi, Loredana Dardi, Fiorenza Infascelli, Simona Izzo, Gabriella Rosaleva, Roberta Torre, and Cinzia Torrini. Cristina Comencini debuted with *Zoo* (1998), a delicate character study of a twelve-year-old girl who lives in Rome's zoo, where her father works as a night watchman. The director achieved popular success with *Va' dove ti porta il cuore* (*Go Where Your Heart Takes You*, 1996), an adaptation of a best-selling romance novel by Susanna Tamaro. Like the novel, the film tells the maudlin story of the unhappy marriage and secret love life of Olga, the matriarch of a family in Trieste, through the hackneyed device of a flashback inspired by Olga's granddaughter's discovery of the old woman's diary. After making a string of undistinguished melodramas early in her career, starting with *Pianoforte* (1983) and continuing through *La luce sul lago* (*The Light on the Lake*, 1988) and *Annabelle partagée* (*Annabelle Divided*, 1991), Francesca Comencini found a more interesting voice in the late 1990s as a documentary filmmaker with *Elsa Morante* (1997), *Shakespeare a Palermo* (1997), and especially *Carlo Giuliani, ragazzo* (*Carlo Giuliani, Boy*, 2002), which narrates the harrowing story of the killing of a young protester at the G8 in Genoa in the summer of 2001. One of the most talented members of the new wave of women directors is Archibugi, whose first film, *Mignon è partita* (*Mignon Has Come to Stay*, 1988), depicts the vicissitudes of first love between a young Roman boy, Giorgio, and his French cousin, Mignon.

The film, which suggests the influences of Truffaut, Scola, and Olmi, won five David di Donatello awards, including best new director.

Archibugi's films mostly examine the relationships between different generations such as the rapport between grandfather and grandson in her second film, *Verso sera* (*Towards Evening*, 1991). Her most ambitious and original film of the period is probably *Il grande cocomero* (*The Great Pumpkin*, 1992), in which she explores forms of violence against childhood through the experience of the famous child psychiatrist Marco Lombardo Radice. Finally, we should note that Roberta Torre's *Tano da morire* (*To Die for Tano*, 1997) won a Nastro d'argento and a David di Donatello award for its comic revision of stereotypes of the Mafia and the South, a project that is made more poignant by the film's use of Neapolitan singer Nino d'Angelo's musical score.

Another important young filmmaker began his career in the late 1990s, namely Matteo Garrone, who released his first and second features, *Terra di mezzo* (*Land in Between*, 1996) and *Ospiti* (*Guests*, 1998), during these years. Eventually, his productions in the new millennium such as *L'imbalsamatore* (*The Embalmer*, 2002) and *Gomorra* (*Gomorrah*, 2008) help to suggest fresh possibilities for Italian film. Along with his contemporary Paolo Sorrentino, whose films include *Le conseguenze dell'amore* (*The Consequences of Love*, 2004), *L'amico di famiglia* (*The Family Friend*, 2006), and *Il divo* (2008), Garrone gives the lie to the words of the filmmaker Carlo Mazzacurati, who at the beginning of the 1990s summed up the plight of Italian directors thus: "There is an enormous pressure that forces you to choose constantly between an absolute refusal of the public in order to pursue a kind of absolute marginality, or an indiscriminate conformism (*omologazione*) to models that, by virtue of their schematism, roughness, and simplification, give the impression of being able to satisfy the public."[28] Along with a handful of predecessors such as Amelio, Archibugi, Martone, and Moretti, Garrone and Sorrentino at least offer viewers some reasons for hope that contemporary filmmakers need not choose between the antipodes of marginality and *omologazione* in order to renew the promise of Italian cinema.

Notes

1 Brunetta, *The History of Italian Cinema*, 247.

2 Brunetta, *The History of Italian Cinema*, 247.

3 Brunetta, *The History of Italian Cinema*, 252–53.

4 Brunetta cites the director Gabriele Salvatores' declaration at the Cannes Film Festival: "We tell minuscule stories that are barely recognizable to foreigners" (*The History of Italian Cinema*, 310).

5 See Rosi, "C'era una volta il cinema," 164.

6 Zagarrio observes that Italy's films of the 1980s and 1990s do not have the same ideal potential as those of the 1960s and 1970s, and that following the lead of such writers, sociologists, and critics as Alessandro Baricco, Enrico Magrelli, Alberto Abruzzese, and Morando Morandini, one can speak of a cultural anemia of the 1980s (*Cinema italiano*, 12). With the advent of Berlusconi's cultural and political monopoly in the 1990s, the author argues, Italy as a society comes to look "agghiacciante" (horrifying) or at best tragicomic (Brunetta, *Cinema italiano*, 55–56).

7 See Miccichè, "L'immagine in movimento e il movimento dell'immagine," conference paper presented at Pesaro on June 18, 1998, cited in Zagarrio, *Cinema italiano*, 12; and Brunetta, *The History of Italian Cinema*, 257. See also Miccichè's anthology of essays for that year's *Mostra Internazionale del Nuovo Cinema* (International Festival of New Cinema), a collection to which he gave the telling title *Schermi opachi* or *Opaque Screens*. For a more optimistic view of the cinema of the 1980s and 1990s, see Marcus, *After Fellini*, 3–12.

8 Gieri, *Contemporary Italian Filmmaking*, 198–99.

9 Gieri, *Contemporary Italian Filmmaking*, 209.

10 In the obituary run by *The New York Times* on the day after Fellini's death in 1993, Flint summed up the reception of the director's later films as follows: "After the mid-1960s, his films often stressed the bizarre, the garish, and the grotesque. Detractors praised some sequences, but variously termed the works excessive, simplistic and self- obsessed" ("Federico Fellini, Film Visionary, Is Dead at 73"). The discomfort of celebrated Italian commentators such as Tullio Kezich and Umberto Eco with the political and satirical thrust of Fellini's late-career masterpiece *Ginger e Fred* (1985) seems exemplary in this regard. Kezich, who was an accomplished screenwriter, film critic, and Fellini biographer, sniffed that the film was an "obvious" social satire, while Eco condemned Fellini's view of commercial television in *Ginger e Fred* because it "is a beautiful piece of grotesque, but goes beyond the satire of customs." See Kezich, *Fellini*, 521; and Eco, cited in Fava and Vigano, *I film di Federico Fellini*, 183.

11 Zagarrio, *Cinema italiano*, 67.

12 Siegel, "Identification of a Medium," 216–32.

13 Canby, "The Sheltering Sky."

14 Brunetta emphasizes Pasolini's persistent influence on multiple generations of filmmakers. However, if we look beyond Italian directors, there is no doubt that Antonioni's cinema has proven decisive for filmmakers as diverse as Wong Kar-Wai and Sofia Coppola. See Brunetta, *The History of Italian Cinema*, 310.

15 Zagarrio, *Cinema italiano*, 65.

16 Gieri, *Contemporary Italian Filmmaking*, 210.

17 We can get an idea of the film's polarized reception from even a selective glimpse of reactions in the United States. Damning appraisals have included, among others, those by David Denby, J. Hoberman, Stanley Kauffmann, Lawrence L. Langer, Stuart Liebman, Richard Schickel, and Alan A. Stone.

Langer notes that Benigni at one point advanced the claim that *La vita è bella* was inspired by Art Spiegelman's graphic novel, *Maus*. To which, Spiegelman replied in an interview: "I'd like to erase his memory of having seen my book ... because he'd misinterpreted what I'd done *as* a fable. [In *La vita è bella*,] Auschwitz becomes a metaphor for a big bummer and the movie becomes 'Man, you really can survive this big bummer as long as you've got a good attitude and can keep your sense of humor.'" See the citation of this interview in Langer, *Using and Abusing the Holocaust*, 31. On the other hand, admiring opinions of the film have been offered by, among others, Roger Ebert, Hilene Flanzbaum, Imre Kertesz, Millicent Marcus, Janet Maslin, and Maurizio S. Viano. Marcus, for example, defends Benigni's approach by pointing out that not even a documentary can be said to represent accurately the historical black hole of the Shoah (*After Fellini*, 269).

18 The phrase is Maslin's from "Giving a Human (and Humorous) Face to Rearing a Boy Under Fascism."

19 Langer, *Using and Abusing the Holocaust*, 32.

20 Kurt Jacobsen, "Camping Out."

21 Gieri, *Contemporary Italian Filmmaking*, 226.

22 On this question, I disagree with Marcus's contention that, in typically postmodern fashion, Moretti in his early films is critically complicit with the society that he satirizes, growing more aware only in the 1990s with *Caro diario*; see Marcus, *After Fellini*, 289–91.

23 Marcus, *After Fellini*, 297.

24 In an interview with the historian Jean Antoine Gili in the French film journal *Positif*, Moretti suggested that "it is possible that the protagonist of *La messa è finita* is named Michele as well. This one is named Don Giulio—Don Michele didn't sound right—but perhaps before becoming a priest his name was Michele" (Gili, "Des film pour exorciser mes obsessions," cited in Mazierska and Rascaroli, *The Cinema of Nanni Moretti*, 70).

25 Zagarrio, *Cinema italiano*, 20.

26 Marcus, *After Fellini*, 157.

27 Marlow-Mann, *The New Neapolitan Cinema*, 18.

28 Zagarrio, *Cinema italiano*, 76–77.

Bibiography

Bondanella, Peter. *The Films of Federico Fellini*. Cambridge: Cambridge University Press, 2002.

Bondanella, Peter and Cristina Degli-Esposti, eds. *Perspectives on Federico Fellini*. New York: Hall, 1993.

Brunetta, Gian Piero. *The History of Italian Cinema: A Guide to Italian Film from Its Origins to the Twenty-First Century*. Trans. Jeremy Parzen. Princeton: Princeton University Press, 2011.

Brunette, Peter. *The Films of Michelangelo Antonioni*. Cambridge: Cambridge University Press, 1998.

Bullaro, Grace Russo, ed. *Beyond "Life Is Beautiful": Comedy and Tragedy in the Cinema of Roberto Benigni*. Leicester: Troubador, 2005.

Burke, Frank. *Fellini's Films*. New York: Twayne, 1996.

Campani, Ermelinda M. *L'anticonformista: Bernardo Bertolucci e il suo cinema*. Fiesole: Cadmo, 1998.

Canby, Vincent. "The Sheltering Sky: Toward the Heart of the Sahara, Chic but Lost in Its Vastness." *The New York Times* (December 12, 1990). http://www. nytimes.com/1990/12/12/movies/review-film-toward-the-heart-of-the-sahara-chic-but-lost-in-its-vastness.html. Accessed January 23, 2016.

Cattini, Alberto. *Le storie e lo sguardo: Il cinema di Gianni Amelio*. Venice: Marsilio, 2000.

De Sanctis, Pierpaolo, Domenico Monetti, and Luca Pallanch, eds. *Non solo Gomorra: Tutto il cinema di Matteo Garrone*. Edizioni Sabinae, 2008.

Fellini, Federico. *Fare un film*. Turin: Einaudi, 1980.

Fava, Claudio and Aldo Vigano. *I film di Federico Fellini*. Rome: Gremese, 1981.

Flint, Peter B. "Federico Fellini, Film Visionary, Is Dead at 73." *The New York Times* (November 1, 1993). http://www.nytimes.com/learning/general/onthis day/bday/0120.html. Accessed January 23, 2016.

Gieri, Manuela. *Contemporary Italian Filmmaking: Strategies of Subversion*. Toronto: Toronto University Press, 1995.

Gili, Jean A. *Nanni Moretti*. Rome: Gremese, 2001.

Hope, William. *Giuseppe Tornatore: Emotion, Cognition, Cinema*. Newcastle: Cambridge Scholars Publishing, 2006.

Jacobsen, Kurt. "Camping Out: Roberto Benigni's *Life Is Beautiful*." *New Politics* 7.3 (new series), whole no. 27 (Summer 1999). http://nova.wpunj.edu/newpolit ics/issue27/Jacsen27.htm. Accessed January 23, 2016.

James, Clive. "Mondo Fellini." *New Yorker* (March 21, 1994): 154–64.

Kezich, Tullio. *Fellini*. Milan: Camunia, 1987.

Langer, Lawrence L. *Using and Abusing the Holocaust*. Bloomington: Indiana University Press, 2006.

Marcus, Millicent. *After Fellini: National Cinema in the Postmodern Age*. Baltimore: Johns Hopkins University Press, 2002.

Marlow-Mann, Alex. *The New Neapolitan Cinema*. Edinburgh: Edinburgh University Press, 2011.

Maslin, Janet. "Giving a Human (and Humorous) Face to Rearing a Boy Under Fascism." *The New York Times* (October 23, 1998). http://movies.nytimes.com/ movie/review?res=9905EFDF113DF930A15753C1A96E958260. Accessed January 23, 2016.

Mazierska, Ewa and Laura Rascaroli, eds. *The Cinema of Nanni Moretti: Dreams and Diaries*. London: Wallflower Press, 2004.

Merkel, Flavio, ed. *Gabriele Salvatores*. Rome: Dino Audino, 1994.

Miccichè, Lino, ed. *Schermi opachi: Il cinema italiano degli anni '80*. Venice: Marsilio Editori, 1998.

Ranucci, Georgette and Stefanella Ughi, eds. *Mario Martone*. Rome: Dino Audino, 1995.

Rohdie, Sam. *Antonioni*. London: BFI, 1990.

Rosi, Francesco. "C'era una volta il cinema." *la Repubblica* (April 20, 1994): 33.

Siegel, Michael Loren. "Identification of a Medium: *Identificazione di una donna* and the rise of Commercial Television in Italy." *Antonioni: Centenary Essays.* Ed. Laura Rascaroli and David Rhodes. London: BFI, 2011. 216–32.

Tonetti, Claretta M. *Bernardo Bertolucci: The Cinema of Ambiguity.* New York: Twayne, 1995.

Vitti, Antonio C. *The Films of Gianni Amelio.* Pesaro: Metauro, 2009.

Zagarrio, Vito. *Cinema italiano anni Novanta.* Venice: Marsilio, 2001.

6

Persistence of Vision

Realism and the Popular in Italian Cinema of the New Millennium

Millicent Marcus

It is no mere coincidence that two of the best films to emerge in the year 2000 were historically based accounts of the lives and premature deaths of little-known anti-Mafia crusaders, and that the Neorealist provenance of these works has been critically acknowledged. Marco Tullio Giordana's *I cento passi* (*The One Hundred Steps*), "a neorealist film beyond neorealism, was said to hover between reality, revolt, and dream,"[1] and Pasquale Scimeca's *Placido Rizzotto* was hailed as a latter-day example of "the best neorealism, that of Rossellini and of the authors who remained close to the facts, without embroidering on them."[2] Though these statements show how elastic the attribution of a neorealist source can be—authorizing in the one case an unadorned, factually rigorous reportage, and in the other, a flight into utopian and even dreamlike transfigurations of the historical record—such recourse to neorealism reveals its enduring hold over Italian filmmaking in the new millennium. Accordingly, recent scholarship has noted the renewed impulse to "dialogue with reality" that has come to characterize current Italian cinema, and has linked this trend to the great filmmaking tradition enshrined by Roberto Rossellini, Vittorio De Sica, and Luchino Visconti in the immediate postwar years.[3] Contemporary cinema's engagement with the Italian collective condition, whether through historical retrospection or an investigative approach to present-day concerns, marks an abrupt shift from the prevalence of films of an "intimist, self-reflexive" nature, restricted "within the confines of their own domestic walls" of the 1980s and early 1990s,[4] when television had usurped the primacy of the cinema as the mass medium par excellence, and the large screen followed the lead of its small-format competitor by diminishing the scope of its thematic and formal concerns.[5]

That the new millennium should be the venue for the reemergence of Italian cinema's commitment to tell the Italian national story is no mere accident of the calendar. If the entrance into the twenty-first century brought with it the heavy symbolism of a rupture in time, that rupture was made literal just twenty months and eleven days later with the attack on the World Trade Center, when the ruling forces of nationalism and globalization gave way to something entirely alien, elusive, and seemingly impossible to combat. But this watershed moment had been preceded by an earlier one that had ushered in a less catastrophic, though no less momentous, reorganization of collective thought: the fall of the Berlin Wall in November 1989, with the subsequent collapse of the Soviet Union and the end of the Cold War. Within the Italian context, these events spelled the death of the First Republic, with the splitting (and fatal weakening) of the once-formidable Italian Communist Party and the demise of the postwar governing coalition led by the Christian Democrats, who had fallen under the weight of corruption charges brought by the judiciary in the so-called *Mani pulite* (Clean Hands) campaign, leaving a power vacuum filled by Silvio Berlusconi and his media empire.

This moment of convulsive change in the Italian sociopolitical order came to coincide with a profoundly symbolic event within the history of Italian film: the 1993 death of Federico Fellini, the last of the great auteurs (De Sica, Visconti, Rossellini, and Pier Paolo Pasolini had all perished in the 1970s, and Michelangelo Antonioni had suffered a debilitating stroke in 1985). "Last Fall, as Federico Fellini's coffin was lying in state in a Cinecittà studio," wrote Daniel Singer in 1994, "people were really mourning the virtual death of Italian cinema."[6] In the words of another critic, Fellini's link to the international pantheon of filmmaking giants Ingmar Bergman, Luis Buñuel, Akira Kurasawa, Yasujirō Ozu, Satyajit Ray, Jean Renoir, and Orson Welles rested in his capacity to get "the whole of their country's life" into each film, and thus to "define the nation's self-image, at home and abroad."[7] Biographer Tullio Kezich summed it up when he pronounced Fellini "the absolute master of a certain kind of filmmaking, *alla grande, all'italiana*."[8]

It is a matter of no small consequence that the year of Fellini's death also saw the release of a film that was to herald the advent of Italian cinematic rebirth: Nanni Moretti's *Caro diario* (*Dear Diary*, 1993), which sought a new form of *scrittura cinematografica* (cinematic language) in this supposed period of abject "afterness." Moretti's search, both linguistic and existential in nature, would ultimately lead to a single human body, the body of the filmmaker himself, which was revealed to be a cinematic sign pointing beyond its status as a mere signifier on-screen. In a shocking segment spliced into the flow of this otherwise meticulously staged cinematic text, Moretti included documentary footage of his own chemotherapy session, in a stark revelation of the fact that his on-screen image, his "body-language" as a cinematic sign, was underwritten by a mortal threat that he was able to avert. The unassailable truth claims of *Dear Diary* in this scene dilate beyond the confines of its two-minute-and-fifteen-second duration to endow the entire film with a testimonial force that anticipates Italian cinema's reinvigorated engagement with the real at the threshold of the new millennium. The strong referential impulse embedded in *Dear Diary* stands as a harbinger of what Christian Uva has called "a documentary idea that manifests itself directly in its way of looking at reality and in the ethical and aesthetic attitude by which it [reality] is given form."[9]

Such a claim runs counter to the common understanding of the postmodernist trend in contemporary culture, characterized by the withering of the referent and the triumph of simulacra, a trend abetted in visual media by the onslaught of CGI technology.[10] This assumption has been vigorously challenged by editors Pierpaolo Antonello and Florian Mussgnug in their groundbreaking volume *Postmodern Impegno*, whose very title announces its aim to align the postwar Italian tradition of committed art with contemporary cultural developments. To do this, they argue for an updated notion of *impegno* or "engagement"—one adapted to our post-ideological age, which replaces monolithic, universalizing, absolutist systems of thought, with flexible, pluralistic, localized, ad hoc approaches to the concerns of the day.[11] Central to Antonello and Mussgnug's definition of postmodern *impegno* is the "turn to ethics,"[12] which has characterized recent advances in the humanities and the social sciences.[13] Where radical programs for the establishment of a more just social order have failed, the sense of responsibility for the well-being of others, enacted on individual and local community levels, and based on a network of "thick relationships" defined by "passional and relational exchange rather than abstract norms," has come to replace the revolutionary projects that have foundered on the shoals of history.[14]

Given the fragmentary, issue-based, open, and contingent nature of *impegno* in our post-ideological age, it should come as no surprise that the Italian cinema's return to its realist vocation, after the torpor of the 1980s and early 1990s, would exhibit a corresponding absence of any kind of unity that would qualify it as a "movement" or "school." The sense of *progettualità*, of utopian longing for national rebirth that fueled filmmakers in the immediate aftermath of the Second World War, and to a lesser extent, the *cinema politico* leading up to and following the revolution of '68, is understandably missing from the cinematic landscape of today. What emerges, instead, is a series of mini-trends, clusters of films that gravitate around thematic questions of the utmost consequence to the contemporary Italian condition. Noteworthy too is the ascension of fresh cinematic talents to public and critical acclaim, as well as the reappearance of established figures whose filmographies take surprising new turns in keeping with their own evolving authorial agendas and the pressures of cultural change. These will be the subjects of the following pages, along with a consideration of popular cinema, including such genres as horror, noir, and especially comedy, the mainstay of the Italian film industry, whose relative inaccessibility to foreign audiences has excluded it from much Anglo-American scholarship to date.[15]

Among the new figures to appear on the filmmaking horizon are Matteo Garrone and Paolo Sorrentino, each of whom won international recognition in 2008, when *Gomorra (Gomorrah)* and *Il divo* were awarded top honors at Cannes. Though diametrically opposed in terms of style, both films make strong claims to a neorealist heritage of *denuncia* (or political exposé), and in their disparate modes of pursuing that goal, they reveal the multiple paths that contemporary film authors can take in fulfillment of neorealism's mandate for civic engagement. Based on Roberto Saviano's sensational inquiry into the workings of the Camorra (the Neapolitan mafia), *Gomorrah* adopts a technically "poor" style, whose unadorned visual imagery, spare musical sound track, settings of the most abject urban degradation, and frequent use of the Steadicam align the film with the documentary, anti-spectacular strain of postwar cinematic realism. Playing against the gangster film genre, *Gomorrah* refuses to glamorize its subject matter, demystifying the iconic figure of the crime boss by employing strategies of estrangement that deny the mechanisms of identification and glamour so assiduously cultivated by the mainstream industry. In the process, Garrone's *Gomorrah* takes the stylistic austerity of the documentary strand to its absolute extreme, endowing the camera with a voyeuristic intrusiveness and ductility that recalls the reigning "reality TV" aesthetic of our current age. Garrone's camera is never still: with restless curiosity it trails characters, prowls the walkways, and probes the hidden recesses of the domestic world within which the *malavita*, underworld, plays itself out. Shot entirely on location, the film devotes a good deal of its footage to events occurring on the premises of Vele di Scampia, the dilapidated housing project situated in the desolate wasteland of suburban Naples. Employing for the most part nonprofessional actors indigenous to the film's physical setting, and allowing them to speak a local dialect that requires subtitles even for Italian audiences,[16] Garrone adopts a directorial style that privileges spontaneity, as he simulates a bottom-up approach to representation. The end result feels as if the profilmic world under scrutiny were inventing its own *sui generis* form, devoid of authorial intervention. This is not to deny the workings of a powerful authorial hand behind the film's pretense of stylistic transparency. On the contrary,

Garrone's signature takes the paradoxical form of a self-concealing aesthetic that, by refusing to call attention to itself, promotes the referential urgency of the film's message. "This world exists," the film asserts, "and it demands our attention."

Diametrically opposed to the immanence and transparency of Garrone's film language in *Gomorrah* is the "extrinsic" and opaque quality of Sorrentino's style in *Il divo*.[17] The Andreottian subject matter, which would lead us to expect a static, understated, highly cerebral approach to representation—characteristics associated with the powerful politician Giulio Andreotti himself—instead produces an audiovisual extravaganza of the most astonishing sort. The film's subtitle, *La vita spettacolare di Giulio Andreotti*, heralds the representational acrobatics to come. The incongruity of pairing *that* adjective (spectacular) with *that* particular noun (Andreotti's life) reveals the magnitude of Sorrentino's challenge: to transform the man variously nicknamed "il gobbo, il Moloch, la volpe, la salamandra, l'eternità, l'uomo delle tenebre" (the hunchback, Moloch, the fox, the salamander, eternity, man of shadows) into the hero of triumphant spectacle. The filmmaker revels in this challenge to his ingenuity, and its dare to the cinematic medium through which that challenge must be met. Andreotti's personal inscrutability means that Sorrentino must entrust the signifying task to what Vsevolod Pudovkin called film's "plastic material," or, in T. S. Eliot's term, the filmmaker must find medium specific "objective correlatives" for Giulio's inner state. Hence, the work of representing Giulio must be displaced onto the externals of mise-en-scène, lighting, music, camerawork, and editing—a requirement that Sorrentino fulfills by making *Il divo* a series of scenes that foreground the prodigious effort of mounting this spectacle, and with it, the "primacy of style" and the "strong directing" that have become his authorial trademark.[18]

What this means is that the viewer of *Il divo* is constantly shuttling between two competing planes of signification: Sorrentino's as he weaves this extravagant and fanciful portrait of the most influential figure in postwar Italian history, and the spectator's own knowledge of Andreotti as gleaned from six decades of current events. The viewing experience of *Il divo* thus involves a recognition in the etymological sense—a re-cognition, or a re-knowing—filtered thought the prism of Sorrentino's exuberant auteurship. Whereas the public, which has lived through the Andreottian era, has experienced the many allegations of his wrongdoing in increments, scattered over the past several decades, the film reports them as a lump sum, and thus not only reactivates the memory within the collective Italian consciousness, but does so in an aggregate whose sheer volume is incriminating. In other words, the film's allusions to his serial misdeeds amount to an archive—the counterpart to the archive that Giulio himself keeps in order to intimidate and silence those who would threaten his hold on power. The source of the protagonist's authority, this documented memory of incriminating information about potential detractors, thus finds in Sorrentino's film an equivalent "dossier" of facts, not secret like Giulio's, but open and accessible to the public that has already been apprised of them over the years. In assembling this counter-archive, Sorrentino delivers the full brunt of his film's satiric blow, as he contests and defeats the protagonist's career-long effort to bridle his critics and to obstruct the workings of an open and democratic society in its pursuit of justice.

While such films as *Gomorrah*, and others including Roberta Torre's *Angela* (2002), Sorrentino's *Le consequenze dell'amore* (*The Consequences of Love*, 2004), Michele Placido's *Romanzo criminale* (*Crime Novel*, 2005), and Davide Barletti and Lorenzo Conte's *Fine pena mai* (*Life Sentence*, 2007) depict organized crime from a perspective internal to its workings, there is a significant mini-trend involving historically based portraits of young martyrs who stand up to injustice, in full awareness of the mortal price to be paid for their temerity.[19] This cluster of films, whose most celebrated example is *The One Hundred Steps*, mentioned above, features protagonists hailing from a variety of institutions and social categories (the judiciary, the Church, the press, the labor movement, countercultural youth). The trend dates back to the early 1990s, as mob violence against legal authorities reached a fever pitch with the murders of trial judges Giovanni Falcone and Paolo Borsellino. In the wake of these atrocities, Alessandro di Robilant released *Il giudice ragazzino* (*The Boy Judge*, 1994) about the final years of Rosario Livatino, a young magistrate of impeccable virtue and intense investigative zeal who ran afoul of the Mafia and refused to surrender to its tactics of intimidation. Six years later, Scimeca's *Placido Rizzotto* recounted the life of his film's title character, a Second World War partisan who returns home to Corleone and becomes a labor organizer dedicated to protecting the rights of the fieldworkers against their exploitation by local bosses. His activism culminates in a campaign for the popular occupation of fields left uncultivated by the wealthy landowners of Corleone, in defiance of Mafia threats, leading to his violent end and the ignominious disposal of his remains. The church becomes the venue for a bold anti-Mafia crusade on the part of Don Puglisi (Roberto Faenza's *Alla luce del sole* [*In Broad Daylight*, 2005]) who volunteers for a pulpit in the crime-infested Palermo neighborhood of Brancacci, where his outspokenness and his attempts to offer local youths an alternative to organized criminality earn him the inevitable assassin's bullet. Rita Atria, who was born into a Mafia family and who later turned state's evidence—a decision that required her to assume a false identity and live in hiding, and that finally drove her to suicide—became the subject of two films by Marco Amenta, one a documentary, *Diario di una siciliana ribelle* (*Diary of a [Female] Sicilian Rebel*, 2002) and the second, *La ragazza siciliana* (*The Sicilian Girl*, 2008), a staged recreation of her life and its tragic denouement. The most recent (as of this writing) installment in the mini-trend of films dedicated to young martyrs in the struggle against organized crime is Marco Risi's *Fort'apasc* (*Fort Apache*, 2009), the story of Giancarlo Siani, an investigative journalist who would not be dissuaded from uncovering the saga of Camorra corruption and collusion in Torre Annunziata and later in Naples itself.

In Hollywood parlance, these films are biopics, though the term lacks the dignity that the mini-genre deserves. What gives them their Italianate specificity is their strong memorialist impulse, which links them to the venerable literary tradition crowned by Ugo Foscolo's "Dei sepolcri" ("On Sepulchers," 1807) and Giacomo Leopardi's "All'Italia" ("To Italy," 1818), where heroic history, properly memorialized, becomes a springboard for activism in the present. The first neorealist films took up this challenge. *Roma città aperta* (*Rome, Open City*, 1945) was made as a tribute to the Roman resistance, eulogizing the populist heroics of its characters Pina, Manfredi, and Don Pietro, while three of the six episodes of *Paisà* (*Paisan*, 1946) memorialize the sacrifices of characters whose martyrdom would otherwise have gone unrecorded: Carmela (Sicilian episode), the anonymous partisan who dies in Harriet's arms (Florentine episode), and Cigolani, Dale, and their comrades (Po River episode). In constructing funerary monuments to warriors in the battle against tyranny and injustice, these early Neorealist works were epitaphic in nature, that is, they served as writings on tombs, speaking to the observer of lives given over to defeating the Nazi-Fascist scourge. The anti-Mafia martyr genre literalizes this epitaphic impulse by ending with written inscriptions on the darkened screen—captions that set forth the details of the characters' death or the judicial aftermath of their assassinations.

Of the films within this mini-genre, *The One Hundred Steps* stands out for the richness and complexity of its attempt to forge a cinematic writing adequate to its memorializing task. The film foregrounds the issue of communication, thanks to protagonist Peppino Impastato's role as founder of Radio Aut, a local offshoot of the *radio libera* movement serving to propagate an alternative, countercultural voice in the politically charged atmosphere of the 1970s.[20] Having appropriated the local airwaves, Peppino's most daring move is to broadcast a satiric rewriting of Dante's *Commedia*, populating the fourteenth-century poet's infernal landscape with the corrupt politicians and Mafiosi operatives of his hometown. But this is not Peppino's only recourse to literary models in his quest for selfhood within the Mafia-affiliated family in which he was raised. As a child, he recites romantic poet Leopardi's "L'infinito" ("The Infinite") to the admiration of his listeners, and especially his uncle, Mafia boss Cesare Manzella, who appoints Peppino as his heir apparent. Later in the film, a recitation of Pier Paolo Pasolini's poem "Supplica a mia madre" ("Prayer to My Mother") offers the occasion for Peppino to communicate his inordinate attachment to his mother, and to acknowledge the sexual alterity that he shared with the author of those same verses. Foreign literary figures—Majakovsky and Cervantes—also enter the picture, but the Italian allusions, and the Dantean one above all, dominate the body of literary work which comes to express the young man's public and private self.

Throughout *The One Hundred Steps*, locality emerges as a decisive factor in Peppino's life story: his father wants to send him to study in neighboring Palermo, but he refuses to leave his home; his friends want him to broadcast far and wide, but he has no desire to reach beyond the confines of the town; and a migrant from Bologna wants to "de-provincialize" the radio, but the protagonist bristles at the idea. Such insistence on the primacy of the local points to a previously mentioned feature of postmodern *impegno*, and it is one that has become an organizing principle of much cinematic production in recent years. I have labeled this phenomenon "neo-regionalism" to characterize a body of films that foreground their "locatedness" in a specific historical-cultural-physical landscape, through such mechanisms as the use of dialect, the prevalence of nonprofessional actors indigenous to the locale, the chorality of the narrative, and the synergy between humans and their natural environment. Especially noteworthy in this regard is the proliferation of regional Film Commissions (the use of the English term is striking here, signaling perhaps the awareness that such a practice is a true departure from previous systems of production). Considerable entrepreneurial energy is emerging from such grassroots structures, and it is producing a film corpus deeply tied to the pluralistic, regional nature of the Italian life. In so doing, this cinema has served to rehabilitate the concept of regionalism after its abuse at the hands of the Northern League, which, in my view, has tethered local interests to the elitist, racist, and xenophobic values of a politics devoted to exclusionary ends.[21] Neo-regionalism poses an alternative idea of what it means to identify with a subnational geography, arguing for a strong sense of local rootedness as the foundation on which to build engagement in ever more expansive spheres of political, social, and moral life.

This line of thinking emerges with special clarity in the words of a character in Nicola Cirasola's *Focaccia Blues* (2009), a documentary about the failure of McDonald's to survive in the Pugliese town of Altamura, where a local bakery triumphed over the temporary allure of fast food and the more permanent economic pressures of globalization. "This is the great cultural theme of today—respect for local identities in the ambit of the great multinationals that by now govern the world. We are fully European, we are fully international, we are fully human, if we are truly *altamurani, pugliesi, italiani*."[22]

Food is no mere synecdoche for the triumph of the local in *Focaccia Blues*. As Carlo Petrini's Slow Food movement has made abundantly clear, gastronomy has served as the literal basis for a rethinking of our contemporary condition in natural and cultural terms, with its emphasis on indigenous culinary traditions, the use of ingredients locally grown, and the focus on sustainability and the general stewardship of the environment. As an offshoot of Petrini's movement, we can point to the new culture of Slowness as a general category. Slowness becomes the philosophical reaction against our obsession with velocity and all that it entails: feverish productivity, overstimulation of the senses and the mind, the hyper-connectedness of our technologically saturated existence, and frenetic mobility aimed at the sheer accumulation of experience and quantitative measures of value in all things.

I am therefore tempted to label the cinema that partakes of this cultural opposition to the reigning values of our globalized and digitized world "slow film." By this term, I do not mean to suggest that all such films are slow-moving in the literal sense (though some of them most decidedly are). The intent of "slow films" is first and foremost experiential: to immerse viewers in a world that challenges the primacy of technologically enhanced movement through time and across space, with all of the philosophical implications that this entails. Michelangelo Frammartino's *Le quattro volte* (*The Four Times*, 2010) is a magisterial example of this trend, where slowness equates with a refusal to concede to any of the audience's expectations for filmic temporality: conventional progress in terms of plot development, cause-and-effect displays of individual human agency, and a linear unfolding of narrative meaning. Instead, the film, set in the countryside of Calabria, enacts a metaphysical parable—the four-stage transmigration of the soul, embodied first in the person of an old goatherd living out his final days among his flock, passing into the body of a newborn kid, then into the trunk of a massive tree, and finally into the life-sustaining heat and resulting smoke that issues from the charcoal to which the tree has been reduced. The film is so devoid of the conventional mechanisms for spectator understanding that it exacts from us an entirely new mode of attention, thwarting our impulse to identify with the characters, and blocking any emotional or intellectual investment in their story. The result is a pure phenomenology, one that places us before the raw spectacle of existence without the necessary filters or defenses to contain its mystery.

A film that shares important features with *Le quattro volte*—a slow-moving, de-dramatized plot, a visual fixation on landscape as both object of contemplation and source of an independent subjectivity, a reverence for the primordial human condition, and (surprisingly) a fascination with goats—is Giorgio Diritti's *Il vento fa il suo giro* (*The Wind Blows Round*, 2005). This unassuming, low-budget feature film, Diritti's first, immediately gained a cult following, and ran for two full years at the Cinema Messico in Milan.[23] Set in the remote recesses of northeastern Piedmont, *The Wind Blows Round* gives hyperbolic expression to the neo-regionalist impulse in Italian film. But it is important to note that the film is hardly an unequivocal paean to provincial life, delivering instead a balanced and at times caustic view of the human fauna that inhabit this spectacular natural landscape. The ideal of a progressive, welcoming, all-embracing collective identity that flows from a firm sense of local rootedness and spreads to ever broader spheres of civic engagement in *Focaccia Blues* meets its negative counterpart in *The Wind Blows Round*. Significantly, Diritti's camera never moves beyond the physical confines of the isolated mountain retreat surrounding the village of Chersogno, and the film's dialogue is spoken, for the most part, in Occitan, a dialect derived from *langue d'oc*, the medieval tongue of southern France. This fossilized language makes explicit the regressive, self-marginalized, and introverted nature of life in Chersogno, whose geographic enclosure within the Valle Maira has allowed this antique dialect to survive. When Philippe Héraud, a French goatherd, chooses the village to settle his family and ply his trade as a cheesemaker, the local populace is taken by surprise. Despite the resistance of some villagers, the municipal leaders embrace this as an infusion of new life into the languishing community. But deeply entrenched suspicions soon surface among a growing number of townsfolk, and the Hérauds are eventually ostracized from their midst.

There is another group of outsiders who instead are warmly welcomed in Chersogno, and these are the seasonal vacationers, the city folk for whom the country sojourn is "time out," and who come to "consume" nature from the comfort of the patios and porches of their rented chalets, while Philippe has come to "live" the nature of Chersogno, to experience fully its year-round biorhythms, and to harvest the fruits of his direct, organic, and participatory relationship with its workings. In the process, he reinvigorates Chersogno's connection to its archaic, agrarian past, exemplifying the folk wisdom of the film's title, derived from an Occitan proverb about the circularity of human experience. But the title also authorizes a more sinister circularity as the villagers' initial animus against their foreign guests reasserts itself by the film's end.

But there is another outcast in the film, this time originating from within the native population, and it is he who bears the brunt of the Héraud's misfortune. The victim is a mentally disabled man—never named, and only occasionally glimpsed throughout the story—who had found acceptance and dignity within the Héraud family circle. Toward the end of the film, as a helicopter flies over Chersogno to shoot a documentary about the natural beauties of the area, a closer, ground-level look reveals the dark underside of life in this spectacular setting. What we learn as the helicopter touches down is that the disabled man has taken his own life in the wake of his adoptive family's expulsion from Paradise. Diritti, however, adds a mitigating coda to the bleakness of this denouement by following the footsteps of Massimo, another young admirer of Philippe, in the immediate aftermath of the suicide's funeral. In the final frames of *The Wind Comes Round*, Massimo enters the abandoned house of the Hérauds, where he proceeds to light the kitchen stove, suggesting that the *giro* of the film's title involves not just the resurfacing of the villagers' intolerance but also includes its possible defeat, through the determination of this young man to keep the legacy of Philippe alive.

Another mini-trend of interest in the Italian cinema of the new millennium may be described in psychoanalytic terms as the "return of the repressed." I am referring to the outpouring of films on the Italian Shoah, "a passage little revisited, and hardly edifying, of our History," wrote Ettore Scola in the preface to the screenplay of his bitter comedy on the 1938 Racial Laws, *Concorrenza sleale* (*Unfair Competition*, 2001).[24] Complicit in the silence surrounding the issues of Fascist anti-Semitism and the Final Solution was the Italian cinema itself, unwilling (with some notable exceptions, Vittorio De Sica's *Giardino dei Finzi-Contini* (*Garden of the Finzi Continis*, 1970) chief among them) to confront this subject matter throughout much of the postwar period. For reasons that I have discussed elsewhere,[25] that was all to change in the 1990s, with Roberto Benigni's *La vita è bella* (*Life Is Beautiful*, 1997) as the most conspicuous example of Italy's new willingness to represent its Holocaust experience on the silver screen. Among the titles in this body of work to appear since 2000 are two films that came out in that very year, *Canone inverso* (*Making Love*, Ricky Tognazzi) and *Il cielo cade* (*The Sky Is Falling*), (Andrea and Antonio Frazzi), followed by the aforementioned *Unfair Competition* (Ettore Scola, 2001), *Senza confini* (*Without Borders*, 2001, by Fabrizio Costa), *Perlasca: Un eroe italiano* (*Perlasca: An Italian Hero*, 2002, by Alberto Negrin), *La finestra di fronte* (*Facing Windows*, 2003, by Ferzan Ozpetek), *Il servo ungherese* (*The Hungarian Servant*, 2004, by Massimo Piesco e Giorgio Molteni), *La fuga degli innocenti* (*The Flight of the Innocents*, 2004, by Leone Pompucci, 2004), *Hotel Meina* (2007, by Carlo Lizzani), and *Il giorno della Shoah* (*The Day of the Shoah*, 2009, by Pasquale Squitieri). Noteworthy in this cluster of films is the rich variety of genres that have converged around the plight of the Jews under Fascism and Nazi rule, from *commedia all'italiana* (Scola) to melodrama (Tognazzi), from portrait of the action hero (Negrin and Costa) to domestic tragedy (the Frazzi brothers), and from travel narrative (Pompucci) to historical allegory (Piesco and Molteni).

Amid this wealth of generic approaches, *Facing Windows* merits special attention for what Ozpetek's particular brand of auteurism has added to our understanding of Italian Holocaust memory. The Turkish-born Ozpetek, who has been active in the Italian filmmaking community for years and is outspoken about his homosexuality, brings a double alterity to his cinema. Within *Facing Windows*, one of the protagonists, Davide Veroli, is also doubly "other"—Jewish and gay—a Holocaust survivor who had to sacrifice his lover, Simone, in order to help save his coreligionists from the Nazi roundup of the Roman ghetto on October 16, 1943. The film in fact begins in the predawn hours of that notorious day, as the young Davide, a bakery worker, struggles with and finally slays his boss, who is collaborating in the planned Nazi raid.

Racing from the scene of the crime, Davide leaves a bloody handprint on a wall flanking the street along which he flees. In a breathtaking lap dissolve, the gory stain modulates into a pale blemish on the same wall in the film's narrative present, some sixty years later. It would be no exaggeration to read into this lap dissolve the interpretive key to Ozpetek's film, and to the generalized historical accountability it portends. Though faint and barely decipherable, the Holocaust past marks the present in ways that require continual revisiting through the arts. As Italy struggles to come to terms with alterity in the effort to absorb the recent tidal wave of immigrants in desperate flight from persecution or material wretchedness, the cinema of Holocaust memory offers a sobering reminder of the extremes to which intolerance can lead.[26]

Closely bound to Italian cinematic interest in Holocaust representation, then, is the ever-increasing number of films to address the issue of migration that has so unsettled Italian collective identity in recent years. In *Terrafirma* (*Mainland*, 2011), a film by one of the most promising auteurs to come to the fore in the new millennium, Emanuele Crialese, the tension between humanitarian impulses and socioeconomic realities reaches crisis proportions in the story of the young man Filippo, resident of Linosa, a tiny Pelagian island located a hundred miles off the coast of Tunisia. Born and raised in the world of fishermen, and obedient to the communitarian ideals of the law of the sea, Filippo willingly helps save a pregnant African fugitive and her young son from the waters of the Mediterranean. As a vacation resort, however, Linosa is subject to modern economic and sociological pressures that conflict with the law of the sea. Infatuated with a sophisticated young tourist from the North, Filippo arranges a romantic moonlight excursion in a stolen boat, and when the outing is interrupted by the onslaught of desperate refugees swimming toward them, the young man beats them off, unable to accommodate their large numbers aboard his tiny craft. Tormented by guilt, Filippo seeks absolution by recommitting himself to the law of the sea. The film ends with his daring, and possibly doomed attempt to save the African woman (who had by now given birth) and her older son from deportation, by sailing away from Linosa toward *terraferma*, the mainland, in search of safety for them and redemption for himself.

While the previous pages have focused extensively on trends that have characterized the changing complexion of Italian cinema in the new millennium, it is important to acknowledge an element of continuity that has underpinned the health and viability of the industry over the years. I am referring to the popular genres that make up the great bulk of domestic production, and constitute the main diet of Italian filmgoers (aside from the inevitable Hollywood fare that takes up a significant share of the menu). Among the genres that flourish in Italian soil are, according to Christian Uva, "il noir, il thriller, l'horror, la detective story" (noteworthy is the international provenance of these labels, revealing perhaps the *frisson* of the foreign that underwrites their appeal).[27] But above all, it is the comic genre that comprises the bulk of domestic production. The spectacular success of Italian film comedy from the very outset of the industry speaks to its deep roots in national culture, recalling the Renaissance *commedia dell'arte* and the other rich comedic traditions native to the country's literary and theatrical history. It is the quintessential *italianità* (Italian-ness) of this genre, its ability to hold up the mirror to the Italian national self and to reflect that image back as the object of therapeutic laughter, which explains the genre's perennial hold on the collective imagination. Within the comic vein, Uva singles out "its most popular (vulgar) version . . . .as the genre phenomenon of the greatest longevity in Italy." Foremost in the subcategories of Italian film comedies is the *cinepanettone* (named after the Italian holiday cake, *panettone*), "whose release is . . . rigidly programmed for the Christmas holidays and whose primary artificer has been, for approximately twenty years, the director Neri Parenti," in collaboration with the "actor-fetish Christian De Sica."[28] The summer equivalent of this phenomenon is the *cinecocomero*, named after the summer fruit par excellence, the watermelon, and referring to the beach movie—a subcategory that overlaps with another popular genre, the "teen movie," crowned by the smash hit *La notte prima degli esami* (*The Night Before the Exams*, 2006) and the sequel that it spawned. Seriality—or in Hollywood terms, the franchise—is key to the success of such popular cinema, contributing to its ritual appeal, which is often tied to seasonal celebrations and promises the assured pleasures of the familiar with enough novelty to keep it from becoming stale and passé.[29] Of considerable critical interest in this regard is the elevation of the popular to the level of serious and sustained study by recent scholars who argue convincingly for the importance of genre films as manifestations of the ideological and psychological issues besetting the Italian collective self.[30] Mary Wood, for example, reads "the continuing narrative and visual tensions in popular cinema," characterized by its "emotional and visual excess," as symptoms of the "impossibility of constructing a completely modern consensus of Italian values."[31]

Early in this chapter, I referred to Nanni Moretti's 1993 *Dear Diary* as the harbinger of a cinematic revival in the run-up to the next millennium, and it therefore seems appropriate that I end with his penaltimate feature film as of this writing, *Habemus Papam* (*We Have a Pope*, 2013), which signals yet another new departure, if not for Italian cinema as a whole then at least for a filmmaker whose body of work has served as a remarkable measure of the cultural shifts that his generation has witnessed over the last forty years. Of the utmost importance for the progress of his filmography is the displacement of the director's on-screen persona from the role of central character to the periphery of the action in *We Have a Pope*.[32] In this film, Moretti plays a psychoanalyst (as he had in *La stanza del figlio* [*The Son's Room*, 2001]) now relegated to a position of comic impotence as the therapist of the story's protagonist, the panic-stricken pope-elect, Melville, who commands center stage both for his world-historical importance in the fiction of the film and his riveting hold on the viewer's attention. Significantly, this is not Moretti's first film to take up matters ecclesiastical—he had done so in 1985 with *La messa è finita* (*The Mass Is Over*), in which he had played the starring role of a priest struggling with his vocation. Deeply interconnected with Moretti's movement toward self-effacement in *We Have a Pope* is the film's focus on the virtue of *humilitas*, humility, presaged in a sermon by a young priest whose parish Melville enters by chance as he wanders the streets of Rome in civilian disguise having momentarily escaped from the Vatican. *Humilitas* functions on several levels in *We Have a Pope*, most obviously in Melville's choice to renounce the papacy, but also in the language of the film itself, which subordinates scenes of lavish spectacle to images of the simplest and humblest sort: facial close-ups of Melville. Despite the great visual appeal of the film's glimpses into the behind-the-scenes workings of the Holy See, nothing compares with the curiosity elicited by the mere image of Melville's face, offered up for our intense scrutiny throughout *We Have a Pope* as we seek to fathom the depths of his ambivalence about accepting the pontifical role. With every close-up of Melville, we are seized by a particular form of attentiveness. His visage becomes a screen-within-the-screen, the privileged surface on which the conflict between the external pressure of events and his internal resistance to them plays itself out. Because Melville is inarticulate to the point of incoherence, we are restricted to reading the disposition of his facial features, their every nuance and shift, in search of clues to his inner state. What complicates our reading of the face in film is its double function as window and mask whose very ambiguity resides at the heart of its signifying power.[33] That power is activated when the face is isolated from the flow of images via the close-up in a liberating gesture that frees it from performing a purely communicative service in the advancement of plot.[34] By freeing the face from its utilitarian role in narration, the close-up parallels, at the level of film language, Melville's own emancipation from the chain of events that would seal his destiny as pope.

In offering us intimate visual access to another human face, the close-up poses the great question of subjectivity itself, and in another sign of Moretti's own humility in *We Have a Pope*, he bows before its mystery.[35] With immense delicacy and tact, the film acknowledges the incommunicability of the essential self, the unrepresentable nature of our interior being. The unreadable face of Melville, caught in the throes of world-historical indecision, has come to replace that of Moretti's on-screen persona, whose subjectivity was an open book culminating in the confessional pages of *Dear Diary*. By withdrawing to the sidelines of his film, Moretti is clearing the stage for a very different kind of cinema, one that takes on the problem of subjectivity in a way no longer limited to the personal and idiosyncratic confines of his earlier work, but in the universal terms personified by Melville. That he focuses his attention on the would-be wielder of the highest authority in the Catholic world raises the stakes of his enterprise and underlines its seriousness. In so doing, however, the film skirts the kind of issues that such subject matter seems to demand—issues of the greatest theological and political consequence.

In *We Have a Pope*, instead, Moretti's interests lead elsewhere: to the existential and humanistic concerns that define our very being. On the threshold of the second decade of the second millennium, this may very well be an indication of the broadening and deepening sense of the "real" that Italian cinema is preparing to address, an *impegno* that transcends the postmodern and projects forward to an age that has yet to be named.

Notes

1 Quilici, "*I cento passi*," 5.

2 Argentieri, "Pasquale Scimeca e il mondo contadino del dopoguerra," 6–7.

3 Uva, "Nuovo cinema Italia," 306.

4 These are the words of Giovanna Taviani, quoted in Uva, "Nuovo cinema Italia," 308.

5 This involution of the cinema, its withdrawal from the arena of historical and civic engagement, has been characterized as "claustrophilia" by Sesti, *Nuovo cinema italiano*, 9. Miccichè lamented this as the era of "unexportable and often invisible little films, cute films, and trash" ("Il lungo decennio grigio," 13).

6 Singer, "Gatt and the Shape of Our Dreams," 54.

7 James, "Mondo Fellini," 164; and Cowell, "Thousands of Italian Mourners File in Homage Past Fellini Bier," C22.

8 Kezich, *Fellini*, 534.

9 Uva, "Nuovo cinema Italia," 307.

10 See Baudrillard, *Simulations*, 4.

11 See Antonello and Mussgnug, *Postmodern Impegno*, 3–4.

12 Antonello and Mussgnug, *Postmodern Impegno*, 9.

13 See, for example, Buell's introduction to "In Pursuit of Ethics."

14 Buell's introduction to "In Pursuit of Ethics," 12. Antonello and Mussgnug go on to explain that this new approach to bettering our world arises from the micro-level of personal experience—concrete relationships with family, friends, neighbors, coworkers, and community members—rather than from abstract, universalizing prescriptions for social change.

15 Exceptions to this rule are the studies by Lanzoni, *Comedy Italian Style*; and Bini, *Male Anxiety and Psychopathology in Film*.

16 Such a practice has a venerable precedent in Luchino Visconti's *La terra trema* (*The Earth Trembles*, 1948), where the fishermen spoke such a pure Sicilian dialect that his film required intertitles and a voice-over narration in standard Italian to be understood by domestic audiences.

17 This overview of *Il divo* is a distillation of my article "The Ironist and the Auteur," 245–57.

18 Luca Malavasi, "Studio cubista di Andreotti," 2–3.

19 For a superb, groundbreaking study of the body of Italian films on Mafia subjects to emerge since 2000 see Renga, *Unfinished Business*.

20 A more extensive critical analysis of this film, together with discussions of *Il giudice ragazzino* and *Placido Rizzotto* may be found in my article "In Memoriam," 290–306.

21 In 2018 under the leadership of Matteo Salvini the *Lega* conveniently shed its modifier *nord* in an illusory appeal to national unity, all the while maintaining its demagogic populist anti-immigrant agenda.

22 These are the words of a local high school principal, interviewed in *Focaccia Blues*.

23 Prior to *Il vento fa il suo giro,* Diritti had directed documentaries, short subjects, and television programs.

24 Scola, *Concorrenza sleale,* 5.

25 See my *Italian Film in the Shadow of Auschwitz*, 18–20.

26 For a fuller analysis of *La finestra di fronte*, see my *Italian Film in the Shadow of Auschwitz*, 140–52.

27 See Uva, "Nuovo cinema Italia," 313.

28 Uva, "Nuovo cinema Italia," 313.

29 Uva, "Nuovo cinema Italia," 314.

30 See, for example, Brizio-Skov, *Popular Italian Cinema*, which includes chapters on the peplum, horror, the Spaghetti Western, comedy, and melodrama. Catherine O'Rawe has written a number of important essays on various facets of Italian popular cinema. For a rigorous and thorough study devoted to the genre of *cinema natalizio*, see O'Leary's *Fenomenologia del cinepanettone*.

31 Wood, *Italian Cinema*, 62.

32 Moretti anticipates this move in *Il caimano* (2006), where he appears on screen at the very end playing the role of Berlusconi.

33 For this insight, see Steimatsky, *The Face on Film*, 13.

34 Steimatsky, *The Face on Film*, 38.

35 Steimatsky, *The Face on Film*, 146.

Bibliography

Antonello, Pierpaolo and Florian Mussgnug, eds. *Postmodern Impegno: Ethics and Commitment in Contemporary Italian Culture*. Oxford: Peter Lang, 2009.

Argentieri, Mino. "Pasquale Scimeca e il mondo contadino del dopoguerra." *Cinemasessanta* 42 (March–April, 2002).

Baudrillard, Jean. *Simulations*. Trans. Paul Foss, Paul Patton, and Philip Beitchman. New York: Semiotext(e), 1983.

Bini, Andrea. *Male Anxiety and Psychopathology in Film. Comedy Italian Style*. New York: Palgrave Macmillan, 2015.

Brizio-Skov, Flavia, ed. *Popular Italian Cinema: Culture and Politics in a Postwar Society*. London: I.B. Tauris, 2011.

Buell, Lawrence. "In Pursuit of Ethics." *PMLA* 114.1 (January 1999).

Cowell, Alan. *The New York Times* (November 3, 1993).

James, Clive. "Mondo Fellini." *The New Yorker* (March 21, 1994).

Kezich, Tullio. *Fellini*. Milan: Rizzoli, 1988.

Lanzoni, Rémi Fournier. *Comedy Italian Style: The Golden Age of Italian Film Comedies*. London: Bloomsbury, 2009.

Malavasi, "Studio cubista di Andreotti." *Cineforum* 476 (2008).

Marcus, Millicent. "In Memoriam: The Neorealist Legacy in the Contemporary Sicilian Anti-Mafia Film." In *Italian Neorealism and Global Cinema*. Ed. Laura E. Ruberto and Kristi M. Wilson. Detroit: Wayne State University Press, 2007.

Marcus, Millicent. "The Ironist and the Auteur: Post-realism in Paolo Sorrentino's *Il Divo*." *The Italianist* 30.2 (2010).

Marcus, Millicent. *Italian Film in the Shadow of Auschwitz*. Toronto: University of Toronto Press, 2007.

Miccichè, Lino. "Il lungo decennio grigio." In *Schermi opach: Il cinema italiano degli anni '80*. Ed. Lino Miccichè. Venice: Marsilio, 1998.

O'Leary, Alan. *Fenomenologia del cinepanettone*. Soveria Mannelli: Rubbettino, 2013.

Quilici, Gianni. "*I cento passi*." *La linea dell'occhio* 39 (Spring 2001).

Renga, Dana. *Unfinished Business: Screening the Italian Mafia in the New Millennium*. Toronto: University of Toronto Press, 2013.

Scola, Ettore. *Concorrenza sleale*. Turin: Lindau, 2001.

Sesti, Mario. *Nuovo cinema italiano: Gli autori, i film, le idee*. Roma: Teoria, 1994.

Singer, Daniel. "Gatt and the Shape of our Dreams." *The Nation* (January 17, 1994).

Steimatsky, Noa. *The Face on Film*. Oxford: Oxford University Press, 2017.

Uva, Christian. "Nuovo cinema Italia: Per una mappa della produzione contemporanea, tra tendenze formule e linguaggi." *The Italianist* 29 (2009).

Wood, Mary. *Italian Cinema*. Oxford: Berg, 2005.

PART TWO

Gender, Genre, Theory

7

The Five Faces of the Italian Femme Fatale

Stephen Gundle

The notion of the femme fatale is not one that is either original to Italian cinema or to Italy. Rather, it is a figure with complex antecedents dating mainly to the late-nineteenth-century international movements of Decadentism and Symbolism. In cinema, France and the United States have produced the most memorable examples. Yet Italy has a claim on the femme fatale that derives primarily from four types of cultural production: the decadent novels and plays of Gabriele D'Annunzio, certain operas (notably Giuseppe Verdi's *La traviata*, 1853, an adaptation of Alexandre Dumas fils's novel *La dame aux camélias*), the performances and personas of a handful of stage performers, and the silent "diva" films of the 1910s and early 1920s. To these may be added some lesser-known manifestations in the cinema of the middle decades of the twentieth century, including some significant and original reworkings of imported examples.

Recent examinations have clarified that the femme fatale cannot be seen purely as a product of a misogynistic imagination.[1] The popularity of this figure between the late nineteenth and early twentieth centuries can be related to pressures for women's emancipation and the anxieties this caused, as well as interest in the classification and regulation of female sexuality, in addition to the emergence of powerful women actor-managers in the theater. It is for this reason that the femme fatale has always had an extratextual resonance. While most, perhaps all, fatal narratives end in tragedy, the visual power, disruptive energy, and intriguing enigmas of the women who are their subjects and the women who are their interpreters cannot be so contained. These have shaped celebrity, fashion, modern advertising, and consumption, which is not surprising since the femme fatale emerged at precisely the moment when the forms of modern capitalism were taking definitive shape. In Italy, as elsewhere, these different impulses were fairly distant from the country's political development but not from patterns of modernization and its impulses to emancipation.

The Italian femme fatale's five faces can be related to five not entirely distinct moments in the history of Italian cinema: the divas of silent cinema; the presence of fatale figures in the cinema of the Fascist period; the phenomenon of the neorealist femme fatale, arguably the richest and most innovative of her incarnations; the transformation experienced by Italian actresses in postwar Hollywood; and finally the presence of "dark ladies" in Italian noir cinema and of Italian actresses in wider noir and neo-noir cinema. As we will see, a number of continuities mark these different figures as the trope of the femme fatale, originally a feature of silent cinema, resonated in Italian culture for many decades.

1 Diva Films of Silent Cinema

The diva of Italian silent cinema was a distinctive feature of a film industry that before the late 1910s was known exclusively for its ancient-world blockbusters. The diva was essentially an adaptation of an invention of Scandinavian cinema but, thanks to domestic literary and cultural antecedents, she soon established her compelling, original presence in Italy. For Angela Dalle Vacche, the Italian diva was "a mixture of Catholic mater dolorosa, of the Northern European femme fatale in literature and in painting and of the new woman of modernity, [who] would move from the roles of prostitute to socialite, or from rags to riches in the very same melodrama, so combining stereotypes of femininity from both the upper and lower classes" ("The Diva Film," 24). Audiences knew that, at the movies, they could expect to be transported into alluring milieus and experience with their diva of choice a range of emotions that would be expressed through signature physical movements and gestures. Before, typically, finishing badly, she took spectators on a psychological and experiential journey of unusual intensity.

The most prominent of them, Lyda Borelli, had appeared on stage from the age of sixteen alongside the great actress Eleonora Duse. Her preeminence was established in the twelve films she made between 1913 and 1918. Like the other leading screen actresses of the 1910s, Francesca Bertini and Pina Menichelli—who were both in their early twenties—Borelli emerged in a context in which the Art Nouveau or Liberty style was the rage, and there was a diffuse artistic involvement with feminine beauty.[2] Borelli belonged to the spirit of her time, Ettore Zocaro notes, by "interpreting a specific style according to which women covered their bare shoulders with ostrich feather boas and wandered across the stage carelessly dragging a mink coat behind them" ("'Prima donna' del teatro italiano," 31). Borelli would be remembered more than her colleagues mainly because she became a social phenomenon. The critic Alfredo Panzini described her particular performance style as "borelleggiare," and "borellismo" soon became a craze. She wore clothes and jewels that caught the eye, practiced new sports, smoked, and offered a repertoire of screen poses and attitudes that were very widely imitated. Between the early war years and 1920, young women copied her looks and gestures, dressed like her, did their hair like hers, and affected attitudes similar to those of the characters she played.[3] This practice was a spontaneous response, the expression of a desire for acknowledgment and emancipation. It was not encouraged by the numerous popular and women's magazines that were published at this time. A close study of the coverage received by Francesca Bertini in some fifty publications has revealed that the attention granted to cinema and its stars was sporadic and irregular.[4]

Italy's early film stars were indirect protégées of D'Annunzio, the writer and poet whose debut novel *Il piacere* (*Pleasure*, 1889) featured the character Elena Muti, a refined and highly eroticized woman of passion and instinct. This author's decadent aesthetic of excess and refinement had an impact on everything from fashion and interior decoration to the treatment of the artistic heritage and politics. This D'Annunzian legacy combined with other literary antecedents of the screen diva to shape every aspect of her being and confirm her as a cultural emblem. This imaginary background has led some to argue that "the world represented on the screen had virtually no links with the real country . . . but many with the literary world and that of the figurative arts."[5] Yet this is not the whole picture. "The diva's unusual contribution to the history of stardom stems from the cultural specificities of Italian modernity," Gian Piero Brunetta argues (*Cent'anni di cinema italiano*, 99). Among these was the fact that modern urban culture was confined to a limited number of large cities and the audience for cinema was much smaller and consequently more bourgeois than in other industrial countries. "The sparkle of a goblet of champagne, the smoke of a cigarette, the hint of a fragrance . . . the revelation of an ankle, the caress of a flower: a wealth of messages is communicated through the exchange of glances and the presence of objects," Brunetta notes (*Cent'anni di cinema italiano*, 99). The spectator was consequently sucked in, to the extent that he or she experienced

> the loss of perception of space and time. A piano, a couch, flowers . . . the appearance of a coach or a chauffeur-driven car, the possibility of entering noble palaces by means of staircases, of being invited to parties and the rites of the aristocratic and high bourgeois worlds: all this works together and makes visible and tangible things that had previously been confined to the imagination or restricted to the few.[6]

Precisely this paradox of accessible exclusivity was one of the cardinal features of glamour, a property that had not yet been fully appropriated by cinema, although steps in this direction were under way in Hollywood.[7] The diva's stardom was constructed through repetition and predictability. As a fact of modern communication, it belonged to the age of mechanical reproduction.

Famously, Antonio Gramsci anticipated Benjamin's reflections on the decline of the auratic aspect of culture by denying Borelli's art, affirming that she "cannot play anyone other than herself."[8] In contrast to historical films, which presented different situations and characters each time, the diva was both constant and mobile in the sense that her character was readily identifiable and guaranteed to evolve. As Vittorio Martinelli confirms: "Malevolent or transparent, fatal or ingenuous, it was always her; she was unmistakable because she carried in her blood the lively fascination of her heroines" ("La Borelli," 28). For this reason she was unforgettable. Even after the Italian film industry collapsed in the early 1920s, memories of her were strong enough still to exercise some influence during the resurrection of stardom in the 1930s and to persist into the postwar years.

2 The Fascist Femme Fatale

By the time the film industry began to revive in the early 1930s, the femme fatale had migrated from Europe to Hollywood. It was no longer the divas of Northern or Southern European cinema who fascinated film audiences but Europeans like Greta Garbo and Marlene Dietrich who had been repackaged by Hollywood.[9] In Italy, the Hollywood model found an adaptation in the person of Isa Miranda. The first case in the sound era of an Italian actor being groomed and launched according to industrial criteria, Miranda's debut in a lead role was as the ill-fated film star Gaby Doriot in Max Ophüls's Italian-produced *La signora di tutti* (*Everybody's Lady*, 1934). The film's complicated plot, recounted mostly in flashback, explores a stream of fatal encounters, beginning with the heroine's expulsion from school after a teacher who has fallen in love with her abandons his family and takes flight. It ends with the suicide of the scandal-tinged Gaby, who, despite being launched as the star of a film, cannot accept that the man she once loved has married her sister and was the father of her children. Like two previous films by the Austrian director, *Liebelei* (1932) and *Divine* (1935), *La signora di tutti* explores the story of an ostensibly ordinary woman who is unaware of the effect she has on the people and world around her. However, Mary Ann Doane argues that, unlike the femme fatales of film noir, she is passive rather than consciously manipulative or scheming. She appears to float in a passive state and wreaks havoc unawares. In this respect, she is "reminiscent of the tradition of the diva in the silent Italian cinema" ("The Abstraction of a Lady," 70). A woman of exceptional beauty who causes catastrophe simply through her presence, the diva often met an end as tragic and final as her lovers, and this is the case with Gaby. But this reminiscence is a matter of echoes since the age of the diva had passed and her exaggerated gestures now seemed absurd. Doane argues that the gestural excess of the diva was replaced by "the hyperbolic strategies of the Ophulsian style—in camera movement, mise-en-scène, and music, which take up in their repetitive *straining*, the thematic of the fatal inevitability of history" ("The Abstraction of a Lady," 71). Indeed, the film can be seen as "an investigation into the birth of a star (in contrast to the diva of the teens)."[10] In Miranda's performance there was a dose of romantic pathos in the Garbo mold. In Italian terms, her character glances backward to the idea of the diva while incorporating a sense of the ordinary girl.

The film was notable for the way it both deployed technique and commented on a variety of media. It won the prize for cinematic technique at the Venice Film Festival on account of its ample uses of dissolves, montage sequences, tracking shots, and voice-overs. "The praise for the film's technical aspect is highly ironic," Susan White comments, "in that the subject of the film is the alienation of woman through technology— including the camera, the printing press, and the auditory devices of telephone, telegraph, and radio" (*The Cinema of Max Ophuls*, 199). Gaby is catapulted into a medium and an industry in which her appearance, voice, gestures and capacity for expression are magnified, exploited, projected, and sold. Even though, as Brunetta has remarked, the film was "a work too sophisticated and distant from the models of popular culture and from any sort of projection-identification at all" (*Storia del cinema italiano, 1895-1945*, 510), it wove a star narrative into Miranda's yet-to-emerge screen persona. Inevitably, over the years, the tragic story of the fall of a young star came to be read back on to Miranda herself, even though there were few biographical overlaps between her and her character.[11] In the mid-1930s, in contrast to the 1910s, there was no desire to see Italian womanhood equated with diva types. A prominent film journalist, Mino Doletti, writing in the newspaper *Il Resto del Carlino*, deplored the fact that, in *La signora di tutti*, Miranda was a "torbid and sick creature, with a disturbed and disquieting sensibility (not stuff of ours, for goodness sake, but imported stuff!)" ("*Passaporto rosso*," 7). He much preferred the more down-to-earth parts she took in films like Mario Camerini's *Come le foglie* (*Like the Leaves*, 1935): "Here she is simply a woman, calm and human, who loves and suffers," he noted: "We dare to underline: an Italian woman of the type who plotted during the Risorgimento, one of those women who know how to be sweet and uncorrupted wives, who dress proudly in mourning when they give up a son to the Fatherland. Isa Miranda should be just as she is, calm and measured, gentle and sweet."

Such remarks show both the shift that had turned cinema from an elite into a mass phenomenon and the sort of pressures that were placed on the medium under Fascism. Cinema's role was, to be sure, to provide mass entertainment, but it was also to act as a promoter of normative types of beauty, gender roles, and social attitudes. While American cinema was admired and envied, and in some respects was copied, it was also seen as a negative model, an example of a sort of cinema that ultimately had no place in the new Italy. Miranda was a problematic case from this point of view, for not only was her appearance similar to that of the foreign "fatales" Garbo and Dietrich (indeed Ophuls probably cast her for this reason), but she was spotted and placed under contract by the American major Paramount and made two films for the company, *Adventure in Diamonds* (1939) and *Hotel Imperial* (1940), before personal issues and the onset of war put an end to her American experience. Italian reactions to this mixed pride in the recognition accorded an Italian star with dismay at her easy incorporation into an alien star system.[12] Following her return to Italy, Miranda struggled to win roles and eventually played tragic women in three films directed by her husband, Alfredo Guarini.

This does not mean that the femme fatale was banished from Italian cinema. The residual influence of D'Annunzianism, the Fascist taste for daring gestures, and the relative liberty of the artistic milieu to which film artistes belonged meant that transgressive femininity still found a place. Clara Calamai and Doris Duranti, two stars of slightly lesser standing than Miranda, engaged in a public rivalry that manifested itself in the pursuit of scandalous images. Calamai specialized in queenly roles that invariably involved elaborate costuming and the construction of a seductive glamour. Duranti, for her part, was often cast as rustic or oriental women, disruptive types who briefly unsettle the stolid men they encounter before being tamed or destroyed. A dark-haired woman of deep complexion, she cultivated a compelling image off-screen. She became the lover of Culture Minister Alessandro Pavolini, a privileged position that she exploited to the full.[13] She even accompanied him north to the infamous Republic of Salò in his final role as secretary of the revived Fascist party after 1943 and only narrowly avoided sharing his fate before a firing squad in April 1945. In the postwar years, she would revel in her image as a dark seductress and unapologetic mistress of the regime. The two actresses both fleetingly went topless, respectively in *La cena delle beffe* (*The Jester's Supper*, 1942) and *Carmela* (1942), with each claiming to have been the first.[14] In the context of each film, Duranti's gesture was the bolder one and was repeatedly cited by her as proof of her indisputable sex appeal.[15] In terms of Italian cinema, this exposure constituted the first sign of a shift from character to body that was already evident in American cinema and that would bloom in the postwar years.[16] It also made sex a more explicit feature of the Italian femme fatale than had previously been the case.

3 The Neorealist Femme Fatale

One of the most dramatic signs of the hybrid nature of neorealism was the persistence within it of the femme fatale. On the face of it, neorealism should have heralded the end of this figure. Yet the filmic current that aimed to abolish the conventional artifice of cinema and explore the everyday was far more heterodox than is commonly acknowledged and elements of melodrama and film noir are present in many even of the best-known films.[17] The question therefore is not why we find femmes fatales in these films, but rather how and in what ways they act as sites of tension between cinematic tropes and innovation and reflect a turbulent social and political moment. The first example is the figure of the adulterous innkeeper's wife-turned-murderess Giovanna in Luchino Visconti's *Ossessione* (1943). Often cited as the precursor of postwar realism, the film presented a series of ruptures with the established conventions of Fascist cinema, while adopting a narrative borrowed from an American pulp novel. Played by Calamai in an unfamiliar disheveled guise, Giovanna induces her indecisive lover Gino to assist her in doing away with her repulsive husband before seeking to make a new life with him and eventually being killed in a road accident. Calamai and her character have been subject to intensive, even obsessive, analysis. Her emphatic acting in the part has even been seen to owe a debt to the diva tradition.[18] In her analysis of the film, Giuliana Minghelli refers to Giovanna as a "black-clad femme fatale" who "belongs" in the dark interiors of the inn, and to Calamai's "gleaming with black brilliance" (*Landscape and Memory in Post-Fascist Italian Film*, 21, 25). These two elements overlap and fuse in Minghelli's analysis when she refers to "glamorous and unhappy Giovanna" (*Landscape and Memory in Post-Fascist Italian Film*, 26). Giovanna is indeed unhappy, but it is Calamai—also unhappy at her transformation at Visconti's hands from queen to rundown skivvy—who is glamorous, though not in this role. For Gilles Deleuze, Giovanna is an outsider, a displaced person, "a sleepwalker [more] than a seductress or lover," who never really wakes up.[19] In fact, she is a force of rebellion that refuses to conform while desiring nothing more than a conventional life. Giovanna is not at all a rooted figure; the only thing we know of her past is that she was, like Gino, a sort of drifter who had ended up on the fringes of prostitution before her portly, middle-aged husband "rescued" her. Her failure to conform fully to the established type of the femme fatale has led some authors to question whether she is "fatale" at all, and even to elaborate a new interpretation of the film according to which it is the handsome vagrant Gino who is the bearer of fatality.[20] These disputes suggest the rich ambiguity of the film text and also some of the ways in which a standard plot was pulled and distorted by a director who wanted to extract from it as many critical perspectives on the Italian reality of the time as possible. There was also a political element to this. From the point of view of the anti-Fascist makers of the film, Giovanna arouses little sympathy as her actions are dictated solely by personal and material concerns. Thus, there is no real point of conflict with the basic borrowed plot that establishes the evil of her act and the need for her to be punished by death. However, her husband Bragana, a brusque man of conventional views who has been a soldier in the Bersaglieri regiment, deserves to die because he is a Fascist, as he reveals during a fleeting moment of banter with Gino.

Calamai would appear in *Due lettere anonime* (*Two Anonymous Letters*, 1945), the first postwar film made by the Mario Camerini, the director of many escapist comedies in the 1930s. The film is unusual because, unlike films belonging to the neorealist canon, it explicitly addresses the guilt of Italians and their complicity with Nazism. The dark fatality of Calamai in this sense was not reduced or overturned by its translation into a simple, everyday context. Rather it was a tool of political and moral judgment. A vocal critic of the whitewashing of Italian responsibilities during the Nazi occupation in Robert Rossellini's iconic *Roma città aperta* (*Rome, Open City*, 1945), Camerini struck a stance that could not but arouse hostility.[21] In this film, Calamai is again a lower class woman who murders a Fascist man—in this case, an upwardly mobile fellow print worker and Nazi collaborator to whom she has given herself after breaking with her dejected, war-worn fiancé. Given the different political context (the film includes footage of the liberation of Rome, which occurs within the film's narrative shortly after her homicidal act), her action cannot be regarded as requiring punishment.

Yet her indirect collaborationism is a stain on her character. Conventional plot developments are discarded in favor of a political solution. The film closes on a close-up of her distraught face staring out from behind the bars of her prison. Even though her one-time fiancé has assured her she will soon be free and will be able to make a new life, she will always be haunted by her past.

The femme fatale would be subject to reworking in several canonical and some less canonical neorealist films. This variety suggests the different ways in which directors deployed this cinematic trope in their efforts to stake out moral and aesthetic positions. In *Roma città aperta* and *Paisà* (*Paisan*, 1946), Rossellini set out three different views of the femme fatale. Two of these appear in the first film, in the person of the female Nazi Ingrid, whose vampirish appearance and make-up and apparent lesbianism mark her out as a character with multiple deviant aspects, and in the figure of the drug-addicted showgirl Marina, whose crass materialism is seen as the main cause of her betrayal of her communist lover, the heroic Manfredi. Whereas Ingrid is endowed with agency, Marina is weak and devoid of power. Maria Michi, who played Marina, reappears in the Rome episode of *Paisà* as Francesca, another good girl turned bad who tries and fails to turn the clock back and recover the innocence she had before she turned to prostitution.

But her conversion does not work for the soldier has also changed and, while he can reminisce, he can no longer "see" her. Significantly, she signals her failed attempt to return to innocence by exchanging the ostentatious external markers of her corrupted status (the lurid clothing that she wore as prostitute) for a simple white outfit. Rossellini's most interesting take on the femme fatale occurs in the Sicilian episode of *Paisà*, and it exemplifies Bazin's well-known remark that the director's cinema was marked by a concern with "a way of seeing" (*What Is Cinema?* 2:62). Carmela is a simple peasant girl who has none of the appearance of a femme fatale, and we, as spectators, do not see her as such; but she is regarded as an evil siren by both the German soldiers, on whom she turns a rifle, and the American troops who believe that she has lured their comrade Joe into a fatal trap. They do not know that she bears no guilt for Joe's death and, on the contrary, has been thrown from a cliff top by the German soldiers at whom she fired the gun in a vain effort to avenge Joe. Such exposure of the dynamics of points of view illustrates the way neorealism upped the stakes of spectatorship in the postwar years.[22]

Rossellini's complex deconstruction of the femme fatale found no followers. Among filmmakers, the trend toward the blending of realism and melodrama that marked *Ossessione* proved a more ready template than his experimentation. Mary Wood has noted that within the subgenre known as *neorealismo nero* the seedier side of life and the fallout from the aftermath of war are explored through the prism of noir, with male and female figures pursuing a complex reconfiguration of gender and genre codes. The femme fatale in these narratives is often symbolic of the rejection of "the exercise of masculinist power" (*Chiaroscuro*, 160). With their sexual assertiveness, expressed often through elaborate costuming and accessorizing—more so than in the dominant current of neorealism itself—and evident pursuit of a measure of freedom and autonomy, the innovative fatale figures of these films were not unrelated to important social and political developments such as the widespread desire for material improvement, the extension of the franchise to women, and the employment opportunities offered to women by the expansion of the service sector.

Anna Magnani, whose persona prior to her extraordinary performance as Pina in *Roma città aperta* had in part been that of a worldly seductress, would take a significant role in this subgenre. For Wood, Lattuada's 1946 film *Il bandito* (*The Bandit*), ostensibly a drama about the difficulties faced by returning soldiers, is exemplary in this sense, since it features Magnani as Lidia, a gangster's moll, whose role helps make the film "much more complex and interesting in its questioning of traditionally held beliefs about social and gender hierarchies."[23] Such processes can be seen in other films too, although in a less marked way. In *La vita ricomincia* (*Life Starts Over*, 1946), one of the younger stars of the late Fascist years, Alida Valli plays a wife forced to prostitute herself during her husband's wartime absence in order to secure medicine for her sick son. In true noir fashion, following the return of her husband and his discovery of her actions, she kills the man who bought her favors. But in a contemporary twist, the husband, who had initially disowned her, changes his mind, forgives her, and steps forward to take the blame for the murder.

Giuseppe De Santis's drama *Riso amaro* (*Bitter Rice*, 1949) was unusual in offering a double take on the femme fatale. At the outset of the film it is the gangster's moll Francesca, played by Doris Dowling, who is the femme fatale. An experienced Hollywood actress, she brought a knowing noir feel to playing a woman with a checkered past who has been involved in a hotel robbery. By contrast, the magnetic young rice worker Silvana, who initially befriends her, is a fundamentally good young woman whose only fault is her naïve weakness for American popular culture. These positions are not fixed, however, and, by the end of the film, Francesca has been redeemed while Silvana has rejected the overtures of a solid army sergeant for those of Francesca's gangster former boyfriend, a fateful choice that leads her to betray her fellow workers by flooding the rice fields. Only when Silvana realizes the enormity of her actions does she repent, but by this point she cannot be redeemed and, in a narrative trajectory compatible with noir conventions, she dies, taking her own life. Only after her death is she accepted back into the community by her fellow women workers, who file past her body, each casting a fistful of rice over it in a collective gesture of pity. Silvana was not truly bad; she was merely rendered defenseless before the material blandishments of a corrupting influence of American culture. As a member of the Italian Communist Party, De Santis employed an eminently political narrative, but the plot and much of the characterization were conventional. However, his reworking of the femme fatale motif to blend it with the more marked physical emphasis of some American female stars (notably Rita Hayworth) left a lasting legacy that was taken up in other films featuring other new female faces of the postwar years. By taking Silvana's youthful and curvaceous body rather than any complex apparatus of accessories as the basis of her seductive appeal, he renewed the connection between "woman and land" that was an established trope of national identity.[24] As several scholars have argued, Silvana was configured as a "body-landscape" of unusual representative power.[25] This representation was a significant development that was of a different order to the wartime bodily exposures of Calamai and Duranti.

4 The Hollywood Template

The conventional view of Italy as a net importer of modern culture has led some to stress the influence of foreign input on the Italian femme fatale.[26] Characterization and at times physical appearance in popular cinema owed something to the impact of Hollywood and French films. What also needs to be studied, however, is the way Hollywood recruited mainstream Italian actresses and turned them, without regard to their original personalities, into exotic femme fatales in accordance with a practice developed in the 1920s. As Alastair Phillips and Ginette Vincendeau explain in *Journeys of Desire* (2006), there was a significant typecasting of nearly all European actresses that was consolidated in the sound era and survived the Second World War. Europeans could not generally be fresh, vibrant, and vigorous; they had to be decadent, complex, and ambiguous in the manner of Garbo and Dietrich. This practice fitted with the American-centric outlook of Hollywood. In the postwar era, this perception was consolidated by the experiences in Italy and Europe of American soldiers who had seen widespread prostitution and social and moral collapse. It would condition the way several Italians, including Gina Lollobrigida and Sophia Loren, would be deployed in some of their American films.

Alida Valli was the first significant Italian screen actress to be recruited by Hollywood after the war. Between the late 1930s and the fall of Fascism, she was one of the most popular actresses in Italy. In the early 1940s, she broadened her repertoire and established herself as a talent of great promise. However, neorealism largely passed her by (in her view, she was too northern and too bourgeois to be of interest to directors associated with the movement).[27] Albeit reluctantly, she accepted the offer of a contract from the prominent Hollywood producer David O. Selznick, who subjected her to an extensive process of remolding and glamorization before launching her in the United States in a manner that recalled the treatment of European actresses in the past.[28] She was first cast in Hitchcock's *The Paradine Case*, a 1947 film that, for legal reasons, would not be released in Italy until 1952. The story concerns the trial of the widow of a wealthy blind man for her husband's murder. The widow is a much younger woman of foreign origin (Danish in the original novel) who is suspected of having killed out of love for her husband's manservant. A mysterious beauty, she exercises a magnetic attraction over her lawyer, who mistakenly trusts her and nearly destroys his marriage in the process.

Initially, Selznick had seen the project as ideal for Garbo and had bought the rights with her in mind. He then moved on to his one-time protégée Ingrid Bergman, before trying to get Vivien Leigh to take the part while her husband Laurence Olivier would be cast as the lawyer. Valli was in a way a last resort, but also a feasible option.[29] There was not a lot for Mrs. Paradine to do, a reality that made the film less than suitable for established stars but ideal for the launch of a new foreign import.[30]

Valli's Mrs. Paradine is of unspecified nationality, although her first name of Maddalena gives a hint of Italy. The construction of a compelling aura around her was crucial to the audience's acceptance of the basic premises of the plot. Valli's beauty was a factor here, but costuming, camerawork, and publicity all played key parts, the latter beginning even before the actress arrived in California. Within twenty-four hours of her arrival, she was being trumpeted as "Europe's most beautiful woman" and her signing as "one of the greatest production coups in American film history."[31] Valli was never seen as marketable to a young audience. Her image was to be sophisticated and adult, in keeping with the questionable history of Maddalena Paradine who, it is suggested, has been rescued from a degrading past of prostitution. As such, a full program of glamorization was ordered with the aim of having her emerge as "a slinky siren in the grand tradition, a tawny female with danger in her eyes."[32] The key person in this process was Anita Colby, a former model who had advised on (and appeared in) the Rita Hayworth vehicle *Cover Girl*, and whose task was to ensure that actresses under contract to Selznick looked sophisticated and behaved accordingly. She produced a list of items from designers and major stores that she suggested should be bought for Valli. These included two fur pieces and several cocktail and evening dresses. In addition, she advised that "Jean Louis of Columbia design some special clothes that have glamour and a foreign look as she lends herself to advanced design."[33] The publicity campaign was subtle and effective, interweaving aspects of the actress's biography and personality with doses of fantasy and artifice.

Despite the successful construction of an intriguing dark aura around Valli, who in the narrative is separately introduced with compelling close-ups by cinematographer Lee Garmes to three male characters, the film did not do well. As a femme fatale, she was utterly conventional; no account was taken either of the intriguing twist on this type that was associated with Hayworth or of the reworkings that were taking place in Italian cinema. Consequently, the film did not lead to further prestigious roles but rather to a series of loan-outs, one of which, however—Carol Reed's Cold War thriller *The Third Man*—would become a classic and establish Valli's name and face with international audiences. In the course of her short-lived Hollywood career, Valli was cast consistently neither as the exotic temptress that was the conventional stereotype for European women nor as a bearer of the type of sexualized candor that Ingrid Bergman had made her trademark. But her characters mostly carried within them the suggestion of a shameful sexual history like that which was bestowed on her character in *The Paradine Case*.

The Italian actresses who would follow Valli to Hollywood found themselves subjected to similar pressures and constrictions. But they would also find themselves working in a new context in which the Italian film industry was able to offer them roles that were more attractive. Indeed, while they might have been inflected with destructive aspects in some contexts, mostly their more "fatale" roles were simply as prostitutes,[34] and their personas reflected the variety of roles they were offered by Hollywood, Italian cinema, and European cinemas. Despite attempts by Hollywood to remold them, they maintained a distinctive identity. This was assisted by the development of an original Italian take on glamour that was related to the emergence of a national fashion industry, changes in the social and economic order, and the rise of a new postwar star system.[35]

5 Dark Ladies

With the internationalization of film production, national distinctions of genre and characterization in popular cinema declined over time. Thanks in part to the injection of foreign capital and coproductions, the Italian industry developed a system of low-cost genres including sword and sandal epics, horror films, and police procedurals. In these films, the femme fatale continued to reverberate. Wood observes, "in contrast to the blonde and wholesome heroines of the aspirational comedies of that time, films of the sword and sandal genre usually included an evil priestess, the antagonist of the passive, blonde heroine whose function was to scream and look decorative. Priestesses were usually played by actors of southern physical type, darkly sensual, active and in authority" (*Chiaroscuro*, 162). Wood is wrong to identify the heroines of popular comedies as "blonde" except sometimes in the Italian use of this term to indicate "light brown." Generally speaking, the actresses of the postwar period, in contrast to their predecessors of the interwar years, were darker haired, in keeping with the popular vocation of cinema and the rapid expansion of audiences among the lower classes and in the South.[36] But it is true that in the sword and sandal films, most of which were international coproductions, conventional typing and casting were required. Blondes, whether foreign, like British actress Belinda Lee, or of the homegrown bottle variety, like Dorian Gray, could never be evil, but it was not unusual to find them endowed with a sophisticated seductive suggestiveness.

The persistence of the femme fatale in popular genres through the 1960s and 1970s testifies, on one level, to the continuing influence of the Catholic Church at a time of rapid secularization. Although the church's censorial influence over the portrayal of the family had diminished sharply by the late 1960s, its general cultural role ensured that suffering remained intrinsic to the idea of Italian womanhood.[37] Catholic culture also explains why, despite the march to prosperity that became especially marked in the 1960s, materialism remained endowed with many negative cultural connotations. In addition, the political ruptures and conflicts of the period created dislocations, interruptions, needs for blame and guilt that could be conferred on femmes fatales who, from the time of the diva, had suffered for the community. Such women were not, however, strongly present in the political thrillers which prospered in the 1970s and afterward.[38] For Francesco Rosi, the absence of women in positions of power meant that they had little place in his screen explorations of the dynamics of power and illegality.[39] "Female bodies do not seem to be able to represent political or social power," Wood writes ("Italian Film Noir," 263–64). "Female power therefore becomes a sign that something is amiss, resulting in characters which constitute the disruption which starts an investigation, or transgressive models of femininity (the prostitute or hypersexual woman) which bear the blame for social malaise. In effect Italian film noirs are male melodramas rehearsing shifting power relationships in Italian society."

An exception of note was the films of Elio Petri, a political director whose explorations of crime, police corruption, and other social themes often involved the use of a femme fatale to hint at darker forces, be they the Fascist past, official collusion with the Mafia, or irrational violence. Nevertheless, these figures lack the embedded quality of the complex and socialized femme fatales of neorealism. They are suggestive on account of the way they mobilize established cinematic conventions to bring forward certain narrative possibilities and crystalize them in visual tropes. The actresses are invariably foreign: Ursula Andress as a homicidal huntress in the sci-fi thriller *La decima vittima* (*The Tenth Victim*, 1965), Irene Papas as the darkly intriguing Luisa in *A ciascuno il suo* (*We Still Kill the Old Way*, 1967), Florina Bolkan as the murdered mistress in *Indagine su un cittadino al di sopra di ogni sospetto* (*Investigation of a Citizen Above Suspicion*, 1970). The location of these women in specific contexts follows different paths in each film, with sexuality and eroticism always playing a part in the determining not only the fatale nature of their contributions to the narrative but also their visual construction. An excess of color, emotion, or—a trademark of Petri's—violence signals their presence and whatever uses they perform in expressing anxieties about unseen threats, female autonomy, or the mystifications of power.

The use by male directors of femme fatales may not be expressly misogynistic, but it bears witness to a willingness to use an established trope to explore contemporary issues. A disjunction can be noted between the very real shifts in the position of women in Italian society over the twentieth century and occasional revivals of the cinematic femme fatale. The femme fatales of films like *Romanzo criminale* (Michele Placido, 2005) and *Notturno bus* (*Night Bus*, Davide Marengo, 2007), both cited by Wood, show a certain lack of imagination on the part of filmmakers as well as the enduring visual fascination of the artificial and unpredictable woman. Of course, the status of women remains problematic in some spheres of Italian society, but the persistence of this trope also testifies to the powerful way in which realist questions and intentions inflected the femme fatale in the 1940s in such a way that she still retains a certain analytical power. Explicit referencing of past fatale figures is rare, although Dario Argento's modern horror classic *Profondo rosso* (*Deep Red*, 1975) features Clara Calamai as a mad murderess, the former actress Marta. Photographs of Calamai's youthful films roles as a femme fatale are deployed to create the now elderly Marta's backstory.[40]

It has been shown how actresses can absorb aspects of their fatale screen roles to different degrees into their personas. Of contemporary actresses, only Monica Bellucci can be said to reference the entire repertoire of the Italian femme fatale.[41] A former model, who featured mostly in advertisements for luxury goods including fur coats, she graced many early films with her beautiful physical presence more than her skills as a performer; she spoke little and appeared self-absorbed. She was said to incarnate "a more complex, allusive and intimate type of beauty, closer to transgression and sin" than her colleagues.[42] Her body was repeatedly made overtly the object of the male gaze, with voyeurism being a key theme of the Sicilian-set *Malèna* (Giuseppe Tornatore, 2000). Regularly cast in French films as a retro femme fatale, she also appeared in a variety of Hollywood productions exploiting her dark good looks, including *The Matrix 2* and *The Matrix Reloaded*, as well as Mel Gibson's *The Passion of Christ* (as Mary Magdalene). In *Sanguepazzo* (Marco Tullio Giordana, 2008), she took the part of Luisa Ferida, a Fascist-period actress who did not escape like Duranti but was executed by partisans. Her embodiment of the disjointed parts of the tradition of Italian cinema testifies to the interconnectedness of the five faces of the femme fatale and to the continuing influence it exercises in Italian culture.

Notes

1 See Hanson and O'Rawe, *The Femme Fatale*.

2 Gundle *Bellissima*, 82–83.

3 Paciscopi, *Cinefollie*, 44.

4 See Caranti, "La diva e le donne"; see also Welle, "The Beginnings of Film Stardom and the Print Media of Divismo."

5 See Caranti, "La diva e le donne."

6 Brunetta, *Cent'anni di cinema italiano*, 99.

7 Gundle, *Glamour*, 159–60, 181–87.

8 Dalle Vacche, *Diva*, 52–55.

9 Magli, "La maschera dell'odio," 58–59.

10 Landy, *Stardom Italian Style*, 45.

11 See Gundle, *Mussolini's Dream Factory*, 123–43.

12 See Gundle, *Mussolini's Dream Factory*, 132–35.

13 See Gundle, *Mussolini's Dream Factory*, 57, 87.

14 See Forgacs, "Sex in the Cinema," 159–61.

15 See Duranti, *Il romanzo della mia vita*.

16 On bodily exposure and the traditional femme fatale, see Scaraffia, *La donna fatale*, 65–66.

17 See Wood "Italian Film Noir," 243–47.

18 See Duncan, "*Ossessione*," 101.

19 Cited in Minghelli, *Landscape and Memory in Post-Fascist Italian Film*, 28.

20 See O'Rawe, "Gender, Genre and Stardom," 130–31.

21 See Germani, "Entretien avec Mario Camerini," 135.

22 See Schoonover *Brutal Vision*, xvii, 142.

23 Wood, *Chiaroscuro*, 159.

24 Gundle, *Bellissima*, 1–27.

25 See Grignaffini, "Il femminile nel cinema italiano," 358; Marcus, "The Italian Body Politic Is a Woman," 338; Buckley, "The Female Film Star in Postwar Italy," 78–102; Gundle, *Bellissima*, 143–47; and Carman, "Mapping the Body," 331–32.

26 See O'Rawe, "Gender, Genre and Stardom," 127–29.

27 See Cova, Un convento aspetta la nomade del cinema, 14.

28 See Gundle, "Alida Valli in Hollywood."

29 See Leff, *Hitchcock and Selznick*, 232.

30 See Gundle, "Alida Valli in Hollywood," 570.

31 Gundle, "Alida Valli in Hollywood," 568.

32 Gundle, "Alida Valli in Hollywood," 569.

33 Cited in Gundle, "Alida Valli in Hollywood," 569–70.

34 See Calabrese, "La donna fatale nel cinema," 71–72.

35 See Gundle, "Hollywood Glamour and Mass Consumption in Postwar Italy"; and Buckley, "Glamour and the Female Film Stars of the 1950s" and "Material Dreams."

36 See Gundle, *Bellissima*, 107–24, 142–63.

37 See Wood, *Chiaroscuro*, 167.

38 See Wood, "Italian Film Noir," 263.

39 See Wood, *Chiaroscuro*, 162–63.

40 See Wood, "Italian Film Noir," 251–52; and Moscati, *Clara Calamai*, 146–47.

41 See Gundle, *Bellissima*, 246–52.

42 Augias, "Vorrei opporre la Bellucci alla Ferilli," 18.

Bibliography

Augias, Corrado. "Vorrei opporre la Bellucci alla Ferilli." *La Repubblica* (February 11, 2002).

Bazin, André. *What Is Cinema?* 2 vols. Trans. Hugh Gray. Berkeley: University of California Press, 2014.

Brunetta, Gian Piero. *Storia del cinema italiano, 1895-1945*. Rome: Editori Riuniti, 1979.

Brunetta, Gian Piero. *Cent'anni di cinema italiano*. Bari: Laterza, 2001.

Buckley, Réka. "The Female Film Star in Postwar Italy." PhD diss. Royal Holloway—University of London, 2002.

Buckley, Réka. "Glamour and the Female Film Stars of the 1950s." *Historical Journal of Film, Radio and Television* 28.3 (2006): 267–89.

Buckley, Réka. "Material Dreams: Costume and Couture Italian Style: From Hollywood on the Tiber to the Italian Screen." In *The Italian Cinema Book*. Ed. Peter Bondanella. London: BFI, 2013. 133–41.

Calabrese, Omar. "La donna fatale nel cinema." In *La donna fatale*. Ed. Grazietta Butazzi and Alessandra Mottola Molfino. Novara: De Agostini, 1991. 63–73.

Caranti, Chiara. "La diva e le donne: Francesca Bertini nella stampa popolare femminile." In *Francesca Bertini*. Ed. Gianfranco Mingozzi. Genoa: Le Mani, 2003. 111–26.

Carman, Emily S. "Mapping the Body: Female Film Stars and the Reconstruction of Postwar Italian National Identity." *Quarterly Review of Film and Video* 31.4 (2014): 322–35.

Cova, Sandro. "Un convento aspetta la nomade del cinema." *Il Giorno*. December 18, 1954. 14.

Dalle Vacche, Angela. *Diva: Defiance and Passion in Early Italian Cinema*. Austin: University of Texas Press, 2008.

Dalle Vacche, Angela. "The Diva Film: Context, Actresses, Issues." In *The Italian Cinema Book*. Ed. Peter Bondanella. London: BFI. 2013. 24–30.

Doane, Mary Ann. "The Abstraction of a Lady: *La Signora di tutti*." *Cinema Journal* 18:1 (1988): 65–84.

Doletti, Mino. "*Passaporto rosso*." *Il Resto del Carlino* (August 23, 1935).

Duncan, Derek. "*Ossessione.*" In *European Cinema: An Introduction*. Ed. Jill Forbes and Sarah Street. Basingstoke: Palgrave, 2000. 95–105.

Duranti, Doris. *Il romanzo della mia vita*. Milan: Mondadori, 2007.

Forgacs, David. "Sex in the Cinema: Regulation and Transgression in Italian Cinema, 1930–1943." In *Re-viewing Fascism: Italian Cinema, 1922–1943*. Ed. Jacqueline Reich and Piero Garofalo. Bloomington: Indiana University Press, 2002. 141–71.

Germani, Sergio Grmek. "Entretien avec Mario Camerini." In *Mario Camerini*. Ed. Alberto Farassino. Locarno: Yellow Now, 1992. 87–146.

Grignaffini, Giovanna. "Il femminile nel cinema italiano: Racconti di rinascita." In *Identità italiana e identità europea nel cinema italiano dal 1945 al miracolo economico*. Ed. Gian Piero Brunetta. Turin: Edizioni della Fondazione Agnelli, 1996.

Gundle, Stephen. "Hollywood Glamour and Mass Consumption in Postwar Italy." *Journal of Cold War Studies* 4.3 (2002): 95–118.

Gundle, Stephen. *Bellissima: Feminine Beauty and the Idea of Italy*. New Haven: Yale University Press, 2007.

Gundle, Stephen. *Glamour: A History*. Oxford: Oxford University Press, 2008.

Gundle, Stephen. *Mussolini's Dream Factory: Film Stardom in Fascist Italy*. Oxford: Berghahn Books, 2013.

Gundle, Stephen. "Alida Valli in Hollywood: From Star of Fascist Cinema to 'Selznick Siren.'" *Historical Journal of Film, Radio and Television* 32.4 (2013): 559–87.

Landy, Marcia. *Stardom Italian Style: Personality and Performance in Italian Cinema*. Bloomington: Indiana University Press, 2008.

Leff, Leonard J. *Hitchcock and Selznick*. Berkeley: University of California Press, 1999.

Magli, Patrizia. "La maschera dell'odio." In *La donna fatale*. Ed. Grazietta Butazzi and Alessandra Mottola Molfino. Novara: De Agostini, 1991.

Marcus, Millicent. "The Italian Body Politic Is a Woman: Feminized National Identity in Postwar Italian Film." In *Sparks and Seeds: Medieval Literature and Its Afterlife*. Ed. Dana E. Stewart and Alison Cornish. Turnhout: Brepols, 2000. 329–47.

Martinelli, Vittorio. "La Borelli." In *Lyda Borelli*. Ed. José Pantieri. Rome: MICS, 1993. 27–28.

Minghelli, Giuliana. *Landscape and Memory in Post-Fascist Italian Film*. London: Routledge. 2013.

Moscati, Italo, ed. *Clara Calamai: L'ossessione di essere diva*. Venice: Marsilio, 1996.

O'Rawe, Catherine. "Gender, Genre and Stardom: Fatality in Italian Neorealist Cinema." In *The Femme Fatale: Images, Histories, Contexts*. Ed. Helen Hanson and Catherine O'Rawe. Basingstoke: Palgrave Macmillan, 2010. 127–41.

Paciscopi, Leopoldo. *Cinefollie: Miti e sregolatezze del "muto."* Milan: Lucini, 1986.

Scaraffia, Giuseppe. *La donna fatale*. Palermo: Sellerio, 1987.

Schoonover, Karl. *Brutal Vision: The Neorealist Body in Postwar Italian Cinema*. Minneapolis: University of Minnesota Press, 2012.

Welle, John. "The Beginnings of Film Stardom and the Print Media of *Divismo*." In *The Italian Cinema Book*. Ed. Peter Bondanella. London: BFI, 2013. 17–23.

White, Susan M. *The Cinema of Max Ophuls*. New York: Columbia University Press, 1995.

Wood, Mary. "Italian Film Noir." In *European Film Noir*. Ed. Andrew Spicer. Manchester: Manchester University Press, 2007. 236–72.

Wood, Mary. "*Chiaroscuro*: The Half-Glimpsed *Femme Fatale* of Italian *Film Noi*." In *The Femme Fatale: Images, Histories, Contexts*. Ed. Helen Hanson and Catherine O'Rawe. Basingstoke: Palgrave Macmillan, 2010. 127–41.

Vincendeau, Ginette and Alastair Phillips, eds. *Journeys of Desire: European Actors in Hollywood—A Critical Companion*. London: BFI, 2006.

Zocaro, Ettore. "'Prima donna' del teatro italiano." In *Lyda Borelli*. Ed. José Pantieri. Rome: MICS, 1993. 12–23.

8

Italian Women's Cinema and the Wounded Filmic Body

Dana Renga

Women's cinema may well be characterized, not necessarily by an outright rejection of voyeuristic and fetishistic desires but by the recasting of those desires so as to open up other possible pleasures for film viewing.

—JUDITH MAYNE

As a body, the vulnerable one remains vulnerable as long as she lives, exposed at any instant to vulnus. Yet, the same potential also delivers her to healing and the relational ontology that decides its meaning.

—ADRIANA CAVARERO[1]

Scholarly work on women's cinema in Italy, that is, films made by women, has been increasing in step with a number of female directors working in the country. Since 2000, Italian women directors have made 316 feature films, documentaries, and shorts compared to 247 features, documentaries, shorts, and animations prior to the new millennium.[2] As a whole, women constitute between 20 and 30 percent of the directors working in the country.[3] Bernadette Luciano and Susanna Scarparo's chapter on "Contemporary Italian Women Filmmakers" from 2012 discusses a "quiet revolution" in the production of films made by women in Italy over the past ten years,[4] and *Studies in European Cinema* from 2011 reevaluates the "agency" and "growing visibility" of Italian women filmmakers in a study that includes essays on Letizia Battaglia, Antonietta De Lillo, Sabina Guzzanti, Alina Marazzi, and Manuela Pellarin.[5] These contributions complement important studies of the last twenty years on the female directors Francesca Archibugi, Katia Bernardi, Francesca Bertini, Liliana Cavani, Cristina Comencini, Emma Rossi Landi and Flavia Pasquini, Alina Marazzi, Susanna Nicchiarelli, Elvira Notari, Costanza Quatriglio, Fabiana Sargentini, Monica Stambrini, Roberta Torre, and Lina Wertmüller.[6] Recent work on these filmmakers speaks to Mary Ann Doane's call to move beyond simply writing women filmmakers into the past and thus filling out a chronology of film history in order to save these women from oblivion. Instead, Doane cites the work of Claire Johnston regarding the need to situate Dorothy Arzner's filmic production within a theoretical discourse: "Women and film can only become meaningful in terms of a theory, in the attempt to create a structure in which films [by women directors] can be examined."[7] For example, simply asserting that Francesca Bertini "really did co-direct" *Assunta Spina* (1915)—until quite recently the director credit went solely to Gustavo Serena, despite Bertini's outspoken assertions regarding the extent of her own involvement in the film— without critically contextualizing the film could risk being reductive and potentially regressive.[8]

"Writing the woman into [Italian] cinema," to cite the subtitle of Janet McCabe's book *Feminist Film Studies*,[9] entails approaching films made by women through the lens of feminist film theory and gender studies so as to "interrogate the power structures at play in the gendered construction of the gaze" and to examine the many contradictions, inconsistencies, and challenges that the films under consideration present to the dominant ideology.[10] To that end, the trope of the wound in selected directors suggests that Italian women's cinema itself can be read as a kind of "wounded body." *Sfregi*, lacerations, lesions, and decapitations, both literal and metaphoric, are rife in these films and emphasize the precarious position of women who threaten the status quo. Although many wounds remain unhealed and bring about the death, incarceration, exile, or abjection of the transgressive female protagonist, in more recent feature films injuries are sutured and the marked body recovers. Indeed, although Bertini as *actress* in *Assunta Spina* is physically disfigured early in the film and then imprisoned for taking blame for a murder committed by her attacker, Bertini as *director* is now, albeit gradually, recognized for her efforts behind the camera.[11]

1 Francesca Bertini, Elvira Notari, and the Disfigured Body

About thirty minutes into *Assunta Spina*, the title character is assaulted in public by her lover Michele who slashes her face so as to produce a "sfregio," a "marker of love and hate." He means to avenge his honor as Assunta was earlier dancing with rival Raffaele at a party and thus publicly humiliated him. Despite the physical and emotional abuse of the attack, Assunta stays by his side, lies under oath in a failed attempt to save him, takes up with Federigo, a vice-chancellor who arranges for Michele to spend his time in prison closer to home, and then ultimately takes the fall for Michele's murderous outburst.

In *'A santanotte* (*The Holy Night*, 1922) and *'E piccerella* (*The Outspoken Girl*, 1922), two of three extant films of Elvira Notari, the plot resolves when main female protagonists Nanninella and Margaretella are murdered by scorned suitors who stab them in the chest. Nanninella, described as a saint, was abused by her drunkard father who falls to his death during an argument with her true love, Tore. She only agrees to marry Carluccio in the attempt to help Tore, whom Carluccio had framed for the crime. In the end, Carluccio murders Nanninella when he discovers that she was manipulating him to save Tore. Contrary to the chaste Nanninella, Margaretella is unruly and sexually active: her mother complains that she cannot sit still and men are drawn to her. Her rejection of Tore earlier in the film enrages him, and one year later he surprises Margaretella, who is enjoying the afternoon riding across town in a carriage, before later stabbing her.

The violent, sudden, and very public attacks on Assunta, Nanninella, and Margaretella underline these women's vulnerability and lack of agency, and much of the behavior of Assunta and Nanninella can be read as an apt

FIGURE 8.1 *Assunta Spina's wound.*

metaphor for the masochism of the female spectator theorized by Laura Mulvey in her foundational essay treating spectatorship, voyeurism, and identification in the cinema.[12] However, as Tania Modleski and Judith Mayne remind us, identification is much more complicated. The female spectator might be "caught up in a double desire," identifying both with the "passive (female) object" and the "active (usually male) subject" (Modleski). Mayne cautions against conceptualizations of "the cinematic spectator" in favor of readings that engage "multiple desires, contradictory effect and multiple stagings."[13]

All three films are clearly melodramatic and conspicuously punish female characters that desire excessively (or in the case Nanninella, desire at all), thus threatening the male subject position. In this way, they are in line with Mulvey's thesis regarding the fetishizing or punishment of the wayward female so as to fend off castration anxiety.[14] In the end, Nanninella and Margaretella are dead and Assunta is imprisoned, a plotline in keeping with that of the melodramatic woman's film going back to the tradition of the cinematic femme fatale. Indeed, Mulvey argues that women protagonists accept masculinization (usurping the gaze, inhabiting center stage, occupying an active rather than passive position) at a very high price (e.g., punishment or death). In the final tally, "masculine identification" is unworkable and ultimately fails.[15]

But what about the men who loved these women? Are these films complicit with the dominant ideology of the male subject? Or, in presenting weak men who are unable to control their emotions, do they undermine the notion of the melodramatic "happy ending," which, as Mulvey argues, affirms "the ideology of the family . . . and reaffirmation of the Oedipus complex"?[16] In all three films, children have no place in the narrative, several male characters have overly close and anguished relationships with aged mothers whom at times they wrong (as does Tore when he steals from his mother to please Margaretella), and fathers are either conspicuously absent or, in the case of Assunta, worthless and brutish. What's more, although it is implied in *Assunta Spina* that Michele will go free after murdering Federigo, his narrative receives no traditional sense of closure (other than vendetta). In the case of *'A santanotte*, Tore is portrayed as ineffective: he is unable to save Nanninella as he arrives on the scene too late, and she dies in his arms while the film ends on a medium shot of Carluccio looking insane as a result of Nanninella's deception and his act of vengeance. Finally, in *'E piccerella*, Tore will spend the rest of his days in prison, haunted by the woman he killed. All of these films, to different degrees, conform to the "fallen man formula" in which men are lured "into wayward paths because of their lack of control."[17] In the films in this cycle, men make bad choices, are unredeemable, and the conclusion is somber.[18] Masochism is certainly at play, but it is not reserved solely for women.

Ultimately, these men are emasculated, brought down by women whom they fail to control.

In the conclusion of *'E piccerella*, Tore is tormented by the apparition of Margaretella as he sits in his cell. She first appears as beautiful and strong. Her back is to him, and she gazes out toward the viewer defiantly. As Tore approaches her, entranced by her allure, a cut reveals a different Margaretella, with unkempt hair and clothing, a despondent gaze, and most poignantly a large gash across her breast. Tore's desire turns to terror and he backs away. Then the specter disappears, and he falls to the ground as the film abruptly concludes.

Giuliana Bruno reads this scene as writing on the body, what she dubs "*corpo*reality": the disfigured breast of Margaretella "bears the mark of lack" and signifies castration and thus "provokes fear and anxiety."[19] Unlike many melodramas in which the threat of castration must be contained so as to leave viewing pleasure intact, here the open wound, and all that it signifies from a psychoanalytic perspective, is emphasized. This abrupt transformation of Margaretella from seductress to bearer of a bleeding wound brings about both the final collapse of the fallen man and the sudden conclusion of the film, recalling Mulvey's claim: "It is as though the fact of having a female point of view dominating the narrative produces an excess which precludes satisfaction."[20] Hence, the viewer is left at an impasse, as identification, at least as it is theorized in the classical cinema, is troubled here, as it is in the other two films under consideration. Indeed, the final images of these films—Federigo's lifeless and bloody body illuminated by a shaft of sunlight (*Assunta Spina*), Carluccio's deranged and joker-like face (*'A santanotte*), Tore's collapsed figure, his head out of frame (*'E piccerella*)—suggest that Bertini and Notari are interested in staging male subjectivities in crisis.

These films, like many melodramas, can be "read against the grain" so as to subvert "the very attitudes that they seem superficially to be endorsing."[21]

2 Gendering the Holocaust

Until fairly recently, Liliana Cavani and Lina Wertmüller were Italy's most renowned and anthologized women filmmakers. They (and to a lesser extent Notari) were frequently the only women filmmakers to appear in histories or studies of Italian film. Within the span of one year, each released what would become a controversial, influential, and seminal film on the Holocaust. Cavani's *Il portiere di notte* (*The Night Porter*, 1974) and Wertmüller's *Pasqualino Settebellezze* (*Seven Beauties*, 1975) are different in genre, tone, and style. Yet they both answer Doane's essential question: "How is it possible for feminist filmmaking practice to represent a female body which has been overcoded, overwritten, overconstructed within mainstream culture and, in particular, mainstream cinema?"[22]

The answer lies in how they represent the female body, which could not be more dissimilar in the two films. Roughly two-thirds into Cavani's film, Lucia plays a game with Max, a former SS officer with whom she was involved in a complicated sexual relationship while she was interned in the camp. Several years later, in 1957 in Vienna, the two meet by chance and are irresistibly drawn to each other. They feel compelled to relive episodes from the past. While in his apartment, after Max forces a child's shoe onto Lucia's foot, she runs from him, locks herself in the bathroom, and shatters a perfume bottle on the floor before letting him in. Upon entering, his foot is pierced by the glass, yet he does not cry out. As Lucia approaches him, she places her hand under his foot, and he immediately steps down upon it, thus propelling her hand against the shards. The non-diegetic theme music begins, and the camera moves upward to capture them staring wordlessly at each other, rapt and content. We then move to the past to see Lucia kissing Max's chest before returning to the present where the pair tend to each other's injuries.

This sequence lays bare one of the film's key concerns: unlike the ex-Nazis who haunt Vienna and put on fake trials so as to purge their guilt while defending their actions during the Final Solution, Lucia and Max represent wounds that are still hemorrhaging. While the ex-Nazis deny the trauma of the Holocaust, and attempt, citing Erik Santner, "to reinvoke prematurely a condition of normalcy," Lucia and Max are fettered by the past.[23] Their inability to move beyond it speaks to the Holocaust as an event that is not over and still must be worked through. Lucia's body frequently is the site of unresolved trauma. Her cabaret dance in the camp troubles notions of

FIGURE 8.2 *Max's and Lucia's mutual wounding.*

complicity and confuses gender paradigms: cross-dressing in a Nazi uniform while bare-chested and emaciated, she connotes both victim and perpetrator, man and woman. Teresa de Lauretis argues that *The Night Porter* is a woman's film because it "deals with female experience from within . . . to investigate the dialectics of the male-female relationship in . . . society."[24] The murder of Lucia and Max at the end of the film while he wears an SS uniform and she a replica of her "little girl dress" from the past, may speak to the audience's unease over ambiguous relationships that scrutinize the status quo.

Like Cavani's film, *Seven Beauties*, which earned Wertmüller an Oscar nomination for Best Director (one of only five women to be so honored), is reluctant to incorporate the viewer into the narrative. The film's protagonist is Pasqualino, a low-ranking mafioso from Naples who, due to his incredible will to survive, ironically ends up in a concentration camp where he seduces the female camp commandant to save his own skin. When the tables are turned, he is ordered to perform sexually or face death at her hands, and is then promoted to Kapo, where his first task is to select six inmates for elimination. *Seven Beauties* foregrounds the politics of survival; closer to our purposes, it genders such politics by exposing Pasqualino, who imagines himself a dandy and ladies' man, as a rapist.

As Kriss Ravetto argues, Wertmüller is interested in debunking essentialist relationships as they relate to "the gendering of power."[25] Throughout his life, Pasqualino objectifies and sexually abuses women. When he is in the mental hospital, he rapes a mentally ill woman who is tied to a bed. Although he is punished for this deviance with electroshock therapy, the female doctor declares him "normal" and sends him off to war. When caught for desertion and sent to the camp, Pasqualino turns from victimizer to victim when he is handed the death threat from the Nazi woman who is physically the antithesis of his traditional conquests.[26] Literally under the gun, Pasqualino envisions a series of women from his past so as to complete the sexual act: Fifi, a cabaret dancer after whom he lusted as a child, appears throughout the fantasy which also includes what come across as two acts of sexual violence committed by Pasqualino as an adult. In the first, a woman is below him with her arms flailing about and she seems to push him away. The second is much less ambiguous: Pasqualino pursues a woman up the stairs, pushes her against a wall and rapes her.

Seven Beauties differs from other films featuring rape narratives in which, according to Sarah Projansky, "rape justifie[s] violent masculine sexual . . . spectatorial pleasure,"[27] by turning the gaze away from these women and back on Pasqualino at the film's conclusion. Reflected in the mirror, his eyes are vacant as he impassively relates that he "is alive." This composition underlines the high price of survival, while suggesting that, like *The Night Porter*, this film too signifies the Holocaust not as "unthinkable Other, but as one distinctly possible effect of" misogynistic culture that Wertmüller and Cavani are so interested in exploring.[28]

3 Mafia Women in the Honored Society

In Wertmüller's *Mimì metallurgico, ferito nell'onore* (*The Seduction of Mimi*, 1972), the title character concocts an elaborate plot to vindicate his wounded honor to face only imprisonment and then be forever in the mafia's debt. As in *Seven Beauties*, here the female body is configured as the ultimate site of castration, and the director is interesting in undermining the traditional process in the mainstream cinema whereby the female character connotes "to-be-looked-at-ness."[29] Mimì, like Pasqualino before him, is punished for his previous objectification of women throughout the film, and both films overturn Mulvey's claim that the cinema is a signifying system predicated on sexual difference where "pleasure in looking has been split between active/male and passive/female."[30]

Roberta Torre's *Angela* (2002), the first Italian mafia movie told through the eyes of a female protagonist, recalls Doane's claim regarding the "violence which is coincident with the attribution of the gaze to the female."[31] Angela Spina is not the typical mafia wife: she is quite involved in her husband's business dealings and active in Cosa Nostra as a drug runner. Yet her autonomy is quite limited as she is surveilled by the police and by her family and is essentially a prisoner, bound to the code of omertà.

Her world falls apart, however, when her affair with Masino, a younger man who works for her husband, is discovered, and her husband orders her to disappear from his life.

Before the arrest that led to her affair being made public, the camera accentuates Angela's sexuality, and the film attempts to represent her subjectivity. Red hues, roving camera, shallow focus, alluring costuming, elaborate mise-en-scène, and an emotive score suggest that Angela wants more than what her proscribed role as mafia wife and mother can give her.

FIGURE 8.3 *Angela's visibility.*

After her arrest, and especially after her transgression is made public, Angela's hair, nails, and makeup are unkempt, and she is frequently shown in a state of breakdown, as white replaces red as the main color with which she is associated. In keeping with melodramas that generate a "medical discourse," Angela's lawyer tells the court that her psychological condition has worsened and refers to her as "of unsound mind."[32] She slips into a depression, and at the film's close it is implied that she perpetually returns to the port to await Masino—where he had promised to meet her so the two could run off together.

The typical heroine of the woman's film is punished for excessive desire and either meets a bad end such as death, or is forgiven and then returned to the dominant patriarchal model. Catherine O'Rawe argues that *Angela* demonstrates "the impossibility of the 'woman's film' in a mafia context" because of the female protagonist's unknowability.[33] Indeed, Angela is doubly punished as she is exiled from both blood and mafia family. Angela connotes a problem: the trauma of the mafia that hangs over Italy, yet is unacknowledged. Indeed, neither killed off nor redeemed, and certainly unmourned, Angela is left ghostlike and clanless: she is an open wound, much like the community that shunned her.[34]

4 Matricide and the Lesbian Road Movie

Most reviews of Monica Stambrini's *Benzina* (*Gasoline*, 2001) compare it to *Thelma and Louise* (Ridley Scott, 1991) because it focuses on two women who, left without options, choose death rather than surrender to the authorities. In both films, an act of violence motivates the narrative, and the two female protagonists must flee from the law and take to the road. *Thelma and Louise* is a rape-revenge film in which rape, both the attempted rape of Thelma and the inferred rape of Louise earlier in her life in Texas, unleashes "desire in the text."[35] Stambrini's film begins with the accidental matricide of Lenni's mother when Lenni's girlfriend Stella strikes her mother during an argument over Lenni's sexual orientation, and the mother falls, gashing her head on the counter before dying.

The couple flees from the gas station owned by Stella with Stella's beloved dog, Clio, and with the cadaver of Lenni's mother in the trunk. During their journey to nowhere, Lenni and Stella attempt to dispose of the body at a dump and are pursued by a trio of sadistic bullies who threaten sexual violence and attempt to steal money that Lenni has inherited and that was brought by her mother. In the end, the couple return to the scene of the crime and set the gas station ablaze in a gesture of protest, igniting themselves along with the corpses of Lenni's mother and Clio, who had been murdered by their assailants.

Benzina thematizes the struggle of the child attempting to break free from the maternal bond and enter the symbolic order.[36] Excessive blood that Lenni cannot clean up, a wounded body that will not go away (and that will not remain quiet, even in death), and the film's circular narrative speak to the difficulties of fully renouncing the mother (read in the film as the Law) and all that she symbolizes in terms of normativity and conformity. In the film's final moments, after Lenni and Stella set the station aflame, a policeman and the three tormentors watch the apocalyptic scene. Rather than conclude on the perspective of those who see the couple as deviant, the film returns to Lenni and Stella, to an earlier unscreened moment when Stella asks Lenni's forgiveness for "everything, even for Clio" before Lenni passionately kisses her and the film ends.

Benzina is an example of the New Queer Cinema, which, as B. Ruby Rich explains, is not a unified genre in terms of aesthetic approach and thematic content. Instead, such films include "appropriation and pastiche, irony, as well as a reworking of history," and are "irreverent, energetic." "Above all," Rich argues, "they are full of pleasure."[37] Despite its somber content, *Benzina* is a different type of road movie that proposes a viewing pleasure well beyond that typically reserved for the heterosexual male viewer, for it creates a space for the development of friendship and the enactment of female desire.

Like other examples of the New Queer Cinema, Stambrini's film is interested in "defiance," in this case, of homophobia, harassment, and intolerance.[38] But at the same time the death of the two women at the film's end underlines "the extent of their vulnerability,"[39] evoking Giovanni Dall'Orto's claim that in Italy homosexuality was repressed for so long that until recently it simply did not exist on the national level.[40] Like many other Italian films released after World Pride 2000 in Rome that centered on the lives of gays and lesbians, Stambrini's *Benzina* actively engages in breaking through such repressions.[41]

5 The Atypical Teen Film

Italy has seen the release of several films over the last ten years or so that address a teenage female audience. Some of these films, such as those by Federico Moccia, can be read "as typically postfeminist products . . . in which feminism is repackaged as commodity," while others open up spaces for the negotiation of sexual exploration, female friendship, and parental conflict—all integral concerns in teen coming-of-age films.[42] Susanna Nicchiarelli's *Cosmonauta* (*Cosmonaut*, 2009) and Roberta Torre's *I baci mai dati* (*Stolen Kisses*, 2010) are two somewhat recent films whose narratives unfold from the perspective of teenage girls reluctant to conform. Both films follow the conventions of the teen movie and include a focus on heterosexuality, a romance narrative, the attempt of families and school to manage adolescents, and child-parent and peer-peer conflict and resolution.[43] Although both films dramatize "incorporation and exclusion among peer groups,"[44] they are more concerned with staging coming-of-age plots that critique the status quo than with depicting teen protagonists who conform to the dominant model. The traditional focus on "virginity, graduation, and the makeover" is upended.[45] Instead, both films challenge Mulvey's claim that "woman's desire is subjugated to her image as bearer of the bleeding wound."[46]

The protagonist of *Cosmonauta* is Luciana, whom we first meet when she flees from her First Communion because, as she announces, she's a communist. The narrative, which develops around her nonconformity and against the backdrop of the Russian-American space race, focuses on Luciana's political activism with the Italian Federation of Young Communists. It also covers her developing infatuation with peer *compagno* Vittorio, her struggles with her brother Arturo who has epilepsy, and her opposition toward her right-wing stepfather. Although the film implies that both Luciana and Arturo's dreams of space travel are motivated by a lacking paternal metaphor, it also appears that Luciana's activism is an attempt to capture the attention of Vittorio, a typical plot line of the teen movie.

Later in the film, everything falls apart after Luciana assaults Vittorio's girlfriend, the popular and pretty Fiorella, and calls her brother a "sick retard who always embarrasses" her, encouraging him to leave so that she can have a normal life. In this way, Luciana acts out and projects her own sense of alterity onto her brother, whose disability makes him an easy target. But ultimately Luciana learns from her mistakes, and after losing her virginity to Vittorio—a customary denouement of the teen film that is quite downplayed in *Cosmonauta*—she makes amends with Arturo. She is even welcomed back into the political fold, and the film moves toward a conclusion with a toast to cosmonaut Valentina Tereshkova, the first woman in space. Luciana's mentor Marisa (fittingly played by Nicchiarelli) states that women would "like to have the freedom to choose their own destiny"—a message conveyed by the film as well.

Although Luciana in the end gets the boy, she also does not have to become another person to do so. *Cosmonauta* suggests that happy endings come not with the protagonist conforming "in the right ways" that lead to reinforcing or instilling conformity in the audience.[47] Instead, the film successfully inscribes "female subjectivity and desire," without suggesting that female fantasy is necessarily masochistic.[48]

In both *Cosmonauta* and *I baci mai dati*, the paternal figure is absent or lacking, and the younger female protagonist clashes with her mother who leads a conventional and consumerist lifestyle—and who prioritizes the man in her life over her children. In *I baci mai dati*, the mother-daughter storyline is central to the plot, and Manuela, the film's thirteen-year-old protagonist,

FIGURE 8.4 *Luciana comes of age into history.*

is desperate for maternal validation. The film opens by underlining a connection between Manuela and a statue of the Virgin Mary newly erected in the town's main piazza. We are positioned from the film's opening to identify with the statue: we see through its eyes and look through the veil that covers it to make eye contact with Manuela who waits, like the rest of the crowd, for the statue's unveiling.

When two boys playing soccer accidentally decapitate the statue, the viewer no longer clearly identifies with the statue. In a cry for attention and love, Manuela attests that the Madonna came to her in a dream; she recovers the hidden pieces, the statue is rebuilt, and Manuela is declared a miracle worker.[49]

The women in the film, excluding Manuela, are obsessed with body image and spend copious amounts of time on hair and physique. Indeed, Manuela's mother Rita ironically "makes her over" from hip to mainstream as is befitting of her new calling, as she attracts the attention of multitudes willing to pay a high price for Manuela's beatitude. Manuela is also an artist, and her Picasso-like designs of women with contorted features haunt her dreams and speak to her creativity and fantasy. *I baci mai dati* also foregrounds recovered vision: of all those who visit her, only one young girl named Ersilia asks for nothing in return, and it is she who is the recipient of the true "miracle." After recounting the story of the moment that she lost her sight as a child when her father was murdered in front of her eyes, Ersilia's vision is miraculously recovered, and Manuela is declared a saint. Miracle or not, the film suggests that giving voice to and working through traumatic injury can restore memory and recover truth to "[set] things right in the self."[50] The film's restorative finale underlines the significance of female bonding and open communication, and thus

FIGURE 8.5 *The female gaze in* I baci mai dati.

threatens "patriarchal structures," which, *I baci mai dati* suggests, are fragile and in crisis.[51]

6 The Documentary and the Beginning of a New History

Italian women filmmakers have made important documentaries in the last decade addressing several wounds to the Italian body politic. Sabina Guzzanti attacks former prime minister Silvio Berlusconi's treatment of the catastrophic 2009 Aquila earthquake that killed roughly 300 people and left approximately 40,000 homeless in the satirical documentary *Draquila—L'Italia che trema* (*Draquila—Italy Trembles*, 2010). Barbara Rossi Prudente's *La bambina deve prendere aria* (*The Baby Needs Some Fresh Air*, 2009) engages with the notorious Garbage Crisis of Campania, and the narrator describes to her baby daughter the items that make up her "Garbage Emergency Kit." The film takes the initial form of a fairy tale, but we soon realize that the fresh "air" that the mother is instructed to provide for her healthy newborn is polluted with the stench of waste, and on a more sinister note we learn that the breast milk of several women in the area is contaminated with dioxin. Rossi Prudente's film emphasizes the fragility of existence in an environment controlled by the mafia.

Gabriella Romano's documentary *Ricordare* (*To Remember*, 2003) treats the experience of internal exile during Fascism for homosexual men. Men interviewed attest to several aspects of delayed response to trauma—and to the pervasiveness of the past and the impossibility of forgetting. Remembering is challenging for several reasons, particularly as Romano's interviewees are asked to address their sexual orientation in a country that has only recently adopted a more tolerant attitude toward homosexuality.

One activist explains that many older gay men feel that they have no right to national history or collective memory, and therefore are incapable of processing their trauma. For these men, there is no forgetting or getting over history, and their mourning is not productive. For example, they miss appointments, do not answer the director's phone calls, or shut the door on her. Many men only agree to be interviewed out of fear, as they believe that the director is planning to blackmail them. Interviewees convey that they relive the anguish of their internment on a daily basis: they feel that they are still in danger and risk deportation. In treating the experience of internal exile for gay men, Romano opens closed doors that many would prefer remained shut.

The wounded body is the focus of photojournalist Lettizia Battaglia's short film *Fine della storia* (*End of the Story*, 2007), which is part documentary and part performance piece. Battaglia is best known for her work chronicling the devastation of the Sicilian Mafia, and this film juxtaposes many of her striking and violent images with footage of Serena Barona, who, in anguish, traverses the city of Palermo. The film is built around a tension: the obligation to remember past traumatic injury and a desire to move beyond it, which the film suggests is impossible because of the extensive injury that the Mafia has caused to individuals and groups. Several photos of women's lifeless bodies, or of women grieving at funerals or hunched over murdered loved ones, are accompanied by the sound of Barona as she sobs. The montage speaks to the precarious position of women in, against, and around the Mafia while underlining the pivotal role that they continue to play in resisting it.

Much remains to be done on the subject of Italian women directors. Because of space, I have omitted a consideration of many established directors, emergent migrant directors, and a long-standing tradition of directors working in experimental film and documentary. What we need is a comprehensive book-length study of Italian women directors, one that explores the different types of viewing pleasures that the cinema allows when a woman occupies both sides of the camera.

Notes

I would like to thank Maria Coletti, Viridiana Rotondi, and Valeria Dalle Donne for granting me access to the film archives in Rome and Bologna, and Danielle Hipkins, Catherine O'Rawe, and Alan O'Leary for their feedback on earlier versions of this chapter.

1 Mayne, *The Woman at the Keyhole*, 5; Cavarero, *Horrorism*, 30.

2 Luciano and Scarparo, "Contemporary Italian Women Filmmakers," 134.

3 In an informal poll taken in 2001, Paternò determined that "le donne sono, o potrebbero essere, poco meno di 30% tra i registi (women number, or could

number, a little less than 30% of all directors), while Emanuela Mascherini states that women constitute 20 percent of Italian directors (no year is given for the study). See Paternò, "Un cinema al femminile," 135; and Mascherini, *Glass Ceiling*, 122.

4   Luciano and Scarparo, "Contemporary Italian Women Filmmakers," 134. Luciano and Scarparo also coauthored *Reframing Italy*, which treats recent films by women directors.

5   The volume, edited by Flavia Laviosa, is entitled "Cinematic Journeys of Italian Women Directors." See Laviosa, "Editorial," 86. The six essays in the volume are: Benini, "A Face, A Name, A Story"; Bonifazio, "Documenting Work"; Boria, "Sabina Guzzanti"; Karagoz, "Palermo Revisited"; Luciano and Scarparo, "Costanza Quatriglio"; and Tabanelli, "An Unstable Body."

6   The first publication interested in looking closely at Italian women's cinema is Bruno and Nadotti, *Offscreen Women & Film in Italy*. In addition to what is already mentioned, recent examples of scholarship on Italian women directors from the last twenty years include Bieberstein, *Lost Diva—Found Woman*; Bruno, *Streetwalking on a Ruined Map*; Bullaro, *Man in Disorder*; Cantini, *Italian Woman Filmmakers and the Gendered Screen*; Dall'Asta, "Il singolare multiplo"; Glynn, "Engendering Occupation"; Harrison, "Smaller and Larger Families"; Hipkins, "Of Postfeminist Girls and Fireflies"; Lanslots, "Exiled Childhood"; Laviosa, "Archibugi's Cinematic Representations of the Socio-Cultural Changes in the Italian Family"; Lucamante, "Road movies and Gas Stations"; Luciano and Scarparo, "The Personal Is Still Political," *Reframing Italy*, and "Vite sospese"; Marrone, *The Gaze and the Labyrinth*; Missero, "Cecilia Mangini"; O'Healy, "Anthropological Anxieties," "Border Traffic," "[Non] è una somala," and "Theatre and Cinema, 1945-2000"; O'Rawe, "Roberta Torre's *Angela*"; Ravetto, *The Unmasking of Fascist Aesthetics*; Renga, "Failed Anarchists and Anti-Heroes in Lina Wertmüller's *Love and Anarchy*," "The Teen Film and the Female Auteur," "Mafia Woman in a Man's World," and "Screening the Italian Mafia"; Ross, "Queering the Habitus"; Torlasco, *The Time of the Crime*; and Waller, "Signifying the Holocaust" and "You Cannot Make the Revolution on Film." The following contain brief entries on some Italian women directors: Morandini Sr. and Morandini Jr., *I Morandini delle donne*; and Sossi, *Dizionario delle registe*.

7   Claire Johnston, cited in Doane, "The Woman's Film," 283.

8   Dall'Asta writes that Bertini's autobiographies and interviews contain "una determinazione della Bertini nel rivendicare uno stato autoriale" (a determination to claim the right to her authorial status) ("Il singolare multiplo," 70).

9   McCabe, *Feminist Film Studies*.

10   Hipkins, "Why Italian Film Studies Needs a Second Take on Gender," 216.

11   See, for example, Luciano and Scarparo, "Contemporary Italian Women Filmmakers," 132–34; Dalle Vacche, *Diva*, 265; Dall'Asta, "Il singolare multiplo"; Nochimson, *World on Film*, 158; Ramirez, "Silent Divas"; and Bruno, *Streetwalking on a Ruined Map*, 110.

12 Mulvey, "Visual Pleasure and Narrative Cinema."

13 Modleski, *The Women Who Knew Too Much,* 2; Mayne, "Paradoxes of Spectatorship," 45, 38.

14 "The female figures . . . connotes something that the look circles around but disavows: her lack of a penis implying the threat of castration and hence unpleasure. . . . The male unconscious has two alternatives of escape from this castration anxiety: preoccupation with the re-enactment of original trauma (. . . demystifying her mystery), counterbalanced by the devaluation, punishment or saving of the guilty object" (Mulvey, "Visual Pleasure and Narrative Cinema," 21).

15 Mulvey, "Afterthoughts on 'Visual Pleasure and Narrative Cinema' Inspired by King Vidor's *Duel in the Sun* (1946)," 37.

16 Mulvey, "Notes on Sirk and Melodrama," 76.

17 Staiger, "Film Noir as Male Melodrama," 73.

18 Staiger, "Film Noir as Male Melodrama," 82.

19 Bruno, *Streetwalking on a Ruined Map,* 327–28.

20 Mulvey, "Notes on Sirk and Melodrama," 79.

21 Landy, "The Melodramatic Context," 32.

22 Doane, *Femmes Fatales,* 12. Although Wertmüller's feminism has been notoriously attacked, her films have been read through the lens of feminist film theory.

23 Santner, "History Beyond the Pleasure Principle," 148.

24 De Lauretis, "Cavani's 'Night Porter,'" 35–36.

25 Ravetto, *The Unmasking of Fascist Aesthetics,* 191.

26 Marcus argues that the female commandant is a site of abjection for Pasqualino, one that must be repressed for the symbolic order to remain intact (*Italian Film in the Shadow of Auschwitz,* 58). For more on the trope of abjection, see Kristeva, *Powers of Horror.*

27 Projansky, *Watching Rape,* 5.

28 Waller, "Signifying the Holocaust," 216.

29 Mulvey, "Visual Pleasure and Narrative Cinema," 19.

30 Mulvey, "Visual Pleasure and Narrative Cinema," 19.

31 Doane, "The Woman's Film," 285.

32 Doane, "The Woman's Film," 285.

33 O'Rawe, "Roberta Torre's *Angela,*" 334.

34 Renga, "Mafia Woman in a Man's World."

35 Projansky, *Watching Rape,* 152.

36 Kristeva, *Powers of Horror,* 12–13.

37 Rich, "New Queer Cinema," 769.

38 Aaron, "New Queer Cinema," 3.

39 Ross, "Queering the Habitus," 243.

40 See Dall'Orto, "La 'tolleranza repressiva' dell'omosessualità.'"

41 For more on films made after World Pride 2000, see Rigoletto, "Sexual Dissidence and the Mainstream," 202–203.

42 Hipkins, "Sorry If I Love You."

43 For more on the generic qualifiers of the teen film, see Driscoll, *Teen Film*, 1–3.

44 Driscoll, *Girls*, 221.

45 Driscoll, *Teen Film*, 2.

46 Mulvey, "Visual Pleasure and Narrative Cinema," 14.

47 Driscoll, *Girls*, 221.

48 Doane, "The Woman's Film," 285.

49 *Corpo Celeste* (Alice Rohrwacher, 2011) is another film by a woman director that focuses on a thirteen-year-old girl named Marta and is interested in the complications of faith and spiritual transcendence.

50 Alexander, "Toward a Theory of Cultural Trauma," 5.

51 Straayer, *Deviant Eyes, Deviant Bodies*, 17. See his discussion of how female bonding in film explicitly threatens patriarchy as "female bonding is a precondition for lesbianism" (17).

Bibliography

Aaron, Michele. "New Queer Cinema: An Introduction." In *New Queer Cinema: A Critical Reader*. Ed. Michele Aaron. New Brunswick: Rutgers University Press, 2004. 3–14.

Alexander, Jeffrey C. "Toward a Theory of Cultural Trauma." In *Cultural Trauma and Collective Identity*. Ed. C. Alexander et al. Berkeley: University of California Press, 2004. 1–30.

Benini, Stefania. "'A Face, A Name, A Story': Women's Identities as Life Stories in Alina Marazzi's Cinema." *Studies in European Cinema* 8.2 (2011): 129–39.

Bieberstein, Rada. *Lost Diva—Found Woman: Female Representations in New Italian Cinema and National Television from 1995–2005*. Marburg: Schüren, 2009.

Bonifazio, Paola. "Documenting Work: Manuela Pellarin's Non-Fiction Films in the Industrial Veneto." *Studies in European Cinema* 8.2 (2011): 141–52.

Boria, Monica. "Sabina Guzzanti: From TV Satire to Political Documentary." *Studies in European Cinema* 8.2 (2011): 101–13.

Bruno, Giuliana. *Streetwalking on a Ruined Map: Cultural Theory and the City Films of Elvira Notari*. Princeton: Princeton University Press, 1993.

Bruno, Giuliana and Maria Nadotti, eds. *Offscreen Women & Film in Italy*. Routledge: London and New York, 1988.

Cantini, Maristella, ed. *Italian Woman Filmmakers and the Gendered Screen*. Basingstoke: Palgrave Macmillan, 2013.

Cavarero, Adriana. *Horrorism: Naming Contemporary Violence*. New York: Columbia University Press, 2009.

Dall'Orto, Giovanni. "La 'tolleranza repressiva' dell'omosessualità: Quando un atteggiamento legale diviene tradizione." In *Omosessuali e stato*. Ed. ARCI GAY nazionale. Bologna: Centro di Documentazione il Cassero, 1987. 37–57.

Dalle Vacche, Angela. *Diva: Defiance and Passion in Early Italian Cinema*. Austin: University of Texas Press, 2008.

De Lauretis, Teresa. "Cavani's 'Night Porter': A Woman's Film?" *Film Quarterly* 30.2 (1976): 35–38.

Doane, Mary Ann. *Femmes Fatales: Feminism, Film Theory, Psychoanalysis*. New York: Routledge, 1991.

Doane, Mary Ann. "The Woman's Film: Possession and Address." In *Home Is Where the Heart Is: Studies in Melodrama and the Woman's Film*. Ed. Christine Gledhill. London: BFI, 1987. 67–82.

Driscoll, Catherine. *Girls: Feminine Adolescence in Popular Culture and Cultural Theory*. New York: Columbia University Press, 2002.

Driscoll, Catherine. *Teen Film: A Critical Introduction*. Oxford: Berg, 2011.

Hipkins, Danielle. "Of Postfeminist Girls and Fireflies: Consuming Rome in *Un giorno speciale*." *Forum Italicum* 50.1 (2016): 166–82.

Hipkins, Danielle. "Sorry If I Love You." In *Directory of World Cinema*. http://wor ldcinemadirectory.co.uk/component/film/?id=958. Accessed February 28, 2013.

Hipkins, Danielle. "Why Italian Film Studies Needs a Second Take on Gender." *Italian Studies* 63.2 (2008): 213–34.

Karagoz, Claudia. "Palermo Revisited: Letizia Battaglia's *Fine della storia*." *Studies in European Cinema* 8.2 (2011): 153–62.

Kristeva, Julia. *Powers of Horror: An Essay on Abjection*. New York: Columbia University Press, 1982.

Landy, Marcia. "The Melodramatic Context." In *Imitations of Life: A Reader on Film and Television Melodrama*. Ed. Marcia Landy. Detroit: Wayne State University Press, 1991. 3–12.

Laviosa, Flavia. "Editorial: Cinematic Journeys of Italian Women Filmmakers." *Studies in European Cinema* 8.2 (2011): 85–88.

Luciano, Bernadette and Susanna Scarparo. "Contemporary Italian Women Filmmakers: Reframing the Past, the Present, and the Cinematic Tradition." In *New Perspectives in Italian Cultural Studies*. Vol. 2. *The Arts and History*. Ed. Graziella Parati. Madison: Fairleigh Dickinson Press, 2013. 131–50.

Luciano, Bernadette and Susanna Scarparo. "Costanza Quatriglio: In Search of the Invisible." *Studies in European Cinema* 8.2 (2011): 115–27.

Luciano, Bernadette and Susanna Scarparo. "The Personal Is Still Political: Films 'By and For Women' by the New *Documentariste*." *Italica* 87.3 (2010): 488–503.

Luciano, Bernadette and Susanna Scarparo. *Reframing Italy: New Trends in Italian Women's Filmmaking*. West Lafayette: Purdue University Press, 2013.

Marcus, Millicent. *Italian Film in the Shadow of Auschwitz*. Toronto: The University of Toronto Press, 2007.

Marrone, Gaetana. *The Gaze and the Labyrinth: The Cinema of Liliana Cavani*. Princeton: Princeton University Press, 2000.

Mascherini, Emanuela. *Glass Ceiling: Oltre il soffitto di vetro: professionalità femminili nel cinema italiano*. Città del Castello: Edimon, 2009.

Mayne, Judith. "Paradoxes of Spectatorship." In *The Film Cultures Reader*. Ed. Graeme Turner. New York: Routledge, 2002. 28-45.

Mayne, Judith. *The Woman at the Keyhole: Feminism and Women's Cinema*. Bloomington and Indianapolis: Indiana University Press, 1990.

McCabe, Janet. *Feminist Film Studies: Writing the Woman into Cinema*. London: Wallflower Press, 2004.

Modleski, Tania. *The Women Who Knew Too Much: Hitchcock and Feminist Theory*. New York: Routledge, 1989.

Morandini, Morando Sr. and Morando Morandini Jr. *I Morandini delle donne: 60 anni di cinema al femminile*. Pavona di Albano Laziali: Iacobelli, 2010.

Mulvey, Laura. "Afterthoughts on 'Visual Pleasure and Narrative Cinema' Inspired by King Vidor's *Duel in the Sun* (1946)." In *Visual and Other Pleasures*. Bloomington: Indiana University Press, 1989. 29-38.

Mulvey, Laura. "Notes on Sirk and Melodrama." In *Home Is Where the Heart Is: Studies in Melodrama and the Woman's Film*. Ed. Christine Gledhill. London: BFI, 1987. 75-79.

Mulvey, Laura. "Visual Pleasure and Narrative Cinema." In *Visual and Other Pleasures*. Bloomington: Indiana University Press, 1989. 14-30.

Nochimson, Martha P. *World on Film: An Introduction*. Malden: Wiley-Blackwell, 2010.

O'Healy, Áine. "'[Non] è una somala': Deconstructing African Femininity in Italian Film." *The Italianist* 29.2 (2009): 175-98.

O'Rawe, Catherine. "Roberta Torre's *Angela*: The Mafia and the Woman's Film." In *Mafia Movies: A Reader*. Ed. Dana Renga. Toronto: University of Toronto Press, 2011. 329-37.

Paternò, Cristiana. "Un cinema al femminile." In *La meglio gioventù: Nuovo cinema italiano, 2000-2006*. Ed. Vito Zagarrio. Venezia: Marsilio, 2006. 135-42.

Projansky, Sarah. *Watching Rape: Film and Television in Postfeminist Culture*. New York: New York University Press, 2001.

Ramirez, Joy. "Silent Divas: The *Femmes Fatales* of the *Cinema Muto*." In *The Femmes Fatales: Images, Histories, Contexts*. Ed. Helen Hanson and Catherine O'Rawe. Hampshire: Palgrave Macmillan, 2010. 60-71.

Ravetto, Kriss. *The Unmasking of Fascist Aesthetics*. Minneapolis: University of Minnesota Press, 2001.

Renga, Dana. "Mafia Woman in a Man's World: Roberta Torre's *Angela*." In *Unfinished Business: Screening the Italian Mafia in the New Millennium*. Toronto: University of Toronto Press, 2013. 51-64.

Renga, Dana. "The Teen Film and the Female Auteur." In *New Visions of the Child in Italian Cinema*. Ed. Danielle Hipkins and Roger Pitt. Oxford: Peter Lang, 2014. 307-29.

Rich, R. Ruby. "New Queer Cinema." In *Critical Visions in Film Theory: Classic and Contemporary Readings*. Ed. Timothy Corrigan et al., New York: Bedford/St. Martin's, 2011. 767-73.

Rigoletto, Sergio. "Sexual Dissidence and the Mainstream: The Queer Triangle in Ferzan Ozpetek's *Le fate ignoranti*." *Italian Studies* 30.2 (2010): 202-18.

Ross, Charlotte. "Queering the Habitus: Lesbian Identity in Stancanelli's *Benzina*." *Romance Studies* 33.3 (2004): 237–50.

Santner, Eric. "History Beyond the Pleasure Principle: Some Thoughts on the Representation of Trauma." In *Probing the Limits of Representation: Nazism and the "Final Solution."* Ed. Saul Friedlander. Cambridge, MA: Harvard University Press, 1992. 143–54.

Sossi, Tiziano. *Dizionario delle registe: L'altra metà del cinema.* Rome: Gremese, 2000.

Staiger, Janet. "Film Noir as Male Melodrama: The Politics of Film Genre Labeling." In *The Shifting Definitions of Genre: Essays on Labeling Films, Television Shows, and Media.* Ed. Lincoln Geraghty and Mark Jancovich. Jefferson: McFarland, 2008. 71–91.

Straayer, Chris. *Deviant Eyes, Deviant Bodies: Sexual Reorientations in Film and Video.* New York: Columbia University Press, 1996.

Tabanelli, Roberta. "An Unstable Body: The Cinema of Antonietta De Lillo." *Studies in European Cinema* 8.2 (2011): 89–100.

Waller, Marguerite. "Signifying the Holocaust: Liliana Cavani's *Portiere di notte*." In *Feminisms in the Cinema.* Ed. Laura Pietropaolo and Ada Testaferri. Bloomington: Indiana University Press, 1995. 206–19.

Filmography

Angela, Dir. Roberta Torre, Italy: Lucky Red. 2002.

Assunta Spina, Dir. Francesca Bertini and Gustavo Serena, Italy: Caesar Film. 1915.

I baci mai dati (Stolen Kisses), Dir. Roberta Torre, Italy: Nuvola Film, Rosetta Film. 2010.

La bambina deve prendere aria (The Baby Needs Some Fresh Air), Dir. Barbara Rossi Prudente, Italy: 19.11 Produzioni. 2009.

Benzina (Gasoline), Dir. Monica Strambrini, Italy: Lion Lantina. 2001.

Corpo Celeste, Dir. Alice Rohrwacher, Italy: Istituto Luce. 2011.

Cosmonauta (Cosmonaut), Dir. Susanna Nicchiarelli, Italy: Fandango. 2009.

Draquila—L'Italia che trema (Draquila—Italy Trembles), Dir. Sabina Guzzanti, Italy: BiM Distribuzione. 2010.

Fine della storia (End of the Story), Dir. Letizia Battaglia, Italy. 2007.

Mimì metallurgico, ferito nell'onore (The Seduction of Mimi), Dir. Lina Wertmüller, Italy: Euro International Film. 1972.

Pasqualino Settebellezze (Seven Beauties), Dir. Lina Wertmüller, Italy: Medusa Distribuzione. 1975.

'E piccerella, Dir. Elvira Notari, Italy: Film Dora. 1922.

Il portiere di notte (The Night Porter), Dir. Liliana Cavani, Italy: Lotar Film Productions. 1974.

Ricordare: un documentario su fascismo e omosessualità (Remember: A Documentary on Fascism and Homosexuality), Dir. Gabriella Romano, Italy. 2004.

'A santanotte, Dir Elvira Notari, Italy: Film Dora. 1922.

Thelma and Louise, Dir. Ridley Scott, USA: Pathé. 1991.

9

The Cinematic Evolution of *Commedia all'Italiana*

Marcia Landy

The *commedia all'italiana* derives from a variety of comic forms that inhere in Italian culture, including the ancient *commedia dell'arte* with its uses of masks and stock types from a range of sources and models.[1] Antecedents to the *commedia all'italiana*, which flourished in the 1950s and 1960s, appear as early as the birth of Italian film. In the silent film era of the 1910s, Italian cinematic comedy was particularly identified with social class (especially lower and upper-middle classes). Comic sketches were aligned to the antics of the mobile body and relied on such elements as dress, disguises, thieving, crime detection, social blunders, and the perils of social climbing. If American film comedians such as Charlie Chaplin and Buster Keaton were able to express social rebellion, silent comedians with such names as Cretinetti (André Deed) and Robinet (Marcel Fabre) were "unable to reach a level of competence that would guarantee integration into the world that [they] parodied but greatly desired."[2] A major exception to this assessment perhaps might be the figure of Maciste, the *divo* of silent historical and adventure films. Played by Bartolomeo Pagano, Maciste was both heroic and comic. The strong man (*uomo forte*) was to maintain his appeal through the early 1920s in action, adventure, and historical films, and he would return in the later "peplum" (sword and sandal) epics as well as the Spaghetti Westerns of the 1960s.[3]

While the comic forms of the 1910s evolved as a popular entertainment medium in Italian cinema, they were less influential internationally in comparison to such historical films as *Quo vadis?* (1913), *Gli ultimi giorni di Pompei* (*The Last Days of Pompeii*, 1913), and *Cabiria* (1914).

Melodrama, a form often linked to the comedic for its physical expressivity, also had its heyday in the pre-First World War cinema and in the period preceding the advent of sound on film. Associated with the charismatic figure of Gabriele D'Annunzio, this poetic and visually expressive cinema was synonymous with a form of acting known as *divismo*. Goddesses of the screen, these female figures incarnated desire, defiance, and passion.[4] This cinema was a transnational phenomenon that saw the emergence of many European divas, including Francesca Bertini, Asta Nielsen, and Eleonora Duse.

After the First World War, much had changed in culture and cinematic production. Attempts were made to revive an Italian cinema mired in financial crises because of the loss of audiences, political conflicts related to the rise of Fascism, and the growing imperialist sway of Hollywood. Other factors included the exorbitant salaries demanded by such divas as Bertini, Lyda Borelli, and Pina Menichelli, pressures to modernize with the advent of sound, and the unsuccessful attempt to recapture former markets in Europe and America. The crisis of cinema was also due to the lack of organization in the many competing production companies as well as the loss of technicians to other countries. Italian cinema sought to woo audiences that no longer responded at the box office.

Thanks to Stefano Pittaluga (1887–1932), who sought to consolidate bankrupt production studios into a few potentially profitable companies (including his own), there were modest signs of amelioration. Slowly, the Fascist regime saw fit to support the cinema via the sponsorship of documentary filmmaking, newsreels, and propaganda through the agency LUCE (L'unione cinematografica educativa) formed in 1924 to enhance through cinema the ideological project of Fascism "as a reformation of culture."[5] Comedy was to play a significant role in the ensuing cinematic productions of the 1930s.

1 The Fascist Era, the Coming of Sound, and Comedy

With the development of sound on film, the Italian Fascist regime recognized that popular cinematic forms contributed to a visual and verbal language conducive to advancing its political interests, and so it offered filmmakers limited assistance. By the mid-1930s, modest signs of improvement in the economic conditions of cinema became apparent. Significantly, these changes can be attributed largely, but not exclusively, to the popularity of comic forms, to what later became labeled as "white telephone" films, a form of light comedy imported from Germany and Hungary. The telephone, whether white or black, played a symbolic role in these films as a modernizing technology that would serve as a bridge between social classes, spaces, and national concerns. These comic films featured the exploits and foibles of the rich. Exemplary works of the genre are such films as *Rubacuori* (*The Charmer*, Brignone, 1931), a domestic comedy centered on a roving husband in need of marital discipline, and *La segretaria privata* (*Private Secretary*, 1931), a romantic musical comedy that starred a young woman (Elsa Merlini) who is in search of work and eventually rewarded for her chastity and industriousness by marriage to a rich and penitent boss.

The most prominent comedies of the 1930s and early 1940s were by director Mario Camerini, who was critically and commercially successful in reviving Italian film stars, most notably Assia Noris and Vittorio De Sica. His films focus largely on the dilemmas of working-class protagonists and dramatize the pleasures and dangers of upward mobility. They also exhibit a fascination with the Hollywood dream factory, but in the final analysis withdraw from it by returning their characters to their original social stations. These films relied on prescribed social rituals, models of desirable bodies, and acceptable forms of leisure and work that portray the parameters of permissible pleasure (as opposed to the decadence of the upper classes).[6] In Camerini, comedy personifies a compromise between what his characters desire and what they could achieve within the constraints of modern urban life. The narratives are presented through physically attractive, young, and mobile protagonists who are instrumental in "negotiat[ing] for the 'new' nation the terms of a naturalized modernity."[7]

2 The Second World War and Signs of Things to Come

If this type of comedy captured the imaginary sense of Fascist modernity, the comedies in the late 1930s and early 1940s, following the German-Italian alliance and its racial and imperialist policies and then the coming of the Second World War, appeared to suggest positions at odds with the regime. For example, *Il cappello a tre punte* (*The Three-Cornered Hat*, Mario Camerini, 1935) is the satire of a lecherous and unscrupulous rural governor intent on seducing a miller's wife, while *I bambini ci guardano* (*The Children Are Watching Us*, Vittorio De Sica, 1943) focuses on disintegrating domestic relations, especially child neglect, and *Le sorelle Materassi* (*The Materassi Sisters*, Ferdinando Maria Poggioli, 1943) is a surreal, satiric film that centers on a reprobate young man who cruelly exploits two elderly women. In keeping with these decidedly non-Fascist themes, the film *Quattro passi fra le nuvole* (*Four Steps in the Clouds*,

1942), directed by Alessandro Blasetti—another major innovative director of the era—features a traveling salesman who lives a ritualized city life and is enlisted to aid a young rural woman who is pregnant out of wedlock. He plays a role in mollifying the dismay of her family and reconciling her with them. This comedy, along with the melodramatic *I bambini ci guardano*, has been linked to the emergence of neorealism because of its use of ordinary people, location shots in the city and countryside, and critical treatment of the violation of familial values.

With the coming of the Second World War, with its food shortages and the disappearance of men on the home front, support for the Fascist regime began to erode. Significantly, filmmakers began to explore new uses of the language of cinema. In their quest for a different form of cinematic production, writers and filmmakers turned to regional landscapes, such as Sicily, that were to play a critical role in Italian film comedy and melodrama in the work of such directors as Luchino Visconti, Giuseppe De Santis, and Pietro Germi. Neapolitan actors including Totò (Antonio De Curtis) and the De Filippo brothers, Eduardo and Peppino, were to become central in the comedies of the 1930s through 1970s. Their comedies, with "double entendres and parodies of everyday life and situations,"[8] were popular with stage and film audiences and bore a relation to the critical movement known as neorealism as well as to an enrichment of Italian comic stardom.

3 The Postwar Cinema, Colorful Neorealism, and Comedy

Identified with the post–Second World War era, neorealism has been tied to the effects of Fascism, world war, and an uncertainty about the fate of the nation and national cinema. For a major writer on neorealism, the movement was "more an ontological position than an aesthetic one. . . . The word neorealist was thrown like a fishing net over the postwar Italian cinema and each director is doing his best to break the coils, in which is it claimed, he has been caught."[9] Despite the ongoing confusion about the meaning of neorealism, there are reasons to stick with the nomenclature for purposes of identifying an important and contentious dimension of its cinematic forms and style as they relate to the evolution of Italian comedy.

Neorealism is not a faithful reproduction of reality. It is not a genre, nor merely a technical reliance on actual locations and nonprofessional actors. It is a form of cinema that has remained contentious, ambiguous, and resistant to definition, though it continues to be a yardstick against which much of Italian film production is still measured—even in considerations of what constitutes *commedia all'italiana*. Tied to conceptions of the everyday, the marginal, and the suffering body, neorealism provides a cinematic language that is self-conscious about narration. The immediate postwar neorealism, exemplified in such films as *Roma città aperta* (*Rome, Open City*, Rossellini, 1945), *Paisà* (Rossellini, 1946), *Sciuscià* (*Shoeshine*, De Sica, 1946), and *Ladri di biciclette* (*Bicycle Thieves*, De Sica, 1948), represented a challenge to conventional forms of realism associated with Fascism that had foregrounded heroism, action, and resolution.

After the triumph of the Christian Democratic Party in 1948 (and later with the burgeoning of the so-called economic miracle), the Italian filmgoer of the late 1940s witnessed a return to genre films, including melodramas, peplum epics, westerns, documentaries, animation, and comedies. Producers' eyes were on the international market and on profitability, and popular comedies were a promising source of income and audiences. In a form of neorealism allied to satiric comedy and fantasy, *Miracolo a Milano* (*Miracle in Milan*, De Sica, 1951) offered a neorealist fairy tale, a comic fable that visualized the poverty and exploitation of the lower classes, the unemployed, and the elderly, ostensibly emphasizing a message of endurance, faith, and solidarity. While critical, if not pessimistic, of social institutions and the upper classes and of their unwillingness to contribute to social transformation, De Sica used satire and humor to shatter the clichés and stereotypes associated with the poor to humanize them through the love lavished on them by the magic of film. It was clear that neorealism eschewed familiar cinematic models, revealing a different design on its viewers that introduced a new type of image to pose "problems at the level of reality" and, hence, put "the image into contact with thought."[10]

Another emergent form of Italian comedy were adaptations from the Don Camillo novels of Giovanni Guareschi.[11] The political and social conflicts in this rural world were largely local and commonplace, often absurd if not satirical, and involved such issues as elections, political meetings, church meetings, and sporting events. Comedies such as *Pane, amore e fantasia* (*Bread, Love, and Dreams*, Comencini, 1953) and *Pane, amore e gelosia* (*Bread Love, and Jealousy*, Comencini, 1954) were set in a sleepy rural village where the most unsettling elements are romance and sexual desire. The films' connections to neorealism have been described as "pink" or "rosy," and reside in their portraits of common folks, community, and social aspirations; they also emphasize the role of the physically vital female who comes to stand in for the revitalization of the nation scarred by Fascism.[12] The rosy neorealist comedies represented one side of the changing landscape of Italy and were presented in sentimental terms.[13] Another important group were the melodramatic films labeled as "black" neorealism that starred the popular Amedeo Nazzari in such films as *Il bandito* (*The Bandit*, Lattuada, 1946), in which he becomes a criminal, "his behavior emblematic of an institutional crisis, the moral turpitude of family members (male and female) and the destruction of the nation."[14]

4 Stardom, Neorealism, and
Commedia all'Italiana

The films of Antonio De Curtis, known familiarly as Totò (1898–1968) in a career spanning from the 1920s to the late 1960s, were popular in postwar cinematic culture. His role as small-time con artist to Aldo Fabrizi's cop in *Guardie e ladri* (*Cops and Robbers*, Monicelli and Steno, 1951) is a forerunner of *commedia all'italiana* in its blurring of the boundaries between thief and law enforcers. Totò's physical appearance, slight body, bent nose, plastic facial grimaces, and bodily gestures endeared him to Italian audiences.[15] His most memorable role was in Pier Paolo Pasolini's *Uccellacci e uccellini* (*Hawks and Sparrows*, 1966), a poetically and stylistically reflexive comic fable on cinema and politics. He was a cultural model for the next generation of comedians, especially for Alberto Sordi who later became an icon of *commedia all'italiana*.

Italian theater and cinema boast a lineage of versatile male comedians such as Sordi, Vittorio Gassman, Nino Manfredi, and Ugo Tognazzi, each of whom convey the ineptitude, braggadocio, and pathos of the comic figures they portray as well as the cultural constraints under which they function. Sordi, like Totò, was a talented comic and was revered by his public as "Albertone," a national monument. His roles include the egregious Nando Moriconi, a sycophantic emulator of Americans (*Un americano a Roma*, Steno, 1953); Alberto the "mammone" (mamma's boy) in *I Vitelloni* (Fellini, 1953); the naïve southerner Antonio Badalamente in *Mafioso* (Lattuada, 1962); and Oreste Jacovacci, the "coward become a hero"[16] in *La grande guerra* (*The Great War*, Monicelli, 1959). While Sordi might be considered an exemplary instance of *commedia all'italiana*, he saw his acting as "a non-dramatic form of neorealism."[17] His observations validate the view of many critics that certain distinguishing qualities of the *commedia* bear connection to conceptions of neorealism.[18] These comedies of the late 1950s and 1960s were largely upbeat, although they also exemplified a growing uneasiness about the emphasis on wealth, consumerism, and American influence in Italian life.

I soliti ignoti (*Big Deal on Madonna Street*, Monicelli, 1958) became for many a landmark film in the emergence of a new form of comedy that introduced the comic protagonist as a rogue, an operator, and a specialist in "the art of getting by" (*l'arte di arrangiarsi*). *Big Deal* belongs to the *giallo-rosa* or "caper film" that focuses on the exploits of a group of incompetents to carry off a big heist. The 1950s witnessed international versions of this subgenre, namely in *The Ladykillers* (Mackendrick, 1955), *Rififi* (Dassin, 1955), and *Bob le flambeur* (Melville, 1956). Fellini's *Il bidone* (*The Swindle*, 1955) also belongs to this seriocomic form. Using an American actor, Broderick Crawford, Fellini's version of the swindle involves a dishonest

Roman Catholic bishop who visits peasants and claims to have access to a hidden treasure. But Fellini's satire becomes an allegory of the good thief[19]: as in *La strada* (1954), the body of the suffering male figure in the film is transformed into an uncertain allegory of conversion and redemption, thus shifting the meaning of *commedia all'italiana* into another stylistic and conceptual register.

Big Deal on Madonna Street joins these other Italian and international caper film comedies in its encyclopedic treatment of Italian social life at the margins. It satirizes the pretensions of the protagonists, their conventional views of courtship and marriage, hostility toward employment, and outmoded familial rituals associated with Sicilian life. The success of the film derives from its selection of actors, including the legendary Totò and accomplished dramatic actor, Vittorio Gassman.

Though the emphasis of the action is on the execution of the heist, the film also links the men's portraits to Italian sexual politics, exemplified in the virtual imprisonment of a young Sicilian woman, Carmela (Claudia Cardinale), by her brother Michele (Tiburio Murgia) to insure her chastity until he finds a suitable husband for her. Michele's plan is thwarted by Mario's (Renato Salvatori) subversive and comical efforts to save her.

Gassman as Peppe also capitalizes on his persona as a swaggering womanizer in other comedies of the 1960s: *Il mattatore* (*Love and Larceny*, Risi, 1960), *Il sorpasso* (*The Easy Life*, Risi, 1962), and *I mostri* (*The Monsters*, Risi, 1963).

FIGURE 9.1 *Vittorio Gassman, left, and Vittorio De Sica in Monicelli's* Big Deal on Madonna Street *(1958).*

5 Masculinity, Femininity, Sexuality, and Family

According to Jacqueline Reich, what differentiates the *commedia all'italiana* from the *film comico* is its exposure of "inept, bumbling, self-absorbed males who fail to assume the role of responsible adults" (*Beyond the Latin Lover*, 15). While the stars of the *commedia all'italiana* are preponderantly male, women also play a significant role in the revelation of this ineptness. *commedia all'italiana* uses caricature, ridicule, and an emphasis on gendered bodies to create a grotesque form of humor that flouts the traditions, rituals, customs, and codes that had imprisoned Italian men in the persona of the *gallo*, preening womanizer. This masculine figure, with his compulsive roving eye and need for real or imagined sexual exploits with women, mirrored the patriarchal, gendered, and sexual politics of Italian society. For example, Pietro Germi's iconic film *Divorce Italian Style* concludes with the camera travelling over the bikini-clad body of Angela as the ostensibly victorious Fefé (Marcello Mastroianni) gazes at her—yet he is becoming a cuckold (*cornuto*) after all, for she is flirting with another man unbeknownst to him as he gazes upon her.

The dark humor in *Divorce Italian Style*, which includes a feigned honor killing of Fefé's wife, ultimately satirizes "the cruelty of a legal system and

FIGURE 9.2 *Portrait of a cuckold:* Divorce Italian Style *(1961), with Stefania Sandrelli as Angela and Marcello Mastroianni as Fefé. Courtesy of Photofest.*

all its gender absurdity [in its] general portrayal of an archaic mentality and its consequences on everyday people."[20]

Another dark comedy also set in Sicily and focusing on the bizarre expectations of male and females comportment is *Il bell'Antonio*, directed by Mauro Bolognini and scripted by Pasolini in 1960. As the title suggests, Mastroianni plays Antonio as the *bella figura*, the beautiful figure, handsome in appearance, respectful to women, and seemingly the ideal spouse—but, alas, he is also impotent before his figure of the ideal woman. The grotesque humor entails his "worship of the female figure," in the form of his wife Barbara (Claudia Cardinale) who presents an inviolate and virginal image to the point of being an obstacle to their sexual consummation. However, with carnal creatures such as the maid Santuzza to whom he will finally be yoked, he can perform sexually. In the dark bitter ending to the film, he gazes at his mirrored image in which he has bitterly, finally become "a man."[21]

The economic miracle, or "Il boom," designates the material prosperity and social mobility that played a critical role in cultural, political, and aesthetic transformations in Italy from late 1950s and 1960s. A growth of per capita income extended to young adults and was apparent in the increased availability of such consumer commodities as motorcars, motorbikes, and motorcycles—in short, a dramatic change in lifestyle that was portrayed in Federico Fellini's *La dolce vita* (1960) and Risi's *Il sorpasso. The Easy Life*, with its emphasis on money, automobiles, fashion, and sex, shows a cynical attitude toward history, tradition, and modernity. In this film, Gassman, the star of so many comedies, becomes the "prototype of the new Italian" in the cinema of "economic miracles."[22]

FIGURE 9.3 *The fantasy of the "mobile" male in* Il sorpasso *(1962), starring Vittorio Gassman (far right) and Jean-Louis Trintignant (far left). Courtesy of Photofest.*

Il sorpasso set the terms for this new figure of an outwardly attractive but unsentimental man who was exploitative, even cruel, in his treatment of others. Gassman's Bruno is a womanizer, a narcissist, a city dude. Though Gassman is a versatile actor, his cynicism and opportunism remain consistently anti-sentimental; while other "softer" actors, like Alberto Sordi and Nino Manfredi, are figures of comic pathos who expose their frailties in such films as, respectively, *Mafioso* and *Pane e cioccolata* (*Bread and Chocolate*, Brusati, 1974), a dark comedy on immigration.

The emphasis on mobility is not restricted to the bourgeois flâneur; it includes workers who appear in films as migrants from southern to northern Italy (e.g., *Mimi metallurgico ferito nell'onore* [*The Seduction of Mimi*, Lina Wertmüller, 1972] and episodes from *Sessomatto* [*How Funny Can Sex Be?* Risi, 1973]). In *Bread and Chocolate*, the migration is from southern Italy to Switzerland, and in *La ragazza con la pistola* (*The Girl with the Pistol*, Monicelli, 1958) from Sicily to the United Kingdom. *La ragazza con la pistola*, starring Monica Vitti, focuses on the violation of the honor code

FIGURE 9.4 *The "new woman": Monica Vitti as Assunta in* The Girl with the Pistol *(1958). Courtesy of Photofest.*

that dooms Assunta Patanè (Vitti) to avenge her and her family's honor by murdering the *gallo* that debauched her. She sets out on a journey to the United Kingdom armed with a gun to find him, and on her travels she begins to inhabit a modern world that serves as a critique of the archaic values that she has left behind.

The film is another instance of how Monicelli uses actors in roles different from their well-known screen personas. In Vitti's case, her character was a contrast to the enigmatic roles that she played for Michelangelo Antonioni in such films as *L'avventura* (1960). Her role for Monicelli was an important exception in a male-dominated genre.

While the stars of the *commedia all'italiana* are preponderantly male, it is evident that women do play a demystifying role in exposing the men's posturing of masculinity. The gun-toting Assunta emancipates herself from the cult of honor and the traditional blandishments of the *gallo*, exposing his strategies to the spectator's ridicule.

6 The *Commedia* and Omnibus Films

An important aspect of the success of *commedia all'italiana* is the episode of omnibus films during the 1950s and 1960s, a form that served actors and producers alike. This type of film was also an opportunity for collaboration among different directors and writers, and was productive in mixing narrative forms, as it combined shorter and longer formats, while maintaining commercial standard length for the entire production. Such films also permitted an opportunity to focus encyclopedically and incisively on a range of social types, sexual behavior, classes, and genders.[23] They featured such stars and directors as Sophia Loren and Vittorio De Sica, who collaborated in *L'oro di Napoli* (*Gold of Naples*, 1954) and *Ieri, oggi, domani* (*Yesterday, Today, Tomorrow*, 1963).

Other notable collaborative works include *Boccaccio '70* (Monicelli, Fellini, De Sica, Visconti, 1962) and *RoGoPaG* (Rossellini, Godard, Pasolini, Gregoretti, 1963). In *How Crazy Can Sex Be?* Dino Risi employed Giancarlo Giannini in all the episodes.

In the quest for expanding audiences, these films cast a wider net in relation to audience tastes and allowed for greater latitude in portraying a world in the throes of wanted and unwanted transformations. They also focused on issues of gender and sexuality. In *The Gold of Naples*, Sophia Loren used her body seductively and transgressively to flout the law and dramatize, publicly and privately, her indifference to rules, as well as her competence in self-consciously performing a role to achieve her desires. Most conspicuously, her loud and disruptive articulations of outrage (characteristic also of Silvana Mangano's role in *La grande guerra* and

FIGURE 9.5 *Inverting, complicating, and exposing sexual taboos: Giancarlo Giannini and Paola Borboni in* Sessomatto *(1973). Courtesy of Photofest.*

Annie Girardot's performance in *I compagni* [*The Organizer*, Monicelli, 1963]) convert the female into a figure of power. These female performers in Italian comedy remove the man's mask for the viewer, as evident in Loren's different personas in films ranging from neorealism to *commedia all'italiana*. While some might say, following Laura Mulvey's early essay "Visual Pleasure and Narrative Cinema," that Loren's feminine image is emblematic of how the female is caged within the male (patriarchal) gaze, Mulvey herself has altered this view in her "Afterthoughts on Visual Pleasure," which seeks to account for the position of women as active and critical spectators within certain narrative forms. In *Ieri, oggi, domani*, Loren preforms a striptease for her panting customer, played by Marcello Mastroianni, as she exposes his voyeurism and reduces him to a childlike position before yet another viewer, the spectator, who laughs at him. This scene becomes a meta-commentary on woman as fetish.

7 The *Commedia* and the Historical Film

A decade later in the 1970s, the comedies and historical films of Lina Wertmüller also expose the ineptness of the Italian male figure, as they involve the female in reinforcing or disrupting his performance. Her *The Seduction of Mimì* and *Film d'amore e d'anarchia* (*Love and Anarchy*,

FIGURE 9.6 *Sophia Loren in her famous "striptease," with Marcello Mastroianni as viewer. Courtesy of Photofest.*

1973) are instances where the agents of exposure are women, played by Mariangela Melato in both films, along with Elena Fiore in the first and Lina Polito in the second. Melato's Salomè, a Roman prostitute, is indeed an "unruly woman" in appearance, behavior, and language, and she is instrumental in conspiring to assassinate Mussolini, thus she challenges the performative dimensions of masculinity as well as the power of the Fascist regime. *Pasqualino Settebellezze* (*Seven Beauties*, Wertmüller, 1975) is a quintessential example of the comic grotesque, a historical film that portrays Nazism, Italian Fascism, their perpetrators and collaborators, and the Holocaust. A small-time operator, Pasqualino (Giancarlo Giannini) is a deserter from the army and then captive in a German concentration camp, where he learns the art of survival at any cost from an imposing female concentration camp attendant. His "onore" (honor) is blatantly exposed as residing literally in his power to perform sexually upon her command as they engage in macabre physical relations. Pasqualino is reduced to an abject figure that sacrifices an ethical life in the name of bare survival.

The comedies of the late 1970s, Wertmüller's films prominently among them, appear during yet another crucial political moment in Italy: the *anni di Piombo*, Years of Lead, so called because of all the bullets fired in this time of political terrorism, culminating in the kidnapping and assassination in 1978 of the leading politician Aldo Moro. Alberto Sordi's role as the distraught father Giovanni Vivaldi in the tragi-comedy *Un borghese piccolo, piccolo* (*An Average Little Man*, Monicelli, 1976) captures the unsettled political climate of the 1970s that produced portraits of "sad aging monsters" indicative of the economic miracle becoming a horror story for many Italians.[24]

Historical narratives were (and continue to be) a rich source for comic scenarios, and Monicelli has provided significant examples of cinematic comedy as counter history in such films as *La grande guerra*, *I compagni*, *L'armata Brancaleone* (*For Love and Gold*, 1963), and *Brancaleone alle crociate* (*Brancaleone at the Crusades*, 1970). In *La grande guerra*, Monicelli treats the First World War in certain ways reminiscent of Kubrick's *Paths of Glory* (1957). If Kubrick's film is a surreal satire of war that highlights the rigidity of the officers and the expendability of the soldiers in the trenches, Monicelli's also highlights the brutality of war, but his comedy focuses on two unwilling draftees who through their wits try to avoid combat. Monicelli's selection of actors for his comedies was based on deglamorizing them and placing then in roles in which they are outcasts. Their ineptness masks cleverness to expose corruptions and undermine clichés and stereotypes. The counter history of Kubrick's *Paths of Glory* resides in its mundane and cynical treatment of protagonists and antagonists, as when Kubrick's General Mireau visits the troops and exposes his ineptness and cynicism in dealing with his oppressed soldiers ("Hello, soldier. Ready to kill more Germans?"). Similarly, the general's opportunism in *La grande guerra* is related to the commonplace manipulations that are part of warfare. Oreste Jacovacci and Giovanni Busacca, Monicelli's two protagonists, have no choice about serving in the army; consequently, they wittingly and unwittingly undermine army regulations, at times to disastrous effect. The comedy offers the viewer a version of history that not only inverts the patriotic myths and sentiments associated with war but also reigning conceptions of human agency, by indicating that even the ultimate heroic "choice" to withhold information from the enemy is fraught with failure.

Working in the generic mode identified with *commedia all'italiana*, Monicelli creates antiheroes, who are "inept, self-centered, shallow, yet often lovable."[25] He places them in absurd situations that often end in failure, portraying a "darker, more ironic, and cynical vision of Italian life."[26] The characters are no longer truthful; they are forgers, thieves, imposters, and confidence men, and truth becomes a matter not of judging their goodness or badness, but of the truthfulness of the storytelling itself. In fact, *commedia all'italiana* is often a saga of failure in contrast to heroic epic and romance.

Perhaps the most ambitious historical comedy identified with Monicelli's *commedia all'italiana* are the two Brancaleone films. Working again with

FIGURE 9.7 *The "rewards" of heroism in* The Great War *(1959), starring Alberto Sordi (front of frame) and Vittorio Gassman (behind him). Courtesy of Photofest.*

Agenore Incrocci and Furio Scarpelli as he had in *I compagni* and *La grande guerra*, Monicelli was able to plan and execute two difficult films that could be described as "mock epics." At the heart of Monicelli's comedy is a cinematic historian at work self-consciously, drawing on numerous canonical and popular literary sources for his medieval imagination: Dante, Cervantes, folklore, romance, and even film (e.g., *The Seventh Seal, Seven Samurai, The Good, the Bad and the Ugly*). The visual sources are eclectic: cartoons, ceremonial tableaux (in a montage of combat, wedding feasts, funeral rituals), and a cornucopia of caricatures of young females, moribund elderly males, as well as diseased and malformed figures derived from literary and cinematic sources. The verbal language is also eclectic, a mixture of various regional (often Sicilian dialects), Latinate and pseudo-Latinate constructions (*deus vult* and *deus non vult*), and foreign phrases.[27] The second Brancaleone film injects poetry into the dialogue: the characters begin to speak in rhymed couplets, another instance of the film's evocation of earlier heroic poems. But the "elevated" poetry is joined to prosaic, colloquial, even obscene language reminiscent of goliardic literature and its crude satiric characterizations. The influence of the *commedia dell'arte* is most obvious in Gassman's portrayal of Brancaleone, a figure reminiscent of the braggart captain. Brancaleone (which means literally the "lion's talon") is a descendant of picaresque literature, of Morgante, of Don Quixote and his squire Sancho Panza.

Adhering to the quest narrative, the films employ a journey form that permits an encyclopedic treatment of characters and situations. Its portrait of the Middle Ages as a parody of quest narratives might lead one to assume that it offers a negative picture of medievalism in contrast to enlightened modernity; but such a view would misconstrue the film's indebtedness to the moral quandaries of the mock epic. The films return to the past to demolish nostalgic portraits of both past and present. Instead of setting them in opposition to the present, the film finds parallels between them. Monicelli's historical comedies create images of the past through memory, recollection, and sensation to address the forms of thinking and behavior that have turned the world into what Gilles Deleuze calls a "bad film."[28]

Fellini's *Amarcord* (1974) is another instance of the differences among the various practitioners of *commedia all'italiana*, particularly in relation to historical film. The film's setting is the town of Rimini during the years of Fascism. It centers on the filmmaker's wary construction of that past, drawing on fragments of history, personal memory, legend, and myth to create a composite portrait of community life, family, sexuality, religion, and education. The figures involved are caricatures of certain social types, and "Fellini builds on their tics and eccentricities to paint a collective portrait of Fascism."[29] Fellini's complex humor resides in avoiding melodramatic binaries between villains and heroes, preferring instead to expose the adolescent, regressed, and repressed grotesque behavior of the populace in a form of comedy. This comedy is a form of counter history that exposes hypocrisy and authoritarianism through Horatian, not Juvenalian, satire, prodding and provoking cruel cinematic portraits of the populace in order to expose the fixated adolescent character of Fascism for contemporary audiences.

In discussions of the *commedia all'italiana*, there seems to be a consensus that the heyday of this comic form had waned by the end of the 1970s. Lanzoni refers to the directors and the comic actors of these films as the "Last of the Protagonists." Despite global production, shrinking funds, and uncertain markets, film directors from the 1980s to the present time like Robert Benigni, Maurizio Nichetti, Nanni Moretti, and Cristina Comencini, among other talented filmmakers, continue to produce comedies that have garnered international attention. All this has occurred despite the endless talk in the last decades about the so-called death of cinema in the digital age. However, to quote Deleuze, "the less human the world is, the more it is the artist's duty to believe and produce belief in a relation between man and the world."[30] The *commedia all'italiana* at its best awakened viewers to that relation, and the task of cinematic comedy in a new incarnation remains the creation of "an ethic or belief that makes idiots laugh, not a need to believe in something else, but a need to believe in this world of which fools are a part."[31]

Notes

1 See Nicoll, *Mimes, Masks, and Miracles*, 215–22.

2 Brunetta, *The History of Italian Cinema*, 39, 42.

3 See Landy, *Stardom Italian Style*, 7–15.

4 See Dalle Vacche, *Diva*.

5 Ricci, *Cinema and Fascism*, 58.

6 See Ben-Ghiat, *Fascist Modernities*, 85.

7 Ben-Ghiat, *Fascist Modernities*, 124.

8 Brunetta, *The History of Italian Cinema*, 115.

9 Bazin, *What Is Cinema*, 2:66.

10 Deleuze, *Cinema 2*, 1.

11 See, for example, *Don Camillo* (Duvivier, 1952) and *Don Camillo e l'onorevole Peppone* (*Don Camillo and the Honorable Peppone*, Gallone, 1955).

12 See Grignaffini, "Female Identity and the Italian Cinema of the 1950s," 278–79.

13 See Bini, "The Birth of Comedy Italian Style," 118–19.

14 Wood, *Italian Film*, 102.

15 See Landy, *Stardom Italian Style*, 140–44.

16 Giacovelli, *Breve storia del cinema comico in Italia*, 33.

17 Gili, *Alberto Sordi*, 59.

18 See Bini, "The Birth of Comedy Italian Style"; Giacovelli, *Breve storia del cinema comico in Italia*; and Lanzoni, *Comedy Italian Style*.

19 Bondanella, *The Films of Federico Fellini*, 25.

20 Lanzoni, *Comedy Italian Style*, 115.

21 Reich, *Beyond the Latin Lover*, 61–65.

22 Restivo, *Cinema of Economic Miracles*, 57.

23 See Lanzoni, *Comedy Italian Style*, 95–99.

24 Brunetta, *The History of Italian Cinema*, 185.

25 Bondanella, *Italian Cinema*, 145.

26 Bondanella, *Italian Cinema*, 145.

27 Brunetta, *The History of Italian Cinema*, 4, 97.

28 Deleuze, *Cinema 2*, 171.

29 Bondanella, *The Films of Federico Fellini*, 128.

30 Deleuze, *Cinema 2*, 171.

31 Deleuze, *Cinema 2*, 173.

Bibliography

Ben-Ghiat, Ruth. *Fascist Modernities: Italy, 1922–1945.* Berkeley: University of California Press, 2004.

Bini, Andrea. "The Birth of Comedy Italian Style." In *Popular Italian Cinema: Culture and Politics in a Postwar Society.* London: I.B. Tauris, 2011. 107–53.

Bondanella, Peter E. *Italian Cinema: From Neorealism to the Present.* New York: Continuum, 2001.

Bondanella, Peter E. *The Films of Federico Fellini.* Cambridge: Cambridge University Press. 2002.

Brunetta, Gian Piero. *The History of Italian Cinema: A Guide from Its Origins to the Twenty-First Century.* Trans. Jeremy Parzen. Princeton: Princeton University Press, 2003.

Dalle Vacche, Angela. *Diva: Defiance and Passion in Early Italian Cinema.* Austin: University of Texas Press, 2008.

Deleuze, Gilles. *Cinema 2: The Time-Image.* Trans. Hugh Tomlinson and Robert Galeta. Minneapolis: University of Minnesota Press, 1989.

Giacovelli, Enrico. *Breve storia del cinema comico in Italia.* Turin: Lindau, 2002.

Gili, Jean. "Alberto Sordi: J'ai toujours cherché à représenter la vie." *Positif* (June 2003): 59–61.

Grignaffini, Giovanna. "Female Identity and the Italian Cinema of the1950s." In *Off Screen: Women and Film in Italy.* Ed. Giuliana Bruno and Maria Nadotti. London: Routledge, 1998. 111–24.

Landy, Marcia. *Italian Film.* Cambridge: Cambridge University Press, 2000.

Landy, Marcia. *Stardom Italian Style: Screen Performance and Personality in Italian Cinema.* Bloomington: Indiana University Press, 2008.

Lanzoni, Rémi Fournier. *Comedy Italian Style: The Golden Age of Italian Film Comedies.* New York: Continuum, 2008.

Mulvey, Laura. *Visual and Other Pleasures.* Basingstoke, Hampshire: Palgrave Macmillan, 2009.

Nicoll, Allardyce. *Mimes, Masks, and Miracles: Studies in the Popular Theatre.* New York: Cooper Square, 1963.

Reich, Jacqueline. *Beyond the Latin Lover: Marcello Mastroianni, Masculinity, and Italian Cinema.* Bloomington: Indiana University Press, 2004.

Restivo, Angelo. *The Cinema of Economic Miracles: Visuality and Modernization in the Italian Art Film.* Durham: Duke University Press, 2002.

Rowe, Kathleen. *The Unruly Woman: Gender and the Genres of Laughter.* Bloomington: Indiana University Press, 2004.

Wood, Mary P. *Italian Cinema,* Oxford: Berg, 2005.

10

Popular Italian Cinema

Catherine O'Rawe

In 2014, the Oscar for Best Foreign Film went to Paolo Sorrentino's *La grande bellezza* (*The Great Beauty*, 2013). It was Italy's first such win since Roberto Benigni's *La vita è bella* (*Life Is Beautiful*) in 1998 and was widely seen as a redemptive moment for Italian cinema, which at the time was often perceived as having fallen into crisis after the artistic heydays of the postwar period and the 1960s. Even before the Oscar win, the status of *The Great Beauty* as art film was affirmed because of its auteur director Sorrentino (renowned for his visual style and previous collaborations with cinematographer Luca Bigazzi), its respected star actor (Toni Servillo), and its self-conscious references to Fellini's classics *La dolce vita* (1960) and *8 1/2* (1963). It is by now clear that the prestige of Italian cinema rests largely on international exports like *The Great Beauty*, which is in keeping with the choice of films screened at festivals, the material included in survey courses at universities (i.e., subtitled films by well-known directors), and academic or institutional interest in great auteurs and moments such as Italian neorealism.[1]

But the history of Italian cinema is not merely the history of the films that have been successfully exported (nor, as we will see, is it merely the history of films per se). As Rosalind Galt and Karl Schoonover remind us, "Art cinema is a resolutely international category, often a code for foreign film. While certain kinds of popular films can circulate globally (Hollywood, Hong Kong action films, Hindi films viewed by Indian diasporic audiences), for most countries, art cinema provides the only institutional context in which films can find audiences abroad."[2] Those films that are consumed primarily by domestic audiences have been relatively neglected in histories of Italian cinema. Yet recently attempts have been made to excavate the histories of Italian popular cinema, and to theorize the "popular" within the

Italian context. Often taught as a timeless and unchanging list of "great" works, the canon of Italian cinema is now being deconstructed, and its highly ideological nature uncovered. If narratives of Italian cinema have often rested on ideas of auteurist prestige and a return to the "masterpiece tradition" of national cinema, it is common today to find attention paid to popular Italian genres: cult genres or *filoni* such as the Spaghetti Western, the *poliziottesco* or cop film, the *giallo* or thriller, and the horror film have been reclaimed and studied.[3] Meanwhile, valuable work on early cinema by the likes of Angela Dalle Vacche and Giorgio Bertellini has demonstrated the international reach of cinema of this period, as well as its hybrid nature and its ability to complicate easy distinctions between art house and popular.[4] We have also seen a widening of the study of film and media to incorporate a broad range of cultural texts: television, new media, porn, and star studies are all expanding fields of research, while there has been welcome attention to cinema as an economic practice and to the relations of branding and consumption it generates.[5]

The move away from the study of the text in splendid isolation and the historical turn in film studies in the last fifteen years have meant that analysis of film reception, exhibition, and audience response can tell us much not merely about the spatial or geographic contexts within which film was produced and consumed, but also about what audiences do or did with films, the meanings they acquire within everyday life, and their place within a broader media flow.[6] In Italy, the interaction between spectator and film had been an object of great interest to left-wing film critics in the postwar period, especially with the decline of neorealism and the affirmation of cinema as the nation's most popular leisure activity in the 1950s. In particular, the influence of Antonio Gramsci has been widely felt within discussions of Italian cinema, particularly his desire for an intellectual caste that "can know and sense the needs and aspirations" of the people, and his regret for the absence of a national-popular culture in Italy, linked to the failure of intellectuals to "elaborate a modern 'humanism' able to reach right to the simplest and most uneducated classes."[7] Although Gramsci did not address cinema specifically, his views on the revolutionary potential of cultural practice were taken up by the left-wing film press of the postwar period, and their legacy has been a tendency to locate the "progressive catharsis," in Gramscian terms, of individual texts, or the precise degree of political commitment or *impegno* they exhibited. The way that, even today, discussions of popular genres and products inevitably spill over into anguished hand-wringing about the tastes of audiences has a long history in Italy and seems to revolve around an idea of the audience as passive and dangerously receptive to the threat of the allegedly toxic popular film. A good example of this is the 1955 debate in the Communist newspaper *L'Unità* on *cinema e popolo* (cinema and the people). The intervention of screenwriter, Gianni Puccini, is telling: "We must not confuse the public with the people, or a 'film for the public' with a 'popular film.'" Although popular production has validity, cautioned Puccini, we must remember that "the public is made up of pensioners, children, housewives, the petit bourgeoisie, and the sub-proletariat, rather than peasants and workers."[8] The problem groups identified (the young, housewives, the old, and petit bourgeoisie, and sub-proletariat) are not the *popolo* in the Gramscian sense of workers and peasants, but rather represent a mass culture that is to be distrusted.[9]

In the contemporary context this distrust still exists, and it is largely through scholarly approaches drawn from Anglo-American cultural studies that debates around popular versus mass culture have emerged. Such approaches "allow one to study how distinctions are produced and reproduced, and the ways in which such distinctions act to legitimate the tastes of dominant social groups."[10] They also enable an understanding of how mass culture itself is seen as "feminized" and often associated with a degraded consumer sphere.[11] The popular itself, in its material forms, is also nearly always nebulous, defined not so much by quantitative measures or by association with a putative *populus* but rather, as John Storey puts it, as "the culture that is left over when we have decided what is high culture." The popular is thus a "residual category, there to accommodate cultural texts and practices which fail to meet the required standards to qualify as high culture."[12]

This residual category of course incorporates the vast majority of the output of the Italian film industry over the course of its history, and it is true that "research and teaching on Italian cinema has predominantly followed the elitist pattern of concentrating on individual art-house auteurs, and on films in the neorealist style, as constituting the traditional canon, thereby ignoring not only most of Italy's film production, but also the viewing habits of the greater part of Italian cinema audiences."[13] When the residual, however, becomes the focus of the investigation, many of the commonsense assumptions of Italian film history are overturned, and we are able to cast a new light on well-worn tropes and categories. Looking at two key moments in Italian cinema, the postwar period and the contemporary one, and analyzing films and generic styles that have been little studied—and that do not fit neatly into art-house or (neo)realist classifications—can give us an insight into the viewing tastes of the Italian public, and help us understand how historical events and political change were and are negotiated. Examining these films through the lens of gender is extremely helpful in understanding some of the functions of the popular in responding to and negotiating political and social change. Although in a less dramatic vein than the postwar films, these contemporary films' engagement with the political is in the realm of affective relations and the domestic sphere, using familial and intergenerational comedy to address governmental crisis. Thus we should not understand the political charge of the popular as residing in its form or content, or indeed in the "engaged" stance of its auteur, but as Alan O'Leary argues, as "a cinema that articulates the concerns of people in their ordinariness."[14]

1 War, Resistance, Aftermath: Beyond Neorealism

A rather reductive critical opposition has prevailed between the neorealist films that documented the war, occupation, and Resistance—for example, *Roma città aperta* (*Rome, Open City*, Rossellini, 1945), *Paisà* (*Paisan*, Rossellini, 1946), *Ladri di biciclette* (*Bicycle Thieves*, De Sica, 1948)— and a popular filmmaking that is assumed to be incapable of intervening in debates on the state of the nation.[15] Most histories of postwar Italian cinema have insisted upon the close connection between neorealism and the representation of the Italian Resistance, neglecting the large amount of genre production that also undertook this representation. The equation between the Resistance and neorealism has been enduring, from French critic André Bazin's designation of the latter in 1948 as "the Italian school of the Liberation,"[16] to Millicent Marcus's more recent affirmation that it was "the cinematic offspring of the Resistance."[17] Gian Piero Brunetta's statement that "for some time, everyone hopped on the neorealist bandwagon [by using war and Resistance themes]" is indicative of the erasure of the many ways that different genres and styles of filmmaking used the Resistance experience.[18]

Due lettere anonime (*Two Anonymous Letters*) was released in November 1945 in an Italy only beginning to recover from the horrors of war and occupation. Directed by Mario Camerini, best known for his popular comedies of the 1930s starring Vittorio De Sica, it opens with the return of soldier Bruno (Andrea Checchi) to Rome from the Russian front after two years away, just prior to the Armistice in 1943. Thus the film anticipates one of the most widespread motifs of the postwar period, the return of the *reduce* or veteran, and his difficult reinsertion into national life. Ruth Ben-Ghiat has written extensively of the *reduce* as "shameful symbol" of the guilt and trauma of Fascism and of Italy's alliance with Nazism, as well as of its failed war.[19] She has discussed how the half a million soldiers deported to camps after the Armistice, and those who were imprisoned abroad, especially in Russia, were regarded as pariahs when they returned, and carried with them the symbolic task of expiating the sins of the Italian nation. Although in Camerini's film Bruno is returning before the Armistice, and thus before Italy's humiliating surrender, as with many other films of the late 1940s and early 1950s, the experiences abroad can never be directly narrated or described: Bruno refers to Russia as "over there," and merely mutters darkly of the German "allies" that "you had to be in Russia to know them."

However, the film's principal device for narrating the ideological conflict of the Armistice period, the choice of whether to become a partisan or a passive collaborator with the occupying Germans, is the melodramatic love triangle. Bruno returns home to find his girlfriend Gina (played by prewar diva Clara Calamai) in a relationship with Fascist collaborator Tullio (Otello Toso). So a political choice is dramatized as a romantic one, and it is for this reason that Brunetta describes the film as a "jumbled story of love, spies, jealousy and revenge."[20] The love triangle is a common device in films depicting the postwar return of the soldier, and works to elide ideological differences (both partisan and collaborator can be brought into complicated proximity through the body of the woman they share) and to encourage a narrative of ideological equivalence that might neutralize and expel a difficult past. The fact that the love triangle is typical of the schemes of melodrama means most of these films have been critically dismissed or ignored because of melodrama's relatively low critical status as a feminized mode. But the film alludes powerfully to the disruption of domestic life and the difficulty for the returning man to understand the new kinds of relations that have sprung up.

Two Anonymous Letters, importantly, gives narrative agency to Gina, who helps Bruno once he becomes a partisan, as women are able to move without suspicion around the city, and she makes a decisive intervention in the Resistance cause, shooting dead the traitor Tullio. Within the film narrative this gesture is misrecognized—in prison the other women laugh at the suggestion that Gina's crime was political and dismiss it as a crime of passion. But the film's ending on a melodramatic close-up of Gina's tear-stained face behind bars, after Bruno thanks her for saving the partisans, suggests that melodrama was a key means of elaborating the trauma and emotional confusion of the postwar period.[21]

Senza pietà (*Without Pity*), released in 1948, has been described as *neorealismo nero* (black or *noir* neorealism). This body of films, which includes Lattuada's *Il bandito* (*The Bandit*, 1946) and *Tombolo, paradiso nero* (*Tombolo*, Ferroni, 1947) mixes *noir* and realist conventions to depict the seedy aftermath of the war, generally featuring prostitutes, GIs, and black marketeers. As Wood says, it is a style in which "characters and mise-en-scène reflect the anxieties accompanying this massive social disruption."[22] The innocent relationship between the prostitute Angela (Carla del Poggio) and Jerry (played by African American ex-GI John Kitzmiller, who appeared in many Italian films) aligns prostitutes and black men as marginal, inferior subjects in postwar Italy. And the strategic use of jazz, boogie-woogie, and African American spirituals to complement the narrative of intermingling and Americanization of the period—also evident in a film like De Santis's much better known *Riso amaro* (*Bitter Rice*, 1949)—helps us think about how the soundtrack can also be a key method for popular film to reach the spectator affectively. As Danielle Hipkins has shown, the extraordinary recurrence of the female prostitute in films of this period is not merely a realist reflection of the state to which Italian women were reduced, but an overdetermined attempt to displace Italian collective guilt over Fascism and Nazism onto the body of the fallen woman, routinely assumed to stand in for the national body politic.[23] The death of outcast Angela in *Without Pity* after she whispers an *Ave Maria*, albeit in a hyperbolic register, references a powerful idea of sacrificial femininity that was also capable of resonating with the everyday wartime experiences of many Italian women.

In Eduardo De Filippo's *Napoli milionaria* (*Side Street Story*, 1950), based on his hugely successful 1945 play, similar ideas of guilt and postwar trauma are at play. In the second part of the film, Gennaro (De Filippo) returns to his home in Naples after over a year in a concentration camp. There he finds that his son has become a thief, his wife a black marketeer, and his daughter is pregnant by a GI. In addition to depicting anxiety about slippages in female behavior when Italian men were absent fighting or imprisoned, the film uses jazz and boogie-woogie, in a similar way to *Without Pity*, to show the threatening influence of American culture in the form of the soldiers stationed in Naples, and represents mixed-race children as an inevitable consequence of this fraternizing. Although it was shot in a studio, the film also shows how comedy mixes with realism by including documentary footage of the liberation of Naples. But the main note of *Side Street Story* is somber: as opposed to other *reduci* of Italian postwar cinema, Gennaro desperately tries to recount what he experienced but nobody wants to listen.

FIGURE 10.1 *Gennaro (Eduardo De Filippo) returns from war in* Napoli milionaria *(1950). Dir. Eduardo De Filippo, Italy. Dino de Laurentiis Cinematografica.*

Gennaro is frequently reminded by others that "the war is over," and their reluctance to confront the past is symptomatic of Italy's attempts to forget Fascism and collaboration with the Germans. The appearance in the film of popular Neapolitan stars Eduardo, Totò, Titina De Filippo, and Dante Maggio doubtless contributed to its success. Yet it is interesting to note that the film remains outside any canon of postwar Italian cinema, presumably because of its generic hybridity, even though its release sparked bitter polemics around the poor image of Naples it portrayed, in a similar vein to the polemics that raged around neorealism following the Andreotti Law of 1949.[24] Neorealism was accused by politicians of painting a negative picture of Italy, yet what is striking is how, in so many different registers and keys, Italian filmmaking was addressing the difficulties of the period, and the use of popular stars, music, and genre conventions should not blind us to the powerful interventions these films were making in contemporary society.

2 Comedy and the Politics of the Popular

Comedy has always been Italy's most popular genre, although only the "golden age" of *commedia all'italiana* of the 1960s has received serious and sustained critical interest. In recent years, comedy is still dominant at the Italian box office: Casetti and Salvemini's 2007 industrial and market analysis of recent Italian cinema claimed that the indigenous film industry was in relatively rude health, and that in fact "Italian cinema seems to be blooming in this new era," thanks largely to Italian-made comedies.[25] In fact, Fabrizio Montanari has argued convincingly that comedy ought to be considered Italy's "national" cinematic genre, based both on its commercial popularity, and on its ability to "touch on themes that are particular to and very close to the culture."[26] As further proof of the popularity of Italian comedy, a study of young Italian spectators in 2008 found that both male and female viewers declared their favorite genre to be "comic films starring Italian actors."[27] More recent reports also confirm that Italian cinema's ability to hold its own at the domestic box office is largely due to films that "have been increasingly successful at satisfying the tastes of the public."[28] Of the thirty top-grossing Italian films between 2010 and 2012, all but one can be described as comedies. Most of these films are "inexportable," including the grotesque, ribald, and hugely popular *cinepanettoni* or Christmas films.[29] In 2016, the vehicle for comic star Checco Zalone (Luca Medici), *Quo vado?* (directed by Gennaro Nunziante) broke Italian box office records with takings of over €60 million, yet few spectators outside of Italy will have heard of Zalone or the film.

In the last few years there has also been a "rediscovery of politics" on the part of Italian comic films,[30] as popular comedies are thought able to "explain the phenomena that even political analysts struggle to interpret."[31] The perceived "crisis" of Italian politics—the left's perennial failure to mount a coherent challenge to Silvio Berlusconi's center-right coalition, and the power vacuum created by the eventual resignation of Berlusconi in 2011—gave rise to several films that take as their premise this idea of political crisis in a variety of comic registers. These films address the recent political upheaval in Italy using familiar comic tropes, but also mobilize a register of male melodrama that is very common to Italian cinema, relying on sympathetic treatments of nostalgia and male melancholy, father-son conflicts, and generational difficulties to suggest a relationship between political crisis (or the crisis of the left) and a diffuse crisis of masculinity.

Viva la libertà (*Long Live Freedom*, Andò, 2013) was the most acclaimed of the three films, not least because it starred Toni Servillo, Italy's most critically praised actor, as the twin brothers Giovanni and Enrico Ernani. The film describes how Enrico, leader of the opposition party (a facsimile of the Italian Democratic Party), becomes depressed at catastrophic personal ratings and escapes to France to visit his old love, Danielle (Valeria Bruni Tedeschi). His philosopher brother, Giovanni, recently released from a mental health facility, takes over his role as party leader, unbeknownst to the electorate, and is, of course, a huge hit. The Pirandellian plot, in which ingenuous Giovanni's uncensored pronouncements win popular support and at the film's end neither his aides nor the audience is sure of which brother is installed as leader, has been likened by critics to *Totò terzo uomo* (*Totò the Third Man*, Mattoli, 1951) as well as to such American films as *Mister Smith Goes to Washington* (Capra, 1939) and *Dave* (Reitman, 1993). The film relies upon a repertoire of high-culture references to cement its serious intentions: Giovanni (improbably) wows a rally by intoning a Brecht poem, plays Schubert on the piano, and quotes Hegel and Epimenedes. Meanwhile, Enrico helps out on a film in France, and Danielle's husband, it transpires, is the revered film director known as "Mung" (Danielle whispers to Enrico that her husband is "worshipped like a rock star"). As Andrea Minuz points out, the film "is the drama of the educated, reflexive, conformist middle class of the last thirty years, which wanted to govern a country that it didn't know . . . [and] which imagined an Italy ready to adapt itself to its habits, to its books, to its films. [An Italy that] exalted Brecht and the films of Mung."[32]

However, the film also offers a vision that is familiar from much Italian cinema, of middle-aged masculinity in crisis, through the mode of male melodrama. Male melodrama foregrounds the suffering man, and takes for granted audience sympathy for him, illustrating that "melancholia has historically been a culturally privileged form of ethos" for men.[33] Giovanni's depression is a source of creativity (inspiring his philosophical treatise, *L'illusione di vivere*, or *The Illusion of Living*), while sad Enrico is inexplicably attractive to a much younger French girl, Marà, who invites him to go swimming naked with her and who admiringly murmurs before they kiss: "You always give the impression that you feel out of place." In fact, Enrico's final epiphany as he leaves France to return from exile centers on the memory of Mara's naked body. This ecstatic flashback is an analog of the epiphanic moment in another acclaimed Italian film, the Oscar-winning *The Great Beauty*, where the middle-aged protagonist, also played by Servillo, ends the film with a melancholy flashback to his youth, and the "great beauty" of the title is, arguably, revealed as the naked breasts of his first love.

The extent to which the crisis of the left, crisis of masculinity, and crisis of Italian cinema *tout court* are felt to be intertwined has been noted by Minuz, and the photo that adorns Enrico's office of former Communist Party leader, of Enrico Berlinguer—the last left-wing Italian leader to enjoy popular consensus in the 1970s and early 1980s—speaks to a feeling of nostalgia for a bygone era of left-wing solidarity. Such nostalgia finds an outlet in a more mainstream comedy *Benvenuto presidente!* (*Welcome Mr. President*, Milani, 2013) starring popular film and TV comedian Claudio Bisio. Bisio's character, Giuseppe Garibaldi, finds himself accidentally elected President of Italy due to his propitious name. Like Giovanni Ernani, he is a truth-telling naïf who represents the innocence of the Italian people that has been corrupted by decades of state vulgarity. Once again, culture is represented as the bulwark against decadence, as we open with Garibaldi, a rural librarian, acting out Alessandro Manzoni's classic nineteenth-century novel *The Betrothed* with some local children. His dream when he becomes president is not to avail of the television actresses or soubrettes laid on for him, but merely to visit the library of the Quirinal, Italy's version of the White House.

The shadow of Berlusconi (again, never mentioned) falls heavy on the film, especially in the scene where secret service agents are desperate to expose Giuseppe in a scandal, and so trail him to the house of an underage scantily clad girl, only to be disappointed when he merely urges her to take her high school exams and reproaches her that at nine years old she was reading the nineteenth-century Italian poet Ugo Foscolo. The film is, however, also playful about the supposed crisis of Italian cinema: when Giuseppe is brought to meet the "Dark Powers" who really run Italy, in place of the shadowy secret service figures he expects—common to Italian political conspiracy films—waiting for him are the directors Lina Wertmüller and Pupi Avati as well as well-known film critics Steve Della Casa and Gianni Rondolino, all playing themselves.

Although Bisio's character stands for a return to family values and the traditions of rural Italy (constantly repeating his grandfather's sententious sayings), the mechanisms of the comedy again revolve around the melodramatized male, as we see conflict with his son, his nostalgic desire to return to the homosocial bonds of his youth, and the film's sympathetic depiction of male crisis and self-doubt. While Giuseppe's popular appeal is dramatized, as in *Long Live Freedom*, by having ordinary Italians watch his speeches delightedly on TV, the alternative Constitution he proposes, that of the *italiano medio* or ordinary Italian man, makes it clear to what extent this "universal" comedy is gendered (and heteronormative): "Article 1, law of the bar: if a woman wearing a skirt climbs a ladder above a man with eyes, the man looks."[34]

The truth-telling in which politicians engage in these films is decidedly nonideological, consisting of humanist maxims or appeals to basic morality. Such is the case also with *Viva l'Italia* (*Long Live Italy!* Bruno, 2012), in which Michele Placido plays Michele Spagnolo, a corrupt politician (this time on the center-right) whose family values platform is exposed as a sham when he suffers a stroke during a night with a call girl, the effects of which are to render him unable to tell lies. The "truth" that Placido's character reveals relates mainly to the practices of corruption, nepotism, and *raccomandazione* that beset Italian politics and public life, a subject also tackled in a recent comedy, *C'è chi dice no* (*Some Say No*, Avellino, 2011). But *Long Live Italy!* tackles quite directly one of the darkest stains of the recent Berlusconi governments, the mismanagement and corruption that hampered the aftermath of the 2009 earthquake in L'Aquila. Placido's character takes his corrupt son to visit the ruins of the town and admits that he took a bribe to award the building contract for one of the jerry-built apartment blocks that collapsed. The episode is a rare (and very dark) direct commentary on recent political events on the part of Italian popular comedy, which generally prefers to remain indirect in its critique.

Like Bisio's character in *Welcome Mr. President!* Placido proposes a new article of the Constitution, this time that "all citizens have the right to know the truth," and again the fractured nation is brought together as they watch his oration on television. As with *Long Live Freedom*, a portrait of Berlinguer looms large over the stage as Placido speaks, though it is also flanked by a portrait of 1970s center-right leader Aldo Moro, perhaps expressing a nostalgia for lost ideological certainties.

FIGURE 10.2 *Michele Placido as politician Michele Spagnolo in* Long Live Italy! *(2012). Dir. Massimiliano Bruni, Italy. Italian International Film/Rai Cinema.*

As with almost all Italian comedy, the film mixes modes, moving from slapstick and the grotesque (it has been dubbed by Guido Vitiello a "civic cinepanettone"), to the generational comedy (stars Raoul Bova and Ambra Angiolini had previously appeared together in hit thirty-something comedies *Immaturi* [*The Immature*, Genovese, 2011] and *Immaturi: Il viaggio* [*The Immature: The Trip*, Genovese, 2012]), and finally to the male melodrama we have already identified in the previous two films examined.[35] So, for example, Placido's male crisis is exposed through his conflictual relationship with his children, as well as his nostalgic revelation that the only woman he ever really loved was his boyhood love Teresa, a girl from his village. What all three films have in common is that in their address to the Italian audience about a corrupt and degraded political system, they postulate that the middle-aged man, the *italiano medio* of the Italian comic tradition, is both the cause of these problems as well as their solution. The male melodrama of Italian cinema reminds us that "to speak of crisis and of crisis-of-the-left is to speak of the same things."[36] I would also argue that to speak of crisis in Italian cinema is always to speak of crisis masculinity.

As we have seen, the popular is extremely difficult to define, and its terms are unstable: "popular" is often used as a synonym for "genre cinema" in academic discourse, the conceptual boundaries of popular and mass culture often become confused, and none of this terminology maps onto industrial practice, or indeed onto audience understanding of films.

The influential American film historian David Bordwell recently argued that film does not reflect social reality, nor a national mood, and that to think so "assumes that popular culture is the audience talking to itself, without interference or distortion from the makers and the social institutions they inhabit."[37] Rather than any "reflectionist" view of the relation between film texts and lived reality, I propose that we should acknowledge the ways in which popular films are often recapitulating, recasting, and intervening in recent events, and how often the filmic representation of those events is cast in gendered terms, and thus demands a gender-informed reading. Emphasis on the gendered dimensions of screen representation and performance helps us to understand how star bodies might articulate or make visible preoccupations with masculinity or femininity that may be circulating in a culture, and might also be shaping those preoccupations in specific directions. Studying two moments of intense social change in Italy—the postwar period and the post-Berlusconi period—demonstrates how inexportable and "marginal" films are often working to present collective experiences.

By using hyperbolic affective and comic registers with popular appeal, the popular film constructs versions of national life that may be contestable, but that are ultimately, for their audiences, recognizable.

Notes

1   See the British Film Institute's Pasolini retrospective in 2013; see also the season run in 2013 by the British Film Institute on The Roots of Neorealism. The enduring hegemony of neorealism has seen seven monographs published in the last few years on the topic by American and UK scholars: see Haaland, *Italian Neorealist Cinema*; Giovacchini and Sklar, *Global Neorealism*; Schoonover, *Brutal Vision*; Gelley, *Stardom and the Aesthetics of Neorealism*; Minghelli, *Landscape and Memory in Post-Fascist Italian Film*; Scala and Rossini, *New Trends in Italian Cinema*; and Coleman, *Filming the Nation*.

2   Galt and Schoonover, "Introduction," 7. As Eagleton argues, "to claim that a work belongs to high culture is to claim among other things that it has an inherent portability, a sort of built-in detachability from its context," whereas popular cultural products are "blatantly particular" (*The Idea of Culture*, 53–54).

3   See, for example, Fisher, *Radical Frontiers in the Spaghetti Western*; Marlow-Mann, "Strategies of Tension"; Koven, *La Dolce Morte*; Willis, "Italian Horror Cinema."

4   Dalle Vacche, *Diva*; and Bertellini, *Italian Silent Cinema*.

5   See Masoero, *Product placement, teenpic e adolescenti 2.0*; Cucco and Richeri, *Il mercato delle location cinematografiche*.

6   See Fanchi and Mosconi, *Spettatori*; and Gennari, Hipkins, and O'Rawe, "In Search of Italian Cinema Audiences in the 1940s and 1950s."

7   Gramsci, "Concept of National-Popular," 367, 369.

8   Gianni Puccini, "È necessaria una critica più profonda e sottile."

9   For further details see O'Rawe, "I padri e i maestri." We could trace an interesting and complex history of attempts to come to terms with the problematic tastes of the Italian mass public: for example, in 1956 and 1958 film journal *Bianco e nero* published a survey by Luca Pinna in response to the supposed crisis of Italian cinema, and sent researchers to rural Sardinia to examine popular taste. What is perhaps most interesting in this fascinating report is that before the detailed questions and interviews about their cinema-going habits, the inhabitants of this town were subjected to a variety of high-culture classic films such as *Paisà* (*Paisan*, Rossellini, 1946), *Battleship Potemkin* (Eisenstein, 1925), and *Man of Aran* (Flaherty, 1934), plus one Italian genre film. The purpose of showing them these films was to ascertain from the get-go whether the public was "capable of judgment based on attention rather than emotion," that is, to see if they were in possession of rational or critical faculties. See Pinna, MacLean, and Guidacci, *Due anni col pubblico cinematografico*. The well-meaning distrust of the public has, in my view, characterized attempts to evaluate popular film taste over the decades.

10   Willis, "Cultural Studies and Popular Film," 175.

11   On mass culture as feminized, see Huyssen, "Mass Culture as Woman."

12   Storey, "What is Popular Culture?" 6.

13 Günsberg, *Italian Cinema*, 18.

14 O'Leary, "Political/Popular Cinema," 108.

15 This opposition is complicated by the fact that the aforementioned films were all relatively successful at the box office, with *Rome, Open City*, in particular, topping the 1945 box office.

16 Bazin, "An Aesthetic of Reality."

17 Marcus, *Italian Film in the Light of Neorealism*, xiv.

18 Brunetta, *The History of Italian Cinema*, 140.

19 Ben-Ghiat, "The Secret Histories of Roberto Benigni's *Life is Beautiful*," 256. On the prevalence of the returning soldier in postwar melodrama, see my "Back for Good."

20 Brunetta, *Cent'anni di cinema italiano*, 2:83.

21 See Wood's view that the "affective charge" of melodrama needs to be considered as a means of restoring complexity in representations of the postwar period (*Italian Cinema*, 207).

22 Wood, "Chiaroscuro," 159.

23 Hipkins, "Were Sisters Doing It for Themselves?"

24 On the Andreotti Law, see Wagstaff, *Italian Neorealist Cinema*, 15–17. On the reception of De Filippo's film, see Montariello, *La Napoli milionaria di Eduardo De Filippo*.

25 Casetti and Salvemini, "Dove va il cinema italiano?" 3.

26 Montanari, "I film nelle sale," 25.

27 See http://www.anica.it/online/attachments/032_anica_doxa_2008.pdf (accessed March 20, 2017).

28 Niola, "Italia, come è cambiato il cinema in 10 anni," *Wired Italia*.

29 See O'Leary, *Fenomenologia del cinepanettone*, for an in-depth analysis of the *cinepanettone*.

30 Morgoglione, "Saggio e naif, Bisio al Quirinale."

31 Roy Menarini, "La commedia del potere," March 24, 2013.

32 Minuz, *Quando c'eravamo noi*, 37. On the film's oblique evocation of Berlusconi, see Lombardi, "*Viva la libertà*," 404.

33 Modleski, "Clint Eastwood and Male Weepies," 140.

34 See Rigoletto, "The Italian Comedy of the Economic Miracle," on the ways in which Italian comedy works to naturalize the specifically gendered (male) and heterosexual *italiano medio*.

35 Vitiello, "Re folli, capri espiatori e spiriti dei defunti."

36 Minuz, *Quando c'eravamo noi*, 6–7.

37 Bordwell, "Zip, Zero, Zeitgeist."

Bibliography

Bazin, André. "An Aesthetic of Reality: Cinematic Realism and the Italian School of the Liberation." Vol. 2. *What Is Cinema?* 2 vols. Tans. Hugh Gray. Berkeley: University of California Press, 2005.

Ben-Ghiat, Ruth. "The Secret Histories of Roberto Benigni's *Life is Beautiful*." *Yale Journal of Criticism* 14.1 (2001).

Bertellini, Giorgio, ed. *Italian Silent Cinema: A Reader*. New Barnet: John Libbey Publishing, 2013.

Bordwell, David. "Zip, Zero, Zeitgeist." In *Observations on Film Art* (August 24, 2014) http://www.davidbordwell.net/blog/2014/08/24/zip-zero-zeitgeist/. Accessed March 20, 2017.

British Film Institute. Pasolini Retrospective. http://www.bfi.org.uk/sites/bfi.org.uk/files/downloads/bfi-press-release-pier-paolo-pasolini-2013-02.pdf. Accessed April 7, 2017.

British Film Institute. The Roots of Neorealism. http://www.bfi.org.uk/news-opinion/sight-sound-magazine/features/deep-focus/roots-neorealism. Accessed March 20, 2017.

Brunetta, Gian Piero. *Cent'anni di cinema italiano*. 2 vols. Bari: Laterza, 2003.

Brunetta, Gian Piero. *The History of Italian Cinema: A Guide to Italian Film from Its Origins to the Twenty-First Century*. Trans. Jeremy Parzen. Princeton: Princeton University Press, 2009.

Casetti, Francesco and Severino Salvemini. "Dove va il cinema italiano?" In *È tutto un altro film: Più coraggio e più idee per il cinema italiano*. Ed. Francesco Casetti and Severino Salvemini. Milan: Egea, 2007.

Coleman, Donatella Spinelli. *Filming the Nation: Jung, Film, Neo-Realism and Italian National Identity*. New York: Routledge, 2012.

Cucco, Marco and Giuseppe Richeri. *Il mercato delle location cinematografiche*. Venice: Marsilio, 2013.

Dalle Vacche, Angela. *Diva: Defiance and Passion in Early Italian Cinema*. Austin: University of Texas Press, 2008.

Eagleton, Terry. *The Idea of Culture*. Oxford: Blackwell, 2000.

Fanchi, Mariagrazia and Elena Mosconi, ed. *Spettatori: Forme di consumo e pubblici del cinema in Italia, 1930–1960*. Venice: Marsilio, 2002.

Fisher, Austin. *Radical Frontiers in the Spaghetti Western: Politics, Violence and Popular Italian Cinema*. London: I.B. Tauris, 2011.

Galt, Rosalind and Karl Schoonover. "Introduction: the Impurity of Art Cinema." In *Global Art Cinema*. Ed. Rosalind Galt and Karl Schoonover. Oxford: Oxford University Press, 2010.

Gelley, Ora. *Stardom and the Aesthetics of Neorealism: Ingrid Bergman in Rossellini's Italy*. New York: Routledge, 2012.

Gennari, Daniela Treveri, Danielle Hipkins, and Catherine O'Rawe. "In Search of Italian Cinema Audiences in the 1940s and 1950s: Gender, Genre and National Identity." *Participations, Journal Of Audiences and Reception Studies* 8.2 (November 2011). http://www.participations.org/Volume%208/Issue%202/3l%20Treveri%20et%20al.pdf. Accessed March 20, 2017.

Giovacchini, Saverio and Robert Sklar, eds. *Global Neorealism: The Transnational History of a Film Style*. Jackson: University Press of Mississippi, 2012.

Gramsci, Antonio. "Concept of National-Popular." In *The Gramsci Reader: Selected Writings, 1916–1935*. Ed. David Forgacs. New York: New York University Press, 2000.

Günsberg, Maggie. *Italian Cinema: Gender and Genre*. Basingstoke: Palgrave, 2005.

Haaland, Torunn. *Italian Neorealist Cinema*. Edinburgh: Edinburgh University Press, 2012.

Hipkins, Danielle. "Were Sisters Doing It for Themselves? The Sister-prostitute and Discredited Masculinity in Post-war Italian Cinema." In *War-Torn Tales: Representing Gender and World War II in Literature and Film*. Ed. Danielle Hipkins and Gill Plain. Oxford: Peter Lang, 2007.

Huyssen, Andreas. "Mass Culture as Woman: Modernism's Other." In *After the Great Divide: Modernism, Mass Culture, Postmodernism*. Bloomington: Indiana University Press, 1986.

Koven, Mikel. *La Dolce Morte: Vernacular Cinema and the Italian Giallo Film*. London: Scarecrow Press, 2006.

Lombardi, Giancarlo. "*Viva la libertà*: Language, Politics, and Consensus." In *Italian Political Cinema: Public Life, Imaginary, and Identity in Contemporary Italian Film*. Ed. Giancarlo Lombardi and Christian Uva. Bern: Peter Lang, 2016. 399–408.

Marcus, Millicent. *Italian Film in the Light of Neorealism*. Princeton: Princeton University Press, 1986.

Marlow-Mann, Alex. "Strategies of Tension: Towards a Re-interpretation of Enzo G. Castellari's *The Big Racket* and the Italian Crime Film." In *Popular Italian Cinema*. Ed. Louis Bayman and Sergio Rigoletto. Basingstoke: Palgrave Macmillan, 2013.

Masoero, Francesco. *Product placement, teenpic e adolescenti 2.0*. Turin: Kaplan, 2012.

Menarini, Roy. "La commedia del potere" (March 24, 2013). http://www.mymo vies.it/film/2013/buongiornopresidente/news/lacommediadelpotere. Accessed March 20, 2017.

Minghelli, Giuliana. *Landscape and Memory in Post-Fascist Italian Film: Cinema Year Zero*. New York: Routledge, 2013.

Minuz, Andrea. *Quando c'eravamo noi. Nostalgia e crisi della Sinistra nel cinema italiano: da Berlinguer a Checco Zalone*. Soveria Manelli: Rubbettino, 2014.

Modleski, Tania. "Clint Eastwood and Male Weepies." In *American Literary History* 22.1 (2009).

Montanari, Fabrizio. "I film nelle sale." In Casetti and Salvemini, *È tutto un altro film*.

Montariello, Carlo. *La Napoli milionaria di Eduardo De Filippo*. Naples: Liguori, 2008.

Morgoglione, Claudia. "Saggio e naif, Bisio al Quirinale." *La Repubblica* (March 13, 2013).

Niola, Gabriele. "Italia, come è cambiato il cinema in 10 anni." *Wired Italia* (July 15, 2013). http://daily.wired.it/news/cultura/2013/07/15/cinema-italiano-numeri-47893.html. Accessed March 20, 2017.

O'Leary, Alan. *Fenomenologia del cinepanettone*. Soveria Mannelli: Rubbettino, 2013.

O'Leary, Alan. "Political/Popular Cinema." In *Italian Political Cinema: Public Life, Imaginary, and Identity in Contemporary Italian Film*. Ed. Giancarlo Lombardi and Christian Uva. Oxford: Peter Lang, 2016.

O'Rawe, Catherine. "'I padri e i maestri': Genre, Auteurs and Absences in Italian Film Studies." *Italian Studies* 63.2 (2008): 173–94.

O'Rawe, Catherine. "Back for Good: Melodrama and the Returning Soldier in Post-war Italian Cinema." *Modern Italy* 22.2 (2017).

Pinna, Luca, Malcolm S. MacLean, and Margherita Guidacci, *Due anni col pubblico cinematografico*. Rome: Edizioni Bianco e Nero, 1958.

Puccini, Gianni. "È necessaria una critica più profonda e sottile." *L'Unità* (April 24, 1956).

Rigoletto, Sergio. "The Italian Comedy of the Economic Miracle: *L'italiano medio* and Strategies of Gender Exclusion." In *Italy on Screen: National Identity and the Italian Imaginary*. Ed. Lucy Bolton and Christina Siggers Manson. Oxford: Peter Lang, 2010.

Scala, Carmela and Antonio Rossini, eds. *New Trends in Italian Cinema: "New" Neorealism*. Newcastle: Cambridge Scholars Press, 2013.

Schoonover, Karl. *Brutal Vision: The Neorealist Body in Postwar Italian Cinema*. Minneapolis: University of Minnesota Press, 2012.

Storey, John. "What Is Popular Culture?" In *Cultural Theory and Popular Culture*. Harlow: Pearson, 2006.

Vitiello, Guido. "Re folli, capri espiatori e spiriti dei defunti. Appunti (quasi) antropologici sui politici nel cinema italiano" (April 30, 2014), https://guidovi tiello.com/2014/04/30/re-folli-capri-espiatori-e-spiriti-dei-defunti-appunti-qua si-antropologici-sui-politici-nel-cinema-italiano. Accessed March 20, 2017.

Wagstaff, Christopher. *Italian Neorealist Cinema: An Aesthetic Approach*. Toronto: University of Toronto Press, 2007.

Willis, Andy. "Cultural Studies and Popular Film." In *Approaches to Popular Film*. Ed. Joanne Hollows and Mark Jancovich. Manchester: Manchester University Press, 1999.

Willis, Andy. "Italian Horror Cinema: Between Art and Exploitation." In *Italian Cinema: New Directions*. Ed. William Hope. Oxford: Peter Lang, 2005.

Wood, Mary. *Italian Cinema*. Oxford: Berg, 2005.

Wood, Mary. "Chiaroscuro: the Half-Glimpsed *Femme Fatale* of Italian *Film Noir*." In *The Femme Fatale: Images, Histories, Contexts*. Ed. Helen Hanson and Catherine O'Rawe. Basingstoke: Palgrave Macmillan, 2010.

Filmography

Due lettere anonime (*Two Anonymous Letters*), Dir. Mario Camerini, Italy. Lux-Ninfa. 1945.

Senza pietà (*Without Pity*), Dir. Alberto Lattuada, Italy. Lux Film. 1948.

Napoli milionaria (*Side Street Story*), Dir. Eduardo De Filippo, Italy. Dino de Laurentiis Cinematografica. 1950.

La grande bellezza (*The Great Beauty*), Dir. Paolo Sorrentino, Italy. Indigo Film/Medusa Film/Babe Films. 2013.

Viva l'Italia (*Long Live Italy!*). Dir. Massimiliano Bruni, Italy. Italian International Film/Rai Cinema. 2012.

Viva la libertà (*Long Live Freedom*), Dir. Roberto Andò, Italy. Bibi Film/Rai Cinema. 2013.

Benvenuto presidente! (*Welcome Mr. President*), Dir. Riccardo Milani. Indigo Film/ Rai Cinema. 2013.

11

Italian Film Theory, 1907–2015

Gabriele Pedullà

The best Italian film theory is still unknown abroad.[1]
—GUIDO ARISTARCO

Compared to its Anglophone, French, and German counterparts, Italian film theory has long suffered from a linguistic marginality, which too often has limited its international circulation. Outside Italy, the best-known theorists are either famous filmmakers (e.g., Roberto Rossellini, Cesare Zavattini, and Pier Paolo Pasolini), renowned philosophers and writers who occasionally devoted some isolated thoughts to cinema (Filippo Tommaso Marinetti, Luigi Pirandello, Antonio Gramsci, Galvano Della Volpe, Umberto Eco, Gianni Vattimo, and Giorgio Agamben), or film critics who at a certain moment of their lives adopted either French or English for their texts (Ricciotto Canudo and Francesco Casetti). Although only partially known to English and American readers, Italian film theory was extremely creative during the twentieth century, and often opened new roads that only later became relevant in international discourse. For this reason, it deserves a fresh look today.[2]

1 The Pioneers

Italian film theory enjoys an undisputed primacy: the first essay on the aesthetics of the new cinematic art published in any Western language appeared in the Turin daily newspaper *La Stampa* on May 18, 1907. It was entitled "Filosofia del cinema" (Philosophy of Cinema) and was signed by a young writer, the Florentine Giovanni Papini (1881–1956), who at that time had won a certain renown for a collection of short stories that would ensure him the honor of being the only Italian selected by Argentine writer Jorge Luis Borges for his famous anthology of fantastic literature. After the First World War, Papini converted to Catholicism and published a heavily anti-Semitic *Storia di Cristo* (*Life of Jesus*, 1922) destined to quickly sell more than a million copies and become an international best seller (for some time even Charlie Chaplin considered the idea of making a film based on it). But in 1907, Papini was still in love with French culture and in touch with modern culture, as would not be the case in subsequent years. "Filosofia del cinema" reflects then the extraordinary openness to the most diverse influences that characterized the first part of his life.

In the face of the growing diffusion of picture houses that "threaten little by little to oust theatres, just as trams have ousted public coaches," Papini's "Filosofia del cinema" discusses the new form of film entertainment coming from France and argues for its importance. First of all, the essay claims, with its "impression of reality" film competes with theater no less than with the news, making "the most unlikely fantasies" possible thanks to special effects.[3] At the same time, however, film satisfies the need to travel and know the world without moving from home.

If for Papini, the moving image was the medium par excellence of modern life in general, his interest for the new art form was not isolated. Until the First World War, the Italian film industry was one of the largest in Europe, and it was in Italy that some great formal innovations were carried out, from the first experiments in abstract cinema by the Futurists Bruno Corra and Arnaldo Ginna to *Cabiria* (1914), Giovanni Pastrone's historical blockbuster that was so important for the evolution of D. W. Griffith's style. In this lively context, two major Italian film theorists of the first half of the century took their first steps: Ricciotto Canudo (1877–1923) and Sebastiano Arturo Luciani (1884–1950).

A native of Bari, Canudo is by far the better known of the two. Dramatist, novelist, essayist, and pianist, Canudo decided to move permanently to Paris around 1902, to what was at the time the cultural capital of the West. In the first twenty years of the twentieth century, many Italian writers (Gabriele D'Annunzio, Ardengo Soffici, Filippo Tommaso Marinetti, Giuseppe Ungaretti, Alberto Savinio) and artists (Medardo Rosso, Amedeo Modigliani, Giorgio De Chirico) also spent much time in France. However, just Canudo chose to write mainly in French and, having become part of the intellectual avant-garde, he soon was recognized as one of the most ardent advocates of the new cinematic art. As the French director Jean Epstein wrote in 1926, commemorating him after his premature death, Canudo deserved more than anyone else the title of "father" of film aesthetics.[4]

If Canudo's best-known texts are undoubtedly those written in French at the beginning of the 1920s, starting with his "Manifeste des sept arts" ("Reflections on the Seventh Art," 1923), all his fundamental ideas date back to the early years of the century and can be found in a series of essays written in Italian. Of great importance is above all "Trionfo del cinematografo" ("Triumph of Cinema"), which appeared in *Nuovo giornale* (November 25, 1908). Here Canudo spoke of cinema as a "New Temple" for the twentieth century, capable of spreading a collective ritual in which religious feast and "aesthetic oblivion" were united. And he had no doubts about the divinity to which this temple should be consecrated: "We have created a new goddess, for our Olympus: this goddess is Speed."[5]

These ideas on modern daily life's mechanization were widespread in the avant-garde and found their most famous formulation in the "Futurist Manifesto" (February 1909). However, Canudo's "Triumph of Cinema" contains two other important theses. One is that art is always stylization and not mere representation, and that the great novelty of cinema consists therefore in its ability to carry out the process of symbolization without renouncing its penchant for movement. While previously art was considered the "stylization of life in immobility" and able to focus only on partial aspects depending on the discipline practiced, in movies "real life is represented in a supreme way, and is carefully 'stylized' in speed." "The bad painter," Canudo argues, "copies the lines and imitates the colors; the great artist lays down a cosmic soul in a plastic form." In the same way, contrary to photography, cinema shows a precise will to go beyond the surface and overcome the limits imposed by mechanical reproduction.

The second key thesis of "Triumph of Cinema" is that cinema has the power to reconcile "theatre and museum, the joy of the show and that of aesthetic contemplation." Here Canudo refers to a famous distinction made by German playwright and philosopher Gotthold Ephraim Lessing, who in his famous *Laocoön* (1766) had divided artistic disciplines into "rhythms of Space" (architecture, sculpture, painting) and "rhythms of time" (music, poetry). In Canudo's view, cinema was finally able to restore unity by creating a new form of aesthetic experience that in his words possesses all the traits of the *Artwork of the Future* (1849) theorized by Richard Wagner for his operas. In fact, such a reconciliation, continues "Trionfo del cinematografo," had already been attempted by the theater, "but it was ephemeral, because the plastic of the theater depends closely on that of the actors and then changes always," show by show, while movies enjoy an unprecedented stability. Cinema was thus seen as the crowning achievement of an aesthetic experience of several millennia.

In his French years, Canudo pushed his intuitions without substantially changing his initial approach. In "Elena, Faust et nous (Précis d'esthétique cérébriste)" ("Elena, Faust, and We [Guide to Cerebral Aesthetics]") from 1920, for example, he developed his anti-mimetic conception of cinema, referencing Cubism and avant-garde music as the model for film directors. But, more importantly, Canudo updated his general theory of the arts by including dance (which in those years was popular in Paris thanks to the

Russian choreographers Leonide Massine and George Balanchine) among the "rhythms of time." This change led him to propose the following diagram, which in the "Manifeste des sept arts" officially proposed cinema as "the Seventh Art."[6]

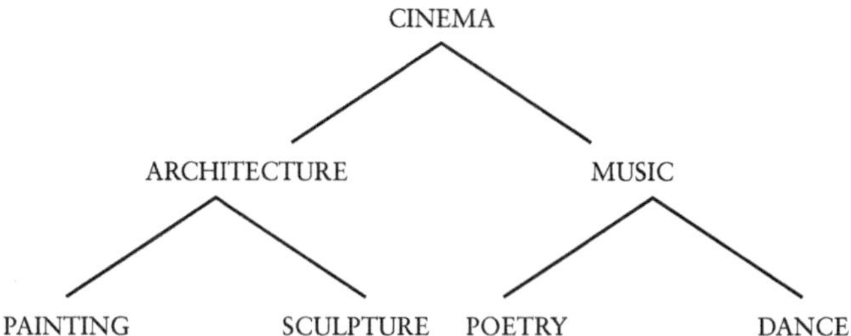

Sebastiano Arturo Luciani's contribution was no less important than Canudo's, even if his works enjoyed less international circulation. A native of Bari (and therefore compatriot of Canudo), Luciani had an excellent musical education and was destined to stand out as a leading music historian and theorist, contributing to one of the manifestos of Futurist music and collaborating in the 1920s with the most important Italian avant-garde stage director, Anton Giulio Bragaglia. Luciani's first works on cinema followed closely on Canudo, starting with two essays that appeared in 1913 in the literary journal *Il Marzocco*: "L'evoluzione della scenografia" ("Evolution of the Scenography") and "Il cinematografo e l'arte" ("Cinema and Art"), both of which were later included in *Verso una nuova arte: Il cinematografo* (*Toward a New Art: Cinema*, 1920). In these texts his musical training was especially evident. For Luciani, silent films must be deciphered through the pictorial and musical sensibility of a spectator willing to recognize the purest essence of cinema in "visual lyricism." As for Canudo, for Luciani movies possess potentialities unknown to photography, even if—on a purely technical level—they depend on the photographic medium. In fact, films are able to "express the invisible through the visible," whereas photography remains condemned to the passive reproduction of reality instead.[7]

In two subsequent essays, "Impressionismo scenico" ("Scene Impressionism") and "Poetica del cinematografo" ("The Poetics of Cinema"), both published in 1916 in *Apollon* and later collected in the already mentioned volume *Verso una nuova arte: Il cinematografo*, Luciani further articulated the difference between the two arts in six distinct points. First, while cinema has a visual, dynamic, and synthetic vocation—and, for this reason, is based on the "rapid succession of innumerable scenes and episodes that integrate in time"—theatrical performances are essentially verbal, static, and analytical. Two, unlike theater, movies do not suffer from the strident contrast between the actor, "who is alive," and more artificial scenes. Three, cinema carries out changes in scene without effort and with extreme rapidity ("What to the theatre is a rare exception, to the cinematograph is the norm. The scene is mobile; its beauty is dynamic. And, as a consequence, the landscape often ceases to be an accessory thing, a background of painting, and becomes the painting itself, in continuous transformation"). Four, a filmmaker does not need the mediation of the actors to express himself because in the movies the actor is "simply something in the hands of the director." Five, the absence of words that characterizes silent movies "focuses . . . all the interest in the visual elements and in particular in the rhythm of life." And finally, film and theater actors require very different acting techniques: "the first is analytical, that is, made up of elements that unfold without interruption and that gradually lead to a culminating effect. The cinema is instead synthetic and impressionistic. Every scene, every part of the action is not developed, but captured in its essential and culminating point, which must illuminate each psychological passage as if in a flash." For Luciani, however, it was not only a question of establishing distinctions, but of formulating a precise ranking. While theater is condemned to being "verbal, static, directed towards the external movement," cinema has the tools to transcend these limits and for this reason can claim a clear aesthetic superiority with respect to its direct ancestor.[8]

Some of Luciani's ideas, as we have seen, were common in Italy and, mainly thanks to Canudo, would spread to France and from there to Europe. Luciani's most original intuition was probably that cinema had a special talent for ellipsis, and that it combined different spaces and times to focus on moments of intensity. This intuition implies an appreciation for editing, which in the following decade would be recognized by Soviet theorists. But Luciani's insight also carries something more with it: a theory of cinema as an art of "net weight," which offers its audience blocks of space and time liberated from all that could weaken the visual and rhythmic composition (metaphorically, the "unladen weight"). At the same time, Luciani formulated a hypothesis that, independently of him, would be taken up again in the 1930s and popularized by the German theorist Rudolf Arnheim: the idea that cinema's artistic nature depends on the technical limits of the camera and its inability to reproduce fully reality, given the absence of color and sound (Arnheim would add other "differentiating factors," including two-dimensionality, the limitation of the frame, the abolition of spatial and sensory continuity, the absence of smell, touch, and taste, and artificial lighting).

A discussion of the first great period of Italian film theory would not be complete without mentioning two other figures: the founder of Futurism, Filippo Tommaso Marinetti (1876–1944) and the playwright and novelist Luigi Pirandello (1867–1936). The proximity between the first formulations of Canudo and Luciani and nascent Futurism is rather evident, as both promoted the rejection of mimetic art, the cult of speed, the praise of synthesis, the desire for an art capable of unifying the various disciplines, and anti-passéism. For this reason, it might be a bit surprising that Futurists waited until 1916 to draw up their manifesto "La cinematografia futurista" ("The Futurist Cinematography"), signed by Marinetti with Ginna, Corra, Emilio Settimelli, Giacomo Balla, and Remo Chiti, where the principles of speed, simultaneity, and dynamism are affirmed with the usual warlike tone in the name of the Wagnerian dream of a "total art."[9] However, this delay is easily explained as soon as one looks at their theoretical production as a whole. Rather than being interested in cinema as a specific art, Marinetti and his associates tended to consider it as a model for every aesthetic experience. Instead of worrying about a Futurist cinema per se, the Futurists believed that film—as an intrinsically modern phenomenon—was the form toward which all the other media must turn, by appropriating it wherever possible (as stated in the "Manifesto del teatro di varietà" [The Variety Theater, 1913]), and above all by transposing its principles into daily creative practice. In other words, despite the attempts to pervert movies by pushing them toward spoken theater, for Marinetti and his collaborators, cinema represented the obligatory point of reference through which to rethink the essence of beauty. Thus film was the alpha and omega of the new, supreme Art toward which Futurists aspired.[10]

Pirandello's case is different, also because his first reflections were not entrusted to a theoretical text but to a literary work, the novel *Si gira!* *(Shoot!)*, first published in the magazine *La nuova antologia* (1915), then collected in volume form (1916) and finally rewritten with a new title as *I quaderni di Serafino Gubbio operatore* (*The Notebooks of Serafino Gubbio, Cinematograph Operatore*, 1925). Pirandello was interested in movies as an emblem of the inauthenticity and mechanization that characterized the modern world, rather than as an aesthetic phenomenon. The "little machine" (as Pirandello called cinema) had, he believed, the power to transform life into automated simulacra even more quickly and radically than the social masks that were one of his main obsessions. Above all, cinema held for Pirandello the tendency to subdue all those who approached it, so that in the conclusion of the novel the protagonist Serafino, after a shock, becomes completely speechless and turns into a sort of appendix of the same camera that he still operates with the movement of the hand.

Because of the author's fame, Pirandello's reflection was destined to have considerable influence also outside of Italy (for instance, Benjamin mentioned it in his essay "The Work of Art in the Age of Mechical Reproduction"). From our perspective, it represents above all a counterbalance to the euphoric attitude of the avant-garde towards the movie-making machine. The story of Serafino Gubbio thus can be seen as an apologue about the dangers of modernity in the same year in which Italy entered the Great War and started experiencing the destructive power of that same technology of which, up to that moment, European intellectuals had mainly grasped only the positive aspects.

2 Italian Idealism and the Advent of Sound Movies

The exploit of Italian theory in the 1910s can be explained by several factors. Among the great European countries, Italy at the beginning of the twentieth century was certainly the one most tied to a classical tradition that was still perceived as a constitutive element of its national identity, embedded as it was in such elements as the Roman legacy, the Latin heritage, the cult of the Renaissance. This privileged relation to the humanistic tradition, however, sometimes fed an attitude hostile to novelties. Thus, the persistence of ancient forms provoked, on the part of many of younger writers, an acute desire to slough off a legacy often perceived as suffocating. That the first European avant-garde, Futurism, was born in Italy can be explained precisely by this psychological attitude, as the perception of a sense of national cultural backwardness (compared to France, Germany, and England) gave Italians an indispensable push to leap forward and cleanse the past.

This particular disposition also helps to understand some of the positions of major intellectuals to cinema. In Italy, the conflict between supporters and opponents of the new filmic art was often more bitter than elsewhere. From the beginning, for instance, some famous authors were involved in writing for cinema, including the Sicilian naturalist novelist Giovanni Verga, author of *I Malavoglia* (*House by the Medlar Tree*, 1881) and the Piedmontese poet Guido Gozzano, author of a screenplay on the life of Saint Francis. Novelists were, in general, happy to collaborate with filmmakers, because cinema (like theater) paid better than writing for the book trade. And yet such figures as Verga and Gozzano were reluctant to see their work credited by filmmakers and preferred their collaboration to remain secret. The exception in this case was Gabriele D'Annunzio, who had Giovanni Pastrone pay him very handsomely just to sign the captions of his colossal *Cabiria* (actually written by Pastrone himself). But in that case the investment paid off because D'Annunzio's renown contributed to the film's international success.

It is not surprising that in this context one of the most frequent questions was the relation between cinema and theater, a connection made even more dramatic by the introduction of sound movies in the late 1920s. As we saw, the film-theater link had been explored with great acumen by Luciani. For others, it was a matter of professional life and death, as in the case of Anton Giulio Bragaglia (1890–1960), who was one of the first Italian thespians to claim for himself the status of director (*regista*) on the model of foreign masters like Konstantin Sergeevič Stanislavskij, Vsevolod Ėmil'evič Mejerchol'd, Adolphe Appia, Edward Gordon Craig, and Jacques Copeau. After having been linked to the Futurist movement in the 1910s, Bragaglia in subsequent years devoted himself above all to staging, by creating a series of avant-garde theaters that were as artistically thought-provoking as they were economically shaky. He found productive stability only in the 1930s, thanks to the support of the Fascist regime, of which Bragaglia had become an ardent supporter. However, Bragaglia never ceased to alternate his activity as a director with that of theorist, and he wrote extensively on cinema as well. For a former Futurist like him, moving images posed a particular challenge to the theater in terms of speed. He saw no alternative but to adapt the theater to the new aesthetic criteria launched by films, and he detected in the technology that threatened older theatrical forms a potential solution, giving him the idea of designing elaborate sets which made it possible to change scenes almost as quickly as on screen. As for the Futurists before him, for Bragaglia cinema was no mere art of the future; it offered a model for all the other arts to follow.[11]

Not everyone reacted with the same optimism to the challenge posed by sound movies. It is worth remembering the position of Pirandello, who in the 1920s, despite his denunciation of the mechanization of life in *I quaderni di Serafino Gubbio operatore*, had become a great admirer of silent films, which he praised as a form of avant-garde art similar to mime. The advent of sound films changed everything. At the beginning of the 1930s, all over Europe there was a proliferation of positions hostile to cinema, but Pirandello's condemnation was particularly violent. In June 1929, the Anglo-American Newspaper Service asked him to write a text on "Whether the Talking Film Will Abolish the Theater," and his bitter answer was immediately spread with great outcry throughout the world.

Pirandello wrote that the theater "can rest assured that it will not be abolished for this very simple reason, that it is not the theatre that wants to become cinema, but it is the cinema that wants to become theatre."[12] Predictably, polemics followed. Above all, Pirandello's rejection of a cinema that limited itself to filming the actors' stage performances without exploiting the creative potentialities of the new medium went hand in hand with his defense of traditional theater. For this reason, his position appeared contradictory to avant-garde thespians like Bragaglia, who believed that Pirandello did not draw the necessary conclusions of his own logic, which should have pushed him to apply to theater his same thinking on film, and thus free the stage from its traditional servitude to the dramatic text. In short, Bragaglia believed that Pirandello should have admitted that, just as a cinema based on dialogue is a sort of "anti-cinema," so a "theatre of words" is in its own turn only "anti-theatre."[13]

The 1920s and 1930s were not as significant as the 1910s for Italian film theory. An obstacle seems to have come from the absolute authority of Benedetto Croce's (1866–1952) and Giovanni Gentile's (1875–1944) neo-Idealistic philosophy. While in the same period in Germany a new generation of thinkers like Benjamin, Theodor Wiesengrund Adorno, and Siegfried Kracauer applied the categories of nineteenth-century classic German philosophy to new media forms—and while already in 1907 a French philosopher like Henri Bergson had been able to use the movie experience to formulate some of his most original theses on human mind—in Italy philosophers seemed to oppose the efforts of those who tried to investigate cinema seriously. Croce and Gentile had collaborated for several years, before going their separate ways because of their opposing political views, which after 1924 led Croce to become one of the symbols of liberal opposition to Mussolini's regime. Gentile, for his part, became a sort of official ideologue of Fascism, assuming the positions of Minister of the Education, Director of the Scuola Normale Superiore of Pisa, and President of the Accademia d'Italia. Despite the discrepancies in their philosophical systems, in many ways Croce and Gentile continued to share a similar approach to aesthetic phenomena and—it must be added—a certain suspicion of novelty. Thus, their prestige contributed significantly to curbing cinematic reflection, especially because at that time all cinephile efforts were directed at proving the legitimacy of a serious study of the new art form—even when, in the 1930s, outside of Italy the question of film's legitimacy was already settled.

In his highly influential *Estetica come scienza dell'espressione e linguistica generale* (*Aesthetics as Science of Expression and General Linguistics*, 1902), Croce defined art as intuition-expression: two inseparable terms in his eyes because it would not be possible to intuit without expressing, or to have a poetic expression without "lyrical intuition."[14] Already within the theater an aporia could arise from this statement, but Croce's claim made the confrontation with cinema even more difficult, as in the case of film the final aesthetic result depends of course not only on the collaboration of a large number of professionals but also on a technical mediation that insinuates itself between the moment of intuition and that of expression. In other words, from a Crocean perspective there is the risk that one can admit the impossibility of talking about an "art" of film.

Croce and Gentile's disdainful silence toward cinema is relevant to Italian film theory mostly because of the enormous influence that they had on younger philosophers and critics. Today, it is difficult to realize the influence that a "yes" or "no" from either of them was able to exert in those years, but otherwise it would be impossible to explain the marginality of Italian theoretical reflection on movies during the 1920s and 1930s after such a promising beginning. However, both Croce and Gentile were eventually induced by their disciples to take a stand and endorse their timid attempts to include officially cinema among the fully recognized artistic disciplines. And, at a certain point, the longed-for legitimation finally came.

The first to break the silence was Gentile—author of, among many other books, a *Filosofia dell'arte* (*Philosophy of Art*, 1931)—who in 1935 agreed to write a brief introduction to the monograph *Cinematografo* by his young pupil Luigi Chiarini. In a couple of pages, Gentile took issue with "the increasing interest of film scholars in technique," because this concern distracts them "from the end to which technique serves and from which it draws its value.[15] Once again, the forest has prevented us from seeing the tree, which is the whole or the essence of the forest. The mechanism has covered the principle that creates it and therefore explains it." Not unlike poetry, painting or music, even at the movies, Gentile continues, genuine art begins only when technique stops. For this reason, "the aesthetic problem of the cinematograph as it derives from the use of a technique containing mechanical elements is the problem of every art; and also in this case the problem is solved by overcoming or erasing the technique: that is, in the show, during which the viewer does not see the mechanism that produces it." In this way Gentile could therefore conclude by reiterating one of his Idealistic aesthetic principles, namely the rejection of any distinction between content and form.

Croce's verdict was much slower in arriving. Only in 1948, in fact, did the elderly philosopher send a letter to the magazine *Bianco e nero* to correct some oral statements on cinema that had been attributed to him by Emilio Cecchi, a well-known literary critic as well as former director of the production company Cines. More than ten years earlier, according to Cecchi, the Idealist philosopher had told him that, "as a fusion of drama or plot and visual images," cinema could not be denied the "full quality of art."[16] Croce was keen to point out that he had always opposed such discourses on the "means of expression" of the individual arts, but then he admitted, magnanimously: "If you feel and judge it beautiful, a movie has its rights, and there is nothing else to say."[17] They were only a few words, but for many they represented a precious approval: cinema could receive the same attention that had been granted to the other arts up to that moment.

The Italian thinkers who in the following years studied cinema from an Idealistic perspective remained largely bogged down in Croce's and Gentile's categories, continuing to focus on problems like the overcoming of technique or the unity of aesthetic intuition, while elsewhere great theoretical progress was being made by thinkers more closely focused on the concrete evolution of film form. The only Idealist theorist of truly international renown in those years was the art historian Carlo Ludovico Ragghianti (1910–87). Despite the orthodoxy of his thought, Ragghianti's interest in cinema as an art form was manifest at a young age in his essay "Cinematografo rigoroso" (Rigorous Cinematography) published in the movie journal *Cine-convegno* in 1933. The fundamental premise of his analysis was the substantial unity of the arts, an open polemic against those who insisted on Lessing's partition into "Arts of space" and "Arts of time." This dispute had a constructive side too. Ragghianti relied on his notion of unity to enhance the pictorial aspects of films and reread cinema as a chapter in the history of theater, all to be understood as an "art of vision" (like painting) and all sharing similar aesthetic principles. For this reason, as he would explain in more detail a few years later, the ideal spectator of cinema ends up looking very much like an art connoisseur.[18] It was not surprising that, among film theorists, Ragghianti felt a special affinity with Ejzenštejn, who had dedicated illuminating pages to the relationship between cinema and painting and read single shots as dynamic compositions of lights, shadows, and figures that editing was called upon to enhance through juxtaposition with other shots of equally charged internal tension.[19]

Ragghianti's "pictorial" interpretation of cinema was convincing above all because it went hand in hand with a parallel "cinematic" interpretation of painting. That is confirmed by one of the most original aspects of his post–Second World War work: namely his commitment to the production of about twenty documentaries on Italian art history, which Ragghianti defined as *crito-film* (critic-film). Here one can see even better than in his essays what he meant by "time of vision." In his documentaries, in fact, specific "filmic tools" such as editing and camera movements are used either to reproduce the movements of the viewer's gaze (both his lingering on details and the unpredictable jumps from one portion of the image to another), or to activate his iconographic and formal memory, with a sudden passage from one work to another. With the same goals, Ragghianti used static or animated superimpositions to bring out the compositional principles of the work and help the less experienced public to set paintings or sculptures in motion according to the visual plan presumably conceived by the author himself.[20]

3 The Poetics of Neorealism

In the second half of the 1930s, as a result of many factors, Italy came to being equipped with the most effective public institutions in the West for the study and promotion of cinema. In the years after 1922, as a result of the march on Rome, Benito Mussolini had demolished liberal institutions, transforming Italy into a Fascist dictatorship. Clearly aware of their potentialities for propaganda, the regime immediately devoted much attention to radio and cinema. From this perspective, Fascist government worked hard to increase Italian film production, imitating Hollywood studios and eventually supporting the entertainment industry with special public funding. As Mussolini repeatedly stated, "cinema is the strongest weapon." This also meant that the Fascist state could not help but control it with a precise policy of intervention that included the creation of the first Film Festival in Venice (1932), the opening of the Centro Sperimentale di Cinematografia (1935), and the founding of Cinecittà (1937), which proved to be decisive also for Italian film theory's development. In the intentions of the regime, the Centro Sperimentale was to promote the training of a new generation of technicians and artists, from film directors and actors capable of performing in front of the camera (often by breaking with the Italian tradition of overacting) to screenwriters, set designers, sound engineers, and directors of photography. At the same time, the Centro Sperimentale, as a propaganda showcase of Italian totalitarianism, also aimed to stimulate a new awareness in the potential of the new art and was given, beginning in 1937, a monthly magazine, *Bianco e Nero*, to which all the major foreign theorists of the period contributed, including Rudolf Arnheim, Béla Balász, Sergej M. Ejzenštejn, and Paul Rotha.

Gentile chose the philosopher Chiarini (1900–75) to head the new Centro Sperimentale. In the following years, before and after the Second World War, Chiarini would become a preeminent figure of Italian film culture, grafting his passionate defense of cinema's aesthetic dignity onto some elements typical of Gentile's thought, such as the insistence on the morality of artistic creation and the artwork's aspiration to totality. This Idealist approach could in fact be maintained only at the condition that the camera did not capture the outside "objective" world, but rather offered a subjective vision of it. And Chiarini never really came out of Gentile-inspired idealism, despite his attempts to update his aesthetic vocabulary (rather than his concepts) after the war.

However, Chiarini was above all a great organizer of culture, and his leadership coincided with a moment of extraordinary activity by the Centro Sperimentale. Alongside *Bianco e nero*, a series of books was also published, soon to become one of the most prestigious in Europe, especially for the great attention it devoted to Soviet film theory. Some of the translations were made by Chiarini's principal collaborator: the eclectic critic, novelist, screenwriter, and (secretly) fervent Communist militant Umberto Barbaro (1902–59), who spoke Russian and German and introduced Vsevolod Illarionovič Pudovkin's writings to the Italian public. Even more than Chiarini, Barbaro gave the decisive imprint to the Centro Sperimentale in those years, not only by making accessible the best foreign works to an Italian audience, but even more so by transforming one of the prime cultural institutions of Mussolini's regime into a nest of anti-Fascist subversives.

It is impossible to exaggerate the importance of the Centro Sperimentale in this period, as in a few years a great number of the young authors destined to form the backbone of the new Italian cinema after 1945 passed through there as students, including Giuseppe De Santis, Pietro Germi, Michelangelo Antonioni, and Luigi Zampa. The watchwords of this new generation of aspiring directors were the rediscovery of Italy and its landscape, the attention to social issues, the recovery of nineteenth-century realism (in particular the legacy of Giovanni Verga), and the rejection of light comedy. In short, it was in the Centro Sperimentale that, thanks mainly to Barbaro's commitment, the theoretical and poetic principles of what would soon be called neorealism were first elaborated.

Barbaro was not an original theorist, though he was up to date on important intellectual trends ranging from German art-historical pure visibility theory and Soviet theory of editing to Italian idealism and the Hungarian Marxist philosopher György Lukács's works on literary realism. Despite that, his work as a teacher, essayist, and translator deeply influenced the intellectual climate of those years. Like all major theorists of his generation, Barbaro also drew on idealism, and in particular Croce, and throughout his life he would not distance himself from some of the Neapolitan philosopher's main theses, such as the fundamental unity of art and the spontaneous fusion of form and content. At the same time, over the years, and as a consequence of his public commitment to Marxism, Barbaro rejected the most questionable elements of Croce's aesthetics, starting with his neglect of collective creation and his tendency to identify creation with lyrical intuition. As one reads in *Film: Soggetto e sceneggiatura* (*Film: Subject and Screenplay*, 1939), "Art can be the result of collaboration; indeed, given the bond between artists over time and the relationship between the artist and his movement, it cannot fail to be so."[21]

In distancing himself from Croce, an important contribution came from Pudovkin. While he was leading a personal quest for a new realism, Barbaro drew from Soviet directors the idea (only apparently contradictory) that the essence of cinema should be sought in editing, and that art relies on selection and reconstruction. Thus, while Italian directors began to emphasize the importance of long shots for their alleged greater adherence to reality, Barbaro did not abandon his old passion for Russian Formalist theories: he merely limited himself to refusing that Soviet reflections on editing could turn into a normative aesthetic. Under these conditions it was possible to reconcile, at least in part, Pudovkin's and Ejzenštejn's cult for the technical moment with Croce's imperative to focus rather on the moment of intuition-expression. But, as for Chiarini, for Barbaro it seems more appropriate to speak of a "Crocean heresy" than of autonomous thought, despite his frequent recourse to Marxist vocabulary in the postwar years.

Curiously enough, together with Ragghianti, the most original figure active in Italy in the 1930s was another art historian: the German Jewish Rudolf Arnheim (1904–2007), who emigrated to Italy in 1933 and remained there until Mussolini's Racial Laws of 1938 forced him to seek refuge first in England and then definitively in the United States. In 1932, Arnheim published a book in Germany in which he had applied the principles of the psychology of perception to the new art, *Film als Kunst* (*Film as Art*); six years later, an updated Italian version of his original theses in the light of the many changes introduced by the talkies appeared in *Bianco e nero* with the title "Il nuovo Laocoonte" ("The New Laocoön"), which eventually became a classic and his most famous theoretical work after it was translated into English.[22] In this book, Arnheim situated his own research under the sign of

Lessing, who had been already taken as a model by Canudo and many others Italian theorists to grasp film's specificity at the intersection of the "Arts of time" and the "Arts of space." Unlike Canudo, Arnheim was more interested in the limits of film technology because they let him draw a powerful argument against those who wanted to reduce cinema to a mere device for reproducing reality. Arnheim's theses had matured in Germany when he worked on the psychology of perception, but in Italy of the 1930s such an insistence on the difference between the arts sounded like a peremptory reply to the Idealists, both the ones influenced by Gentile (Chiarini) and ones tied to Croce (Ragghianti and Barbaro).

The war years and especially the period between September 1943 and April 1945, when Italy found itself torn apart by a civil war between Fascists and anti-Fascists and subject to the presence of German and Anglo-American troops, represented a moment of profound change in consciousness. It was then that the ideas developed at the Centro Sperimentale and in the journal *Cinema* (whose contributors included Giuseppe De Santis, Mario Alicata, Carlo Lizzani, and Mario Puccini) quickly spread everywhere. With Luchino Visconti, Roberto Rossellini, and Vittorio De Sica, the cinema dreamed up by Barbaro and his students at the Centro Sperimentale became a reality thanks to a series of revolutionary works in terms of screenplay (which got much more open-ended than in the past), editing (either more elliptical or reduced to a minimum, depending on the case, with a clear primacy of long shots), choice of the actors (often nonprofessionals), photography (with an increasing use of deep focus), and production practices (movies were shot outside the studios).

The emergence of neorealism upon the ashes of the Fascist period's more entertainment-based cinema also implied a radical change in film theory. Rather than thinking abstractly about the essence of the Seventh Art or imagining a cinema to come, directors and critics found themselves engaged in explaining the profound changes that were taking place right in front of them. Neorealism seemed to usher in a new way of using the camera, but in what terms exactly could this novelty be described?

If today one compares Italian reflection on postwar cinema with their French counterpart, and in particular with André Bazin's essays, one has to acknowledge the greater theoretical depth of the critical approach associated with the *Cahiers du cinéma*. In France, neorealism was analyzed in its formal aspects, and attention was drawn to the philosophical implications of the shift from a closed to an open screenplay—which required the active participation of the viewer—and on Neorealist directors' quest for a new kind of audience that was willing to explore the movies instead of being led along by the flow of images. In Italy, the discourse on neorealism focused rather on its themes and contents, so that the movement was seen principally as a denouncement of social injustices. The prevalence of such a reductive attitude was also the effect of the intense politicization of the postwar period, particularly acute in the years between 1945 and 1948, when, with little scruple and even at the highest level of Italian bureaucracy, many former Fascists were restored to power in an anti-Soviet atmosphere. If, therefore, the couple "cinema and politics" (but also "literature and politics" and "art and politics") marked the whole of postwar Italian culture, in the first decade after Mussolini's fall such a link was tighter than ever. It was only in 1956 that this situation would partly soften, following the Hungarian uprising, when the Soviet military invasion of a friendly socialist state compelled Italian intellectuals, at that time mostly Marxist, to break away from the Communist Party and decry "cultural Stalinism."

Given the subordination of much of Italian theory to immediate political goals, it is not strange that in those years the contributions destined to have the greatest impact outside Italy were by the filmmakers. Egged on by their success, the masters of neorealism (and, later, of the new generation that came to the scene in the 1960s) left a lasting trace on international film theory. Not all filmmakers, of course, had the same urgency to reflect in an abstract way on their work and on the new art's potentialities. Of the five directors who gained international renown immediately after the war—Visconti, De Sica, Rossellini, Antonioni, and Federico Fellini—only Rossellini conceived of his writings (and even his interviews) as an extension of his creative work, only supported in his tireless theoretical elaboration of neorealist principles by De Sica's main collaborator, the novelist Cesare Zavattini (1902–89).[23]

Rossellini (1906–77) was the most arguably radical neorealist filmmaker, and his idea that cinema should "show and not demonstrate" was very influential worldwide both among film directors and critics. However, his theoretical proclamations are often disappointing and do not go far beyond a generic humanitarianism, which often results in edifying banalities.[24] Zavattini's theoretical writings, on the contrary, are much more interesting.[25] If, as a screenwriter, Zavattini was at his best when working with a director like De Sica, who was careful not to lose contact with the general public and even eager to rebuild a relationship with the star system after the early stages of neorealism, Zavattini's reflections took on a much more extreme form. Zavattini started from the idea that

> the first and most superficial reaction to everyday reality is boredom. As long as we cannot overcome our intellectual and moral laziness, reality seems to us to be devoid of any interest. It is not surprising, therefore, that cinema has always felt the need for "a story" to be inserted into reality as natural and inevitable, to make movies exciting and "spectacular."[26]

The main merit of neorealism was therefore its capacity to teach the audience how to look at everyday life, reducing the gap between existence and art.

This pedagogy of the gaze has also a political aim. Without knowing each other, men and women cannot form communities, and it was precisely this additional knowledge that, according to Zavattini, one should ask of the cinema. This basic idea determines all the fundamental precepts of Zavattini's "poetics of witness": reducing the role of scripts and screenplays (almost a paradoxical statement in the mouth of a great screenwriter like him), exalting the "duration" of reality, and rejecting tidy endings ("neorealism does not offer solutions, it does not indicate roads. The endings of neorealist films are open to the maximum").[27] Fittingly, Bazin nicknamed Zavattini "the Proust of the present tense of the indicative mood."[28]

Such an interpretation of neorealism was subjected to severe criticism by the most authoritative film critic of those years, the Marxist Guido Aristarco (1918–96). For Aristarco, who starting in 1952 directed the journal *Cinema nuovo*, true realism had nothing to do with a pure and simple "shadowing of actual life," but was linked to the director's ability to go beyond the simple mirroring of reality by drawing on the example of nineteenth-century novels. Author of an anthology of classic works on the theory of cinema, *L'arte del film* (*The Art of Film*, 1950), and of a very successful *Storia delle teoriche del cinema* (*History of the Theories of Cinema*, 1951), Aristarco was well aware of the many debates held during the previous decades and came to the conclusion that, now that the artistic potentialities of the new medium had been finally recognized, it was necessary to end the artistic isolation of cinema by linking it more closely to other forms of expression. Even neorealism for Aristarco was only a moment of passing, while—in the light of Lukács's ideas—the time had come to fight for an "integral realism," with no more prefixes. According to Aristarco, Rossellini's films from the 1950s were already a step backward, and in *Cinema nuovo* a bitter controversy against Italian directors arose, also involving Bazin in the part of the defender of what remained of the neorealist movement.

While *Cinema nuovo* quickly started opposing Italian cinema as a whole and initiated against Hollywood a sort of intellectual embargo, a much more open approach characterized the other major film journal of those years, *Filmcritica*, founded in 1950 by a young film critic, Edoardo Bruno (born in 1928), together with Rossellini, Barbaro, and the Marxist philosopher Galvano Della Volpe. The journal was from the beginning close in principles to the *Cahiers du cinéma* (and thus less hostile to American cinema). In the short run, Aristarco's conformity to the Italian Communist Party's official line seemed enticing to many left-leaning Italian intellectuals. Soon, however, *Cinema nuovo* ended up placing itself increasingly in positions of disdainful rearguard and to fight all new developments (with a few exceptions: some movies by Visconti, Antonioni, the Taviani brothers, Jean-Marie Straub, and Danièle Huillet). Meanwhile, *Filmcritica* quickly became the most appreciated Italian film journal.

The last important figure of this period was one of the contributors to *Filmcritica*, Galvano Della Volpe (1895–1968). Della Volpe was a professor of aesthetics and, like Chiarini, he too had been trained in Gentile's philosophy (*attualismo* or actualism), but during the Second World War he had become increasingly critical toward neoidealism (much more than his friend Barbaro). In an attempt to free himself from Gentile's and Croce's influence, he turned back to the lessons of Aristotle, Hume, and then Kant, to endorse ultimately an eclectic form of Marxism. For this reason, Della Volpe's intellectual struggle was conducted simultaneously on a double front: on one side, against Italian idealism and, on the other side, against the "vulgar Marxism" of figures such as Georgij Valentinovič Plechanov and Lukács, whom Della Volpe considered to be lacking any "gnoseological analysis of the technical-structural or formal processes of art."[29]

For Della Volpe, any philosophical inquiry had, first, to start from the observation of the human being's unprecedented condition in modern society and, two, to abandon mystical residues and romantic legacies (which were still very present in Italian neoidealism). In such a context, it was obvious that Della Volpe turned to cinema as an inevitable test of his ideas, so that this new cinematic art form occupies an important place in what is considered his philosophical masterpiece, *La critica del gusto* (*Criticism of Taste*, 1960), a work that appeared after the composition of his *Il verosimile filmico* (*Filmic Verisimilitude*, 1954).[30] Since, against the Idealists, Della Volpe was convinced that the artistic nature of film, just like that of any other art form, resides in its technique, he gave a place of particular importance to Pudovkin's works, where a general reflection on the medium is never separated from a meticulous analysis of creative practices (a principle that led Della Volpe to develop his own "Laocoonte 1960" in the last part of *La critica del gusto*).

In the Russians, Della Volpe also appreciated the central role given to editing as a vehicle for finding new ideas. With a series of examples from Ejzenštejn's most famous movies, the Italian philosopher interpreted editing in the light of metaphor and tried to demonstrate how, through the juxtaposition of images, cinema was able to express abstract symbols and concepts no less than literature and philosophy. This is probably one of the most original aspects of Della Volpe's thought, which—in contrast to Croce's notion of art as "pure intuition"—refuses any categorical distinction between art and science. Poetry too, Della Volpe maintains, is a discourse and as such uses image-concepts, even if it clearly organizes them in a different way from philosophy or science. Simply put, by establishing links, metaphors allow readers to grasp similarities between what at first glance would seem dissimilar.

Such a perspective was not without problems, first of all because it devalued poetry's rhythmic and musical aspects, so that Della Volpe reached the paradoxical conclusion that any literary text was perfectly translatable into other languages, in line with his ancient mentor Gentile who—unlike Croce, a thinker interested mainly in "pure" poetry—had a special taste for Italian poet-philosophers, such as Tommaso Campanella and Giacomo

Leopardi. However, from a strictly cinematic perspective, Della Volpe's hyper-rationalistic attitude had the merit of opening cinema to an abstract and frankly conceptual dimension that few theorists had granted it up to that moment and that would return later in Gilles Deleuze's works (even if the French philosopher never acknowledged his debt toward Della Volpe).

The history of Italian film theory in the 1945–56 period can also be described as the history of a missed encounter. Between 1949 and 1951, the many notebooks written by Antonio Gramsci (1891–1937) when he was locked up in a Fascist prison (1926–37) were published. It was soon clear to everyone that the former Secretary of the Italian Communist Party was also a thinker of the highest order and that his *Quaderni del carcere* (*Prison Notebooks)* were one of the greatest achievements of Italian modern philosophy.[31] In Italy, Fascism had been defeated by force of arms and not philosophy, but the categories elaborated by Gramsci in prison offered very useful tools for the interpretation of society and culture in the postwar period. Notions such as that of "hegemony," "national-popular culture," and "passive revolution," and reflections such as those on Taylorism and Fordism, on the "Southern Question," or on the slight popular participation in the Risorgimento all quickly became central to Italian cultural and political debate. Moreover, with Gramsci the Communists now seemed to have an intellectual point of reference capable of competing with Croce (to whom Gramsci dedicated many critical pages), and it was with this precise objective that the new Secretary of the Italian Communist Party, Palmiro Togliatti (a very refined intellectual), had personally edited the posthumous writings of his predecessor.

Curiously, however, although Gramsci had dedicated several brilliant notes to cinema (as a young man, he had also been theater critic for socialist daily newspaper *Avanti!*), Italian film theorists seemed to be unaware of the many fruitful ideas contained in the *Quaderni del carcere*. It is particularly significant that the greatest film theorist of the 1950s, Della Volpe, was a Marxist but not a Gramscian (while, in the same period, Aristarco limited himself to paying occasional homage to Gramsci with some minor quotations). Thus, it was only in the 1990s, after the fall of the Berlin Wall (1989), that Gramsci became an unavoidable point of reference for Italian cultural studies and film theory, mainly in the wake of Anglo-American postcolonial production.

4 Semiotics and the Debate on Cinematic Language

Between the end of the 1950s and the beginning of the 1960s, Italy experienced one of the greatest changes in its history. Within five years or so, the country transformed from a predominantly agricultural country into one of the world's major industrial powers, but the transformation was marked by a huge and often painful internal emigration from the poorer South to the developed North. The so-called economic boom (or economic miracle) was accompanied by an extraordinary cultural dynamism in all fields: from poetry to fiction, and from art (with the so-called *Arte povera* or "Poor Art" movement) to cinema, where within a few years many new talents made their debut: Marco Ferreri (1958), Ermanno Olmi (1959), Pier Paolo Pasolini (1961), the Taviani brothers (1962), Bernardo Bertolucci (1964), and Marco Bellocchio (1965).

This quick metamorphosis inevitably affected Italian culture. A new generation of intellectuals, mostly gathered in the avant-garde movement known as Gruppo 63, was severely polemical about the neorealist period and complained of Italy's cultural backwardness vis-à-vis other nations. As Alberto Arbasino, one of the main exponents of Gruppo 63, provocatively said, it would have been enough for Italian writers to cross the border into Switzerland and buy some books at the first gas station in Chiasso to broaden their vision.[32] It was, of course, a polemical joke, but his aggressive charge illustrates well the desire to make a clean break with traditions now perceived as too self-referential.

At the theoretical level, the fathers-to-be-killed bore the names of Benedetto Croce and Antonio Gramsci, the two tutelary deities of the then dominant Italian historicism. In order to achieve such a parricide, the most fruitful suggestions came from France, where a series of young authors had begun to subvert the literary field by applying the lessons of linguistics to poems and novels and by replacing historical study with a structural approach to the texts.

Above all, a new discipline was emerging, destined to influence profoundly theoretical reflection on cinema: semiotics (or the "science of signs"), inspired by the hitherto neglected works of two great nineteenth-century linguists: the American Charles Sanders Pierce (1839–1914) and the French-Swiss Ferdinand de Saussure (1857–1913). The spread of semiotics beyond specialist boundaries was largely linked to French literary critic Roland Barthes who, at the end of the 1950s, had adopted Saussure's lesson in order to interpret a series of very different phenomena. The signs, of course, were not only verbal, and already in *Mythologies* (1957), Barthes started discussing images and photographs. And, although he was not specifically interested in cinema, it was clear that many of his insights were clearly applicable to it too.

The leap was made by a young scholar initially trained as a classicist, Christian Metz, who, in the closing of a 1964 essay published in issue 8 of the journal *Communications* ("Le cinéma, langue ou langage?"), launched the challenge: "We need to make the semiology of cinema." Metz's challenge sounded both new and old. If "classic" film theory, not only in Italy, had sought the essence of cinema in the confrontation with photography, theater, painting, and music, then semiotics, at the very moment in which it presented itself as a fresh starting point, did nothing but look for the "specific filmic" in the comparative analysis between verbal signs and iconic signs. The challenge was taken up above all in Italy, where between 1965 and 1967, in connection with the Mostra Internazionale del Nuovo Cinema di Pesaro organized by the film critic Lino Miccichè (1934–2004), three important conferences were held and attended by critics, theorists, and important filmmakers like the Taviani brothers, Milos Forman, and Lindsay Anderson. France was represented by Barthes (in 1966) and Metz (in 1966 and 1967); among the Italians, in addition to the aged Della Volpe, two young philosophers stood out: Umberto Eco (1930–2016), then a member of Gruppo 63 and already famous for one his most important books (*L'opera aperta* [*The Open Work*, 1962]), and the Kantian Emilio Garroni (1925–2005).

The real star at Pesaro, however, was undoubtedly Pier Paolo Pasolini (1922–75). Invited in the double role of film director and public intellectual, Pasolini participated in all three conferences with texts of considerable theoretical commitment, progressively widening the scope of his interventions (later collected in 1972 in *Empirismo eretico* [*Heretical Empiricism*]).[33] The first, "Il 'cinema di poesia'" ("The 'Cinema of Poetry'"), is still halfway between a statement of poetics and an abstract reflection on the cinematic medium's potentialities. Pasolini adopts semiotic jargon to argue that, compared to verbal communication, "visual communication" (like the one that is "at the base of cinematographic language") is "extremely rough, almost animal," and that "the linguistic instrument on which cinema is based is therefore of an irrational type: and this explains the oneiric depth of cinema." With such views, Pasolini placed himself at the extreme opposite of the rationalization of cinematic language through editing and metaphors that had been proposed by Della Volpe only a few years earlier. Above all, Pasolini argued, while writers have at their disposal a dictionary, so that they compose their sentences with the words contained in it, a hypothetical dictionary of images would be infinite. The objects, Pasolini continues, are not organized in a grammar, but "have a pre-grammatical history already long and intense," which directors must take into account. The irrational element of cinema should "make us think that the language of cinema is basically a 'language of poetry.' Instead, historically . . . the cinematographic tradition . . . seems to be that of a 'language of prose'": a tradition constantly trying to conceal "the fundamentally irrational element of cinema," which nevertheless remains inexorable.

The peculiarity of the so-called "new cinema" of the 1960s was therefore for Pasolini its desire to recover this marginalized tradition of a "cinema of poetry." But Pasolini did not stop there and—with a series of vertiginous analogies—established a presumed parallel between some stylistic means of the novels and cinema. For Pasolini, "direct discourse" would correspond to the subjective film shot, while so-called free indirect discourse (which represents in the third person the words and thoughts of a character, combining them with the same character's linguistic and stylistic peculiarities) would refer to an alleged "indirect free subjective film shot," capable of expressing "the psychological state of mind" of a "sick, abnormal protagonist." For Pasolini, this was a way of linking his own novels *Ragazzi di vita* (*The Ragazzi*, 1955) and *Una vita violenta* (*A Violent Life*, 1959), which made great use of free indirect discourse to give voice to the underclass from Rome's outskirts, to his movies. But his views aimed also to describe a more general trend, and he included such directors as Antonioni, Bertolucci, Godard, the Brazilian Glauber Rocha, and the Czechoslovakian Milos Forman in his analysis. In short, "Il 'cinema di poesia'" aspired to a truly theoretical dimension.

The following year, in the presence of Metz, Pasolini went on the attack with "Il linguaggio scritto della realtà" ("The Language Written by Reality").[34] To the French theorist, who aspired to construct a semiotics of cinematic images, Pasolini opposed a much more ambitious project: a "semiotics of reality," made possible precisely through cinema. Convinced that "the minimum unity of the cinematographic language are the various real objects of which a shot is made up," and that cinema communication is not based so much on the shot's "impression of reality" as on "reality tout court," he developed a very peculiar cinematic ontology. Pasolini himself defined the outcome as "the most concrete of the possible philosophies." Reality, the Italian director said, "is nothing but cinema in nature," so that "the first and main of human languages can be considered the action itself: as a relationship of mutual representation with other people and with physical reality." In this perspective, "we do cinema by living." Conversely, "the whole of life, in all its actions, is a natural and living cinema: in this, it is linguistically the equivalent of the oral language in its natural or biological moment"; whereas, on the contrary, "cinema is only the written moment of a natural and total language, which is living." In short, through cinema the "'language of action' found a means of mechanical reproduction, similar to written language's convention with respect to oral language." As Pasolini himself said in the years following, reality is therefore a sort of "Code of Codes," to quote the title of one of his subsequent essays ("Il codice dei codici").

Although highly suggestive, such a position was easily questionable, and the following year Eco himself highlighted the main contradictions on which Pasolini's theory was based, starting with the naïve idea that "we can speak of a reality and an action in its purest state, free and virgin from any conventionalizing intervention of culture" (a Rousseau-like myth very dear to Pasolini, as a novelist and as a filmmaker).[35] Moving one's eyes, raising one's arm, posing one's body, laughing, dancing are, in the words of Eco's "Sulle articolazioni del codice cinematografico" ("On the Articulations of Cinematic Code"), "acts of communication," and thus the result of "convention and culture": "so much so that there is already a semiology of this language of action, and it is called kinesics."

Pasolini replied to Eco's criticism through an analysis of the famous amateur film by Abraham Zapruder on the 1963 assassination of American president

John F. Kennedy ("Osservazioni sul piano-sequenza" ["Observations on the Long Take"]). Here Pasolini identified cinema and life even more than in his preceding essays, to the point that he described reality as a kind of "Great Being" who constantly speaks to himself through the silent language of facts and actions. Pasolini's idea was that if one summed up all the hypothetical shots of a given event (from every perspective and angle) one could—at least theoretically—reconstitute the original event in its entirety. And just as the meaning of an existence becomes comprehensible only after the death, when no supplementary element can be added, so, in the same way, is it the editing that makes a film meaningful ("after death, this continuity of life no longer exists, but its meaning is there. The alternative is: or to be immortal and remain unexpressed or to express oneself and die").[36]

Because of its tendency to naturalize language and cancel any distinction between life and communication, Pasolini's position was harshly criticized by semiologists in the following years, in the tradition of Eco's withering critique. However, it is worth noting that at the beginning of the 1980s, Pasolini's notions were given a new life by French philosopher Gilles Deleuze, who used some of Pasolini's ideas to elaborate his own original ontology of film in *Cinéma 1: L'image-mouvement* (*Cinema 1: The Movement-Image*, 1983) and *Cinéma 2: L'image-temps* (*Cinema 2: The Time-Image*, 1985). Also thanks to Deleuze, and despite the great number of contradictions on which the essays collected in *Empirismo eretico* are based, Pasolini gradually has become probably the most widely read Italian film theorist in the world in the last thirty years or so.

As far as Eco was concerned, in addition to his discussion of Pasolini's positions, his 1967 essay anticipated a series of potential theoretical developments on cinematic thinking that were only partially realized in subsequent works. Eco had learned from the masters of linguistics that all verbal languages have a "double articulation." In the disciplinary jargon, that simply meant that if sentences can be broken down into words, in turn words can be broken down into arbitrary phonemes. Unlike Metz, who in his early research—in the absence of a double articulation of images— had argued that cinema could not be a codified language and that therefore it was only an idiom, for Eco the images on the screen had not two but even three articulations. In each photogram there are in fact "iconic semes" (e.g., tall and dark girl), which in turn can be broken down into smaller "iconic signs" (e.g., nose, eye, hair) and "iconic figures" (corners, lines, and curves devoid of meaning, and so forth). But, as soon as one moves from the isolated photogram to the frame, Eco believed, one has to consider a "third articulation," in which the single portions of a gesture (defined as "kines") come to compose actions (defined as "kinemorphs").

After "Sulle articolazioni del codice cinematografico" (collected in *La struttura assente* [*The Absent Structure*, 1968]), Eco rarely returned to cinema. If one excludes his Pesaro statements, film never played an important role in his semiotic thinking, which preferably drew its examples from literature

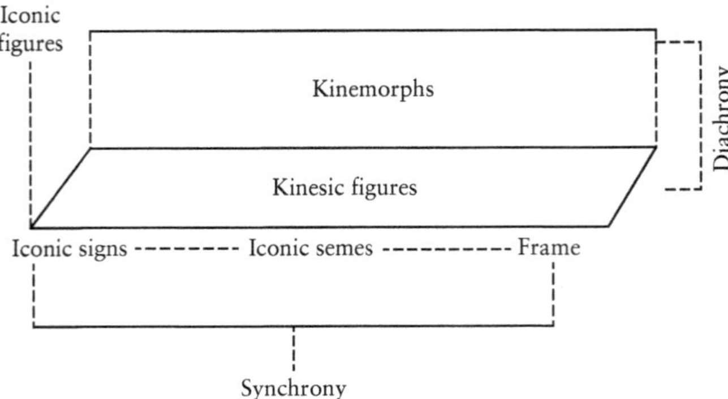

and music (and sometimes from figurative art), with the partial exception of the *Trattato di semiotica generale* (*Treatise on General Semiotics*, 1975). Nevertheless, film does appear in his more socially engaged writing, where Eco seems fascinated by Hollywood's ability to create modern myths and forge a global collective imagination, by reworking ancient plots of proven effectiveness again and again. With the exception of "*Casablanca* o la rinascita degli dei" ("*Casablanca*, or Rebirth of the Gods"), which was dedicated to the genesis of cult films, his film writing was generally limited to occasional pieces, often brilliant but ultimately of little theoretical commitment. Tics, manias, clichés, and tendencies of contemporary collective imagination, all of them discussed through movies—thus was Eco's work on film, compelling but with little organic reflection on cinema itself as a medium.

5 Academic Theory and the Encounter with History

It is difficult to establish exactly when the second great era of Italian film theory came to an end. After the exciting conferences in Pesaro, the 1970s were certainly a two-faced decade. On the one hand, the decade coincided with great efforts to deepen and systematize the ideas of the 1960s. On the other hand, it was easy to perceive in the 1970s a growing annoyance for theoretical reflection on film, which was increasingly considered a dry alternative to socially engaged criticism and the practice of filmmaking itself. A leading role in undermining the certainties of the past decade and its tendency to interpret cinema as verbal language can be attributed to Garroni, who explicitly targeted Metz, Pasolini, Eco, Barthes, and Deleuze in important essays from *Semiotica ed estetica* (*Semiotics and Aesthetics*, 1968) and *Ricognizione della semiotica* (*Semiotics Reconsidered*, 1977).

In part, the departure of critics and directors from theory also turned on a change in the professional status of the theoreticians. Before the 1970s, not a single teenager in love with movies could have answered the question

"What do you want to do when you grow up?" by saying "film theorist." But with the spread of film studies programs at universities, a hypothetical exchange of this kind suddenly became possible (albeit unlikely). Thus, while until then Italian theorists had been journalists, writers, directors, screenwriters, and only occasionally professors, from the 1970s onward there appeared a new and well-defined professional figure that could often find a home inside an academic discipline. If, as Cecchi said in the 1930s, "cinema is the Foreign Legion of intelligence," the 1970s coincided with the enlistment of many of former legionaries into a regular army.

The first university courses had already begun at the end of the 1950s. An adjunct professor since 1961, Chiarini in 1968 became the first Italian professor of film history and film criticism along with Aristarco. Eventually the most authoritative critics and journalists also migrated to the university without abandoning their socially engaged writing (e.g., Edoardo Bruno and Miccichè). And the foundation of the first Department of Art, Music, and Spectacle (DAMS) in Bologna in 1970, located within the Faculty of Literature and Philosophy, also played an important role in this process.

With the academic institutionalization of film studies, newspaper critics gradually began to leave theoretical questions to the professors. No example seems more appropriate than the one offered by Enzo Ungari (1948–85). Essayist, cultural organizer, and screenwriter (credits include Bernardo Bertolucci's *The Last Emperor*), Ungari was the best film critic of his generation and had a clear penchant for theory. Nevertheless, it is enough to browse his two collections of essays, *Schermo delle mie brame* (*Screen of My Desires*, 1978) and *Proiezioni private* (*Private Projections*, 1996), to see how in the end he always avoids generalizing concepts. In his pages, there is no shortage of general ideas, as in his brilliant essays about the directors of photography's artistic status ("I piaceri dell'occhio: Grandi cacciatori di luce a cavallo" ["The Pleasures of the Eye: Great Hunters of the Light In-Between"]), or about the relationship between remake and flashback ("I film che abbiamo già visto" ["The Films That We Have Already Seen"]). But Ungari clearly conceived of theory as something too cold and too professorial for his tastes, and preferred to insist on the subjective experience of vision rather than on the film itself, in line with a shift toward the moment of artistic reception that marked the decade on an international level (see, for example, the work of literary theorists like Hans Robert Jauss and Wolfgang Iser). As a result, Ungari's criticism moves more and more toward autobiography and diary, as in the opening essay of *Schermo delle mie brame*, "Confessioni di un amatore di film di provincia" ("Confessions of a Lover of Provincial Films"), with its allusion to the famous book by Thomas De Quincey, *Confessions of an English Opium-Eater*.

Although there are many exceptions, late twentieth-century Italian film theory seems less incisive. Various reasons can be given for this general trend: for example, the crisis of film journals, the difficulties of Italian cinema itself after the American producers left Cinecittà, and the decline of the nexus between aesthetics and political engagement that had been so strong in earlier decades. Moreover, the constant closing of film theaters (and in particular of the art-house circuit), the absence of public structures to keep alive the memory of the past, and the invasion of Silvio Berlusconi's commercial broadcasting have all contributed to the impoverishment of Italian cinephile culture. This marginality of film culture in Italy today also explains the substantial absence of Italian philosophers. Unlike France, where leading figures such as Alain Badiou, Jean-Jacques Nancy, and Jacques Rancière usually write about audiovisuals from their disciplinary perspectives, nothing similar tends to happen in Italy, where, to mention only the most internationally renowned, scant references to the universe of moving images can be found in the writing of philosophers Mario Perniola, Paolo Virno, Tony Negri, and Roberto Esposito.

There are exceptions. For instance, in some work from the 1980s the new spectacular regime of cinema and television plays an important role in the analysis by Gianni Vattimo (born 1936) of contemporary daily life, in particular his work on the "transparent society" in which, in the name of continuous "disorientation" and "play," mass media will finally redeem men from the "principle of reality" (*La società trasparente* [*The Transparent Society*, 1989]).[37] But even here, Vattimo does not further develop such questionable intuitions in his following books.

The most famous Italian thinker in the generation after Eco, Giorgio Agamben (born 1942), deserves special mention. As in Vattimo's case, his incursions into cinema and the audiovisual are sporadic: an essay on Guy Debord ("Difference and Repetition: On Guy Debord's Films"), some pages on Bill Viola in *Ninfe* (*Nymphs*, 2007), a very short text on Orson Welles's *Don Quixote* ("I sei minuti più belli della storia del cinema" ["The Six Most Beautiful Minutes in the History of Film"] from *Profanazioni* [*Profanations*, 2005]), but not much more. But two of Agamben's obsessions with moving images bear mentioning. The first relates to his long devotion to the writings of Walter Benjamin and Aby Warburg, resulting in his interest in the "fragment" or single photogram, the minimal unit of film. Agamben's second recurring topic is pornography, an element that suddenly emerges from time to time in the most varied of his texts.[38] However, also in this second case it should be stressed that in his longest works, such as "Elogio della profanazione" ("Praise of Profanation" from the already mentioned *Profanazioni*), Agamben's principal attention is focused on photography, in which he locates an anti-narrative option that finds its perfect counterpart in Agamben's limited interest in the novel compared to his passion for poetry.

Should one therefore conclude that Italian film studies are going through a crisis at the same time when so-called Italian theory in philosophy is enjoying worldwide recognition? One does not have to be so pessimistic. For example, in younger theorists there seems to a great willingness to set up a dialogue beyond national borders, overcoming that linguistic gap that all the great Italian film critics, from Canudo onwards, had to confront. The fact that in 2009 the most famous Italian film scholar, Francesco Casetti (born 1947), left the Università Cattolica del Sacro Cuore in Milan to teach at Yale University on a permanent basis is a clear sign that something is changing, and that Italian film theory is becoming more and more part of a global discussion on film.

Beyond this biographical detail, Casetti's intellectual path is very telling of the fate of Italian film after the 1960s. A pupil of Gianfranco Bettetini (one of the pioneers of the new film studies in the 1960s and one of the few Italian scholars translated into English),[39] Casetti graduated in the years of the rise of semiotics and, predictably, his first theoretical works still reflect that climate: *Dentro lo sguardo: Il film e lo spettatore* (*Inside the Gaze: The Film and the Spectator*, 1986) and *Analisi del Film* (*Analysis of Film*, 1990, coauthored with Federico di Chio). But not surprisingly, Casetti's first internationally acclaimed work was *Teorie del Cinema. 1945-1990* (*Theories of Cinema, 1945-1990*, 1993), where that semiotic experience was the subject of a dispassionate historical reconstruction. It is not difficult to see in Casetti's choice the need to take stock, retrospectively, of the developments made by two or three generations of scholars before looking for new paths forward.

In fact, Casetti's subsequent book was completely different, and has to be considered as the result of a real change of direction: from French semiotics to American cultural studies. *L'occhio del Novecento* (*The Eye of the Twentieth Century*, 2005) abandons pure theory for an inquiry on the ways in which cinema has observed the world, reflected on its own gaze and gradually reshaped the basic categories of aesthetic experience and— even more importantly—of experience tout court. Dedicated to the present process of "relocation" of films from the movie theater to the unstable universe of "individual media" and the internet, Casetti's most recent work, *The Lumière Galaxy: Seven Key Words for the Cinema to Come* (2015, written directly in English), goes somehow in the same direction.[40]

Casetti's trajectory can thus engender a more positive analysis. Perhaps, rather than being impoverished, Italian film theory has simply undergone a rapid metamorphosis under the pressure of cultural studies and the impact of a renewed historiography. Some of the best works published during the last years have a clear historical approach, but, already in their topics (such as war cinema and film nostalgia), they declare a strong theoretical vocation. In other words, it is not that Italian film theory has abdicated its task, but that it is merely questioning works, authors, styles, and motives in ways so different from earlier generations as to seem unrecognizable to predecessors. It would not be the first time that something of this nature happened. And the disorientation of those who judge today's Italian film theory with the categories of the past could then be—paradoxically—the best proof of its persistent vitality.

Notes

1 See Giunta, "Interview with Guido Aristarco," 225.

2 For a short survey, see Bertellini, "Film Theory and Criticism."

3 References to this essay are to Papini, "Philosophy of Cinema," 47–50.

4 See Epstein, *Le cinématographe vu de l'Etna*.

5 References to the essay are to Canudo, "Triumph of Cinema," 66–74.

6 See Canudo, "Reflections on the Seventh Art."

7 See Luciani, *Verso una nuova arte*.

8 See Luciani, "Scene Impressionism" and "The Poetics of Cinema."

9 See Marinetti et al., "The Futurist Cinematography."

10 See Marinetti, "The Variety Theater."

11 See, for instance, Bragaglia, "The Proscenium Arch of My Cinema."

12 See Pirandello, "Whether the Talking Film Will Abolish the Theater."

13 See Bragaglia, *Nuovi orizzonti della cinematografia*.

14 See Croce, *Aesthetics*.

15 References are to Gentile, Preface.

16 See Croce, *Aesthetics*.

17 See Croce, *Aesthetics*.

18 See Ragghianti, "Il verbo di Dreyer."

19 See Ragghianti, "Ejzenštejn, cinema e arte."

20 See Scotini, *Carlo Ludovico Ragghianti and the Cinematic Nature of Vision*.

21 See Barbaro, *Film*.

22 See Arnheim, "A New Laokoon."

23 For views of these directors on film, Fellini, *Fellini on Fellini*, *Interviews*, and *Making a Film*; and Antonioni, *The Architecture of Vision* and *Interviews*.

24 For an English selection of Roberto Rossellini's work, see his *My Method*.

25 Some of Zavattini's texts are collected in *Sequences from a Cinematic Life*.

26 See Zavattini, "Alcune idee sul cinema."

27 See Zavattini, "Alcune idee sul cinema."

28 See Bazin, "De Sica and Rossellini," 174.

29 See Della Volpe, *Critique of Taste*.

30 See Della Volpe, *Critique of Taste*.

31 See Gramsci, *Prison Notebooks*, 339–40 and 346–48.

32 See Arbasino, *Il Giorno*.

33 References to the essay are to Pasolini, *Heretical Empiricism*.

34 References to the essay are to Pasolini, *Heretical Empiricism*.

35 References to the essay are to Eco, "Articulations of the Cinematic Code."

36 References to the essay are to Pasolini, *Heretical Empiricism*.

37 See Vattimo, *The Transparent Society*.

38 See Agamben, *The Idea of the Prose*.

39 See Bettetini, *The Language and Technique of the Cinema*.

40 On a similar topic, see Pedullà, *In Broad Daylight*.

Bibliography

Agamben, Giorgio. *The Idea of the Prose*. New York: SUNY Press, 1995.

Antonioni, Michelangelo. *The Architecture of Vision*. Chicago: University of Chicago Press, 2007.

Antonioni, Michelangelo. *Interviews*. Jackson: University Press of Mississippi, 2008.

Arnheim, Rudolf. "A New Laokoon: Artistic Composite and the Talking Film." In *Film as Art*. Berkeley: University of California University Press, 1957. 199–230.

Arbasino, Alberto. "La gita a Chiasso." *Il Giorno*, January 23, 1963.

Barbaro, Umberto. *Film: Soggetto e sceneggiatura*. Rome: Bianco e nero, 1939.

Bazin, André. "De Sica and Rossellini." In *André Bazin and Italian Neorealism*. Ed. Bert Cardullo. New York: Continuum, 2011. 172–76.

Bettetini, Gianfranco. *The Language and Technique of the Cinema*. The Hague: Mouton, 1973.

Bertellini, Giorgio. "Film Theory and Criticism." In *Encyclopedia of Italian Literary Studies*. Ed. Gaetana Marrone, Paolo Puppa, and Luca Somigli. 2 vols. New York: Routledge, 2007. 1:722–28.

Bragaglia, Anton Giulio. "The Proscenium Arch of My Cinema" (1919). In *Early Film Theories in Italy, 1907–1922*. Ed. Francesco Casetti, Silvio Alovisio, and Luca Mazzei. Amsterdam: Amsterdam University Press, 2017. 47–50.

Bragaglia, Anton Giulio. *Nuovi orizzonti della cinematografia: Il film sonoro*. Milan: Corbaccio, 1929.

Canudo, Ricciotto. "The Birth of a Sixth Art" (1911). Trans. Richard Abel. In *French Film Theory and Criticism: A History/Anthology (1907–1929)*. Ed. Richard Abel. Princeton University Press, Princeton 1988. 58–65.

Canudo, Ricciotto. "Triumph of Cinema." In *French Film Theory and Criticism: A History/Anthology (1907–1929)*. Ed. Richard Abel. Princeton University Press, Princeton 1988. 66–74.

Canudo, Ricciotto. "Reflections on the Seventh Art" (1923). In *French Film Theory and Criticism: A History/Anthology (1907–1929)*. Ed. Richard Abel. Princeton University Press, Princeton 1988. 291–302.

Casetti, Francesco. *Inside the Gaze: The Fiction Film and Its Spectator*. Bloomington: Indiana University Press, 1998.

Casetti, Francesco. *Theories of Cinema, 1945–1995*. Austin: University of Texas Press, 1999.

Casetti, Francesco. *Eye of the Century: Film, Experience, Modernity*. New York: Columbia University Press, 2008.

Croce, Benedetto. *Aesthetics: As Science of Expression and General Linguistic*. London: McMillan, 1909.

Della Volpe, Galvano. *Critique of Taste*. London: Verso, 1978.

Eco, Umberto. *A Theory of Semiotics*. Bloomington: Indiana University Press, 1978.

Eco, Umberto. "Articulations of the Cinematic Code." In *Movies and Methods: An Anthology*. Ed. Bill Nichols. Berkeley: University of California Press, 1985. 590–607.

Epstein, Jean. *Le cinématographe vu de l'Etna*. Paris: Les Écrivains Reunis: 1926.

Fellini, Federico. *Fellini on Fellini*. Cambridge, MA: Da Capo, 1996.

Fellini, Federico. *Interviews*. Jackson: University Press of Mississippi, 2006.

Fellini, Federico. *Making a Film*. New York: Contra Mundum, 2015.

Gentile, Giovanni. Preface to Luigi Chiarini, *Cinematografo*. Rome: Bianco e Nero, 1935.

Giunta, Edvige. "Interview with Guido Aristarco." *Differentia: Review of Italian Thought* 8-9.19 (Spring/Autumn, 1999). 225–32. https://commons.library.s tonybrook.edu/di erentia/vol8/iss1/19. Accessed February 28, 2019.

Gramsci, Antonio. *Prison Notebooks*. New York: Columbia University Press, 2011.

Luciani, Sebastiano Arturo. "Scene Impressionism" and "The Poetics of Cinema." In *Early Film Theories in Italy, 1907–1922*. Ed. Francesco Casetti, Silvio Alovisio, and Luca Mazzei. Amsterdam: Amsterdam University Press, 2017. 321–24 and 329–32.

Luciani, Sebastiano Arturo. *Verso una nuova arte: Il cinematografo*. Rome: Ausonia, 1920.

Marinetti, Filippo Tommaso. "The Variety Theater." In *Futurism: An Anthology*. Ed. Lawrence Rainey, Christine Poggi, and Laura Wittman. New Haven: Yale University Press 2009, 159–65.

Marinetti, Filippo Tommaso et al. "The Futurist Cinematography." In *Early Film Theories in Italy, 1907–1922*. Ed. Francesco Casetti, Silvio Alovisio, and Luca Mazzei. Amsterdam: Amsterdam University Press, 2017. 341–45.

Papini, Giovanni. "Philosophy of Cinema." In *Early Film Theories in Italy, 1907–1922*. Ed. Francesco Casetti, Silvio Alovisio, and Luca Mazzei. Amsterdam: Amsterdam University Press, 2017. 47-50.

Pasolini, Pier Paolo. *Heretical Empiricism*. Ed. Louise K. Barnett. Trans. Ben Lawton and Louise K. Barnett. Washington, DC: New Academia Publishing, 2005.

Pedullà, Gabriele. *In Broad Daylight: Movies and Spectators after the Cinema*. London: Verso, 2012.

Pirandello, Luigi. "Whether the Talking Film Will Abolish the Theater." *New York Times* (July 28, 1929).

Ragghianti, Carlo Ludovico. "Il Verbo di Dreyer" (1955). In *Arti della visione*. Turin: Einaudi, 1975. 89–100.

Ragghianti, Carlo Ludovico. "Ejzenštejn, cinema e arte." In *Arti della visione*. Turin: Einaudi, 1975. 185–215.

Rossellini, Roberto. *My Method: Writings and Interviews*. New York: Marsilio, 1992.

Scotini, Marco, ed. *Carlo Ludovico Ragghianti and the Cinematic Nature of Vision*. Milan: Charta, 2000.

Vattimo, Gianni. *The Transparent Society*. London: Polity Press, 1992.

Zavattini, Cesare. "Alcune idee sul cinema" (1952). In *Neorealismo, ecc*. Ed. Mino Argentieri, Milano: Bompiani, 1979. 95–107.

Zavattini, Cesare. *Sequences from a Cinematic Life*. Englewood Cliffs: Prentice-Hall, 1970.

PART THREE

Relations and Debates

12

Film Music

Kaos and the Tavianis

Daniela Bini

Despite the recent upsurge in scholarship on music's relation to film, this subject still occupies a subordinate role in the immense and growing field of film studies.[1] One of the reasons for delayed interest in the topic has been the difficulty of finding a common ground of discussion for musicologists and film scholars, since the former are for the most part not familiar with film criticism, and the majority of the latter have little knowledge of musicology. But recently film scholars have paid more attention to the treatment of music by emphasizing that it should be considered on the same level as the other media employed in cinema. In their introduction to *Beyond the Soundtrack*, Golmark, Kramer, and Leppert write that we should look at music "as an agent, a force, an object engaged in ongoing negotiations with image, narrative, context. So conceived music operates . . . on an equal footing with its negotiation partners" (3). Rudolf Arnheim argued for an all-embracing approach: music, image, and narrative must complement each other because they deal, albeit differently, with the same subject. Each medium must treat the subject in its own way.[2] Adorno and Heisler criticized the "Mickey Mouse" use of music, that is, the mimicking action of music in many Hollywood films. They ask instead for something like counterpoint to emphasize the disjuncture between sound and image.[3] Finally, the musician Nino Rota added that music in cinema must express the spirit of the film (echoing the overall approach of Max Steiner) rather than the materiality of individual images. Music must keep itself apart, and not submit to the story line.[4]

In Italy, it was the exceptional pairing of Federico Fellini and Nino Rota that brought the centrality of film music to the attention of the public. A composer of operas, sonatas, chamber, symphonic, vocal music, and hundreds of soundtracks, Rota was already famous when he met a young Fellini at the start of his career. From 1952 to 1979, Rota composed the soundtracks of almost all Fellini's films and created the musical style that became their signature. The tunes of Gelsomina in *La strada* (1954), the musical motifs of *La dolce vita* (1960) and *8 1/2* (1963), are inextricably connected with their characters and stories and recognized by thousands. A mixture of the grotesque and melancholic, Rota's music for Fellini exemplifies a quality of many Italian films and of the Italian character in general—a combination of the tragic and the comic.[5] A completely different but almost equally effective pair was that of Sergio Leone and Ennio Morricone, who created the popular Spaghetti Western films. The eerie musical phrases that accompany many long scenes with no dialogue in films like *The Good, the Bad, and the Ugly* (1966) or *Once Upon a Time in the West* (1968) function like a character in the plot. Leone was well aware that in certain situations music speaks much more effectively than dialogue.[6]

A major obstacle in this late interest in film music is the difficulty of speaking of the effects of music on an audience in general. It derives from the nature of music, which is also the reason for our fascination with it. Speaking of opera, Mary Ann Smart writes, "Because of music's expressive slipperiness, the stories told by opera have a special strength, full of ambiguity" (*Siren Songs*, 19). Even though music has a smaller role in film than in opera, we can certainly see similarities between music in film and opera. Slipperiness and elusiveness are characteristics of all music; they create ambiguity in the message that is therefore perceived and interpreted by the audience in various ways. This ambiguity is part of music's power and attraction, and has shaped the way we consider music in film. The composer Ennio Morricone, in fact, considers film the heir of opera

> because—precisely like in musical theater [film] has shown the ability to speak to the hearts of both simple people as well as the intellectuals. . . . Cinema is capable of transforming itself from time to time in chamber work and in opera buffa, in tragedy and in comedy . . . in popular spectacle and in a work for a small elite. (*Comporre per il cinema*, 304–305)[7]

More interesting yet is what Morricone has to say about music's role in film: "I believe that music must intervene when the action stops, crystallizes; just as in musical theater there are recitative and aria . . . music in film must take the place of the aria, when the action stops and we deal with the thought and the interior world of the protagonist, not when the action has its narrative dynamics" (*Musica e cinema nella cultura del Novecento*, 479). When music for the composer intervenes in film, it obviously has the role of protagonist.

When we discuss music in film, we must distinguish between the use of preexisting music and the original film score, and between diegetic and extra-diegetic music. Diegetic (Sergio Miceli prefers to call it "internal") music "emanat[es] from a clearly visible source"[8] and "possesses clear-cut narrative functions."[9] Extra-diegetic—or for Miceli "external"—music accompanies the narrative, commenting on or underscoring it. It "can relax or intensify the pacing of a scene, it can reflect emotion or create atmosphere, it can evoke social or ethnic stereotypes." It can also mimic the actions performed on the screen to reinforce them.[10] What composers prefer to create or work with, however, is neither type of music. They especially like to compose or arrange music that participates "in the primary semantic level of the film by adding referential or narrative dimensions missing from the imagetrack" (*Music and Cinema*, 13). It is the music, to use Miceli's expression, for the "mediated level," the "situation in which the character of a film expresses him/herself not only and not so much through verbal language, but through music—a music that in this case does not appear as thought and imposed from the external level . . . as a musical comment, but that belongs to the character" (*Comporre per il cinema*, 109).[11]

Film critics have had a hard time dealing with the eternal debate about musical expression. Generally, we can say that music expresses feelings. But what feelings? Those that images and dialogues suggest? In film, the tendency generally is that music is "serving," by accompanying the narrative underscoring and emphasizing its message.

More rarely, music can serve as a counterpoint to the narrative, as Adorno and Heisler would have it, almost challenging it. Still, the answer cannot fully satisfy, for as Richard Dryer aptly put it, "whatever feelings music expresses, they go beyond those that can be labeled; the feelings in music often fall through the gaps in our crude vocabulary for describing emotions" (*Beyond the Soundtrack*, 248). Dryer continues, "All these phenomena imply that music is effective yet also indicate that the way in which it is cannot be reduced to the kinds of emotions that words and narratives most readily and commonly deal with" (*Beyond the Soundtrack*, 248–49). To underline the ambiguity of music's message, Slavoj Žižek cites the example of the prelude of Wagner's *Lohengrin* used in Chaplin's *The Great Dictator* in two totally different scenes—Hitler/Hinkel's playing and embracing the balloon representing the world, and the moving final speech Hitler/the Barber delivers before an enormous German crowd. "In so far as it externalizes our inner passions music is potentially always a threat."[12] Žižek sees music as the voice of the id that can be positively liberating but also negatively destructive.

Claudia Gombar is a pioneer in the study of music in film, and in her essay "Music Auteur" she identifies a group of "*mélomanes* directors"—those who consider music as "a key thematic element and a marker of authorial style" (*Beyond the Soundtrack*, 149). Although she includes in her list the best-known Italian directors with their faithful composers—Fellini-Rota and Leone-Morricone[13]—she does not mention the true *mélomanes* of Italian cinema: the Taviani brothers, who use both preexisting and original musical scores and, with their faithful composer Nicola Piovani, have created a particular style recognizable in their different films. In the Taviani brothers' own words, "For Pasolini cinema was above all painting; for Fellini, mise-en-scene, for Visconti, literature, for Eisenstein, editing. . . . For us every aspect is important, but the keystone lies in the relation between image and sound. This is the moment in which the power, the magic, the mystery and the strange miracle of cinema are experienced."[14] Music is for the Tavianis the language of cinema, and its central role is already obvious in their first film, *Padre padrone* (1977), where not only music but also sound in general is its moving force. Sound is both the protagonist and "connective force of this work."[15] Its function is not merely that of commenting and underscoring the images, but often and more interestingly, that of "contradicting" them "with the result that the 'naturalistic' identification with what is happening on the screen is immediately discouraged." When music behaves in this manner, realizes a "Brechtian distantiation" that involves and challenges the audience to take a critical and active role in interpreting the scene.[16]

The Taviani had already worked with Piovani on *La notte di San Lorenzo* (*The Night of the Shooting Stars*, 1982). "The composer," said Piovani, "does not have at his disposal nouns and verbs [as does the writer]—with notes you cannot say: 'Mario leaves the house'—but he possesses in his dictionary an almost infinite variety of adjectives and adverbs. He can say *how* [Mario] leaves the house" (*Concerto fotogramma*, 17). It is an enlightening statement that underscores, as Richard Dryer wrote, the difficulty, if not impossibility of labeling the feelings expressed by music, which "often fall through the gaps in our crude vocabulary for describing emotions" (*Beyond the Soundtrack*, 248).

Even better, Piovani's statement elaborates on Suzanne Langer's suggestion that music may not express joy or sorrow, but certainly the tonalities of a variety of feelings. "Music is a tonal analog of emotive life."[17] For Piovani, music "is necessary to narrate the invisible"—and, we could add, what is inexpressible with verbal language (*Concerto fotogramma*, 17).

The composer of film music, continues Piovani, must set aside his or her own personal poetics and enter those of another. He is an actor who must empty himself of his ego and enter that of the character he plays.[18] It is a great challenge that, if successful, is accompanied by an equally great satisfaction. Indeed, if the composer is a successful musician, he will often create a style that will be recognizable in different films, even by different directors. Not only can Piovani's style be recognized in the music he composed for the Taviani brothers, but also in Giuseppe Tornatore's *Il camorrista* (*The Camorra Man*, 1986), whose soundtrack echoes the dramatic beat of the episode "L'altro figlio" ("The Other Son") in the Tavianis' film *Kaos* (*Chaos*, 1984).

The Night of the Shooting Stars has two main musical themes, an elegiac one and another that mimics, with its beat and rhythm, the marching steps of the inhabitants of San Martino who abandon the city before it is blown up by the Nazis. The long march becomes increasingly dramatic as the film progresses, and the music evokes images of danger and horror that provoke feelings of fear, dread, and exhaustion in the audience. Its echo will resound in an equally, if not more dreadful, episode of *Kaos*, "The Other Son," in which Maragrazia recounts to the town's doctor her dramatic search for her husband and its tragic conclusion.

The film, moreover, features opera, a great love of the Taviani brothers. In *Kaos*, opera is present only in one moving aria from Mozart's *The Marriage of Figaro*. It will reappear several times, becoming the narrative thread of the film. This opera had already had an important role in *Ruffo 60*, a Taviani brothers' radio play of the 1960s, and would be a meaningful presence in *Tu ridi* (*You Laugh*, 1998), the second film of theirs derived from Pirandello's stories. Why, one wonders, is Pirandello important in a discussion on music in film? Luigi Pirandello was fascinated by and involved with film from its inception, which coincided with his early career. His doubts about the arrival of the "talkie" decades later in the early 1930s are well documented.[19] They can in part be explained by his fear that film would compete with the theater and eventually reduce its appeal. His article "Se il film parlante abolirà il teatro" ("Whether the Talking Film Will Abolish the Theater") in *Corriere della Sera* (June 16, 1929) revealed the playwright's worries for his theater and for theater in general. His doubts were legitimate. In the poor early performance of sound film, voices were not synchronized and had a mechanical quality. Pirandello attempted to find a specific space for sound in this new cinema, and elaborated the idea of "cinemelografia," whose specific object was the sound-image connection: images that must spring out of the sound. He was absolutely sure of the powerful function of music in film. "Cinema must leave narration to the novel, and drama to theater. Literature is not its proper element; its element is music" (*Saggi*, 1035). Italy's directors, though many agreed with the importance he gave to music, were to prove him wrong by successfully combining literature (including Pirandello's work) and music.

The Sicilian playwright would probably have been fascinated by a work in which the inspiration was precisely a literary text that, instead of being translated into images accompanied by words, would be realized in images commented on by music. For an author who wrote extensively about the inadequacy of verbal language and the impossibility of communicating with it, the idea that an ambiguous message could be entrusted to visual and musical language would certainly have been attractive. That sound or the absence of sound could achieve a greater effect by intensifying the message— the idea being that music speaks directly to the soul without the intellectual mediation that accompanies the reception of words—would have appealed greatly to Pirandello.

Paolo and Vittorio Taviani had thought of adapting Pirandello's stories as early as 1970, when they proposed "Berecche alla guerra" ("Berecche Goes to War") to RAI. The project was rejected because it would have been too expensive. A few years later, the directors had the idea, also never realized, of making a series of episodes from Pirandello's short stories again for RAI. *Kaos* was finally born out of their desire to make a film on Sicily after having done one on Sardinia, *Padre padrone*, and another on Tuscany, *The Night of the Shooting Stars*.[20] Much has been written on *Kaos*. It consists of four episodes, as well as a prologue and epilogue, taken from six short stories. In a few of the stories, the role of music is central.[21]

In *Kaos*, a work on Sicily that describes the passions, beliefs, and superstitions of a primitive world, the music is intense and direct, and its message immediately reaches the audience. Piovani drew on Sicilian folk tradition and connected the various episodes with a musical motif that I would call the aria of the moon. The moon is the tutelary deity of this primitive world, mistress of the ocean tides and of woman's procreative cycle, but it is also the virgin goddess of Greek tradition. With her multifarious and mysterious nature, she is both omnipotent and worshipped by all.

The film begins with an image of a dry mountainous area of Sicily where the only accompanying sound is that of the wind and soon the shrieking call of a crow that has been captured by shepherds. They are laughing at the male bird sitting on eggs in a nest. Some of the shepherds mistreat the bird, until one takes him and puts a bell around his neck. As he lets him free in the sky and shouts the word "Musica," the sound track begins. The directors are faithful to the literary source, "Il corvo di Mizzaro" ("The Crow of Mizzaro"). It is Pirandello himself, therefore, who offers his music to them. The musical flight of the crow will connect all the episodes, thus music acts as the backbone of the entire narrative. Only in the final episode, the epilogue, will the meaning of the musical crow be explained. It will metamorphose in the beautiful, young body of Pirandello's mother, and her soprano voice will take the place of the bell and sing a Mozart aria from *The Marriage of Figaro*. The epilogue sheds retrospective light on the previous episodes. The old writer needs to return to his physiological mother, Caterina, and his geographical one, Sicily, to be able to write his stories. He will need to remember his mother's story and song to be able to narrate his own.[22]

There are two episodes in the second story "Mal di luna" ("Moon Sickness") where music is exploited to complement the images. The first is the confession of illness that the character Batà makes to the inhabitants of the town who listen in fear, locked up inside their homes. His words are taken almost verbatim from Pirandello's text:

My mother when young used to search for wild greens. That time she had not found enough during the day. It was summer and there was a full moon. My mother kept searching all night long. [She] had left me in the grass in the open exposed to the moon. And poor innocent [baby that I was,] I played with the beautiful moon all night long. And the moon bewitched me. (*Kaos*, 50–51)[23]

The Tavianis show the enchantment of the "bedda luna" ("beautiful moon" in Sicilian dialect) with images and sound so powerful that they make us spectators equal victims to the enchantment. The pure silver light of the moon reflected in baby Batà's eyes and in the water of the nearby pond reveals the power of the goddess Diana and our helplessness, like that of young hunter Actaeon, whom she had killed by his own hounds for his arrogant pride in daring to behold her naked, virginal body as she bathed. But to achieve such intense power, the image needs the help of music. The magical chords of a clarinet, similar to the double flute of Dionysus, develop in a slow, enchanting phrase, soon to be joined by the string instruments. It is extra-diegetic music that, however, becomes, to use Miceli's words, "mediated," in so far as it is recognized as the voice of the moon. Piovani creates her theme that will appear again in the episode "La giara" ("The Jar"). There, too, the moon will display her power albeit in a comical fashion. In this moment, we understand more than ever, as the directors say, that "music arrives in the most telling moments, when it becomes a character in the scene" (*La bottega Taviani*, 15). Words would have been inadequate, and Pirandello would have agreed.

The second episode in "Moon Sickness" that exemplifies the powerful working together of images and sound is the three long minutes without words that serve to describe the passing days between the new and full moon. After Batà's wife, Sidora, refuses to spend another night of full moon near her ill husband, her mother promises her that she and Saro (a young man to whom Sidora is still attracted) will come and keep her company at each full moon when Batà is taken over by moon sickness. The Tavianis show us a limpid day where the first pale crescent of the new moon appears in a clear August sky. A male voice starts singing a slow-moving song in dialect that addresses the moon. The camera slowly closes in on Sidora and Batà plowing as she raises her head to look nervously at the moon. The only words we hear in these three minutes are those that Batà naïvely and ironically (without knowing) uttered to reassure Sidora: "Don't be afraid. There is still time. The trouble will be when the moon loses its horns" (*Kaos*, 56). In the second musical phrase, a female voice joins in the male voice in counter melody.

Slowly the instruments come in, first the violins then a guitar that accompany the voices in an intensely passionate serenade. The music develops in a slow crescendo that mirrors the slow waxing of the moon and the erotic arousal of the lovers. Despite (or because of) the distance that still separates them, their erotic dialogue intensifies with the music. The camera shows Saro in a fishing boat, rowing with excessive intensity as he looks at the waxing moon, while Sidora with equally excessive intensity polishes the floor of her humble home. The frenetic motion of her hips and legs becomes the objective correlative of the sexual act. Three minutes of images without dialogue, where the erotic tension finds only in music its adequate expression.

Much has been written on the last scene of this episode that concludes with the iconic image of *Pietà*, when Sidora holds the head of her wounded husband on her lap. Sidora's erotic love metamorphoses into a sentiment of *pietà*, and Saro is the agent inspiring this change. It is he who goes to help Batà as his illness attacks, and keeps him from hurting himself by holding and restraining his body. The position of the two men creates the first image of *pietà*, the upright one, holding the body of Christ in Michelangelo's Palestrina and Florence *Pietà*.[24] The erotic love of Sidora and Saro is transformed into this new sentiment. In this scene, without dialogue, music is once again the agent of metamorphosis. The passionate Sicilian song that had accompanied the waxing of the moon and the erotic expectations of Sidora and Saro reappears here, but now the intense and vibrant sound is toned down, as the volume is lowered, and the tempo is slowed down. The passionate serenade has become a soft lullaby. The lover has been transformed into the mother-nurse, and once again words surrender to music.

A triumphal march opens the episode "The Jar," where again dialogue is very scarce. The scenic comic space is entrusted to the transport of the splendid new jar to Don Lollo's farmhouse. The notes we hear are the same that will mark the steps of the artisan Zi' Dima, when he arrives to fix the broken jar. In this comic scene, the music underscores the close relationship and complicity between artisan and artifact. It will become Zi' Dima's motif, the real protagonist, magician, and architect of the plot.

The Tavianis' most original addition and contribution to Pirandello's story is with the image of the moon—that same moon whose power we had already seen at work. Here too we have a scanty script, no dialogue, and only a few images of the jar and the moon, the goddess and protector of this primitive world against the greedy representative of the materialistic philosophy of "la roba" (property). And the moon will punish Don Lollò by breaking his treasured possession. Between the arrival of the jar and the discovery of it broken nothing happens in Pirandello's text. The writer describes Don Lollò at length and with humor to underline his greed and stinginess and then, in a new paragraph, the workers' discovery of the broken jar and their consternation. Between these two phases, the directors include a magical and mysterious nocturnal scene. It is introduced by the fading in of the image of Don Lollò hugging his beloved jar in the middle of his farmyard before his workers. He knocks on it, eliciting a bell-like sound: "It sounds like the bells of Santo Stefano," is his comment as he demonstrates his faith in the religion of "la roba" (*Kaos*, 78). This image fades into that of a full moon taking central stage and occupying the entire screen. Light clouds pass over it, accompanied by string music, which we will recognize shortly after as Zi' Dima's theme. As the camera moves inside, it shows Don Lollò tossing in bed, at his feet a little cot with Sara, placed there like a dog, also tossing around. Their sleep is disturbed and the agent of this disturbance is clearly the moon. The camera moves outside focusing on the beautiful jar that now takes center stage. Suddenly the music changes, and we hear the tune of "Moon Sickness" brought about by the clarinet—a very effective piece of "mediated" music. It is the moon's voice we are hearing, and she is about to punish greedy Don Lollò. Once again, the white goddess intervenes to teach men a lesson. Dark clouds cover the scene, and when light makes the jar visible again, it is no longer the formidable vessel of life and abundance, but just two broken pieces. When words are inadequate the message is entrusted to music, which once again becomes protagonist in the story's central play. There is of course no proof that the moon was the culprit. The message therefore can only be hinted at, and this is done by the cooperation of music and images.

Zi' Dima, the artisan who is called in to fix the jar, represents the primitive culture in opposition to Don Lollo's materialistic and precapitalistic one. Close to nature, he is not a man of words but action, and he expresses himself mainly through his formidable facial and body mimicry, brilliantly portrayed by the actor Franco Franchi. To accompany his comic mimicry and slow steps, Piovani arranged the music—which in the scene of the moon was a mysterious slow chant—in syncopation with Zi' Dima's motions. As the miraculous glue appears, however, the same tune is expanded in longer and slower phrases, and is then presented with a crescendo that reaches its climax in the elevation of the chalice that contains it. It is music that accompanies a sacred rite, as Sara's crossing herself shows.

The culminating scene in the working together of music and image is Zi' Dima's "rebirth" out of the broken jar at the end of the story. As the peasants, fearing for the artisan's life, threateningly close in on Don Lollò who broke the jar, a trill of the flute— the same we had heard during Zi' Dima's inspection of the jar—directs our gaze to his coiled-up body. Once again no words are uttered, only the trill of the flute accompanying the mimicry of Zi' Dima who slowly gets up and starts to move his first jerking steps, like a chick hatching. What had Pirandello given to the Tavianis to inspire such a clever scene? Very little: "Rolling down accompanied by the peasants' laughter the jar hit an olive tree and broke to pieces. And Zi' Dima won" (*Novelle per un anno*, 2:279).[25] Once more, we see how the Taviani brothers enrich a brief, telegraphic sentence in Pirandello with meaningful images. They create a narrative through images and sound; what the scene tells us could not have been told with equal effectiveness with words. The episode ends with Zi' Dima carried away in triumph by the peasants while his music is transformed in a triumphal march that makes clear that "Zi' Dima won"—the same triumphal march that accompanied the arrival of the beautiful jar at the beginning of the episode. Zi' Dima and the jar belong to the same world and speak the same language.

The "Dialogue with the Mother" that the directors call the epilogue must be read as a proleptic device. The encounter with his mother, in fact, is what must happen for the stories to be written. The return to his origin is necessary to enable Pirandello's creative "flight." The return, however, is not enough. The writer has to acquire the ability "to open up," as Caterina tells him, and "look at life with the eyes of those who no longer see" (170). To be able to write Pirandello must become humble, and learn to listen, remember, and recount the family journey to Malta to join their father in his exile— the journey that his mother had told him about many times. Not so much the journey but the *pause* matters, the stop during the trip on the island of pumice. It is the pause that escaped him during the important episode, as well as the song that accompanies it—"your song," as he tells her.

As he stepped off the train at a desolate Sicilian station, Luigi had noted two children playing on a mound of dirt with open arms imitating birds in flight. Their motions were accompanied by sad, chanting chords that will be recognized only later. Piovani is here competing with Mozart, arranging his music to make it unrecognizable at first. Only after the apparition of Caterina in the family home when she starts recounting the old story again will "her song" be played again, but this time with words and as Mozart had composed it. The aria accompanies the boat to the island of pumice where they stop, waiting for better winds to pick up again. The first sound we hear on the island is that of our musical crow that has accompanied us during our journey. It is this parenthesis, this magical pause that Pirandello finally remembers and that will inspire his imagination to take flight again and create. We realize this right away, when we see the children and Caterina in particular as they climb up the mound of pumice and then, with open arms that imitate the flight of the crow, jump down to the transparent, aquamarine waters below. No words can accompany this poetic scene. The music of the crow picks up again briefly only to leave center stage to Mozart and the aria of Barbarina from Act 4 of *The Marriage of Figaro*. But what is Barbarina's singing? "L'ho perduta, me meschina" ("I lost it, wretched me"). It is the aria that Pirandello had lost so many times, because he could not look at things with the eyes of others. If, as Millicent Marcus has noted, this episode allows us to reread retrospectively the stories we have just watched, Barbarina's aria allows us to interpret the music of the playing crow. Only after having rediscovered Mozart, that is, the memory of childhood, can Pirandello create his music. And what does Barberina cry for, alone in the dark garden (beyond the literal loss of the count's pin), if not for the loss of her youthful purity?

Piovani creates for *Kaos* a soundtrack that is both original and also uses preexisting music. Music thus has a double function: of pure sound closely connected to the primitive world that the film represents, and intertextual allusion that presupposes the knowledge of the operatic narrative. Opera plays a large role not only in the cinema of the Taviani brothers—for example, in *Allonsanfan* (1974), *Good Morning Babilonia* (1987), and *Fioril* (1993)—but also in Italian cinema in general, from Luchino Visconti to Marco Bellocchio.

Opera, and once again Mozart's *The Marriage of Figaro*, together with Rossini's *The Girl of Algiers*, reappear in the episode "Felice" of *You Laugh*, the second film where the Taviani adapted Pirandello's stories.[26] In yet another artistic departure from the literary source, the directors make Pirandello's character of Mr. Anselmo, a pathetic, sad state employee, into Felice, a baritone who had to abandon his singing career because of a heart condition, and who finds only in music an escape from his wretched life of humiliation at work and home. The setting is Fascist Rome, his work is that of accountant in an opera theater that keeps him at least close to his beloved past life. At home, his jealous, irascible Bulgarian wife does not understand him and eventually leaves him. Although his male superiors constantly make fun of his best friend because of his disability, Felice has no courage to intervene to defend him. Only in front of his photograph in the costume of Taddeo can he escape for a few minutes his self-contempt and depression.

The power of music, and in particular opera, does more than serve Felice as an escape. Just as in *Kaos*, it acts as a truth-revealing agent. The aria from Rossini's *The Girl from Algiers* that had brought a moment of glory to our protagonist—and at times returns to him as a helpful memory—will also make Felice discover the truth about himself. *The Girl from Algiers* is an opera buffa, and Taddeo is one of its comic characters. In love with Isabella (the protagonist) he acts almost as her servant and follows her as far as Algiers in the search for her beloved Lindoro. Why would the Tavianis choose this opera as part of the sound track to adapt Pirandello's stories? A possible answer can be found in the character of Taddeo. Felice identifies with him as he obtained his greatest success in that role. Taddeo's comic character becomes humoristic, in the Pirandellian sense. We can no longer laugh, but we feel pity and compassion for him. In the opera, in fact, he must accept compromises to escape impalement.[27] In life, Felice does not have the courage to stand up to the bullish arrogance of his Fascist superiors. The famous aria "Ho un gran peso sulla testa" ("I have a heavy weight hanging over me"), in which Taddeo's confession takes place, ends with the line "O Taddeo, quant'era meglio che finissi in fondo al mar" ("Oh Taddeo, how much better it would have been if you had ended up at the bottom of the sea")—a suggestion that Felice will take literally with his eventual suicide. The aria that brought him success will thus function as the vehicle through which he becomes aware of his cowardice and weakness. As he sings it for the last time in a restaurant at the request of his old friend Nora, the camera alternates between shots of his present singing and images of him on stage in costume as Taddeo. When for the last time the camera frames Nora's face, her expression has changed: from joyful and playful at the beginning of the aria to somber at its conclusion, her eyes filled with sadness. Felice's heart has spoken to hers.

An early scene tells us much about music's role in film. Working in the theater as an accountant, Felice often hid behind the curtain to listen to opera rehearsals. He was there when Figaro tried his famous aria "Se vuol ballare, Signor Contino" ("If you want to dance, Count") from Act 1 of *The Marriage of Figaro*. The baritone singing the aria was frustrated because the maestro who accompanied him on the piano was never satisfied with his interpretation and told him to sing the aria in a different way every time. To make the baritone understand, the maestro confessed the difficulty of performing Mozart's music, which consists precisely in its constant mutability—one moment clear, the next mysterious. "Mozart is clear and incomprehensible, as nature. He is white and then, if you look well between the chords, he is black." He who plays Mozart must perform a process of discovering the truth, a process that will always fail (70).[28] This brief scene does not have much relevance to the plot of the story. Yet it is emblematic of music's function and its essence. It is music's ambiguity that constitutes its power, and when it accompanies images, as it does in film, it opens them up to a variety of nuances and of meanings that ask for the active participation of the audience in deciphering them. But the truth, if it exists, will never be revealed.

Notes

1 Some of the relevant studies on film music are: Pendergast, *Film Music*; Burt, *The Art of Film Music*; Brown, *Overtones and Undertones*; Mera and Burnand, *European Film Music*; Miceli, *Musica e cinema nella cultura del Novecento*; Powerie and Stilwell, *Changing Tunes*; Cano, *La musica nel cinema*.

2 Deyer, *Beyond*, 250.

3 Deyer, *Beyond*, 250.

4 Deyer, *Beyond*, 251. A detailed description of the Mickey Mouse and "over all" approaches are in Dyer, "Side by Side."

5 Gieri's seminal *Contemporary Italian Filmmaking* traces the influence of Pirandello's humor in a great number of Italian directors. For an overview of the films of "commedia all'italiana," see A. Bini, "The Birth of Comedy Italian Style."

6 In "Cinemelography," Harrison convincingly discusses music's function in the famous "triello" scene at the end of *The Good, the Bad, and the Ugly*.

7 All translations from Italian are mine, unless otherwise stated.

8 Pendergast, *Film Music*, 24.

9 Buhler and Flinn, *Music and Cinema*, 6.

10 Buhler and Flinn, *Music and Cinema*, 13.

11 One of the best examples is Giuseppe Tornatore's *La leggenda del pianista sull'oceano* (*The Legend of 1900*, 1998).

12 In Žižek, *The Pervert Guide to Cinema*.

13 Among the most relevant studies of these two famous film pairs are: Miceli, *Morricone, la musica, il cinema*; Burlingame, Crowdus, and Morricone, "Music at the Service of the Cinema"; Dyer, "Nino Rota"; Van Order, *Listening to Fellini*; and Gorbman, "Music As Salvation." For a comprehensive study, see Miceli, *Musica per film*.

14 Ferrucci and Turini, *Paolo and Vittorio Taviani*, 11.

15 Graham, "*Padre Padrone* and the Dialectics of Sound," 29.

16 Graham, "*Padre Padrone* and the Dialectics of Sound," 29.

17 Dyer, *Beyond the Soundtrack*, 249.

18 When Piovani composed the music for Fellini's *La voce della luna* (*The Voice of the Moon*, 1990), but even more *Intervista* (*Interview*, 1987), he entered the spirit of Fellini to the point of creating a music that clearly echoed that of Nino Rota.

19 Among the many studies on Pirandello and cinema, see Callari, *Pirandello e il cinema*; Nichols and Bazzoni, *Pirandello and Film*; and Gieri, *Contemporary Italian Filmaking*.

20 This information is from an interview Bonsaver had with the director on October 20, 2006 in Rome, published in his book *Kàos*.

21 Among the many studies on *Kaos*, see Marcus's pioneering "*Kaos*'s Pirandello *liberato*," reprinted in English with the title "The Taviani's *Kàos*: The Poetics of Adaptation"; and the recent *Kàos* by Bonsaver, already quoted. For a more extensive discussion of the music, see D. Bini, "Pirandello e la musica del *Kaos*."

22 Pirandello's story has a tragic end. The "musical" crow will cause the death of the farmer who had captured and tortured it and of the donkey that was pulling the farmer's cart. But the "musical" crow, the story ends, "nell'azzurro della bella mattinata, sonava di nuovo pei cieli la sua campanella, libero e beato" ("in the beautiful blue morning, was playing again his bell through the skies, free and blessed"; *Novelle*, 1:1019).

23 "Batà . . . prese adagio adagio a narrare la sua sciagura: che la madre da giovane, andata a spighe, dormendo su un'aja al sereno, lo aveva tenuto bambino tutta la notte esposto alla luna; e tutta quella notte, lui povero innocente, con la pancina all'aria, mentre gli occhi gli vagellavano, ci aveva giocato con la bella luna . . . E la luna lo aveva 'incantato'" ("Batà . . . slowly began to tell his misfortune: that his mother when young, having gone to collect herbs and sleeping outdoors during a clear night, had left him all night long exposed to the moon; and all night long, he, poor innocent, with his

little belly in the air, while his eyes were wandering, had played with the beautiful moon . . . and the moon had bewitched him"; *Novelle*, 1:1301).

24 Bini, "Pirandello e la musica del *Kaos*," 9–10.

25 "Rotolando, accompagnata dalle risa degli ubriachi, la giara andò a spaccarsi contro un olivo. E la vinse Zi' Dima" ("rolling down, accompanied by the laughter of the drunk peasants ended up broken against an olive tree. And Uncle Dima won.").

26 *The Marriage of Figaro*, and in particular the aria "Là ci darem la mano" ("There we will take each other's hands"), was central in an early work by the Tavianis, the radio drama *Ruffo 60* (1965). In this work Mozart appears as character-shadow, similar to those shadows that used to visit Pirandello in his study and of his very mother in the episode used in *Kaos*. For a description of this radio drama, see Accialini and Coluccelli, *Paolo e Vittorio Taviani*, 91–97. For the first episode of *Tu ridi*, the Tavianis adapted at least four of Pirandello stories: "Tu ridi" ("You Laugh"), "L'imbecille" ("The Imbecile"), "Sole e ombra" ("Sun and Shadow"), and "L'illustre istinto" ("The Illustrious Extinct"), as well as indirectly "C'è qualcuno che ride" ("Someone Is Laughing") and "La realtà del sogno" ("The Reality of Dream").

27 It is not a coincidence that in Felice's laughing dreams, the scene that presents itself over and over is that of his poor handicapped friend attempting to climb a staircase. After his friend falls down on the steps, his bully boss pretends to insert the disabled man's cane in his behind.

28 "Mozart è chiaro e incomprensibile . . . come la natura . . . È bianco e poi, se guardi bene qui fra le note, è nero." For a complete study of *Tu ridi*, see my "Umorismo e tradimento in *Tu ridi* dei Taviani."

Bibliography

Accialini, Fulvio and Lucia Coluccelli. *Paolo e Vittorio Taviani*, Florence: La Nuova Italia, Il Castoro Cinema, 1979.

Bini, Andrea. "The Birth of Comedy Italian Style." In *Popular Italian Cinema: Culture and Politics in a Postwar Society*. Ed. Flavia Brizio-Skov. London: I. B. Tauris, 1979. 107–52.

Bini, Daniela. "Pirandello e la musica del Kaos." In *Il cinema di Pirandello*. Ed. Enzo Lauretta. Agrigento: Centro Nazionale Studi Pirandelliani, 2003. 243–56.

Bini, Daniela. "Umorismo e tradimento in *Tu ridi* dei Taviani." In *L'angelo di fuoco*. Turin: Edizioni DAMS, 2003–2004. 101–19.

Bonsaver, Guido. *Kàos: Pirandello e i fratelli Taviani*. Palermo: L'Epos, 2007.

Buhler, James, Carol Flinn, and David Neumeyer, eds. *Music and Cinema*. Middletown: Wesleyan University Press, 2000.

Brown, Royal S. *Overtones and Undertones: Reading Film Music*. Berkeley: University of California Press, 1994.

Burlingame, Jon, Gary Crowdus, and Ennio Morricone. "Music at the Service of the Cinema: An Interview with Ennio Morricone." *Cinéaste* 21.1–2 (1995): 76–80.

Burt, George. *The Art of Film Music*. Boston: Northeastern University Press, 1994.

Callari, Francesco. *Pirandello e il cinema: Con una raccolta completa degli scritti teorici e creativi*. Venice: Marsilio, 1991.

Cano, Cristina. *La musica nel cinema: Musica, immagine, racconto*. Rome: Gremese, 2002.

Caramia, Donatella. *La musica e oltre: Colloqui con Ennio Morricone*. Brescia: Morcelliana, 2012.

Nichols, Nina Da Vinci and Janice O'Keefe Bazzoni. *Pirandello and Film*. Lincoln: University of Nebraska Press, 1995.

Dyer, Richard. *Nino Rota: Music, Film and Feeling*. New York: Palgrave, 2010.

Dyer, Richard. "Side by Side, Nino Rota, Music and Film." In *Beyond the Soundtrack. Representing Music in Cinema*. Ed. Daniel Goldmark, Lawrence Kramer, and Richard Leppert. Berkeley: University of California Press, 2007. 246–59.

Ferrucci, Riccardo, ed. *La bottega dei Taviani*. Florence: Usher. 1987.

Ferrucci, Riccardo and Patrizia Turini. *Paolo and Vittorio Taviani. Poetry of the Italian Landscape*. Trans. Patricia E. Fogarty and Charles Nopar. Rome: Gremese, 1995.

Gieri, Manuela. *Contemporary Italian Filmmaking: Strategies of Subversion*, Toronto: University of Toronto Press, 1995.

Gorbman, Claudia. "Auteur Music." In *Beyond the Soundtrack. Representing Music in Cinema*. Ed. Daniel Goldmark, Lawrence Kramer, and Richard Leppert. Berkeley: University of California Press, 2007. 149–162.

Gorbman, Claudia. "Music as Salvation: Notes on Fellini and Rota." *Film Quarterly* 28.2 (Winter 1974–75): 17–25.

Graham, Mark. "*Padre Padrone* and the Dialectics of Sound." *Film Criticism* 6.1 (1981): 21–30.

Harrison, Thomas. "Cinematography: Pirandello, Leone, and Sonorous Critiques of Realism Cinema." Unpublished paper.

Marcus, Millicent. "Pirandello liberato." In *Il cinema di Pirandello*. Ed. Maria Antonietta Grignani. Florence: La Nuova Italia, 1992. 77–92.

Marcus, Millicent. *Filmmaking by the Book: Italian Cinema and Literary Adaptation*. Baltimore: Johns Hopkins University Press. 1993.

Mera, Miguel and David Bernard, eds. *European Film Music*. Aldershot: Ashgate, 2006.

Miceli, Sergio. *Morricone, la musica, il cinema*. Modena: Mucchi, 1994.

Miceli, Sergio. *Musica e cinema nella cultura del Novecento*. Milan: Sansoni, 2000.

Miceli, Sergio. *Musica per film: Storia, estetica, analisi, tipologie*. Lucca: LIM. 2009

Morricone, Ennio and Sergio Miceli. *Comporre per il cinema: Teoria e prassi della musica nel film*. Venice: Biblioteca di Bianco e Nero, 2001.

Pendergast, Roy M. *Film Music: A Neglected Art: A Critical Study of Music in Films*. New York: Norton, 1977.

Piovani, Nicola. *Concerto Fotogramma*. Milan: BUR. 2005.

Pirandello, Luigi. *Saggi, Poesie e Scritti vari*, Milan: Mondadori, 1965.

Pirandello, Luigi. *Novelle per un anno*. 2 vols. Milan: Mondadori, 1969, 1978.

Powrie, Phil and Robyn Stilwell. *Changing Tunes: The Use of Pre-existing Music in Film*. Aldershot: Ashgate, 2006.

Smart, Mary Ann. *Siren Songs: Representations of Gender and Sexuality in Opera*. Princeton University Press, 2000.

Taviani, Paolo and Vittorio Taviani. *Kaos: Sceneggiatura liberamente ispirata da Novelle per un anno di Luigi Pirandello*. Mantua: Circolo del Cinema, 1997.

Taviani, Paolo and Vittorio Taviani. *Tu ridi. Sceneggiatura originale e integrale dell'omonimo film*. Mantua: Circolo del Cinema, 1999.

Van Order, Thomas. *Listening to Fellini: Music and Meaning in Black and White*. Madison: Fairleigh Dickinson University Press, 2009.

Žižek, Slavoj. *The Pervert Guide to Cinema*. http://beanhu.wordpress.com/2009/12/07/the-perverts-guide-to-cinema/.

Filmography

Kaos. Dir. Paolo and Vittorio Taviani, Italy: RAI-Channel 1-Filmtre Co-Production. 1984.

La notte di San Lorenzo. Dir. Paolo and Vittorio Taviani: RAI-AGER Cinematografica. 1982.

Padre Padrone. Dir. Paolo and Vittorio Taviani: Cinema S.r.l. / RAI 2. 1977.

Tu ridi. Dir. Paolo and Vittorio Taviani: Filmtre, Tele, RAI Cinemafiction, and Dania Film. 1998.

13

Film and Photography

Sarah Carey

Cinema owes its life to the photographic image. It is the sequence of photograms, after all, that produces a moving picture. When photographs (as objects) appear in a film—as they often do—they are subtle references to film's material origins. Less subtle is the fact that a photograph in a film often denotes the object of a character's affection, shows something about a character's past, or (most often in documentary films) functions as historical "proof." What is noteworthy about critical work on photography in cinema is that most scholars point to an Italian film as the ur-text: Michelangelo Antonioni's *Blow-Up* (1966), which features a photographer in the central role and a storyline that revolves around a series of photographic prints.[1]

Why might an Italian film be the case study par excellence? The history of photography in Italy, which is unique with respect to other countries, helps answer this question.[2] The invention of photography in 1839 and its rise in popularity coincided with the years leading up to national unification, the so-called Risorgimento. The Italian peninsula could already boast of the world's oldest photographic firm, established by the Fratelli Alinari in 1852; it was employed to extol Italy's rich legacy by photographing its most iconic monuments and masterpieces of art.[3] Photography served as a way to tell the story of the nation's birth—especially in the light of its fertile cultural history—and thus contributed to Italian national identity from its very beginnings.

As an instrumental part of collective memory in Italy, photography would prove attractive to the other arts even before the age of cinema. For example, Italian writers at the end of the nineteenth century such as Giovanni Verga and Luigi Capuana incorporated photography into the literary and artistic movement of *verismo*, a highly naturalistic form of realism that dominated the cultural landscape in Italy at the time.[4] At the beginning of the twentieth century, photography found itself drawn into artistic movements of a much different sort, most notably that of Futurism.[5] Led by the dynamic Filippo Tommaso Marinetti, Italian Futurists were initially wary of the medium of photography, which they considered to be a "cold" art that froze the energy of modernity. In order to assimilate photography into the movement, Futurists relied instead on montage—not coincidentally, one of the most fundamental components of cinema. Anton Giulio and Arturo Bragaglia (early experimenters in photography who were never fully integrated into the Futurist movement) can be credited with what was called "montaggio in sandwich": the superimposition of two or three photographic negatives, the result of which was an image with an entirely new meaning. The Bragaglias thus anticipated Sergei Eisenstein's famous theory of montage in Soviet cinema by almost a decade.

It was not until 1916 that Marinetti and other Futurists collectively published the "Manifesto della cinematografia futurista" ("Manifesto of Futurist Cinematography," 1916). As opposed to photography, cinema embodied the very notion of movement, a critical component of Futurism's exaltation of velocity and vitality. Though there were several early experiments in Futurist cinema, as well as the production of the "official" movie of the movement, *Vita futurista* (*Futurist Life*, 1916), only photograms of these still exist. The one film still extant is actually Bragaglia's silent film *Thaïs* (1917).[6] The rather conventional, melodramatic plot is not the work's point of interest. It is instead its bold use of black-and-white lines and geometric shapes that adorn the set and costumes, along with its innovative use of montage, that mark this film as a visual powerhouse on both the photographic and the cinematic level.

Futurism had a great impact on avant-garde movements around the world, but it was especially influential for the aesthetics of Italian Fascism at home.[7] In the multimedial system employed by the Fascist regime, photography cultivated its *fratellanza*, kinship, with cinema ("l'arma più forte," or "strongest weapon," according to Benito Mussolini's famous slogan). The most important development in this regard was the creation of the Istituto LUCE, whose job was to produce documentary images of Fascist Italy. It also harnessed the power of mainstream films (often Hollywood imports) by prefacing each feature with newsreel footage that LUCE produced, which put the underlying message of Fascist ideology right next to an easily consumable product.

Despite the flood of images that accompanied Mussolini's ideological grip on the country, there are few films from the period that confront this inundation. The notable exception is Max Ophüls's *La signora di tutti* (*Everybody's Lady*, 1934), which narrates the rise and fall of a film diva. One scene from the film shows a printing press spitting out identical images of the star onto posters—the preferred media of the Fascist regime. The actress's fall from celebrity and untimely death are represented metaphorically as a now-distorted image of her emerges from a broken printing machine. Ophüls's film, despite its focus on cinematic culture rather than politics, alludes to the power of the photograph both to promote public personality and to manipulate it.[8]

Both Futurism and Fascism relied on photography's "otherworldly" qualities in order to further their artistic and ideological aims. With the fall of Mussolini and the end of the Second World War, there was a pressing need to take photography and cinema in another direction: to offer up a true, unmanipulated image of the country. This endeavor was taken up by the artistic movement of Italian neorealism, which is remembered most poignantly through film stills from its greatest movies.[9] Major film directors such as Roberto Rossellini, Luchino Visconti, Vittorio De Sica, and Michelangelo Antonioni were all attracted to photography's realistic qualities, and were further enthralled with the idea that the raw photographic or cinematic image could say just as much as conventional voice-over or dialogue.

The Neorealist turn to photography played out in two ways. On the one hand, directors were compelled toward a more photographic aesthetic in their films. This was achieved by privileging the visual composition of individual shots over traditional modes of cinematic narration that often relied on rapid-fire editing. The result was a preference for the long take, which gave the viewer time to gaze at the scene on the screen without the interruption of a cut, thus producing a more "natural" way of seeing the world of the film. Many neorealist films also featured expansive establishing shots of both urban and rural landscapes, often with very little human movement in them. For the spectator, the experience is more akin to looking at a still photograph than a moving picture. Antonioni became the master of this first technique. By the 1960s, films such as his *L'avventura* (1960), *La notte* (1961), *L'eclisse* (1962), and *Il deserto rosso* (*Red Desert*, 1964) would be both commended and criticized for being more visually stunning than plot-driven (more photographic, in other words, than filmic).

The second, equally important attraction of photography for neorealist directors was the role of the photographic object in the lives of everyday people. Some prime examples of this use of photography are Rossellini's *Roma città aperta* (*Rome, Open City*, 1945) and *Paisà* (*Paisan*, 1946), and Visconti's *La terra trema* (1948). In the first film, the romantic relationship between Resistance leader Manfredi and the showgirl Marina (who is now colluding with the Nazis) is solidified through the placement of a photograph of them in the edge of her dressing room mirror. This same image, along with other ID photographs, leads to Manfredi's capture, his torture, and his untimely death.

With *Paisan*, the spectators never see the contents of a photograph directly, but the object serves as the lynchpin in the conclusion of the Sicilian episode

FIGURE 13.1 *The American soldier Joe and the Sicilian Carmela in Roberto Rossellini's* Paisan *(1946).*

of the film. It features American soldier Joe as he tries to talk to a native girl, Carmela, despite the fact that neither of them speaks the other's language. In an innocent moment of show-and-tell that is prompted by their inability to communicate, Joe tries to show Carmela some photographs of his family that are in his wallet, even though the nighttime setting makes discerning them difficult. What is most striking about *Paisà* is that the confusion over the contents of the photograph and Joe's attempt to illuminate the image with his cigarette lighter cause his death: the momentary light signals his location to a German sniper.

While Rossellini's films feature photographs as potentially deadly, *La terra trema* uses a family portrait as an object of hope able to fill the vacancy left by death or departure. The very first scene of the film, in fact, features the Valastro's family photograph as it is viewed by the women of the family. The absence of the men (some are indeed deceased, while the others are fishermen away at sea) is compensated for by their photographic images. The circumstances of the photograph's production are also important to Visconti's narrative: the sister Lucia alludes to the novelty of the image, since it was taken on a rare trip to the big city. In the photograph, the family's poses are formal and sober, and behind them one can make out the drapes and fake background image of a snow-covered Etna that would have been a familiar arrangement in a photographic studio of the time. This initial scene posits the photograph as a solid and unwavering fixture in the home, despite the changes that will come to the family.

The brother Cola's eventual departure near the end of the film, for example, is marked by the reappearance of the family portrait, which now seems to hang on in its own vain hope that the family unit will remain intact. When

FIGURE 13.2 *Cola views the family photograph one last time before leaving home in Visconti's* La terra trema *(1948).*

Cola grabs his last belongings and a piece of bread for the journey, he walks by the photograph on the wall and says goodbye to his family through the image rather than in person, easing the pain of his pending separation. The photograph remains central in the shot as Cola's reflection passes over it, followed by the shadow of the door closing behind him. Indeed, a door has been closed on the family as it was, and the rest of the Valastros must now face an uncertain future.

Besides their personal import, photographs also serve a public purpose as objects used for identification. As such, they often function as part of official investigations (as in *Rome, Open City*). Italian neorealism should not be considered unique in this regard; the American tradition of the film noir had previously established photographic objects as integral parts of detective stories.

Michelangelo Antonioni's *Cronaca di un amore* (*Story of a Love Affair*, 1950) fits easily into both the neorealist and the noir genres. Its opening sequence is structured around a stack of photographs that give two investigators (hired by a jealous husband) a visual reconstruction of the female person-of-interest's past. Presented as they are—one after another in rapid succession on top of a desk—the effect is one of reconstructing this woman's identity through a kind of flip-book, like a miniature film. With this early film, Antonioni announces that the photographic image will be central to his aesthetic. The film stands as one of the first Italian works to use photographs metatextually—to allude to the art of filmmaking within the film itself.

By far the most meta-cinematic film of this period, however, is Rossellini's *La macchina ammazzacattivi* (*The Machine That Kills Bad People*), which

FIGURE 13.3 *A sequence of photographs in Antonioni's* Story of a Love Affair *(1950).*

FIGURE 13.4. *Celestino (left) and the mysterious visitor in* The Machine to Kill Bad People *(1952).*

started production in 1948 but was not released until 1952. Though it is virtually forgotten in most considerations of Rossellini's oeuvre, the fantastical tale of a small-town photographer who discovers that his camera has the ability to kill bad people remains as an almost postmodern reflection on the power (and danger) of photographic reproduction.[10] The protagonist, Celestino, uncovers this phenomenon after the mysterious arrival of an old man who shows him how it works.

The unique part of the complicated storyline (which includes profound examinations of the cultish nature of both religion and photography, moral judgment, and charity) is that Celestino carries out his own strange philanthropy by photographing the photographs of the so-called bad people.

In other words, it is not the act of photographing that is itself deadly, but the *reproduction* of the original print that proves deadly. Given the film's production, in the early 1950s, this is a subtle allusion to the fact that the endless reproducibility of the photographic object will trump its status as the unique trace of a singular event.

Photographic reproduction and print culture became more interdependent during this transitory historical period. One of the most popular types of reading material in the postwar years, for example, was the photographic novel or *fotoromanzo*. Most of the stories in these works were reductions of popular films into printed stills, though some were original narratives that posed characters on studio sets.[11] The popularity of these publications can be seen in several postwar films that feature them as social and cultural phenomena, including Giuseppe De Santis's *Riso amaro* (*Bitter Rice*, 1949), Antonioni's short film *L'amorosa menzogna* (*Lies of Love*, 1949), and, most importantly, Federico Fellini's *Lo sceicco bianco* (*The White Sheik*, 1952), which gives a backstage look at how these magazines were produced.

In the 1950s, Italian films also began to address outright the culture of film production. Visconti's 1951 work *Bellissima*, for example, centers on a mother, Maddalena (played by Anna Magnani, the iconic star of *Rome, Open City*), who hopes for her young daughter Maria to be chosen in a beauty contest, the prize for which will be a part in a movie. Upon being told that she should have professional photographs taken of Maria, Maddalena is quick to pay a visit to a local studio. The photographer is played by none other than Anton Giulio Bragaglia, the aforementioned director of the Futurist era film *Thaïs*. The comic tone of the scene suggests a complete reversal of Bragaglia's former status as a member of the avant-garde, now appropriated by mainstream cinema. The scene—with its intricate

FIGURE 13.5 *The photographer, played by filmmaker Anton Giulio Bragaglia, in Visconti's* Bellissima *(1951).*

positioning of the camera and a system of mirrors on the set—also suggests that Visconti is considering the inner-workings of the photographic and filmic apparatuses on a profound level.

Fellini's internationally acclaimed *La dolce vita* from 1960 stands as a cultural benchmark with respect to how images and the media had become embedded in Italian culture by the end of the 1950s. It also can be credited with the coining of the now widespread term "paparazzo." Fellini modeled the character of the hounding photographer on Tazio Secchiaroli, a real photojournalist of the time.

The omnipresence of paparazzi in the film reveals society's thirst for public spectacle and alludes to the power of photography to recreate or, more spectacularly, to *create* an event outright.[12] Fellini's later, more self-reflexive film *8 1/2* (1963) is an insider's look at the filmmaking process and the frustration of a director struggling to produce another hit. As in *Bellissima*, the photographic headshot is foregrounded in the process of casting a movie. After the protagonist, Guido, wakes up from the initial dream that begins the film—notable too for its use of stop-motion photography, which gives us brief, filmic "snapshots" of some of the characters that populate his unconscious and future film—the struggling director enters his hotel bathroom where stacks of headshots litter the floor, inundating the most intimate of spaces. In another post-oneiric scene, Guido wakes up, engulfed on his bed by the glossy prints as if drowning in the faces from which he has to choose. Every inch of the walls of the hotel room that serves as the film's production hub likewise features casting photographs, or even cutouts of individual body parts, suggesting the extremity of Guido's indecision as well as a pathological attention to detail that might be the very cause of his professional crisis.

In addition to Fellini, the early 1960s witnessed a number of directors tackling the changing face of visual culture in Italy. The use of photography

FIGURE 13.6 *Fellini's invention of the "paparazzo" in* La dolce vita *(1960).*

in Visconti's *Rocco e i suoi fratelli* (*Rocco and His Brothers*, 1960), for example, plays upon the clash between private, family photographs and the public images of mass advertising—a juxtaposition that mimics the clash of tradition with the postwar economic miracle. Visconti's first shot of the Parondi family's rudimentary dwelling in their adopted city of Milan features a family portrait (much like the one in his earlier *La terra trema*) hanging above the sideboard of the kitchen. Near this older image of the Parondis are photographs of the family's "new" identity: boxing photographs that feature oldest brother Vincenzo as the hope of the family's success.

Once the younger siblings, Simone and Rocco, decide to start boxing, the traditional images of the past fade into the background as commercialized images take center stage. This is best exemplified in the final shot of Visconti's film, which shows youngest brother Luca looking up at a city wall that is covered with publicity images of the now-famous Rocco. When Luca affectionately keeps his hand running along the posters as he begins to walk down the sidewalk, the effect turns the series of stills into a moving picture, subtly suggesting how film will surpass the older art of photography.

Indeed as the 1960s wore on, photographic objects within films came to symbolize a certain degree of backwardness, even as directors (paradoxically) demonstrated a preference for a more photographic, self-reflexive approach to filmmaking. Three films that revealed this shift were Bernardo Bertolucci's *Prima della rivoluzione* (*Before the Revolution*, 1964), Marco Bellocchio's *I pugni in tasca* (*Fists in the Pocket*, 1965), and Pier Paolo Pasolini's *Teorema* (*Theorem*, 1968). In *Before the Revolution*, it is incest that figures into the protagonist Fabrizio's revolt against the paternal order of the nuclear family. The mentally unstable character of his aunt (and lover) Gina is the center of this ultimately failed rebellion, but what is most notable about the

FIGURE 13.7 *Rocco's proliferating public image in Visconti's* Rocco and His Brothers *(1960).*

FIGURE 13.8 *Gina absorbed in gazing at photos of herself in Bertolucci's* Before the Revolution *(1964).*

film is how Bertolucci relies on still photographs within the film to create a nuanced portrait of a troubled woman.[13]

In a scene following Gina's arrival to the family enclave, she sits on her bed and looks at old photographs of herself, suggesting a nostalgia for the certainty of the past. But Bertolucci goes a step further by making explicit the connection between still and moving images. The family photographs that Gina examines on her bed are arranged in a linear fashion and each is filmed in a series, without cuts, through the movement of the camera from right to left. This is cinema in its simplest form. But the camera's movement from right to left produces the strange effect of moving backward—a visual regression that coincides with Gina's misdirected interest in her much younger nephew, and in a younger version of herself.

Like Bertolucci's work, Marco Bellocchio's *Fists in the Pocket* portrays a dysfunctional, incestuous, and violent family through the disruptive presence of photographic images. The family's first dinner takes place under a number of family portraits, which dominate the entire space of the home and transport it backward in time, freezing it in a temporal no-man's-land. When the sister Giulia vainly looks for her own reflection in the glass pane of a family photograph, the effect—layering a present reality on top of an image of the past—emphasizes an embeddedness in familial ties that is exemplified by the incestuous attachment between Giulia and her brother Ale. When their blind mother "accidently" dies after falling off a cliff, Ale systematically destroys the family photographs in the house, tearing them down in an attempt to escape the vestiges of their sick past. The act is a futile one, however, since the picture frames have left their outline on the fading color of the wallpaper; the shadows of the past endure even after the photographic objects have been taken down.

Pasolini's *Teorema* also centers on the disintegration of a typical bourgeois family. More importantly, it quite possibly features the first female photographer in Italian cinema.[14] The film begins by revealing the daughter

FIGURE 13.9 *Ale (left) destroying family photos in Bellocchio's* Fists in the Pocket *(1965).*

Odetta's perverse obsession with a photographic album, the contents of which are almost exclusively of her father. The family soon receives an unexpected, unnamed "Guest," a young man who transforms each of the members of the family through a series of erotic encounters. In the case of Odetta, both her act of photographing him and her later exhibition of her album to him will play a role in the erotic tension between them. The importance of the album is made explicit after the Guest's sudden departure from the family. In her state of emotional turmoil, Odetta turns to the album as her only source of comfort, since it now also contains the photographs of the Guest. Her fascination with his photographic likeness becomes apparent as she traces the Guest's body with her finger, allowing her to tactilely relive the past by touching an iconic representation of her sexual awakening. Such nostalgia, however, soon reveals itself to be the first clear sign of Odetta's increasingly disturbed mental state, as the album comes to symbolize a futile coping mechanism.

The most famous photographer in Italian cinema remains the protagonist of Antonioni's film *Blow-Up*. The work explores several thematic considerations with regard to photography, most notably the darkroom process of developing and enlarging photographic prints and—like *Teorema* just two years later—the photographic act as a metaphor for sexual domination. What resounds most strongly in this intensely studied work is how photographic manipulation and interpretation contribute to the protagonist's sense of identity as a photographer, and how this character embodies an Antonionian investigator of the visual world.[15] Set in bustling London, the film's protagonist (Thomas) is a high-powered fashion photographer whose studio is visited daily by hordes of beautiful young

FIGURE 13.10 *Photography and Odetta's sexual awakening in Pasolini's* Theorem *(1968).*

models. But once Thomas leaves his studio, it is clear that he is likewise drawn to the quotidian: the humble inhabitants of a community shelter in the beginning of the film and, later, the natural beauty of a park punctuated by an amorous couple strolling through it.

This latter interest is the main part of the film's plot: Thomas voyeuristically captures the couple's private interaction by spying on them with his camera and then, once he develops the photographs, he believes to have inadvertently captured a murder scene. The sequence in which Thomas enlarges the negatives provides an insider's look at a photographer in and out of the darkroom while simultaneously showcasing Antonioni's own inventive camera work. Thomas tacks up the prints in his living room and tries to recreate the story's timeline. After showing Thomas in profile as he looks at the images, a cut places Antonioni's camera behind the backs of the photographs; Thomas's face is now framed between the spaces of the prints as they seem to stare back at him. Antonioni uses this setup three times in the extended sequence, emphasizing the stark contrast between the black-and-white images from Thomas's camera and the color of the moving picture—differentiating the worlds of the photographed and the filmic while also enmeshing them.

As Thomas continues to reconstruct the story through the photographs, Antonioni shifts his approach by removing Thomas from the frame altogether and presenting the photographs as a series of stills. But the camera does not remain motionless, since some images are presented with a zoom-in or with a subtle pan as if to mimic the act of looking. Although it seems as if the viewer is given the "raw" material of photography, the effect actually makes the spectator all the more aware of the cinematic apparatus. This is further heightened by the overlay of extra-diegetic noise—the rustling of the leaves in the trees that eerily accompanied the real events back in the park. The effect is one of a cinematic recreation of the earlier filmic material, a juxtaposition that emphasizes the gray area between photographic and cinematic creation. *Blow-Up* is not just a film about photographs; it is a film about *photographing*. And Antonioni is just as important a photographer in this film as Thomas.

Like *Blow-Up*, Antonioni's film *Professione: reporter* (*The Passenger*, 1975) takes place abroad and is in English, and it also examines notions of personal and national identity. The plot centers on David Locke (a journalist documenting political developments in Africa). Locke assumes the identity of another man, Robertson, whom Locke befriends and who is later revealed to be a gunrunner for a group of African rebels. When Locke discovers Robertson dead in Robertson's hotel room, he decides to switch all of his clothing and personal belongings with the deceased. But it is only through their respective passport photographs that Locke can fully take on Robertson's identity.

The critical scene in which this takes place shows Locke sitting down at a table with the two passports in front of him. What follows is a confusing set of filmic events that accentuate the fragile balance between past and present (which is also at the heart of the photographic object). First, a knock at the door seems to be diegetic sound (a noise that originates within the world of the film). But the conversation then heard is between Locke and Robertson, which *must* have taken place in the past. A cut shows the presence of a tape recorder near Locke's table, revealing the source of the soundtrack. This detail is crucial, since it reveals that the recording is a reproduction of a past event, much like a photograph itself. As their conversation continues, the camera lingers on Locke's process of switching the passport photos. Antonioni then creates an unusual flashback sequence in which the camera and the audio tape recording segue seamlessly into a shot that shows the two men talking in the past. When the film finally exits this visual flashback, the camera returns to a shot of Locke as he finally puts his photograph into the dead man's passport—the proof of his new identity. The fluidity of this temporal shift suggests just how easily photographs can move between past and present.

With the dawn of digital photography, visual manipulation became possible on a whole different level. Jumping ahead in the timeline of Italian cinema, the film *Cover boy: L'ultima rivoluzione* (*Cover Boy . . . Last Revolution, 2007*) by Carmine Amoroso, like *The Passenger*, examines the question of identity and its malleability. Rather than a switch of ID photographs, however, this time it is photographic montage that creates the fiction. The film's use of still photography begins when a young illegal Romanian immigrant, Ioan, gets involved with a female photographer whose job as a photojournalist documenting national revolutions has shifted to the more lucrative world of fashion. In a reversal of the gendered relations of *Blow-Up*, this time it is the woman who turns the man into a model on the Milan runways. After his initial success, the woman takes advantage

FIGURE 13.11 *A seesaw between identity, in the form of passport photographs, in Antonioni's* The Passenger *(1975).*

of one of their sexual encounters to snap some naked photographs of him. Without his knowledge, she digitally adds his figure to one of her earlier, "real" images of the Romanian revolution and tags it with a caption in red that says "Exile: Wear the Revolution," which turns the image into a provocative type of advertisement under the guise of high art. Ioan sees it for the first time at her gallery opening party, and he leaves in disgust at the thought of how his vulnerability (both in the sense of his nudity and in his status as the foreign "other") has been exploited for aesthetic purposes.

A portion of Amoroso's film also includes real documentary film footage from Romania in 1989. This harkens back to a montage technique employed by a film from just a few years earlier by Marco Bellocchio: *Buongiorno, notte* (*Good Morning, Night*, 2003). Based on the kidnapping and murder of prominent politician Aldo Moro in the late 1970s by the left-wing terrorist group the Red Brigades, the film features television coverage of the event as well as a famous photograph taken and distributed by the captors as proof of their still-living prisoner. Rather than recreate the photograph using the actor who plays Moro, Bellocchio inserts the real image into the film, which serves as an essential, iconic document of Italian history. This artistic decision is crucial; Bellocchio wants to ensure that historical proof is "real" rather than "recreated." It harkens back to the neorealist desire to use photography and cinema for their proximity to reality.

What these last two films ultimately reveal is the fine line that photography straddles between fact and fiction: it is at once objectively tied to real life and yet beholden to the subjective eye behind the lens. Italian filmmakers have harnessed this paradox in ways that are unique to the history of cinema. As mentioned at the outset, it is not coincidental that the most famous film about photography (*Blow-Up*) is an Italian one. Italian identity itself is enmeshed in the history of photography like no other: Italy as a nation saw its birth at the same moment as photography's explosion as a technology and an art form. Just as one has that uncanny realization when looking at a photograph of oneself—"Oh, look, that's me!"—a nascent nation was able to see itself for the first time. Italian cinema has likewise thrived on the photographic image's self-reflexivity, not only in terms of its natural fraternity with film but also in its dexterity in serving as both document and storyteller within a moving picture.

Notes

1   The most recent and relevant studies in this field include: Beckman and Ma, *Still Moving*; Campany, *Photography and Cinema*; Green and Lowry, *Stillness and Time*; Røssaak, *Between Stillness and Motion*; and Sutton, *Photography, Cinema, Memory*.

2   On the unique history of photography in Italy, see my own "The Image/ Imagining of Italy." I rely in part on the analysis of Bollati in the collaborative work *Fotografia dell'800* as well as his introductory essay "Note su fotografia e storia" in *L'immagine fotografica (1845–1945)*. For more on the early decades of photography and the Risorgimento, see also Vitali, *Il Risorgimento nella fotografia*; and the first volume of Zannier, *Segni di luce*.

3   On the Alinari firm, see *Una storia della fotografia italiana nelle collezioni Alinari*; Quintavalle and Maffioli, *Fratelli Alinari, fotografi in Firenze*; and Colombo and Sontag, *Italy*.

4   See Hill, "Il grande enigma del vero"; Nemiz, *Capuana, Verga, De Roberto*.

5   The foremost critic on the subject continues to be Lista. See his most recent work from 2009 and his two publications from 2001.

6   The best works on *Thaïs* remain Marcus, "Anton Giulio Bragaglia's *Thaïs*"; and Re, "Futurism, Film and the Return of the Repressed."

7   See Falasca-Zamponi, *Fascist Spectacle*.

8   See Doane, "The Abstraction of a Lady."

9   Key critical texts about neorealist photography and cinema are Taramelli, *Viaggio nell'Italia del neorealismo*; and Viganò, *NeoRealismo*.

10   My analysis draws upon the excellent work of Bondanella, *The Films of Roberto Rossellini*.

11   On visual culture in the post-war period, see Forgacs and Gundle, *Mass Culture and Italian Society*. For a more specialized analysis of the *fotoromanzo*, see Bravo, *Il fotoromanzo*.

12   See Gundle, "Hollywood Glamour and Mass Consumption in Postwar Italy."

13   One critic to address the importance of photography in Bertolucci's work is Kline ("The Absent Presence" and *Bertolucci's Dream Loom*).

14   See Marcus, *Italian Film in the Light of Neorealism*, for an analysis of photography in the film.

15   Important full-length works on Antonioni that include discussions of this seminal film include Brunette, *The Films of Michelangelo Antonioni*; Chatman, *Antonioni*; and Rohdie, *Antonioni*. A seminal collection of essays about *Blow-Up* (as well as its initial reviews) is Huss, *Focus on Blow-Up*. The most recent works on the film are Tomasulo, "You're Tellin' Me You Didn't See"; Torlasco, *The Time of the Crime*; and Williams, "A Surface of Forgetting."

Bibliography

Beckman, Karen and Jean Ma, eds. *Still Moving: Between Cinema and Photography*. Durham: Duke University Press, 2008.

Bollati, Giulio. "Note su fotografia e storia." In *L'immagine fotografica 1845–1945*. Ed. Carlo Bertelli and Giulio Bollati. Part 2, Vol. 1 of *Storia d'Italia*. Torino: Einaudi, 1979. 5–55

Bondanella, Peter. *The Films of Roberto Rossellini*. Cambridge: Cambridge University Press, 1993.

Bravo, Anna. *Il fotoromanzo*. Bologna: Il Mulino, 2003.

Brunette, Peter. *The Films of Michelangelo Antonioni*. Cambridge: Cambridge University Press, 1998.

Bugli, Maria et al. *Fotografia italiana dell'Ottocento*. Florence: Palazzo Pitti, 1979.

Campany, David. *Photography and Cinema*. London: Reaktion, 2008.

Carey, Sarah. "The Image/Imagining of Italy." *La Fusta* (2012): 1–16.

Chatman, Seymour. *Antonioni, or The Surface of the World*. Berkeley: University of California Press, 1985.

Colombo, Cesare and Susan Sontag. *Italy: One Hundred Years of Photography*. New York: Rizzoli, 1988.

Doane, Mary Ann. "The Abstraction of a Lady: 'La Signora di tutti.'" *Cinema Journal* 28 (1988): 65–84.

Falasca-Zamponi, Simonetta. *Fascist Spectacle: The Aesthetics of Power in Mussolini's Italy*. Berkeley: University of California Press, 1997.

Forgacs, David and Stephen Gundle. *Mass Culture and Italian Society—From Fascism to the Cold War*. Bloomington: Indiana University Press, 2007.

Green, David and Joanna Lowry, eds. *Stillness and Time: Photography and the Moving Image*. Brighton: Photoworks/Photoforum, 2006.

Gundle, Stephen. "Hollywood Glamour and Mass Consumption in Postwar Italy." *Journal of Cold War Studies* 4.3 (Summer 2002): 95–118.

Hill, Sarah. "'Il grande enigma del vero': Photographic and Literary Realisms in Late Nineteenth-Century Italy." *Spunti e ricerche* 19 (2004): 64–70.

Huss, Roy, ed. *Focus on Blow-Up*. Upper Saddle River: Prentice-Hall, 1971.

Kline, T. Jefferson. "The Absent Presence: Stendhal in Bertolucci's 'Prima della rivoluzione.'" *Cinema Journal* 23.2 (1984): 4–28.

Kline, T. Jefferson. *Bertolucci's Dream Loom: A Psychoanalytic Study of Cinema*. Amherst: University of Massachusetts Press, 1987.

Lista, Giovanni. *Cinema e fotografia futurista*. Milan: Skira, 2001.

Lista, Giovanni. *Futurism and Photography*. London: Merrell, 2001.

Lista, Giovanni. *Il futurismo nella fotografia*. Florence: Fratelli Alinari, Fondazione per la Storia della Fotografia, 2009.

Marcus, Millicent. "Anton Giulio Bragaglia's *Thaïs*; or, The Death of the *Diva* + The Rise of the *Scenoplastica* =The Birth of Futurist Cinema." *South Central Review* 13.2/3 (Summer–Autumn, 1996): 63–81.

Marcus, Millicent. *Italian Film in the Light of Neorealism*. Princeton: Princeton University Press, 1986.

Nemiz, Andrea. *Capuana, Verga, De Roberto: Fotografi*. Palermo: Edikronos, 1982.

Quintavalle, Arturo Carlo and Monica Maffioli, eds. *Fratelli Alinari, fotografi in Firenze: 150 anni che illustrarono il mondo, 1852-2002*. Florence: Alinari, 2003.

Re, Lucia. "Futurism, Film and the Return of the Repressed: Learning from *Thaïs*." *MLN* 123.1 (2008): 125–50.

Rohdie, Sam. *Antonioni*. London: BFI, 1990.

Røssaak, Eivind, ed. *Between Stillness and Motion: Film, Photography, Algorithms*. Amsterdam: Amsterdam University Press, 2011.

Sutton, Damian. *Photography, Cinema, Memory: The Crystal Image of Time*. Minneapolis: University of Minnesota Press, 2009.

Taramelli, Ennery. *Viaggio nell'Italia del neorealismo: La fotografia tra letteratura e cinema*. Turin: Società Editrice Internazionale, 1995.

Tomasulo Frank, P. "'You're Tellin' Me You Didn't See': Hitchcock's *Rear Window* and Antonioni's *Blow-Up*." In *After Hitchcock: Influence, Imitation, and Intertextuality*. Ed. and Trans. David Boyd and R. Barton Palmer. Austin: University of Texas Press, 2006. 145–72.

Torlasco, Domietta. *The Time of the Crime: Phenomenology, Psychoanalysis, Italian Film*. Stanford: Stanford University Press, 2008.

Williams, Megan Rowley. "A Surface of Forgetting: The Object of History in Michelangelo Antonioni's *Blow-Up*." *Quarterly Review of Film and Video* 17.3 (2000): 245–59.

Viganò, Enrica, ed. *NeoRealismo: La nuova immagine in Italia*. Milan: Admira, 2006.

Vitali, Lamberto. *Il Risorgimento nella fotografia*. Turin: Einaudi, 1979.

Zannier, Italo. *Segni di luce*. 3 Vols. Ravenna: Longo, 1991–93.

Zannier, Italo et al. *Una storia della fotografia italiana nelle collezioni Alinari: 1841-1941*. Florence: Alinari, 2006.

Filmography

8½, Dir. Federico Fellini. Italy: Cineriz, Francinex. 1963.

L'amorosa menzogna (Lies of Love), Dir. Michelangelo Antonioni. Italy: Filmus, Edizioni Fortuna. 1949.

L'avventura, Dir. Michelangelo Antonioni. Italy: Cino del Duca, Produzioni Cinematografiche Europee (P.C.E.), Societé Cinématographique Lyre. 1960.

Bellissima, Dir. Luchino Visconti. Italy: Film Bellissima. 1951.

Blow-Up, Dir. Michelangelo Antonioni. Italy: Bridge Films, Carlo Ponti Production, Metro-Goldwyn-Mayer (MGM). 1966.

Buongiorno, notte (Good Morning, Night), Dir. Marco Bellocchio. Italy: Filmalbatros, Rai Cinemafiction, Sky. 2003.

Cover Boy, Dir. Carmine Amoroso. Italy: Paco Cinematografica, Filand, Ministero per i Beni e le Attività Culturali (MiBAC). 2007.

Cronaca di un amore (Story of a Love Affair), Dir. Michelangelo Antonioni. Italy: Villani Film. 1950.

Il deserto rosso (Red Desert), Dir. Michelangelo Antonioni. Italy: Film Duemila, Federiz, Francoriz Production. 1964.

La dolce vita, Dir. Federico Fellini. Italy: Riama Film, Cinecittà, Pathé Consortium Cinéma. 1960.

L'eclisse, Dir. Michelangelo Antonioni. Italy: Cineriz, Interopa Film, Paris Film. 1962.

La macchina ammazzacattivi (The Machine That Kills Bad People), Dir. Roberto Rossellini. Italy: Tevere Film, Universalia Film. 1952.

La notte, Dir. Michelangelo Antonioni. Italy: Nepi Film, Sofitedip, Silver Films. 1961.

Paisà (Paisan), Dir. Roberto Rossellini. Italy: Organizzazione Film Internazionali (OFI), Foreign Film Productions. 1946.

The Passenger, Dir. Michelangelo Antonioni. Italy: Metro-Goldwyn-Mayer (MGM), Compagnia Cinematografica Champion, Les Films Concordia. 1975.

Prima della rivoluzione (Before the Revolution), Dir. Bernardo Bertolucci. Italy: Cineriz, Iride Cinematografica. 1964.

I pugni in tasca (Fists in the Pocket), Dir. Marco Bellocchio. Italy: Doria. 1965.

Riso amaro (Bitter Rice), Dir. Giuseppe De Santis. Italy: Lux Film. 1949.

Rocco e i suoi fratelli (Rocco and His Brothers), Dir. Luchino Visconti. Italy: Titanus, Les Films Marceau. 1960.

Roma città aperta (Rome, Open City), Dir. Roberto Rossellini. Italy: Excelsa Film. 1945.

Lo sceicco bianco (The White Sheik), Dir. Federico Fellini. Italy: OFI, P.D.C. 1952.

La signora di tutti (Everybody's Woman), Dir. Max Ophüls. Novella Film. 1934.

Teorema, Dir. Pier Paolo Pasolini. Italy: Aetos Produzioni Cinematografiche. 1968.

La terra trema, Dir. Luchino Visconti. Italy: AR.TE.AS Film, Universalia Film. 1948.

Thaïs, Dir. Anton Giulio Bragaglia. Italy: Novissima Film. 1917.

Vita futurista (Futurist Life), Dir. Arnaldo Ginna. Italia Futurista. 1916.

14

Film and Television in Italy

Stefano Baschiera

It is impossible to overemphasize the impact that television has had on Italian culture and society. In fact, since its birth on January 3, 1954, the history of Italian television has been deeply intertwined with political and cultural debates in the nation, starting with the era of the economic boom. This period of fast-paced economic growth (from 1958 to 1963) was characterized by a new upward social mobility, and the development of Italian television mirrored and mapped the changes in the geography of consumption.[1] Even more, television has shaped the language and the tastes of Italians, creating new myths and stars and stealing the role that for decades was cinema's almost exclusive domain.

The impact that television had on Italian cinema could indeed be described as devastating, as it contributed to the crisis of the national film industry in the 1970s and has in a wholesale manner reshaped cinematic modes of production, viewing habits, and even the films themselves. The history of television in Italy, and consequently its relationship with cinema, can be divided in three main stages: first, the RAI (Radiotelevisione italiana) monopoly (1954–72); second, the rise of private channels (1972–90); and third, the duopoly (1990–present).

1 RAI's Monopoly

RAI's monopolistic position was a continuation of that of EIAR (Ente Italiano per le Audizioni Radiofoniche), which was active under Fascism.[2] In 1951, the government granted RAI a monopoly on radio and future television broadcasting services, which was to last until December 15, 1972. The monopoly was the brainchild of the Christian Democrat Party, the political majority, which conceived of television as an opportunity to inform, entertain, and educate, with the goal of protecting its audience from what it believed to be the "pure entertainment" embodied by cinema.[3] Therefore, the educational vocation of the medium was the dominant argument for keeping it under the exclusive control of the state as a public service, and for avoiding opening it to the free market and private investments. The result of this choice was positive for Italian cinema, as it resulted in protection from the competition of television, which instead occurred in other European countries at that time. In fact, in Italy the amount of films on television was limited by RAI's monopoly and by the agreement between the public broadcaster and ANICA (Associazione Nazionale Industrie Cinematografiche Audiovisive e Multimediali).[4]

The only films that were actually broadcasted by RAI were of no real appeal to audiences. They were "low-quality," old films not included in the main distribution circuit, and were only used to fill the television programing schedule.[5] Aldo Grasso argues that the complex of inferiority that television suffered vis-à-vis the cinema in its early stages was overcome only as recently as the 1960s. In that decade, in fact, cinema was celebrated, screened, and reviewed on television to the extent that the small screen became "Italy's cine-club."[6] The quality of TV programs was considered part of the educational mission of the public broadcasting service. This view was behind the creation of the first connections between the film industry and TV broadcasting, both in the matter of distributing films considered of cultural significance and in exchanging expertise and production resources. For instance, it is in this period that renowned filmmakers began to collaborate with television productions. Rossellini, for example, made his documentary program *L'India vista da Rossellini* (*India as Seen by Rossellini*, 1959) for RAI.[7] While Rossellini was tempted to engage with the potential of the new medium in his desire to reach new audiences, Italian television tried to legitimize itself by featuring one of the most influential directors of the time. However, these rare events of collaboration did not work out as expected, and the distance between the two media ultimately widened.

During the 1960s, one of the consequences of the economic boom was that television sets became more affordable. The small screen grew in popularity and began to be a serious competitor to cinema as the preferred form of entertainment. Despite the fact that Italy was one of the last European countries to face the crisis of cinemagoing (thanks to protective measures and state aid),[8] the decline of cinema audiences was unstoppable. In particular, the second- and third-run circuits as well as the cinema theaters of the urban peripheries had suffered because of the competition represented by film programing on TV. A further repercussion of the crisis of film attendance regards the financing of national cinema, which, with the decrease in audience share, progressively lost the support of tax breaks, further aggravating its economic position.

The lack of state financing was soon covered by the financial opportunities derived from television distribution, thus planting the first seeds of dependency of the big screen on the television industry. The ability of Italian cinema to resist the competition represented by the new medium thus weakened progressively.

As the crisis of Italian cinema deepened during the 1960s, RAI became progressively more involved in film production and financing. In order to hew to its educational vocation, RAI started to support struggling auteurs and offer visibility to "difficult," highbrow films. By the end of the 1960s, the public broadcaster played an important role in the attempt to maintain the international reputation of Italy's art cinema. RAI, in fact, focused on auteur cinema, producing such films as *Francesco D'Assisi* (directed by Liliana Cavani, 1968), *Diario di una schizofrenica* (*Diary of a Schizophrenic Girl*, Nelo Risi, 1968), *I clowns* (Federico Fellini, 1970), *La strategia del ragno* (*The Spider's Stratagem*, Bernardo Bertolucci, 1970), and *San Michele aveva un gallo* (*St. Michael Had a Rooster*, Taviani brothers, 1972).[9] RAI's commitment to art cinema, indeed, reached beyond these famous examples. Starting in 1969, it produced a series of experimental low-budget, medium-length films intended exclusively for broadcast on prime time, including *La fine del gioco* (*The End of the Game*, Gianni Amelio, 1970).

Therefore, not only was RAI directly involved in the attempt to renovate and consolidate the Italian cinematic landscape (at least partly in response to the emergence of European New Wave film in the 1960s),[10] but it also broadcast in prime viewing time films about social issues during an era of significant cultural and economical transformation.

Overall, the exchange between cinema and television during the years of RAI's monopoly was characterized by the educational vocation of the medium, which differentiated cinema from pure entertainment, and by the diffidence of cinema toward the new medium. Eventually, cinema began to move slowly toward television, first through a shy exchange of expertise and then by recognizing its potential role in financing, broadcasting, and production.

2 End of the Monopoly and Rise of Private Channels

The next important date for Italian television was 1972. In that year, the term of the monopoly of televisual services, guaranteed to RAI by a law from 1952, came to an end. The government extended the convention for some months, while trying to find a solution to the problem. However, nothing happened in the implementation of a regulation of the television landscape until 1976. In July 1976, the Constitutional Court claimed that

RAI did not have the monopoly at the regional level, creating in this way the opportunity for the legal introduction of private television stations, which had been illegally broadcasting since the early 1970s. However, this attempt to regulate the TV landscape was not particularly successful. Schlesinger points out that the "Court's decision had opened a big loophole because precisely what 'local' meant was not defined. . . . The legal vacuum that emerged also meant an absence of rules concerning the use of frequencies, the ratio of advertising to programmes, the proportion of domestically-produced to imported product . . . and the concentration of ownership and control."[11]

Such lack of regulation opened the doors of broadcasting to hundreds of regional television stations eager to exploit this commercial opportunity while "the RAI remained tightly regulated."[12] The national broadcaster was indeed ill-prepared to cope with the new and uncontrolled competition that did not have to abide by the same strict censorship rules. This led to a significant fall of audiences for RAI (50 percent by 1982),[13] and the need to change in order to be competitive. The educational model could not survive against the business plan of private channels, which was based on the often unregulated selling of advertisement space and the consequent new flow of programing in a hectic rhythm that was the opposite of the "slowness" of RAI. In this new landscape, the broadcasting of films on television played a central role. Schlesinger points out that one of the areas of intense struggle and fierce competition was that of American imports: "the pressure to import was further reinforced by the crisis in the Italian film industry which had seen a 50 per cent fall in film production between 1974 and 1980, falling returns from seats sold and the closure of half of Italy's theatres between 1978 and 1982."[14] While television profited from selling advertising spaces, the programing of free films on the new television channels became the principal cause of film attendance, from 514 million spectators in 1975 to 195 million in 1982.[15] With the crisis of theatrical releases, there was a significant reduction in the distribution money that went back to the production, based on the system of the minimum guarantee.[16] In this way, broadcasting rights became an increasingly important form of financing for the film industry. In sum, the offering of private channels swept away the second- and third-run cinema as well as all the industry of low-budget genre films that had relied on those channels of distribution. On a deeper level, the lack of regulation of advertisement and the use of cinematic products widely (and wildly) broadcasted on regional private channels created large disparity between the financial possibilities of the two media.[17] We should remember that the rise of TV led to a significant change in the production landscape, with producers like Dino De Laurentiis and Alberto Grimaldi who moved to the United States in order to cope with the new direction of the industry, leaving a void that the public broadcaster tried to fill.

Following the end of its monopoly, RAI plowed ahead with the production of "quality films" alongside made-for-television works that were broadcast both on TV and distributed in a shorter version in international cinema theaters. The Cannes Palme d'Or award for Ermanno Olmi's *L'albero degli zoccoli* (*The Tree of Wooden Clogs*, 1978) and the Taviani brothers' *Padre e padrone* (*Father and Master*, 1977) proved the international critical success of RAI productions and rewarded the convergence policy of the film and television started two decades earlier. Adriano D'Aloia rightly remembers that the double success at Cannes confirmed the conviction of RAI (and of private channels) that it ought both to produce and broadcast films, thus creating a strong dependency of the film industry on broadcasters.[18] In fact, during the 1980s, RAI continued to produce art films for the big screen. Auteurs like Michelangelo Antonioni, Cavani, Fellini, Ermanno Olmi, and Ettore Scola were supported by RAI, as was a new generation of emerging young filmmakers including Marco Tullio Giordana, Daniele Lucchetti, Carlo Mazzacurati, Gabriele Salvatores, and Giuseppe Tornatore. And yet RAI's cultural investment in art cinema, which underlined once again the educational role of the medium, limited the possible development of television language and the progress of the industry.[19] This situation left the public broadcaster ill-prepared to face the competition by private channels during the advent of the *neotelevisione* (new television).[20]

3 Era of Duopoly and Multimedia Empires, 1990–Present

By 1984, the Italian TV landscape was dominated by a multitude of small regional TV stations, which filled their schedules with as many films as possible. This inevitably led to the creation of multimedia empires aimed at controlling the entire life cycle of the film, from the development, production, and theatrical release to the television runs.[21] This condition of duopoly enabled RAI and Silvio Berlusconi's Fininvest to share in developing two multimedia empires. In particular, 1990 was a decisive year because of the so-called Mammí's Law that left RAI and Fininvest with three channels each, while demanding that all other private broadcasters apply for a concession. The law strengthened the duopoly of Italian mass communication and spelled out the role of cinema in these multimedia empires, allowing, for instance, the broadcasters to coproduce films.[22]

The first private multimedia empire was Silvio Berlusconi's company Fininvest, which in 1984 formed Reteitalia, its film-producing branch.[23] As Barbara Corsi argues, even from its name we can grasp the direct connection and continuity between the film production branch and Publitalia, the company founded in 1979 to collect advertisements for Fininvest's

Canale 5.[24] Reteitalia, in fact, embodied Fininvest's approach to television as a form of entertainment aimed at generating advertisement revenues, while the big screen was relegated to an ancillary role. Significantly, "from 1984 to 1995, the year when its name became Mediaset and then Medusa, Reteitalia produced 155 films, more than any other Italian production company in the history of Italian cinema."[25] These films were clearly conceived with television in mind, and were aimed at a generic public. Corsi defines this as "nice cinema," in the sense that it aims to be average, does not involve any deep thinking, and tries at all costs to avoid controversy and complications. It is a "pre-digested" cinema, ready to be fed to an audience that, it is assumed, does not want to be challenged. Despite ranging in different genres (from comedy to the ghost story), these productions were characterized by their listless cinematic language, which could cope with the many commercial interruptions. Soon, however, this national comedic style imposed itself as the dominant genre, the only one able to compete against Hollywood productions at the box office, while maintaining a strong appeal for television distribution. In this context, the new generation of comedians and television celebrities who debuted on the private channels in such light-entertainment shows as *Non Stop* (1977–79) found in the big screen the natural next step for their careers (e.g., such actors/directors as Claudio Verdone, Francesco Nuti, Lello Arena, Massimo Troisi, Alessandro Benvenuti, and Jerry Calà). In this way, Fininvest promoted their television stars in order to exploit their success in the film industry and the subsequent broadcasting of their films on television.

A similar multimedia empire could also be found with the public broadcaster, even though the official constitution of RAI Cinema, a company specialized in the production of films, took place only in 1997. The crucial role that RAI played in the development of national cinema was stressed in the period's legislation. In 1998, a series of laws were designed to cope with the rising crisis of cinema audiences, to update cinema theaters, and to promote film attendance in Italy as a form of entertainment. But these interventions ultimately encouraged television companies to save cinema. For instance, the law established that a quota of income derived from the placement of advertisements on television, or from related licensing fees, had to be reinvested in the production, marketing, and distribution of films. Consequently, the same television duopoly was now strongly present in the Italian film industry, in the form of RAI Cinema and Medusa. Both companies, in fact, were responsible for the financing of films, the management of film rights, and the relationship with distribution companies.[26] As in television programing, in film production the aligned interests of the two media empires tended to converge. While RAI Cinema tried to add a commercial side to its auteur base, Medusa offered a generic mix, which, however, also included art cinema (e.g., the works of Pupi Avati, Bertolucci, and Tornatore).

4 Small Screen to Big Screen: Representation of TV and Its Viewers in Italian Cinema

Despite the important role that TV played in Italian culture, national cinema has only in a few occurrences depicted the world of television and its audience, and even more rarely done so in a positive way. On the one hand, cinema arguably did not want to offer too much credit to its young competitor, which film enthusiasts considered a "minor" and "trivial" form of entertainment. Television, when not completely ignored by cinema, was only present in the background of films, through the gaze of a distracted spectator mindlessly looking at the television screen. On the other hand, the Italian cultural elite considered television as the embodiment of the negative changes that occurred in society in the years of the economic boom. Therefore, many films engaging with the new medium represented it as an empty and fake world able to distract, alienate, and corrupt society. In order to offer an overview of this relationship, I will focus on three particular cinematic approaches. The first is that of the *commedia all'italiana*, Italian-style comedy, which was the popular genre that most engaged with the representation of television, primarily in order to mock its consumers. This is hardly a surprise, as the *commedia all'italiana* was known for being at the front line in the portrayal of the radical social and cultural changes in Italy during the Boom. The second is the auteur film, which was a dominant cultural force in Italy and the flagship of Italian cinema. Finally, I will look at some contemporary examples, focusing on the role that television plays as a reality index.

A Italian Comedy

In the *commedia all'italiana*, television was represented as a vane status symbol, a way for quick celebrity and success, and an addictive corruptor of morality and community, as we see in *I tartassati* (*The Overtaxed*, 1959). The film tells the story of Mr. Pezzella (played by the legendary comic Totò), the well-off owner of a clothing store who employs every stratagem in order to avoid paying taxes. However, one day his shop is under the scrutiny of the revenue office and the incorruptible investigator Topponi (Aldo Fabrizi), who struggles to pays his bills but promptly rejects all the bribery attempts made by Pezzella. One of these attempts consists in the delivery of expensive modern items, such as a fridge and a TV set to what Pezzella believes to be Topponi's apartment but which turns out to be the home of a relative. The television set represents, along with the fridge, a luxury object that seems to be more important as a status symbol than as an everyday utility. Topponi considers it a pastime of which he is not particularly fond (or at least he would have us believe), but which apparently his wife likes. For the Topponi family, watching television is a collective experience focused on a few particular shows, during a given time frame. In fact, they go to the neighbor's apartment and squeeze their chairs in front of the screen. A different experience of television viewing is that of the Pezzella family, which owns a television set and can watch it comfortably in their living room. In short, what emerges from this film is that television broadcasts some popular shows that for an active and productive person can be a waste of time, and that in the end reflects its status as a luxury item. We do not see any images of the television screen, and after those early references the television disappears from the film.

One year later in 1960, another comedy focused on television's power of creating celebrities in order to offer everyone their fifteen minutes of fame. In Luigi Zampa's *Il vigile* (*The Traffic Policeman*, 1960), a member of local police Otello Celetti (played by another celebrated comic, Alberto Sordi) does not fine the film star Sylvia Koscina for driving without her license while going to the RAI studios to be the host of the popular program *Il musichiere* (a series from 1957–60 based on *Name That Tune*). Otello asks for a favor in return: to mention his name during her interview with the presenter, Mario Riva. The same evening, Otello gathers with his wife to the local bar to see the show.

When Koscina thanks Otello on air (and on screen) for his kindness to let her go without a fine, all the customers of the small bar look at him with envy, while his wife becomes angry and jealous. Television viewing is represented as a collective and popular act. However, a movie star is the object of desire on the small screen.

In comedies of the 1960s, the protagonist often figures as a participant in quiz shows, such as in *Domenica è sempre domenica* (*Sunday Is Always Sunday*, 1958), and in *C'eravamo tanto amati* (*We All Loved Each Other So Much*, 1975). In these cases, television was a fast route to celebrity and success, conditions that the *commedia all'italiana* eventually attributed to desires of the petite bourgeoisie that made characters lose important values, such as solidarity and a sense of community. The world of TV was represented as an integral part of the commodification of everyday life, in this way the *commedia all'italiana* mirrored the judgment on the new medium by cultural critics. As Marcia Landy argues, "Television has been blamed for the decline of family values, the dissolution of community, the rise of terrorism, the triumph of Americanism, and the resurgence of Fascism (among other things)."[27]

This depiction did not change a decade later, even when the Italian comedy was increasingly dominated by actors and characters who emerged from the small screen. An example was Fantozzi, the character created by Paolo Villaggio in his monologues on the TV show *Quelli della domenica* (*Those from Sunday*), who became the main character of a best-selling book (1971) and the star of ten films in twenty-four years, from 1975 to 1999. In these films, television viewing was represented as one of the few vices of the lead character, in particular when broadcasting sporting events. In *Il secondo tragico Fantozzi* (*The Second Tragic Fantozzi*, 1976), for instance, Fantozzi and his colleagues are in despair because they have to attend an art-cinema night organized by their employer instead of staying at home in front of the television set to watch religiously a football match of the Italian national team. However, it is in *Fantozzi contro tutti* (*Fantozzi Against Everybody*, 1980) that the depiction of Italian television in the private channels was most acidly satirized. The protagonist, as every other Italian, rushes back home from work in order to sit in front of the television set, where he handles his remote control and changes channels incessantly until reaching the record of "three hundred sixty changes in a minute." The dinner table is arranged so as to allow all the family members to watch the television set. However, only the head of the family has the right to handle the remote.

From the courtyard we can see the constant flicking of television lights through all the apartments windows and hear the recurring complains of the wives. The television set is hypnotic and addictive not for its contents but for its endless and fragmented offerings. The only time a program successfully captures Fantozzi's attention and keeps him from changing channels is when a stripper performs, a comedic representation of the new freedom from censorship enjoyed by the unregulated private channels during the 1970s. On this occasion, Fantozzi moves closer to the screen and hugs the television set, imploring the stripper to take her panties off. Once more, the television is the source of nothing more than mindless petit bourgeois entertainment.

B Auteur Film

Art cinema kept its distance from the new medium of television or used it to mirror the alienation of its actors. If television appeared in auteur films, it did so only in the background, as if in embarrassment. Gianni Canova engages with this apparent absence in the three masterpieces produced by Italian cinema in 1960: *Rocco e i suoi fratelli* (*Rocco and His Brothers*, 1960) by Luchino Visconti, *La dolce vita* (1960) by Fellini, and *L'avventura* (1960) by Antonioni.[28] As Canova points out, in *L'avventura* the television appears only in one scene, and we can grasp it only for its reflection on the thoughtful face of Sandro (Gabriele Ferzetti). So the object of Sandro's vision is not even seen.

Overall, in the three films the television seems an empty object, which does not engage our gaze and which does not (as in the case of *La dolce vita*) shape our reality.[29]

The most significant depiction of the television world made by an Italian auteur was Fellini's *Ginger e Fred* (1986). Bondanella argues that, in Fellini's opinion, "Television represents a threat to the creative expression of the individual artist . . . not merely because it employs an impoverished technical language, but, more importantly, because it destroys the ritualistic nature of the cinematic experience."[30] The film refers to Ginger Rogers and Fred Astaire as cinematic icons now aged and constrained to fit in the small box that is the television world.[31] Television appears as a poor imitation of the social life and the richness of popular culture. It is an entertainment dominated by banality and commercialization. It is flat, repetitive, predictable, and unpleasant.

Everything on the small screen is a bad copy of other forms of entertainment: film celebrities, popular genres, and the *varietà* or variety shows (which are the subject of the film). Television cannot compare with the "real" thing of the popular theater and the music hall.[32]

The same shallowness of the television world is represented decades later in Gabriele Muccino's *Ricordati di me* (*Remember Me*, 2003). One of the characters of the film is a teenage girl who dreams of becoming one of the half-naked dancers who populate Italian shows, as if it were the only way for her to be "someone." *Ricordati di me*, on the one hand, shows squalid auditions and the emptiness of the television world, which in truth seems to be the only "functional" world among those portrayed. On the other hand, it represents the backstage of television production, with the audiences in studio who brainlessly follow basic orders, such as clapping their hands or laughing on cue. *Ricordati di me* is one of the few films that shows the objectification of the body on television. Recently some nonfiction films have focused on this aspect of Italian television culture, again representing the empty shallow dreams portrayed by television. Lorella Zanardo's *Il corpo delle donne* (*The Body of Women*, 2009) and Erik Gandini's *Videocracy* (2009) tell the stories of youngsters dreaming to become television celebrities and engage with their desire to be on screen. Moreover, both documentaries depict the exploitation of the female body made by television shows since the end of the RAI monopoly and the looseness of Italian censorship. Interestingly, these films had independent production and mainly online distribution, suggesting that there are alternative forms of financing outside of the television realm.

C Contemporary Approach: Television as Shared Reality

Television as documentation of the real is a trend that it is increasingly present in Italian cinema. Canova, for instance, notes how a film like Marco Bellocchio's *Buongiorno, notte* (*Good Morning, Night*, 2003) relies on television archival materials to stress elements of Italian history, recognizing in this way the role of TV as a recipient of the collective memory of the nation. The television is always on in the Red Brigades hiding spot, where they keep former prime minister Aldo Moro in captivity. It is through the screen that all the representations of the events happening outside the apartment (and outside the film) become part of the diegesis or narrative. Canova defines this new use of "television as collective memory archive," and points out that this puts a sort of end to the fifty years of cinema's hostility toward television.[33]

Television as the authentic depository of collective memories increasingly features outside of auteur cinema, and specifically in the middlebrow productions made in the new millennium that focus on the representation of the Italian past, in particular the 1970s. Films such as Marco Tullio Giordana's *La meglio gioventù* (*The Best of Youth*, 2003), Michele Placido's *Il grande sogno* (*The Great Dream*, 2009), and *La prima linea* (*The Front Line*, Renato De Maria, 2009) not only portray characters watching television—usually programs that help to contextualize the film in a particular time frame—but also make use of televised archival images, often mixed with the reenactment of the events. Television becomes the witness of choice for Italian history, and its programming is depicted as a real imprint on the collective memory. And the screening of former television anchors and celebrities framed by old television sets with the family religiously watching the news in silence (as happens in *Il grande sogno*) works alongside props and soundtrack to create a nostalgic feeling. This feeling of nostalgia tends to disappear when the events represented occurred after the RAI monopoly.

Most recently, the film of a new Italian auteur highlighted the role of television in contemporary Italy. In *Reality* (2012), the acclaimed director of *Gomorra* (*Gomorrah*, 2008), Matteo Garrone, engaged with reality TV, its participants, and its viewers in a film coproduced by RAI Cinema. *Reality* tells the story of a Neapolitan fishmonger who takes part in some auditions to become a participant on the program *Big Brother*. During the long wait to know if he made the cut, his perception of life and the boundaries between reality and fiction changes. This lead character transforms his life into a realty show. He believes that the television is spying on him, checking on his behavior in order to establish whether or not he will be fit to be part of the program. Garrone thus depicts the extreme consequences that the new forms of television have created in their attempt to capture the "normality" of everyday life.

4 Television-Funded Cinema

In contrast to what happened in other national cinemas, since the 1970s the Italian film industry has lost more than its leading role in the entertainment world. The lack of regulation that occurred during the end of RAI's monopoly allowed the television industry to become consistently richer at the expenses of the structurally weak film industry. As a result, the contemporary landscape of Italian cinema is now strongly dependent on the television industry, to the extent that it might well be considered an appendix of the small screen. Italian film production is financially sustained by the publicly funded RAI or the private Mediaset, the two media conglomerates that for more than three decades have dominated the television and audiovisual market. They control the entire life of Italian film, from its production to its companies RAI Cinema and Medusa, and to its final broadcasting on one of their channels.

The competition between the two media outlets is characterized by convergent trajectories, to the extent that it is impossible not to find strong similarities between their two film catalogues. Most of the production is made with particular attention to the final television audience, and so—apart from some art-cinema exceptions aimed at the prestige market of the film festivals—the end result is in general easily accessible works, often filled with television celebrities who move back and forth between the small and the big screens. The employment by film and television of the same actors, directors, comedians, presenters, producers, and screenwriters further blurs and weakens the boundaries between the two media. The television medium that was first understood both as an educational tool and as a corruptor of the masses has now been superficially infused with cinematic personnel, plotlines, and moralism. In fact, television was mainly portrayed as background noise or as a commodity that disrupted the strength of community and society. Television was truly "the other," its alterity able to bend the audience's minds and to dwell on the surface of the real. Despite some exceptions (most notably Nanni Moretti and Fellini) Italian cinema has failed to engage with the impact of television, a medium that eventually became at once its savior and its master.[34]

Notes

1 See Ginsborg, *A History of Contemporary Italy*; and Forgacs and Gundle, *Mass Culture and Italian Society*.

2 EIAR changed name to RAI by legislative decree on October 26, 1944.

3 See, among others, Ortoleva, "Cinema e televisione"; and Zagarrio, *L'anello mancante*.

4 On the role of ANICA, see Corsi, *Produzione e produttori*, 41.

5 Grasso, *Storia della televisione italiana*, 723.

6 Grasso, *Storia della televisione italiana*, 723.

7 Caminati, *Roberto Rossellini documentarista*, 87.

8 Corsi, *Con qualche dollaro in meno*, 117.

9 See D'Aiola "Piccolo grande schermo."

10 See Baschiera, "New Wave Italian Style."

11 Schlesinger, "The Berlusconi Phenomenon," 272.

12 Schlesinger, "The Berlusconi Phenomenon," 272.

13 Venturini, "TV."

14 Schlesinger, "The Berlusconi Phenomenon," 275

15 Corsi, *Produzione e produttori,* 42.

16 Corsi, *Produzione e produttori,* 42.

17 Corsi, *Produzione e produttori,* 43.

18 D'Aloia, "Piccolo grande schermo," 275.

19 D'Aloia, "Piccolo grande schermo," 276.

20 The *neotelevisione* is a term minted by Umberto Eco to define the "new television," with its use of color, its multitude of channels, and its private ownership. For more on the *neotelevisione,* see Ortoleva, "Cinema e televisione"; and Eco, "A Guide to the Neo- Television of the 1980s," 245.

21 Ortoleva, "Cinema e televisione," 1011.

22 D'Aloia, "Piccolo grande schermo," 279.

23 On the role played by Berlusconi in shaping the Italian media landscape during the 1980s and beyond, see Barra and Scaglioni, "Berlusconi's Television."

24 Corsi, *Produzione e produttori,* 44.

25 Corsi, *Produzione e produttori,* 44. My translation.

26 On the Italian media empires, see D'Aloia, "Piccolo grande schermo."

27 Landy, *Italian Film,* 367.

28 Canova, "L'etere e il nulla."

29 Canova, "L'etere e il nulla," 259.

30 Bondanella, *The Cinema of Federico Fellini,* 220.

31 Landy, *Italian Film,* 371.

32 Landy, *Italian Film,* 372.

33 Canova, "L'etere e il nulla," 267.

34 See D'Aloia, "Piccolo grande schermo," 288–89.

Bibliography

Barra, Luca and Massimo Scaglioni "Berlusconi's Television, Before and After: The 1980s, Innovation and Conservation." *Comunicazioni sociali* 1 (2013): 78–89.

Baschiera, Stefano. "New Wave Italian Style." *Italian Studies* 67.3 (November 19, 2012): 360–74.

Bondanella, Peter. *The Cinema of Federico Fellini.* Princeton: Princeton University Press, 1992.

Caminati, Luca. *Roberto Rossellini documentarista: Una cultura della realtà.* Rome: Carocci, 2012.

Canova, Gianni. "L'etere e il nulla: La rappresentazione della tv nel cinema italiano." In *Storie e culture della televisione italiana*. Ed. Aldo Grassi. Milan, Mondadori, 2013. 258–68.

Corsi, Barbara. *Con qualche dollaro in meno*. Rome: Editori Riuniti, 2001.

Corsi, Barbara. *Produzione e produttori*. Milan: Il Castoro, 2012.

D'Aiola, Adriano. "Piccolo grande schermo" Quando la televisione fa il cinema." In *Storie e culture della televisione italiana*. Ed. Aldo Grassi. Milan, Mondadori, 2013. 269–82.

Eco, Umberto. "A Guide to the Neo-Television of the 1980s." In *Culture and Conflict in Postwar Italy*. Ed. Zygmunt G. Barański and Robert Lumley. New York: St. Martin's Press, 1990.

Forgacs, David and Stephen Gundle. *Mass Culture and Italian Society: From Fascism to the Cold War*. Bloomington: Indiana University Press, 2007.

Ginsborg, Paul. *A History of Contemporary Italy: Society and Politics, 1943–1988*. London: Palgrave and Macmillan, 1990.

Grasso, Aldo. *Storia della televisione italiana*. Milan: Garzanti, 2000.

Landy, Marcia. *Italian Film*. Cambridge: Cambridge University Press, 2000.

Ortoleva, Peppino. "Cinema e televisione." In *Storia del cinema mondiale I*. Ed. Gian Piero Brunetta. Turin: Einaudi, 1992. 993–1112.

Schlesinger, Philip. "The Berlusconi Phenomenon." In Barański and Lumley, *Culture and Conflict in Postwar Italy*.

Venturini, Renato. "TV: Verso un sistema misto." *Studi sociali* 12 (July 11, 1983).

Zagarrio, Vito. *L'anello mancante: Storia e teoria del rapporto cinema-televisione*. Turin, Lindau, 2004.

15

Italian Documentary and the Predicaments of the Auteur

Nonfiction Films of Michelangelo Antonioni, Pier Paolo Pasolini, and Roberto Rossellini

Luca Caminati and Mauro Sassi

Over the past twenty years or so, film and media scholars have increasingly focused their attention on documentary and its limits—particularly in the wake of groundbreaking studies by Michael Renov, Bill Nichols, and other theorists, who grappled with a firm definition of documentary film.[1] Italian documentary studies are no exception to this critical trend, as they have been triggered by an unexpected explosion of nonfiction filmmaking across a variety of media platforms, from traditional methods of distribution to emergent interactive media experiments. This resurgence of nonfiction films is slowly eroding the bad reputation of *il documentario* in Italy. In fact, documentaries made after the end of the Second World War and up until the late 1960s—when the government substantially reduced its support for film—were mass-produced objects, generally considered overtly didactic and unbearably boring. Indeed, one often thought of them as dose of necessary albeit bitter medicine before the feature fiction film. Italy never had a public-funded body, like the Canadian National Film Board or the General Post Office film unit in Great Britain, which took charge of financing and promoting a real documentary culture and creating nonfiction films that would stand the test of time. In addition, before the documentary form could evolve into something that would accrue critical respect, its visibility began to shrink dramatically in the 1980s. In other words, film scholars have always valued Italian *fiction* films far above the corpus of Italian documentaries, and thus there has been a paucity of work about Italian documentary film in Italian. Things were even worse in the anglophone world, where the topic was almost never mentioned.

However, a new wave of Italian directors—spearheaded by Gianfranco Rosi, Pietro Marcello, and Michelangelo Frammartino—have been producing nonfiction films that have garnered international praise, making the history of this genre both interesting to scholars and ripe for reconstruction. Yet this potential for a newfound engagement with the Italian documentary film has not yet produced any definitive or canonical reappraisal. English-speaking scholars still do not have access to a reliable and up-to-date history of Italian documentary.

An even more problematic aspect of this lack of interest in nonfiction film in Italy has to do with the predominant Crocean aesthetic of most of the Italian intelligentsia in the postwar years. Film criticism imbued with Benedetto Croce's Idealist aesthetics perceived documentary as "non-art," since it was not the product of personal inspiration. And given cinema's status as a craft in search of a proper place in high-art circles, there was an attempt to keep film and its theories uncontaminated by such "low" forms as documentary. The insistence of early Italian film historians (such as Carlo Lizzani) on literary and painterly indigenous sources reflects precisely this anxiety regarding artistic hybridity and miscegenation. In short, meddling with the real was not for "real" artists and scholars. It would take a while—mostly thanks to Marxist Galvano Della Volpe's groundbreaking *Il verosimile filmico e altri scritti* (*Verisimilitude in Film and Other Writings*, 1954) and, more influentially in terms of film practice, to the ethnographic film culture triggered by Ernesto De Martino's research in the Mezzogiorno in the early 1950s to bring nonfiction back into the cultural debate.[2]

Without explicitly venturing into the territory of documentary theory, this chapter wishes to recount the critical response to the documentaries of three famous auteur directors: Michelangelo Antonioni, Pier Paolo Pasolini, and Roberto Rossellini. Through our analysis, we intend to identify some of the preconceptions surrounding Italian documentary practice, which—until very recently—stifled the development of a respected and prosperous documentary sector in Italy. We aim to bring to life a moment of Italian intellectual history that could shed some light on problems as diverse as the definition of the documentary form and the role of the documentary in postwar Italy.

According to an established narrative,[3] Italian documentaries made from the postwar period up until the 1980s were generally considered a "means to an end." They were the pedagogical appendage of other disciplines at best.

However, already by the 1950s, there were films recognized as autonomous contributions to the genre. The first milestones of this path toward a redefinition of the genre were the documentaries made in the 1950s by Ermanno Olmi, Cecilia Mangini and Lino Del Fra (keen collaborators on early field works by Ernesto De Martino), and Vittorio De Seta. In the 1960s and 1970s, the end of state subsidies for documentary films, together with the radicalization of Italian politics, created a new contentious space for experimentalism in both stylistic form and production methods. These experiments prepared the field for the true renaissance of Italian documentary filmmaking, which started with the first auteur documentaries of Silvano Agosti, Daniele Segre, and the more experimental work of Yervant Gianikian and Angela Ricci Lucchi. This trend continues nowadays with the works of Pietro Marcello as well as the experimental narrative nonfiction of Michelangelo Frammartino and Gianfranco Rosi, among others. The recent resurgence of documentary as a genre in its own right owes something to the documentary work of Antonioni, Pasolini, and Rossellini. Their status as star auteurs in the Italian film industry compelled the attention of film critics, who were prodded to explore a more complex approach to the documentary genre. The critical reception of these directors' documentaries is of the utmost interest not only in terms of the development and history of auteur cinema, but also for its implications in the wider history of documentary practice.

Maria Orsini's 2002 collection *Michelangelo Antonioni: I film e la critica (1943-1995)* is a good starting point for an analysis of the critical reception of Antonioni's documentaries, since it gathers all the articles and reviews written on Antonioni's fiction and nonfiction films. Specifically, the study shows how Antonioni's documentaries drew attention exclusively when they included the same themes and motifs that populate his fictional masterpieces. In other words, his nonfiction films were never discussed in terms of the documentary genre, as such. For example, amid the critical responses to *Gente del Po* (*People of the Po*, 1947)—Antonioni's first documentary, shot in 1943 but only completed in 1947, a work that focuses on the people who live along the banks of the Po River—Orsini selects a review by Aldo Bernardini. In his 1967 monographic study on Antonioni, Bernardini stresses the subjective character of the gaze the filmmaker directed at the Po Valley landscape and "la tendenza ad un racconto che, più che in funzione strettamente documentaria, serve a precisare una verità umana e ambientale" (the desire to produce a narrative that, rather than strictly documentarian, aims at portraying a human and environmental truth).[4] Bernardini's notion of the "strictly documentarian" is never spelled out; instead, he judges the documentary in a constant reference to the value categories developed for fiction cinema. Apparently, Antonioni's authorial subjectivity, which permeates the filmic text, suffices to elevate the documentary to the list of Antonioni's "true" films. Interestingly, Orsini's book includes an article on *Gente del Po* that is written by Antonioni himself. Entitled "Per un film sul Po" ("For a Film on the Po"), Antonioni's piece elaborates on the genesis of the project. The director states that at the beginning he was not sure whether he was going to shoot a documentary or a fiction film; the documentary would have been more attractive, because of the kind of footage he already had at his disposal, but it was also dangerous, because it could fall prey to the "rhetorical attitude" of the genre.[5] This is a very revealing note because it shows that Antonioni was well aware of the problems associated with the documentary-style of the period. At the same time, the fact that he felt he could make a documentary that would transcend the usual standard of the genre means that he did understand the documentary form as having intrinsic qualities not fully expressed in its instrumental or propagandistic form. Orsini also includes articles written by Antonioni about his second documentary, on street cleaning in Rome, *N.U.* (1948). In one of these articles, entitled "La malattia dei sentimenti" ("The Malady of the Sentiments"), which appeared in the journal *Bianco e nero* in 1961, Antonioni criticizes the schematic composition of Italian documentaries of that period, particularly their narrative structure, which he defines as "blocchi di sequenze, che avevano un loro principio, una loro fine, un loro ordine; questi blocchi messi insieme costituivano una certa parabola che dava al documentario una sua unità" (sets of shots in a very strict order, with a clear beginning and a clear end; these sets when put together became an arc that gave the documentary its unity).[6] By contrast, he reserves for himself a total freedom over how he edits his sequences, leaving them disconnected if necessary and even stressing their separateness in order to give a more mediated idea of what he intends to express. The critic Carlo di Carlo drew on this suggestive idea, and even expanded its range by identifying it as the signature style of the director in both his documentaries and fiction films. Di Carlo argues that in all Antonioni's movies, this peculiar editing technique transforms the landscape into an event or a character—to the degree that the meaning of any sequence is only partially the result of its order in a narrative structure. Predominantly, meaning arises from the relationships established between characters and the environment.[7] The identification of a consistent style in Antonioni's fiction and documentary films seems to preoccupy those critics who have analyzed his films. An influential study of Antonioni's work, the collection edited by Lorenzo Cuccu, *Antonioni: Il discorso dello sguardo e altri saggi* (1970), offers an analysis of this topic in the section dedicated to documentary, where Cuccu also refers to Seymour Chatman's reading of Antonioni's films.[8] Like Carlo di Carlo, Chatman sees continuity between the fiction and documentary films of the director, particularly within the composition of the images, the tension between characters and background, and the preference for long shots. All of these stylistic elements denote a keenness for description. In Cuccu's view, two apparently opposite aspects are at work in Antonioni's documentaries: the first one is the closeness to the aesthetics of neorealism, or to Zavattini's theory of *fare i film attraverso il buco della serratura* (shooting the film through a keyhole).[9] The second aspect is the desire to intervene and modify the reality confronting the director. These two opposing strategies result in a tension for the director, between immersing himself in a reality within which his film forms a creative component and the desire to underline a sense of distantiation. For Cuccu, the most curious and original aspect of Antonioni's filmmaking is that these two attitudes are at work in both fiction films and documentaries, where, given the stereotype of documentaries as representing the filmic real, they lend a new dimension to the genre. Following this thesis, Cuccu argues for a new definition of documentary and fiction film, in which fiction film images are mainly defined in relation to what they leave off-screen, because it is the operation of hiding something from the visual field of the spectator that creates the presupposition on which the narration can develop.

Documentary, on the other hand, is predominantly *descriptive*, which means that nonfiction images do not leave anything off-screen.[10] By Cuccu's own admission, Antonioni's documentaries challenge his definition; however, it is extremely revealing to examine how the critic interprets this challenge. He focuses principally on one of Antonioni's latest documentaries, produced by RAI (Radiotelevisione italiana), *Ritorno a Lisca Bianca* (*Return to Lisca Bianca*, 1983). Enrico Ghezzi, the producer, intended the film as an example of "cinema archaeology," because it is set on the same island where Antonioni directed *L'avventura* (1960). Cuccu acknowledges that there is nothing descriptive in the film, which resembles a *sguardo assoluto* (absolute gaze), disconnected from reality; its images refer neither to an off-screen narration, nor to a descriptive syntax, but they are *vuota contemplazione* (empty contemplation).[11] In other words, he does not concede that Antonioni's fiction films may have a documentary nature—as an orthodox semiotic approach would entail; rather, he maintains that Antonioni's documentaries are actually disguised fiction films.[12] Cuccu's book is important because, unlike those of most other Italian scholars, it makes a real effort to avoid subordinating the documentary to the fiction film. Indeed, it seems that it is precisely his appraisal of Antonioni's documentaries that pushes Cuccu to attempt a redefinition of the genre that would modify the usual balance between the two forms. Yet it is precisely his honesty and intelligence that, by contrast, make the bias of the Italian film critics toward the documentary even more evident.

Pier Paolo Pasolini is another director who has attracted a vast secondary literature, some of which is specifically dedicated to his documentary production. A few scholars have taken an original and innovative approach to the relationship between his fiction and documentary films. For example, in a fascinating article entitled "How Much Does It Cost for Cinema to Tell the Truth of Sex? Cinéma Vérité and Sexography," Nicholas De Villiers compares *Comizi d'amore* (*Love Meetings*, 1965) with other documentaries from different regions and periods in order to analyze how a realist cinema—which he defines as one engaged with the notion of truth—treats sex as a site where truth is revealed. *Comizi d'amore* is composed of a series of interviews that Pasolini personally conducted throughout Italy, from the south to the north. He recorded conversations with people on the street, in front of schools and factories, and he also interviewed intellectuals—such as Alberto Moravia, Camilla Cederna, and Oriana Fallaci—to provide a meta-analysis of the interviews collected on location. De Villiers notes that in this film Pasolini deals with many social issues: women's freedom, machismo, prostitution, homosexuality, divorce, and conformism, all of which can be grouped under the heading of "sex." This implies an expansion of the social and semantic category of sex, which casts a novel light on the biases and taboos in the Italian society of the 1960s. In order to prove his point, De Villiers compares *Comizi d'amore* to other more recent documentaries, like those by Polish filmmaker Wiktor Grodecki: *Body Without Soul* (1996) and *Not Angels but Angels* (1994). In the former, Grodecki interviews young male prostitutes in Prague about their sexual habits. There are some striking connections to Pasolini's film—including the topic and the technique of the interview—and yet De Villiers argues that the intention is totally different. While Pasolini wanted to perform a sociological survey and contribute to a political debate on the economic and cultural condition of Italian society, Grodecki isolates his interviewees and records their conversations in private rooms, not on the street, as Pasolini had done. Consequently, he has the power to control the situation, and as a result his interviewees are more inclined to tell him what he wants them to say, which is that homosexuals are victimized and have a subordinated role in society.[13] De Villiers examines other films about sexuality, some driven by a Manichean ethics and an inauthentic confessional style (including Larry Clarck's *Kids*, 1995), others apparently driven by a pure pleasure for the deconstruction of taboos about sexuality, such as Paul Morrissey's *Flesh* (1968). But none matches Pasolini's ability to present the ambiguities that accompany any discourse about sexuality, nor is any guided by Pasolini's consciousness of the fact that freedom to talk about sex is not always a reliable sign of a more advanced and free society. De Villiers's conclusion is important because it stresses the often-overlooked anthropological vein of Pasolini's work. At least in the earlier part of his career, he was an extremely inquiring artist, willing to spend hours eavesdropping on conversations in order to reconstruct the vitality of the Roman dialect, and eager to talk to strangers about their habits and thoughts—as *Comizi d'amore* testifies. In the introduction to the 1999 collection of Pasolini's filmscripts, Vincenzo Cerami maintains that Pasolini did not describe the Italian society "realistically," but instead reverted continually to allegories, myths, or parables as heuristic models.[14] In Cerami's view, as the Italian society was becoming "market-oriented" and consumerism was destroying the old peasant culture, Pasolini's movies became increasingly detached from reality and more oriented toward mythical visions.[15] We believe that this interpretation overlooks Pasolini's documentary work—which was not a parenthesis in his career or a sideline, but something that occupied him until the very end of his life in such works as *Le mura di Sana'a* (*The Wall of Sana'a*, 1971), about the ancient Yemeni city and *Pasolini e . . . la forma della città* (*Pasolini and . . . the Form of the*

City, 1974), a documentary on the cities of Orte and Sabaudia. Cerami's view also risks misinterpreting Pasolini's commitment to history in general and his oppositional position to trends in Italian society in particular.

Another fruitful approach to Pasolini's documentary is to read them through a postcolonial lens, in the light of the representations of alterity and otherness in Western art, as has been recently done by Luca Caminati and Giovanna Trento.[16] This approach can lead us to a better comprehension of the complex set of motivations behind Pasolini's fascination for Africa, India, and other areas of recent decolonization. First, we have his ideological and political beliefs, which are rooted in the connection between the Third World and a premodern era, which Pasolini construed as an idealized period of full contact with nature that preceded the alienation brought by consumerism and industrialization. Second, we have his artistic and psychological desires, through which Pasolini experienced the so-called Third World as the ultimate space of the "uncanny" (in a Freudian sense). Third, we have his understanding of the Third World as the last space for revolutionary potential. These intentions are well-exemplified in those documentaries combining political manifesto, ethnographic focus, and an experimental form, such as *Le Mura di Sana'a*, *Sopralluoghi in Palestina* (*Location Hunting in Palestine*, 1965), *Appunti per un film sull'India* (*Notes for a Film on India*, 1968), and *Appunti per un'Orestiade africana* (*Notes Toward an African Orestes*, 1970). Collectively, this work radically transforms the genre of the exotic documentary into something that is not in principle the translation of the "other" for a Western audience, but is rather a meditation on the process of observation and its parameters as well as a consideration of the film apparatus. In any event, it is possible to look at Pasolini's documentaries and essays as precursors to a cinematic realism that fuses the instinctive attraction to reality of the neorealist directors with the gestures of self-reflection, irony, appropriation, and non-closure that would come to permeate auteur filmmaking.

Roberto Rossellini is the least studied of the three directors that contributed to the Italian documentary history.[17] Although Rossellini's career began and ended shooting nonfiction films, his critical bibliography contains few entries dedicated to this aspect of his work. Rossellini started his career as an animal documentary filmmaker—the *Green Porno* series in which his daughter Isabella Rossellini was recently involved is, in a manner of speaking, part of the family business. This pioneering director of neorealism had a large aquarium built on the rooftop of the family house in order to shoot *Fantasia sottomarina* (*Undersea Fantasy*, 1938), a six-minute narrative documentary about fish "falling in love" accompanied by a saccharine orchestra soundtrack.[18] *Fantasia sottomarina* was the first in a series of short films on animals that parallel the narrative structure of contemporary Disney films, although they were in clear dialogue with the concomitant underwater experiments of Jean Painlevé, which Rossellini might have seen in Venice in 1935 and 1936.[19] In these first shorts—*Il ruscello di Ripasottile* (*The Brook of Ripasottile*, 1940), *La vispa Teresa* (*Lively Teresa*, 1940), and *Il tacchino prepotente* (*The Bullying Turkey*,

1940)—one already finds in a nutshell the narrative themes and moral concerns that will reappear in Rossellini's early cinema: the fight against oppression, friendship and love, the sense of community and communal effort, and the clash of personal beliefs and institutions. All these seminal concerns are all first enacted in the animal world before being transplanted to the human one. The career of Rossellini as a documentary filmmaker seemed to grind to a halt as he gained success with a long list of acclaimed fiction films, from the newsreel-style realist cinema of early works—*Roma città aperta* (*Rome, Open City*, 1945), *Paisà* (*Paisan*, 1946), and *Gemania anno zero* (*Germany Year Zero*, 1948)—to the more complex modernist narratives of alienation in his later "Bergman period" with *Stromboli* (1950), *Europa '51* (1952), and *Voyage to Italy* (1954). The revival of Rossellini's documentary career began in Paris in 1954, when he met with Jean Rouch, whose filmmaking proved to be one of the major influences for the Italian director's work during his trip to India, and more generally, for most of his nonfiction cinema in the years to come. Rouch's "ethno-fictions"—or "*cine-fictions*" as he called them—culminated in the summer of 1960, when Rouch and sociologist Edgar Morin made *Chronicle of a Summer*, signaling Rouch's move beyond "observational cinema" into "participatory anthropology." While *India: Matri Bhumi*—the fiction film shot by Rossellini in India between 1956 and 1957—certainly does not take the anthropological discourse to that extreme, Rossellini employs a style not too different from Rouch's participatory anthropology. Rouch's influence on Rossellini is evident in the narrative structure of the stories located in India, wherein the contamination between fiction and documentary images is embraced rather than resisted. *India* is the most blatant example of how an appropriately scaled historical analysis of Rossellini's long-lasting commitment to the documentary can help us understand both the cultural field in which the unquestionably innovative first neorealist movies were able to appear and the transnational environment at the core of much of Italian cinema.

Italian documentary emerged from the twenty-first century's industrial and technological media revolutions with substantial modifications to its institutional role and aesthetic ambitions. Wherever documentaries are made, they are frequently employed as a tool to gauge, describe, and vindicate social and political themes. But the political role of Italian documentary is less ideologically predictable in the current environment than it was in the 1970s, when considerations of the mediations between image and reality were often put aside in the name of a political urgency that aspired toward a radically simplified agenda to score points, raise outrage, and make history. In the meantime, documentary's role as a technology of perception and as an art form has become more relevant in light of a renewed autonomy from ideological, cultural, and economic pressures. Nowadays, even if the documentary is not more commercially successful than it was in the 1960s and 1970s, there is certainly a sense—at least in Italy—that documentary filmmakers are more convinced about the validity of the genre. For this reason, we argue, the historical background of the documentary in the Cold War era deserves a more careful critical examination. This chapter has attempted to reveal and destabilize one of the most common clichés of Italian film criticism, which is that auteur films are—for lack of a better word—*better* than documentary films and that when auteurs make documentaries, they transform the genre into something comparable to their fiction cinema. We have argued that Antonioni's documentaries are not as foreign to the documentary tradition as many scholars—obsessed by the search for a unified reading of his works—would suggest. Similarly, Pasolini's documentarian attitude—which is at play not only in his documentaries but also in many of his works—has been generally downplayed by the Italian critics in favor of a reading that is more consistent with the label of the auteur traditionally ascribed to his cinema. Finally, Rossellini's documentaries also connect with an influential European wave of innovative documentary filmmaking, of which he was not only aware but indeed overtly supportive. Our research conclusively suggests that Antonioni's, Pasolini's, and Rossellini's documentaries are not mere appendages to their creative work, but rather essential works in and of themselves. They are also key components in a documentary history that takes into account all the potentials of the documentary narrative form. By recognizing these major functions of the nonfiction films of Antonioni, Pasolini, and Rossellini, we can open up a more profitable critical approach to the Italian documentary tradition—one that understands it in terms of its own undeniable achievements and successes.

Notes

1 A proper history of documentary theory has not been written yet. A concise but polemical summary of the main problems and positions is in Bruzzi, *New Documentary*, 2–10.

2 See Marano, *Il film etnografico in Italia*, 12.

3 For a brief history of the work of professional documentarists, see Caminati and Sassi, "Notes on Italian Non-Fiction Film."

4 Orsini, *Michelangelo Antonioni*, 29.

5 Orsini, *Michelangelo Antonioni*, 30.

6 Orsini, *Michelangelo Antonioni*, 38.

7 Orsini, *Michelangelo Antonioni*, 39.

8 Cuccu, *Antonioni*, 196.

9 Cuccu, *Antonioni*, 198.

10 Cuccu, *Antonioni*, 205–206. See also Gaudreault, *From Plato to Lumière*, 47–50.

11 Cuccu, *Antonioni*, 207.

12 This notion of documentary as "disguised fiction" recalls Christian Metz's theory that both "fictional" and "nonfictional" film statements consist of

denotative frames of identical nature, which are subsequently assembled together to form discourses (*Film Language*, 108–11).

13 De Villiers, "How Much Does It Cost for Cinema to Tell the Truth of Sex?" 348.

14 Pasolini, *Saggi sulla letteratura e sull'arte*, xxvii–xxviii.

15 Pasolini, *Saggi sulla letteratura e sull'arte*, xliv.

16 Two volumes dedicated to this topic are Caminati, *Orientalismo eretico*; and Trento, *Pasolini e l'Africa*.

17 For a thorough analysis of Rossellini's documentaries, see Caminati, *Roberto Rossellini documentarista*.

18 See Rondolino, *Roberto Rossellini*, 27.

19 See Castello and Bertieri, *Venezia 1932–1939*, 64. Another source for Rossellini's "aquatic" filmmaking was the scientific cinema of filmmaker Roberto Omegna, especially his underwater film *Uno sguardo al fondo marino* (*A Look at the Seabed*, 1936), which won a special prize at the Venice Film Festival. See Bertozzi, *Storia del documentario italiano*, 64.

Bibliography

Bertozzi, Marco. *Storia del documentario italiano: Immagini e culture dell'altro cinema*. Venice: Marsilio, 2008.

Bruzzi, Stella. *New Documentary*. New York: Routledge, 2006.

Caminati, Luca. *Orientalismo eretico: Pier Paolo Pasolini e il cinema del Terzo Mondo*. Milan: Mondadori, 2007.

Caminati, Luca. *Roberto Rossellini documentarista: Una cultura della realtà*. Rome: Carocci, 2012.

Caminati, Luca and Mauro Sassi. "Notes on Italian Non-Fiction Film." In *Blackwell Companion to Italian Cinema*. Ed. Frank Burke and Peter Brunette. Oxford: Wiley-Blackwell, 2014, 361–74.

Castello, Giulio Cesare and Claudio Bertieri. *Venezia 1932–1939: Filmografia critica*. Rome: Bianco e Nero, 1959.

Cuccu, Lorenzo. *Antonioni: Il discorso dello sguardo e altri saggi*. Pisa: ETS, 1997.

De Villiers, Nicholas. "How Much Does It Cost for Cinema to Tell the Truth of Sex? Cinéma Vérité and Sexography." *Sexualities* 10.3 (2007): 341–61.

Gaudreault, André. *From Plato to Lumière: Narration and Monstration in Literature and Cinema*. Toronto: University of Toronto Press, 2009.

Lizzani, Carlo. *Il cinema italiano*. Florence: Parenti, 1953.

Marano, Francesco. *Il film etnografico in Italia*. Bari: Pagina, 2007.

Metz, Christian. *Film Language: A Semiotics of the Cinema*. New York: Oxford University Press, 1974.

Orsini, Maria. *Michelangelo Antonioni: I film e la critica*. Roma: Bulzoni, 2002.

Pasolini, Pier Paolo. *Saggi sulla letteratura e sull'arte*. Ed. Walter Siti and Silvia De Laude. Milan: Mondadori, 1999.

Rondolino, Gianni. *Roberto Rossellini*. Torino: UTET, 1989.

Trento, Giovanna. *Pasolini e l'Africa, l'Africa di Pasolini. Panmeridionalismo e rappresentazioni dell'Africa postcoloniale*. Milan: Mimesis, 2010.

16

The Global Impact of
Italian Neorealism

Laura E. Ruberto and Kristi M. Wilson

For me, [neorealism] is above all a moral position. It then became an aesthetic position, but at the beginning it was moral. . . . Ideas, not images, are important.

—ROBERTO ROSSELLINI[1]

Neorealism is the cinema that discovers the Italy of underdevelopment, discovers in a country that apparently has the clothing, the tinsel, and what's more, the rhetoric of development, another reality, a hidden one, that of underdevelopment . . . it was the cinema of the humble and offended. It was possible everywhere.

—FERNANDO BIRRI[2]

We begin with the premise that Italian neorealism is the kind of term that film scholars all know, and yet many of its nuances are rarely brought to the surface. It's a messy term at best.[3] Here we define neorealism in its original political and cultural context and point out some of the ways it has blossomed throughout world cinema. Our interest is in highlighting how the concept of neorealism has been adapted and adopted by filmmakers invested in constructing local as well as national film traditions, and how seminal neorealist films are sometimes referenced in their work.

Italian neorealism generally refers to a group of films produced in Italy in the immediate post–Second World War era. Sometimes these years are given in specifics: 1945 to 1952. Although using these dates is, in our view, problematic, it remains a tidy way to make sense of what is a politically and artistically complicated set of films.[4] The year 1945 refers to the release of Roberto Rossellini's *Roma città aperta* (*Rome, Open City*) and the year 1952 to the release of Vittorio De Sica's *Umberto D*, traditional cinematic "bookends" of the national movement. More importantly, though, 1945 refers to the end of the Second World War and a film, *Open City*, which triumphantly marked that end for Italians who had lived under a Fascist dictatorship.[5] The film, made by filmmakers who had in some cases worked in Italy's Fascist film industry, documents the occupation of Rome by Nazi Germany vis-à-vis the urban Resistance movement and the everyday lives of Rome's working class. *Open City's* style exemplifies some of the qualities commonly associated with Italian neorealism, or, as Millicent Marcus suggests, some of the "rules governing [it]": "location shooting, lengthy takes, unobtrusive editing, natural lighting, a predominance of medium and long shots, respect for the continuity of time and space, use of contemporary, true-to-life subjects, an uncontrived, open-ended plot, working-class protagonists, a nonprofessional cast, dialogue in the vernacular, active viewer involvement, and implied social criticism."[6]

On the other end of the timeline is *Umberto D.*, a film about a retired state employee without enough money to rent even the simplest of rooms in postwar Rome. He is surrounded by similarly down-and-out people: other pensioners, local soup kitchen visitors, a young maid. The film illustrated in stark ways the rampant poverty of the immediate postwar years and the futile or nonexistent efforts by institutional and social organizations to help rebuild Italy. As a result, *Umberto D.* was openly criticized by the government—most notably by the Minister of Culture, Giulio Andreotti, who disparaged De Sica for "washing Italy's dirty laundry in public," and instituted enough changes in how films were funded and scripts screened to put an end to state sponsorship of neorealist-style filmmaking in the strictest sense of the word.[7] That said, neorealism in Italy did not come to a screeching halt in 1952, but rather meandered its way through successive film styles to its place of continued cinematic influence today.[8] Although the most prominent trends in Italy in the era immediately after *Umberto D.* were either hyper-stylized, art-house films (like those of Federico Fellini or Michelangelo Antonioni), or *commedia all'italiana* (for example, by Mario Monicelli or Pietro Germi), the sensibility learned from neorealism was still apparent. For example, a film like Gillo Pontecorvo's *La battaglia di Algeri* (*Battle of Algiers*, 1966), with its emphasis on nonprofessional actors, true-to-life narrative, vernacular language, and heavy social critique, stems directly from its neorealist precursors. This neorealist legacy has continued in Italy, as scholars including Millicent Marcus, Pasquale Verdicchio, Bert Cardullo, and others have discussed.[9]

Between 1945 and 1952, dozens of Italian films shared a similar style and sensibility to both *Open City* and *Umberto D.* All housed under the same umbrella of neorealism, these films were not the only ones made in that short seven-year period, nor were they the most lucrative or popular. But they have had an unusually far-reaching stylistic impact on global cinema. It is in fact the legacy of neorealist films that contemporary Italian filmmakers, some seventy years later, most commonly and most explicitly respond to in their own artistry. Beyond any particular Italian director who has arguably influenced filmmaking internationally, it is indeed the loosely gathered set of films called "neorealist" that have most widely and deeply left their mark beyond Italy. Such acclaimed filmmakers as Satyajit Ray, Fernando Birri, Abbas Kiarostami, Martin Scorsese, among others, have all been linked to neorealism in one way or another.

So, then, what is unique about the style and sensibility of neorealist films, and why do they continue to influence filmmaking? To answer this question, one must understand the political milieu of the Italian film industry in which neorealism developed. Early on in film's mass-production history, Italy had been at the forefront with such large-scale productions as the film *Cabiria* (1914), where director Giovanni Pastroni first used crane shots to capture expansive sets and scenes. Benito Mussolini, who came to power in 1922, was invested in seeing the industry grow and support his political aims. His interest in new media ran deep (building Cinecittà, starting LUCE, the Union for Cinematic Education, supporting film production), and he was particularly keen on docudramas—fictionalized narratives that relied on documentary-style formalism to develop a cinematic Fascist aesthetic. It should come as no surprise, then, that Rossellini's *Open City* had such a documentary-like feel to it, since Rossellini's previous "Fascist trilogy," a group of films made under Mussolini that glorified the military and celebrated the war efforts, took advantage of similar formal strategies (especially the first film of the trilogy, *La nave bianca* [*The White Ship*], from 1941, which favored an objective camera point of view, nonprofessional actors, and on-location sets).

When the war ended, the industry's infrastructure was suffering. In a quite physical sense this occurred because the studios at Cinecittà were off-limits to filmmakers because they were being used by the Allies as a refugee camp. Noa Steimatsky places this history in relation to the development of neorealism, arguing that one of the reasons neorealist filmmakers chose to shoot on-location was less about an aesthetic or ideological choice and more about a practical one: the studios-turned-refugee-camps meant that they could not be used for film production.[10] After *Open City*, a film that made great use of location shooting, came a series of films that echoed it in style, thematics, and ideological intent.[11] While the biggest names as far

FIGURES 16.1 and 16.2 *Scenes from Roberto Rossellini's neorealist classic,* Paisan *(1946).*

as international impact goes are Roberto Rossellini, Vittorio De Sica, and Luchino Visconti, there were in fact dozens of other filmmakers who made Neorealist films: Renato Castellani, Giuseppe De Santis, Pietro Germi, Aldo Vergano, and Luigi Zampa, to name just a few.

In detailing some of the ways in which neorealism came to influence filmmakers—especially those outside of Italy—one does well to study one of the most popular and well-known Italian neorealist films, De Sica's *Ladri di biciclette (Bicycle Thieves*, 1948). The movie tells the simple story of a man's search through Rome for his stolen bicycle. But under this straightforward narrative lies a story of a disjointed community, broken social system, working-class struggle, critique of US imperialism, and questioning of religion and the family. Many lessons about neorealism can be learned from the film. First, the basic formal traits most associated with this style of filmmaking are present in De Sica's masterpiece: the use of nonprofessional actors, on-location shooting, diegetic sound, and dialect. Second, the narrative is set in the present moment (in the here and now, as opposed to a particular historical period), and it focuses on the working class, with an emphasis on children (especially young boys) as well as urban decay. In other words, the narrative strives to achieve a social impact—a hope that audiences might recognize the need for change (Figures 16.1 and 16.2).

Bicycle Thieves' broader ideological position clearly outlines the way that neorealist films were generally interpreted. In fact, a shared ideology, perhaps more than any shared formal characteristics, helps group together films in the postwar era as neorealist and, similarly, suggests connections to films beyond that time and place. In *Bicycle Thieves*, it is no accident that protagonist Antonio Ricci finally escapes the grip of long-term unemployment by being offered a job hanging Hollywood movie posters.

The film was released shortly after the momentous 1948 elections that ostensibly barred communists from having power in Italy and inaugurated the official beginning of the Marshall Plan (although US involvement was already strong since, and most likely even before, the 1943 Allied invasion). De Sica refashions this American deployment into a cultural one (through the impending reestablishment of the Hollywood industry in Europe), making a direct connection between the Ricci family's economic state and the United States. That De Sica, an Italian Communist Party (PCI) member, constructs this critique of US cultural imperialism is not surprising. And using film as a form of cultural criticism illustrates one of the ways in which neorealism could be seen as useful to a nation whose political and cultural identity was in flux. In 1945, filmmaker Alberto Lattuada was not shy about affirming the potential of cinema to present an honest picture of postwar Italy:

> Are we in rags? Then let us show our rags to the world. Are we defeated? Then let us acknowledge our disasters. How much do we owe to the Mafia? To hypo-critical bigotry? To conformity? To irresponsibility, to poor upbringing? Let us pay our debts with a fierce love of honesty and the whole world will join in, moved by this great contest with the truth. This confession will display our incredible hidden virtues, our faith in life, our superior Christian brother-hood.
> We will meet with understanding and respect. There is nothing better than cinema for revealing a nation's basic character.[12]

As described here, the political bent found in neorealist films has most readily been associated with communist filmmakers (De Sica, De Santis, and Cesare Zavattini) working in the new democratic Italy after Fascism. However, not all neorealist filmmakers were committed communists (Rossellini was not), nor are such socialist-leaning positions only associated with postwar filmmaking. Instead, the idea of making politically conscious films predates the end of the war. In fact, during Fascism, among the thinkers interested in shaping Italy's national identity were those who wrote for the journal *Cinema*, edited by one of the Duce's son, Vittorio Mussolini. Many of these writers came together informally, naming themselves the Verga Group, after the nineteenth-century realist Italian writer, Giovanni Verga. On the pages of *Cinema*, we can see much of the theory that would later be seen in the productions we now call neorealist. For instance, Giuseppe De Santis characterized the need for a specific kind of realism in cinema: realism is "the true and eternal measure of every narrative significance—realism intended not as the passive homage to an objective, static truth, but as the imaginative and creative power to fashion a story composed of real characters and events."[13] For De Santis and other postwar Italian filmmakers, the movie camera could capture the expressivity and vibrancy of real life during a moment of deep trauma and transition in Western Europe.

Thus, it comes as no surprise that neorealism's most obvious impact has been on filmmakers working within contexts under political and social imbalance: postcolonial India, Cold War Eastern Europe, postrevolutionary

Iran, and post-dictatorship Latin America, to name a few examples. In many instances, it is the United States, or Western cultural imperialism more broadly, that is being critiqued and opposed. Similarly, the United States en masse has not in a sense *needed* neorealism as intensely as other nations; it is, instead, among minority filmmaking circles that the Italian movement's legacy is most apparent.

Let us jump to 1952 London, where a young Satyajit Ray goes to work. He recounts seeing De Sica's film:

> Within three days of arriving in London I saw *Bicycle Thieves*. I knew immediately that if I ever made *Pather Panchali* [1955]—and the idea had been at the back of my mind for some time—I would make it in the same way, using natural locations and unknown actors. All through my stay in London, the lessons of *Bicycle Thieves* and neorealist cinema stayed with me. On the way back I drafted out my first treatment of *Pather Panchali*.[14]

Film scholars have linked Ray's oeuvre explicitly to neorealism, and De Sica's work in particular. This kind of epiphanic conversion to neorealist filmmaking strategies can also be seen in the work of many other filmmakers. Ray's reaction—the "lessons of *Bicycle Thieves*"—might be better understood by studying the words of De Sica's main collaborator, the screenwriter Zavattini, who is sometimes called the "theorist of neorealism" and whose words clarify how in and of themselves the experiences of everyday life offer the most compelling narratives for cinematic stories:

> We are now aware that reality is extremely rich. We simply had to learn how to look at it. The task of the artist—the neorealist artist at least— does not consist in bringing the audience to tears and indignation by means of transference, but, on the contrary, it consists in bringing them to reflect (and then, if you will, to stir up emotions and indignation) upon what they are doing and upon what others are doing; that is, to think about reality precisely as it is.[15]

Typically, Zavattini skewers classic Hollywood notions here. At its core, neorealism showed filmmakers that they had options beyond what they saw most prominently being exported from the US market. The neorealist option—to film with little money, to rely not on studios or professional actors, to construct plausible stories from everyday occurrences, and to create a kind of cinema of everyday life—was easily adaptable to filmmakers' specific national and cultural needs. As we have argued elsewhere, the influence of neorealism was not, though, merely an exercise in mimicry.[16] Others have reached a similar conclusion as well.[17] In explaining the connection between postwar Italian cinema and Iranian filmmakers like Kiarostami (*Where Is the Friend's Home?* 1986), Mohsen Makhmalbaf (*The Cyclist,*

1987), and Majid Majidi (*The Color of Paradise*, 1989), Bahman Farmanara observes ways in which Iranian filmmakers made Italian neorealism their own in the wake of the 1979 Islamic Revolution: "Here the circumstances have forced us to take a new look at this cinema, and sex and violence have been taken out. You have to go back to basic human stories that are very much elements of Italian neorealism. Now, we are using it in a different sense."[18] Indeed, an attack on the Iranian film industry by Islamic fundamentalists during the final years of the Shah's reign made many outside of Iran think pessimistically about the ability of the film industry to survive the new regime. Yet, as Stephen Weinberger points out, by the early 1990s, Iranian film was declared by *The New York Times* as one of the most exciting examples of world cinema. The practice of an entirely Iranian spin on neorealism continues up to today. For instance, in 2010, Jafar Panahi, whose films like *The White Ballon* (1995) or *The Circle* (2000) have been described as neorealist, was arrested in Iran and later sentenced to six years in prison and a twenty-year filmmaking ban. Panahi's response was to find ways, *neorealist* ways, to make films reflective of his everyday life, i.e., *This is Not a Film* (2011) was shot mostly with an iPhone and offers a realistic cinemascape that is critical of his house arrest.

On the other hand, while neorealism influenced politically engaged filmmakers all over the world, they were often critical of the limitations of that influence. This dynamic can best be understood in a Latin American context, through the work of Fernando Solanas and Octavio Getino, whose ideas about "Third Cinema" (*tercer cine*) sought to produce a subversive film form, one which attempted to decolonize cinema through a removal of Western imperialist and colonial influences, as in Hollywood productions ("First Cinema") and European auteur cinema ("Second Cinema"). They argued:

> The anti-imperialist struggle of the peoples of the Third World and of their equivalents inside the imperialist countries constitutes today the axis of the world revolution. *Third cinema* is, in our opinion, the cinema that *recognizes in that struggle the most gigantic cultural, scientific, and artistic manifestation of our time*, the great possibility of constructing a liberated personality with each people as the starting point—in a word, the *decolonization of culture*.[19]

The connections between radical Latin American filmmakers and Italian neorealism are not just conceptual. Both Fernando Birri, the founder of the Santa Fe School of Cinema in Argentina and director of the Argentine "neorealist" classic film *Tire Die* (*Throw a Dime*, 1958), and later Nobel Prize-winning author Gabriel Garcia Márquez studied under Zavattini at the Centro Sperimentale di Cinematografia (CSC) in Rome. Inspired by the films of De Sica, Garcia Márquez abandoned his career as a film critic to study screenwriting under Zavattini at the CSC. On the other hand, Birri came to understand neorealism as a prototype to cinema of what he called "underdevelopment," as the epigraph to this essay demonstrates: "Neorealism is the cinema that discovers the Italy of underdevelopment, discovers in a country that apparently has the clothing, the tinsel, and what's more, the rhetoric of development, another reality, a hidden one, that of underdevelopment . . . it was the cinema of the humble and offended. It was possible everywhere."[20] These early connections between prominent Latin American artists and Italian neorealism set the stage for many Latin American films that would follow (and follow still) under the heading of New Latin American cinema. Latin American filmmakers were, for the most part, passed over on the world stage until the 1960s, when films emerged in Argentina, Brazil, and Cuba that responded to increases in underdevelopment as well as economic and cultural dependency in the region.[21] Not unlike neorealism, New Latin American cinema is likewise a flexible term that corresponds to a style of filmmaking and film production that contrasts with notions of capitalist exploitation and foreign domination. At the same time, though, New Latin American cinema thought to uphold and support national and popular examples of cultural expression. Some of the most well-known New Latin American cinema directors include Glauber Rocha (Brazil), Fernando Solanas (Argentina), Fernando Birri (Argentina), Julio Garcia Espinosa (Cuba), and Tomás Gutiérrez Alea (Cuba).

David Martin-Jones looks at some of the more recent examples of New Latin American cinema as they relate to an Italian neorealist staple: the child's point of view.[22] He compares Roberto Rossellini's *Germania anno zero* (*Germany Year Zero*, 1948) to *Machuca* (Chile/Spain/UK/France, 2004), *Kamchatka* (Argentina, 2002), *O Ano em Que Meus Pais Saíram de Férias* (*The Year My Parents Went on Vacation* [Brazil, 2006]), and *Paisito* (Uruguay/Spain/Argentina, 2008), but there are countless examples one could draw upon. According to Gilles Deleuze, "The role of the child in neorealism has been pointed out, notably in De Sica (and later in France with Truffaut); this is because, in the adult world, the child is affected by a certain motor helplessness, but one which makes him all the more capable of seeing and hearing (Figure 16.3)."[23] As Martin-Jones reminds us, the child seer, a neorealist character type who develops out of the ruins of postwar Europe, "encounters history in the making [or, as he also calls it "mutation"] and this is very often a national history."[24] The new, often disjointed, history that evolves out of the loss of a coherent whole has particular appeal to the post-dictatorship landscape in Latin America. Thus, this character type has special narrative appeal where New Latin American cinema is concerned.

Colombian director Víctor Gaviria's film *Rodrigo D: No Future* (1990) is especially indebted to Italian neorealism and makes use of the child's

FIGURE 16.3 *Scene from Rossellini's* Germany Year Zero *(1948).*

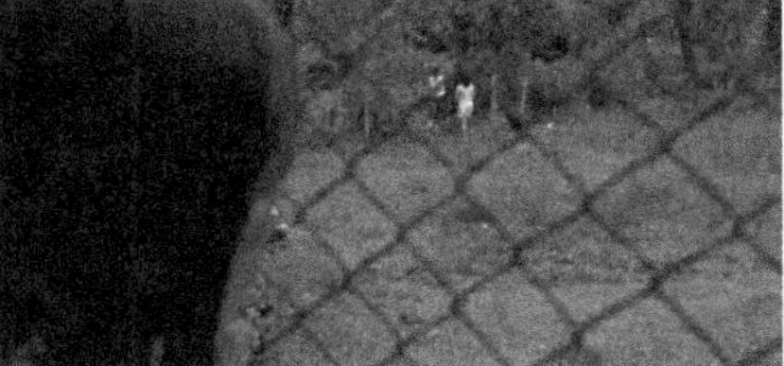

FIGURES 16.4 and 16.5 *From Lucrecia Martel's* The Swamp *(2001).*

perspective. The film's entire cast was made up of nonprofessional youth from the impoverished neighborhood in Medellin. The collective of actors helped conceptualize the script, which was in essence the story of their lives. By the time the film was released many of the young actors had perished from the various forms of violence and drug addiction depicted in the film. *Rodrigo D* was shot almost entirely on location in a Medellin shanty town, whose half-finished houses resemble the ruins of postwar Europe that make up the sets of certain Italian neorealist films.[25]

The connection between Latin American cinema and neorealism continues to the present. For example, Argentina director Lucrecia Martel—director of *La Ciénega* (*The Swamp*, 2001), *La Niña Santa* (*The Girl Saint*, 2004), *La Mujer sin Cabeza* (*The Headless Woman*, 2008) and *Zama* (2017) is one of New Latin American cinema's recent superstars and has been described by some critics as a modern neorealist (Figures 16.4 and 16.5). She has not adopted neorealism wholesale, but rather uses it to guide the emotional perspective of her films and how audiences engage with her films' narratives.

Her films are stark, poetic depictions of life in the North of Argentina that emphasize local cultures and class conflict between affluent white and poor nonwhite local populations.

Another recent Latin American film that stands out as having a particular affinity with Italian neorealism is Uruguayan filmmaker Federico Veiroj's *La Vida Útil* (*A Useful Life*, 2010). In this film, as in De Sica's *Umberto D.*, the central protagonist faces eviction and life on the streets. *La Vida Útil* is simultaneously about the transnational capitalist market forces that ruthlessly disenfranchise everyday working people, and the death of a certain type of cinema spectatorship: going to the local movie theater. Like Umberto in *Umberto D.*, Jorge fights a losing battle to preserve his place in the world, as the director of the local Cinemateca movie theater, a Montevideo cultural institution for over fifty years. The fact that the actors in *La Vida Útil* are real-life film critics and historians, and more importantly, that the Cinemateca is a real theater in Montevideo, makes the message of this neorealist-style film all the more urgent.[26]

As we have suggested throughout, neorealism was especially well suited to filmmakers in nations under political and cultural flux. As artists who were politically engaged with the cultural ideas of getting their people invested in change and in reflecting on society's problems, neorealism offered them cultural options. Karl Schoonover argues that, where global spectatorship is concerned, neorealism encourages a

> spectatorial experience in which multiple modes of engagement might coexist without contradiction ... the neorealist image actually lies precisely at the intersection of sensational rawness and world understanding, and . . . the humanist spectatorial mode it encourages tracks between the supposedly antithetical poles of affective engagement and reasoned ethical judgment.[27]

As demonstrated in the works of directors from a range of countries, including Senegal, Hong Kong, and Brazil, neorealism has not lost its penchant to push beyond the national boundaries of Italy, to entertain with a socially conscious narrative, and to suggest variations and alternatives from the mainstays of Hollywood exports.[28]

Given neorealism's fundamental political bent and its repeated adoption as the backbone of a filmmaking style that could counter Hollywood imports, it is confusing at best to suggest that Hollywood filmmakers make neorealist films. However, even Hollywood productions have at times favored a formal approach in line with neorealism—especially in films that use on-location settings or vernacular language like Elia Kazan's *On the Waterfront* from 1954. Similarly, certainly Hollywood films have been known to offer social or political critiques à la neorealist films (such as Mike Nichols's *Silkwood*, 1983). But Hollywood films that do both (achieve a neorealist formal style and ideological take) are few and far between. Instead, US filmmakers who seem most invested in adopting neorealism as both a formal and an ideological choice come from independent production and distribution circles.[29] Such films share an interest in socially conscious reflections on disenfranchised people and communities across the United States, often using an urban landscape to explore how specific ethnic/racial communities interact with or against dominant culture. For instance, Kent Mackenzie's *The Exiles* (1961) documents in a fictionalized way the struggles of Native American youth in Los Angeles by relying on nonprofessional actors and not using sets. Meanwhile, Lionel Rogosin's *On the Bowery* (1956) follows desperate, impoverished men for three days on Manhattan's skid row. This film was only partially scripted and was shot entirely along the Bowery. Similarly, in Morris Engels's *Weddings and Babies* (1958) the characters are well drawn (in this case Italian Americans on the Lower East Side) and the acting is naturalistic, with a script that is mainly improvised. In fact, Engels's entire oeuvre has been described as a kind of "New York neorealism."[30] By and large, such independent films were never widely distributed when first released. In some cases, they were banned (Herbert Biberman's *Salt of the Earth*); in other cases they never found a distributor (*The Exiles*).

Some US filmmakers with more widespread audiences and visibility—and who have made films both within and beyond Hollywood infrastructures—have also been connected to neorealism (for instance, John Cassavetes, Martin Scorsese, and Gus Van Sant). Scorsese's neorealist style can best be seen in early films. For example, *Mean Streets* (1973) favors little-known actors, a rough kind of realism and (apparently) on-location shooting (although memorable scenes were shot on the streets of New York City, the majority of the film was shot in Los Angeles). The film, a gritty story about low-level street criminals in Manhattan, carries with it a subtle critique of contemporary urban decay. Although strictly speaking *Mean Streets* (a Warner Brothers production) was not an independent film, it did follow both in form and concept a neorealist sensibility. And yet, beyond a few superficial examples, the connection between Scorsese and neorealism can be made perhaps most powerfully by recognizing the work that he has done not as a filmmaker but as an activist and advocate for film preservation, most directly through his World Cinema Foundation, which helps restore rare films from countries lacking the resources to undertake such preservation.[31] Scorsese's actions on behalf of international cinema suggest a global worldview, one that he has associated with childhood screenings of Italian neorealist films. In *My Voyage to Italy* (1999), Scorsese recollects his childhood exposure to Italian films in his family's New York City apartment, stating that "all of a sudden it [my world] became much bigger" through screening films like *Paisà* or *Bicycle Thieves* (*My Voyage to Italy*). The aesthetic alternative that Scorsese watched as a child and that Satyajit Ray experienced in a theater in London is neorealism's staying power, a power that filmmakers have implemented to bring local stories to the screen, to effect social change, and ultimately to construct new directions in cinematic styles.

Notes

1   Roberto Rossellini as quoted in Verdone, *Storia del cinema italiano*, 43. Unless otherwise noted all translations are our own.

2   Fernando Birri as quoted Hess, "Neo-Realism and New Latin American Cinema," 110.

3   See our Introduction to *Italian Neorealism and Global Cinema*, 5. See also Sorlin, *Italian National Cinema*.

4   The post–World War II start date is useful but problematic for a number of reasons. It emphasizes a clean break from Fascism when in fact neorealist-like filmmaking was already in place to a large extent during the dictatorship (for example, *Osessione* and *Children Were Watching Us*). It also gives little space to even earlier neorealist-like filmmaking practices in Italy, such as that of the silent-era Neapolitan filmmaker, Elvira Notari. See Bruno, *Streetwalking on a Ruined Map,* who warns against understanding Italian neorealist films strictly as a response to Fascism. See also Bondanella, *Italian Cinema*; Brunetta, *Cent'anni di cinema italiano*; and Sitney. *Vital Crisis in Italian Cinema.*

5   For an analysis of *Open City* that speaks to the less-well-known relationship between the United States and the making of *Open City*, see Wranovics, "Spooks Behind the Lens," 22–28.

6   Marcus, *Italian Film in the Light of Neorealism*, 22.

7   Sitney, *Vital Crisis*, 107.

8   See Ruberto and Wilson, *Italian Neorealism and Global Cinema.*

9   See Cardullo, *After Neorealism*; Marcus, *Italian Film in Light of Neorealism*; and Marcus and Verdicchio in Ruberto and Wilson, *Italian Neorealism and Global Cinema.*

10   See Steimatsky, "The Cinecittà Refugee Camp (1944–1950)," 22–50.

11   Although Rossellini constructed some sets, the film relies on the Roman geography in many ways—from shots taken from above rooftops to long shots of the city's famous cityscape.

12   Weinberger, "Neorealism, Iranian Style," 5–16.

13   In Overbey, *Springtime in Italy*, 131.

14   Ray, *Our Films, Their Films*, 9–10.

15   In Overbey, *Springtime in Italy*, 67–68.

16   See Ruberto and Wilson, *Italian Neorealism*, 2007.

17   In Giovacchini and Sklar, *Global Neorealism*, 2011.

18   In Weinberger, *Neorealism*, 11.

19   In Ames, *Third World Filmmaking at the West*, 37.

20   See Crowder-Taraborrelli, "A Stonecutter's Passion"; and Hess, "*Bicycle Thieves* and *Blood of the Condor.*"

21   See Martin, *New Latin American Cinema.*

22 For further discussions of children in neorealist films, see Fisher, "On the Ruins of Masculinity"; Traverso, "Migrations of Cinema"; and Ruberto, "Neorealism and Contemporary European Immigration."

23 Deleuze, *Cinema 2*, 3.

24 Martin-Jones, *Deleuze and World Cinemas*, 74.

25 See Wilson, "From Pensioner to Teenager."

26 See Wilson, "On the Decay of the Art of Going to the Movies." For more on New Latin American cinema, see Martin, *New Latin American Cinema*; and Lopez, *Mediating Two Worlds*.

27 Schoonover, *Brutal Vision*, 72.

28 See, for example, the Senegalese films *Xala* (1975), *Ceddo* (1977), *Camp de Thiaroye* (1987), and *Guelwaar* (1992) by filmmaker Ousmane Sembene; the *1997 Trilogy* of Hong Kong filmmaker Fruit Chan; and the more recent Brazilian blockbusters *Central do Brasil* (*Central Station*, Walter Salles, 1998), and *Cidade de Deus* (*City of God*, Kátia Lund and Fernando Meirelles, 2002).

29 See such films as *Killer of Sheep* (Charles Burnett, 1977); *Nothing But a Man* (Michael Roemer, 1964); *Salt of the Earth* (Herbert Biberman, 1954); *La Ciudad* (David Riker, 1998); *The Exiles* (Kent MacKenzie, 1961); *On the Bowery* (Lionel Rogosin, 1956); *Dark Odyssey* (Bill Kyriakis, 1961): and *Weddings and Babies* (Morris Engel, 1958). See Chris Norton on Charles Burnett and other independent African American filmmakers working within a neorealist tradition ("Black Independent Cinema and The Influence of Neo-realism," 5).

30 Hoberman, "New York Neo-Realism."

31 See Ruberto, "Italian Films, New York City Television, and the Work of Martin Scorsese."

Bibliography

Ames, Roy. *Third World Filmmaking and the West*. Berkeley: University of California Press, 1987.

Bondanella, Peter. *Italian Cinema: From Neorealism to the Present*. New York: Continuum Press, 1991.

Brunetta, Gian Piero. *Cent'anni di cinema italiano*. Vol. 2. *Dal 1945 ai giorni nostri*. Rome-Bari: Laterza, 1995.

Brunetta, Gian Piero, *Storia del cinema italiano*. Rome: Riuniti, 1993.

Bruno, Giuliana. *Streetwalking on a Ruined Map: Cultural Theory and the City Films of Elvira Notari*. Princeton: Princeton University Press, 1993.

Cardullo, Bert. *After Neorealism: Italian Filmmakers and Their Films: Essays and Interviews*. London: Cambridge Scholars Publishing, 2009.

Crowder-Taraborrelli, Tomas F. "A Stonecutter's Passion: Latin American Reality and Cinematic Faith." In *Italian Neorealism and Global Cinema*. Ed. Laura E. Ruberto and Kristi M. Wilson. Detroit: Wayne State University Press, 2007. 128–43.

Deleuze, Gilles. *Cinema 2*. London: Continuum, 2005.

Fisher, Jaimey. "On the Ruins of Masculinity: The Figure of the Child in Italian Neorealism and the German Rubble-Film." In *Italian Neorealism and Global Cinema*. Ed. Laura E. Ruberto and Kristi M. Wilson. Detroit: Wayne State University Press, 2007. 128–43. 25–53.

Giovacchini, Saverio and Robert Sklar, eds. *Global Neorealism: The Transnational History of a Film Style*. Jackson: University of Mississippi Press, 2011.

Hess, John. "Neo-Realism and New Latin American Cinema: *Bicycle Thieves* and *Blood of the Condor*." In *Mediating Two Worlds: Cinematic Encounters in the Americas*. Ed. J. King, A. M. López, and M. Alvarado. London, BFI, 1993. 104–18.

J. Hoberman. "New York Neo-Realism: From Coney Island to Rye Playland." *Village Voice* (June 17, 2008). www.villagevoice.com/2008-06-17/film/old-n-y-on-dvd/. Accessed January 20, 2013).

Lopez, Ana, John King, and Manuel Alvarado, eds. *Mediating Two Worlds: Cinematic Encounters in the Americas*. London: BFI, 1993.

Marcus, Millicent. *Italian Film in the Light of Neorealism*. Princeton: Princeton University Press, 1987.

Martin, Michael T. *New Latin American Cinema. Volume One: Theory, Practices, and Transcontinental Articulations*. Detroit: Wayne State University Press, 1997.

Martin-Jones, David. *Deleuze and World Cinemas*. London, New York: Continuum, 2011.

Norton, Chris, "Black Independent Cinema and The Influence of Neo-realism: Futility, Struggle, and Hope in the Face of Reality." 1997. *Images: A Journal of Film and Popular Culture*, www.imagesjournal.com. Accessed March 23, 2017.

Overbey, David, ed. and trans. *Springtime in Italy: A Reader on Neorealism*. Hamden: Archon Books, 1978.

Ray, Satyajit. *Our Films, Their Films*. Calcutta: Orient Longman 1976.

Ruberto, Laura E. "Neorealism and Contemporary European Immigration." In *Italian Neorealism and Global Cinema*. Ed. Laura E. Ruberto and Kristi M. Wilson. Detroit: Wayne State University Press, 2007. 242–58.

Ruberto, Laura E. "Italian Films, New York City Television, and the Work of Martin Scorsese." In *A Companion to Martin Scorsese*. Ed. Aaron Baker. New York: Wiley-Blackwell Press, 2015. 53–70.

Ruberto, Laura E. and Kristi M. Wilson. *Italian Neorealism and Global Cinema*. Detroit: Wayne State University Press, 2007.

Schoonover, Karl. *Brutal Vision: The Neorealist Body in Postwar Italian Cinema*. Minneapolis: University of Minnesota Press, 2012.

Sitney, P. Adams. *Vital Crisis in Italian Cinema: Iconography, Stylistics, Politics*. Austin: University of Texas Press, 1995.

Sorlin, Pierre. *Italian National Cinema*. New York: Routledge, 2012.

Steimatsky, Noa. "The Cinecittà Refugee Camp (1944–1950)." *October* 128 (Spring 2009): 22–50.

Traverso, Antonio. "Migrations of Cinema: Italian Neorealism and Brazilian Cinema." In *Italian Neorealism and Global Cinema*. Ed. Laura E. Ruberto and Kristi M. Wilson. Detroit: Wayne State University Press, 2007. 165–86.

Verdone, Mario. *Storia del cinema italiano*. Rome: Tascabili Economici Newton, 1995.

Weinberger, Stephen, "Neorealism, Iranian Style." *Iranian Studies* 40.1 (February 2007): 5–16.

Wilson, Kristi M. "On the Decay of the Art of Going to the Movies. Federico Veiroj's *La Vida Útil* (2010)." *Latin American Perspectives* (March 2013).

Wranovics, John. "Spooks Behind the Lens: U.S. Psychological Warfare and the Birth of Neo-Realism." *Noir City* 10.4 (2016): 22–28.

Filmography

Cabiria, Dir. Giovanni Pastroni. Italy: Itala Films. 1914.

Camp de Thiaroye, Dir. Ousmane Sembene. Senegal: Films Domireew. 1987.

Ceddo, Dir. Ousmane Sembene. Senegal: Films Domireew. 1977.

Central do Brasil (*Central Station*), Dir. Walter Salles. Brazil: Audiovisual Development Bureau. 1998.

Cidade de Deus (*City of God*), Dir. Kátia Lund and Fernando Meirelles. Brazil: 02 Films. 2002.

Dark Odyssey, Dir. Bill Kyriakis. USA: Era KM Films. 1961.

Germania anno zero (*Germany Year Zero*), Dir. Roberto Rossellini. Italy: Tevere Film. 1948.

Guelwaar, Dir. Ousmane Sembene. Senegal: Films Domireew. 1992.

Kamchatka, Dir. Marcelo Piñeyro. Argentina: Alquimia Film. 2002.

Killer of Sheep, Dir. Charles Burnett. USA: Unknown. 1977.

La battaglia di Algeri (*Battle of Algiers*), Dir. Gillo Pontecorvo. Algeria and Italy: Casbah Film. 1966.

La Ciénaga (*The Swamp*), Dir. Lucrecia Martel. Argentina: 4 K Films. 2001.

La Ciudad, Dir. David Riker. USA: Journeyman Pictures. 1998.

La Mujer sin Cabeza (*The Headless Woman*), Dir. Lucrecia Martel. Argentina: Aquafilms. 2008.

La nave bianca (*The White Ship*), Dir. Roberto Rossellini. Italy: Scalera Film. 1941.

La Niña Santa (*The Girl Saint*), Dir. Lucrecia Martel. Argentina: La Pasionaria. 2004.

La Vida Útil (*A Useful Life*), Dir. Federico Veiroj. Uruguay and Spain: Cinekdoque. 2010.

Ladri di biciclette (*Bicycle Thieves*), Dir. Vittorio De Sica. Italy: Produzione De Sica. 1948

Machuca, Dir. Chile/Spain/UK/France. Wood Producciones. 2004.

Mean Streets, Dir. Martin Scorsese. USA: Warner Brothers. 1973.

My Voyage to Italy, Dir. Martin Scorsese. USA: Media Trade. 1999.

Nothing But a Man, Dir. Michael Roemer. USA: Du Art Film. 1964.

O Ano em Que Meus Pais Saíram de Férias (*The Year My Parents Went on Vacation*), Dir. Cao Hamburger. Brazil: Gullane. 2006.

On the Bowery, Dir. Lionel Rogosin. USA: Rogosin Films. 1956.

On the Waterfront, Dir. Elia Kazan. USA: Columbia Pictures. 1954.

Paisà (Paisan), Dir. Roberto Rossellini. Italy: Organizzazione Film Internazionale. 1946.

Paisito, Dir. Ana Diez. Uruguay/Spain/Argentina: Haddock Films. 2008.

Pather Panchali, Dir. Satyajit Ray. India: Government of West Bengal. 1955.

Rodrigo D: No Future, Dir. Víctor Gaviria. Colombia: Compañía de Fomento Cinematográfico. 1990.

Roma, città aperta (Rome, Open City), Dir. Roberto Rossellini. Italy: Excelsa Film. 1945.

Salt of the Earth, Dir. Herbert Biberman. USA: Independent Productions, International Union of Mine, Mill and Smelter Workers. 1954.

Silkwood, Dir. Mike Nichols. USA: ABC Motion Pictures. 1983.

The Circle, Dir. Jafar Panahi. Iran, Italy, and Switzerland: Jafar Panahi Productions. 2000.

The Color of Paradise, Dir. Majid Majidi. Iran: Varahonar Film. 1989.

The Cyclist, Dir. Mohsen Makhmalbaf. Iran: Bonyad Mostazafan. 1987.

The Exiles, Dir. Kent MacKenzie. USA: Unknown. 1961.

The White Balloon, Dir. Jafar Panahi. Iran: Ferdos Films. 1995.

Tire Die (Throw a Dime), Dir. Fernando Birri. Argentina: Instituto de Cinematografía de la Universidad Nacional del Litoral. 1958.

Weddings and Babies, Dir. Morris Engel. USA: Morris Engel Associates. 1958.

Where Is the Friend's Home? Dir. Abbas Kiarostami. Iran: Kanon. 1986.

Xala, Dir. Ousmane Sembene. Senegal: Films Domireew. 1975.

PART FOUR

Films in Focus

17

Cabiria

Robert Rushing

Widely regarded as the most important Italian film of the silent era, *Cabiria* (1914) tells two alternating stories that intersect near the film's end. The first is the history of the Second Punic War (218–201 BC) between Rome and Carthage, a war that eventually made Rome the dominant power in the Mediterranean. The actual history depicted in the film includes not only epic-historical figures (Hannibal crossing the Alps with elephants, the determined Roman general Scipio who will eventually defeat Hannibal) but also a love triangle between the Carthaginian princess Sophonisba and the two Numidian kings, Massinissa and Syphax. The romance had a particularly melodramatic twist—Sophonisba committed suicide rather than surrender to the Romans, an act of courage that made her a legend in classical times. *Cabiria*'s second, and entirely fictional, storyline gives a smaller and more human view of these historical events: it tells the story of a little Roman girl who is separated from her family during an eruption of Mount Etna, is abducted by pirates, nearly sacrificed to the god Moloch, and ends up (after a ten-year gap in the narrative) as a servant to Sophonisba in Carthage. She is rescued from death and danger by Fulvius Axilla, a Roman nobleman as well as soldier and intelligence agent, and his extraordinarily strong and loyal slave, the mixed-race Maciste. The film ends shortly after the definitive Roman victory and Sophonisba's suicide, with Fulvius and Cabiria, in love, sailing back to Roman lands while Maciste smiles on their union and serenades them.

1 *Cabiria* and Its Context

Like most films of the early silent period, *Cabiria* is part of what Tom Gunning has called "the cinema of attractions" that has close ties to the circus or vaudeville show.[1] While the film tells a coherent story, it never lets that stand in the way of a spectacular sequence that, strictly speaking, is not necessary. When Fulvius Axilla returns to Carthage after years away, Roman soldiers form an enormous human pyramid that allows him to climb over the city's massive walls, an impressive if unnecessary stunt. In one of the film's most striking sequences, we cut away to the city of Syracuse, under siege by the Romans. We watch the famous Greek engineer Archimedes devise a "heat ray" of mirrors that focus sunlight onto the attacking Roman ships and make them burst into flames—an astonishing spectacle (and at least somewhat based in history), but without any relevance to the film's double plot.

Cabiria was also quite typical of Italian film industry in the 1910s. It was part of a large number of Italian-made historical epics set in ancient Rome that were extremely popular both in Italy and abroad, such as *Quo vadis?* (Enrico Guazzoni, 1913) and *Gli ultimi giorni di Pompei* (*The Last Days of Pompeii*, Mario Caserini, 1913).[2] The Italian film industry enjoyed certain advantages in making such films, particularly the presence of widely varied landscapes, good weather (and hence abundant sunlight in an era when film stock was not particularly light sensitive), and numerous classical ruins that could be incorporated into sets or used as background. Like many Italian films of the period, *Cabiria* also featured a diva, or female superstar, part of a star system known as *divismo* in Italy. These women were not simply stars, but specialized in a particular kind of role: in a still-conservative post-Victorian era, they played sexually assertive femmes fatales who would then, obligatorily, meet a bad end, often through suicide.[3] Italia Almirante Manzini played Sophonisba as a classic diva—seductive, fickle, enigmatic, languorous, and dangerous to the men around her—and it made her career. *Divismo* as a star system was not limited to women, and the actor who played Maciste (Bartolomeo Pagano) became one of early Italian cinema's best-known stars. Unlike the typical *divo* (the masculine form of diva), however, Pagano was known less for his good looks and more for his impressively muscled massive body.[4]

In its quality, length, epic scope, filming techniques, and attention to detail, *Cabiria* was not a typical film of the era. The film's director, Giovanni Pastrone, was determined to make a work of spectacular and lavish magnificence, in a manner that would virtually come to define the so-called quality film.[5] Marga Cottino-Jones notes "the sumptuousness of its images and its costumes" as well as Pastrone's use of "the most famous Italian composer of the time," Ildebrando Pizzetti, for the score, which was executed at the film's premiere with "a one hundred twenty-member orchestra."[6] Perhaps Pastrone's most ingenious decision was to enlist the help of Gabriele D'Annunzio, one of the most highly regarded poets of the era, to work on the intertitles for the film (D'Annunzio was so famous that the film's initial posters only mention his name, and not the director or any of the actors; see Figure 17.1). The film was even epic in length, with a running time virtually unheard of in the 1910s. The commercial versions available today are just over two hours, but the Museo Nazionale del Cinema in Turin has a nearly complete copy that runs slightly over three hours.[7]

Even today, viewers are surprised by the film's quality and sheer opulence. The Temple of Moloch sequence, in which little Cabiria is about to be sacrificed to one of the Cathaginian gods, has passages that

FIGURE 17.1 *Poster for* Cabiria *prominently featuring D'Annunzio rather than Pastrone.*

are enigmatically beautiful (chiaroscuro shots of hands emerging from darkness, lit only by the sacrificial fire) as well as sets that are breathtaking in their size. When Maciste, Fulvius Axilla, and Cabiria escape from the temple, we watch their tiny figures climb down the exterior of the temple and realize that it is not a miniature—the exterior of the temple was built in its entirety. While some of the special effects sequences appear dated today, Pastrone's use of miniatures and matte shots are often convincing: as Roman ships burn in one battle sequence, we can see tiny human figures moving inside. Similarly, when Etna erupts the attentive viewer will notice a parade of tiny refugees moving down its slopes. *Cabiria* has also long enjoyed a reputation as the first film to feature a moving camera, allowing the director to "push in" on emotionally important action, and to follow the movements of actors. In short, Pastrone ably makes a case throughout *Cabiria* for the potential of film as an art and, more specifically, as an ideal medium for the epic.

Cabiria enjoyed enormous success both in Italy and abroad. It was the first film shown at the White House, and it saw multiple re-releases throughout the 1920s and—in a version that had synchronized sound added to it—into the early 1930s. But its success in Italy had to do with more than simply its quality and grandeur. As Cottino-Jones notes, "the film highlights the power and glory of Rome as a world-conquering institution" (12), and it does so precisely at the moment when Italy was somewhat belatedly attempting to establish itself as a colonial power—in the exact same part of the world where *Cabiria* is set. The film paints a straightforward victory and a successful empire in the historic past that Italian audiences in 1914 could easily project onto their country's present circumstances, a "clear analogy between past and present."[8] In imagining Cabiria's abduction from Italy and her mortal danger in North Africa, *Cabiria* suggests that Italy's modern imperialism was justified as a symbolic rescue of a "damsel in distress." Finally, the film depicts Maciste as the ideal colonial subject. He is immensely strong, but even more intensely loyal to his master. His leopard-print loincloth and blackface makeup mark him as an African "other," but he wears a Roman toga (see Figure 17.2), and turns up his nose at the African serving woman in the inn in Carthage. After Fulvius Axilla and Maciste rescue the child Cabiria from her ritual sacrifice, Fulvius gets away, but Maciste is caught by the Carthaginians. He is chained to a millstone, and forced to turn it for ten long years before Fulvius returns to Carthage. When Maciste sees his old master, the titles inform us that "the joy of unexpected freedom increases his strength," allowing Maciste to break his iron chains.

The film is almost Orwellian here, since the freedom that elates Maciste is the freedom of being a slave to his "proper" master, Fulvius the Roman, rather than to the Carthaginians.

FIGURE 17.2 *Maciste's first appearance in* Cabiria.

2 The Legacy of *Cabiria*

Cabiria has inspired generations of filmmakers. Its technical innovations (such as the dolly shot) became a permanent part of the language of cinema, while the huge, opulent epic set in ancient Rome has remained a favorite up through Ridley Scott's *Gladiator* (2000). When *Cabiria* was first released, it had an enormous impact, most famously on D. W. Griffith, who modeled the Babylonian sections of *Intolerance* (1916) on *Cabiria*'s vision of the ancient world.[9] The Temple of Moloch sequence has been widely imitated over the years, particularly in science fiction and fantasy. In Fritz Lang's *Metropolis* (1927), a young man witnesses a terrible industrial accident on a giant machine that injures dozens of workers. The machine briefly transforms, in the young man's eyes, into a bestial temple based on *Cabiria*'s temple of Moloch (Lang thus cleverly implies that both the barbaric Carthaginians and modern factory owners practice a form of human sacrifice). The temple reappears, now called the Temple of Vaal, in an even more overt visual homage, in an episode of *Star Trek* from 1967.[10] The temple sacrifice sequence is referenced once again, not surprisingly, in Steven Spielberg's *Indiana Jones and the Temple of Doom* (1984).

Cabiria's most influential character, however, was certainly Maciste. He was one of numerous strongman acts in early cinema, but, unlike most, Maciste attained an enduring popularity. The actor, Bartolomeo Pagano, went on to star in some two dozen Maciste films between 1914 and 1926, and his trademark character appeared as a modern-day Italian soldier in the First World War, a big-game safari hunter in Africa, a sailor in the Middle East, and even a traveler to the depths of hell in one of his final films.[11] He rescued damsels in distress and performed feats of strengths in a series of films that were populist (Maciste's strength contrasts with "the decadence and languor of upper-crust figures"[12]), and often explicitly imperialist and nationalist. These films left a lasting legacy in the form of action films in which the star's extraordinary muscled and massive body is the principal attraction. Italy produced over a hundred such films in the early 1960s, starring American bodybuilders like Steve Reeves as super-strong heroes from antiquity, from the Greek Hercules to the biblical Samson. This genre is now called "peplum" films by critics, in reference to the scanty silk dresses worn by the female actors, or more popularly, "sword and sandals" films, alluding to the ancient heroic garb of the male stars. The plots were often ludicrous, and the films shot on the cheap, but they were also extremely popular for a brief while. The hero of these films was often named Maciste— indeed, some of the movies had the same titles as Maciste films of the silent era, and even some of the same directors.

One might imagine that Maciste disappeared as a character after the peplum craze died out in 1965, but he has survived in other forms in the years since. In the 1970s, he reappeared as a character in Mike Grell's *Warlord* comics (which ran up to 2010), once again with darkened skin and a leopard-skin loincloth, but with his name changed to "Machiste," the English spelling of the Italian pronunciation.[13] In the 1980s, Machiste had his own action figure in the United States, and today the name in its original Italian form remains in a Brazilian line of protein supplements for bodybuilders, an Italian beer, and even as a character in a novel by the award-winning Chilean writer Roberto Bolaño. Ultimately, of course, we recognize something of Maciste in all of the hard-bodied fantasy heroes that have populated our screens since the 1980s, from Conan the Barbarian to King Leonidas of Zach Snyder's *300* (2007). At times, the connection is quite deliberate: the adult Conan (Arnold Schwarzenegger) first appears in *Conan the Barbarian* (1982) chained to a giant millstone that he is forced to turn for ten years, a scene that appears nowhere in Robert Howard's short stories and novels—but which is taken directly from Pastrone's *Cabiria*.

Notes

1 See Gunning, "The Cinema of Attraction."

2 Solomon gives a detailed list of almost forty Italian films of this type, just between 1908 and 1914 (Solomon, *The Ancient World in the Cinema*, 4–5).

3 On the female diva in Italian cinema, see Dalle Vacche's comprehensive *Diva*.

4　For the definitive study in English of Maciste as a character and of Pagano as an early film star, see Reich's *The Maciste Films of Italian Silent Cinema*.

5　On Pastrone's desire to make "quality films," see Alovisio, "The 'Pastrone System.'"

6　Cottino-Jones, *Women, Desire, and Power in Italian Cinema*, 12.

7　On the difficulties of establishing a definitive version of the film (written before the discovery of the three-hour version), see Usai, "*Cabiria*, an Incomplete Masterpiece."

8　Bondanella, *A History of Italian Cinema*, 10.

9　Bondanella, *A History of Italian Cinema*, 9.

10　See the *Star Trek* episode "The Apple."

11　On the transformation of Maciste from a mixed-race slave in the ancient world to a modern-day Italian, see Reich, "The Metamorphosis of Maciste in Italian Silent Cinema."

12　Hay, *Popular Film Culture in Fascist Italy*, 226. Ricci also notes Maciste's populist strength in *Cinema and Fascism*, 81–83.

13　See *The Warlord*.

Bibliography

Alovisio, Silvio. "The 'Pastrone System': Itala Film from the Origins to World War I." Trans. Giorgio Bertellini. *Film History* 12.3 (2000): 250–61.

Bondanella, Peter. *A History of Italian Cinema*. New York: Continuum, 2009.

Cottino-Jones, Marga. *Women, Desire, and Power in Italian Cinema*. New York: Palgrave, 2010.

Dalle Vacche, Angela. *Diva: Defiance and Passion in Early Italian Cinema*. Austin: University of Texas Press, 2008.

Gunning, Tom. "The Cinema of Attraction: Early Film, Its Spectator and the Avant-Garde." *Wide Angle* 8.3–4 (1986): 63–70.

Hay, James. *Popular Film Culture in Fascist Italy: The Passing of the Rex*. Bloomington: Indiana University Press, 1987.

Reich, Jacqueline. "The Metamorphosis of Maciste in Italian Silent Cinema." *Film History* 25.3 (2013): 32–56.

Reich, Jacqueline. *The Maciste Films of Italian Silent Cinema*. Bloomington: Indiana University Press, 2015.

Ricci, Steven. *Cinema and Fascism: Italian Film and Society, 1922–1943*. Berkeley: University of California Press, 2008.

Solomon, Jon. *The Ancient World in the Cinema: Revised and Expanded Edition*. New Haven: Yale University Press, 2001.

Usai, Paolo Cherchi. "*Cabiria*, an Incomplete Masterpiece: The Quest for the Original 1914 Version." *Film History* 2.2 (1988): 155–65.

The Warlord. Vol. 1. No. 2. Written by Mike Grell. Art by Mike Grell. DC Comics. April, 1976.

Filmography

300, Dir. Zack Snyder. USA: Warner Brothers. 2007.

Cabiria, Dir. Giovanni Pastrone. Italy: Itala Film. 1914.

Conan the Barbarian, Dir. John Milius. USA: Universal Pictures. 1982.

Gladiator, Dir. Ridley Scott. USA: DreamWorks. 2000.

Gli ultimi giorni di Pompei, Dir. Mario Caserini. Italy: Società Anonima Ambroisio. 1913.

Indiana Jones and the Temple of Doom, Dir. Steven Spielberg. USA: Paramount. 1984.

Intolerance, Dir. D. W. Griffith. USA: Triangle Distributing Corporation. 1916.

Metropolis, Dir. Fritz Lang. Germany: UFA. 1927.

Quo vadis? Dir. Enrico Guazzoni. Italy: Cines. 1913.

Star Trek. "The Apple." Directed by Joseph Pevney. Written by Max Ehrlich. NBC, October 13, 1967.

18

Bitter Rice

Charles L. Leavitt IV

When Giuseppe De Santis's *Riso amaro* (*Bitter Rice*) was released in Italian theaters in December 1949, controversy soon followed. In the nation's leading newspapers and magazines, critics, politicians, and concerned filmgoers debated what many saw as the film's excessive pessimism, its insufficient realism, and most problematically its contrived "Americanism."[1] *Bitter Rice* was accused of transgressing against some of postwar Italy's most cherished political and cultural convictions. In such films as *Roma città aperta* (*Rome, Open City*, Roberto Rossellini, 1945) and *Ladri di biciclette* (*Bicycle Thieves*, Vittorio De Sica, 1948), critics were beginning to identify a new direction in Italian cinema, which they baptized "neorealism." Yet neorealist films often struggled to compete with their Hollywood counterparts, more than 600 of which flooded into Italian theaters in the first years after the war. As a result, many critics believed themselves to be engaged in a cultural struggle against a foreign invader, a struggle tinged by the burgeoning Cold War opposition between the American and Soviet spheres of influence. *Bitter Rice* fit uneasily into such a schematic opposition: politically, the film promoted collective action rooted in Marxism; thematically, it relied on the appeal of American consumerism; stylistically, it blended neorealist reportage and Hollywood spectacle. *Bitter Rice* thus transcended the boundaries—political as well as artistic—that distinguished Italy's nascent art cinema from American popular culture, and De Santis was accused of having betrayed neorealism.

What troubled the critics, it would seem, was that *Bitter Rice* flouted expectations. After all, De Santis was thought to belong to the neorealist camp, having assisted Luchino Visconti on the set of *Ossessione* (*Obsession*, 1943), a harbinger of neorealist cinema, and having gone on to direct his own neorealist showpiece, *Caccia tragica* (*Tragic Hunt*, 1947). What is more, as a critic at the journal *Cinema*, he had helped to define neorealism from its infancy, championing some of the aesthetic principles that *Bitter Rice* seemed to abandon.

The film thus struck many as a compromise, if not an outright betrayal. Because of *Bitter Rice*'s commercial appeal, which helped it to become one of the highest grossing films of 1949–50, De Santis was accused of pandering to his audience and of forsaking the rigor of neorealism for the promise of financial success.

Yet such a reflexive critique of the film's popularity obscures both its narrative sophistication and its cultural connotations. Notwithstanding the charges against it, *Bitter Rice* presents a trenchant critique of America's outsized influence on postwar Italian culture. Indeed, in a 1953 interview De Santis asserted that "the theme of *Bitter Rice* is this: the condemnation of the corruption that a certain American ideology has disseminated, with apparently innocent means, across Western Europe."[2] Yet the critics were not entirely mistaken in charging *Bitter Rice* with glamorizing the American lifestyle. At the heart of the film's appeal is a kind of equivocation: trading on Italians' fascination with American culture, *Bitter Rice* simultaneously repudiates that American fascination and its deleterious influence on Italian society. In a sense, De Santis was taking his audience to task, forcing them to recognize their complicity in the impoverishment of Italian popular culture that had resulted from the influx of American customs. But to reach that audience in the first place, he was drawing them in by depicting—even romanticizing—those same American customs.

Viewers who might have avoided a more austere or programmatic neorealist film flocked to *Bitter Rice*, only to find themselves engrossed by a narrative whose protagonist is brought down because she gives in to the same desires that had brought these same audiences to the theater.

Bitter Rice opens in a railway station. As the trains fill with migrant laborers departing for the rice paddies of northern Italy, the gangster Walter (Vittorio Gassman) awaits his girlfriend and accomplice Francesca (Doris Dowling), while attempting to avoid the policemen who are trailing him as a suspect in a recent jewel heist. When the officers close in on him, he leaves his loot with Francesca, who boards a train bound for Vercelli, in Piedmont. Concealing Walter's stolen necklace, Francesca introduces herself to Silvana (Silvana Mangano), a young laborer who has witnessed the gangster's escape and who is clearly fascinated by the mysterious couple. From behind her copy of *Grand Hotel*, a popular *fotoromanzo* (photographic love story), Silvana gives Francesca a sly glance. Perhaps motivated by *Grand Hotel*'s version of opulent sophistication and high-society romance, and with a mischievous gleam in her eye, Silvana offers to help the enigmatic Francesca find clandestine work in the rice paddies. Her intentions, it seems clear, are not entirely altruistic. Indeed, once the two women are settled in the dormitory with the other workers, Silvana manages to steal the necklace from under the blankets on Francesca's bed (see Figure 18.1).

FIGURE 18.1 *Francesca (left) and Silvana dreaming together in the rice workers' dormitory.*

Despondent after the loss of Walter's loot, Francesca becomes more desperate still when she learns that only those in the union will be allowed to join in the harvest. She and her fellow clandestine workers can expect no more than a paid ticket home. In response, she encourages the others to join her in harvesting rice at twice the rate of their union competitors in an attempt to prove their worth, only to be branded as a scab by Silvana. More than promoting the union cause, Silvana is attempting to force her opponent's departure so that she might keep the stolen necklace for herself. But this is not to be. Angrily pursued by the union harvesters, Francesca is saved by Marco (Raf Vallone), an army sergeant, who calms the vengeful crowd with talk of worker solidarity. As it happens, Marco is Silvana's boyfriend and is surprised to learn that it was she who led the charge against Francesca. He entreats the two women to reconcile, prodding Silvana to return the stolen necklace. Only a short while later, however, Silvana is compelled to steal again, so that when the gangster Walter returns, he finds the necklace not in Francesca's hiding place but around Silvana's neck as she seductively dances the boogie-woogie before an admiring crowd (see Figure 18.2).

Among the most famous scenes in the history of Italian cinema, Silvana's dance was a prominent point of contention in the long polemic over *Bitter Rice*. As one of the debaters, a union leader, put it, "the rice harvesters aren't all like the film depicts them. In the farmyards they dance to the traditional rhythms of the regions of their birth, with their fellow workers, with other

FIGURE 18.2 *Silvana dances her iconic boogie-woogie.*

laborers; they are not possessed by sensual pleasures and Americanism."[3] Silvana's dance, in other words, struck many of *Bitter Rice*'s critics as inauthentic and unrealistic, a concession to audiences accustomed to Hollywood products. That may well be true, but in my view it misses the point. Within the moral logic of the film, Silvana, the kind of girl who reads *Grand Hotel* and dreams of wealth and glamour—and the kind of girl who falls for the latest American dance craze—is also the kind of girl who would steal from a friend and betray the cause of worker solidarity. Silvana's dancing thus incriminates her, signaling the frivolous American desires that have led her to forsake her community.

Recognizing Silvana's moral failings does not preclude us from enjoying the eroticism of the boogie-woogie, and the cinematographer Otello Martelli's camera lingers on Silvana's shimmering body even as the glittering necklace alerts us to her thievery. We are encouraged to delight in Silvana's grace even as we are inspired to deplore her crime.

And yet, are we spectators not also implicated by our delight, and led to recognize our complicity in Silvana's desire? After all, the same allure that draws the audience to Silvana destroys her in the end. The coveted necklace, it emerges, is false, worthless. Walter has returned not for his loot but for a hideout, a place to avoid the police. Here he hatches a new plan, a bid to steal the rice that Silvana, Francesca, and their fellow workers have gathered in the storeroom. He also steals Silvana away from Marco, making her an accomplice in his plot. On the last night of the harvest, as Walter fills his trucks with stolen rice, Silvana floods the fields in order to distract the other workers. Meanwhile, those same workers chant her name, celebrating her as the winner of the harvesters' beauty pageant and inviting her to claim the title of "Miss Mondina 1948" (*mondina* was the name given to seasonal female rice workers). Wearing her crown and cheered on by the crowd, Silvana seems for an instant to possess the glamour that she has long desired. Her reverie is broken, however, by shouts from the fields as the workers discover the rising floodwaters. Alone on the stage, Silvana is finally forced to recognize the implications of her desires and the consequences of her actions. As the workers struggle to salvage the crops, she removes her crown and runs to Walter. Yet by the time she has reached him, so too has Marco, who is wounded by Walter's knife, and Francesca, who manages to shoot the gangster with Marco's gun. In the end, it is Silvana who finishes the deed, firing on Walter as he tries to flee, then leaping to her demise from a nearby tower. Although she meets a tragic fate, Silvana receives in death something that trumps the transient glory of a beauty prize: the pardon and acceptance of her fellow workers, who pour some of their hard-earned rice over Silvana's body in a gesture freighted with symbolism. Despite her crimes, and despite her aberrant and exotic desires, Silvana is finally returned to the community.

Similarly, despite *Bitter Rice*'s drive to satisfy the audience's desire for Hollywood excitement, the film ultimately returns to its moral center, reinforcing its emphasis on the workers' shared sacrifice and class struggle. Even as we thrill to gangsters, shootouts, and sensual dances, we are led to witness the rice harvesters' backbreaking labor, their exploitation at the hands of indifferent landowners, and their triumphant solidarity in the face of systemic injustice. Some of De Santis's critics saw the film's two aspects, spectacle and social engagement, as fundamentally opposed, decrying what they believed to be the director's abandonment of neorealism. In fact, *Bitter Rice* transcends this simplistic opposition, utilizing stylish cinematography, alluring narrative, and compelling drama to draw a wider audience to witness its moving depiction of the workers' struggle. In the final tally, therefore, the film's social and political mission is inseparable from its popular appeal.

De Santis clearly hit upon a winning formula. In his wake, there followed a wave of films that sought similarly to bridge the apparent gap between neorealism and Hollywood, adapting the innovations of Italy's realist cinema for use in more popular genres. Soon, new, composite film styles began to emerge: *neorealismo rosa* (pink neorealism), uniting social realism with romantic drama; *neorealismo nero* (black neorealism), with its atmosphere of *film noir*; and *neorealismo giallo* (yellow neorealism), with its plots lifted from mystery novels, called *gialli* in Italian because of their characteristic yellow spines. The emergence of these spinoff genres only tells part of the story. Not only did *Bitter Rice* introduce a certain "Americanism" into Italian neorealism, it also helped to introduce neorealism into the American consciousness. In an iconic episode of *I Love Lucy*, America's most-watched television program in the 1950s, Lucy (Lucille Ball) is spotted in Rome by an Italian director who invites her to star in his upcoming film about the grape harvest. And what was the title of Lucy's "Italian Movie," which was meant to evoke social realism, European sophistication, and exotic glamour for its American audience? *Bitter Grapes*.

Notes

1   On this debate, see Farassino, *Giuseppe De Santis*, 24.
2   De Santis, "Confessioni di un regista," 227. All translations from the Italian are my own.
3   For this and other entries in the polemic over *Bitter Rice*, see Carotti, *Alla ricerca del Paradiso*, 75–85.

Bibliography

Carotti, Carlo. *Alla ricerca del Paradiso: L'operaio nel cinema italiano 1945–1990*. Genoa: Graphos, 1992.
De Santis, Giuseppe. "Confessioni di un regista [1953]." In *Rosso fuoco: Il cinema di Giuseppe Santis*. Ed. Sergio Toffetti. Turin: Lindau, 1996.
Farassino, Alberto. *Giuseppe De Santis*. Milan: Moizzi, 1978.

19

Senso

Brendan Hennessey

When the historical film *Senso* was released in 1954, it created a firestorm of debate over official accounts of the Risorgimento, the wars for Italian unification fought during the nineteenth century. Instead of celebrating the Risorgimento as a moment of national triumph, director Luchino Visconti emphasized how Italian patriotism had been undermined by the self-interest of the country's ruling elites, who united with foreign occupiers rather than compatriots of the lower classes. By locating the film in the context of foreign occupation, Visconti conjured Italy's experience in the Second World War, when it was first occupied by Nazi Germany then by Allied forces. Exposing the origins of rifts in Italian society, *Senso* continued to reference the recent conflict, including the bloody civil war it set in motion between Fascists and anti-Fascists. This discourse on history was not limited only to Italy's political history, but also to its *cinematic* history. Visconti's decision to direct a large-scale historical film broke with the cinematic conventions of postwar neorealism that were still relevant in discussions of Italian cinema at the time. Neorealism, with its gritty depictions of poor Italians and unmediated look at contemporary society, was a universe apart from the aristocratic characters, grand historical events, and allusions to high art in *Senso*.

Senso features one of the most iconic opening sequences of any Italian film of the 1950s—a scene that establishes dramatic touchstones for the narrative to come. The film begins in Venice's storied La Fenice opera house during a performance of *Il trovatore* (*The Troubadour*, 1853), one of Giuseppe Verdi's best-known operas. As the camera tilts toward the stage, a dramatic moment of Verdi's third act unfolds: the hero Manrico abandons his fiancée to aid his mother, who has been captured and is about to be tortured. The performance seems to hint at the broader heroism of Italy's birth as a modern nation, reinforced by an establishing text that appears on screen, "Venice—Spring 1866, the final months of Austrian occupation of the Veneto." When the camera pans away from the stage to a group of Austrian soldiers seated in the audience, the chorus ("To Arms!") infects the Italians in the crowd, who hail chants of "Foreigners out of Venice!" and "Viva l'Italia!" down upon the Austrian foreign occupiers seated below. Here, opera stages a fundamental component of the Italian character, a "national condition, a refusal of critical and progressive engagement in life for the indulgent pleasures of emotional fantasy."[1]

In the place of an anthem to Italy's intrepid patriotism that one might expect to follow this stirring incipit, *Senso* substitutes a lament on infidelity that centers on the ignoble transgressions of the Countess Livia Serpieri (Alida Valli), a married Italian aristocrat. The arc of the narrative interlaces her affair with Austrian lieutenant Franz Mahler (Farley Granger) together with the national cause of unification, concluding with her betrayal of both. Throughout, Livia plays a dual role, melding the "fallen woman" of nineteenth-century European literature (not unlike Madame Bovary or Anna Karenina) with the cinematic femme fatale: a woman with disruptive powers of seduction. By situating this dangerous female protagonist in the final years of Italian unification, Visconti confounds traditional historical films, often defined by their attention to the great deeds of great men. As he would throughout his career, Visconti emphasizes how positive narratives of joy and rebirth eventually dissolve, leaving only death and damnation.[2]

Intertwining literary and cinematic figures generates a tension between art and life that sets in motion the tale of passion and betrayal. The film is based on an eponymous 1883 novella by author Camillo Boito and features many marks of its literary ancestor. Both film and novella delineate Livia's affair with an Austrian soldier, and both are set in northern Italy at the end of the Third War of Independence (1866). Despite many essential similarities between book and film, Visconti also makes numerous significant alterations. Boito's self-absorbed young countess is transformed into the older, more politically conscious female protagonist of the film. Unlike the book, where history remains in the background, Visconti sets Livia's illicit liaison firmly in 1866, on the eve of the Austrian victory at the Battle of Custoza.

Visconti and his screenwriters added the character Roberto Ussoni (Massimo Girotti) as Livia's cousin and the leader of a clandestine group of Italian nationalists. Ussoni is the film's ideological contrast to the self-centered Livia and the narcissistic Franz, as he is willing to sacrifice personal interest and safety for the good of the new Italian state. When Ussoni entrusts Livia with vital funds for supporting the anti-Austrian resistance, she deceives the Italian cause to bribe a doctor who will designate Franz unfit for battle. Her circle of treachery is completed when she discovers that

Franz has taken up with a prostitute: she denounces him as a deserter, and brings about his execution after the Austrian victory has been sealed.

When *Senso* was released in 1954, admonishments soon radiated from across the Italian political spectrum. On the right, objections from the ruling Christian Democrats centered on Visconti's radical reinterpretation of unification history. Indeed, *Senso* offers provocative commentary on Italian independence as an example of political *trasformismo* (transformism): "the process where-by seemingly dangerous elements were 'transformed' into stable parts of the system."[3] The Risorgimento was a prime historical example of *trasformismo* analyzed by such thinkers as Antonio Gramsci, a Marxist who viewed unification in the nineteenth century as a perpetuation of upper-class dominance, not a popular revolution. Along these lines, *Senso* depicts Italian independence as a royal conquest, with Livia and her husband sharing more allegiance to aristocratic Austrians than to fellow Italians of a lower class. This same Marxist viewpoint would persist into Visconti's next Risorgimento film, *Il Gattopardo* (*The Leopard*, 1963), the story of a Sicilian prince whose lofty position in the hierarchy of Italian society crumbles under the weight of the independence movement. Censors required numerous cuts to *Senso* that successfully moderated the scope of Visconti's historical critique. While the film concludes with Franz's execution, Visconti originally wanted to close on Livia's encounter with an Austrian soldier, whose triumphant cries of "Viva l'Austria!" spotlighted the disloyalty to her native Italy. Despite the censorship, main themes such as military defeat, *trasformismo*, and treason were hotly debated in the years immediately following the Second World War, when Italy was just beginning to process its recent wartime memory. The fall of Fascism, the shifting alliance between the Nazis and the Allies, and the civil war fought between Resistance members and Nazi-Fascist collaborators all represented raw, untreated wounds on the postwar Italian psyche.

Intellectuals on the left also took issue with the film. They viewed *Senso*'s focus on aristocratic characters engaged in epic-historical events as a betrayal of cinematic neorealism, famous for its attention to the everyday struggles of the Italian everyman in the wake of the Second World War. Seminal neorealist works like Roberto Rossellini's *Roma città aperta* (*Rome, Open City*, 1945), Vittorio De Sica's *Ladri di biciclette* (*Bicycle Thieves*, 1948), and Visconti's own *La terra trema* (1948) depicted experiences of the poor in the aftermath of the war, unearthing the mechanisms of social and political injustice that they faced. *Senso*'s grandiose portrait of nineteenth-century Italy, with its sprawling cinematography and complex historical setting, was condemned as a withdrawal from neorealism's concentration on contemporary Italians and their dire conditions.[4] And Visconti's emphasis on spectacle, theatricality, and melodrama recalled Italian film production under Fascism, at the time negatively associated with Mussolini's regime.

While influential editor Guido Aristarco famously defended *Senso* as a transition from neorealism to realism, many still regarded Visconti as a traitor to Italy's most exalted cinematic moment.

In retrospect, *Senso* was just one of many innovative alternatives to neorealist convention taking place across Italy in the 1950s. The same year that *Senso* was released saw Rossellini's *Viaggio in Italia* (*Voyage to Italy*, 1954) and Federico Fellini's *La strada* (1954), landmark films in their bold display of subjectivity, fantasy, and dream. Together with the biting satires of the so-called *commedia all'italiana* (Italian-style comedies), and the widely popular melodramas by director Raffaello Matarazzo, the Italian film industry of the 1950s exemplified a combination of artistic acumen and industrial infrastructure. For Visconti, *Senso* marked the beginning of a post-neorealist phase, with productions on a larger scale reflecting his expanded artistic ambitions. Lux, the production house that funded *Senso*, was unabashed in its desire to top the lucrative domestic market with a blockbuster film.[5] Lux wagered that a Visconti film could also generate interest from global audiences, who flocked to big-budget pictures cast with international stars and directed by famous Italian auteurs. Sharing this international vision, Visconti originally wanted Marlon Brando and Ingrid Bergman cast in the starring roles. He also shot the film in richly saturated Technicolor, a process associated with Hollywood spectacle at the time. In Visconti's hands, colors express moods and help contour the peaks and valleys of Livia's romantic involvement with Franz, and the shifting hues of her veils and attire reflect her changing psychological states. Visconti's use of color also echoed nineteenth-century painting, from his direct imitation of Francesco Hayez' famous *Il bacio* (*The Kiss*) to the war scenes by painter Giovanni Fattori and the "Goya-esque" atmosphere of Franz's final execution. These intertextual references made *Senso* arguably Visconti's most pictorial film.[6] Expressive colors were aided by the film's lighting, which accentuates the visual effects of the colors themselves, contrasting settings in brightness and darkness to delineate the shadow of death as it progressively casts across the film. This trajectory from light to dark can be witnessed by comparing the film's beginning with its conclusion. The bright, ornate interiors of La Fenice that commence the film, where the polychromatic Italians deride the Austrians clad in monotone military white, introduce the hopeful, insurgent tone of *Senso*'s beginning section. These colors will be steadily bled of their vibrancy, giving way to the tattered insides of Franz's Verona apartment, with its shabby furniture and tawdry decorations mirroring the dwindling glow of the nationalist spark. Light and darkness are most boldly contrasted during Franz's shadowy nighttime execution at the very end of the film.

Like Visconti's other historical films or films set in the past—*The Leopard*, *La caduta degli dei* (*The Damned*, 1969), *Morte a Venezia* (*Death in Venice*,

1971), *Ludwig* (1972), and *L'innocente* (*The Innocent*, 1975)—musical variations shape history's vanishing and reappearing in *Senso*, giving cadence to the whims of the film's often irrational and unstable characters. Historical scenes such as the ambitious battle sequence toward the end are accompanied by an absence of music that highlights diegetic sound.[7] In as intensely musical a film as *Senso*, with the raucous opening performance of *Il trovatore* and the repetition of Anton Bruckner's Symphony No. 7 (originally composed as a funereal ode to Richard Wagner), these moments of silence are conspicuous. Beyond these specific compositions, *Senso*'s narrative is structured around a series of solos, duets, quartets, and choral performances that order actions and interactions on screen. As the film can reasonably be split into four "acts," one might tie *Senso* to Visconti's extra-cinematic activities in opera and theater during the same period in which the film was made.[8]

One of Italy's greatest historical films, *Senso* introduced the Risorgimento counter-narrative that persists in Italian cinema today. From Visconti's own *The Leopard* to more recent films like Roberto Faenza's *I Viceré* (*The Viceroys*, 2007) and Mario Martone's *Noi credevamo* (*We Believed*, 2010), Italian filmmakers continue to question the mythology surrounding the Risorgimento, pondering how disappointment and delusion were absent in official accounts of independence. Just as Verdi's melodrama incites the crowd into action at the beginning of the film, *Senso* inspired a renewed discussion on the nation's past that cleared a path to rethinking the rhetoric of Italy's grand historical narratives. Yet *Senso* must also be appreciated as a unique response to a call for innovation at a time when Italian cinema was attempting to redefine itself as something more than a mirror of contemporary reality. With *Senso*, Visconti demonstrated the artistic and ideological potential of looking to the past to unearth compelling images that would become synonymous with a national cinema of international appeal.

Notes

1 Bayman, *The Operatic and the Everyday in Postwar Italian Film Melodrama*, 173.

2 Miccichè, *Luchino Visconti*, 79–80.

3 Nowell-Smith, *Luchino Visconti*, 78.

4 Marcus, "Visconti's *Senso*," 282.

5 Rondolino, *Luchino Visconti*, 291–92.

6 Blom, *Visconti and the Visual Arts*, 14.

7 Pellanda, *Senso*, 63–64.

8 Miccichè, "Visconti e il melodrama," 229.

Bibliography

Bayman, Louis. *The Operatic and the Everyday in Postwar Italian Film Melodrama*. Edinburgh: Edinburgh University Press, 2015.

Blom, Ivo. *Visconti and the Visual Arts*. Milan: Olivares, 2006.

Marcus, Millicent. "Visconti's *Senso*: The Risorgimento According to Gramsci or Historical Revisionism Meets Cinematic Innovation." In *Making and Remaking Italy: The Cultivation of National Identity around the Risorgimento*. Ed. Albert Ascoli and Krystyna von Henneberg. Oxford: Berg, 2001. 277–96.

Miccichè, Lino. *Luchino Visconti: Un profilo critico*. Venice: Marsilio, 2002.

Miccichè, Lino. "Visconti e il melodramma." In *Storia del cinema italiano, Volume IX, 1954/1959*. Ed. Sandro Bernardi. Venice: Marsilio, Edizioni di Bianco e Nero, 2011. 227–39.

Nowell-Smith, Geoffrey. *Luchino Visconti*. London: BFI, 2003.

Pellanda, Marina. *Senso*. Palermo: L'EPOS, 2008.

Rondolino, Gianni. *Luchino Visconti*. Turin: UTET, 2003.

Filmography

Roma, città aperta, Dir. Roberto Rossellini. Italy: Excelsa Film. 1945.

Ladri di biciclette, Dir. Vittorio De Sica. Italy: ENIC. 1948.

La terra trema, Dir. Luchino Visconti. Italy: Universalia Film. 1948.

Viaggio in Italia, Dir. Roberto Rossellini. Italy: Italia Film. 1954.

La strada, Dir. Federico Fellini. Italy: Ponti-De Laurentiis Cinematografica. 1954.

La caduta degli dei, Dir. Luchino Visconti. Italy: Italnoleggio. 1969.

Morte a Venezia, Dir. Luchino Visconti. Italy: Alfa Cinematografica. 1971.

Ludwig, Dir. Luchino Visconti. Italy: Mega Film. 1972.

L'innocente, Dir. Luchino Visconti. Italy: Rizzoli Film. 1975.

I Vicerè, Dir. Roberto Faenza. Italy: Jean Vigo Italia. 2007.

Noi credevamo, Dir. Mario Martone. Italy: Palomar. 2010.

20

La strada

Federico Pacchioni

Released in 1954, *La strada* was the third solo directorial work of Federico Fellini and followed the critical and commercial success of *I vitelloni* (1953). Together with the films that preceded *La dolce vita* (1960), *La strada* represented a more traditional narrative and sober visual style that contrasted with Fellini's later experimental work. It is also an important film for understanding Fellini's reputation and evolution as an auteur director, especially in the light of the debate that it triggered among the Italian and French critics of the time regarding the true "calling" of Italian neorealism. The idea for *La strada* (which literally means the "road" or "way," in reference to the lengthy journeys that the film's characters take) came from Fellini and his screenwriter Tullio Pinelli, both of whom had observed traveling artists making their way across the Italian Apennines.[1] One of the recurring characteristics of Fellini's cinema was its focus on the forms of popular entertainment, a trait that is reflected in *La strada*'s poignant and careful portrait of the unique world of nomadic street entertainers in Italy.

The film's plot centers around the story of Gelsomina, a poor young girl (played by a childlike Giulietta Masina), whose "services" are purchased by a traveling strongman named Zampanò (Anthony Quinn), who basically makes Gelsomina his domestic and sexual servant as well as fellow performer. While Zampanò treats Gelsomina as a half-wit and useless girl, she sincerely commits to their relationship and reveals a resilient and rare sensibility. Gelsomina's meeting with an acrobat known as Il Matto (The Fool), who performs in an angel costume, is instrumental to her discovery of self-worth and acceptance of her role as Zampanò's caretaker. However, because of the Fool's habit of vexing and antagonizing Zampanò, who eventually kills him in a fight, an event that leads Gelsomina to lose her sanity and then be abandoned by Zampanò. Years later, upon learning of Gelsomina's death,

Zampanò is awakened for the first time to his humanity by overwhelming emotions of guilt and loneliness.

The allegorical and archetypical weight of the film is based on the Christlike figure of Gelsomina—portrayed with saintlike innocence, purity, and spontaneous spiritual perceptiveness—who undergoes her martyrdom at the hand of the beastly, thoughtless, and materialistic Zampanò. The presence of the character of Gelsomina places the film within the Franciscan cinematic lineage that Fellini had begun to explore in connection with certain humble minor characters in earlier films, who are all endowed with a peculiar kind of wisdom, such as Frate Ginepro and Giovanni il Semplice (from his collaboration with Roberto Rossellini in *Francesco Giullare di Dio [The Flowers of St. Francis]* in 1950) as well as Giudizio (from *I vitelloni* in 1953).[2]

The religious and mythical tone of *La strada*, which has been analyzed by a good deal of scholarship that often attempts to demonstrate how the film expanded the neorealist canon, actually has its direct roots in the context of Christian literature and theater.[3] Pinelli, the main screenwriter of *La strada*, was an accomplished playwright in his own right and author of several plays focusing on such intimate themes as guilt and everyday redemption, often through allegories. Pinelli wrote the first draft of the script and brought much of his own creative world to the film—at times to the dismay of another one of Fellini's screenwriters, Ennio Flaiano, who criticized the film's "peculiar obscure atmospheres" and "the affectation of its characters," while insisting that "the too-beautiful fable may have come down to earth, and its symbolism may have melted into the plot."[4] Even Fellini was not entirely in favor of the tragic tone and overt Christian symbolism at the base of *La strada*, so he attempted to balance these extreme characteristics.[5] As a result, the film serves as an example of Fellini's eclectic and pantheistic form of spirituality as well as his undying comedic vein. The director's efforts to render the bitter tale more lighthearted can be evinced from the diminished cruelty of Zampanò's violence in comparison to the original script, as well as by Fellini's insertion of unscripted comic and lyrical scenes, such as Gelsomina playfully imitating the shape of a tree, awkwardly falling into a hole while arguing with Zampanò, listening to the hum of electricity in the telephone pole, and playing with ants.

The spontaneous spiritual perceptiveness of Gelsomina often leads to a compelling use of the subjective shot, as we see in Gelsomina's encounter with Osvaldo, the paralytic child relegated to a farmhouse attic. Osvaldo is a character with whom Gelsomina empathizes because of his eccentricity and vague mediumistic inclinations.

The subjective shot is also employed with regard to the locales of *La strada*, in ways that invoke the tenets of symbolism rather than naturalism. For example, Fellini uses different sets to embody the emotional change in Gelsomina before and after the death of the Fool: he uses sunny and bucolic vistas at first, then shifts to wintry and desolate landscapes after the Fool's death.

The complex function of music deserves special attention in the film, as it is one of the secrets of its powerful yet subtle religious inspiration. Fellini employs music in order to convey the growing consciousness of Gelsomina and the transmission of the moral lesson inherent in her sacrifice to Zampanò. Nino Rota, Fellini's faithful composer, crafted an unforgettable and haunting melody for *La strada*, which resonates with both simple joy and sorrowful longing. The melody embodies the spiritual truth of Gelsomina's story as it travels across different characters and grows in legendary significance. The melody is first heard when played by the Fool on the violin. Once Gelsomina accepts the angel-acrobat's "Parable of the Pebble," teaching her that even the smallest and most humble thing in the universe has its purpose and place, the melody becomes Gelsomina's favorite piece, which she often plays on the trumpet. Eventually, the woman who informs Zampanò of Gelsomina's death sings the same melody, having learned the tune while acting as caretaker to Gelsomina during her last days. At the close of the film, the melody evolves into a symphonic movement, suggesting that Gelsomina's sacrifice has reached another, higher level of signification, moving fully to the realm of hagiography and allegory.

The spiritual orientation of the film and its emphasis on Gelsomina's apparently troubled inner life was received with drastically conflicting opinions. The Mostra del Cinema of Venice in 1954 was particularly heated. Supporters of Luchino Visconti's *Senso* (1954), an historical film on the Risorgimento appealing to such socialist critics as Guido Aristarco, were appalled by the jury's decision to deny an award to *Senso* in favor of *La strada*. The universal and legendary qualities of the Fellini's film were perceived by Aristarco as being "outside of time," therefore leading him to accuse the film of being a return to prewar Fascist cinema: escapist and unengaged.[6] In 1955, Massimo Puccini published a public letter to Fellini in the left-wing magazine *Il contemporaneo*, accusing *La strada* of lacking in social commitment and dangerously departing from the ethical path of neorealism. A month later, Fellini published a letter of reply in *Il contemporaneo*, most likely written with the help of his close collaborator, the existential philosopher Brunello Rondi. The reply explained that the film was actually in line with the higher ambitions of neorealism, as it addressed social issues, though by tackling them at their essence and core. Fellini proposed that he was exploring the issue of "personal and spiritual communication" between individuals, and between man and woman in particular. Critics have since elaborated the basic and mythical quality of the film's characters. *La strada* certainly marked a turning point in neorealist criticism, forcing critics to uncover the limitation of a strictly political understanding of the movement.

The religious discourse of *La strada* and its success among auteurist critics are intrinsically connected. As John Hess noted, the idea of the cinematic auteur was unexpectedly made available to the young French critics of *Cahiers du cinéma*—who yearned to become directors in their own right—by the Christian-realist movement of the journal *Esprit*. And a major theorist of auteur cinema, André Bazin, was especially interested in art's capacity to reveal transcendent reality.[7] *La strada*, whose release in 1954 coincided with the publication of François Truffaut's influential article "A Certain Tendency in French Cinema" in *Cahiers du cinéma*, became a model of film's capacity to capture inner life, turning Fellini into a prime example of film auteur and establishing his work as a major influence on the French New Wave. The attention received by *La strada* in Europe was finally sealed by the American Academy of Motion Picture Arts, which awarded it the Oscar for Best Foreign Language Film in 1955.

Some of the narrative and stylistic elements touched on in this chapter (Christian allegory, subjective shot, and musical motifs) had certainly encouraged Bazin to employ such notions as "neorealism of the person" or "phenomenological realism" in order to describe *La strada* and the film's ability to expose the soul of its characters. Bazin's 1955 article in *Esprit* demonstrates that he quickly understood that the subjective depth of the film was not merely psychological but also spiritual.[8] Because of their unabashed interest in messages worthy of comparison with classic authors of literature, the French critics were quicker to celebrate the importance of *La strada* than the Italians were. With its seamless capacity to elevate realism to an allegorical level, the film was considered a masterpiece in the eyes of those who were calling for an art capable of reinterpreting Christian values as well as rejuvenating the Italian and European spirit in the aftermath of the war.

A director influenced by Fellini, Pier Paolo Pasolini, once identified a genealogical line between Roberto Rossellini and Fellini, celebrating the transmission of a mystical stance that was to him the chief force behind the creation of a new level of lyrical dynamism in Italian cinematography. Pasolini explained how the representation of the world of Rossellini and Fellini is "transfigured by an excess of love for their reality," a state that leads them to film with an obsessive intensity where "even the air is photographed."[9] Neorealism has traditionally been seen as a primarily political movement; but the sublime rhetoric of religion is actually at the heart of its cinematic language. In this sense, *La strada*, which could be catalogued both as a representative of modern Christian art and postwar cinema, still has important lessons to teach film historians about the role of religious discourse in neorealism.

Notes

1 See Fellini, *Fare un film*, 58–60; and Zambelli and Acone, *Campane nel pozzo*, 43.

2 For an earlier analysis of the Franciscan threads within the film, see Aubier, "Mythologie de La Strada."

3 See, for example: Pecori, *Federico Fellini*; Bondanella, *The Cinema of Federico Fellini*; and Marcus, "Fellini's *La strada.*"

4 Flaiano, "Ho parlato male de 'La strada.'"

5 For more information on the genesis of *La strada*, see my *Inspiring Fellini*, 21–48.

6 Aristarco, "La strada."

7 Hess, "Auteurism and After," 29.

8 Bazin, "*La strada*," 54–59.

9 Pasolini, "Nota su 'Le notti,'" 702–704.

Bibliography

Aristarco, Guido. "La strada." *Cinema nuovo* 3.46 (November 10, 1954).

Aubier, Dominique. "Mythologie de La Strada." *Cahiers du cinéma* 49 (July 1955): 3–9.

Bazin, André. "La strada." In *Federico Fellini: Essays in Criticism*. Ed. Peter Bondanella. Oxford: Oxford University Press, 1978. 54–59. Originally in *Esprit* 23.226 (May 1955): 847–51.

Bondanella, Peter. *The Cinema of Federico Fellini*. Princeton: Princeton University Press, 1992.

Fellini, Federico. "Letter to a Marxist Critic." In *La strada*. Ed. Peter Bondanella and Manuela Gieri, Trans. Isabel Quigly. New Brunswick: Rutgers University Press, 1987. 211–14. Originally in *Il contemporaneo* 2.15 (April 9, 1955).

Fellini, Federico. *Fare un film*. Turin: Einaudi, 1993.

Flaiano, Ennio. "Ho parlato male de 'La strada.'" *Cinema* 139 (August 10, 1954): 449.

Hess, John. "Auteurism and After: A Reply to Graham Petrie" *Film Quarterly* 27.2 (1973): 28–37.

Marcus, Millicent. "Fellini's *La strada*: Transcending Neorealism." *Italian Film in the Light of Neorealism*. Princeton: Princeton University Press, 1986. 144–63.

Pacchioni, Federico. *Inspiring Fellini: Literary Collaborations Behind the Scenes*. Toronto: University of Toronto Press, 2014.

Pasolini, Pier Paolo. *Per il cinema*. Ed. Walter Siti and Franco Zabagli. Milan: Mondadori, 2001.

Pecori, Franco. *Federico Fellini*. Florence: La Nuova Italia. 1974.

Puccini, Massimo. "Lettera aperta a Federico Fellini." *Il contemporaneo* 2.12 (March 19, 1955).

Truffaut, François. "A Certain Tendency in French Cinema." In *The New Wave: Critical Landmarks*. Ed. Peter Graham and Ginette Vincendeau. London: BFI, 2009. 39–63. Originally in *Cahiers du cinéma* 6.31 (1954): 15–29.

Zambelli, Massimo and Giuseppe Acone, eds. *Campane nel pozzo: La voce della luna; Il testamento spirituale di Federico Fellini*. Rimini: Il Cerchio, 1997.

Filmography

Francesco, giullare di Dio, Dir. Roberto Rossellini. Italy: Cineriz. 1950.
La dolce vita, Dir. Federico Fellini, Italy. Riama Film. 1960.
La strada, Dir. Federico Fellini. Italy: Ponti-De Laurentiis. 1954.
Senso, Dir. Luchino Visconti. Italy: Lux Film. 1954.
I vitelloni, Dir. Federico Fellini. Italy: Cité Films. 1953.

21

L'avventura

John David Rhodes

In *L'avventura* (1960), Antonioni creates a situation in which the film's spectators are given too little and thus too much to do. Even when we are attending to the film's details, there is always the problem that we are looking at the wrong details, or looking at them in the wrong way. In other words, the film stages a problem of economy. What is enough, too little, or too much? Moreover, enough, or too little, or too much of *what*? Presumably the sensation of not being adequately employed in a recognizably productive mode of spectatorship is what so annoyed its first hostile spectators at Cannes, many of whom jeered at it. Time expands as the film blooms gorgeously in black and white. But the rare beauty that the film expends in such abundance might feel incommensurate with the events that act as the pretext for the production of such beauty. The two main characters, Sandro (Gabriele Ferzetti) and Claudia (Antonioni's muse, Monica Vitti) seem to forget, or else will themselves to ignore, what they are meant to be doing in the precious hours and days after the disappearance of Anna (Lea Massari). By forgetting and thus not finding Anna—if indeed she could ever have been found—Sandro and Claudia make time expand. They create closet dramas of temporal duration: a song sung on a hotel bed, a pointless trip up a *campanile* (church bell tower), a moment spent clowning in front of a mirror.

Time is brought into the rhythms of the body and its pleasures and sensations, and thus time is enlarged, but also simply wasted: nothing happens as a result of anything that all this dawdling makes happen. The film is long, and despite the portentousness of the final shot—a disgraced man, Sandro, and a consoling woman, Claudia, facing the immensity of Mount Etna—the ending itself feels contingent and even peremptory, even after two hours and twenty-some minutes. Really, it could have just kept going on, taking up more time by sending its characters through more spaces.[1]

L'avventura offers a lot of not much, we could say, or else a surplus of a series of highly controlled deficits. The metaphoric register I summon is meant to resonate metonymically—to resonate, that is, with the period of economic surplus that was (for many, but not for all) Italy's "economic miracle," a time of astonishing economic growth in the 1950s through the 1970s (fueled to a great extent by the American anti-communist Marshall Plan) that led to the creation of Italy's middle class. This film preoccupies itself with the languorously awkward scenes of frenetic social climbing—scenes of frigid expenditure and calculated nonchalance—that characterize this period in Italian history.

The film keeps us guessing about who and what matters. It plays this trick from its very beginning. The first image is a long shot of a dark-haired woman in a white dress, Anna, leaving a building (an aristocratic villa, we discover shortly). As she approaches the camera, it begins to dolly backward in order to record the entirety of her exit from the house and its grounds through a front gate. Finally, it holds her in medium close-up at the threshold of the outside world. Already the film has taken more time and expended more labor than are strictly necessary in showing us something of no significance: a woman leaves a house. (More specifically, a beautiful and elegantly dressed young woman leaves a house of some size.) The film's manner of summoning its narrative world proceeds by way of minimalist excess: it gives us a bit too much of something that is not terribly essential, in terms of the plotline. The same could be said for the short scene in which Anna converses with her father about the weekend trip that has occasioned her leave-taking. The tone of the conversation is strained and vaguely hostile, but we come away with few details regarding the actual nature of their relationship. He seems to be a retired diplomat, a widower perhaps, skeptical of her relationship with a man (Sandro) referred to only as a "that sort of guy." "Quel tipo non ti sposerà mai, bambina mia," he tells his daughter, "That sort of guy will never marry you, my child." The entire exchange is acerbic, and the few words that are said point to a vast quantity that are not. We could nearly say that the film takes pains to let us know that information is being imparted, but to impart only enough so as to let us know that it is exercising some restraint in not imparting more.

At the same time, in structural terms, these opening moments give us an excess of visual information. A woman leaves home and in so doing pauses uncertainly on the border between home and world. She bids farewell to her father, who must embody the family as a structural unit, the law, the state even (because he has identified himself as a diplomat). She is on the brink of marriage and, we infer from the father's advice, is already sexually active—in his traditional view, giving the milk away for free. Thus, in terms of the richly generic nature of this scene—in some sense this is a melodrama, a "woman's film," after all—what could be taken at first glance for sparseness is also overabundance, and this is before we have even taken into account the profusion of metonymic details that populate these early moments in the film.

When Anna reaches the gate to the villa and looks up, the film cuts to a medium long shot of an elegantly dressed man—her father, we learn when she hails him seconds later. He is talking to a laborer, complaining about the new buildings going up in the area, also visible in the shot. The camera has framed the men from a moderate distance that allows us to see their entire bodies. But behind and all around them the world radiates out in radical extension. Deep, deep in the furthest plane of the image, just to the right of center, we see the dome of Saint Peter's. To the left, we see the new constructions that have just been lamented: a row of apartment buildings, several notably under construction and obscured by scaffolded exoskeletons, extending orthogonally toward Saint Peter's. The film, wordlessly and once again, gives us too much: this is Rome, and thus this is Italy, the Italy of a postwar economic boom in which, as the exchange between the father and the laborer indicates, new construction displaces countryside. Anna steps into a shot of her father, and this shot will run for more than forty seconds without a cut—nearly four times the average shot length for a film made around 1960. As the shot endures the camera will move, dollying in to frame them in medium close-up. The characters move as well, trading their positions screen left and screen right. Saint Peter's, which is between them in the background at the beginning of the shot, becomes obscured by the father's body at other times, and disappears briefly into off-screen space when the camera pans left to follow the father's movement. Following this pan, the new apartment buildings appear behind Anna and her father. When Anna moves back to the right, Saint Peter's reappears behind her left shoulder, just before the film finally ends this long take by cutting to the father who is now framed with one of the new apartment houses immediately at his back.

The alignment of architecture with character (father=old; daughter=new) is impossible to maintain, given Anna's, her father's, and the camera's movements during the shot's duration. Instead, we have a collection of semantic pairings—old/new, father/daughter, male/female, sacred/profane. We have too much metonymic data regarding our location in time and space, and a too-loaded dramatic situation, but not enough *narrative* information to allow these things to gel comfortably into the pudding of story. In other words, try as we might to take all of this in, there will be less than we need to make sense of everything; what remains instead is the imperative to keep watching as the film endures.

We would be forgiven for mistaking Anna for the film's main character. As she moves to kiss her father goodbye, a man in livery who is followed by a smartly dressed blonde woman passes behind them in the middle distance, while, deeper in the background, a woman wearing a dark dress, sunglasses, and a scarf tied under her chin exits the apartment building. A laborer can be seen going about his business around the raw space surrounding the building. We might think: so much contingency passes through this shot. The turgid exchange between daughter and father is aerated by these fleeting inconsequentialities of everyday life. But the camera pans left, and we see the blonde woman again who, in an attitude of insecure beseeching, says hello to the father who barely acknowledges her. This woman is Claudia, and she (not Anna) will be our main character, though we will continue to think otherwise for some time. For the moment she is the sidekick—less privileged than Anna, it seems, but perhaps more strikingly beautiful. Their contrasting hair colors already indicate yet another register of structural oppositions. The film will preoccupy itself by playing with appearances (the appearance of a set of narrative expectations generated by the *appearance* of one character, Anna, in advance of the other, Claudia) and *disappearance* (the evaporation of this first character from the film, on whose surface she leaves no trace). But long before Anna actually disappears, and even in these early, fleeting but no less slow-going moments, the film has declared an interest in dramatizing its regulation of an abundance of one possibility or material in relation to the scarcity of another. In this sense, *L'avventura* quietly declares its critical attachment to neorealism's widely publicized love affair with contingency.

When Anna goes missing on the tiny island of Lisca Bianca, one of the Aeolian Islands off the coast of Sicily, she really goes missing. Leading up to her disappearance, the film spends time establishing a set of social relations in the cramped quarters of a modest if expensive yacht. The foreground of the film in these scenes is cluttered with bodies, but behind them the Mediterranean extends in all directions. Anna wants a swim and so jumps impulsively off the boat, on the kind of impulse that a spoiled rich person is quite used to feigning. But her movements, as jaded as they are, open up the film to possibilities that have hovered immanently but that have been foreclosed by the yacht's close quarters. When the party goes ashore on Lisca Bianca, she and her boyfriend Sandro argue. Time is shown to pass by way of an ellipsis, a narrative gap in time. When the members of the party wake up from their siestas, Anna is nowhere to be found.

The initial search for Anna that ensues is hapless and desultory in narrative terms, but it also occasions one of the fullest expressions of what we could call Antonioni's mature style. Most notably, he offers several instances of what will become a trademark stylistic gesture: a shot of a landscape is offered to the spectator; a character will walk into the shot in medium close-up then wander into the deeper planes off the image; at some subsequent point another character will enter the frame in close-up. In other words, figure and ground keep changing places. First, the landscape is figure—that is, it is all that we see and thus what occupies our interest. Next, the entry of the first character renders the landscape as the ground against which the character appears as figure. Then, as that character moves into the distance, the new character enters the frame to usurp the position of figure and relegate the first character to ground, a mere part of the landscape.

These formal operations are what we mean when we say that something is "Antonionian." Through such techniques, Antonioni establishes an economy, creating a pattern of economic relations between presence and absence, between figure and ground, and between two competing figures. These shots never tell us anything, nor do we discover the mysteries of Anna's disappearance in them. But insofar as her first appearance in the film was occasioned by the film's dramatization of a visual-narrative-symbolic economy, her disappearance (which we never see) merely restages the film's ontological investment in economic distribution.

Claudia and Sandro's meandering pursuit of Anna leads them to Noto, a Baroque stage-set of a town, built ex novo in the eighteenth century to replace Noto Antica, which was destroyed by an earthquake in 1693. The setting itself rehearses the film's interest in staging absence and presence. At one point, while Claudia rests in her hotel, Sandro wanders around the town's center. After admiring the façade of one of the Baroque churches, his attention is drawn to a pen-and-ink drawing of a detail of the facade that has been temporarily abandoned, apparently, by a young man who stands a few meters away in conversation with another man.[2] Apparently acting out of churlishness, jealousy, or resentment, Sandro knocks over the ink bottle sitting on the drawing, causing a black stain to spread across the careful rendering of the church.

The young man confronts Sandro who defends himself rather stupidly and unconvincingly. Just following this exchange, the film shows a stream of young students, all dressed in black, accompanied by priests in black soutanes pouring out of the church's white facade into the white of the piazza. Sandro's intentions here are illegible, and his pretend accidental upsetting of the ink has rendered the drawing illegible, abstract, or a combination of representational and abstract elements. The long shot that shows the boys and priests issuing from the white mouth of the church is intelligible as action, but radically abstract as an image. The drawing stained by spilt ink, the piazza stained by the black-garbed bodies spilling into it: both are formal operations that do not denote so much as materialize an economic relation of presence and absence, figure and ground, representation and abstraction.

The film's insistence on an abstract formal language is not itself merely abstract. This is not to say that the film's abstract picturing of the world is really "about" something else. Rather, Antonioni offers a vision of the world that strains to see it abstractly, that seeks to organize it around an insistent patterning of less and more, too little and too much, as a means of organization itself. This is an economic vision that emerges across the film as a means of staging a story of appearance and disappearance, one that is set in an actual historical period of radical (financial, capitalist) economic expansion, Italy's economic miracle. The film's dedication to an abstract economy of less and more, and more and less, is thus Antonioni's intuitive solution to the problem of narrating a story that is consubstantial with this period of economic activity.

Notes

1 My thinking here is influenced by Schoonover, "Wastrels of Time."
2 The detail is that of sculptural niche of the sort often found on Baroque facades and intentionally left empty. The drawing's incompletion is thus mirrored by the intentional incompletion or emptiness of the niche.

Bibliography

Schoonover, Karl. "Wastrels of Time: Slow Cinema's Laboring Body, the Political Spectator, and the Queer." *Framework* 53.1 (Spring 2012): 65–78.

22

Once Upon a Time in the West

Mary Ann McDonald Carolan

The *western all'italiana* emerged as a major phenomenon in the early 1960s, just as the success of American Westerns was on the wane. Whereas the American Western celebrates the pursuit of civilization into previously uncharted lands, the Italian-style Western seeks to debunk such positive notions of expansionism. Critics' use of the derogatory appellation Spaghetti Western reflected a disdain for the European appropriation of this most American of genres.[1] Between 1964 and 1974, approximately 400 Spaghetti Westerns were released. Many were filmed in Italy, while others including Sergio Leone's highly successful Dollars Trilogy starring Clint Eastwood (*Per un pugno di dollari* [*A Fistful of Dollars*, 1964]; *Per qualche dollaro in più* [*For a Few Dollars More*, 1965]; and *Il buono, il brutto, il cattivo* [*The Good, the Bad, and the Ugly*, 1966]) were shot on location in the Tabernas Desert in Spain's Andalusia, with multinational casts speaking a variety of languages.[2] *Once Upon a Time in the West*, Leone's epic fairy tale that offers a darker interpretation of frontier life, was one of seventy-two Italian-style Westerns released in 1968.[3]

The Spaghetti Western has proved to be remarkably enduring. In 2012, New York's Film Forum presented a retrospective that included works by Leone and Sergio Corbucci, the most successful directors of the genre, as well as films by such less familiar directors as Carlo Lizzani, Sergio Sollima, and Tonino Valerii.[4] Anton Corbjin (*The American*, 2010) and Nico Cirasola (*Focaccia Blues*, 2009) acknowledge Leone's contributions to filmmaking by suturing scenes from *Once Upon a Time in the West* into their films. One of the stars of the genre, Franco Nero, the protagonist of Corbucci's *Django* (1966), appears in Quentin Tarantino's Oscar-winning *Django Unchained* (2012) as a Mandingo by the name of Amerigo Vessepi (a wordplay on

Amerigo Vespucci, the Italian explorer whose name was applied to the New World) who encounters his African American reincarnation in Django (Jamie Foxx), the male lead.[5]

Spaghetti Westerns use motifs and symbols of the Western to parody and subvert the message of the traditional genre. The *western all'italiana* seeks to repudiate American westward expansion as a civilizing phenomenon by highlighting the violence on which such supposed progress is predicated. Unlike the traditional version, in which bloodshed results primarily from the epic struggle between good and evil, justice and injustice, the Spaghetti Western demonstrates that carnage can occur outside such neat parameters. The brutality inherent in the Spaghetti Western led Corbucci to draw this comparison:

> Our Westerns are more emotional and more realistic [than the American version], but let's face it, they are also more perverse. There is everything: drugs, savage cruelty. We kill babies too. Soon the Americans will understand how things are. For the time being, they remain attached to honest fights and legal duels.[6]

In this way, the genre reflects what Gian Piero Brunetta calls "a systematic loss of the moral and ideal center," resulting in the destruction of taboos associated with the representation of death.[7] The Western also alludes, through analogy and metaphor, to the massacres of the same period, and to the atrocities committed in the course of the Vietnam War in particular.[8]

In *Once Upon a Time in the West*, Leone reveals the railroad as a vehicle for the expression of greed. Instead of propelling society forward, these technological advances destroy it. The connection between the train and death begins as the credits roll. In the first sequence of the movie, which lasts approximately ten minutes, there is little dialogue or action. Ennio Morricone's score of a ticking telegraph, buzzing flies, dripping water, and a creaking windmill establishes the film's languorous pace as three gunmen wait at a deserted station to ambush Harmonica (Charles Bronson). Meanwhile, at a ranch outside the fictional town of Flagstone, Frank (Henry Fonda) and his posse kill Brett McBain (Frank Wolff) and his children because the rapacious railroad baron Morton (Gabriele Ferzetti) needs their property in order to extend his railway to the Pacific. Morricone's soundtrack merges the gunshot by which Frank kills Timmy McBain, at point blank range, with the train whistle that announces the arrival in Flagstone of Jill (Claudia Cardinale), the woman whom McBain had married in New Orleans unbeknownst to Morton. She has little time to mourn her husband and stepchildren because Frank and his men will do whatever it takes to acquire the land, which contains the area's only water and which Jill has inherited. The mysterious Harmonica (who recites the names of men Frank has killed, but never his own killings) and his more loquacious sidekick, Cheyenne (Jason Robards), protect Jill despite the initial suggestions that they are bandits. Frank and Harmonica finally face off on the range, with the dramatic duel recorded by Tonino Delli Colli's sweeping circular camera work and Morricone's soaring score. Before the dying Frank takes his last breath, we learn that he was responsible for the hanging of Harmonica's brother years earlier. That revelation makes sense of the mysterious flashbacks of a murky figure that appear, accompanied by Frank's melody, at critical moments in the film. The station town of Sweetwater has taken a heavy toll: the McBain family, Frank, Morton, Cheyenne, and many others have died so that Jill might realize her husband's entrepreneurial dream.

Weapons provide a matrix for the comparison of the American Western and its Italian interpretation. In the classical Western, guns identify and define heroes. But the Spaghetti Western employs firearms, which are loaded with totemic value, in curious and surprising ways. Riding precariously atop a railway car, Cheyenne shows how a leg can literally become an "arm" when he shoots a gun through his boot to liberate Harmonica from Frank's men. Yet in the unabashedly capitalist society of this Spaghetti Western, weapons lose their value relative to money, as Frank notes when he spies a drawer filled with cash in Morton's office aboard the train. Even Harmonica, who is decidedly unmoved by the promises of financial success that motivate Morton to lay tracks from coast to coast and that compel Jill to build a station town, partakes in the capitalist equation. In order to preserve Jill's claim on Sweetwater, Harmonica surrenders Cheyenne to the authorities for a bounty. This money enables Harmonica to outbid Frank at the auction of the McBain property, but since Cheyenne has escaped repeatedly from jail in the past, we understand that no real betrayal of friendship has occurred.

The Spaghetti Western diverges from the American Western in terms of casting as well.[9] Leone mastered the art of placing familiar faces in unfamiliar roles to underscore the difference between his interpretation of the genre and that of Hollywood. When called to audition, Henry Fonda assumed that the director wished to cast him according to type, as the "good guy." But Leone had other plans. In *Once Upon a Time in the West*, Fonda plays the scruffy, villainous Frank while Charles Bronson, who began his career under his birth name, Frank Buchinsky, in the role of a renegade Indian warrior in *Drum Beat* (1954), is Harmonica, the silent but honorable cowboy who plays his eponymous instrument more than he speaks. The opening credits for *Once Upon a Time in the West* list Woody Strode and Jack Elam, veteran Western actors who play two of Frank's men, Stony and Snaky, as guest stars. When Harmonica kills them in the first scene, we understand the famous American actors' abbreviated time on the screen as part of Leone's larger program to introduce then eliminate vestiges of the traditional Western.

While critics acknowledge Leone's subversive adaptation of the Western, they ignore his evident critique of the marginal role women play in the genre.[10] As André Bazin explains, in the Western, two women, a bad one (saloon girl) and a good one (virginal rancher's daughter, virtuous wife, or schoolteacher), often compete for the hero's attention.[11] After the hero alienates the honorable woman, he must then save her from imminent danger in order to regain her affection. The saloon girl, who also loves the hero, vindicates herself and satisfies the audience's expectations by sacrificing her life for him. In *Once Upon a Time in the West*, there is only one woman, Jill, who is both bad (former prostitute) and good (loving widow). She attracts Frank's (mostly professional) attention, as well as Cheyenne's, while the one man who interests her, Harmonica, remains aloof.

In *Once Upon a Time in the West*, Jill does not fit the model of woman as "vestal of the social virtues," responsible for bringing order to the essentially male world of the West.[12] Nor does she bear children that would lead her to represent, according to Bazin, "the physical future, and by way of the institution of the family to which she aspires as the root is drawn to the earth, its moral foundation."[13] *Once Upon a Time in the West* portrays the rise of a single, childless career woman in a society in which familiar bonds disintegrate and extra-familial relationships based on friendship (Cheyenne, Harmonica, and Jill) or economic collaboration (Frank and Morton) emerge.[14] The new West is no longer dominated by men, according to Leone: "With *Once Upon a Time in the West* I have shown the birth of the matriarchy and the beginning of the world without balls."[15] Leone imbues the female role with more complexity and power. In fact, Jill enjoys a masculine sort of independence since, as Robert Warshow indicates, "nobody owns her, nothing has to be explained to her, and she is not, like a virtuous woman, a 'value' that demands to be protected."[16] When Cheyenne tells Jill that she reminds him of his mother, "the biggest whore in Alameda and the finest woman that ever lived," he both intuits her past and underscores her embodiment of the exemplary mother (Madonna) and the fallen woman (prostitute).

As the singular female presence in *Once Upon a Time in the West*, Jill is both object and subject. Her baroque hairstyle, exotic eye makeup, and revealing bodices seduce viewers, who, like the men in the film, want to ogle her. At the end of the film, Cheyenne confirms Jill as object of male desire when he suggests how she might reward the train crew: "If I were you, I'd go give those boys a drink. You can't know how good it makes a man feel to see a woman like you. . . . And if one of 'em should pat your behind . . . make believe it's nothin.' They earned it."[17] Clearly, Cardinale's status as a sex symbol plays into this voyeuristic dynamic, yet we should consider the casting of this bombshell actress in light of the film's other reversals. If Bronson and Fonda play against type, why would one not assume the same for Cardinale, who had already played the role of the independent-minded Maria in *The Professionals* (Richard Brooks, 1966)? The actress's iconic sensuality should not limit our assessment of her character's agency.

After all, Jill's narrative connects the two subplots of revenge (Harmonica) and greed (Frank), while her intimate association with the water that she drinks, draws from the well, bathes in, and supplies to the men who build the railroad underscores her elemental power.[18] Jill represents the new West in Leone's retelling of history, yet her centrality escapes most critics who fail to see her as someone with whom the spectator, assumed to be male, might identify in such an overtly macho genre.[19] Perhaps for these critics Jill embodies the threat of castration, which Mulvey theorizes in terms of spectatorship and sexual difference—in Leone's terms, a "world without balls."[20] As Christopher Frayling points out, the Spaghetti Western, as an example of critical cinema, shocks the spectator into questioning what is on the screen, and challenges the viewer to think about it afterward.[21] Yet most refuse to challenge the gender roles characteristic of the traditional Western. Hence, these critical musings, with their disconsolate theme of vague dissatisfaction, at once underscore and miss the point: as Leone bids farewell to the West and its cinematic genre, he looks forward to the future with a new paradigm, at the center of which is his lone lady: Jill.

Notes

These ideas are adapted from Chapter 4, "The Evolving Western: From America to Italy and back in *Once Upon a Time in the West* (Leone, 1968) and *Kill Bill: Volumes 1 and 2* (Tarantino, 2003 and 2004)," in my book, *The Transatlantic Gaze: Italian Cinema, American Film* (Albany: State University of New York Press, 2014).

1 Frayling discusses the terminology applied to the Western (*Spaghetti Westerns*, xi.) See also Brunetta, *Storia del cinema italiano dal 1945 agli anni ottanta*, 777; and Miccichè, *Il cinema italiano degli anni '60*, 110.

2 In "Mini Hollywood," the area in which many large-scale Spaghetti Westerns were shot, former studios are now theme parks with such names as "Oasys Park," "Fort Bravo," and "Western Leone." The latter two still function as film locations.

3 See Miccichè, *Il cinema italiano degli anni '60*, 114.

4 For a description of the series, see Cox, "A Spaghetti Western Roundup at Film Forum," 16.

5 Tarantino, in an interview with Charles McGrath ("Quentin's World," 18–20), acknowledged the importance of the Spaghetti Western for his work: "I've

always been influenced by the spaghetti western. I used to describe 'Pulp Fiction' as a rock n' roll spaghetti western with the surf music standing in for Ennio Morricone. I don't know if 'Django' is a western proper. It's a southern. I'm playing western stories in the genre, but with a southern backdrop."

6 Quoted in Liehm, *Passion and Defiance*, 187.

7 Brunetta, *Storia del cinema italiano dal 1945 agli anni ottanta*, 780: "una programmatica perdita del centro morale e ideale" (my translation).

8 In his critique of this film, Hamill identifies American involvement in Vietnam as one of the extenuating circumstances contributing to the lack of popularity of *Once Upon a Time in the West* in the United States, since in 1969, "all notions of good and bad, or redemption through violence, were being widely questioned" (*"Once Upon a Time in America,"* 22).

9 French notes how casting offers clues to reading the film: "Taken along with familiar plots and recurrent situations, these well-known, and increasingly well-worn faces serve to give the Western its quality of dejà vu and reinforce the sense of ritual. The physical presence and established properties of these actors have become part of the genre's iconography, to be accepted literally or to be worked into new patterns or mined for fresh meanings. Alone or in conflict with each other they determine the tone of a picture, and most directors are intuitively aware of the way an actor's image and attributes can be manipulated and within what limits" (*Westerns*, 58).

10 Frayling, who sees the Spaghetti Western as an example of critical cinema that forces spectators to question the film during and after their viewing, does not extend this analysis to the treatment of women (*Spaghetti Westerns*, xv).

11 Bazin, "The Western, or the American Film par excellence," 143–44.

12 Bazin, "The Western, or the American Film par excellence,"145.

13 Bazin, "The Western, or the American Film par excellence,"145.

14 Cumbow, *Once upon a Time*, 66. Frayling argues that many of the Spaghetti Westerns exhibit "amoral familism," a term coined by Edward Banfield in *The Moral Basis of a Backward Society* (1958), his study of the root causes of abject poverty in southern Italy in the 1950s (*Spaghetti Westerns*, 59–61). Citing Luigi Barzini's best-selling book *The Italians* (1964), Frayling compares the growth of families of bandits in Westerns to the Mafia in southern Italy.

15 Noel Simsolo, *Conversations avec Sergio Leone*, 163: "Avec *Il était une fois dans l'Ouest*, j'avais montré la naissance du matriarcat et l'arrivée d'un monde sans couilles"; translation mine.

16 Warshow, "Movie Chronicle," 46.

17 Cumbow appears to have taken this suggestion seriously when, after acknowledging the importance of Cheyenne and Harmonica as well as "strong, but flexible people like Jill," he shifts credit from the female protagonist to the male masses: "In the end, though, credit goes to the diggers (not to the heroes)—the Boys who built the West, the Boys who occasionally need a drink and the touch of a woman" (*Once upon a Time*, 68). These critiques resonate

with Budd Boetticher's rejection of female agency in film: "What counts is what the heroine provokes, or rather what she represents. She is the one, or rather the love or fear she inspires in the hero, or else the concern he feels for her, who makes him act the way he does. In herself the woman has not the slightest importance" (quoted in Mulvey, "Visual Pleasure and Narrative Cinema," 750).

18 See Wright for a discussion of variations of the vengeance tale (*Six Guns and Society*, 154–63).

19 Sarah Hill is the exception; while rejecting the notion that Leone has created a feminist character, she considers the problem of Jill's classification outside the traditional binary classification of the Western ("Sergio Leone and the Myth of the American West," 206).

20 According to Mulvey, "the meaning of woman is sexual difference, the absence of the penis as visually ascertainable, the material evidence on which is based the castration complex essential for the organisation of entrance to the symbolic order and the law of the father. Thus the woman as icon, displayed for the gaze and enjoyment of men, the active controllers of the look, always threatens to evoke the anxiety it originally signified" ("Visual Pleasure and Narrative Cinema," 753).

21 Frayling, *Spaghetti Westerns*, xv.

Bibliography

Bazin, Andrè. "The Western, or the American Film par excellence." In *What Is Cinema?* Vol. 2. Trans. Hugh Gray. Berkeley: University of California Press, 1971. 2:140–48.

Brunetta, Gian Piero. *Storia del cinema italiano dal 1945 agli anni ottanta*. Rome: Editori Riuniti, 1982.

Cox, Alex. "A Spaghetti Western Roundup at Film Forum." *New York Times* (June 3, 2012): AR, 16.

Cumbow, Robert C. *Once Upon a Time: The Films of Sergio Leone*. Metuchen: The Scarecrow Press, 1987.

Frayling, Christopher. *Spaghetti Westerns: Cowboys and Europeans from Karl May to Sergio Leone*. London: Routledge and Kegan Paul, 1981.

French, Philip. *Westerns: Aspects of a Movie Genre*. London: Secker and Warburg, 1977.

Hamill, Peter. "*Once Upon a Time in America*." *American Film* (June 1984): 20–25.

Hill, Sarah. "Sergio Leone and the Myth of the American West: *Once Upon a Time in the West*." *Romance Languages Annual* 9 (1998): 202–10.

Liehm, Mira. *Passion and Defiance: Film in Italy from 1942 to Present*. Berkeley: University of California Press, 1984.

McGrath, Charles. "Quentin's World: From 'Reservoir Dogs' to 'Django Unchained,' How Tarantino Concocted a Genre of His Own." *New York Times* (December 23, 2012): AR1, 18–20.

Miccichè, Lino. *Il cinema italiano degli anni '60*. Venice: Marsilio, 1979.

Mulvey, Laura. "Visual Pleasure and Narrative Cinema." *Film Theory and Criticism*. Ed. Gerald Mast et al. New York: Oxford University Press, 1992. 746–57.

Simsolo, Noël. *Conversations avec Sergio Leone*. Paris: Stock, 1987.

Wagstaff, Christopher. "A Forkful of Westerns: Industry, Audiences and the Italian Western." *Popular European Cinema*. Ed. Richard Dyer and Ginette Vincendeau. London: Routledge, 1992. 245–61.

Warshow, Robert, "Movie Chronicle: The Westerner." In *Focus on the Western*. Ed. John G. Nachbar. Englewood Cliffs: Prentice-Hall, 1974. 45–56.

Wright, Will. *Six Guns and Society: A Structural Study of the Western*. Berkeley: University of California Press, 1975.

23

Theorem

Robert S. C. Gordon

Shot in spring 1968 and first shown at the tumultuous Venice Film Festival in September of the same year, *Teorema* (*Theorem*) was Pier Paolo Pasolini's sixth full-length feature film.[1] *Theorem* features a cluster of acclaimed Italian and international screen actors—Terence Stamp, Silvana Mangano, Massimo Girotti—as well as Pasolini regulars Ninetto Davoli and Laura Betti. It is a troublingly strange, allusive work: part allegorical Mystery play, part reworked Greek tragedy, and part abstract "report" on modernity. The film mixes sexuality, ideology, poetry, and high intellectualizing as perhaps only European art cinema of the 1960s could. For much of its ninety-eight minutes (ninety-four minutes on DVD), it is wordless; but its every move, its every cool line of controlled vision, is studiedly laced with meaning and patterned meaningfulness.

Pasolini had only turned to film-directing in the late 1950s, having established himself in the preceding decade as one of the most intense, experimental, and contrarian young literary intellectuals of his generation. He was also one of its most eclectically talented and productively original minds: he had published collections of poetry both in Italian (*Le ceneri di Gramsci* [*The Ashes of Gramsci*, 1958]) and in the northeastern Italian dialect of Friulan (*La meglio gioventù* [*The Best of Youth*, 1954]); novels and stories steeped in Roman street slang and dialect (*Ragazzi di vita* [*The Ragazzi*, 1955]); *Una vita violenta* [*A Violent Life*, 1959]); and a rich body of literary criticism and anthologies informed by the ideas of Antonio Gramsci and Leo Spitzer, among others. He had also taken on bit-part work as a screenwriter, including contributions for Federico Fellini. He was steeped in the literary traditions of the classics, and of the Italian and European canon, but this classicism came coupled with a fierce Marxist political commitment forged in the years of the anti-Fascist Resistance and with a never-quite-resolved struggle with his homosexuality. In the late 1950s, his peers were grappling with the intense crisis prompted by the fading of the euphoric neorealist moment of the 1940s. Pasolini's response to this crisis in literature and the role of the intellectual was to turn to what he saw as the deeper, more radical realism of the cinematic medium.

His early films, however, were quite unlike *Theorem*. They extended his Roman novels and stories into film, forging a sublime, almost sacred vision of the *borgate*, the slum peripheries of the capital (*Accattone*, 1960; *Mamma Roma*, 1962), and then extending and adapting this "peripheral" aesthetic into his bold, austere restaging of the story of Christ, shot against the rocky landscapes of the Italian South (*Il vangelo secondo Matteo* [*The Gospel According to Matthew*, 1964]). *Theorem* marks a shift at several levels from this first phase of his film work: from the underclasses to the middle classes; from the worn, rugged faces of the urban and rural poor to a troupe of professional and polished actors; and from Rome or rugged Basilicata to Milan and the Po plains.

Elements of the sublime and the sacred nevertheless survive, but they are now the scaffold on which to hang the film's principal protagonists, the haute bourgeoisie, embodied in the comfortable, complacent family of a Milanese industrialist. Husband, wife, son, daughter: one by one, *Theorem* watches— and it is a film built on insistent looking—as each one is driven to distraction and destruction. Only the family Maid makes for a strange exception to the rule, reaching a kind of transcendence ("trasumanar," "transhumanizing," was the Dantesque term Pasolini used in his later poetry), in contrast to the others' abjection, although she pays for this anomalous triumph with a kind of martyrdom.

In *Theorem*, we have a cinema of clinical dissection, even hatred of its principal subjects, presented by Pasolini with the clean inevitability and apparent geometric objectivity that its lapidary title implies. The theorem— "if A, then B"—is easily extracted, its demonstration embodying the very substance and style of the film: "*If* brought into contact with the 'sacred,' *then* the bourgeoisie will catastrophically and irreversibly collapse under its own contradictions." Hence Pasolini stages a theorem of revolution.

The central plot of the film is neat, symmetrical, opaque but relentless, segmented into regularly patterned, parallel temporal slots and staged in coldly filmed sequences.

First, we meet the four family members and their house servant: the Father (Girotti) emerges from his factory, the Son (Andres José Cruz) and the Daughter (Anne Wiazemsky) from their respective and highly respectable Milanese high schools, and the Mother (Mangano) sits in her luxury boudoir, served by the Maid (Betti). The four come together for a stiff dinnertime scene (Figure 23.1) interrupted by a mysterious telegram delivered by a hopping and bouncing, mercurial delivery boy (Davoli). It says, simply, "I arrive tomorrow."

FIGURE 23.1 *Pier Paolo Pasolini,* Theorem *(1968). A rare shot of all the family together, held in rigid spatial near-symmetry, repressively respectable, as the news of the Guest's arrival reaches them.*

Along comes the serene, icy blue-eyed, and vacantly wondrous presence of Terence Stamp, casually dressed in cream. Stamp will take up his place as Guest in the family villa and, over approximately thirty minutes of screen time, will encounter and have sex with all five of its denizens. Sexuality— pure, transcendent, carnal, and yet also strangely abstract—is the Guest's (and Pasolini's) weapon with which the certainties and conformities of this ideal family will be destroyed.

After each character's fateful sexual encounter, the delivery boy returns, another telegram in hand, and the Guest leaves. Act I is complete. A brief interlude gives us rambling free-verse monologues by each character, seared by loss and confusion: the Guest has shown them something transcendentally beyond themselves and his departure has left them shattered. Act II, and the remainder of the film, gives us the mathematical proof of the theorem, the void into which each in turn is projected, helpless. The Maid leaves the family and returns to her rural origins to become a saint, a miracle worker, and eventually a martyr, buried alive beneath the building-site rubble of neo-capitalist Milan. The Daughter is lost to a form of fetishistic obsession with photography and then to a hysterical catatonia. The Son returns to his pathetic attempts at art, his paintings degraded eventually into mere scatology (he pisses onto his canvases). The Mother heads out into the city periphery and then into the flatlands of the Po Valley, cruising for empty sex with bland, interchangeable young men. And, finally, the Father abandons his factory and strips naked—bare life in its raw essence—in Milan Central Station. His cry of agony, a desperate, primal scream like that of Joseph

Conrad's character Kurtz in *The Heart of Darkness* ("The horror! The horror!"), closes out the film.

In between the symmetries and neat parallels of this iterative plot line, there are several temporal inversions and spatial disturbances that give the film much of its resonance and power, a viscerally troubling depth beneath the cool surface. The spatial disturbances center on a sequence of interruptions (fourteen in all) that suddenly and in flashes take us from the emblematic urban bourgeois spaces of Milan and its hinterland—the space of modernity and culture, we might say—to a terrifying, wild, black sand, volcanic landscape. For much of the film, this space is empty, biblical, awesome, and unexplained until the closing shots, when Massimo Girotti's Father, naked in body and spirit, is projected from the Milan Central Station to the volcano to utter his final scream.

The flashes, we realize, have been *flash-forwards*, proleptic glimpses of the endpoint or corollary of the theorem, of a future apocalypse. They also help us to decipher the careful interplay of spaces in the rest of the film, spread between artificial interiors (bedrooms, apartments, chapels, car, or ambulance interiors) and natural exteriors (gardens, river parklands, marshes, and farm courtyards). In a parallel inversion, *Theorem* opens with what in retrospect looks like another film, another genre entirely: a *cinéma vérité* documentary set in a factory, with street interviews, workers, pans over industrial architecture (Figure 23.2), questions analyzing capitalist labor.

Once again, only at the end do we realize that this is the Father's factory and that he has, in a prelude to his and the film's final crisis, given up

FIGURE 23.2 *Pier Paolo Pasolini,* Theorem *(1968). Framing the film as an allegory of capitalist modernity,* Theorem *opens with a black-and-white mock-documentary of a Milanese factory (shot at Industria Innocenti, Lambrate).*

ownership of the factory to its workers, ceding the means of production in a hyper-literal Marxist gesture. In this conjunction of Marx and eschatology (the factory and the apocalyptic volcano), *Theorem* is perhaps not as far removed as it initially seemed from Pasolini's biblical film *The Gospel According to Matthew*.

Theorem also works to layer its meanings through an obsessive accumulation of citations, of allusions to books, art, music, other films.[2] The books we see as physical objects on screen include work by Konrad Lorenz, Arthur Rimbaud, and Leo Tolstoy, as well as a legal textbook, and there are quotations from the Bible (Exodus, Jeremiah) and allusions to Pasolini's own poetry. The art includes Francis Bacon (in tellingly hypermediated form: we look on through film as the Guest and the Son look through some catalogue reproductions of Bacon's work), and the music references work by Ted Curson, Mozart, and an original score by Ennio Morricone. But the key intertext that complements and explains *Theorem* more than any other is one that takes us back to the film's genesis in the mid-1960s and to its position in Pasolini's career as he shifted into a newly charged final phase of his career responding to dramatic transformations in the culture and society around him.[3]

In an interval from his hyperactive, eclectic pattern of work, in 1966 Pasolini was convalescing from an operation and spent weeks planning and writing a cycle of verse tragedies. These either built on ancient Greek texts or forged modern equivalents. Six were completed, and this new mythical mode would form the basis of a cluster of ancient and modern myth films of the following years (*Edipo re* [*Oedipus Rex*, 1967]); *Medea*, 1969; *Porcile* [*Pigsty*], 1969). *Theorem* was part of this new cluster of films, and was also part of the writing project. It was originally conceived as a seventh play, but morphed between 1966 and 1968 into the film as well as an elaborate mixed prose-and-verse book of the same title, also published in 1968. This work is neither a screenplay nor a novel, but a complex parallel text that accompanies the film at every step, in which its every silence, its every move and cut and look, are expressed in a parallel medium of words.

So paradoxically, out of an arcane project to renew Greek verse tragedy and an exceptional experiment in mixed media text-and-film, came a work that plunged into the white-hot moment of political radicalism of 1968. As the film was being shot between March and May 1968, violent clashes between police and students were taking place in Rome, Paris, and elsewhere. Drawing in part on the book of *Theorem*, Pasolini published an infamous, typically contrarian poem entitled "I hate you, dear students!" and sided with the police, sons of the poor, as they beat up the students, who were for Pasolini sons of the bourgeoisie playing at revolution. The film—with its chaste allusions to the naked body, to homo- as well as heterosexual sex, and its close-ups of Terence Stamp's crotch—was prosecuted for obscenity. It was nonetheless awarded a Catholic film prize at the 1968 Venice festival;

yet the Vatican and even Pope John VI himself denounced the film. At Venice in September, the festival was heavily disrupted by protests, just as Cannes had been earlier that year, and Pasolini tried to withdraw the film from competition. But his producers entered it anyway. He set up alternative meetings amid the general chaos, and organized a boycott of the major literary prize, the Premio Strega, for which the book had been entered. Despite its abstractions, *Theorem*'s radical anti-bourgeois position and taboo-breaking clearly touched countercultural nerves.

At a distance of nearly fifty years, *Theorem* looks dated in some aspects of its politics and aesthetics. But it also looks like a film of exceptional, seminal importance: for Pasolini's trajectory as an artist, but more broadly still, for European auteurist cinema and film form. Pasolini extracted from a remarkable group of actors a series of genuinely enigmatic performances, denying them the opportunity to build a fiction based on character, suspense, or naturalistic psychology. Instead, he forged a new model of film as allegory and as argument, what we might call the narrative essay-film, and it stands foursquare alongside some of the most influential and transformative film experiments of its era, from Chris Marker to Jean-Luc Godard to Orson Welles.

Notes

1 Prior to *Theorem*, Pasolini had also made seven shorter episode films and documentaries.

2 Pasolini's last film, *Salò* (1975), which shares several features with *Theorem*, would actually offer a bibliography of further reading on screen.

3 Pasolini was to die, brutally murdered outside Rome, in November 1975.

24

The Conformist

Michael Cramer

Il conformista (*The Conformist*, 1970), Bernardo Bertolucci's fourth and for many his best feature film, adapts Alberto Moravia's novel of the same name. The "conformist" of the title is Marcello Clerici, a young man who dedicates himself to Fascism in an effort to relieve his own sense of abnormality. As he tells his friend, Fascist ideologue Italo, he feels different from others when he looks in the mirror each morning, and so seeks "an impression of normality . . . stability, security." Marcello's pathological desire for normality stems at least partly from a traumatic childhood sexual encounter with a chauffeur, Lino, whom he shot. Upon the eve of his marriage to Giulia, a woman who represents the normality and mediocrity to which he aspires, he accepts a mission to track down and aid in the assassination of his former professor Luca Quadri, an anti-Fascist activist who has fled to Paris. Through this act, he explains to a priest, "one sin atones for another." But after meeting Quadri and his beautiful wife, Anna, Marcello begins to have second thoughts about his mission, and hopes to save the life of Anna, with whom he has fallen in love. While Bertolucci takes the film's main plot and some of its dialogue from Moravia's novel, he also incorporates his own preoccupations, both erotic and political, and engages in a self-reflexive use of film style in order to comment on both the seductive appeal of Fascism and its underlying brutality.

The film, which was shot by cinematographer Vittorio Storaro—who also worked on Bertolucci's *Last Tango in Paris* (1972) and Francis Ford Coppola's *Apocalypse Now* (1979)—is famous for its striking stylistic flourishes. Breaking from mentors Jean-Luc Godard (who had adapted Moravia's *Contempt* seven years earlier) and Pier Paolo Pasolini (who wrote Bertolucci's directorial debut, *La commare secca* [*The Grim Reaper*,

1962]), Bertolucci formulates a flamboyant film style in *The Conformist* that is marked by bravura camera movements, meticulously balanced compositions, and a symbolic use of light and color. Bertolucci's strong foregrounding of style, noticeable here to the point that it threatens to overwhelm all else, contributes to the film's often surreal or dreamlike feel, as though it were aiming not for a realistic depiction of the Fascist era but rather a kind of subjective memory, laden with symbolic meaning. This subjective perspective is motivated by the film's structure, which unlike the novel casts much of the action in flashback form, remembered by Marcello as he pursues the Quadris to Savoy with his Fascist handler, Manganiello. The point of view, however, is never fully Marcello's; instead it is mixed with that of Bertolucci, who adds layers of visual symbolism to his protagonist's memories, both adopting his perspective and remaining at arm's length in a fashion that resembles Moravia's use of free indirect discourse in the novel.

Through the eyes of Marcello (and Bertolucci), the Fascist era appears here as meticulously polished, full of symmetry, straight lines, and right angles. Upon his visit to a government building, Marcello finds himself in the center of a vast, polished marble hall, shot from above as though to emphasize the geometric precision and symmetry of its layout. Bertolucci also makes recurring use of windows and frames: the flashback sequence begins with Marcello placed against the backdrop of a rectangular pane of glass opening onto a radio studio, as though the performance of Fascist modernity taking place inside (and encapsulated in the synchronized gestures of three female singers in identical dresses and hairstyles) represented the world he wished to enter. Later, a painting briefly stands in for the landscape when Marcello stops off in Ventimiglia. Much like the perfectly symmetrical government building, these carefully composed and "framed" environments suggest both the manicured and meticulous aesthetic of Fascism and its underlying status as an artful contrivance, incommensurable with a far less orderly reality—a reality filled with trauma and neurosis that Marcello seeks to escape through his own political commitment.

But just as Marcello's efforts to normalize himself through adherence to Fascism run up against the obstacle of his attraction to Anna and his doubts about killing Professor Quadri, the seemingly perfect spaces of Fascism are easily troubled and disrupted. Their surface majesty carries along with it a sense of coldness and soullessness, reminiscent of Michelangelo Antonioni's sanitized, dehumanized landscapes. Perhaps even more importantly, Bertolucci's Fascist tableaux recall the uncanny atmosphere of a De Chirico painting, a reference underscored by repeated appearances of Fascist statuary. Menace, it seems, lurks beneath the film's smooth and polished settings.

Bertolucci conveys the theme of disruption or threat to seemingly composed and orderly surfaces not only through such visual connotations but also through the figure of Dominque Sanda, who appears in the film in three roles, like an apparition periodically disturbing Marcello's itinerary. Marcello first sees her in the office of the Fascist minister whom he meets before embarking on his mission to kill Quadri, reclining provocatively on the minister's desk as though to suggest both the "abnormal" sexuality barely concealed by the superficial propriety of Fascism and Catholicism as well as Marcello's own repressed urges. Appearing a second time as a prostitute in a Ventimiglia brothel, Sanda takes on a more tender cast: her luminous gaze toward Marcello prompts him to embrace her like a child embracing his mother, as though she incarnated a kind of innocent, maternal femininity, disavowed by the brutal masculinity of Fascism. Finally, Sanda appears as Anna Quadri. This time, however, her character takes on a more complex and layered symbolic significance: she represents not only the possibility of true love (a possibility forbidden to Marcello by his own psychic repression and his submission to Fascist discipline) but also non-normative sexuality (she is bisexual and at times presents herself in masculine fashion, first appearing in trousers, with a cigarette hanging from her lips) and an alternative political order. These three elements clearly converge in one of the film's key scenes, in which Quadri and his wife join Marcello and Giulia for a night out at a Joinville dancehall. Here, a dance between Giulia and Anna that initially appears as purely erotic in character transforms into an expression of community, as the working-class crowd dances in a series of concentric circles, evoking both traditional May Day festivities and communist pageantry. The erotic abnormality that Marcello seeks so violently to repress, both in his own marriage and in his submission to Fascism, thus takes on a positive cast, suggesting the possibility of a political order based on erotic drive rather than its repression, on love rather than violence. Another scene draws similar connections, but refers more explicitly to Bertolucci's own background: after Marcello exits his hotel, having discovered Anna and Giulia in a quasi-erotic embrace, he is confronted by a woman selling Parma violets outside. Bertolucci, a Parma native, thus appears by proxy in the form of the flower seller, who is joined by two street children in singing a communist anthem, the Internationale, just as Anna emerges from the hotel. As the couple walks off, the flower seller and the children follow them, still singing, as though in encouragement: another order is indeed possible, if one can only accept both oneself and individuals like the working-class flower seller and the bisexual Anna who, in a Fascist society, represent untolerated difference.

Bertolucci's film thus avoids any facile equation of Fascism with repressed homosexuality, and allows Marcello's sense of abnormality to take on the character of a more abstract sense of guilt, taintedness, or mere difference, casting Fascism as the quotidian violence necessary to disavow it. It is Fascism's drive toward normality, and not Marcello's sexuality, that is the true aberration or disruptive element here. Indeed, despite the fact that Marcello's trauma does indeed result from a reprehensible act—an attempted rape and his violent response to it—Bertolucci, with his characteristic appeal to psychoanalysis, recognizes the polyvalence of the repressed forces of the id and identifies them just as much with potential liberation as with trauma. Indeed, Marcello literally dreams of his own redemption at the hands of Quadri, whom he imagines as a surgeon curing his blindness, as though it were only acceptance by a "foreign" element—in this case, an anti-Fascist and implicitly communist hunchback who lives outside of Italy with his bisexual wife—that could truly grant him the sense of peace he seeks. The metaphor of blindness also connects to the film's symbolic use of lighting. In one pivotal scene, absent from Moravia's novel, Marcello recounts to Professor Quadri Plato's myth of the cave, in which a group of prisoners in a cave mistakes the shadows of the world outside, inaccessible to them, with reality itself. It is this theme, Quadri recalls, on which Marcello had initially planned to write his doctoral thesis. This scene differs from the bulk of the film in that it takes place almost in the dark, after Marcello closes one of the windows of the professor's office. It is only by shutting out the light, it seems, that one can escape the flashy, seductive surface of Fascism, which constitutes nothing more than a false shadow-world, one that obscures the reality that lies beneath.

This metaphor of light and visibility, associated with deception, enables Bertolucci to make cinema itself a key thematic element of the film. Plato's myth has often been used to describe cinema, most famously by theorist Jean-Louis Baudry, usually to express its illusory nature and its deceptive ideological function. By referencing this myth, Bertolucci makes clear that the overly lit images of his film draw a parallel between cinema and Fascism. Just as Fascism, for Marcello, substitutes a perfect, seamless world for the complex and fractured one that he fears, so does cinema present us with an ideal that we risk mistaking for the real, as we construct normative identities with which we mistakenly seek to reconcile our own. The film's thematization of cinema is further underscored in the scene in which Giulia and Marcello first make love, as their train travels toward France: a surreal orange light envelops them, as landscapes pass across the window behind them like frames of a film strip. As they enter into what appears to be a tunnel, the "film strip" behind them displays only an intermittently flashing light, unmistakably the light of a film projector. This thematization of cinema provides a motivation for the seemingly excessive, flamboyant style that permeates the film. If this world is overly stylized, improbably perfect, and at once seductively and disturbingly beautiful, it is because it is, Bertolucci seems to say, a cinematic fantasy, as seductive and ultimately hollow as Fascism itself, the site of a violence that tries to master and transform the real.

Truth emerges in the dark, then, when appearances no longer matter. Bertolucci's counterintuitive valuations of light and darkness are perhaps most explicit in a scene in which Marcello, having second thoughts about his mission, struggles with Manganiello in the back room of a Chinese restaurant. As the two confront each other, Marcello swings a hanging lamp and moves into the darkness to draw his gun; he fails to act, though, and Manganiello draws him back into the light of Fascism. Darkness also plays a key role in the film's nocturnal epilogue, in which Fascism falls and Marcello ventures out into a Roman night to find his panicked Fascist friend, Italo. As they walk through the passages of the Coliseum, they happen upon a man, whom Marcello recognizes as his childhood aggressor Lino, and who is speaking to a young male prostitute. Lino's appearance is clearly improbable—indeed, both the novel and the film suggest that Marcello did indeed kill him as a boy—but its symbolic meaning is clear: now that the ordering structure of Fascism has crumbled, trauma resurfaces. But Marcello does not take this opportunity to join the ranks of the anti-Fascist protesters in the street. Instead he denounces both Lino, accusing him of Quadri's murder, and Italo. Rather than accept his own difference and confront his misguided actions in an act of restitution that would be a gesture of both psychic and political liberation, Marcello once again flees from his psychoses. Illuminated only by a small fire, he gazes back into the darkened niche of the young prostitute solicited by Lino, as though considering a possible liaison. His own perceived abnormality thus persists. But rather than being integrated into any form of political action—like that of the march that literally passes him by—his psychic and sexual difference remains nestled deep in an ancient ruin, at once subterranean and foundational.

25

Love and Anarchy

Bernadette Luciano

The first woman ever nominated for an Oscar in the Best Director category, Lina Wertmüller is among the very few Italian women filmmakers who appear in histories of Italian cinema and whose films have been widely distributed internationally. After a background in theater, Wertmüller began a long career as a film director and screenwriter in the 1960s that stretches to the present, with close to thirty films to her credit.[1] With her signature white-rimmed glasses and cropped hair, Wertmüller boasts a unique cinematic style that combines poignant political satire and a revisionist take on the *commedia all'italiana* (Italian-style comedy).

Film d'amore e d'anarchia (*Love and Anarchy*, 1973) is often grouped together with her other 1970s films: *Mimì metallurgico ferito nell'onore* (*The Seduction of Mimì*, 1972), *Tutto a posto e niente in ordine* (*All Screwed Up*, 1974), *Travolti da un insolito destino nell'azzurro mare d'agosto* (*Swept Away*, 1974), and *Pasqualino settebellezza* (*Seven Beauties*, 1975), which was awarded the Oscar for Best Foreign Film. These films explore topical political issues through exuberant imagery influenced by Federico Fellini, with whom Wertmüller had worked on his *8 1/2* (1963). Her films also probe the conventions of Italian grotesque comedy, including its vulgarity, stock characters, and attacks on tradition.[2] In the United States, Wertmüller's 1970s films met with public and critical acclaim while they received a cooler reception in Italy. Italian critics did not agree that the films were original and bold, but rather scathingly accused Wertmüller of rehashing the social critique themes of the *commedia all'italiana* of the 1960s while indulging in clichéd treatment of situations and stock characters typical of the *commedia dell'arte*.[3] Recognizing that many of her critics were disturbed by the popular nature of her films, Wertmüller declared that her aim as a left-wing Italian filmmaker was to make movies with a political message that would appeal to the masses.[4] And in response to the many critics who denounced her use of comedy in dealing with serious political issues, Wertmüller, in keeping with the spirit of Italian *commedia all'italiana* filmmakers, maintained that a serious approach to the representation of political problems could be much less effective than a comic one.[5]

Love and Anarchy exploits a comedic technique present in many of her films, one described by Millicent Marcus as "the politics of polarity."[6] This strategy juxtaposes ideological opposites: super-feminist versus feminism in the case of *All Screwed Up*; the Italian North-South dichotomy in *The Seduction of Mimi*; Nazi idealism versus Mediterranean survival strategy in *Seven Beauties;* and capitalist slave-driver versus communist slave dialectic in *Swept Away*.[7] But *Love and Anarchy*, which Marcus sees as Wertmüller's best film, goes beyond the juxtaposition of ideological opposites and presents "a highly nuanced complex study of the interrelationship between emotional and political commitments."[8] The film's representation of love and anarchy both applies and dismantles oppositional dualities of male and female characters and gendered spaces. In confronting historical events in this way, *Love and Anarchy* repositions our understanding of traditional ideological discourses and pressing sociopolitical issues past and present.

Set in the years of Fascism, *Love and Anarchy* launches a resounding condemnation of its political ideology. Giancarlo Giannini, a mainstay of Wertmüller cinema, won the Cannes Best Actor Award for his role in the film as Tunin, a peasant-turned-anarchist not so much out of political conviction but in response to the brutal murder of his anarchist friend Michele Sgaravento by the Fascist police. Tunin travels to Rome to a high-class brothel to meet his contact, the prostitute Salomé (Mariangela Melato). Salomé's anarchist nature and hatred for Fascism, we soon discover, is also personally rather than politically motivated. Her former lover, Anteo Zamboni, like Tunin's friend, was also murdered by the Fascist squads. As Tunin and Salomé plot the assassination of Mussolini, another love intervenes. Tunin falls for Tripolina, a prostitute in the brothel, who will ultimately prevent Tunin from carrying out the anarchist deed. With the politics of the assassination plot revolving around avenging the deaths of friends and lovers, the film weds love and politics and reconsiders the motivation behind anarchist acts.

Love and Anarchy begins in the style of the oral tradition, featuring a ballad about the film's hero, which asks where Tunin is going and questions the purpose of fighting wars. Close-ups of the freckle-faced, wide-eyed peasant alternate with long shots of Michele Sgaravento, the sprightly anarchist daredevil prancing across the countryside, living up to the meaning of his last name (Figures 25.1, 25.2 and 25.3). A subsequent shot of Sgaravento's body hanging from a tree reveals the anarchist's fate, and confirms in a flashback Tunin's mother's definition of what an anarchist is,

FIGURE 25.1 *Close-up of Tunin.*

FIGURE 25.2 *Long shot of Sgaravento.*

FIGURE 25.3 *Sgaravento running through the countryside.*

namely "someone who kills kings and throws bombs, someone who ends up with a rope around his neck."

The contrast between freedom (the peasant anarchists) and tyranny (the Fascist police) is mirrored in the subsequent cut from the open spaces of the countryside of Lombardy to the imperial and monumental architecture of Rome. A triumphal march provides the musical backdrop to shots of Rome taken from the imposing Victor Emmanuel monument, one which appears numerous times in the film and which is joined by later images of the Forum, Coliseum, and Campidoglio, as well as by images of the modernist, Fascist architecture of the town of Latina. The character most directly associated with Fascist Rome is, not surprisingly, the chief of the Fascist police, Giacinto Spatoletti. Spatoletti, whose name means "little spade" (a sexually reductive diminutive), functions as the antithesis of Tunin, or little Antonio (an endearing diminutive) in the film. As Spatoletti drives his motorcar through the Lazio countryside, one is reminded of the association of machines with Modernism, Futurism, and Fascism. Loud and boastful, Spatoletti flaunts his masculinity while Tunin, the country boy, sits uncomfortably in the backseat holding onto his hat.

Spatoletti is repeatedly associated with aggressive sexual behavior, Tunin with romantic love. Their drunken encounter at night in the Campidoglio, where Spatoletti designates Mussolini and Fascism as the natural inheritors of Roman glory, is challenged by Tunin's declaration that desperation can move people to rise up and rebel against tyranny. Ultimately the scene that epitomizes the contrast between the two is their final meeting. With the city of Rome in the background and the statue of the she-wolf suckling the twins Romulus and Remus in the interrogation space, the ordered, groomed, authoritarian chief of the Fascist police aggressively questions the beaten, disheveled Tunin who responds with dignity, repeating the words that will lead to his death, "Long live anarchy!"[9] But the scene's visual imagery is a tragic reminder that the film's hero, like so many heroes of the Italian Resistance movement, will not survive to participate in the forging of post-Fascist Italy.

If the public spaces of Rome are where masculine tensions are played out, the interior space of the labyrinthine and ornate brothel, the film's other major space, is occupied by the film's two female main characters. Wertmüller's juxtaposition of exterior monumentality and ornately decorated interiors replicates similar contrasts employed by Elio Petri and Francesco Rosi's political films of the 1970s. In the cinematic spaces of those films, institutional and monumental sites clash with baroque architecture of visual excess, creating a tension between power and revolt, order and disorder, and Fascism and anarchy.[10] The visual excess of the interiors of the brothel, along with the colloquial meaning of the word *casino* ("chaos" as well as "brothel"), suggests a space that rejects stability and order, or more specifically, patriarchal order.

At the same time, some feminist readings of the film see Wertmüller's choice of space and representation of the prostitutes in *Love and Anarchy* as antifeminist. With the women mirroring the brothel's broken statues and thus functioning as objective correlatives of disintegration and fragmentation, such readings see the women as trapped in a patriarchal world, objects of the male gaze.[11]

While the scene of the prostitutes parading down the brothel's staircase to the tune of the love song "La petite Tonkinoise" is said to borrow extensively from Fellini's brothel scene in *Roma* and to be emblematic of Wertmüller's antifeminism, it can also be argued that the scene mocks the very situation of feminine display that it represents.[12] While the women are framed in a number of alluring positions, the male clients are far from images of masculine power: many are fat, bald, inexperienced, or old, and one client indeed meets his death, completely overpowered by the prostitute that hosts him. The prostitutes' domineering presence and high-angle shots of Salomé empower the women. Likewise, Madame Aida and her assistants join other women of Wertmüller's films, who are empowered specifically because they are not configured as objects of male desire, but rather as key components of her "feminism of despair."[13] The representation of Wertmüller's brothel differs significantly from Fellini's brothel precisely because it is not presented exclusively from the point of view of the male gaze. Allowed access in the after-hours, the viewer also experiences it as a female space that features female solidarity, sympathy, conspiracy, and protection.

The brothel, a female microcosm of Italy inhabited by women speaking in a range of accents and dialects, also provides a space for female reinvention, visible in the self-selection of new names. Salomé from Bologna chooses a name that highlights her position as icon of female seduction, while another of the film's main characters, Tripolina, chooses a name associated with the exoticism of Africa featured in silent cinema (e.g., *The Sheik* from 1921 starring Rudolph Valentino), and is oblivious to its association with Mussolini's colonial agenda.[14] One of the film's most important brothel scenes is when Salomé and Tripolina argue about whether or not to wake Tunin in time to carry out the planned assassination. The scene begins by positioning Salomé and Tripolina as the antitheses of each other, as they apparently represent the two terms of the film's title, love (Tripolina) and anarchy (Salomé).

Convinced that Tunin will die pointlessly in the assassination attempt, Tripolina refuses to wake him on the morning of the scheduled assassination. Convinced that the political mission must go ahead as planned and that love and politics don't mix, Salomé intervenes: "Feelings are a luxury and this is war! What would happen if all women stopped their soldiers at the door during war?" Through her response to this seemingly rhetorical question ("It would be great if every mother did that, why not?"), Tripolina advocates an empowering, subversive female politics that suggests that it is indeed by obstructing patriarchal politics that one could bring an end to the useless dying, and that has persisted since "the creation of the world." Salomé gives in to Tripolina's reasoning, reconfiguring the two women not as opposites but as coconspirators in this new feminist politics. As a result, Salomé and Tripolina appear as Wertmüller herself has defined them: "very strong women [who] instinctively rebel against militarism and the patriarchal order." Salomé and Tripolina stand in stark contrast to the many men in her films who, like Spatoletti, are portrayed as "all vain, arrogant and stupid, real chauvinists who believe in the superiority of the penis."[15] This new politics, however, cannot reign in a film that reflects on an historical situation that left a negative legacy. Tunin, it can be argued, dies because he rejects the politics that Salomé and Tripolina propose. While the plan Salomé and Tripolina concoct for his escape would save him—and the feminine, labyrinthine, womblike brothel might protect him from the authorities—a confused Tunin first cowers then chooses to fight violence with violence, wildly shooting at the *carabinieri* who have entered the brothel.[16]

As he runs out into the street, out of the film's feminine space and into the public space of Rome, he becomes inevitably subject to the prevailing Fascist authorities. He is eventually captured, imprisoned, and beaten to death by the police, meeting a similar fate to that of his friend Sgaravento and of Salomé's lover. The arrest of Tunin and the women retreating back into the brothel signal the conquest of female politics in the public space. As the film draws to a close, we listen to an official typing the words that appear on the screen and that comprise the subtitle of the film, "This morning at ten, on Via dei Fiori in a noted brothel." The use of this press release announcing the death of an unnamed man, who was arrested and then supposedly committed suicide, reveals to the audience the cover-up surrounding Tunin's death and highlights Fascist violence and censorship.

The film ends with an on-screen quotation by Enrico Malatesta, an anarchist tolerated by the Fascists, who comments thusly on the attempts made on Mussolini's life: "I would like to stress my horror at the attempted assassinations. These gestures are not only evil but they hinder the cause they are meant to serve. . . . One must admit, though, that these murderers are heroes as well. . . . When their extreme gesture is forgotten, we shall celebrate the ideal that spurred them." The paradoxical quote, which both condemns and eulogizes violent anarchists, mirrors Wertmüller's own conflicted feelings about responses to tyranny. While the film is a clear condemnation of Fascist ideology and therefore supports those who rise against it, it also warns against what happens when ideology leads to the very kind of violence it condemns.

In that vein, *Love and Anarchy* can be considered an historical film that is as much about the *anni di piombo* (Years of Lead), the terrorist years in which it was made, as it is about the past it represents. While Wertmüller leads the viewer to sympathize with the film's protagonist, the peasant-turned-anarchist Tunin, she also leaves the viewer questioning the assassination attempt that translates into violence and results in the protagonist's own death and failure to bring about change. Tunin's ideologically motivated behavior can thus be seen to prefigure, and at the same time condemn, the many terrorist attacks by political radicals on both the extreme right (clandestine Fascist groups) and extreme left (those fighting the failed battle of the Resistance) during the bloody and politically paralyzed Years of Lead.[17] In essence, such terrorist activities are viewed by Wertmüller as the tragic perversion of the ideologically motivated behavior exhibited by Tunin, who acts to preserve his dignity and put an end to the dehumanizing conditions of Fascism. In an interview discussing the parallel between the film's historical moment and the Years of Lead, Wertmüller articulated what was clearly for her an irresolvable but dangerous tension between anarchy and terrorism:

> My film *Love and Anarchy* gives a sense of what Italy was like as an agricultural country, a poor country that the Fascists tried to change into another thing. It's full of feeling. Afterwards, anarchy became terrorism, right action was deformed into mass murder. The film has become very contemporary today. It was meant as a warning about all this passion for justice.[18]

Love and Anarchy joins the many Italian political films that reinterpret national history and events, and in so doing provide a revisionist account of history while also commenting on the present. The image of a bludgeoned Tunin at the end of *Love and Anarchy* is one that recalls cinematic images from neorealist films, most notably the martyred Manfredi in Roberto Rossellini's *Roma città aperta* (*Rome, Open City*, 1945).[19] The brutal image also recalls other cinematic protagonists marginalized from institutional power in the defiant political films of Elio Petri and Francesco Rosi of 1960s and 1970s and prefigures Marco Bellocchio's haunting image of an Aldo Moro roaming free at the end of *Buongiorno, notte* (*Goodmorning, Night*, 2003), as well as the images of the silenced and incarcerated Ida Dalser, unacknowledged wife of Mussolini in *Vincere* (*Victory*, 2009).[20] Considered by many to be Wertmüller's greatest film, *Love and Anarchy*, rather than love *or* anarchy, challenges the polarity of the two terms. The film affirms the need to fight tyranny and uphold liberty while promoting an anti-ideological humanitarian view of the world and a future based on an alternative feminist politics.

Notes

1   For an updated list of films directed and written by Wertmuller, see the IMDb database: http://www.imdb.com/name/nm0921631/?ref_=tt_ov_dr.

2   Bondanella, *Italian Cinema*, 354.

3   Bullaro, *Man in Disorder*, xv.

4   Haskell, *Holding My Own in No Man's Land*, 83.

5   Georgakas and Rubenstein, *The Cineaste Interviews*, 132.

6   Marcus, "Wertmüller's *Love and Anarchy*," 314.

7   Marcus, "Wertmüller's *Love and Anarchy*," 315–17.

8   Marcus, "Wertmüller's *Love and Anarchy*," 319.

9   Marcus, "Wertmüller's *Love and Anarchy*," 337.

10 Wood, *Italian Cinema*,189.

11 Consolati, "Grotesque Bodies, Fragmented Selves," 39.

12 Bondanella, *Italian Cinema*, 357.

13 Diaconescu-Blumenfeld, "Regista di clausura," 399.

14 Marcus, "Wertmüller's *Love and Anarchy*," 321–22.

15 Georgakas and Rubenstein, *The Cineaste Interviews*, 26.

16 Consolati, "Grotesque Bodies, Fragmented Selves," 41.

17 The period is broadly defined as the years between the bombing of Milan's Piazza Fontana in 1968 and the Moro kidnapping and killing in 1978.

18 Oumano, *Film Forum*, 286–87.

19 Marcus, "Wertmüller's *Love and Anarchy*," 338.

20 For a discussion of Wertmüller as a political filmmaker of the 1970s, see Michalczyk, *The Italian Political Filmmakers*, 1986.

Bibliography

Bondanella, Peter. *Italian Cinema: From Neorealism to the Present*. New York: Continuum, 2001.

Bullaro, Grace Russo. *Man in Disorder: The Cinema of Lina Wertmüller in the 1970s*. Leicester: Troubador, 2006.

Consolati, Claudia. "Grotesque Bodies, Fragmented Selves: Lina Wertmuller's Women in *Love and Anarchy* (1973)." In *Italian Women Filmmakers and the Gendered Screen*. Ed. Maristella Cantini. New York: Palgrave Macmillan, 2013. 33–52.

Diaconescu-Blumenfeld, Rodica. "Regista di clausura: Lina Wertmüller and Her Feminism of Despair." *Italica* 76.3 (1999): 389–403.

Georgakas, Dan and Lenny Rubenstein. *The Cinéaste Interviews: On the Art and Politics of the Cinema*. Chicago: Lake View Press, 1983.

Haskell, Molly. *Holding My Own in No Man's Land: Women and Men and Film and Feminists*. New York: Oxford University Press, 1997.
Marcus, Millicent. "Wertmüller's *Love and Anarchy*: The High Price of Commitment." In *Italian Film in the Light of Neorealism*. Princeton: Princeton University Press, 1986. 313–38.
Michalczyk, John J. *The Italian Political Filmmakers*. Rutherford: Fairleigh Dickinson University Press, 1986.
Oumano, Elena. *Film Forum: Thirty-Five Top Filmmakers Discuss Their Craft*. New York: St. Martin's Press, 1985.
Wood, Mary P. *Italian Cinema*. Oxford, New York: Berg, 2005.

Filmography

8 1/2, Dir. Federico Fellini. Italy/France: Cineriz, Francinex. 1963.
Buongiorno, notte (*Goodmorning, Night*), Dir. Marco Bellocchio. Italy: Filmalbatros, RAI Cinemafiction. 2003.
Film d'onore e d'anarchia (*Love and Anarchy*), Dir. Lina Wertmüller. Italy/France: Euro International Film, Labrador Films. 1973.
Mimi metallurgico ferito nell'onore (*The Seduction of Mimi*), Dir. Lina Wertmüller. Italy: Euro International Film. 1972.
Pasqualino settebellezza (*Seven Beauties*), Dir. Lina Wertmüller. Italy: Medusa. 1975.
Roma, Dir. Federico Fellini. Italy/France: Ultra Film, Les Productions Artistes Associés. 1972.
Roma città aperta (*Rome, Open City*), Dir. Roberto Rossellini. Italy: Excelsa Film. 1945.
The Sheik, Dir. George Melford. USA: Paramount Pictures. 1921.
Travolti da un insolito destino nell'azzurro mare d'agosto (*Swept Away*), Dir. Lina Wertmüller. Italy: Medusa. 1974.
Tutto a posto e niente in ordine (*All Screwed Up*), Dir. Lina Wertmüller, Italy: Euro International Film. 1974.
Vincere (*Victory*), Dir. Marco Bellocchio. Italy/France: Offside, RAI Cinema, Celluloid Dreams. 2009.

26

The Best of Youth

Alan O'Leary

La meglio gioventù (*The Best of Youth*, 2003) is a television miniseries produced by RAI, the Italian public broadcaster, which had its postponed first broadcast on RAI Uno, the largest national channel, in December 2003. The film had already been shown in cinemas in Italy that summer, and it was given an international cinema release in two parts after winning a major prize at the 2003 Cannes Film Festival (it was picked up for US distribution by Miramax).[1] A historical saga built around the tale of two brothers, *La meglio gioventù* echoes such films in the Italian tradition as *Rocco e i suoi fratelli* (*Rocco and His Brothers*, 1960) and *Novecento* (*1900*, 1976). It spans a period from the mid-1960s to the new century as it follows the lives of the two main characters, Matteo and Nicola Carati, and their Roman family.

The film begins with the brothers as university students, Matteo in literature and Nicola in medicine, both keen to improve society. It registers public events and historical processes and jumps around the peninsula and islands of Italy (with two significant digressions to northern Europe) as the brothers' paths inevitably diverge. The handsome and sexually ambiguous Matteo, disappointed with his inability to help Giorgia, a mentally ill woman who reappears at intervals in the narrative, opts to join the army and then the police. He becomes all but estranged from his family and, incapable of emerging from his carapace of loneliness, eventually commits suicide, ignorant of the fact that the beautiful Mirella is pregnant with his son. If *La meglio gioventù* asserts Matteo's career and life choices as symptomatic of his frustration, then the film invests heavily in the tenacious activism of his brother Nicola. After medical school, Nicola becomes a campaigning psychiatrist and survives the desertion of his first partner—Giulia, who abandons him and their daughter to engage in clandestine armed struggle against the state—to help Giorgia, and to find happiness in his declining years with the same Mirella whose son has been deprived of a father by the suicide of Matteo.

On Italian television, *La meglio gioventù* attracted nearly 8 million viewers and provoked massive discussion and celebration in the Italian press. One (non-film) magazine, *Il diario del mese*, devoted its entire December 2003 edition to the heroes of the 1960s generation portrayed in the film, while the website of the left-leaning daily *la Repubblica* made space for dozens of testimonial accounts by those who found their experience echoed in the tale of the two brothers. The political context in Italy at the time is key to understanding the rapturous response to the miniseries.

Following the demise in the early 1990s of the Italian First Republic (the political system in place since the late 1940s), and the collapse or fragmentation of the parties that had been most powerful within that system (especially the Christian Democrats), a new right came to prominence in Italy. This was led, of course, by Silvio Berlusconi and his center-right party Forza Italia, but it also included the federalist/secessionist Lega Nord as well as the Alleanza Nazionale, the reincarnation as a post-Fascist center-right party of the neofascist Movimento Sociale Italiano. The entrance into the political mainstream and accession to power of these parties was accompanied by a revisionist attitude to the history of unified Italy, focusing especially on the civil war that occurred in northern Italy in the latter years of the Second World War and on other moments of internecine contestation in Italian society.

The late 1960s and early 1970s were one of those periods. Internationally, this was a time of protest and widespread aspiration to social and political change, particularly among the young. Nowhere was this truer than of Italy, which saw a student and worker movement agitate for social equality and reform, for the control of resources by workers rather than capitalists, and sometimes even for revolution. In pursuit of this last goal, some made the move, as the 1970s progressed, to the sort of violent direct action that is described as terrorist. Was this move to terrorism a betrayal of the protest movement's democratic ideals, or was it the inevitable outcome of a wholesale rejection of the status quo? The second interpretation came to be widespread with the rise to power of the new right, and the aspirations and activities of the 1960s generation were tainted by association.

La meglio gioventù offers the alternative, positive view of that generation: for the makers of the film, political violence was a betrayal of the movement's hopes and ideals.[2] So it is that the film's narrative and affective investment is in the modest but determined reformism of Nicola, who is seen to work *within* state institutions—especially the health service and legal systems—rather than try to abolish them from without, and to be effective and successful in doing so. In its paean to Nicola's cautious tenacity, the film pays homage to a hero who might ordinarily be unsung.

Sandro Petraglia and Stefano Rulli, scriptwriters of *La meglio gioventù* and themselves quintessentially of the 1960s protest generation, described their undertaking in the film as follows:

> We wrote *La meglio gioventù* for Carlo, for Gioia, for Stefano, for Giovanna, for Rico and Romeo, for Ely and Piero, for Sergio who has passed on but will always be with us, and for many others who were twenty in 1968. They're our companions from that time: they don't bother with gossip, they don't appear on TV, they're not famous. They went to help after the floods in Florence [in 1966]; they hitchhiked their way towards the North Cape [in Norway]; they read furiously and debated just as furiously; they fell in love; and they went to the cinema. They got angry and they said as much. Sometimes they shouted as much. Because—sometimes—you have to shout to make yourself heard. They still do so. They work in the schools, in the health centers, in the courts, in the libraries, in the hospitals, in the factories. They keep the best of this country on its feet, getting their hands dirty saving the good things from the mud, today just as they did in Florence in '66: loyalty, consistency, courage, and determination. We wrote it for them, *La meglio gioventù*. And for ourselves among them.[3]

La meglio gioventù addresses and celebrates those protagonists of civil society, including the scriptwriters themselves, known as the reflexive middle classes: "those [Italians] who had traversed the dramatic experiences of the late '60s and early '70s, and had emerged the other end neither in total despair nor with total cynicism."[4] In the address to the reflexive middle classes, *La meglio gioventù* is unabashedly melodramatic, while its makers' formal choices are as self-effacing in the service of the tale as befits the film's broadcast venue on the most watched and most conservative of the three Italian state television channels. Marco Tullio Giordana, director of *La meglio gioventù*, is highly regarded in the anglophone academy because his work tends to deal admirably with themes of political or historical importance. But the consolatory tone and televisual aesthetic of *La meglio gioventù* means that it has an ambiguous status in Italian film studies, which prefers to celebrate formally ambitious or markedly authorial products (films that bear the identifiable stamp of a renowned director). David Forgacs, in an otherwise sympathetic account of *La meglio gioventù*, regrets that the film slides "into a sentimentalism that blunts the political edge of its chronicle of a generation."[5] Actually, one might suggest that its sentimentality is essential to the politics of *La meglio gioventù*: the film employs a nostalgic and middlebrow mode in order to address its audience as a *constituency*, as a group aware of itself in political terms.[6] It formulates its account of recent Italian history on behalf of this intended audience, and hopes to reproduce it by articulating and celebrating its experience.

The reproduction of the reflexive constituency is figured symbolically in the film by the reconfiguration of the nuclear family around Nicola, Mirella, and Andrea, the son Mirella has conceived with Matteo. Indeed, political reproduction and familial reconfiguration are enabled by Matteo's purgative suicide: political disappointment has been invested in Matteo in order to be expunged. His choice of career as soldier and policeman is shown in the film to be pathological (even if the institutions of army and police are not represented unsympathetically), a distortion of his early idealism into an evasion of personal and political responsibility. The doomed Matteo's emotional intransigence and alienation are mirrored in the fate of Giulia, whose choice of clandestinity and terrorist action is likewise implied to be pathological. The film's inability to investigate her choices signals the disavowals involved in providing a sharable myth of the recent past to the constituency addressed and celebrated by the film.

I have characterized the aesthetics of *La meglio gioventù* as self-effacing but I do not mean that its makers' formal decisions were anything but deliberate. Consider the employment of extended takes made with dolly or crane: for example, the shot along the portico of the Uffizi, an hour and fifteen minutes into the film, that follows the line of young volunteers rescuing precious books from the Florence 1966 flood (Figure 26.1). The shot emphasizes the communal effort of cultural salvage even as the line is shown to culminate in Nicola, narrative avatar of selfless "best of youth." The preservation of Italian heritage, both cultural and environmental, is a key theme in *La meglio gioventù*—Nicola saves books from the flood, his sister works against industrial pollution, his daughter studies the restoration of frescoes—and a good part of its political charge is its own heritage appeal, an aspect of the flattering address to a reflexive middle class proud of the look and legacy of the best of Italy.[7]

FIGURE 26.1 *Saving treasures from the flood in* La meglio gioventù.

FIGURE 26.2 *The uncanny love triangle staged in a long take in* La meglio gioventù.

FIGURE 26.3 *A dialogue in two-shot in* La meglio gioventù.

The fifty-second take outside the Uffizi also presages the reuniting of Nicola with his brother when Matteo arrives (in a subsequent shot) with a unit of soldiers to aid the salvage operation.[8] Some hours later in the film another long take heralds Matteo's reappearance when his ghost materializes to expedite the union between Nicola and Mirella (Figure 26.2). The staging of this late scene represents the development and culmination of a formal device employed throughout *La meglio gioventù*, in which conversations are filmed in two-shot (rather than the more typical shot/reverse shot) with one of the characters located behind the other (Figure 26.3). The tableau staggering of the figures (and not their division through the editing) seems to declare that the individual always has others "behind" him or her, and it stresses that the tale is one of relationships rather than monads. The staggered two-shot becomes a group shot in the scene with Nicola, Mirella, and the undead Matteo; significantly accompanied by music from François Truffaut's *Jules et Jim* (*Jules and Jim*, 1962), it is one of the more candid examples in Italian cinema of the homosocial configuration whereby a woman is the token of exchange between men and their heterosexual alibi.[9] As Catherine O'Rawe has argued of *La meglio gioventù* and other "middlebrow commitment" films by the scriptwriters Petraglia and Rulli, the erotic triangle routes narrative interest *through* the woman but it never rests *with* her, and the story asserts "the fundamental irrelevance of women" to politics.[10]

It is important to note this scene's precise place in the narrative: it ends the film's penultimate sequence and releases a coda that grants the tale a circular structure and sense of extra-political and ahistorical closure. In order to account for that sense of closure, some mention should be made of the ravishing long shots that introduce each episode and location in the film, images that thematize the urban and environmental heritage of Italy even as they function as narrative markers. We are shown, for example, the crowded historical cityscape of Rome and the bourgeois city rooftops of Turin, while the landscapes range from cultivated Tuscan hinterland to the natural splendor of the Aeolian Islands. Such vista shots offer a collage

FIGURE 26.4 *Basiluzzo, one of the Aeolian Islands, in* La meglio gioventù.

vision of a picturesque Italy that represents the national heritage that the film is fighting to preserve. But if the uncanny geological phenomena of Basiluzzo (Figure 26.4) and the Stromboli volcano seem beyond history, then the film's Norwegian landscapes are "not Italy" when represented in two trips, the first by Nicola as a young man, and later by Mirella and Matteo's son, Andrea, when he realizes Nicola's abortive plan to reach Norway's North Cape in the sequence that ends *La meglio gioventù*.[11] The circular reprise of Nicola's trip north and the closing words of the film (spoken by Andrea), "everything is truly beautiful," place the narrative in a space beyond history.[12] Perhaps it was felt that such a suspension represented the only way to provide, at the time, a consolidating memory of a still fresh and painful past.

Notes

1 I will use the term "film" rather than miniseries for convenience, but it is important to bear in mind that *La meglio gioventù* was made for television rather than the cinema.

2 For more on this theme, see Luzzi, *A Cinema of Poetry*, 154–58.

3 Petraglia and Rulli, *La meglio gioventù*, 295.

4 Ginsborg, *Italy and Its Discontents*, 120. The term "reflexive" indicates awareness of economic and cultural privilege as well as a reformist concern with society and the state.

5 Forgacs, "Our Friends from Turin."

6 For an analysis of the film's address to an Italian left-wing constituency, see the section "The Terrorist and the Olive Tree" in O'Leary, *Tragedia all'italiana*, 207–27.

7 We can group *La meglio gioventù* with films like *Piazza delle Cinque Lune* (*Five Moons Plaza*, 2003), *Romanzo criminale* (2005) and *Tre fratelli* (*Three Borthers*, Francesco Rosi, 1981) which, like it, employ ravishing images of Italy that "owe as much to the iconography of advertising, tourism and the heritage industry, as to the inheritance of neorealism" (Wood, *Italian Cinema*, 198).

8 There may be a concealed edit halfway through the shot when the camera passes close to a pillar.

9 "Heterosexual alibi" is a term used in gender criticism to indicate a trope or character (for example, a female love interest who "comes between" two men) that functions to "guarantee" the heterosexuality of a given relationship or character—or at least to disavow a possible homosexual reading.

10 O'Rawe, "Brothers in Arms," 157. O'Rawe's important article is also sensitive to the implications of the sibling relationship as vehicle and metaphor for history in *La meglio gioventù* and other films.

11 The use of "another country" to close the film recalls the ending of *La seconda volta* (*The Second Time*, 1995), another film that deals with Italy's recent experience of political discord and violence.

12 It allows, as O'Rawe puts it, "a suspension of the political, and the potential erasure of the intervening events" ("Brothers in Arms," 161).

Bibliography

Forgacs, David. "Our Friends from Turin." *Sight and Sound* 76 (2004), http://old.bfi.org.uk/sightandsound/feature/76. Accessed April 13, 2014.

Ginsborg, Paul. *Italy and Its Discontents: Family, State, Society*. London: Allen Lane, 2001.

Luzzi, Joseph. *A Cinema of Poetry: Aesthetics of the Italian Art Film*. Baltimore: Johns Hopkins Press, 2014.

O'Leary, Alan. *Tragedia all'italiana: Italian Cinema and Italian Terrorisms, 1970-2010*. Oxford: Peter Lang, 2011.

O'Rawe, Catherine. "Brothers in Arms: Middlebrow *Impegno* and Homosocial Relations in the Cinema of Petraglia and Rulli." In *Intellectual Communities and Partnerships in Italy and Europe*. Ed. Danielle Hipkins. Oxford: Peter Lang, 2012.

Petraglia, Sandro and Stefano Rulli. *La meglio gioventù*. Rome: RAI Eri, 2004.

Wood, Mary P. *Italian Cinema*. Oxford: Berg, 2005.

Filmography

Jules et Jim, Dir. François Truffaut. France: Cinédis. 1962.
La meglio gioventù, Dir. Marco Tullio Giordana. Italy: 01 Distribution. 2003.
La seconda volta, Dir. Mimmo Calopresti. Italy: Rizzoli Corriere della Sera Home Video (RCS). 1995.
Novecento, Dir. Bernardo Bertolucci. Italy: 20th Century Fox. 1976.
Piazza delle Cinque Lune, Dir. Renzo Martinelli. Italy: Istituto Luce. 2003.
Rocco e i suoi fratelli, Dir. Luchino Visconti. Italy: Titanus Distribuzione. 1960.
Romanzo criminale, Dir. Michele Placido. Italy: Warner Bros. 2005.
Tre fratelli, Dir. Francesco Rosi. Italy: Gaumont Italia. 1981.

PART FIVE

Behind the Scenes

27

Sound and Soundtrack
in Italian Cinema

Monica Facchini

A mother who sees her son dying in her arms will desperately cry. . . . Lips uttering the true words of love and pain will move the audiences.[1]

With these words, the Italian film producer Stefano Pittaluga welcomed the advent of sound in film in 1929. As his statement suggests, Pittaluga considered the new technological addition to cinema to be a "truer" and more effective means to convey emotions to film audiences. With sound, cinema would sing and talk of pain and love, of feelings that until that moment had been delivered only through the actors' facial expressions and toneless descriptive captions. And indeed, although the advent of sound would eventually revolutionize the aesthetic of films and radically change our way of conceiving cinema, the first use of sound in Italian films mostly fulfilled the function formerly assigned to music accompaniment in silent films.

In silent films, music and sound were employed to illustrate the images on the screen and magnify the inner feelings of the characters. The first Italian composer who committed to writing original music score for a film was Pietro Mascagni (1863–1945), best known for his operas and his greatest success *Cavalleria rusticana* (1860). When Mascagni decided to compose the music for *Rapsodia satanica* (*Satan's Rhapsody*, 1915), directed by Nino Oxilia, he did not simply adapt a preexisting score to the film, but actively collaborated with the film director. In so doing his music would aptly interpret the inner feelings and emotions of the actors and the actions on the screen, "blend[ing] each gesture in a homogeneous arc that only music was able to organize."[2] Unfortunately, the collaboration between Mascagni and Oxilia was so troubled that the composer decided not to write for films anymore.

With the advent of sound films, the role of sound and music was not much different. The first Italian sound film to be released was Gennaro Righelli's *La canzone dell'amore* (*The Song of Love*) screened in Rome on October 6, 1930. The plot, based on Luigi Pirandello's short story "In silenzio" ("Silence," 1923), recounted the story of a troubled love with a romantic happy ending. Despite the modest budget and the poor quality of the acting, directing, and sound, the film was a great success, thanks to the excellent cinematography, the tear-jerking plot, and above all the melody of the songs, written by Cesare Andrea Bixio, Armando Fragna, and Pietro Sassoli. As Pittaluga had predicted and intended, music in Righelli's film "moved the audiences," by singing the love and the pain of the characters on the screen. "The film struck a deep chord in the hearts of moviegoers," Gian Piero Brunetta points out, "and was met with enthusiasm and the sense of marvel that always accompanies the birth of a new technological miracle."[3]

Three years later, Mario Camerini directed a film that brought him great success, *Gli uomini che mascalzoni . . .* (*What Scoundrels Men Are!* 1933), starring a young Vittorio De Sica. The film's success was due not only to the director's light style and narrative but also to the novelty of staging everyday people and proletarian characters, who eventually earned the love of their beloved and a respectable position in society. As in Righelli's *The Song of Love*, in Camerini's film the strategic use of love songs was crucial for its success: the film launched one of the best-known Italian love songs, *Parlami d'amore Mariù* (*Speak to Me of Love, Maria*), written by Cesare Andrea Bixio and Ennio Neri, and sung in the film by De Sica.

Besides music, the most striking element of the first sound films was undoubtedly the advent of the "spoken word," welcomed with enthusiasm by many directors and audiences, but also seen as a menace to the specificities of (silent) cinema and the power of visual language by some film critics.[4] The use of spoken language acquired a special significance in Italian films, because for the first time it was possible to reproduce on the screen the linguistic heterogeneity of the nation. Conscious of the variety of Italian dialects and regional accents, as well as of the influence of foreign words on the national language, screenwriters worked in two directions: on the one hand, they aimed at showing off Italy's wealth of linguistic possibilities (even when this meant transgressing the regime's promotion of a unified national language); on the other, they created an accessible language for daily communication that soon would become a model for interpersonal and professional relationships in society.[5]

The first masterful example of the employment of regional accents and dialect in film is Alessandro Blasetti's *1860: I mille di Garibadi* (*1860: The Thousand of Garibaldi*, 1934), a film on Garibaldi's military campaign in Sicily interwoven with the stories of local peasants who participated in it. Although the Fascist government prohibited the use of dialects, Blasetti's film passed muster with the censor, because his political use of different Italian idioms "encouraged audience identification and highlighted the national scope and scale of the enterprise of Italian unification."[6]

The use of regional accents and dialects played an even greater role as a way for neorealist cinema to set itself against Fascist film production and represent reality in a more accurate manner. The most extreme sound and linguistic experiment in cinema in this regard was easily Luchino Visconti's *La terra trema* (1948), inspired by Giovanni Verga's *I Malavoglia* (*The House by the Medlar Tree*, 1881).

The first sound novelty in Visconti's *La terra trema* concerns the use of direct sound at a time when the general tendency was post-synchronization. While, indeed, Italian films were usually shot with direct sound recording, the original soundtrack was not used in the finished film because of its poor quality. It rather served as a guide-track at the dubbing stage. In some exceptions, films were even shot with no sound, because of the higher costs incurred by direct recording at the developing stage. This was true in the case of Roberto Rossellini's *Roma città aperta* (*Rome, Open City*, 1945) and De Sica's *Ladri di biciclette* (*Bycicle Thieves*, 1948).[7] The use of post-synchronization was dictated by different factors. During the Fascist regime, it served the national cause of promoting a standardized Italian language (actors' strong regional accents were replaced by the proper diction of the actors who did the dubbing), while in neorealist cinema it helped meet the low budget of film productions. However, post-synchronization continued to be a tendency in Italian cinema even later and was employed to pursue artistic effects, as in the films of Michelangelo Antonioni, Federico Fellini, and Pier Paolo Pasolini. In *La terra trema*, the use of direct sound and the Sicilian dialect was both an aesthetic and political choice for Visconti.

As the opening titles announce, the Sicilian fishermen in the film speak their dialect because "they do not know another language to express their rebellion, suffering, and hope. In Sicily, Italian is not the language spoken by the poor."[8] The use of Sicilian dialect in *La terra trema* is not a mere naturalistic element aiming at faithfully representing the reality of the South, but rather serves a political motive, expressing the sociocultural separation between subaltern realities and dominant cultures in Italy.

However, Visconti's linguistic choice also has aesthetic purposes, grounded in his personal fascination with the sounds of the Sicilian dialect.[9] In *La terra trema*, indeed, the director aimed at recovering a lost ancient language, a "religious and fatal tone of ancient tragedy,"[10] and at turning the dialect of the Aci Trezza fishermen into a mythical perspective and an original music score.[11] To this end, Visconti worked on dialect on different levels and stages, hearing it from the local fishermen and polishing its sounds and expressions into a musical language. The result was so different from the real local dialect that the Italian film critic Pio Baldelli argued that if it was true that Italian was not the language of Sicilian fishermen, neither was Visconti's language.[12]

A talented composer trained in cello, Visconti had excellent technical-musical skills and knowledge that inform each of his cinematic and theatrical works. Music plays a crucial role in his films not merely as accompaniment of the images but also as a leading element that guides the characters, sets the environments, gives rhythm to actions, and determines events. As the music scholar and Visconti's niece, Cristina Gastel Chiarelli, emphasizes, Visconti's cinema is imbued with his love of music and particularly, of melodrama. "I love melodrama—he used to say—because it is at the border between theater and life."[13] His love for this musical genre is visible in the ways in which his films obey melodramatic conventions: a screenplay structured in "acts," characters trapped in fixed roles, dialogues inextricably connected with music and silence, and extremely spectacular situations and emotions represented through an operatic mise-en-scène of the events.[14]

The most conspicuous example of his melodramatic style is certainly *Senso* (1954), a film in which the love affair between the Italian Countess Livia Serpieri and the Austrian lieutenant Franz Mahler intersects with the historical events of the Italian Risorgimento.[15] Inspired by Camillo Boito's novella of the same name, *Senso* is according to Lino Miccichè, "read, narratively structured, and stylistically represented as an operatic *score*."[16] In this film, more than any other, Visconti notably merges music and life, melodrama and history, as the analysis of the very first sequence demonstrates.

The film opens with a long shot of the stage at the Teatro La Fenice in Venice in 1866, during a performance of the duet scene between Leonora and Manrico from Giuseppe Verdi's *Il trovatore* (*The Troubadour*, 1853). While the story on the stage unfolds, the film follows the offstage actions of Livia and Franz. The dialogues, emotions, extreme situations, dramatic acting, costumes, and settings on the opera stage all reflect and match the dialogues, the characters, and the environments in the rest of the film. This entangled connection between opera and the film story is immediately suggested by the superimposition of the opening film credits on the performance on stage.

In the first sequence of *Senso*, music performs many functions: it introduces the characters on and off stage, accompanies the romantic and political themes in both the opera performance and the opera theater, and illuminates the main characters' actions and personalities. In the first images that open the film, the duet between Leonora and Manrico (*Ah, sì ben mio*) has reached its climax, with the two characters on stage giving in to their passion and foreshadowing the love story that will soon be presented off stage. But the idyllic moment is quickly interrupted by the arrival of Manrico's army bearing the tragic news of his mother's impending death. Manrico's determination to save his mother is accompanied by the film titles that inform the spectators that the opera on the screen is taking place in Venice in the Spring 1866 when "the war for the Italian liberation [from Austrian rule] is imminent." The juxtaposition of the opera performance and the film titles once again hints at the melodramatic nature of the film and the close connection between the love story we are about to witness off stage and the political history of the Italian Risorgimento.[17] The stage actor's direct address to the theater audience during his performance of *Di quella pira l'orrendo fuoco* visually reinforces this connection between opera and politics. When he finally exhorts his soldiers to prepare for the battle, the choral *All'armi, all'armi* becomes a clear exhortation for the nineteenth-century theater audience to get ready for the battle against the Austrian invader. It is only at this point that the camera finally pans on the theater parterre and balconies, underscoring the political implications of the opera's performance. Verdi's aria also introduces the first film character, the Marquis Roberto Ussoni, Livia's cousin and a fervent patriot, who is ready to risk his life in the name of the Italian independence from the Austrians. He scans the theater with a circumspect look, until his fellow patriots shout their slogans against the Austrian soldiers and launch white, red, and green propaganda leaflets and tricolor flower bouquets from the balconies. The protest becomes more and more vehement until Ussoni, provoked by the derisory words of lieutenant Mahler, challenges him to a duel. Determined to help him, Livia invites Mahler to her balcony: her intercession for her cousin is once again visually and aurally echoed by Leonora's performance on stage expressing her own plans to save Manrico (*Salvarlo io potrò forse*; *Deh pietosa, gli arreca i miei sospiri*). Leonora's performance, portrayed in crisp focus in the balcony's archway next to Livia, acts as a mirror to the countess's actions and words. Opera finally meets life in the dialogue between Franz and Livia. When he asks her whether she likes opera, she tellingly replies: "I like opera very much, but not when it happens off stage."[18] While Livia's words aim at discouraging the lieutenant to accept Ussoni's challenge to a duel, they presage the tragic consequences of her own melodramatic passion for Franz and her consequent dismissal of her political responsibilities.

The ensuing love story between Livia and Franz is presented on screen in a clear operatic style: the use of high-angle camera shots reproduces the gaze of a theater audience from their balconies, the grandiosely decorated interiors and fairy-tale Venice outdoors replicate the stage-painted backgrounds, and the melodramatic acting of Alida Valli and Farley Granger recalls the passionate characters from Verdi's and Giacomo Puccini's operas.[19] And yet Visconti confines opera's music to the opening sequence of the film, preferring the symphonic music by the Austrian composer Anton Bruckner

(1824–96) to accompany and unravel the romantic and political webs of Livia and Franz's love affair. While the Austrian lieutenant's name in the film, Franz Mahler (Remigio Ruz in Boito's original novella), echoes the famous nineteenth-century Austrian composer Gustav Mahler (1860–1911), Visconti would employ Bruckner's Symphony No. 7 as a counterpoint to the initial patriotic and nationalistic music of Verdi. A controversial figure during his time, Bruckner was greatly admired by the next generation of composers, including his friend Mahler, to whom he is often compared. However, despite their musical similarities, the history of the popularity of these two composers reveals wide contrasts. A well-renowned conductor and composer during his lifetime, Gustav Mahler and his music was neglected and even banned in much of Europe during the Nazi era. Bruckner, by contrast, became a cultural icon for National Socialism, culminating with the installation of his bust in the Walhalla in 1937, at the site honoring the titans of Germanic culture. Hitler's preference for Bruckner's music was determined by its "Teutonic aspects," as highlighted by Friedrich W. Herzog in 1934, and by his own identification with the composer, who shared his same Austrian and peasant origins.[20] Whereas Mahler's music gained wide popularity again only after 1945, Bruckner's music would be associated with German occupation for much of Europe throughout the late 1940s and 1950s.[21]

Visconti was certainly aware of the political repercussions of Bruckner's music in the postwar era, and his use of the Austrian composer's symphony in *Senso* therefore acquired an ideological value, commenting and amplifying the various layers of interpretations of the images and actions on screen. The sudden musical change, from the Italian patriotic Verdi's *Il trovatore* to the Austrian Bruckner's symphony with its ominous echoes for the 1954 European film audience, unveils the political message underneath the melodramatic love story between Livia and Franz. Livia's private love for the Austrian enemy corresponds to her (and her Italian aristocratic class's) betrayal of the liberation cause. "I'm like my cousin . . . a true Italian," says Livia to Franz, but, as Roger Hillman noted, "the music says otherwise: we hear not Verdi but Bruckner, signaling the gradual erosion of both her personal and national allegiances."[22]

The elaborate musical editing in *Senso*, and in other Visconti films, was the product of the skillful work of Nino Rota.[23] An extremely prolific composer (he was only eleven when he composed his first oratorio, *L'infanzia di San Giovanni Battista* (*The Childhood of Saint John the Baptist*), Nino Rota graduated from the National Academy of Santa Cecilia in Rome, attended the Curtis Institute in Philadelphia, and earned a *laurea* in Italian literature at the University of Milan. He composed symphonies, sacred and chamber music, concertos, and music scores for films. Before his collaboration with Visconti, Rota worked with many Italian and American film directors, such as Raffaello Matarazzo, Mario Soldati, Luigi Zampa, Mario Camerini, Alberto Lattuada, Mario Monicelli, and Francis Ford Coppola, receiving numerous awards, including the Academy Award for Best Original Score for *The Godfather: Part II* (1974). But his fame in cinema is mainly related to his prolific collaboration with Federico Fellini.

Fellini and Rota worked very closely together. Fellini usually had a clear idea about the music that should accompany his films, mostly music from his childhood or variety shows. Rota adapted Fellini's musical ideas and turned them into original pieces that went well beyond the images, unveiling narrative cues and symbolic meanings. As Sergio Miceli maintains, music in Fellini's cinema is a physical presence within the filmic narration, acting as a real character and contributing to the film's multilayered structure and content: "If there is a way to conceive of a kind of cinema in which [music] proves to be *indispensable* (not even as a comment, but rather as an *actress*), that is Fellini's cinema."[24]

In Fellini's films, music is characterized by elaborate synchronic and diachronic variations and an enigmatic use of diegetic and extra-diegetic music. Repetitions and themes often become leitmotifs to mark the development of a character and reveal meaning beyond the images and dialogues, as in the last scene of *La strada* (1954),[25] or act as a nonverbal moral statement, as in *Le notti di Cabiria* (*Nights of Cabiria*, 1957).[26] But it is with *La dolce vita* (1960) and *8 1/2* (1963) that Fellini/Rota's music best expresses the world of Fellini's cinema: spectacular and grotesque, burlesque and nostalgic, lighthearted and bitter, always blurring the boundaries between dreams, memories, and everyday life. All this is reflected in Rota's music through a combination of motifs from the circus, variety theaters, 1930s melodramas, Charlie Chaplin's cinema, cartoons, and musicals. Music exalts the ambiguity of the images and actions on the screen, and unveils the many intricate levels of the filmic narration toward a final synthesis, as in the last sequence of *8 1/2*. Here, the circus music magically transcends the question of its diegetic and non-diegetic sources, imposing itself as a part of the spectacle (diegetically), while revealing and commenting on it and its complicated relations with real life (non-diegetically).[27] In this scene, music is not just a character: it is Fellini himself with his world of dreams and memory and his conception of cinema and life.

As Maurice Jaubert claimed, music in film is that "unreal element that bends the game and breaks the 'primordial realism' [of cinema]."[28] Jaubert's words well describe the role of music in Fellini's films. While music in neorealism never had any autonomous expressive power, and was instead used to support the verisimilitude of the visual narration, Fellini and Rota's music emerges as a poetic stance, transcending the limits of a realist narrative dimension and reaching toward a symbolic realm made of ancestral and irrational values.[29]

Denying the traditional use of music in films, Michelangelo Antonioni also elaborated an original poetic use of sound, and more specifically of noises, aiming at defying the real and our perception of it.

> Music accompaniment in its traditional function has no place in cinema
> anymore. . . . It is true that there are . . . "musical" moments . . . when it
> is necessary to detach from reality and force it. In these moments music
> has its function. In other moments it is necessary to use noises, even if
> not used in a realistic way, but rather as sound effects, in a poetic spirit.[30]

In his early films, Antonioni still relied on a traditional use of music. In his
documentary *N.U.—Nettezza urbana* (1948), music by Giovanni Fusco and
the prelude by Johann S. Bach accompany and comment on the images of the
street cleaners. In later films beginning with *Il grido* (1957), and even more
with *L'avventura* (1960), Antonioni largely reduced commentary-style music
and, finally, eliminated it completely in *Deserto rosso* (*Red Desert*, 1964).
Here, the director replaced a more traditional use of music with a symbolic
and interpretive use of noises that are employed throughout the film almost
as an "extension of the central nervous system" of the protagonist.[31]

The initial scene of *Red Desert* is a clear example of this. The images of
factories and colored smoke are accompanied by industrial noises, obtained
by the use of electronic sounds (Vittorio Gelmetti), and a soprano voice
singing a wordless song (composed by Giovanni Fusco and sung by his
daughter, Cecilia Fusco). It is only in the following scene, when an electronic
whistling invades the private space of Giuliana's house in the middle of the
night, that their hermeneutic and diegetic function appears clear. As Gelmetti
explained, they are "the sounds of the subconscious."[32] While the electronic
sounds seem to signal the imminence of Giuliana's mental breakdowns, the
disembodied female singing that will reappear later to accompany Giuliana's
narration of an idyllic story of a young girl on the beach (possibly a memory
of her childhood), seems rather to represent Giuliana's longing for a realm
far from the industrial city.[33] Through the use of electronic sound for both
the industrial site and Giuliana's troubled mental state, Antonioni comments
on the rise of the new industrial society of the 1960s and its effects on the
Italian people.

If in *Red Desert* the use of noises and sounds outside the real provides
a key to interpreting the character's emotional state and social uneasiness,
in Antonioni's *Blow-Up* (1966) they go as far as to defy "reality" and our
own perception of it. The story revolves around a young photographer who,
by repeatedly enlarging (or "blowing up") his photographs of two lovers in
a park, believes he has captured a murder on film. But he will never know
whether the crime actually happened, and in the final sequence of the film
he will have the ultimate proof of the deceptiveness of his perceptions of
the real, when he "hears" the sound of a fictitious tennis ball volleyed by
a group of mimes. As Jurij Lotman states, if "in the beginning he did not
see what was happening . . . in the end he heard what was not happening,"
confirming Antonioni's idea that reality escapes us.[34] The choice of an artist
as the protagonist of the film is not irrelevant in this regard, since it raises

the entire story on a meta-cinematic level, where the question of what is real and what is not is subordinate to artistic representation of it and, in this case, to the potentialities of visual and sound elements of cinema. In *Red Desert* and *Blow-Up* more than in any other film, Antonioni epitomizes and carries to an extreme the essence of what Michel Chion defines as "acousmatic sounds," that is, "those sounds and voices that are not completely inside or definitely outside [and] that are our main interest: because it is perhaps through these sounds and voices meandering on the screen that the power of cinema comes into place."[35]

It is not by chance that Pier Paolo Pasolini chose *Red Desert* as one of the most relevant examples of what he would call "cinema of poetry." As Pasolini states, with *Red Desert*:

> Antonioni has freed his most deeply felt moment: he has finally been able to represent the world seen through his eyes, *because he has substituted in toto for the worldview of a neurotic his own delirious view of aesthetics.* . . . It is clear that the "free indirect point-of-view shot" is a pretext, and Antonioni took advantage of it, possibly arbitrarily, to allow himself the greatest poetic freedom.[36]

The free indirect point-of-view shot is a key element of Pasolini's elaboration of a "cinema of poetry." Drawing on the free indirect discourse used in literature to merge two different voices, the narrator's and the character's, Pasolini advocated a free indirect point-of-view shot in cinema, through which the director could appropriate the gaze of his/her characters to express his/her own view. But while Antonioni selected his "pretextual characters" from his own social class (these "exquisite 'flowers of the bourgeoisie'" share the director's cultural, linguistic, and psychological characteristics),[37] Pasolini's use of the free indirect point-of-view shot aimed at portraying the worldview through the gaze of the sub-proletariat that until then had been represented only through the mythicized and paternalistic gaze of bourgeois directors.

According to Pasolini, it is exactly in this "contamination"—in the "collision" between the two profoundly different souls of the bourgeois director and the sub-proletarian character—that poetry arises.[38]

Pasolini's "heretical" poetic choices often earned him the disapproval of film critics as well as accusations of defamation, of the State's religion, especially when the director-poet associated the images of brutal violence and vulgar pettiness of marginal worlds with the highest forms of Christian iconography and sacred music. The most exemplary case of his poetic contamination in cinema was undoubtedly his use of Johann S. Bach's *Passion According to Saint Matthew* in his first film *Accattone* (1961), to accompany the images of the savage fight between a pimp (Accattone) and his brother-in-law. The contrapuntal association of sound and image in this scene was harshly criticized by film and music experts of the time. But as Pasolini explained, his decision to juxtapose those brutal images with such elevated music obeyed his intentions to contaminate two different views, the sub-proletarian and the bourgeois intellectual, and to sacralize and eternalize those marginal realities that were disappearing in the new capitalistic society. While Gelmetti commented on Pasolini's "dehistoricized use" of Bach's music,[39] the German composer Hans Werner Henze recognized in it the deepest understanding of Bach's *Passion*, which aims at empathizing with human misery, forgiving it, and crying for it.[40] Music was certainly not the only stylistic device that Pasolini employed to express his poetic approach to cinema and his "epical-religious" worldview, but it was nonetheless "the focal element, the sensational element, almost the exterior trappings of the internal stylistic approach, of a given way of shooting, of seeing things, of feeling the character."[41]

Far from what he defined as a "horizontal application" of music to the visual sequence of a film—that is, a music that accompanies the images only "on the surface," following their pace and adding rhythmic values—Pasolini applied music to his films "vertically," an approach technically similar to the horizontal one, but having the function of acting upon the meaning of the images. It is through the vertical application of music, Pasolini argued, that it is possible to add real depth to the illusory flatness of the visual world. "The musical source—which is not recognizable on the screen and starts from a physical 'somewhere else' that is 'deep' by its nature—breaks through the flat, or deceptively profound, images of the screen, opening them to the confused and borderless depth of life."[42] But music in Pasolini's films is not just explanatory; it is also deeply emotional, thanks to its capacity to "conceptualize the emotions . . . and sentimentalize the concepts," as confirmed by his use of Bach to comment on a world that no longer was.[43]

Six years after *Accattone*, Gillo Pontecorvo would use the same notes from Bach's *Passion* for the initial sequence of *La battaglia di Algeri* (*The Battle of Algiers*, 1966). As in Pasolini's film, Pontecorvo's use of Bach's mourning music sets up a strong counterpoint to the violent images it accompanies of a group of French soldiers torturing an Algerian man. Bach's music in this scene not only betrays Pontecorvo's sympathy for the Algerian cause but also serves as a strong comment on the two sides of European civilization, represented both by its artistic production of elevated and compassionate music and by the brutal violence of its colonizing forces.

In the rest of the film, music serves different functions. The use of the same mourning theme for the Algerian and the French victims of the battle, for example, is intended to deliver the director's condemnation of any form of violence, whether perpetrated by the French or Algerian fighters. In other instances, sound serves to convey the film's inner story that cannot be told with visual images or dialogues.[44] This is most evident in a scene in which three Algerian women disguise themselves as European to pass unnoticed through the French checkpoints and plant their bombs in the

French quarter of the city. Originally the scene contained a joke and some light conversation among the women, but Pontecorvo was not happy with this plan and decided to cut all the dialogues and accompany the scene with only a percussion piece. The result was a very tense scene. While the images tell the story of three women making themselves up in French fashion, the music reveals the story behind the actions, that of the Algerian fight for independence. Pontecorvo's percussion motif, recorded before the beginning of the film and used in many scenes, was so impressive that even the eminent Ennio Morricone, who worked with him on the soundtrack for the film, has often praised it.[45]

The Battle of Algiers is only one of many films for which Morricone has composed the music score. Born in 1928 and a graduate of the National Academy of Santa Cecilia in Rome, Morricone is a trumpet player, composer, orchestrator, and conductor. He has composed more than a hundred classical pieces and served as a successful arranger for RCA. But he is best known worldwide for his original film scores, composing over 500 scores for cinema and television, and receiving numerous awards, including the David di Donatello, BAFTA, Golden Globe, Grammy, AFI, and two Academy Awards (the Honor Academy Award in 2007 and Best Original Score Award in 2016). Morricone has contributed music to a great variety of films and has collaborated with a number of film directors, including Pontecorvo, Pasolini, Bernardo Bertolucci, Dario Argento, Brian De Palma, John Carpenter, Mike Nichols, Oliver Stone, and Quentin Tarantino. He started writing music for Italian light comedy films, such as Dino Risi's *Il successo* (*The Success*, 1963) and Lina Wertmüller's *I basilischi* (*The Lizards*, 1963), but it was his collaboration on Italian Westerns with Sergio Leone that brought him worldwide success.

There are numerous elements that distinguish what would be known as Spaghetti Westerns from their American counterparts: the absence of Native Americans and the "righteous sheriff," the extremely stereotyped characters, a large employment of graphic violence, and the use of exhaustingly slow shots and extreme close-ups. But the real novelty of this new genre was arguably its use of music, which became, alongside the images that it accompanied, an autonomous narrative text. Through the juxtaposition of classic and unusual instruments and sounds—such as the flute and the Sicilian *maranzano* (jaw harp), the violin and the bells, the soprano vocals of Edda dell'Orso and the whistling—Morricone created a unique style which became a *maniera*, a defined style imitated by and inspiring to numerous film directors and music artists. Morricone's music for Leone's films accomplished many functions. It was often a "caricatural soundtrack," but its dramatic and humorous elements also served to highlight "the importance of . . . vague, unfocused memories at key moments in the development of the plot."[46] It contributed to characters' personality on the screen, especially in their ironic aspects,[47] and, as Leone himself would reveal, helped the actors identify with their characters.[48]

Leone's films have been compared to operatic and melodramatic films, but Leone defined himself as a *cantastorie* (literally "story-singer"), and he would accept the comparison only with regard to the music in his films: "If it is true that I conceived of a new kind of Western, creating picaresque characters in epic situations and original characters, it was Ennio Morricone's music that gave them voice," he used to claim.[49] The most sonorous example of this is without doubt the main character of *C'era una volta il West* (*Once Upon a Time in the West*, 1968), Harmonica, named after the musical instrument that he does not just play, but rather uses to talk: "When he oughta talk, he plays," exclaims one of the characters in the film. As the story unfolds, it will be clear that his harmonica not only identifies the character, but is also a symbol for death and vindication, around which the whole film revolves and through which the actions on the screen acquire meaning.

More recently, Morricone has regularly worked with the Italian director Giuseppe Tornatore, writing the music for all of his films, notably for the Academy Award-winning *Nuovo Cinema Paradiso* (internationally released as *Cinema Paradiso*, 1988) that earned the composer the BAFTA Award for Best Music Film. Other examples of their collaboration include *Malèna* (2000), *Baarìa* (2009), and *La migliore offerta* (*The Best Offer*, 2013). For Tornatore's films that are set in Sicily, Morricone's music blends original thematic motifs with Sicilian sounds, translating characters' emotions and the local atmosphere into music. But with *La leggenda del pianista sull'oceano* (*The Legend of 1900*, 1998), the Italian composer created a totally new experience.[50] Morricone wrote the music for the film before seeing it, aware that he had to write a music completely different from all he had composed before: an immortal, enchanting music played by a talented pianist who never heard any other kind. "I thought of something by Mozart," explains Morricone. "Mozart is an immortal genius. . . . Then I realized: 1900 [the protagonist of *The Legend*] is not registered at the Civil Registrar. So he was not born and thus cannot die: he is immortal. With this in mind I thought of him as a child playing a Mozart's theme in the night of his first apparition."[51]

Born on an ocean liner, the *Virginian*, the character 1900 spent his whole life on the ship, using music as a privileged source of knowledge of the outside world. To convey this idea, Morricone blended music from different genres, mainly jazz and ragtime, but also Italian folk music along with powerful virtuoso pieces, such as the eight-hand piece played by 1900 in the duel scene with the jazz piano player Jelly Roll Morton. Even the love theme, which the protagonist plays when he first sees and falls in love with a girl on the ship, is not just the expression of a romantic passion, but is the means through which 1900 learns "love." This is confirmed by the non-diegetic use of the same theme in the scene in which 1900 first attempts to leave the *Virginian* to see the world with his own eyes. The music theme does not merely illustrate and comment on 1900's love for the girl, which would supposedly motivate him to climb down the stairs of the ocean liner. It rather suggests that music is his only way to experience love and life. This is why he will eventually decide not to step off of the ship.[52] Morricone's score for this film earned him the Nastro d'Argento Speciale, the David di Donatello, and the Golden Globe Award.

In the same year that *The Legend of 1900* was released, the Italian composer Nicola Piovani received the Academy Award for Best Original Dramatic Score for Roberto Benigni's *La vita è bella* (*Life Is Beautiful*, 1997), which also earned the director the Academy Award for Best Foreign Language Film and Best Actor. A graduate of the Conservatory "Giuseppe Verdi" in Milan, Piovani composed musical scores for many directors, including Fellini, Bertolucci, Marco Bellocchio, Mario Monicelli, Nanni Moretti, and Paolo and Vittorio Taviani. In Benigni's *Life Is Beautiful*, Piovani's score succeeds in conveying the essence of the film, highlighting the lightness of its comic aspects, while announcing the tragic progression of the plot by introducing elements of uneasiness. If the first Italian sound films had launched what would become successful love songs (such as *Parlami d'amore Mariù* in Camerini's *What Scoundrels*), with *Life Is Beautiful* the wordless famous tune with the same name composed by Piovani became a song only after the film's release and success. The Israeli singer Achinoam Nini, alias Noa, and the lyricist Gil Dor wrote the English lyrics for the music and recorded it with the title "Beautiful That Way" (2000), further confirming the crucial role of music in the film and beyond it.

Music and sound have accomplished various roles and functions in Italian cinema, from accompanying and commenting on events to providing a key to interpreting and developing characters and plots, to even unveiling new meanings beyond the images on the screen. Whatever their role within specific film narrations, sound and soundtrack in film possess an enchanting aura, providing "a subliminal echo chamber of magical power to touch remote and forgotten chords."[53]

Notes

1   "La madre a cui muore tra le braccia il figliuolo darà un urlo disperato. . . . Le labbra diranno, per la commozione dei pubblici, le vere parole d'amore e di pena" (Pittaluga, quoted in Redi, "Ti Parlerò . . . d'amor," 7). All translations from Italian and French are mine unless otherwise stated.

2   ". . . fondere i singoli gesti in un arco unitario che solo alla musica era dato di organizzare" (quoted in Simeon, *Per un pugno di note*, 146).

3   Brunetta, *The History of Italian Cinema*, 78.

4 On this regard, see Rudolf Arnheim, *Film as Art* and *Art and Visual Perception.* He claimed that "the silent film possessed great artistic purity of expression. Therefore . . . sound and dialogue are not suitable for promoting the image formation on the film screen; rather, they significantly limit the expression of the image" (Grundman and Arnheim, "The Intelligence of Vision").

5 Brunetta, *The History of Italian Cinema*, 85.

6 Ben-Ghiat, "*1860*," 25.

7 Wagstaff, *Italian Neorealist Cinema*, 105.

8 "Essi non conoscono lingua diversa dal siciliano per esprimere ribellioni, dolori, speranze. La lingua italiana non è in Sicilia la lingua dei poveri" (*La terra trema*).

9 As he himself states in an interview about his project to make a film based on Verga's novel, "il solo suono di quei nomi—padron 'Ntoni Malavoglia, Bastianazzo, la Longa, Sant'Agata, 'La Provvidenza'—e di quei luoghi—Aci Trezza, il Capo dei Mulini, il Rotolo, la Sciara—servirà a spalancare uno scenario favoloso e magico dove le parole e i gesti dovranno avere il religioso rilievo delle cose essenziali alla nostra umana carità." (the mere sound of those names— padron 'Ntoni Malavoglia, Bastianazzo, la Longa, Sant'Agata, La Provvidenza— and of those places—Aci Trezza, il Capo dei Mulini, il Rotolo, la Sciara . . . will open onto a fabulous and magical scene where words and gestures will have the religious relevance of things essential to our human compassion). Luchino Visconti, "Tradizione e invenzione," in Miccichè, *Luchino Visconti*, 97.

10 Miccichè, *Luchino Visconti*, 96.

11 See Parigi, *Cinema*, 53.

12 Baldelli, *I film di Luchino Visconti*, 97.

13 "Amo il melodramma perché si situa tra il teatro e la vita" (Visconti in an interview with Henry Chapler, *Arts* [1958], quoted in Chiarelli, *Musica e memoria nell'arte di Luchino Visconti*, 110).

14 Chiarelli, *Musica e memoria*, 98. As Visconti once put it: "La forma più completa di spettacolo, secondo me, resta il melodramma, dove convergono parole, canto, musica, danza, scenografia" (Melodrama is for me the most complete artistic form, for in it lyrics, singing, music, dance, and scenography converge; Visconti, "Vent'anni di teatro," quoted in Miccichè, *Luchino Visconti*, 120–21).

15 In this same year, Visconti debuted as opera director at La Scala in Milan.

16 "Letta, narrativamente strutturata e stilisticamente rappresentata come una *partitura* operistica" (Miccichè, *Luchino Visconti*, 81; italics in the original).

17 On Visconti's reinterpretation of Risorgimento through a Gramscian lens, see Marcus, "Visconti's *Senso*," 164–87; and Bacon, "*Senso*," 60–82.

18 Chiarelli, *Musica e memoria*, 111–12.

19 Visconti had initially thought of Maria Callas for the role of Livia. See Stefano Albertini, Peter Brunette, and Wayne Koestenbaum, "Viva Verdi: Visconti and Opera," in Luchino Visconti, *Senso* (Criterion Collection, 2010), DVD 2.

20 See Friedrich W. Herzog, "Was ist deutsche Musik? Erkenntnisse und Folgerungen," *Die Musik* 26 (1934): 802 (quoted in Gilliam, "The Annexation of Anton Bruckner," 590).

21 Gilliam, "The Annexation of Anton Bruckner," 598.

22 Hillman, "Pivot Chords: Austrian Music and Visconti's *Senso* (1954)," 154. Hillman's analysis of the role of music in *Senso* extends to the use of folksongs sang by the Austrian soldiers that serve as a Greek chorus commenting on the development of Livia and Frantz's love story (160–61).

23 Nino Rota worked with Visconti on *Le notti bianche* (*White Nights*, 1957), *Rocco e i suoi fratelli* (*Rocco and His Brothers*, 1960), *Il lavoro* (*The Job*, 1962), and *Il Gattopardo* (*The Leopard*, 1963).

24 "se esiste un modo di pensare il cinema in cui essa risulta *indispensabile* (neppure come commento bensì in quanto *attrice*) questo è proprio il cinema di Fellini" (Miceli, *Musica e cinema nella cultura del Novecento*, 411).

25 Gorbman, "Music as Salvation," 18.

26 Gorbman, "Music as Salvation," 22–25.

27 The multiple levels in which music is employed in Fellini's films go well beyond the standard characterization of diegetic and extra-diegetic music. Sergio Miceli analyzes its multiple symbolic values in Fellini's cinema through the categories of "internal," "mediated," and "external" music. As Miceli recounts, this method of levels "was born not as an independent theoretical formulation, but out of the necessity to fashion adequate and coherent tools for the study of a specific case: the association of Federico Fellini and Nino Rota." See Miceli, "La musica nel film e nel teatro di prosa," 223–30, English translation "Miceli's Method of Internal, External, and Mediated Levels: Elements for the Definition of a Film-Musical Dramaturgy," 2.

28 "Parmi tous les matériaux bruts dont use le film et dont, seule, la juxtaposition donne lieu à création artistique, la musique apporte un élément d'irréalité qui va fausser le jeu et détruire ce 'réalisme primordial' [du cinéma]" (Jaubert, "Petite école du spectateur," 116).

29 Miceli goes so far as to affirm that a neorealist music never existed (*Musica e cinema*, 407), while Comuzio questions the effectiveness of the music used in some neorealist films, such as *The Bycicle Thieves*, in which music seems to compromise the social message of the film ("Alessandro Cicognini, un musicista italiano per il cinema," 41). See also Van Order, *Listening to Fellini*, 16.

30 "L'accompagnamento musicale dei film, nella sua funzione tradizionale, non ha più ragione di esistere ... È vero che esistono dei momenti ... 'musicali' ... in cui si ha più bisogno di staccarsi dalla realtà, di forzarla. In quei momenti la musica ha una sua funzione. In altri momenti, si deve ricorrere ai rumori, anche se non utilizzati con spirito di realismo, ma piuttosto come effetti sonori, naturalmente con poesia" (Antonioni, *Fare un film è per me vivere*, 240–41).

31 McLuhan, *Understanding Media*, 302. While McLuhan's words refer to radio, I believe they accurately describe the use of sounds in Antonioni's films.

32 "Le sonorità elettroniche ... si qualificano, nel continuo ambiguo trapasso tra esse e altri rumori, come sonorità dell'inconscio e come tali vengono percepite dallo spettatore" (Gelmetti, "La qualità 'inaudita' del suono al computer," 184).

33 Chatman, *Antonioni*, 135.

34 Lotman, *Semiotics of Cinema*, 103. See also Antonioni, *Tecnicamente dolce*, xxviii.

35 "Ces sons et ces voix que ne sont *ni tout à fait dedans, ni clairement dehors* [et] qui nous intéressent le plus: parce que c'est là peut-être, avec ces voix et ces sons laissés *en errance à la surface de l'écran*, qu'entre en jeu la puissance du cinéma en tant que tel" (Chion, *La voix au cinema*, 18).

36 Pasolini, *Heretical Empiricism*, 179–80; italics in the original.

37 Pasolini, *Heretical Empiricism*, 181.

38 Pasolini, *Heretical Empiricism*, 89.

39 Gelmetti, "La musica nei film di Pasolini," 57.

40 Henze, "Johann Sebastian Bach e la musica del nostro tempo" (*Henze*, 391).

41 Pasolini, "An Epical-Religious View of the World," 32.

42 Pasolini, *La musica per film*, 154–55.

43 Pasolini, *La musica per film*, 115.

44 Pasolini, *La musica per film*, 7.

45 See Morricone, *Lontano dai sogni*, 145. Morricone also worked on the soundtrack of Pontecorvo's *Queimada* (*Burn!* 1969) and *Ogro* (1979).

46 Frayling, *Spaghetti Westerns*, 170.

47 Interview with Sergio Leone released to Christopher Frayling (February 1982), quoted in Frayling, "The Making of Sergio Leone's *A Fistful of Dollars*," 20.

48 Caravetta, "Il western di Leone-Morricone," 144.

49 "Se è vero che ho creato un nuovo tipo di western, inventando i personaggi picareschi in situazioni da epopea e nuovi personaggi, è stata la musica di Ennio Morricone a farli parlare" (Leone, *I western all'italiana*). With regard to the operatic aspects of Leone's films, see Staig and Williams, *Italian Western*.

50 For this film, Morricone was awarded the Golden Globe for Best Original Score.

51 "Pensai a qualcosa di mozartiano, quel genio immortale di Mozart . . . Feci una riflessione: il protagonista, Novecento, non è inscritto all'anagrafe. Non nasce quindi, e dunque non può morire: è immortale. È da questa considerazione che nasce l'idea di vedere il bambino, nella prima apparizione, suonare di notte il tema mozartiano" (Morricone, *Lontano dai sogni*, 84).

52 The same theme is also played when 1900 sneaks into the dormitory in third class to see the girl sleeping. In this case, as Morricone explains, the music is played with dissonances to emphasize the crisis. The same motif will appear in Gabriele Muccino's *Seven Pounds* (2008).

53 McLuhan, *Understanding Media*, 302; McLuhan's original quote refers to radio.

Bibliography

Antonioni, Michelangelo. *Tecnicamente dolce*. Ed. Aldo Tassone. Turin: Einaudi, 1976.

Antonioni, Michelangelo. *Fare un film è per me vivere: Scritti sul cinema*. Venice: Marsilio, 2001.

Aristarco, Guido and Teresa Aristarco, eds. *Il nuovo mondo dell'immagine elettronica*. Bari: Dedalo, 1985.

Arnheim, Rudolf. *Art and Visual Perception: A Psychology of the Creative Eye*. Berkeley: University of California Press, 1974.

Arnheim, Rudolf. *Film as Art*. Berkeley: University of California Press, 1957.

Baldelli, Pio. *I film di Luchino Visconti*. Manduria: Lacaita, 1965.

Ben-Ghiat, Ruth. "Alessandro Blasetti's *1860*." In *The Cinema of Italy*. Ed. Giorgio Bertellini. London: Wallflower Press, 2004. 21–30.

Bertini, Antonio. *Teoria e tecnica del film in Pasolini*, Rome: Bulzoni, 1979.

Brunetta, Gian Piero. *The History of Italian Cinema: A Guide to Italian Film from Its Origins to the Twenty-First Century*. Trans. Jeremy Parzen. Princeton: Princeton University Press, 2009.

Caravetta, Masina. "Il western di Leone-Morricone." In *La musica del cinema*. Ed. Enzo Kermol and Mariselda Tessarolo. Rome: Bulzoni, 1996.

Chatman, Seymour Benjamin. *Antonioni, or, The Surface of the World*. Berkeley: University of California Press, 1985.

Chiarelli, Cristina Gastel. *Musica e memoria nell'arte di Luchino Visconti*. Milan: Archinto, 2006.

Chion, Michel. *La voix au cinema*. Paris: Édition de l'Étoile, 1982.

Comuzio, Ermanno. "Alessandro Cicognini, un musicista italiano per il cinema." In *Trento Cinema 1990. Incontri Internazionali con la Musica per il Cinema*. Trento: Provincia autonoma di Trento, 1990. 35–70.

Frayling, Christopher. "The Making of Sergio Leone's *A Fistful of Dollars*." *Cinéaste* 25.3 (2000): 14–22.

Frayling, Christopher. *Spaghetti Westerns: Cowboys and Europeans from Karl May to Sergio Leone*. London: Routledge and Kegan Paul, 1981.

Gelmetti, Vittorio. "La musica nei film di Pasolini." *Filmcritica* 151–52 (1964): 570–73.

Gelmetti, Vittorio. "La qualità 'inaudita' del suono al computer." In *Il nuovo mondo dell'immagine elettronica*. Ed. Guido Aristarco and Teresa Aristarco. Bari: Dedalo, 1985.

Gorbman, Claudia. "Music as Salvation: Notes on Fellini and Rota." *Film Quarterly* 28.2 (1974–75): 17–25.

Grundman, Uta and Rudolf Arnheim. "The Intelligence of Vision: An Interview with Rudolf Arnheim." http://www.cabinetmagazine.org/issues/2/rudolfarnheim.php. Accessed December 9, 2017.

Henze, Hans Werner. "Johann Sebastian Bach e la musica del nostro tempo." In *Henze*. Ed. Enzo Restagno. Turin: EDT/Musica, 1986. 386–92.

Hillman, Roger. *Unsettling Scores. German Film, Music, and Ideology*. Bloomington and Indianapolis: Indiana University Press, 2005.

Jaubert, Maurice. "Petite école du spectateur: La Musique." *Esprit* 43 (1936): 114–19.

Kermol, Enzo and Mariselda Tessarolo, eds. *La musica del cinema*. Rome: Bulzoni, 1996.

Leone, Sergio. *I western all'italiana*. Milan: Selezione dal Reader's Digest, 1974.

Lotman, Jurij. *Semiotics of Cinema*. Trans. Mark E. Suino. Ann Arbor: University of Michigan, 1976.

McLuhan, Marshall. *Understanding Media. The Extensions of Man.* Cambridge, MA: MIT Press, 1994.

Miccichè, Lino. *Luchino Visconti. Un profilo critico.* Venice: Marsilio, 2002.

Miceli, Sergio. "La musica nel film e nel teatro di prosa: L'avvento dello specialismo." In *Italia millenovecentocinquanta*, Ed. Guido Salvetti and Bianca Maria Antolini. Milan: Guerini e Associati, 1999. 283–300.

Miceli, Sergio. "Miceli's Method of Internal, External, and Mediated Levels: Elements for the Definition of a Film-Musical Dramaturgy." In Gillian Anderson and Ron Sadoff, eds., *Music and the Moving Image* 4.2 (Summer 2011): 1–29.

Miceli, Sergio. *Musica e cinema nella cultura del Novecento.* Milan: RCS, 2000.

Morricone, Ennio. *Lontano dai sogni: Conversazione con Antonio Monda.* Milan: Mondadori, 2010.

Parigi, Stefania. *Cinema—Italy.* Trans. Sam Rohdie. Manchester: Manchester University Press, 2009.

Pasolini, Pier Paolo. "An Epical-Religious View of the World." Trans. Letizia Ciotti Miller and Michael Graham. *Film Quarterly* 18.4 (Summer 1965): 31–45.

Pasolini, Pier Paolo. *Heretical Empiricism.* Ed. Louise K. Barnett, Trans. Ben Lawton and Louise K. Barnett. Bloomington: Indiana University Press, 1988.

Redi, Riccardo. *Ti Parlerò . . . d'amor: Cinema italiano fra muto e sonoro.* Turin: ERI, 1986.

Simeon, Ennio. *Per un pugno di note: Storia, teoria, estetica della musica per il cinema, la televisione e il video.* Milan: Rugginenti, 1995.

Staig, Laurence and Tony Williams. *Italian Western: The Opera of Violence.* London: Lorrimer Publishers, 1975.

Van Order, Thomas. *Listening to Fellini: Music and Meaning in Black and White.* Madison: Fairleigh Dickinson University Press, 2009.

Wagstaff, Christopher. *Italian Neorealist Cinema: An Aesthetic Approach.* Toronto: University of Toronto Press, 2007.

Filmography

1860: I mille di Garibaldi (1860: *The Thousand of Garibaldi*), Dir. Alessandro Blasetti. Italy: Società Anonima Stefano Pittaluga. 1934.

8 1/2, Dir. Federico Fellini. Italy: Cineriz. 1963.

Accattone, Dir. Pier Paolo Pasolini. Italy: Cino del Duca. 1961.

Baarìa, Dir. Giuseppe Tornatore. Italy: Medusa. 2009.

Blow-Up, Dir. Michelangelo Antonioni. USA: Premier Productions. 1966.

C'era una volta il West (*Once Upon a Time in the West*), Dir. Sergio Leone. EIA. 1968.

Deserto rosso (*Red Desert*), Dir. Michelangelo Antonioni. Italy: Cineriz. 1964.

Gli uomini che mascalzoni . . . (*What Scoundrels Men Are!*), Dir. Mario Camerini. Italy: Società Italiana Cines-Pittaluga. 1933.

I basilischi, Dir. Lina Wertmüller. Italy: Cineriz. 1963.

Il grido, Dir. Michelangelo Antonioni. Italy: CEI Incom. 1957.

Il successo, Dir. Dino Risi. Italy: Incei Film. 1963.

L'avventura, Dir. Michelangelo Antonioni. Italy: Cino del Duca. 1960.

La battaglia di Algeri (*The Battle of Algiers*), Dir. Gillo Pontecorvo. Italy: Magna. 1966.

La canzone dell'amore, Dir. Gennaro Righelli. Italy: Società Anonima Stefano Pittaluga. 1930.

La dolce vita, Dir. Federico Fellini. Italy: Cineriz. 1960.

La leggenda del pianista sull'oceano (*The Legend of 1900*), Dir. Giuseppe Tornatore. Italy: Medusa. 1998.

La migliore offerta (*The Best Offer*), Dir. Giuseppe Tornatore. Italy: Warner Bros. 2013.

La strada (*The Road*), Dir. Federico Fellini. Italy: Dino De Laurentiis. 1954.

La terra trema, Dir. Luchino Visconti. Italy: CEIAD. 1948.

La vita è bella (*Life Is Beautiful*), Dir. Roberto Benigni. Italy: Cecchi Gori. 1997.

Ladri di biciclette (*Bicycle Thieves*), Dir. Vittorio De Sica. Italy: ENIC. 1948.

Le notti di Cabiria (*Nights of Cabiria*), Dir. Federico Fellini. Italy: Paramount Films of Italy. 1957.

Malèna, Dir. Giuseppe Tornatore. Italy: Medusa. 2000.

N.U.—Nettezza urbana, Dir. Michelangelo Antonioni. Italy: ICET. 1948.

Nuovo Cinema Paradiso (*Cinema Paradiso*), Dir. Giuseppe Tornatore. Italy: Titanus. 1988.

Rapsodia satanica (*Satan's Rhapsody*), Dir. Nino Oxilia. Italy: Società Italiana Cines. 1915.

Roma, città aperta (*Rome, Open City*), Dir. Roberto Rossellini. Italy: Minerva Film. 1945.

Senso, Dir. Luchino Visconti. Italy: Lux Film. 1954.

The Godfather: Part II, Dir. Francis Ford Coppola. USA: Paramount Pictures. 1974.

28

Screenwriting

Cosetta Gaudenzi

Screenwriting has been a major chapter in the history of Italian cinema. But regrettably, its impact on films has been only occasionally addressed and recognized by critics, primarily because of the various challenges posited by the very nature of screenplays. They are difficult to study because of their fluctuating and unstable character, with such alterable mixed and intermediary forms as story, screenplay, and storyboard[1]; their ephemeral status, with words that lead to a different kind of finished product (Pasolini, "La sceneggiatura come 'struttura che vuol essere altra struttura'"); their relative anonymity, that is, the difficulty of attributing to a particular writer any aspect of a screenplay completed by more than one; and their questionable literary quality as a working script.[2]

Historically, screenwriting has been characterized in Italy by a meaningful relation to the literary world and an extensive use of original stories. As far as the Italian screenplay format is concerned, while silent movies typically utilized a shooting script that divided screenwriting into *quadri* or "scenes,"[3] the script page of sound films was later divided into two columns: the one on the left placed the visual information for the story, and the one on the right added the sound data. Nowadays, because of the influence of global transformations and mobility within the world's film industry, the format of an Italian script is less detailed and has become similar to an American one, which is usually organized in spatiotemporal units (master scenes).

Here, I will present an historical overview of the forms and traits of screenwriting as it has developed from the early years of Italian cinema. Between 1908 and the early 1920s, there was increased recognition of the story writer (*soggettista*), the person who wrote plot outlines for the movies, and the screenwriter (*sceneggiatore*) who produced a longer format of film summary, including instructions on how to act and film a movie.[4] With the rising popularity of feature films, screenwriting became more and more the domain of Italian literati as well as other intellectuals who worked as paid professionals for both theater and cinema. By the mid-1910s, many famous writers offered their services as story writers or screenwriters and sold their works for the screen (e.g., Grazia Deledda, Guido Gozzano, Luigi Pirandello, Matilde Serao, and Giovanni Verga). An especially significant moment for Italian screenwriting was Gabriele D'Annunzio's participation in Giovanni Pastrone's *Cabiria* (1914), for which he helped write the intertitles. By then a supremely famous Italian writer, D'Annunzio contributed to the reputation of Italian cinema by bestowing on it the authority of canonical literature.[5]

But many early screenwriters were ordinary paid professionals, like Arrigo Frusta, who had an eclectic but not necessarily profound knowledge of his craft. Frusta's screenplays are helpful for understanding the typical characteristics of early screenwriting, which aimed to appeal to both elite and mass culture: they included intertitles and specific gestures and moods, and they called attention to landscape and space in general (e.g., a bridge, a window, curtains) for an Italian cinema that was still quite connected to theatrical representation.[6]

Another momentous development for screenwriting in Italy was the introduction of sound film in the 1930s, which made the writing of a screenplay an even more critical stage in movie production, and resulted in the establishment of precise criteria for scripts and the screenwriting process. Contracts were often arbitrary, and the concept of intellectual property was not yet well defined, which led to legal disputes.[7] Writers worked at their scripts in pairs or groups, and often came from theatrical and literary fields. When heading the production house Cines (1932–33), Emilio Cecchi hired as story writers and screenwriters such playwrights as Pirandello, Aldo De Benedetti, Alessandro De Stefani, and Raffaele Viviani, as well as the novelists Giacomo Debenedetti and Mario Soldati. In general, screenwriters in the 1930s made significant contributions to popularizing the idea of Italian identity.[8] From the comedy writer Aldo De Benedetti to the erudite Debenedetti—and from Aldo Vergano to Sergio Amidei, Eduardo De Filippo, and Cesare Zavattini—they all created a cinematic language that made space for the growing aspirations for unity in the Italian peninsula, while also exploring its regional traditions and contact with other cultures.

Because of the impact of the work of several notable contemporary screenwriters, and because of the additional attention on scripts brought by the recent introduction of sound, in the mid-1930s journals including *Cinema* and *Bianco e nero*, as well as Alberto Consiglio's *Cinema: Arte e linguaggio*, began to recognize the academic value of screenplays and initiated a systematic theoretical discussion of them.[9] These studies were partly rooted in Umberto Barbaro's 1932 translation of some of Vsevolod

Pudovkin's essays in *Il soggetto cinematografico*, a publication regarded by critics as the theoretical text that began the concept of cinematographic creation as linguistic process in Italy (for an English version, see Taylor's *Vsevolod Pudovkin*).

Pudovkin's work advocated a close collaboration among scriptwriters, directors, and editors, and it was an essential source for the contribution of neorealist screenwriters to the postwar rebirth of Italian cinema.[10] Indeed, neorealist scriptwriters worked closely with directors, meeting in cafés or crowded apartments to come up with a well-defined story with innovative narrative techniques, such as those displayed in Roberto Rossellini's *Roma città aperta* (*Rome, Open City,* 1945) and *Paisà* (*Paisan,* 1946): a fragmentary, episodic structure, with a tragic ending and the occasional use of comic relief—techniques that derived from the diverse experiences neorealist screenwriters gained in both mass and elite cinema.

The most representative and recognized of the neorealist scriptwriters was Sergio Amidei, who, besides contributing to *Roma città aperta*, scripted more than a hundred films in a long and varied career during which he was nominated four times for an Oscar for Best Original Screenplay. As a typical neorealist screenwriter, Amidei was an experimentalist able to work with any of his peers and with different film genres and directors (not only neorealists). Other important scriptwriters of the period included Zavattini and Suso Cecchi d'Amico. Zavattini collaborated frequently with Vittorio De Sica (*Sciuscià* [*Shoeshine,* 1946], *Ladri di biciclette* [*Bicycle Thieves,* 1948], *Miracolo a Milano* [*Miracle in Milan,* 1951], and *Umberto D.* [1952]), and worked on a great number of other Italian movies, ranging from historical films to comedies, musicals, and even propaganda films. Suso Cecchi served as screenwriter in notable neorealist works like *Roma città aperta* and *Ladri di biciclette*, and, among other accomplishments, later became a close assistant to Luchino Visconti in *Bellissima* (1951), *Senso* (1954), *Rocco e i suoi fratelli* (*Rocco and His Brothers,* 1960), and *Il Gattopardo* (*The Leopard,* 1963).

Screenwriting of the 1950s might be described as transitory, anonymous, and formulaic. It was transitory because the 1950s was an age of transition between the Second World War and the economic boom of the 1960s, and for this reason there was a tendency in the scripts of the time to transform the past in memory. It was anonymous because many screenwriters, especially those working in popular cinema, often cowrote scripts in groups, making it difficult to identify the single contribution of each of them (as in Pietro Germi's *Divorzio all'italiana* [*Divorce Italian Style,* 1961]). This may have been an expedient that writers employed to keep a low profile in films where they were trying to free themselves from the old neorealist model, or attempting to change a conservative Italian society.[11] Finally, 1950s screenwriting was also formulaic in that it promoted narrative formulas generally in line with audience's expectations, as exemplified by several of the scripts of Ennio De Concini (Academy Award for *Divorzio all'italiana*) and Ettore Maria Margadonna (Orso d'argento at the Berlin Festival for *Pane amore e fantasia* [*Bread, Love, and Dreams*, 1953]).

In the 1960s, a lively period for Italian cinema, screenwriting underwent a substantial change. First, screenwriters who had reached high recognition at that time helped to steer productions toward original stories, moving away from traditional Italian cinematic ties to literature.[12] Second, because of the increasing power of auteurs like Federico Fellini, Luchino Visconti, and Michelangelo Antonioni, there was a redrawing of the relation between filming and screenwriting, where the latter lost part of its creative force. For instance, Fellini relied in his films more on the power of montage than of the script.[13]

In addition to the earlier director-screenwriter pair of Visconti-Suso Cecchi, in the 1960s, we witnessed the combination Fellini-Ennio Flaiano (a collaboration started in the 1950s), and Antonioni-Tonino Guerra. Guerra also worked with many other directors till the 1990s, making notable contributions to the *cinema d'inchiesta* or investigative cinema of Elio Petri and Francesco Rosi. Finally, a unique 1960s figure was Pier Paolo Pasolini, who entered the film industry as a screenwriter invited by Mario Soldati, and eventually became a celebrated film director. Pasolini's essay "La sceneggiatura come 'struttura che vuol essere altra struttura'" ("The Screenplay as a 'Form That Wants to Be Another Form,'" 1966) is a key work highlighting the symbolic value of the written signs of a screenplay. This essay regards a screenplay as form in movement, connecting verbal language with the cinematographic one: the written signs of a screenplay allude to their cinematographic production, compelling their reader to lend the text a visual completeness through the creation of mental images. Pasolini's view of screenplay as "form in movement" made an important contribution to the philosophy of cinema, while shedding light on the development of his own varied career: in each genre and medium he employed, he envisioned potential development into other genres and media.[14]

Next to the auteur cinema was the comic cinema and Italian-style comedy of the 1960s and 1970s. Comic films, which had their roots in 1940s and 1950s cinema, were commonly performed by Franco Franchi, Ciccio Ingrassia, and the still active Totò. Its screenwriters, including Vittorio Vighi and Dino Verde, had often worked for the satirical magazine *Marc'Aurelio*, which was also a source for many screenwriters of the comedy Italian style (e.g., Ruggero Maccari and Luigi Magni). The latter usually worked in pairs or in groups connected to production houses (e.g., Giorgio Arlorio, Luciano Vincenzoni, and Stefano Strucchi, all employed by Dino De Laurentis). Among the most recognized pairs of the time were Age and Scarpelli (the assumed names of Agenone Incrocci and Furio Scarpelli, respectively), Vittorio Metz and Marcello Marchesi, and Castellano and Pipolo (the assumed names of Franco Castellano and Giuseppe Moccia, respectively).

Age and Scarpelli wrote economic boom comedies (e.g., Dino Risi's *I mostri* [*Opiate '67*, 1963]), where the illusory miracle of the 1960s was explained in comic terms.[15] Other notable contemporary screenwriters were Rodolfo Sonego, who worked almost exclusively for Alberto Sordi; and the Tuscans Leo Benvenuti and Piero De Bernardi, who wrote Mario Monicelli's *Amici miei* and Luciano Salce's *Fantozzi*, whose scripts mark a passage from the realistic costume satire of the 1960s to the cynical, noncommittal attitude and the hyperbolic grotesque of some 1970s comedies.

Starting in the late 1970s, screenwriting was affected in Italy by a fourfold major crisis: first, the increased authority of film directors; second, the growing distance between difficult-to-interpret film auteurs and their audiences; third, the rise of private television, which rapidly undercut the economic power of cinema; and last, the producers' reluctance to invest in young screenwriters.[16] In this context, film screenwriting was regarded as almost superfluous: some moved either to work for the growing television business or, like Enzo Monteleone, became directors. Among the most recognized screenwriters of the decade were representatives of the older generation (Benvenuti, De Bernardi, De Concini, and Guerra) and some of the younger generation (Roberta Mazzoni, Enrico Oldoini, Sandro Petraglia, and Stefano Rulli). Particularly significant was the work of Vincenzo Cerami, who collaborated both in auteur films like those by Gianni Amelio and Marco Bellocchio, and in such star-driven films as those with Antonio Albanese and Roberto Benigni.

This screenwriting crisis was followed by a period of transition and search for change. Starting in the late 1980s, there were several meetings and public events where professionals expressed the need to bring new energy to Italian cinema through a generational transformation. For instance, the Premio Solinas for Best Screenplay, awarded on Maddalena Island, developed in 1993 into a movement (Movimento Maddalena '93), and focused the public's attention on attempts at renewal within Italian cinema. Because of budgetary constraints, contemporary screenwriters often set their scripts in small environments, frequently treating the themes of journey, drugs, and the cultural "other," as well as the psychoanalytical exploration of family, politics, mafia, and landscape.[17] Some scriptwriters from the 1990s became directors (e.g., Umberto Marino and Paolo Virzì); others came from the field of literature (Niccolò Ammaniti and Carlo Lucarelli); and still others had just started promising careers (Francesco Bruni and Doriana Leondeff).

Although critics agree that attempts in the 1990s to provide new energy to Italian cinema have not been completely successful, it is also true that the screenwriting profession has enjoyed a growing interest in the twenty-first century, as evident in a new generation of screenwriters who studied in the late 1980s and in the 1990s at such private institutions as the Benvenuti and De Bernardi Independent Screenwriting School at ANAC (Associazione Nazionale Autori Cinematografici), Alessandro Baricco's Scuola Holden, and the Centro Sperimentale di Cinematografia. In the 2000s, a common script theme was fracture (i.e., the fracture within families, at work, or between the generations), and landscape and location have also become important contexts for the discussion of diverse identities.[18] For the 2000s, notable work has been done by the pairs Laura Sabatino and Vincenzo Terracciano, Leonardo Fasoli and Gianluca Maria Tavarelli, and Massimo Gaudioso and Matteo Garrone.[19] And for the 2010s, one may add Paolo Bonifacci, a very popular contemporary screenwriter who, with his free online course on how to become a screenwriter (http://www.bonifacci.it), seems to incarnate perfectly the twenty-first-century return to the screenwriting profession.

The chronological narrative outlined in this chapter shows that screenwriting has been a significant part of Italian cinema from the beginning. Various categories of professionals, including established authors, less-recognized writers, and intellectuals like Pasolini, have contributed to its development and have highlighted its pivotal functions. Accordingly, one may hope that screenwriting will become a less marginal field in future studies of Italian cinema.

Notes

1 Rondolino and Tomasi, *Manuale del film*, 5–6.

2 Tinazzi, "La sceneggiatura, zona di mezzo," 24.

3 Alovisio, "Scenari," 55.

4 Alovisio, "Scenari," 33.

5 Brunetta, *Cent'anni di cinema italiano*, 1:55.

6 Alovisio, "Scenari," 55–59, 65.

7 Mazzei, "Prima e dopo l'immagine," 71–77.

8 Brunetta, *Cent'anni di cinema italiano*, 1:85.

9 Mazzei, "Prima e dopo l'immagine," 99–103.

10 Muscio, "Le ceneri di Balzac," 109–14.

11 Villa, "Cordoglio ed euforia," 147.

12 Brunetta, *Il cinema italiano contemporaneo*, 77.

13 Manzoli, "Al servizio dell'autore," 168.

14 Kilian, "Pasolini's Aesthetics of Will," 106.

15 Pergolari, "Commedia e dintorni," 199.

16 Zagarrio, "Morte e rinascita del 'mestiere,'" 223–24.

17 Zagarrio, "Morte e rinascita del 'mestiere,'" 256–57.

18 Comand, "Finale aperto," 269–83.

19 Comand, "Finale aperto," 268–69.

Bibliography

Alovisio, Silvio. "Scenari. La sceneggiatura nel cinema muto." In *Sulla carta: Storia e storie della sceneggiatura in Italia*. Ed. Mariapia Comand. Turin: Lindau, 2006. 33–70.

Barbaro, Umberto. *Il soggetto cinematografico*. Rome: Le Edizioni d'Italia, 1932.

Brunetta, Gian Piero. *Cent'anni di cinema italiano*. 5th ed. 2 vols. Bari: Laterza, 2003.

Brunetta, Gian Piero. *Il cinema italiano contemporaneo. Da "La dolce vita" a "Centochiodi."* Bari: Laterza, 2007.

Brunetta, Gian Piero. *The History of Italian Cinema: A Guide to Italian Film from Its Origins to the Twenty-First Century*. Trans. Jeremy Parzen. Princeton: Princeton University Press, 2009.

Comand, Mariapia. "Finale aperto. Narrazioni di inizio millennio." In *Sulla carta: Storia e storie della sceneggiatura in Italia*. Ed. Mariapia Comand. Turin: Lindau, 2006. 265–85.

Kilian, Sven Thorsten. "Pasolini's Aesthetics of Will" (2013), http://www.arabeschi.it/pasolini-aesthetics-of-will/. Accessed December 28, 2017.

Manzoli, Giacomo. "Al servizio dell'autore: La sceneggiatura nel cinema dei 'Maestri' degli anni '60 e '70." In In *Sulla carta: Storia e storie della sceneggiatura in Italia*. Ed. Mariapia Comand. Turin: Lindau, 2006. 163–91.

Mazzei, Luca. "Prima e dopo l'immagine: Percorsi fra testo letterario e film nel cinema degli anni '30." In *Sulla carta: Storia e storie della sceneggiatura in Italia*. Ed. Mariapia Comand. Turin: Lindau, 2006. 71–108.

Muscio, Giuliano. "Le ceneri di Balzac: Sceneggiatura e sceneggiatori nel neorealismo." In *Sulla carta: Storia e storie della sceneggiatura in Italia*. Ed. Mariapia Comand. Turin: Lindau, 2006. 109–41.

Pasolini, Pier Paolo. "La sceneggiatura come 'struttura che vuol essere altra struttura.'" In *Empirismo eretico*. Ed. Walter Siti and Silvia De Laude. Milan: Mondadori, 1999.

Pergolari, Andrea. "Commedia e dintorni: La scrittura di genere negli anni '60 e '70." In *Sulla carta: Storia e storie della sceneggiatura in Italia*. Ed. Mariapia Comand. Turin: Lindau, 2006. 193–219.

Rondolino, Gianni and Dario Tomasi. *Manuale del film*. Turin: UTET, 2011.

Taylor, Richard, ed. *Vsevolod Pudovkin: Selected Essays*. Chicago: University of Chicago Press, 2006.

Tinazzi, Giorgio. "La sceneggiatura, zona di mezzo." In *Sulla carta: Storia e storie della sceneggiatura in Italia*. Ed. Mariapia Comand. Turin: Lindau, 2006. 21–32.

Villa, Federica. "Cordoglio ed euforia: La sceneggiatura negli anni '50." In *Sulla carta: Storia e storie della sceneggiatura in Italia*. Ed. Mariapia Comand. Turin: Lindau, 2006. 143–62.

Zagarrio, Vito. "Morte e rinascita del 'mestiere'. Sceneggiatori e sceneggiature anni '80-'90." In *Sulla carta: Storia e storie della sceneggiatura in Italia*. Ed. Mariapia Comand. Turin: Lindau, 2006. 221–63.

29

Outdoor Cinema

Allison Cooper

The phenomenon of *cinema all'aperto*, open-air or outdoor cinema, is deeply inscribed in Italian film history and culture. Indeed, the nation's first narrative film, Filoteo Alberini's *La presa di Roma—20 settembre 1870 (The Capture of Rome*, 1905), had its public debut outdoors. The film presented in several vignettes the events surrounding Rome's 1870 annexation by the Kingdom of Italy and contained scenes shot in the same locations that they depicted, including Porta Pia, the gateway in the Aurelian walls through which the Italian Army entered when it claimed the city.[1] Porta Pia was also the setting for the film's open-air premier, organized in 1905 to celebrate the thirty-fifth anniversary of Rome's annexation. It was projected onto a cloth screen hung in front of the gateway, where thousands of enthusiastic spectators reportedly viewed it and called for repeated screenings late into the evening.[2]

The story of *The Capture of Rome*, with its intertwined histories of Italian cinema and the consolidation of the modern Italian state, has been cited by generations of film students and scholars in support of diverse accounts of Italian cinema.[3] While these tend to foreground *The Capture of Rome*'s subject matter or formal traits rather than the circumstances of its debut, the open-air, communal nature of the film's initial presentation provides an important point of departure for understanding Italy's tradition of *cinema all'aperto*. As this chapter will show, *cinema all'aperto* offers a distinctly (if not uniquely) Italian experience of cinema, particularly when considered within the context of Italy's cinemagoing audiences and Italian film spectatorship. Taking place in the heart of a town or city and transforming the *piazza* into a public screening area, Italy's open-air cinema immerses the spectator in a lively community of filmgoers and fellow citizens. This latter point distinguishes it from its nearest American analog (at least in terms of popularity): the drive-in movie theater. The drive-in, located on the periphery of the city to accommodate as many vehicles as possible, effectively transforms the spectator's automobile into a private screening room, whereas *cinema all'aperto* breaks down distinctions between the private and the public, the personal and the communal.

As the example of *The Capture of Rome* demonstrates, open-air cinema has coexisted alongside dedicated film exhibition spaces (i.e., theaters) in Italy since the latter were constructed in the first years of the twentieth century. The appeal of the outdoor viewing experience may be ascribed to a number of factors, including Italy's Mediterranean climate, which has encouraged particular film distribution and release patterns. Film screenings traditionally move outdoors during the summer months, when stifling heat drives many Italians outside in search of fresh air. Businesses, including cinemas, close as annual seaside holidays empty cities of their inhabitants. The temporary closure of first-run theaters attending this exodus contributes to a seasonal increase in alternative viewing spaces such as those hosting open-air cinema.[4]

The attraction of *cinema all'aperto*, however, is as social as it is seasonal. Moviegoers enjoy a greater freedom of expression and movement outdoors, where they are liberated from the physical constraints of traditional theaters and more formal expectations of etiquette. Popular cinema scholar Dimitris Eleftheriotis, who notes the commonalities between Greek and Italian open-air cinema, observes that the outdoor viewing experience is characterized by audience interjections, including "exclamations, whistling, clapping, laughing or sobbing, reciting well-known lines, and asking or answering questions on behalf of the characters."[5] Audience members in outdoor settings, he remarks, are likely to offer running commentary on a film's characters and its overall quality, often as part of an (at times contentious) dialogue with other members of the audience.[6] Open-air cinema suggests a model of spectatorship, then, in which the viewer's dynamic relationship with the surrounding environment significantly shapes her experience of the film. This participatory model stands in contrast to the transcendent viewing experience theorized by traditional apparatus theory, which posits an idealized spectator whose subjectivity is constituted through her immersion into the film text. Instead, *cinema all'aperto*, as Eleftheriotis argues, is where "the apparatus meets the audience."[7] It is an exhibition practice in which spectatorship is conditioned as much by the social interactions taking place among real viewers as it is by the film itself.

Outdoor cinema offers a different perspective on spectatorship and cinema audiences, yet we know relatively little about the phenomenon in Italy. Historically, sites hosting *cinema all'aperto* have not been purpose-built venues, which makes it difficult to trace their histories, attendance figures, or programming. The fact that they often screen second- or even third-run films means that they do not register in data tracking box office grosses, an otherwise useful source of information for understanding movie theaters, film distribution patterns, and release strategies.[8] Ephemeral by nature, their history is preserved in the accounts of those who frequent them and in their representation in films about Italians' relationship with cinema—a phenomenon that is especially present in two landmark Italian films, Luchino Visconti's *Bellissima* (1952) and Giuseppe Tornatore's *Nuovo Cinema Paradiso* (*Cinema Paradiso*, 1988), works that offer insight into the psychological and social aspects of spectatorship in Italy.

In *Bellissima*, Anna Magnani plays Maddalena Cecconi, a working-class Roman mother in post–Second World War Italy whose singular ambition to launch her young daughter, Maria, in an acting career threatens to destroy her family's financial and emotional well-being. Exhausted by her preparations for Maria's approaching audition before famed (real-life) director Alessandro Blasetti (*La corona di ferro* [*The Iron Crown*], 1941; *Prima comunione* [*Father's Dilemma*], 1950), Maddalena takes solace in a film being screened in the courtyard of her apartment block one evening: Howard Hawks's *Red River* (1948).[9] So taken is she with Hawks's vision of the American West and with the film's famous actors, John Wayne and Montgomery Clift, that she misses its cautionary message about the threat posed to the family by individual ambition. *Red River*'s story unexpectedly parallels her own as rancher Thomas Dunson (Wayne) tests his own limits and those of his adopted son, Matthew Garth (Clift), with his determination to drive his herd of cattle from Texas to Missouri. Maddalena's inattentiveness to the correspondence between Dunson's all-consuming ambition and her own is symptomatic of a tunnel vision that will eventually cause her and her family great trouble as the film progresses.

Bellissima's surprising association, through the figure of Maddalena, between the American West in the post-Civil War era and post–Second World War Rome serves as a critique of the Italian moviegoing public's fascination with American cinema and its relative indifference to domestic genres like neorealism, with which *Bellissima* has traditionally been identified. As Maddalena declares her preference for the far-off world depicted on-screen over the relative squalor of her surroundings, her husband gently admonishes her to forget the movies and reminds her that the stories they depict are just fantasies. Visconti underscores Maddalena's rejection of her own social reality as a working-class wife and mother through the scene's mise-en-scène, which has her seated apart from her neighbors and fellow film-viewers in the crowded courtyard, refusing to participate in the communal spectatorship that defines *cinema all'aperto*. She may be a *popolana* or woman of the people, the setting suggests, but she is a wayward one whose apparent misunderstanding of her maternal and wifely obligations, along with her refutation of her own class and even national identity (metonymically represented here through her implied rejection of the tenets of neorealism), will be corrected in the film's denouement. *Bellissima*, then, does more than just document *cinema all'aperto* as a cultural practice of postwar Italy: its simple study of Maddalena's relationship to the phenomenon presents a space in which, to borrow the words of scholar Kay Armatage, "issues of identity, morality, mimetic identification and national pride are on public display and open for all to contest."[10]

In *Cinema Paradiso*, an impoverished Sicilian boy, Totò (played as a child, teenager, and adult by, respectively, Salvatore Cascio, Marco Leonardi, and Jacques Perrin) befriends the projectionist of his local village movie theater, Alfredo (Philippe Noiret). After Alfredo loses his eyesight in a projection-booth fire, the precocious young cinephile Totò takes over his duties and eventually goes on to become a renowned film director. The film's narrative, set primarily in the decades immediately following the Second World War, follows Totò's star-crossed love for the unattainable Elena (Agnese Nano); its real love story, however, concerns Totò, Alfredo, and the cinema. *Cinema Paradiso*'s memorable final sequence—composed of censored on-screen kisses that the village priest had Alfredo remove—makes this fact apparent; but a pivotal earlier scene in which the village piazza becomes an improvised open-air movie theater highlights the film's interest in the social dimension of spectatorship in Italy.[11]

Italian moviegoers in the postwar period regarded the cinema as a microcosm of their social world, a "natural extension of the road, the bar and the square."[12] Tornatore affectionately presents the Cinema Paradiso—the parish cinema at the center of *Cinema Paradiso*—in precisely this way, as a cherished gathering place whose patrons feel free to engage under the cover of darkness in activities ranging from innocent to scandalous.[13] All of this takes place against the backdrop of classic and contemporary films and newsreels—*Stagecoach* (John Ford, 1939), *La terra trema* (Luchino Visconti, 1948), *City Lights* (Charlie Chaplin, 1931), and *Ulisse* (*Ulysses*, Mario Camerini, 1954), to name just a few—that frequently provide commentary on the events and characters depicted in *Nuovo Cinema Paradiso* itself. For example, patrons viewing *La terra trema*, Visconti's drama about poor, uneducated Sicilian fisherman, complain ironically that they can't read the film's opening titles because they are illiterate. In this and similar vignettes, Tornatore underscores the communal aspect of spectatorship as his characters actively inhabit the physical space of cinema and create (or, as in the example above, disregard) a multitude of meanings from a variety of filmic texts.

The *cinema all'aperto* scene, in which Alfredo manipulates the filmic image from the projection booth and causes it to travel outside the theater and onto the wall of a palazzo in the town square, further illustrates the primacy of the audience. Outdoors, Totò's *I pompieri di Viggiù* (*The Firemen of Viggiu*, Mario Mattoli, 1949) is freely available to a group of rowdy moviegoers who have been ejected from the Cinema Paradiso in order to accommodate the next audience for the evening's double feature. The improvised outdoor screening is symbolic of cinema's potential to create solidarity, an interpretation that receives confirmation in a humorous exchange in which an usher's attempt to collect money for the screening is met with derision from the crowd and the exclamation that "La piazza è di tutti!" ("The square belongs to everybody!"). In contrast to its fixed function in an idealized exhibition and reception context, the cinematic apparatus here is entirely fluid, from the mobile projector and image to the improvised outdoor "theater" that utilizes the repurposed wall of a *palazzo* for a screen (figuratively torn via the unwelcome intrusion of one of the building's irritated and sleep-deprived inhabitants), to the haphazard arrangement of standing and seated spectators.

In lieu of historical data, *Bellissima* and *Cinema Paradiso* offer a record of *cinema all'aperto* that is more cultural than it is empirical. The films demonstrate nonetheless the rewards of considering Italian cinema from a social perspective. Both make use of the communal space of outdoor cinema to present particularly Italian social relationships to film, putting on view for us as spectators the processes by which characters like Maddalena and Totò come to understand, question, or reject, their places in post–Second World War Italy. With their recourse to *cinema all'aperto*, both films stage cinema at the heart of a certain kind of *italianità*: a national identity formed collectively in the triangulation of individual spectator, film text, and audience that had its historical precedent in the premier of *The Capture of Rome*. The latter film contributed to the making of the nascent modern Italian state through its narrative of Italian unification, but it also "made Italians"—to echo a well-known axiom attributed to Italian statesman Massimo d'Azeglio—through its distinctive form of public exhibition: *cinema all'aperto*.

Notes

1   Lasi, "Early Italian Cinema," 245.

2   Lasi, "Early Italian Cinema," 248.

3   See, for example, Gieri, "Reflections of the Risorgimento in Italian Cinema," 655–56; and Bertozzi, "Visualizing the Past," 322.

4   For more on the development of open-air cinema in Italy from its origins through the post–World War II period in Italy, see Mosconi and Piredda, "Oltre la sala," 113–25.

5   Eleftheriotis, *Popular Cinemas of Europe*, 190.

6   Eleftheriotis, *Popular Cinemas of Europe*, 190.

7   Eleftheriotis, *Popular Cinemas of Europe*, 180.

8   For more on the habits of Italian cinemagoers in the post–World War II period, see the Italian Cinema Audiences project directed by Gennari et al., which

contains an updated list of books, articles, and book chapters produced by Gennari and her fellow researchers: "Outputs," *Italian Cinema Audiences*, accessed March 29, 2017, http://italiancinemaaudiences.org/. See as well Casetti and Fanchi, "Le funzioni sociali del cinema e dei media," 135–71.

9 For more on the representation of cinema within Italian films, and, in particular, in *Bellissima*, see Casetti, "Cinema in the Cinema in Italian Films of the Fifties," 375–93.

10 Armatage, "Screenings by Moonlight," 40.

11 See Eleftheriotis, *Popular Cinemas*, 196–202, for a rich reading of *Cinema Paradiso* in light of apparatus theory and cinephilia and, in particular, for the author's analysis of the scene also discussed here. My reading emphasizes the role of *cinema all'aperto* in the film, but it is indebted to Eleftheriotis's work.

12 Casetti and Fanchi, "Le funzioni sociali del cinema e dei media," 154.

13 For more on the role of the Catholic Church in the distribution and exhibition of films in postwar Italy, see Gennari, *Post-War Italian Cinema*, 68–72.

Bibliography

Armatage, Kay. "Screenings by Moonlight." *Film International* 6.4 (2008): 34–40.

Bertozzi, Marco. "Visualizing the Past: The Italian City in Early Cinema." *Film History* 12.3 (2000): 322–29.

Casetti, Francesco. "Cinema in the Cinema in Italian Films of the Fifties: *Bellissima* and *La signora senza camelie*." *Screen* 33.4 (1992): 375–93.

Casetti, Francesco and Mariagrazia Fanchi. "Le funzioni sociali del cinema e dei media: Dati statistici, ricerche sull'*audience* e storia di consumo." In *Spettatori: Forme di consumo e pubblici del cinema in Italia*. Ed. Mariagrazia Fanchi and Elena Mosconi, 135–71. Venice: Marsilio, 2002.

Eleftheriotis, Dimitris. *Popular Cinemas of Europe: Studies of Texts, Contexts, and Frameworks*. New York: Continuum, 2001.

Gennari, Daniela Treveri. *Post-War Italian Cinema: American Intervention, Vatican Interests*. New York: Routledge, 2009.

Gennari, Daniela Treveri et al. "Italian Cinema Audiences: A Collaborative Research Project on Cinema-Going in 1950s Italy." *Italian Cinema Audiences*, http://italiancinemaaudiences.org/. Accessed November 27, 2017.

Gennari, Daniela Treveri and John Sedgwick. "Memories in Context: The Social and Economic Function of Cinema in 1950s Rome." *Film History: An International Journal* 27.2 (2015): 76–104.

Gieri, Manuela. "Reflections of the Risorgimento in Italian Cinema: 1905–1955." *Italica* 91.4 (2014): 654–65.

Lasi, Giovanni. "Early Italian Cinema: Risorgimento and National Identity." *Journal of Modern Italian Studies* 18.2 (2013): 244–55.

Mosconi, Elena and Maria Francesca Piredda. "Oltre la sala: Il cinema all'aperto." In *Spettatori italiani: Riti e ambienti del consumo cinematografico (1900–1950)*. Ed E. Mosconi and F. Casetti. Roma: Carocci, 2006. 113–25.

Filmography

Bellissima, Dir. Luchino Visconti. Italy: Film Bellissima. 1951.
The Capture of Rome, Dir. Filoteo Alberini. Italy: Alberini & Santoni. 1905.
Cinema Paradiso, Dir. Giuseppe Tornatore. Italy: Cristaldifilm. 1988.
City Lights, Dir. Charles Chaplin, USA: Charles Chaplin Productions. 1931.
Father's Dilemma, Dir. Alessandro Blasetti. Italy: Universalia Film. 1950.
The Firemen of Viggiù, Dir. Mario Mattoli. Italy: Lux Film. 1949.
The Iron Crown, Dir. Alessandro Blasetti. Italy: Ente Nazionale Industrie Cinematografiche. 1941.
Red River, Dir. Howard Hawks. USA: Monterey Productions. 1948.
Stagecoach, Dir. John Ford. USA: Walter Wanger Productions. 1939.
La terra trema, Luchino Visconti. Italy: AR.TE.AS Film. 1948.
Ulysses, Mario Camerini. Italy: Lux Film. 1954.

GLOSSARY

Mattia Acetoso

adaptation

An adaptation is the transposition of a work, usually of literary or theatrical fiction, into film. Many early Italian films were adaptations of both classical and contemporary authors. Early adaptations included Enrico Guazzoni's *Gerusalemme liberata* (*The Crusaders*, 1911), inspired by Torquato Tasso's eponymous epic poem, and Giuseppe de Liguoro's *L'Inferno* (*Dante's Inferno*, 1911), based on Dante's celebrated canticle.

Among the popular writers who contributed to the newborn film industry were Gabriele D'Annunzio and Luigi Pirandello, several of whose novellas and plays were adapted into film. Literary adaptation remains a cornerstone of Italian cinema to this day and is a central subject of contemporary film scholarship, most notably in the work of Millicent Marcus, whose most influential study is *Filmmaking by the Book: Italian Cinema and Literary Adaptation* (1993).

ANICA

ANICA is the acronym for Associazione Nazionale Industrie Cinematografiche Audiovisive e Multimediali (National Association of Audiovisual Film Industries). Established in 1944, it represents the Italian film industry abroad and is a founding member of one of the most prestigious Italian film awards: the David di Donatello, first conferred in 1956.

auteur

From the French word for "author," the auteur is a director whose artistic vision is reflected in his or her work, and who exercises his or her control in all aspects of a film's production. In 1954, the French director and film critic François Truffaut wrote an article, "Une certaine tendance du cinéma français" ("A Certain Tendency in French Cinema"), where he described French New Wave film directors as auteurs. The essay helped pave the way for auteurist theory. Italy developed its own auteurist cinema in the 1950s and 1960s in the work of such directors as Michelangelo Antonioni, Federico Fellini, and Pier Paolo Pasolini. That seminal auteurist period ended in the late 1980s. In recent years, new auteurs have surfaced in Italian cinema, among them Nanni Moretti, Matteo Garrone, and Paolo Sorrentino.

Cinecittà

The most important film studio in Italy, Rome's Cinecittà was inaugurated on April 28, 1937, by Benito Mussolini The symbol of Italian cinema worldwide, Cinecittà became wildly popular after the Second World War, when it was the set for many comedies and other productions. Cinecittà was the favorite setting of Federico Fellini, who filmed the vast majority of his films there, most notably in the studio Teatro (Theater) 5.

Cines

Established in 1906, the Società Italiana Cines is one of the earliest and most influential Italian film production and distribution companies. Cines produced several masterpieces of early Italian cinema, including Guazzoni's *Quo vadis?* (1913) and Gennaro Righelli's *La canzone dell'amore* (*The Song of Love*, 1930). Among other accomplishments, it is known for being the first company to manufacture blank film in Italy. The company went through different managements and was liquidated in 1958. But Cines was revived in 2006, and it currently focuses on home entertainment and art films under the artistic direction of theatrical director and essayist Leonardo Bragaglia.

cinepanettone

A subgenre of comedy inaugurated by Carlo Vanzina's *Vacanze di Natale* (*Christmas Vacation*, 1983), *Cinepanettone* usually designates films that are designed for commercial success and released during the holiday season. The term derives from the panettone, a famous Italian dessert usually served for Christmas. These films are often based on multiple, interlacing stories of average Italians vacationing in exotic locations, and tend to focus on romantic situations and feature international film stars as part of their commercial hook. In spite of their repetitiveness, clichés, and generally stale comedic routines, *cinepanettone* films can place an unforgiving mirror to Italian society. This trend is the subject of much recent critical attention, most notably by Alan O'Leary in *Fenomenologia del cinepanettone* (*Phenomenology of the* Cinepanettone, 2013).

commedia all'italiana

Translated as comedy Italian style, this label designates a wide variety of bittersweet comedies produced from the 1960s onward. Among the masters of this genre are Mario Monicelli, Ettore Scola, and Pietro Germi. The name of the movement was inspired by the title of Germi's *Divorzio all'italiana* (*Divorce Italian Style*, 1961). The first film in this trend is usually considered Monicelli's *I soliti ignoti* (*Big Deal on Madonna Street*, 1958), the tale of a group of clumsy small-time burglars. Many critics consider the *commedia all'italiana* to be the defining genre of Italian cinema because of its capacious rendering of many aspects of Italian life, from the crude and cruel to the laughable and absurd. But the very expansiveness of the genre makes it difficult to reduce it to a single definition.

crisis

To some critics, postwar Italian cinema is defined by a permanent state of crisis. Throughout its history, Italian cinema was affected by several plights, such as the lack of funding and proper infrastructure. The first notable emergency dates back to the First World War, when the economic and social disruption brought by the conflict crippled the entire Italian silent film industry. Another major crisis occurred during the 1980s and, to some extent, still plagues today's film industry. It was caused mostly by, one, the success of commercial television, which permanently modified Italians' moviegoing habits; and two, by the ever-widening rift between art film and commercial productions (see *Cinepanettone*).

divismo

This term refers to the star system and is derived from the Italian word *diva*, which originally meant "female deity." It is the process through which a public personality becomes a celebrity, a popular idol. The term was born in the heyday of Italian silent cinema, when actors and actresses became wildly popular with film audiences. In early films, the role of the female lead became prominent, intensifying the notion of the femme fatale that transformed women actors into divas in the eyes of adoring spectators. Among the early divas of Italian cinema are Lyda Borelli (1884–1959) and Francesca Bertini (1892–1985), stars of some of the most successful productions of their time.

erotic cinema

Also known as Italian sexy comedy, erotic cinema became a popular genre for more than a decade in Italy, between the 1970s and 1980s. The actors were usually professional comedians, and the plot involved a repertoire of gags and comedic situations. An erotic subtext was prominent in these films, and the female characters were usually voluptuous actresses that inspired the fantasies of male characters. Among the most popular films are Mariano Laurenti's *Quel gran pezzo della Ubalda tutta nuda e tutta calda* (*Ubalda, All Naked and Warm*, 1972) and Sergio Martino's *Giovannona Coscialunga disonorata con onore* (*Giovannona Long-Thigh*, 1973). Recent scholarship has been reassessing the intellectual value of these films as irreverent commentaries on Italian society of the 1970s and its rigid moralism, and as forward-thinking works that jolted the conservative sexual attitudes of Italians.

Felliniesque

The adjective *Felliniesque* is named after the director Federico Fellini (1920–93). It usually indicates a quixotic, dreamlike, often psychosexual element found in some of Fellini's most famous cinematic sequences.

Futurist Cinema
"Il manifesto della cinematografia futurista" ("Manifesto of Futurist Cinematography," 1916) is the title of a document signed by a group of notable Futurist artists, including the founder of the movement, Filippo Tommaso Marinetti (1876–1944) and the painter Giacomo Balla (1871–1958). In the early days of cinema, Italians considered cinema merely a hybrid art form, neither drama nor photography. The Futurist manifesto recognized for the first time the complete autonomy of cinema as an art form and laid out the premises for the birth of film theory in Italy. While active theoretically, the Futurists struggled to produce actual Futurist films. The critically acclaimed *Thaïs* by Anton Giulio Bragaglia (1917) is the only surviving film associated with the movement.

giallo
Also known as Spaghetti Thriller, the *giallo all'italiana* is an Italian interpretation of classic detective stories. Stylistically, Italian detective stories mix the conventional situations of thrillers with horror-like elements, such as a profusion of graphic violence and references to the supernatural. Among the practitioners of this genre are Mario Bava and Pupi Avati. The name comes from a series of crime-mystery pulp novels called Il Giallo Mondadori from the 1920s, books that came with a trademark yellow *(giallo)* cover.

historical epic
In the early days of Italian cinema, one of the most popular film genres was the historical epic, which consisted of costume films inspired by the mythology and history of ancient Rome. The aesthetics of this genre were elaborate sets and large crowd scenes, characteristics that were highly influential in later Hollywood historical productions. Among the most popular historical epics were Mario Caserini's *Gli ultimi giorni di Pompei* (*The Last Days of Pompeii,* 1913) and Guazzoni's *Quo vadis?* (1913). The masterpiece of the genre was Giovanni Pastrone's *Cabiria* (1914), which set the gold standard for early Italian film productions.

Hollywood on the Tiber
In the 1950s, many American production companies moved to Cinecittà to reduce cost. Both American filmmakers and actors worked in Rome and enjoyed the easy lifestyle of the Italian *dolce vita,* sweet life. These Hollywood figures were also fodder for the press and media-scandal machine.

horror Italian style
During the 1970s and 1980s, Italy produced many horror films that were widely successful both nationally and internationally. The most recognizable master of this trend was Dario Argento, whose best-known work is *Profondo*

rosso (*Deep Red*, 1975), a detective story with supernatural undertones. This genre often overlaps with the *giallo* for themes, settings, and narrative tropes.

impegno

During the social unrest of the 1970s, a series of directors made films about political and civic issues. They are known as the directors of *impegno* (engagement), whose films tackle social and political themes (exponents include Francesco Rosi, Elio Petri, Gillo Pontecorvo, and the Taviani brothers). A well-known actor in this movement was Gian Maria Volontè (1933–94), who starred in Petri's *Indagine su un cittadino al di sopra di ogni sospetto* (*Investigation of a Citizen Above Suspicion*, 1970), Rosi's *Uomini contro* (*Many Wars Ago*, 1970), and Marco Bellocchio's *Sbatti il mostro in prima pagina* (*Slap the Monster on Page One*, 1972).

LUCE

Located in Rome, L'Unione Cinematografica Educativa (The Educational Cinematic Union), later known as Istituto LUCE, is the oldest institute for news broadcast in the world. It was founded in 1924 by Benito Mussolini and became a powerful instrument for Fascist propaganda. After the war, several notable directors—including Mario Monicelli, Liliana Cavani, and Ettore Scola—produced documentaries and films for LUCE, which is now a vast depository of archival material on Italian life, history, and costume design.

Macaroni War

During the 1960s, many European productions mimicked the success of contemporary American war movies, creating a popular subgenre. While the definition of Macaroni War refers almost exclusively to Italian war films, in Italy this type of film is known as *Euro-War*. One of its most influential films was Enzo Castellari's *Quel maledetto treno blindato* (1978), which was released internationally as *Inglorious Bastards* and inspired several aspects of Quentin Tarantino's *Inglorious Basterds* (2009).

Magic Lantern

Invented in the eighteenth century, an early device for the production of moving pictures was known as the Magic Lantern. Synonymous with the origins of cinema, it was part of the early development of moving images, predating even photography. These devices are the direct progenitors of modern film projectors, as they use a source of light projected onto moving slides to give the illusion of movement to a live audience.

neorealism

Arguably the most important and influential movement in the history of Italian cinema, neorealism is a documentary-style approach to filmmaking. Its chronological life was brief and consists of only a handful of films (roughly 1945–52), but it is a trend that changed the course of film history. neorealism developed an aesthetic of reality: after the Second World War, neorealist directors sought to record the nation's physical and moral reconstruction after twenty years of Fascism. While premises for a new form of realism had emerged in Fascist cinema in such landmark films as Luchino Visconti's *Ossessione* (*Obsession*, 1943), arguably the official beginning of neorealist cinema was Roberto Rossellini's *Roma città aperta* (*Rome, Open City*, 1945).

neorealismo rosa

This was a genre of realist films that focused on romantic and mundane narrative situations. Pink neorealism maintained some of the characteristics of neorealist cinema: the use of nonprofessional actors, on-location shootings, and socially engaged themes. But it diverted the genre toward comedy and reflected the improving economic and social conditions of Italy during the postwar reconstruction. The first popular film of the genre was *Pane, amore e fantasia* (*Bread, Love, and Dreams*, 1953) by Luigi Comencini. Pink neorealism is also known to have inspired the first examples of the postwar star system.

peplum

Peplum comes from the Greek word for "tunic." Peplum or sword and sandal epic is a historical genre of Italian cinema that was very popular between the mid-1950s and the mid-1960s. Despite their low budgets, peplum films enjoyed international popularity, especially in the United States.

poliziottesco

A subgenre of action fiction, also known as Italian crime film, the *poliziottesco* was popular in the 1970s and inspired by American crime fiction, such as the *Dirty Harry* franchise. The *poliziottesco* offered an original angle on the social unrest of the 1970s, with its sympathetic portrayals of criminals, juxtaposed with corrupted cops. The genre was controversial for the alleged Fascist undertones of its screenwriting. The first example of this genre was Carlo Lizzani's *Banditi a Milano* (*The Violent Four*, 1968).

propaganda

Benito Mussolini believed in the power of cinema for propaganda purposes. During the inauguration of Cinecittà, Mussolini had himself immortalized on a billboard behind a camera. Under the picture the caption was "Cinematography is the most powerful weapon" (see the figure below). Despite this belief, propaganda films were a small fraction of all films produced during the Fascist regime. Propaganda was mostly relegated to LUCE documentaries and to the so-called *cinegiornali*, news broadcasts that were projected in film theaters before screenings.

science fiction

Italy has a long tradition of low-budget sci-fi film productions, which originated as early as the 1920s and 1930s. Italian science fiction is also known as Spaghetti Sci-Fi. In its heyday, the 1960s, it mimicked mainstream American productions, although it was not able to replicate their popular success and only occupied a small niche in the Italian film market. The most popular sci-fi film was perhaps Mario Bava's *Terrore nello spazio* (*Planet of the Vampires*, 1965). Other major film directors used science to explore social and political themes. A classic example was Petri's *La decima vittima* (*The 10th Victim*, 1965), a spy story set in a dystopian Rome of the future. Petri mocked the clichés of sci-fi films, while at the same time attacking capitalism and the intrusion of mass media in people's daily lives. A more recent example of authorial sci-fi is Gabriele Salvatores' *Nirvana* (1997).

Silent Cinema

The origins of Italian cinema are in *cinema muto*, silent film. The first Italian sound film was Righelli's *The Song of Love*. Before then, Italian silent cinema enjoyed worldwide popularity and was a commercial power worldwide. From 1910 to 1914, a period often called the First Golden Age of Italian Cinema, Italy challenged the supremacy of the richer and more powerful Hollywood productions. Among the masterpieces of the genre were de Liguoro's *Dante's Inferno*, Caserini's *The Last Days of Pompeii*, and Pastrone's *Cabiria*.

Spaghetti Western

Sergio Leone revived the American Western with *Per un pugno di dollari* (*A Fistful of Dollars*, 1964), redefining the original characteristics of the genre by playing with clichés and offering a grittier and dirtier version of earlier American films. Leone sparked a series of imitations and followers that helped popularize the genre worldwide. Filmed in the remotest regions of Spain and southern Italy, Spaghetti Westerns have influenced many foreign directors, including Quentin Tarantino. While Spaghetti Western films were produced late into the 1980s and enjoyed a large popular following, Leone is also said to represent the official end of this movement with his *C'era una volta il West* (*Once Upon a Time in the West*, 1968).

telefoni bianchi

Telefoni bianchi (white telephones) is a genre of Fascist comedies popular between 1936 and 1943. Primarily written in imitation of American films, these films were set in glamorous art deco settings. Actors were dressed stylishly and mimicked American film stars of the time. The label comes from the images of the opulent white telephones that would prominently appear on screen as status symbols of the characters' social prestige and wealth.

CONTRIBUTORS

Mattia Acetoso
Assistant Professor of Italian
Department of Romance Languages and
  Literatures
Boston College

Stefano Baschiera
Senior Lecturer in Film Studies
Queen's University Belfast

Daniela Bini
Professor of Italian Studies and
  Comparative Literature
Department of French and Italian
University of Texas
Austin

Luca Caminati
Professor of Film Studies
Mel Hoppenheim School of Cinema
Concordia University

Sarah Carey
Executive Director of Product
  Management
McGraw-Hill Education

Mary Ann McDonald Carolan
Professor of Modern Languages and
  Literature
Fairfield University

Allison Cooper
Assistant Professor of Romance
  Languages and Literatures and
  Cinema Studies
Bowdoin College

Antonio Costa
Professor of Cinema and
  Visual Arts
Dipartimento dei Beni Culturali
Università di Padova

Michael Cramer
Assistant Professor of Film
  History
Sarah Lawrence College

Monica Facchini
Associate Professor of Romance
  Languages and Literatures and
  Film and Media Studies
Colgate University

Robert S. C. Gordon
Serena Professor of Italian
University of Cambridge

Stephen Gundle
Professor of Film and Television
  Studies
University of Warwick

Cosetta Gaudenzi
Associate Professor of Italian
Department of World Languages
  and Literatures
University of Memphis

Brendan Hennessey
Assistant Professor of Italian
Department of Romance Languages
  and Literatures
Binghamton University

Marcia Landy
Distinguished Professor Emerita of
  English and Film Studies with
  Secondary Appointment in French
  and Italian
University of Pittsburgh

Charles L. Leavitt IV
Assistant Professor of Italian
University of Notre Dame

Bernadette Luciano
Professor of Italian
Head of School of Cultures, Languages
  and Linguistics
University of Auckland

Joseph Luzzi
Professor of Comparative Literature
Faculty Member in Italian Studies
Bard College

Millicent Marcus
Professor of Italian
Faculty Member of Film and Media
  Studies Program
Yale University

Giuliana Minghelli
Associate Professor of Italian
Faculty Member in Italian and World
  Cinema Studies
McGill University

Alan O'Leary
Professor of Film and Cultural Studies
Faculty Member in the Centre for
  World Cinemas and Digital Cultures
University of Leeds

Catherine O'Rawe
Professor of Italian Film and Culture
University of Bristol

Federico Pacchioni
Sebastian P. and Marybelle Musco
  Endowed Chair of Italian Studies
Department of World Languages and
  Cultures
Chapman University

Gabriele Pedullà
Professor of Italian Literature
Departmento di Studi Umanistici
Università di Roma Tre

Dana Renga
Associate Professor and Chair
The Department of French and Italian
Co-director, The Film Studies Program
Affiliate Faculty in Comparative
  Studies and Women's, Gender,
  and Sexuality Studies
The Ohio State University

John David Rhodes
Reader in Film Studies and Visual
  Culture
Director, Centre for Film and Screen
University of Cambridge

Alessia Ricciardi
Professor of Italian and Comparative
  Literature
Director of Graduate Studies in the
  Program of Comparative Literary
  Studies
Northwestern University

Laura E. Ruberto
Chair, Arts and Cultural Studies
Faculty in Humanities
Berkeley City College

Robert Rushing
Professor of Italian and Comparative
  Literature
University of Illinois
Urbana-Champaign

Mauro Sassi
Ph.D., McGill University
Independent Scholar
Florence, Italy

Michael Syrimis
Associate Professor of Italian
Faculty Associate in Film Studies
Tulane University

Dr. Kristi M. Wilson
Director of the Writing Program
Associate Professor of Rhetoric and
 Communications
Affiliate in the Humanities
Soka University of America

Vito Zagarrio
Professor of Film, Television,
 and Photography
Department of Philosophy
 Communication, and Performing Arts
Università Roma Tre

INDEX